PUBLIC COMPANIES AND EQUITY FINANCE

PUBLIC COMPANIES AND EQUITY FINANCE

Alexis Mavrikakis MA (Cantab), Solicitor

Published by

College of Law Publishing,
Braboeuf Manor, Portsmouth Road, St Catherines, Guildford GU3 1HA

© The College of Law 2010

All rights reserved. No part of this publication may be reproduced, stored in a retrieval system, or transmitted in any way or by any means, including photocopying or recording, without the written permission of the copyright holder, application for which should be addressed to the publisher.

British Library Cataloguing-in-Publication Data

A catalogue record for this book is available from the British Library.

ISBN 978 1 905391 92 9

Typeset by Style Photosetting Ltd, Mayfield, East Sussex

Printed in Great Britain by Ashford Colour Press Ltd, Gosport, Hampshire

Preface

This book traces the life of a public company from birth (and its planned conception too), through adolescence and its growth into maturity until its demise, or at least the possibility of its demise, for immortality of course may beckon for this legal form of person. In doing so it concentrates on the public company listed on the London Stock Exchange. It is the mightiest of all companies, the biggest and the most high-profile. As such it operates subject to a whole raft of additional rules and regulations (advice on which provides many a fat cheque for lawyers and other advisers), and is required to expose itself to unparalled public scrutiny (providing rich pickings for newspaper and television journalists with unending column inches or minutes to fill).

This book has been written to explain the issues a lawyer may encounter when advising a public company. It seeks in particular to explain the principles behind the rules and to decipher the jargon which lawyers like to use in relation to those rules.

This book should be useful to law students and trainees in corporate seats, as an overview of public company work and as a guide to using the primary sources more effectively. It may also be of interest to the other professionals who work alongside public company lawyers, such as lawyers who undertake corporate support work, accountants and stockbrokers, as an insight into just what public company lawyers do.

To achieve an overview of public company issues, the best way to read this book is to start at Chapter 1 and read through to Chapter 24. This will guide you in a logical manner through the issues which face a public company, from registration, through flotation, to complying with continuing obligations, raising funds and entering into transactions. However, the book is also suitably cross-referenced to enable it to be used in practice as a reference book.

As a result of tremendous regulatory activity in the field of public companies over the past couple of years, primarily provoked by a raft of EU legislation and the global financial crisis, there have been plenty of significant amendments to primary sources. In addition, the Companies Act 2006 is at last fully in force at the time of writing (1 October 2009). All these amendments have been incorporated into the main body of the text.

I am most grateful to Alastair MacQueen, Robert Nisbet-Smith, Catherine Shephard, David Stott and Peter Watson for variously their bequest, forbearance in the face of deadlines stretched, scrupulous attention to detail and lawyerly insight.

Please free to e-mail any comments to alexis.mavrikakis@lawcol.co.uk.

The law is stated as 1 October 2009.

Alexis Mavrikakis
The College of Law
Washington DC

For Robert and Daisy

and in memoriam

Alistair MacQueen

Contents

Table of Cases

Table of Statutes

Table of Secondary Legislation

Glossary

ABI	Association of British Insurers (which represents the interests of the UK's insurance industry)
ABI Guidelines	See **14.5.7**. Reproduced in **Appendix 3**
accounting reference date	The date on which the financial year of a company ends
Admission and Disclosure Standards	Rules made by the Stock Exchange in relation to admission to trading and disclosure of information (see **2.9**). Reproduced in **Appendix 1**
ADS	Admission and Disclosure Standard
AGM	An Annual General Meeting of shareholders and directors held pursuant to s 336 of the CA 2006
AIM	The Alternative Investment Market of the London Stock Exchange: a global market for smaller and growing companies
AIM Rules	Rules published by the Stock Exchange for AIM-quoted companies
AIM Rules for Nominated Advisers	Rules published by the Stock Exchange for Nomads of AIM-quoted companies
analyst	Person employed by an investment bank or stockbroking firm to study a company or sector's performance
analyst's report	Report produced by an analyst, rating a company's shares as a buy, sell or hold. Often the report will coincide with the release of the company's results, and can influence the decision of investors as to whether to buy or sell shares in that company
audit committee	A committee of the board of directors, concerned with matters relating to the company's accounts and auditing (see **8.3.6.3**)
Authorisation Manual	A manual published by the FSA, which forms part of the FSA Handbook and which gives guidance about authorisation under the FSMA 2000
BIS	Department for Business, Innovation and Skills (formerly the Department for Business, Enterprise and Regulatory Reform (DBERR))
bonus issue	See capitalisation of reserves
bookbuilding	See **4.4.2.1**
BVCA	British Private Equity and Venture Capital Association
CA 1985	Companies Act 1985 (which ceased to be in force on 1 October 2009)
CA 2006	Companies Act 2006 (fully in force from 1 October 2009)
Cadbury Report	The 1992 report of the Committee on the Financial Aspects of Corporate Governance under the chairmanship of Sir Adrian Cadbury (see **8.3.2.1**)
call option	See options

capitalisation of reserves	An issue of securities, credited as fully paid, out of the issuer's reserves, to existing shareholders in proportion to their existing shareholdings (also known as a 'bonus' or 'scrip' issue) (see **13.5.5**)
CARD	Consolidated Admissions and Reporting Directive 2001/34/EC
CBI	The Confederation of British Industry (the UK's leading employers organisation)
certificate of approval	See **6.11**
City Code	City Code on Takeovers and Mergers, issued by the Panel (see below)
CJA 1993	Criminal Justice Act 1993
Combined Code	The Combined Code on Corporate Governance (Financial Reporting Council, June 2008) (see **8.3**)
CoMC	Code of Market Conduct. A code produced by the FSA, pursuant to s 119 of the FSMA 2000, to assist on the question whether particular behaviour is market abuse (see **10.1.2**). Contained in MAR1 of the Market Conduct (MAR) part of the FSA Handbook of Rules and Guidance
Company Reporting Directive	Directive 2006/46/EC (on accounts and the need for a corporate governance statement)
Conduct of Business Sourcebook	An FSA sourcebook which forms part of the FSA Handbook
continuing obligations	Obligations set out in the Prospectus Rules, the Listing Rules and the Disclosure and Transparency Rules to which a company becomes subject when its securities are admitted to the Official List (see **Chapter 7**)
contract for differences	See **21.8.10.5**
Corporate Governance Rules	Rules published by the FSA relating to the establishment of an audit committee and the inclusion of a corporate governance statement in a listed company's annual report
CREST	The electronic settlement system for uncertificated securities trading (see **2.5.3.1**)
DBERR	Department for Business, Enterprise and Regulatory Reform (now replaced by BIS)
dematerialisation	The process of replacing paper share certificates and stock transfer forms with an electronic system (see **2.10.2**)
derivative	A financial instrument whose value depends on the performance of an underlying asset or security. Examples include futures, options and swaps (see **21.8.10.5**)
Disclosure Rules	Rules published by the FSA relating to the disclosure of inside information and transactions by PDMRs and their connected persons
DTR	Disclosure and Transparency Rule
EA 2002	Enterprise Act 2002
EC Merger Regulation	Council Regulation 139/2004/EC
EEA	European Economic Area, a trading area comprising the Member States and Iceland, Liechtenstein and Norway

EFTA	European Free Trade Association: a free trade area established in 1960. Its current members are Iceland, Liechtenstein, Norway and Switzerland
equity securities	As defined in s 560 of the CA 2006, ordinary shares in a company or rights to subscribe for or to convert securities into, ordinary shares in the company
equity shares	As defined in s 548 of the CA 2006 and the Listing Rules, shares comprised in a company's equity share capital, that is, the issued share capital excluding any part of that capital which, neither as respects dividends nor as respects capital, carries any right to participate beyond a specified amount in a distribution
Euroclear UK & Ireland Limited	The operator of CREST, owned by Euroclear SA/NV
European Union (EU)	An economic and political union of European Member States created on 1 November 1993 by the Treaty on European Union (the 'Maastricht Treaty')
FPO 2005	Financial Services and Markets Act 2000 (Financial Promotion) Order 2005 (SI 2005/1529)
FRC	Financial Reporting Council. An independent regulator which has responsibility for accounting standards in the UK and promotes high standards of corporate governance
financial year	The period for which a company must prepare statutory accounts pursuant to the CA 2006
FSA	Financial Services Authority
FSA Handbook	A handbook published by the FSA, and updated monthly, of the rules and guidance issued by the FSA under the FSMA 2000, including the Part 6 Rules, the Authorisation Manual and the Code of Market Conduct
FSAP	The European Commission's Financial Services Action Plan
FSMA 2000	Financial Services and Markets Act 2000
FTSE 100	A Stock Exchange index of the largest (by market capitalisation) 100 companies admitted to trading on the Stock Exchange
gap	general accounting practice
GC100	The Association of General Counsel and Company Secretaries of the FTSE 100, which produces guidelines to assist its members in complying with the Part 6 Rules
gearing	The ratio of a company's debt to its equity (see **18.9.1**)
GM	General Meeting of the company
Greenbury Report	The 1995 report of the Committee on Directors' Remuneration under the chairmanship of Sir Richard Greenbury (see **8.3.2.1**)
Hampel Report	The 1998 report of the Committee on Corporate Governance under the chairmanship of Sir Ronald Hampel (see **8.3.2.1**)
Higgs Review	The 2003 review of the role and effectiveness of non-executive directors made by Derek Higgs
ICSA	Institute of Chartered Secretaries and Administrators (the leading professional body for company secretaries)

IMA	Investment Management Association (the trade body for the UK's asset management industry)
inside information	See **7.5.2.1**
International Accounting Standards	Accounting standards adopted for use in the EU in accordance with art 3 of the IAS Regulation (EC) No 1606/2001
IPCs	Investment Protection Committees (representative bodies of major institutional investors)
IPO	Initial public offering (of shares), also known as flotation. This refers to the company's first offer of shares on a stock market
irrevocable undertaking	See **21.10**
ISC	Institutional Shareholders' Committee (a forum to allow the UK's institutional shareholders to exchange news and co-ordinate their activities)
leverage	The opportunity to create profit by financing a business through debt which is entitled to only a finite return (see **18.2.2**)
liquidity	The ease with which a security can be traded on a market
listing particulars	A marketing document published, in terms acceptable to the FSA, as a condition of admission of certain specialist securities to listing (see **6.3**)
Listing Regulations 2001	Financial Services and Markets Act 2000 (Official Listing of Securities) Regulations 2001(SI 2001/2956)
Listing Rules	Rules published by the FSA, relating to the admission of securities to listing on the Official List and the continuing obligations of listed companies
long-form articles	See **1.9.3.1**
LR	Listing Rule
MAD	Market Abuse Directive 2003/6/EC
MAD Regulations 2005	Financial Services and Markets Act 2000 (Market Abuse) Regulations 2005 (SI 2005/381)
Main Market	The Stock Exchange's principal market for listed securities
Market Abuse Directive	Directive 2003/6/EC (to tackle market manipulation and update the insider dealing regime)
market capitalisation	See **13.3.6**
Markets in Financial Instruments Directive	Directive 2004/39/EC (sets the legislative framework for investment firms and securities markets in the EU)
market-makers	A member of the Stock Exchange offering the market a two-way price (ie, buying and selling) in particular securities (see **2.5.2**)
member firms	See **2.5.1**

Member States	The 27 Member States of the European Union, namely Austria, Belgium, Bulgaria, Cyprus, Czech Republic, Denmark, Estonia, Finland, France, Germany, Greece, Hungary, Ireland, Italy, Latvia, Lithuania, Luxembourg, Malta, the Netherlands, Poland, Portugal, Romania, Slovak Republic, Slovenia, Spain, Sweden and the UK
MiFID	See Markets in Financial Instruments Directive
Misleading Statements Order 2001	Financial Services and Markets Act 2000 (Misleading Statements and Practices) Order 2001 (SI 2001/3645)
Model Code	A code regulating dealings by directors and certain others in the shares of their own companies. Listed companies must comply with this code or some other no less exacting in its terms (see **7.8**)
NAPF	National Association of Pension Funds (the UK representative body for organisations providing pensions)
NASDAQ	A stock market based in New York
Nomad	The nominated adviser of an AIM Company (see **24.4.1**)
offer period	See **22.3.4**
Official List	The list of securities which have been admitted to listing, maintained by the FSA under s 74(1) of the FSMA 2000
OFT	Office of Fair Trading
PAL	Provisional allotment letter, which is a negotiable document issued by a company which notifies the recipient that securities have been allotted to him on a provisional basis (see **17.7.3.1**)
Panel	Panel on Takeovers and Mergers (which regulates public company takeovers in the UK and issues the City Code)
Part 6 Rules	The Listing Rules, the Prospectus Rules, the Disclosure Rules, the Transparency Rules and the Corporate Governance Rules
Perimeter Guidance Manual	A regulatory guide, forming part of the FSA Handbook, about the circumstances in which authorisation is required under FSMA 2000
PDMR	Person discharging managerial responsibility. See **7.8.2.1**
PD Regulation	EC Regulation 809/2004
PERG	Perimeter Guidance Manual
PIP	Primary Information Provider
PIRC	Pensions & Investment Research Consultants (the UK's leading independent research and advisory consultancy, providing services to institutional investors on corporate governance)
PMQI Order 2001	Financial Services and Markets Act (Prescribed Markets and Qualifying Investments) Order 2001 (SI 2001/996)
poison pills	See **22.4.9**
Practice Statements	Informal guidance issued by the Panel Executive (see **20.5.6.1**)

Pre-emption Group Statement of Principles	See **14.6.16**
Primary Information Provider	See **7.5.2.7**
private equity house	See venture capital company
Professional Securities Market	The Stock Exchange's market for listing debt, convertibles and depositary receipts. Debt securities can be listed on either the Main Market or on the Professional Securities Market
profit forecast	See **22.4.5.1**
prospectus	A marketing document, published in terms acceptable to the FSA. See **Chapter 6**
Prospectus Directive	Directive 2003/71/EC (sets out the need for a prospectus for the issuers of securities on regulated markets across the EU)
PR	Prospectus Rule
Prospectus Regulations	SI 2005/1433
Prospectus Rules	Rules published by the FSA setting out the form, content and approval requirements for a prospectus
QCA	The Quoted Companies Alliance (a UK representative body established to protect the interests of the smaller quoted company (that is, outside the FTSE 350))
QCA Guidelines	The corporate governance guidelines for AIM published in February 2007 by the Quoted Companies Alliance (see **24.7**)
Regulated Activities Order 2001	Financial Services and Markets Act 2000 (Regulated Activities) Order 2001 (SI 2001/544)
Regulatory Information Service	See **7.5.2.6**
remuneration committee	A committee of the board of directors with responsibility primarily for determining or recommending the remuneration of the executive directors (see **8.3.6.2**)
responsibility statement	See **6.5.2.1** and **22.4.5.2**
RIE	Recognised Investment Exchange (includes the Stock Exchange)
rights issue	An issue to existing holders of securities of rights to subscribe or purchase further securities pro rata their existing holdings made by means of the issue of a PAL or other negotiable document (see **17.7.1**)
RIS	Regulatory Information Service (includes RNS)
RNS	Company news service of the Stock Exchange (an RIS)
rump	Those shares not taken up by the shareholders on a rights issue which it is sought to place in the market (see **17.7.5**)
scrip issue	See capitalisation of reserves

SEAQ	The Stock Exchange Automated Quotations System, a computer screen system enabling Stock Exchange members to advertise share prices for AIM-quoted securities that are not traded on SETS (see **2.5.2**)
Secondary Information Provider	See **7.4.2.2**
Second Company Law Directive	Directive 77/91/EC
settlement	See **2.5.3**
SETS	The Stock Exchange Electronic Trading Service, an order-driven electronic trading system for FTSE 100 securities and for the most traded AIM-quoted securities (see **2.5.2**)
SETSqx	The Stock Exchange Electronic Trading Service – quotes and crosses. A trading system for securities less liquid than those traded on SETS
short-form articles	See **1.9.3.1**
SIP	Secondary Information Provider
SLC	substantial lessening of competition
Smith Report	The report of an independent group, chaired by Sir Robert Smith, to clarify the role and responsibility of audit committees (see **8.3.2.2**)
Societas Europaea (SE)	A European public limited liability company, which must be registered in a Member State with a share capital of at least €120,000
sponsor	A person approved by the FSA to sponsor an application for listing of securities and to assist the issuer in fulfilling its continuing obligations
stamp duty reserve tax	A tax introduced by the Finance Act 1986 to cover paperless share transactions (which fall outside the ambit of stamp duty)
Statutory Audit Directive	Directive 2006/43/EC (on statutory audits of annual accounts)
stick	Those shares not taken up by shareholders on a rights issue, nor subsequently placed in the market, and which, therefore, fall to the underwriters or sub-underwriters (see **17.7.5**)
Stock Exchange	The London Stock Exchange plc
sub-underwriter	A person to whom the underwriters have laid off some or all of the underwriting risk on a marketing of securities
Takeovers Directive	Directive 2004/25/EC (regulating the takeovers of companies trading on a regulated market in the EU)
Transparency Directive	Directive 2004/109/EC (to enhance transparency on EU financial markets by requiring disclosure of periodic financial reports and of major shareholdings for companies trading on a regulated market in the EU)
Transparency Rules	Rules published by the FSA setting out the requirements for periodic financial reporting for listed companies and the disclosure of major shareholdings
Turnbull Report	Guidance, published by the Financial Reporting Council, for directors of listed companies regarding internal controls (see **8.3.4.1**)

UK GAAP   Generally Accepted Accounting Principles in the UK

UKLA   The UK Listing Authority, being a division of the FSA acting in its capacity as the
                    competent authority for the purposes of Pt VI of the FSMA 2000

underwriter   In insurance terms, a person who takes on an insurance risk; in terms of the marketing
                    of securities, a person who agrees to take up shares not purchased or subscribed for

venture capital   A company which specialises in investing, typically, in unlisted, high risk businesses. The
company   venture capital company helps to develop the business, often with a view to listing, with
                    the aim of achieving significant return on its investment

Walker review   An independent review by Sir David Walker of corporate governance in the UK banking
                    industry carried out in 2009

Part I
BECOMING A LISTED COMPANY

Chapter 1
Public Companies

1.1 Introduction

There are more than two million companies registered in England and Wales. Fewer than 15,000 are public companies. Of those public companies, approximately 2,750 have floated on the London Stock Exchange. Around 1,400 are listed on the London Stock Exchange's principal market for larger, more established companies (the 'Main Market'), with approximately a further 1,350 quoted on the Stock Exchange's international market for smaller, growing companies (the Alternative Investment Market or 'AIM').

This book is concerned with the small minority of companies which are public, and with that even smaller minority of public companies which have floated on the London Stock Exchange.

1.2 What is a public company?

A public company is defined by s 4(2) of the Companies Act 2006 (CA 2006). It is a company limited by shares or by guarantee and having a share capital, which has complied with the requirements of the CA 2006 (or former Companies Acts) to enable it to be registered or re-registered as such.

How a company can achieve public company status is explained at **1.9**.

1.3 What is a listed company?

There are several specific definitions of a listed company in company law legislation, some of which are explored in more depth elsewhere in this book. However, broadly, a listed company is a public company any of the shares in which are officially listed and trade on a stock market.

The stock market which is the focus of this book is the London Stock Exchange's 'Main Market'. The London Stock Exchange's other market, AIM, is considered in more detail at **2.4** and in **Chapter 24**. Companies may also be listed on stock markets based overseas, such as the Deutsche Börse in Germany, NASDAQ and the New York Stock Exchange in the USA, NYSE Euronext in Amsterdam, Brussels, Lisbon and Paris, or NASDAQ OMX Nordic Exchange covering Scandinavia and the Baltic countries.

Obviously, when working with specific legislation, care must be taken to analyse the specific definition of 'listed'. For example, under some legislation a company which has its shares quoted on AIM rather than the Main Market will be a listed company, while under other legislation the same company will fall outside the definition of a listed company.

The words 'quoted' and 'listed' are usually used interchangeably, both by the layperson and by the practitioner. However, again, care should be taken to use appropriate terminology in relation to specific markets; the London Stock Exchange, for example, defines shares listed on the Main Market as listed (but not quoted) and shares listed on AIM as quoted but unlisted. Furthermore, the CA 2006 definition of 'quoted company' in s 385 refers to companies listed on 'regulated markets' including the Main Market but not AIM!

This can, of course lead to confusion. The key is to not take for granted the meaning of the terms 'listed' and 'quoted', but to examine (if interpreting such terms) or explain (if using such terms) the context in which they are used, taking account of the differing definitions.

For the purposes of this book, 'listed' is used to mean ordinary shares of an English company admitted to listing on the Official List of the FSA and admitted to trading on the Main Market of the London Stock Exchange.

1.4   The distinction between 'public' and 'listed'

Just because a company is a *public* company, it does not automatically follow that it is a *listed* company. There is some correlation between public companies and listed companies, in that a company must be a public company to become a listed company (private companies cannot become listed companies). However, we already know that only about 10% of public companies are listed.

The distinction between the terms is important, because a company's status will determine how that company is regulated. Public companies are more heavily regulated than private companies; listed public companies are significantly more heavily regulated than unlisted public companies. The question therefore arises, why would investors wish to put their money in a company which is subject to additional restrictions and cost, imposed as a result of greater regulation? The answer rests on a consideration of the advantages (**1.5** and **1.7** below) and disadvantages (**1.6** and **1.8** below) of becoming a public company and a listed company.

1.5   Advantages of public company status

1.5.1   Ability to offer shares to the public

It is prohibited for a private company to offer its shares to the public under s 755 of the CA 2006. The main reason for registering or re-registering as a public company, therefore, is to enable a company to offer its shares to the public. The ability to offer shares to the public is an advantage, as it provides a company with a new source of finance (the consideration received for the shares) and opens up new opportunities for raising finance which otherwise may be unavailable to the company.

If s 755 is breached the court has the power to re-register the offending private company as a public one under s 758 of the CA 2006. If, though, the company does not meet the requirements to become a public company then the court either may order that the company is wound up (s 758), or it may make a remedial order under s 759 of the CA 2006. The remedial order seeks to put a person affected by a breach of s 755 back in the position he was in before the breach. The court has wide-ranging powers to achieve this. The application to court for a s 758 or s 759 order can be made by a shareholder or creditor of the offending company, or by the Secretary of State for Business, Innovation and Skills (BIS).

1.5.2   Prestige

A secondary reason for a company to register or re-register as a public company is to benefit from the prestige conferred by the letters 'plc' ('public limited company'). Some companies therefore opt for public company status even if they have no immediate plans to offer shares to the public. Subsidiaries of public companies are often public companies too, for this reason.

1.6 Potential disadvantages of public company status

As noted at **1.5.1** and **1.5.2** above, public company status brings with it the financial advantage of being able to offer shares to the public, and a certain element of commercial respectability. However, these advantages mean (in theory at least) that any public company, even if unlisted, can be owned by members of the public who have little day to day involvement in the company's business, and who therefore require greater statutory protection than the owners of a private company, who typically are more involved in the running of their companies, often as directors. For this reason, public companies are much more strictly regulated than private companies. This will add to the cost of running the company, and may restrict what it wishes to do and how it seeks to operate. **Table 1.1** below summarises the main differences between the regulation of public companies and private companies.

Table 1.1: Public companies compared to private companies

	Public company	Private company
Accounts	Must file with Companies House within 6 months after end of accounting reference period (CA 2006, s 442(2)(b)).	Must file within 9 months after end of accounting reference period (CA 2006, s 442(2)(a)).
	Must file full accounts with Companies House (CA 2006, ss 446 and 447 and ss 384 and 467).	Requirements to file full accounts can be relaxed for small and medium-sized companies (CA 2006, ss 444 and 445).
	Accounts must be laid before a General Meeting no later than 6 months after end of accounting reference period (CA 2006, s 437).	No requirement to do so.
Administration	Must hold an Annual General Meeting (AGM) (CA 2006, s 336).	No requirement to hold an AGM unless articles require it (SI 2007/2194, Sch 3, para 32(11)).
	The requisite percentage for holding a General Meeting on short notice is 95% (CA 2006, s 307(6)(b)).	The requisite percentage for holding a General Meeting on short notice is 90% (CA 2006, s 307(6)(a)).
	Cannot use the written resolution procedure (CA 2006, s 288).	Can use the written resolution procedure (CA 2006, s 288).
Directors	Minimum of 2 (CA 2006, s 154(2)).	Minimum of 1 (CA 2006, s 154(1)).
	Restrictions apply on voting for the appointment of more than one director in just one resolution (CA 2006, s 160).	No equivalent restriction applies.

	Public company	Private company
	A public company can only make a quasi-loan and a credit transaction with one of its directors provided prior shareholder approval has been obtained (CA 2006, ss 198 and 201).	The need for shareholder approval for quasi-loans and credit transactions with a director will be required only if the private company is 'associated with a public company', as defined in CA 2006, s 256 (CA 2006, ss 198(1) and 201(1)).
Financial assistance	Prohibited (CA 2006, s 678), subject to CA 2006, ss 681 and 682. See **Chapter 16**.	Generally permitted. Restrictions apply to private companies which are subsidiaries of public companies.
Secretary	A secretary is required (CA 2006, s 271). Section 273 sets out qualifications required.	A secretary is not compulsory (CA 2006, s 270(1)). If a company chooses to have one, there are no qualification requirements.
Share capital	The company must have allotted share capital at least up to the value of the authorised minimum (currently £50,000 – CA 2006, s 763 permits a euro equivalent to this amount, set at €57,100 (SI 2009/2425)) to register (CA 2006, s 761) or re-register (CA 2006, s 91(1)). The company must maintain this as its minimum share capital (CA 2006, ss 650 and 662).	No restriction on allotted share capital.
	Each share allotted must be paid up to at least one-quarter of its nominal value together with the whole of any premium on it (CA 2006, s 586).	No equivalent restriction applies. Can allot shares nil paid, partly paid or fully paid.
	Section 561 pre-emption rights on allotment can be disapplied under s 570 or 571 by special resolution or excluded and replaced by articles conferring a corresponding right under s 568.	Section 561 pre-emption rights on allotment can be disapplied under s 569 (by special resolution or provision in the articles), under s 570 or 571 by special resolution or excluded under s 567 (by provision in the articles).
	Restrictions apply on consideration for allotment of shares (ss 585, 587 and 598).	These sections do not apply.

	Public company	Private company
	Valuer's report required to value non-cash consideration for the allotment of shares (s 593).	No equivalent requirement applies.
	GM required in the event of a serious loss of capital (s 656).	No equivalent requirement applies.
	Charges on own shares are void, subject to certain exceptions (s 670).	Subject to certain requirements in s 670(2), charges on own shares are permitted.
	Can redeem and purchase shares out of distributable profits or the proceeds of a fresh issue, but not out of capital (ss 687 and 692).	Can redeem and purchase shares out of distributable profits, the proceeds of a fresh issue, or out of capital (ss 687 and 692).
Shareholders	Has disclosure obligations under DTR 5 and CA 2006, Pt 22 (see **Chapter 15**).	No equivalent restrictions apply.
Takeovers	Subject to the City Code on Takeovers and Mergers.	Typically not subject to the City Code (but see exceptions at **20.5**).

1.7 Advantages of listing

If obtaining public company status enables a company to offer shares to the public, what further advantage is there in listing?

1.7.1 Providing a market for the company's shares

A listing will provide access to a market on which members of the public and financial institutions can buy and sell shares in the company. As the shares can be bought at a pre-agreed price and sold relatively easily (the shares are said to be 'liquid'), they will be an attractive investment, particularly for members of the public who may not be familiar with the (usually more complicated) methods of buying and selling shares off the stock market. This market also enables the original owners of the company or private equity or venture capitalist investors to sell their shares and exit from the company, thereby reaping the rewards of their investment (although they may be restricted from exiting for a period of time immediately following the listing, to promote confidence in the company).

An extract from a newspaper article (below) gives an example of what this can mean in practice (whilst at the same time making you question your choice of career . . .).

Flotation makes Sports Direct founder a billionaire

Julia Finch

SPORTSWEAR entrepreneur Mike Ashley joined the ranks of the super-rich yesterday after his Sports Direct retail empire floated on the Stock Exchange.

Mr Ashley sold 43% of his wholly-owned business – which includes 465 Sports World discount stores, Lillywhites in London and brands like Dunlop, Donnay and Slazenger – to institutional investors, netting £929m in cash. He retains a 57% stake worth more than £1bn.

Source: *Guardian*, 28 February 2007

At the time of writing, you can feel slightly more comfortable about your chosen career. Sports Direct's share price has dropped by almost two-thirds since its IPO, reflecting the global economic recession. As a consequence, Mike Ashley's shareholding was worth hundreds of millions of pounds less. This may well shrink further following raids by the OFT and Serious Fraud Office in relation to allegations of price-fixing and fraud at Sports Direct in September 2009.

As we know from **1.5** above, those same members of the public and financial institutions can buy and sell shares in an unlisted public company if that company chooses to offer them its shares. Although both unlisted and listed companies need to take account of the same rules regarding how the shares are offered to the public (see **Chapter 6**), the shares in an unlisted company will not be listed or trading on a stock market. Therefore, the process of buying the shares, and subsequently finding people to sell them to, will not be as easy (the shares are not as 'liquid') and so members of the public, in particular, will be less inclined to invest in them.

1.7.2   Easier access to capital

A listing enables the company to raise finance through issuing new shares ('equity finance'), both at the same time as the initial listing and afterwards, from the huge supply of capital available through the stock market. See **4.4** and **Chapter 17**. A large number of companies, particularly banks, were taking advantage of this equity finance to raise money in light of the much more restricted access to debt finance (ie, lending) as a result of the 'credit crunch'.

1.7.3   Access to acquisition opportunities

As a result of its access to the stock market and to its ready supply of capital, a listed company can often more easily raise cash or offer new shares in itself as consideration, thereby generally affording it the opportunity to expand through acquisition of other companies or businesses. Unlisted companies do not have the same access to this capital, not being part of a stock market, and, as explained in **1.7.1** above, unlisted company shares are not as attractive a form of consideration from a seller's perspective.

1.7.4   Prestige

The prestige attached to public company status (see **1.5.2**) can be enhanced further if the company lists successfully. In order to list, a company has to receive regulatory approval following considerable investigation into the company's suitability for listing. As listed companies have had their affairs scrutinised yet still obtained this approval, potential customers and suppliers can perceive listed companies to have greater financial standing than unlisted companies. This may help a listed company to negotiate better terms on which to conduct its business.

1.7.5   Profile

The press usually focuses its coverage on listed rather than unlisted companies, and listed companies will also be the subject of analysts' reports (produced by investment banks which rate a company's shares as a buy, sell or hold in order to assist investors with their investment decisions), so the profile of the company and its products will be raised. This can help create and sustain demand for, and therefore liquidity in, its shares.

1.7.6   Employee incentives

Listed companies can offer share ownership schemes to employees. While share ownership schemes are available to private companies, and are commonly used to motivate senior staff, listed companies have the additional advantage of being able to offer employees shares which have an identifiable value (as they are listed on a stock market). If employees own part of the company, the hope is that their commitment to the business will increase. The company should, therefore, benefit from being able to recruit and retain key employees.

1.7.7 Increased efficiency

Listed companies are strictly regulated (see **1.8.1** below). To comply with regulatory requirements, listed companies often have to improve their existing internal regulatory checks and controls. These improvements can, in turn, improve the operating efficiency of the company as a whole.

1.8 Potential disadvantages of listing

1.8.1 Increased regulatory regime

As **Table 1.1** above shows, even an unlisted public company's regulatory regime is much stricter than that of a private company, to reflect the fact that any public company can offer shares to the public at large. However, once a public company is listed, the regime becomes even stricter than that set out in **Table 1.1**. This is because, as noted in **1.7.1** above, the ready market in listed company shares means that, in practice, members of the public tend to invest in listed companies, rather than in unlisted public companies, and therefore it is the shareholders of listed companies who require the most protection. The increased level of regulation involves higher costs for the company, a greater administrative burden, and places restrictions on what the company and its directors can do and how they do it. So what extra rules, over and above those summarised in **Table 1.1**, are imposed on a listed company?

1.8.1.1 Prospectus Rules, Listing Rules, Disclosure Rules, Transparency Rules and Corporate Governance Rules

The Prospectus Rules, the Listing Rules, the Disclosure Rules, the Transparency Rules and the Corporate Governance Rules, introduced in response to EU legislation, apply to any listed company. Such companies must consider the Prospectus Rules and the Listing Rules when first seeking a listing and subsequently when raising equity finance, and the Prospectus Rules, the Listing Rules, the Disclosure Rules, the Transparency Rules and the Corporate Governance Rules for their continuing obligations while listed on the Stock Exchange. **Chapters 5** and **6** consider the listing process; **Chapter 17** examines equity finance. **Chapter 7** looks at continuing obligations in more detail.

1.8.1.2 Statutory provisions

Certain statutory provisions apply to listed companies only:

(a)   *The CA 2006.* For example, pursuant to s 420, the directors of a listed company are required to prepare a remuneration report on their pay, bonuses, share options and other related matters for inclusion in the company's Annual Report. It is a criminal offence for a director to fail to do so.

(b)   *The FSMA 2000.* The market abuse provisions in Pt VIII of the Financial Services and Markets Act 2000 (FSMA 2000) apply to shares listed on various markets, including the Main Market. **Chapter 10** explores the market abuse provisions in more detail.

(c)   *The CJA 1993.* Part V of the Criminal Justice Act 1993 (CJA 1993) provides that it is a criminal offence for a person who holds knowledge as an insider to deal, or encourage someone else to deal, in shares listed on a regulated market (which includes the Main Market). This is known as 'insider dealing'. **Chapter 11** considers insider dealing in more detail.

1.8.2 External forces

External forces beyond the control of a listed company, such as market conditions, rumour or developments in a certain market sector, can affect the company's value. Sometimes external forces can have a positive effect on share price, such as a cut in interest rates which may push up the share price of a heavily indebted company if its interest payments are reduced as a result;

but on other occasions external forces work to depress the share price (consider, for example, the effect of the increased restrictions on carbon emissions on the share price of companies in the power generation industry). The fact that the value of the company can be so affected by forces outside its control can be a source of frustration to management.

1.8.3   Increased shareholder power

A large number of outsiders will become shareholders in the company when it lists. An extreme example is BT plc, which has approximately 1.20 million shareholders. Not only will any equity held by management be diluted by the influx of these shareholders, but listed companies are required to obtain shareholder approval of certain transactions and decisions which, in unlisted companies, would fall to management alone. The inevitable consequence is a decrease in management's level of control over the company. Furthermore, the pressure to keep shareholders happy with, for example, continually increasing dividend payments can cause management to focus on short-term rather than long-term performance. There is also the risk that shareholders will sell to unwelcome buyers seeking to take over the company.

1.8.4   Loss of privacy

The listing process under the Prospectus Rules and the Listing Rules, and the continuing obligations of the Prospectus Rules, the Listing Rules, and the Disclosure and Transparency Rules (referred to at **1.8.1.1** above), the higher profile of the company (referred to at **1.7.5** above), and the greater accountability to shareholders (referred to at **1.8.3** above) mean that decisions of the management of a listed company are subject to much greater scrutiny than an unlisted company. If the company is underperforming, this loss of privacy can be very unwelcome.

1.8.5   Cost and time

The cost and time spent on the listing process, raising equity finance, complying with the continuing obligations of a listed company and maintaining good relations with investors can be onerous, and the company must decide before listing whether this time and money would be better directed towards running the business.

1.8.6   De-listing

These factors may equally apply to companies already trading on the Stock Exchange. Mainly because of the global financial crisis, a number of companies have decided to de-list from the Stock Exchange. In other words they are leaving the Stock Exchange and reverting to being unlisted public companies. A recent example is Culver Holdings plc which announced its intention to de-list in April 2009. Its board of directors argued that the costs and regulation of a listing outweighed the benefits, particularly as the recession had led to a depressed share price which it felt undervalued the company.

1.9   Achieving public company status

A company can achieve public company status in three ways:

(a)   registering as a public company on original incorporation;

(b)   registering as a private company on original incorporation then re-registering as a public company; or

(c)   registering as a Societas Europaea (SE), a European public limited company.

The procedures under (a) and (b) ensure that the resulting public company complies with the CA 2006 requirements relating to a public company's articles, name and share capital.

The SE must comply with EC Regulation 2157/2001 on the Statute for a European Company and related legislation.

1.9.1 Incorporation of a company

Under s 9 of the CA 2006, the following must be sent to the Registrar of Companies to incorporate any company, private or public:

(a) memorandum of association (in the form set out in Sch 1 to the Companies (Registration) Regulations 2008 (SI 2008/3014));

(b) an application for registration (Form INO1) containing:

  (i) a statement of share capital and initial shareholding (content requirements set out in s 10);

  (ii) a statement of the proposed first officers of the company (content requirements set out in s 12);

  (iii) a statement of the intended registered office;

  (iv) copy articles of association (unless the new model articles are adopted unamended); and

  (v) a statement of compliance that all requirements of the CA 2006 have been met (further requirements set out in s 13); and

(c) a registration fee.

1.9.2 Registration as a public company on original incorporation

In addition to sending the documents referred to at **1.9.1** above to the Registrar, there are the following extra requirements to register as a public company on original incorporation:

(a) *Articles.* The articles must be in a form suitable for a public company. Under s 20 of the CA 2006, on registration of a public company a default set of model articles will apply, save to the extent that they are excluded or modified. These public company model articles can be found in Sch 3 to the Companies (Model Articles) Regulations 2008 (SI 2008/3229).

(b) *Name.* The company name must end with 'public limited company' or the Welsh equivalent (CA 2006, s 58), or with the abbreviation 'plc' or its Welsh equivalent 'ccc' (CA 2006, s 58(2)).

(c) *Allotted share capital.* The allotted share capital of the company must be not less than the 'authorised minimum' (CA 2006, s 761(2)). Currently the authorised minimum is £50,000 (CA 2006, s 763). In addition, each share allotted must be paid up to at least one-quarter of its nominal value together with the whole of any premium on it (CA 2006, s 586).

1.9.2.1 Certificate of incorporation

If the company meets all the requirements set out at **1.9.1** and **1.9.2** above, then it will be able to obtain a certificate from the Registrar that the company has been registered as a public company on original incorporation. However, although this certificate of incorporation will prove that the public company exists (CA 2006, s 15(1)), and details of the company will now be recorded at Companies House, the public company needs to obtain one other certificate before it can commence business – a trading certificate.

1.9.2.2 Trading certificate

A company which has been registered as a public company on original incorporation must not begin business or exercise any borrowing powers until it has a trading certificate, issued under s 761 of the CA 2006, confirming that the company has met the *allotted* share capital requirements of the CA 2006 (see **1.9.2** above). The certificate is proof that the company can trade and borrow. To obtain this certificate, an application must be made (accompanied by a statement of compliance) to the Registrar under s 762 of the CA 2006.

The allotted share capital requirements are that the company must have allotted shares at least up to the value of the authorised minimum (CA 2006, s 761), which, as stated in **1.9.2** above, is currently £50,000 (s 763) or the euro equivalent – currently €57,100 (Companies (Authorised Minimum) Regulations 2009 (SI 2009/2425)). Each allotted share must be paid up to at least one-quarter of its nominal value together with the whole of any premium on it (CA 2006, s 568).

What does this mean in practice? Well, if 50,000 shares with a nominal value of £1 each are allotted at nominal value with no premium, the minimum consideration which must be paid to the company is one-quarter of the nominal value of each share, that is 0.25p per share, making a total minimum payment of £12,500 for 50,000 shares.

If, however, the shares are allotted for, say, £3 each, then each share has a premium (the amount by which the price exceeds the nominal value) of £2. This premium must be paid to the company together with a minimum of a quarter of the nominal value of each share, which is £2 plus 0.25p, that is £2.25 per share, making a total minimum payment of £112,500 for 50,000 shares.

1.9.3　Re-registration as a public company

A company which has registered as a private company on original incorporation (by complying with the requirements detailed at **1.9.1** above) can re-register as a public company pursuant to ss 90–96 of the CA 2006. The company must pass a special (or written) resolution, meet the specified conditions and submit an application in a prescribed form to the Registrar (s 90(1)).

1.9.3.1　Resolution

The special (or written) resolution must:

(a)　approve the re-registration of the company (CA 2006, s 90(1)(a));

(b)　alter the company's name so it is in a form suitable for a public company. Section 58(1) of the CA 2006 requires that the name must end with 'public limited company' or 'plc' (or the Welsh equivalent – s 58(2)); and

(c)　alter the articles so that they are in a form suitable for a public company. It is probable that the existing private company articles will require substantial amendment; it is often easier to adopt an entirely new set of articles rather than to amend the existing articles. If the company is re-registering as a public company as a preliminary step to listing in the immediate future, it may be appropriate to adopt a set of articles suitable not only for a public company but also for a public company which is listed. In this case the articles will probably disapply the model articles in their entirety and will be bespoke. These are known as long-form articles (as opposed to articles which apply the model articles either in its entirety or with some amendment, which are referred to as short-form articles).

1.9.3.2　Share capital requirements

The resolution deals with the requirements as to a public company's articles and name. What about the share capital requirements of a public company? This is dealt with by s 90(2). *At the time the shareholders pass the special resolution* (see **1.9.3.1**) the company must have satisfied certain conditions as to its share capital, namely that the company must have allotted shares at least up to the value of the authorised minimum (s 91(1)(a)), which is currently £50,000 (CA 2006, s 763) or the euro equivalent, currently €57,100, and that each allotted share must be paid up to at least one-quarter of its nominal value together with the whole of any premium on it (s 91(1)(b)).

(These requirements reflect the requirements which must be satisfied when a company originally incorporated as a public company applies for a trading certificate, set out at **1.9.2.2** above. A trading certificate therefore is not required for a private company which re-registers as a public company; the certificate of incorporation is all the company requires.)

Note that s 91(1)(c) and (d) provide some further requirements as to shares which have been allotted in consideration of an undertaking. Note also that some shares can be disregarded for the purposes of satisfying the share capital requirements (see s 91(2), (3) and (4)).

1.9.3.3   Application for re-registration

The special resolution must be delivered to the Registrar together with an application for re-registration on Form RR01, which has been signed by a director, the company secretary or a person authorised by the directors under s 270 or s 274 of the CA 2006. If the existing private company does not have a company secretary, one must be appointed and details included in the application. This is because under s 271 of the CA 2006, a public company must have a company secretary, whereas this is not a requirement for a private company. The application must be accompanied by the fee for re-registration (currently £20, together with £10 for any change of name; there is a same-day service available for an increased fee) and the following documents:

(a)   the revised articles (s 94(2)(b));

(b)   a balance sheet prepared not more than seven months before the application, containing an unqualified report by the company's auditors (s 94(2)(c), s 92(1)). If the company's accounting reference date is within this seven-month period, this requirement can be met by the end of year balance sheet; if not, then an interim balance sheet must be prepared and must be audited, which can prove time-consuming and expensive. The auditors must also provide a written statement regarding the level of the company's net assets (as revealed by the balance sheet) in comparison to the company's called-up share capital and undistributable reserves (s 92(1)(c));

(c)   a valuation report on any shares which have been allotted for non-cash consideration between the date of the balance sheet (referred to at (b) above) and the date the special resolution was passed (s 93(1)(a), s 93(2)(a)). This ensures that a private company seeking to re-register is brought into line with the general requirement under s 593 that public companies seeking to allot shares for non-cash consideration must have such consideration valued before allotting the shares; and

(d)   a statement of compliance in the prescribed form (s 90(1)(c)(ii)).

1.9.3.4   Certificate of re-registration on incorporation as a public company

If the Registrar is satisfied with the application, he will issue the company with a certificate of re-registration on incorporation as a public company (CA 2006, s 96). The private company becomes a public company, and the revised articles and change of name will take effect on the issue of this certificate, which is proof of public company status.

1.9.3.5   Trading disclosures

The Companies (Trading Disclosures) Regulations 2008 (SI 2008/495) made under s 82 of the CA 2006 set out the requirements for a company to identify itself, at certain locations (including any place of business), on certain documents (including letters and order forms) and on its websites. The company must state its registered name and certain other registation details depending on the circumstances. Breach of these requirements can result in a fine for the company and any officer of the company who is in default. The company must update its websites and order new signs and company documentation, which will reflect its new identity, in advance of re-registration to ensure that it can meet these requirements with effect from the date the certificate of incorporation on re-registration is issued.

1.9.4   Registration as a Societas Europaea

The SE, the European public company, can be formed in any EEA Member State in accordance with EC Regulation 2157/2001 on the Statute for a European Company. In the UK this is supplemented by the European Public Limited Liability Company Regulations 2004 (SI 2004/ 2326). An SE can be formed in one of five ways but only by existing companies.

Since their introduction in October 2004, very few SEs have been formed in the EEA (the German insurance giant, Allianz, being a notable exception in 2005). This is partly because an SE is not just subject to EU law but also to the domestic company law of the Member States in which it is registered and operates. Another reason is the need for the SE's operations to have been subject to the laws of at least two Member States before it became an SE. For example, an English public company can transform into an SE provided it has for two years had a subsidiary company governed by the laws of another Member State.

An SE registered in England would be subject to the rules of formation, dissolution, reporting and management under the EC Regulation but also to much of the law which applies to English plcs.

We will not consider the SE any further in this book, but it should be noted that proposals presented by the European Commission in 2008 for the creation of a European private company is likely to result in an increase in popularity in the SE should the European private company become a reality. The Swedish Presidency of the EU hopes to reach agreement on this by the end of 2009.

1.10   Achieving listed company status

When a company which does not have any shares listed on the stock market decides to list shares for the first time, the listing process is known as flotation or an IPO. There are different methods of flotation, the main methods for a company new to listing being by a public offer, placing or an introduction. Deciding to float is a serious step for a public company; the process is much more complex (and expensive) than that required for a private company to achieve public company status. **Chapters 4, 5** and **6** examine the complexities of flotation in more detail.

Chapter 2
The London Stock Exchange

2.1 What is the London Stock Exchange?

London Stock Exchange plc (the Stock Exchange) is a listed company. It has four principal areas of business:

(a)   a market place for trading in company securities;

(b)   a provider of trading platforms on which brokers can buy and sell securities;

(c)   a supplier of market information to the financial community, and

(d)   a market place for trading in equity derivatives.

The focus of this book is on the Stock Exchange's role as a market place for trading in a specific type of company securities – shares.

The Stock Exchange is at the centre of one of the world's three main financial centres – London, New York and Tokyo – with over 2,800 companies listed on it worth an estimated £3,200 billion, and is the most international stock market in the world, with companies from over 60 countries and territories, from the USA and China to Malawi, Bangladesh, Papua New Guinea and the Marshall Islands, listed on it. It also has one of the world's largest pools (and Europe's largest pool) of capital, with an estimated £2,500 billion available from UK-based sources, such as pension and insurance funds.

2.2 The market place

The Stock Exchange has two markets, the Main Market and AIM. Both markets serve two main functions. First, they enable companies to raise funds by issuing new shares to the public. This is referred to as the primary market for shares. Secondly, they allow those issued shares to be traded (bought and sold) by the public. This is referred to as the secondary market for shares. The Main Market has both a primary and secondary market, therefore, as does AIM.

2.3 The Main Market

The Main Market is the Stock Exchange's principal market for listed companies and is what the layman will think of as 'the stock market'. This is the market on which the shares of many household-name companies, such as Vodafone, BP, HSBC and Marks & Spencer (as well as a host of lesser-known companies), are listed. Within the Main Market, there are specific groupings for certain sectors: techMARK for innovative technology companies; techMARK mediscience for healthcare companies; and landMARK for UK regional companies. There are currently about 1,450 companies listed on the Main Market, which includes not only UK companies but also approximately 330 overseas companies.

The 100 largest companies make up the FTSE100, which is used as a measure for judging the market value of these Main Market companies at any one given time. It is this FTSE100 value which is used in the press to describe the current market, for example when a newspaper headline states, 'The FTSE100 has dropped below 4,000'. The 100 largest companies are selected every three months. The article below was written when the stock market was at its lowest during the recession and demonstrates how market values of companies plummeted on the Main Market.

The billionaire club that lost its lustre

Torrid two years leave UK's main stock market a shadow of its former self

David Teather

Being a member of the Britain's main stock market index, the FTSE 100, isn't what it used to be.

Two years ago, before the credit crunch began to wreak havoc on the world's financial markets, a company had to be worth at least £2.6bn to make the list of the nation's top 100 companies. The firm at the bottom of the list then was Cairn Energy.

Today, the smallest firm, before it was ejected in last night's quarterly change of FTSE constituents, was the private equity group 3i, which had a market capitalisation of £743m.

The changing make-up of the FTSE 100 provides a telling snapshot of what has happened to the wider economy and to British business in the past two tumultuous years. The value of the entire index has fallen dramatically as share prices have tumbled amid the worst global downturn in decades.

The total value of the FTSE has dropped from £1.55tn to £943bn. But the most glaring change has been the demolition of the banking sector, which two years ago was still regarded by many, including the government, as the champion of modern Britain. Few, if any, could have predicted what followed.

Bank rout

There were nine banks in the FTSE 100 in March 2007, worth £325bn. The banks accounted for almost 21% of the value of the FTSE and were easily the largest sector.

Since then, Bradford & Bingley and Northern Rock have been fully nationalised, HBOS has been bought by Lloyds in haste - regretted at leisure - and Alliance & Leicester has been acquired for a knock-down price by Santander of Spain, one of the few banks to have emerged from the credit crunch relatively unscathed. Lloyds and Royal Bank of Scotland are still listed, but both are majority-owned by the taxpayer. Today the banks account for only 8.5% of the FTSE 100 and are worth a combined £85.5bn.

RBS, worth £66.9bn two years ago, is now worth £8.3bn; Barclays,

despite avoiding a government bailout, has seen its value shrink from £47.5bn to £5.6bn; and even HSBC, which had been regarded as the steadiest of the British banks before it announced plans for a record-breaking rights issue, has more than halved in value, from £105bn to £47.9bn.

The insurance sector has also taken a battering, with the value of the sector dropping by almost two-thirds, from £76bn to £28.4bn.

Instead, more than one-third of the value of the FTSE is accounted for by what Robert Parkes, equity strategist at HSBC, calls the resources block - oil and gas and mining.

"Clearly the reduction in the financial weighting is the obvious point," he said. "That is true of most indices around the world, although the FTSE did have a higher financial weight than most. The FTSE is now very exposed to the resources block and, in turn, to the health of the global economy."

BG, the oil and gas exploration and pipeline group formed from the old British Gas, is one of the rare companies to increase in value, from £23.8bn to £33.6bn.

Resilience

The blue-chip index is far less a reflection of the British economy than it used to be. Parkes said that about 60% of the revenue booked by FTSE 100 companies was now generated overseas. "The link between the FTSE and the domestic economy is a very loose one and that has got to be a very good thing in the current environment."

The resilience of the oil and mining sectors may at first glance appear surprising given the sharp falls in oil and commodity prices from their peaks as demand, particularly from emerging economies, has slowed. In oil especially, the relative robustness is partly due to the strength of the big companies' balance sheets, comparably low debt and the widely held view that the likes of BP and Shell will maintain their dividends while firms in other sectors cut theirs.

"If you are thinking about where to put your money, you can see a revenue stream with oil and mining, there will always be a demand," said Joshua Raymond, a market strategist at IG Index. "With the banks it is more about capital strength, over-leveraging and toxic debts. Oil is not in the strictest sense of the word a defensive stock, but it is compared to the other heavy-weighted stocks."

Other "defensive" sectors less sensitive to recession, such as healthcare and utilities, are also worth a bigger percentage of the FTSE than two years ago.

Disappeared

In the intervening two years, it is not just big banking names that have disappeared from the top flight.

ITV, struggling to cope with the worst advertising downturn in memory along with continuing structural changes in media, fell out of the FTSE in September and matters have only got worse since then. Last week it announced a £2.7bn loss for 2008.

A number of once world-beating names in British business have also dropped off the list as they were acquired by overseas firms - a reminder of the frenzy of deals at the height of the market froth. They grabbed headlines and angered politicians and trade unions but have since dried up as the funding to do deals has all but disappeared.

Corus, the former British Steel, was bought by Tata of India, the tobacco group Gallaher was acquired by Japan Tobacco, Scottish Power bought by Iberdola and ICI by Akzo Nobel.

The tables also neatly tell another story of the past two years: the rise and fall of private equity. A fixture of the FTSE back in 2007 was the high street chemist Alliance Boots. The retailer was taken out in the largest private equity deal ever seen in Europe, in June 2007, as the buccaneers of private equity became increasingly brazen. As 3i - the only quoted private equity group in the UK - slips from view, so too have the industry's ambitions.

Source: *The Guardian*, 11 March 2009

2.4 AIM

The AIM is the Stock Exchange's alternative investment market. It is a global market for smaller and growing companies. The AIM is a separate market from the Main Market and, while some companies may choose to move from AIM onto the Main Market at some point (such as Domino Pizza Group Ltd in May 2008), there is no obligation to do so. In fact, lately, the trend has been for Main Market companies to move to AIM, where the regulatory burden is lower than on the Main Market, or to leave it altogether to avoid the regulatory burden and costs.

There are currently more than 1,350 companies listed on AIM (such as Coffee Republic, Milwall FC and Majestic Wine), which includes over 250 overseas companies. The AIM has been a rapidly expanding market, but over the last couple of years the number of new admissions has slumped as a result of the global recession.

As stated at **1.3** above, the focus of this book is on companies which are listed on the Main Market. However, **Chapter 24** provides a brief overview of the regulation of AIM companies, compares AIM with the Main Market, and considers the advantages and disadvantages of joining AIM.

2.5 Dealing on the markets

Dealing (ie, buying and selling shares) is not an area in which a corporate lawyer typically will have much involvement. The focus of the lawyer's role is to help to bring a client company to the market successfully, and then ensure that the company is advised of the regulatory regime it must follow in order to maintain its listing. However, the corporate lawyer's clients may well have an in-depth knowledge of dealing and the markets, and those clients may be unsettled if the lawyer helping to bring the company to market has no comprehension of how that market works. The following, therefore, is intended to provide some basic information on the mechanics of dealing.

There are two elements to buying and selling shares. The first is usually referred to as 'trading', and this is the process by which a seller is matched with a buyer. The second element is 'settlement', which is the process of paying the purchase price and transferring the shares.

2.5.1 Member firms

Member firms carry out most of the trading on the Stock Exchange's markets. They are investment firms (banks, stockbrokers and fund managers) which trade either on behalf of clients, or on behalf of their firms. Examples of current member firms are Barclays Bank plc, Citigroup Global Markets, Crédit Suisse Securities, Deutsche Bank AG, Merrill Lynch International and UBS.

2.5.2 Mechanics of trading

The Stock Exchange has fully automated trading systems. This means that any pictures you may see of people shouting and waving on a trading floor are either very out-of-date (this was discontinued in London in 1986 after the 'Big Bang'), or show one of the stock exchanges abroad (eg NYSE) which retains that system.

The Stock Exchange has devised various electronic systems for trading shares. These apply regardless of whether the shares are held in paper form (with a share certificate) or electronically (via CREST, see **2.5.3.1**). For the large Main Market-listed companies, including those on the FTSE 100 index, and for the most highly traded AIM-quoted companies, there is the Stock Exchange Electronic Trading Service (SETS), which is known as the order book. This electronic system matches 'buy' and 'sell' orders for the same shares and executes the trade automatically. A further system, SETSqx, supports the trading of shares in companies with turnover which is insufficient for the SETS system (such as the least liquid Main Market companies and most AIM companies). Finally, there is the Stock Exchange Automated Quotations (SEAQ) system for AIM securities not traded on SETS or SETSqx. With this system certain member firms act as competing 'market makers' in relation to certain shares. They will set the 'buy' and 'sell' prices for these shares, using current news about the company, the market sector and the strength of demand for shares as a guide. Member firms acting as 'brokers' will then buy and sell the shares when they think the price set by the market makers is right.

On average, over 600,000 trades a day are executed on the Stock Exchange's markets.

2.5.3   Settlement

Once a share has been traded on the market, it needs to be transferred from the seller to the buyer, and the consideration monies need to be transferred from the buyer to the seller. This process is known as 'settlement'. There is a risk during the time between the trade being struck and settlement being made that the transaction will fail (for example, if one of the parties is declared bankrupt).

The settlement system discussed in **2.5.3.1** covers shares held in uncertificated form only, as these represent the vast majority of shares traded on the Stock Exchange.

2.5.3.1   CREST

CREST was introduced in 1996 and is a paperless (that is, the shares are held in electronic form and no share certificates exist, ie they are uncertificated) share settlement system through which trades on the Stock Exchange's markets can be settled. The system has legal backing under the Uncertificated Securities Regulations 2001 (SI 2001/3755). Euroclear UK and Ireland Limited operates this system. As the system is electronic and paperless, settlement can be made swiftly (within three business days of any trade), so the risk period between trade and settlement is reduced. Approximately 85% of the UK share market's value is voluntarily traded through CREST. There are various options for a shareholder wishing to hold shares through CREST.

CREST member

A CREST member must be linked up to CREST by computer network, so typically it is the member firms of the Stock Exchange (see **2.5.1** above) who have this type of membership. CREST members hold shares as nominees for individual clients (institutional or private investors), so the name of the CREST member, rather than the client, will be entered into the company's register of members as legal owner. The client will be the beneficial owner of the shares.

Each CREST member has an identification number for itself ('participant ID') and at least one other identification number for specific accounts it holds, such as an account for shares beneficially held on behalf of a specific institution ('member account ID').

CREST 'sponsored member'

This type of membership is designed to attract private investors (institutions and individuals). The benefit to the private investor is that its name will appear on the company's register of members (in contrast to the position if it holds shares through a CREST member, where the CREST member's name will feature on the register). Sponsored members who are individuals are known as 'personal members' to distinguish them from sponsored members which are corporate bodies. However, one drawback is that the CREST personal member does not have the required computer link-up to CREST. A CREST sponsor, who will be a CREST member, will provide this for the sponsored member, and will charge for the service.

Nominee shareholder

Other investors who are not CREST members or sponsored members, who hold their shares in electronic form, will hold them as nominees. This means that the shareholder will be the beneficial owner of their shares rather than the legal owner, and the name of the nominee (usually a CREST member) will appear on the share register.

The corporate lawyer and CREST

In practice, the impact of CREST for the corporate lawyer is not dramatic. For example it may involve ensuring that some standard wording is drafted into certain documents, such as how CREST shareholders can accept an offer and receive consideration (in a takeover) or take up shares (when raising equity finance), or being aware of CREST shareholders when considering the mechanics of an AGM. Some standard wording is available on the Euroclear website. The lawyer should be aware that Stamp Duty Reserve Tax is collected on paperless share transactions such as the transfer of shares within CREST. CREST itself, however, is responsible for collecting this tax.

2.6   Investors in the markets

2.6.1   Members of the public

Members of the public have significant involvement with the Stock Exchange. They can invest directly in shares listed on the Main Market or on AIM, either in the primary market (by subscribing for new shares issued by a company on flotation) or in the secondary market (by buying or selling shares which are already in issue). They can also invest indirectly (because, for example, their pensions, other savings schemes or employment incentive schemes are tied up in the Stock Exchange's markets). Obviously, the aim of the member of the public who invests is to realise a healthy profit on the sale of the investment but, as has been seen all too clearly in the current recession, what is intended and what is achieved can be very different.

2.6.2   Institutional investors

Institutional investors (also known as institutional shareholders), such as pension funds and investment funds, have sizeable funds available for investment. The amount they have available to invest means that institutional investors have considerable influence over the companies in which they invest. By way of example, BT plc has approximately 22,800 institutional investors who own around 87% of its issued share capital. One hundred and eighty of them hold over 5 million shares each. By contrast, the remaining 1.14 million plus shareholders (mainly members of the public) own 13%.

The main institutional investors have formed their own representative bodies called Investment Protection Committees (IPCs). Well known IPCs include the Association of British Insurers (ABI) and the National Association of Pension Funds (NAPF). The IPCs have also joined together to form one representative body, the Institutional Shareholders' Committee (ISC). The IPCs issue guidelines as to how members should exercise their shareholder vote. While these guidelines do not have the force of law, listed companies do generally treat them as binding, such is the influence of the institutional shareholders.

Chapter 14 looks at some of these guidelines in more detail. **Chapter 8** also considers the role of institutional investors in relation to corporate governance.

2.7   Regulation of the Stock Exchange

The FSMA 2000 prohibits any person from carrying on any regulated activity unless that person is either authorised or exempt. This is known as the general prohibition (see **9.4**). The Financial Services Authority (FSA) has granted a recognition order to the Stock Exchange under s 290 of the FSMA 2000. This means that the Stock Exchange is a 'recognised investment exchange', and therefore, under s 285 of the 2000 Act, is exempt from the general prohibition. To remain a recognised investment exchange, the Stock Exchange must continue to satisfy various requirements drafted pursuant to s 286 of the FSMA 2000, including the Financial Services and Markets Act 2000 (Recognition Requirements for Investment Exchanges and Clearing Houses) Regulations 2001 (SI 2001/995), as amended, and the FSA Handbook of Rules and Guidance. These requirements include that the Stock Exchange must:

(a)   ensure that business conducted by means of its facilities is conducted in an orderly manner and so as to afford proper protection to investors;

(b)   make arrangements for the provision of pre-trade and post-trade information about share trading;

(c)   make clear and transparent rules concerning the admission of securities to trading on its financial markets; and

(d)   be able to promote and maintain high standards of integrity and fair dealing in the carrying on of regulated activities by persons using facilities provided by the Stock Exchange.

2.8   The role of the Stock Exchange in the flotation process

The Stock Exchange used to have responsibility for the official listing of securities in the UK. This role was transferred to the FSA on 1 May 2000. **Chapter 3** considers this role more closely; however the effect of the transfer of this role is that while the Stock Exchange continues to have responsibility for admitting shares to trading on its markets, the FSA has responsibility for overseeing the listing process. Any company seeking to be a listed company (as defined in **1.3** above) must seek to have its shares:

(a)   admitted to *listing* on the Official List (for which it must liaise with the FSA); and

(b)   admitted to *trading* on the Main Market (for which it must liaise with the Stock Exchange).

Chapter 5 considers this process in more detail.

2.9   Admission and Disclosure Standards

The Stock Exchange has its own set of rules for companies joining the Main Market (they do not apply to companies joining AIM). These rules are called the Admission and Disclosure Standards, and they set out the requirements for companies seeking admission to trading, as well as the continuing obligations for companies already admitted to trading. Extracts from the Admission and Disclosure Standards as at 1 October 2009 are reproduced in **Appendix 1**. The full set of Standards is available on the Stock Exchange's website.

2.10   Future developments

2.10.1   Trading

Under ss 783 to 790 of the CA 2006, there is the power to make regulations to enable shares to be owned or transferred without written documentation. This could even be made compulsory. At the time of writing, no such regulations have been proposed by BIS. Replacing paper share certificates and stock transfer forms with an electronic system is known as 'dematerialisation'.

The Institute of Chartered Secretaries and Administrators' (ICSA) Dematerialisation Reference Group conducted a consultation process on dematerialisation for all share transactions in listed UK companies in 2006, details of which are available on the ICSA website. In 2004 the European Securities Forum, a representative body of the securities industry (now known as the SIFMA European Securities Services Forum), also advocated compulsory dematerialisation of all UK securities. At the time of writing the latest indication of when compulsory dematerialisation might be implemented came in a letter from HM Treasury to ICSA. It mentioned a target date of 2012.

Use of the CREST name is under review by Euroclear UK & Ireland, but it is expected to be maintained at least until 2010.

Chapter 3
The Financial Services Authority

3.1 Background

The regulatory framework governing the listing of companies on the Stock Exchange in the UK has its basis in EU law. In 1999 the European Commission adopted a Financial Services Action Plan (FSAP), with the aims of creating a single market in financial services across all Member States of the EU by the end of 2005 and strengthening regulatory supervision. Over 40 measures have been implemented to achieve the FSAP, mostly in the form of directives (requiring implementing national legislation) and regulations (not requiring further national legislation).

The original regime regulating the listing of companies was established by the Consolidated Admissions and Reporting Directive (CARD) in 2001. This has been radically overhauled by three more recent directives, namely the Prospectus Directive, the Market Abuse Directive (deliciously abbreviated to MAD) and the Transparency Directive. A fourth directive, the Markets in Financial Instruments Directive (MiFID), came into force on 1 November 2007. Although important in practice, it is very technical in its subject matter and is of only limited relevance to this book.

As a consequence of the implementation of the Prospectus Directive and MAD in the UK, coupled with the results of a review by the FSA, substantial changes were made to the UK's listing regime on 1 July 2005. Three new sourcebooks were introduced which together form part of the FSA's Handbook, 'Listing, Prospectus and Disclosure'. The Transparency Directive came into force in the UK on 20 January 2007. In order to implement its provisions, new Transparency Rules were introduced by the FSA. The Disclosure Rules were renamed the Disclosure and Transparency Rules (DTRs) as a result.

In June 2008 amendments were made to the FSA Handbook (Chapter 9 of the Listing Rules and the DTRs) to implement the Statutory Audit Directive and the Company Reporting Directive and to introduce the Corporate Governance Rules (see **3.5.3** below).

The Prospectus Rules, Listing Rules, Disclosure Rules, Transparency Rules and Corporate Governance Rules are collectively referred to as the 'Part 6 Rules' by s 73A of the FSMA 2000.

3.2 The competent authority for listing in the UK

The Directives referred to at **3.1** required each Member State to nominate an authority which is competent (the 'competent authority') to undertake the tasks which are set out in the Directives. Section 72(1) of the FSMA 2000 nominates the FSA as the competent authority for listing in the UK. This is not the FSA's only role. In fact, it regulates the entire financial services industry in the UK. The FSA has created a separate division, therefore, to perform the specific role of competent authority for listing in the UK, and this is called the UK Listing Authority (UKLA).

Neither the FSMA 2000 nor the Listing Rules refer to the term 'UK Listing Authority' or 'UKLA'; they both refer to the FSA as the competent authority for listing. Note, however, that in practice the FSA does still operate through its UKLA division in relation to all things to do with listing, and the FSA website has a separate section for UKLA matters. The FSA Handbook online also describes the Listing Rules as the UKLA listing rules on its contents page (similarly, it adds 'UKLA' for the Prospectus Rules and DTRs). In this book, to avoid confusion, the UKLA is not referred to when describing these rules.

3.3   What does the FSA (in its capacity as the UKLA) do?

The FSA (in its capacity as the UKLA) has responsibility for the official listing of securities under Pt VI of the FSMA 2000. This includes:

(a)   maintaining the Official List (s 74(1));

(b)   drafting the Prospectus Rules, the Listing Rules, the Disclosure Rules, the Transparency Rules and the Corporate Governance Rules (s 73A);

(c)   determining applications for admission to listing, which includes reviewing the documentation which a company must produce to have its shares listed (s 75);

(d)   ensuring that listed companies comply with their continuing obligations under the Listing Rules, the Disclosure Rules, the Transparency Rules, the Corporate Governance Rules and the Prospectus Rules, which includes approving documentation prepared by listed companies, such as circulars; and

(e)   having the power to sanction any listed company which does not comply with the Prospectus Rules, the Listing Rules, the Disclosure Rules, the Transparency Rules and the Corporate Governance Rules (or any director of such a company).

Chapter 5 looks at the listing process in more detail and considers how the FSA is involved in that process in practice.

3.4   Relationship between the FSA and the Stock Exchange

As stated at **2.8** above, the FSA and the Stock Exchange have different roles in the flotation process. The FSA oversees the admission of shares to *listing* and the Stock Exchange oversees the admission of shares to *trading*. A listed company needs to have its shares admitted both to listing and to trading. **Chapters 4, 5** and **6** consider how a company can do this.

3.5   Prospectus, Listing, Disclosure, Transparency and Corporate Governance Rules

As referred to at **3.3**, the FSA has responsibility for five sets of rules, discussed at **3.5.1** to **3.5.3** below.

References to the Prospectus Rules and Listing Rules are prefaced with 'PR' and 'LR', and the Disclosure, Transparency and Corporate Governance Rules with 'DTR'. The paragraph number is suffixed with 'R' to indicate if this is a rule, or 'G' to indicate if this is guidance.

3.5.1   The Prospectus Rules

The Prospectus Rules (together with the PD Regulation and the Prospectus Regulations 2005 – see **3.5.1.1** and **3.5.1.2**) implement the Prospectus Directive in the UK. They contain provisions about the content of, and approval process for, a marketing document called a prospectus.

These Rules apply to companies:

(a)   seeking to *offer* shares *to the public in the UK*. This includes offers of shares by companies seeking admission to AIM or the Main Market for the first time, or which are already admitted; and/or

(b)   seeking to *admit* shares to *trading on a regulated market in the UK* (which includes the Main Market but not AIM) (even where there is no offer to the public referred to at (a) above).

The fact that the Prospectus Rules apply both to companies which are quoted on AIM and companies listed on the Main Market is a break with the tradition of having separate regulatory regimes for AIM companies and Main Market companies. The focus of this book, however, remains with listed companies as defined at **1.3** above.

The Prospectus Directive was drafted as a 'maximum harmonisation' measure, meaning that the UK was unable to set higher standards (known as 'super-equivalent' measures) for the issues covered by the Directive.

While the Directive covers the requirements relating to the content of, and approval process for, a prospectus, it does not cover the issue of eligibility of a company for listing. The UK therefore has retained revised super-equivalent eligibility criteria from the former listing regime in the new Listing Rules (see **3.5.2** below). **Chapters 5** and **6** consider the Prospectus Rules in more detail.

3.5.1.1   The Prospectus Directive Regulation (PD Regulation)

The Prospectus Directive took the form of a framework directive. Much of the detail required for implementation is contained in an EC Regulation, the PD Regulation. Its articles and annexes specify in detail the form and content requirements of a prospectus. Helpfully for the practitioner, the Prospectus Rules, which, as explained above, implement the Prospectus Directive in the UK, replicate the contents of the Regulation (the articles are set out at PR 2.3.1EU and the annexes at Appendix 3). This means that the lawyer needs to be aware of the existence of the PD Regulation (it is referred to in the Prospectus Rules), but he will have all he requires in the Prospectus Rules.

3.5.1.2   The Prospectus Regulations 2005

The Prospectus Regulations (SI 2005/1433) are UK legislation which effected necessary changes to existing UK legislation in order to implement the Prospectus Directive. In particular, they amended parts of the FSMA 2000, the CA 1989 and the Companies (Audit, Investigations and Community Enterprise) Act 2004, and revoked the Public Offers of Securities Regulations 1995 and the Financial Services and Markets Act 2000 (Offers of Securities) Order 2001 (SI 2001/2958).

3.5.2   The Listing Rules

The Listing Rules contain the following key provisions:

(a)   six Listing Principles (see **3.5.2.1** below);

(b)   the eligibility criteria for listing;

(c)   the listing application process;

(d)   rules regarding sponsors;

(e)   the cancellation and suspension of listing; and

(f)   the continuing obligations of a listed company (supplemented by some continuing obligations in the DTRs and one continuing obligation in the Prospectus Rules).

The Listing Rules apply to shares which trade on a regulated market, so they will apply to shares which trade on the Main Market but *not* to shares which trade on AIM. The Listing

Rules also apply to companies which are the subject of an application for listing but whose shares are not yet trading on a regulated market.

The Listing Rules are divided into 19 chapters. Chapters 1 to 5 apply to all securities; Chapters 6 to 16 apply to equity securities; and Chapters 17 to 19 apply to debt securities, depositary receipts and derivatives respectively (and so are not referred to again in this book).

3.5.2.1 The Listing Principles

One of the fundamental changes implemented on 1 July 2005 was the introduction to the Listing Rules of six Listing Principles. The Principles, set out at 7.2.1R of the Listing Rules, are as follows:

Principle 1   A listed company must take reasonable steps to enable its directors to understand their responsibilities and obligations as directors.

Principle 2   A listed company must take reasonable steps to establish and maintain adequate procedures, systems and controls to enable it to comply with its obligations.

Principle 3   A listed company must act with integrity towards holders and potential holders of its listed equity securities.

Principle 4   A listed company must communicate information to holders and potential holders of its listed equity securities in such a way as to avoid the creation or continuation of a false market in such listed equity securities.

Principle 5   A listed company must ensure that it treats all holders of the same class of its listed equity securities that are in the same position equally in respect of the rights attaching to such listed equity securities.

Principle 6   A listed company must deal with the FSA in an open and co-operative manner.

The Principles are intended to ensure adherence to the spirit as well as the letter of the Listing Rules, and it is intended that they will work much like the general principles of the City Code (see **20.5.5** below). The Listing Rules must be interpreted in line with the Listing Principles. The FSA has provided guidance on the application of the Principles (most recently in issue 22 of the FSA's newsletter, *List!*, available in the UKLA section of the FSA's website) and has stated that it does not intend that they will apply any different standards to companies than are expected under the Listing Rules. The Principles are, however, enforceable like any other Listing Rule, and breach can lead to sanction by the FSA (see **3.6** below). In issue 22 of *List!*, the FSA confirmed that it is prepared to take enforcement action on the basis of breach of the Listing Principles alone.

3.5.3 The Disclosure, Transparency and Corporate Governance Rules

These three sets of rules are contained in one FSA sourcebook, the Disclosure and Transparency Rules (DTRs). DTRs 1–3 contain the Disclosure Rules and DTRs 1A and 4–6 set out the Transparency Rules. DTRs 1B, 4 and 7 contain the Corporate Governance Rules.

The Disclosure Rules (together with amendments made to the FSMA 2000) implement the Market Abuse Directive in the UK and seek to prevent insider dealing and market manipulation.

These Rules contain rules and guidance about a listed company's continuing obligation to:

(a)   inform the market about new developments and its financial condition and performance (that is, to disclose 'inside information'); and

(b)   disclose transactions in shares by directors and senior executives and persons connected to them.

They are examined in detail in **Chapter 7**. The Code of Market Conduct (see **10.1.2**) and the Model Code (see **7.6**) should also be considered in addition to the Disclosure Rules and the FSMA 2000.

The Transparency Rules (together with amendments made to the FSMA 2000) implement the Transparency Directive in the UK. They seek principally to improve investors' access to information about companies trading on the UK financial markets, to enable them to invest more efficiently.

The Transparency Rules require more financial information to be revealed publicly about companies listed on the Stock Exchange more regularly than before. They also require the disclosure of significant shareholdings in listed companies, to ensure that these companies are aware of who is building up a significant stake in them, which may be a precursor to a takeover. They are considered in greater detail in **Chapters 7** and **15**.

As with the Listing Rules, DTRs 1–4 and 6–7 apply to companies whose shares trade on a regulated market, so they will apply to companies whose shares trade on the Main Market but *not* to companies which are quoted on AIM. Note, however, that DTR 5 applies to both types of company. The Disclosure Rules also apply to companies which are the subject of an application for trading but whose shares are not yet trading on a regulated market.

The Corporate Governance Rules came into force on 29 June 2008 and were made under s 89(O) of the FSMA 2000. The Rules implement part of the Statutory Audit Directive and the Company Reporting Directive in the UK. Among other provisions, the Statutory Audit Directive requires listed companies to establish an audit committee in compliance with the Directive's terms. Rules relating to the establishment of an audit committee were already in existence for listed companies in the UK under the Combined Code on Corporate Governance but on a non-statutory basis (see **8.3**). The Statutory Directive requires harmonisation of the rules across the EU and, in the UK, for the existing rules to be put on a statutory basis. The Company Reporting Directive, in order to help promote credible company financial reporting and to prevent financial malpractice, requires listed companies to include a corporate governance statement in their annual reports. The Corporate Governance Rules are considered in greater detail in **Chapters 7** and **8**.

3.6 Sanctions for breach of the Part 6 Rules

The FSA can impose a variety of sanctions under powers granted by the FSMA 2000, depending on the particular set of Part 6 Rules breached. The sanctions may apply to securities other than just shares, such as debt securities, but as these are beyond the scope of this textbook they are not discussed. If necessary, reference should be made to the FSMA 2000 and the relevant definitions.

For breaches of *any of the Part 6 Rules* (Listing Rules, Prospectus Rules, Disclosure Rules, Transparency Rules and Corporate Governance Rules) the FSA can:

(a)   privately or publicly censure:

    (i)   the listed company (FSMA 2000, s 91(3)), and/or

    (ii)   a director or former director of the listed company knowingly concerned in the breach (FSMA 2000, s 91(3)).

(b)   impose an unlimited fine on:

    (i)   the listed company (FSMA 2000, s 91(1), (1ZA), (1A) and (1B)), and/or

    (ii)   a director or former director of the listed company knowingly concerned in the breach (FSMA 2000, s 91(2)).

In addition, for a breach of the *Listing Rules only* the FSA can:

(a)   suspend the *listing* on the Official List of a listed company's shares (FSMA 2000, s 77(2) and LR 5.1.1R and LR 5.1.2G);

(b)   cancel the *listing* on the Official List of a listed company's shares (FSMA 2000, s 77(1) and LR 5.2.1G);

(c)   publicly censure the sponsor for a breach of its responsibilities (FSMA 2000, s 89(1) and LR 8.7.19R).

Further, for a breach of the *Prospectus Rules only* the FSA can:

(a)   suspend or require the withdrawal of the offer of shares to the public (FSMA 2000, s 87K(2) and (3));

(b)   suspend *trading* or prohibit *trading* in the listed company's shares (FSMA 2000, s 87L).

In addition, for a breach of the *Disclosure Rules only* the FSA can:

(a)   privately or publicly censure (FSMA 2000, s 91(3) and DTR 1.5.3(1)R):

    (i)   Persons Discharging Managerial Responsibility (PDMRs) as defined in s 96B of the FSMA 2000; and/or

    (ii)   a connected person of a PDMR as defined in s 96B of the Act (DTR 1.5.3(1)R);

(b)   impose an unlimited fine on (FSMA 2000, s 91(1ZA) and DTR 1.5.3(2)R):

    (i)   PDMRs, and/or

    (ii)   a connected person of a PDMR;

(c)   suspend *trading* in the listed company's shares (FSMA 2000, s 96C and DTR1.4.1(R)).

In addition, for a breach of the *Transparency Rules only* the FSA can suspend or prohibit the *trading* on the Main Market of a listed company's shares (FSMA 2000, s 89L).

In addition, for a breach of the *Corporate Governance Rules only*, the FSA can suspend or prohibit the *trading* on the Main Market of a listed company's shares (FSMA 2000, s 87L).

Breaches of the Part 6 Rules may also give rise to the civil liability set out at **6.7.1** and the criminal liability set out at **6.7.2**.

The FSA has prepared an Enforcement Guide which can be found in the Regulatory Guides section of the FSA Handbook on the FSA's website. It provides useful guidance on the approach the FSA will take regarding enforcement of breaches of the Part 6 (and other) Rules.

3.7 Future developments

There are currently reviews under way of some of the fundamental rules constituting the regulatory framework for listed companies and for the enforcement of penalties for breaches of the rules.

3.7.1 Prospectus Directive review

As part of its Action Programme for Reducing Administrative Burdens launched in 2007 the European Commission published a consultation document on proposals to simplify and improve the application of the Prospectus Directive in 2009 with the aim of reducing unnecessary burdens and costs on companies and their intermediaries. Although broadly happy with the implementation of the Directive, the EC is concerned that there may be excessive administrative burdens affecting the operation of the prospectus regime which need to be addressed.

One of the stated aims of the Swedish Presidency running until the end of December 2009 is to advance the review of the Prospectus Directive.

3.7.2 Listing Rules review

The FSA has completed a consultation into amendments to the listing regime in the UK in order to maintain the UK's competitiveness for company listings in the global market. It will introduce on 6 October 2009 a dual listing system for UK companies. Companies can either seek a Primary Listing, which will comply with the highest level of regulation as currently, or a new Secondary Listing, which will comply with the minimum requirements of the EU's listing regime, currently only available to overseas companies. As mentioned at **3.5.1** above, the UK introduced so-called 'super-equivalent' provisions which exceeded the requirements of the EU legislation. The FSA has also announced that Primary Listings will be replaced by Premium Listings and Secondary Listings will be replaced by Standard Listings with effect from 6 April 2010.

3.7.3 Market Abuse Directive review

The European Commission is conducting a review of MAD to reduce the burdens imposed on business and to make it operate more effectively in light of perceived deficiencies which came to light during the global financial crisis. Following a consultation earlier in the year, Commission proposals are expected in October 2009.

3.7.4 Review of the enforcement of financial penalties

The FSA is consulting on changes to its policy on determining the level of financial penalties that it can impose in enforcement cases. This will include penalties imposed for breaches of the Part 6 Rules and for market abuse. The proposed changes seek to increase transparency, lead to greater consistency and, perhaps most importantly of all, will lead to an increase in the level of fines imposed. The new rules are expected to take effect in the first quarter of 2010.

Chapter 4
Initial Public Offerings: Preparation

4.1 What is an Initial Public Offering?

An Initial Public Offering (IPO), also known as a flotation, is the process by which a company becomes a listed company (for our purposes as defined at **1.3** above). The terms 'IPO' and 'flotation' are used interchangeably. As **Chapters 2** and **3** established, any company seeking to become such a listed company must undergo a parallel admission procedure to have its shares:

(a) admitted to *listing* on the Official List (for which it must liaise with the FSA and comply with the Prospectus Rules and the Listing Rules); and

(b) admitted to *trading* on the Main Market (for which it must liaise with the Stock Exchange and comply with the Admission and Disclosure Standards).

While lawyers and other advisers need to be aware of the distinction between admission to listing and admission to trading, in practice the FSA and the Stock Exchange co-operate to ensure that the process is seamless. In fact, the layman would probably not be aware that, technically, IPO involves two admission procedures. **Chapter 5** considers the actual IPO process in more detail. This chapter looks at the preparatory steps a company should take in the year (or two) preceding the IPO.

4.2 Appointing a team of advisers

An IPO is a very complex transaction and good corporate advisers are vital to a successful float. In the year before the IPO the company must consider carefully who to appoint as its advisers. Usually it will seek preliminary advice on this matter from its current advisers (typically its lawyers and accountants). These advisers may not have the necessary expertise to advise in relation to the IPO itself, but they should be able to recommend suitable advisers who can provide guidance to the company. The company will sign engagement letters with some of the key advisers to govern the terms and conditions of their appointment specifically in relation to the IPO.

Any company seeking to float requires professional advice in relation to a wide range of issues. Lawyers advising on the legal aspects of the IPO form just part of a considerably larger team of advisers, who each take responsibility for various aspects of the float. Lawyers advising on an IPO cannot expect to work in isolation. They need excellent communication and project management skills. They also need a good understanding of the roles and responsibilities of the rest of the team. So who does what?

4.2.1 The company and the directors

As set out in **Chapter 6** below, the main marketing document for a float is the prospectus, and this must contain a substantial amount of information about the company. It is the directors who have primary responsibility for the accuracy of this information. While the directors cannot delegate this responsibility, practically they cannot supply all the information required in the time provided. Instead they enlist the help of the company secretary and key managers to locate, and provide to the advisers drafting the prospectus, accurate information about the company. Obviously this diverts many of the company's senior employees and directors from their usual role of day-to-day management and ensuring that the company is profitable. Companies need to be made aware of this hidden cost and distraction from their usual roles.

Hidden cost to preparing prospectus

4.2.2   Sponsor

Listing Rule 8.2.1R provides that any company applying for a listing which requires the publication of a prospectus must have a sponsor (see **4.3.1.1** below). Chapter 8 of the Listing Rules contains the rules relating to the sponsor. Listing Rule 8.3 sets out the responsibilities and principles for a sponsor, including the duty to act with due care and skill (LR 8.3.3R). With the exception of LR 8.3.5 (requiring sponsors to deal with the FSA in an open and co-operative manner and to deal promptly with FSA enquiries), which applies to sponsors at all times, LR 8.3 only applies to sponsors in connection with the provision of 'sponsor services', that is when they have to act under LR 8.2. Advice given by a sponsor outside of this definition is not within the Listing Rules and subject to other legal rules.

Any company requiring a prospectus must have a sponsor

owes duty to FSA

Listing Rule 8.4.1R to LR 8.4.4G set out the specific duties of the sponsor in relation to a float. The sponsor owes duties to the FSA, and a firm must take up an appointment as sponsor only once it is satisfied of the company's suitability for listing. Of course, no sponsor would want to be associated with an unsuccessful float in any event.

Sponsor only interested in IPO's when suitability; Reputation to uphold.

The sponsor has a crucial role in guiding the company and its management through the flotation process and advising the company on the interpretation of the Listing Rules. It will liaise with the FSA and, to a lesser extent, the Stock Exchange on behalf of the company, and will relay any comments back to the company. The sponsor also co-ordinates the team of advisers and will advise them on the timetable for the IPO. The lawyers in particular will have day-to-day contact with the sponsor as the flotation process progresses.

Sponsors role to guide company through IPO.

Usually an investment bank, a stockbroker or an accountancy firm will adopt the role of sponsor, but it must be approved by the FSA. Listing Rule 8.6 sets out the criteria for sponsor approval. A list of approved sponsors is available from the UKLA section of the FSA website (LR 8.6.1G). The sponsor must abide by rules in LR 8.3 to ensure that conflicts of interest which may arise do not adversely affect its ability to perform its functions properly.

UKLA approved list of sponsors

4.2.3   Broker

The broker advises the company with a view to ensuring that there is sufficient demand for the company's shares once the company has floated. The broker will analyse market conditions, liaise with potential investors to market the shares and advise the company on the best method of flotation (see **4.4** below) and other tactical issues, such the price of the shares to be marketed and the timing of the IPO. If the firm appointed as sponsor (see **4.2.2**) has stockbroking capability then it may also take on the role of broker.

Demand, time, price of flotation

4.2.4   Financial adviser

The financial adviser will advise on a wide range of tactical issues, such as the timing of the IPO, how the offer should be structured (see **4.4** below) and the offer price. Again, this role is usually adopted by the firm acting as sponsor.

4.2.5   Reporting accountants

The reporting accountants review the company's finances. This is an important role, because whatever the company states in the prospectus about its financial situation will influence potential investors as to whether the company is an attractive investment. The company will want to present as positive a financial picture as possible, but the reporting accountants must ensure that this picture is accurate.

The reporting accountants will produce three main reports. The lawyers will have little involvement in the production of these, but they do need to know what they are (there will be frequent references to them in meetings). The first report is the 'long-form' report, which is not published but forms the basis of the financial information required to draft the prospectus. The second report is the 'short form' report. This is based on the long-form report, but it is published; it forms part of the prospectus. The third report is the 'working capital' report. The reporting accountants prepare this so that the sponsor can ascertain the company's anticipated working capital position for a period following the IPO (see **4.3.1.1(j)**).

The reporting accountants may also provide 'comfort letters' to the directors, to enable the directors to make certain statements in the prospectus about the financial status of the company which are required by the Listing Rules (the directors cannot, however, delegate responsibility for making such statements to the accountants). The reporting accountants may also advise on taxation issues.

Note that the role of reporting accountants is separate from the role of the company's existing auditors. Often the same accountancy firm does adopt both roles, but allocates a different team to each. The sponsor, however, may prefer that the role of reporting accountant is adopted by an entirely different firm, so that it is seen to be independent.

4.2.6 Lawyers

There are usually two teams of lawyers, from different firms, involved in a flotation. They will be specialists in corporate finance. One team advises the company and one team advises the sponsor. Both teams must work closely together to provide a seamless service. The requirement for two teams reflects the fact that, while both the sponsor and the company have the common aim of a successful IPO, there are issues on which their needs conflict. The sponsor owes certain duties to the FSA (see **4.2.2**) which the company does not owe. The sponsor will be highly sensitive about the risks of being involved with an unsuccessful IPO, or one which generates bad publicity, and the impact this will have on its ability to obtain work in the future. It may, therefore, wish to exercise a more cautious approach than the company in certain areas. The company and the sponsor are also likely to have conflicting interests regarding underwriting (see **4.2.7** below).

In addition to the company's lawyers and the sponsor's lawyers, there may also be other lawyers representing any selling shareholders, if there is a conflict of interest between the company and such shareholders. If there is no conflict, the company's lawyers may also act for any selling shareholders.

4.2.6.1   The company's lawyers

The company's lawyers draft all the documentation relating to the IPO. This includes not only the prospectus but also any ancillary documents, including any preparatory documentation required to restructure the company (see **4.5** below), such as changing the articles of association, drafting new service contracts for the directors and re-registering the company as a public company (see **1.9.3** above). The company's lawyers are also responsible for the verification process (see **5.3.5** and **6.8** below). The workload of the lawyers is examined in more detail at **5.3**.

4.2.6.2   The sponsor's lawyers

The sponsor's lawyers work with the company's lawyers to negotiate the agreements between the sponsor and the company and its shareholders (for example, the underwriting agreement). While the company's lawyers will have primary responsibility for processing the IPO documentation, the sponsor's lawyers will also contribute towards drafting. They will keep a

[handwritten margin note: sponsor not wish to be involved with failure]

close eye on the company lawyers' progress regarding the legal documentation and the verification exercise (see **5.3.5** and **6.8**) and advise the sponsor accordingly. Remember, the sponsor will not wish to be involved with a failure; if anything is not progressing as planned, the sponsor's lawyers must alert the sponsor.

4.2.7   Underwriters

[handwritten margin note: underwriters take up leftover shares in the IPO in the event that the float is undersubscribed]

The underwriters take up any shares left over after the IPO (in the event that the float is 'undersubscribed') in return for a negotiated fee, which is typically around 3 to 4% of the amount underwritten. If the IPO is 'fully subscribed' and there are no shares left over, the underwriter has no liability to take any shares. This arrangement is recorded in an underwriting agreement. The underwriter will usually allocate some or all of the risk of the offer being undersubscribed to sub-underwriters, by way of a sub-underwriting agreement (the company will not be party to any sub-underwriting agreement). Often the sponsor will adopt the role of underwriter. Occasionally the broker (if different to the sponsor) will be the underwriter. Usually the sub-underwriters will be other banks and brokers, and the large institutional investors.

4.2.8   Receiving bank

If the IPO is by way of an offer for sale and/or subscription (see **4.4.1.1** below), the receiving bank deals with the application forms (see **5.4.2.2**) and consideration for shares. Often the company's clearing bank fulfils this role.

4.2.9   Registrars

The registrars manage the company's share register. They send the share certificates to the successful applicants. This can be a considerable task if the offer is sizeable. Often the company's clearing bank takes this role in addition to the role of receiving bank.

4.2.10   Financial public relations consultants

It is important for a company to have a positive public profile before, during and after the IPO. Financial PR consultants liaise with the media and analysts to heighten the profile of the company. They also ensure that the company's communications are effective.

For reasons explained in **Chapter 6**, it is important from a legal perspective that the company's communications are not misleading and can be verified by the company (see **5.3.5** and **6.8** below). The lawyers, therefore, have a role in ensuring that the financial PR consultants take into account these legal requirements. There can, in a process which is ultimately about selling a company and its management to investors, be a tendency towards emphasising exuberant unqualified statements, such as 'we are the biggest/the fastest/the best'; these, while being excellent selling messages, rarely survive the lawyers' red pens.

Good financial PR consultants will be aware of the legal limitations on the company's sales pitch from the outset, and can manage the company's expectations in this regard. It is not just pre-prepared communications which need to be handled cautiously, though. The consultants and the lawyers may also provide the directors with media training, so that when the directors are marketing the IPO they do not say anything ('we are the biggest/the fastest/the best') which might have adverse legal implications because it cannot be verified.

4.2.11   Printers

The IPO documentation will be created initially by word processor, but ultimately the final version will be professionally printed. Once each document is in substantially final draft form, it will be taken to print. Thereafter, each draft will be printed rather than take the form of a word-processed document. The printers need to turn around the documentation quickly, accurately and securely. Towards the end of the IPO the lawyers will spend some time, often well into the night, at the printers, checking *in situ* the final amendments to the draft.

4.3   Is the company ready to float?

The company may consider that it is ready to float, but the advisers, and particularly the sponsor, will need to ensure that the company has taken account of all relevant factors in reaching this conclusion. There are two main considerations, namely:

(a)   Will the company meet the regulatory requirements for an IPO laid down by the FSA (in relation to listing) and the Stock Exchange (in relation to trading) (see **4.3.1** below)?

(b)   Will investors perceive the company to be an attractive investment opportunity (see **4.3.2** below)?

4.3.1   Regulatory requirements

The company may not have considered any regulatory requirements at the time it appoints its advisers. However, as soon as the advisers are on board they will go through the regulatory requirements with the company and discuss the extent to which the company fulfils them. The company can then take action to remedy any problems.

4.3.1.1   Regulatory requirements for admission to listing

Under s 75(4) of the FSMA 2000, the FSA cannot grant an application for listing unless it is satisfied that the requirements of the Listing Rules have been complied with.

The FSA has the following requirements which a company must meet before its shares can be admitted to listing. The IPO team must be aware of these requirements and ensure that, by the time the FSA hears the listing application, the company is capable of meeting all of them.

Sponsor

Listing Rule 8.2.1R provides that any company seeking a listing must appoint a sponsor. The sponsor's role is discussed in more detail at **4.2.2** above; however, the key role of the sponsor from the FSA's point of view is to ensure that the company is suitable for listing, to act as a link between the FSA and the company, and to advise the company in relation to the application for admission to listing and in relation to the Listing Rules.

Eligibility criteria (or 'conditions for listing')

Chapter 2 of the Listing Rules sets out the conditions which a company must satisfy before it can admit any type of security to the Official List. Chapter 6 of the Listing Rules sets out additional conditions which must be satisfied by companies wishing to list equity securities, such as shares. A company wishing to list shares on the Official List, therefore, must fulfil the conditions for listing in both Chapter 2 and Chapter 6 of the Listing Rules. (Chapters 15 to 19, rather than Chapter 6, set out the additional conditions if the securities to be listed are other than equity securities. As the focus of this book is on equity securities, and in particular shares, these chapters are not considered further.)

The conditions in Chapters 2 and 6 are discussed below, although the Rules, and particularly the Guidance to the Rules, should be consulted for further detail:

(a)   *Incorporation (LR 2.2.1R)*. The company must be duly incorporated and operate in conformity with its constitution. For UK companies this means being a public company (as referred to at **1.5.1**, a private company cannot offer shares to the public). The methods by which a company can achieve public company status are discussed at **1.9** above.

(b)   *Validity of securities (LR 2.2.2R)*. The securities (for our purposes, shares) of the company must comply with all legal requirements and be authorised under the company's memorandum and articles. This means that the company must comply with all the provisions of the CA 2006 relating to the issue of shares, such as ss 551 and 561 (see **14.3** and **Chapters 13** and **14** generally).

(c)   *Admission to trading (LR 2.2.3R)*. Shares must be admitted to trading in order to be admitted to listing. As explained at **4.1**, companies seeking to float must not only apply to have their shares listed on the Official List, they must also apply to have their shares admitted to trading (for our purposes, on the Main Market). It is this condition to listing which links the two requirements and ensures a company cannot have shares which are admitted to listing but not to trading.

(d)   *Transferability (LR 2.2.4R)*. In order to list successfully, shares must be marketable. Therefore they must be freely transferable. This means that rights attaching to shares which are common in private companies, such as rights of pre-emption on transfer and the right of directors to refuse to register share transfers, generally are not permitted in the articles of any company seeking to list. (Note, for the avoidance of confusion, that s 561 of the CA 2006 provides a right of pre-emption on the *allotment*, not *transfer*, of shares, and so does not affect this condition in any way.)

(e)   *Market capitalisation (LR 2.2.7R)*. Market capitalisation refers to the number of issued shares in a company multiplied by the current market value of each share. In other words, it represents how much the company is worth. It is a condition to listing that the expected aggregate market capitalisation of the shares to be listed should be at least £700,000. In practice, given the amount of time and costs a company must invest in an IPO, the market capitalisation of shares to be issued on flotation is usually considerably in excess of this figure (for example, the Standard Life IPO in July 2006 valued the company at over £4.5 billion). From 1 January 2009 to 31 August 2009 there was only one IPO of a UK company on the Main Market reflecting the tremendous damage inflicted by the global recession. It was valued at just over £500 million. Nevertheless, the FSA has discretion to accept a lower threshold if it is satisfied that there will be an adequate market for the shares (LR 2.2.8G).

(f)   *Whole class to be listed (LR 2.2.9R)*. If a company has different classes of share (eg, ordinary shares and preference shares), it can choose to list one class and not another (eg, list only the ordinary shares), but it cannot choose to list only part of one class (eg, half of the ordinary shares); all shares of that class must be listed.

(g)   *Prospectus (LR 2.2.10R)*. A marketing document, known as a prospectus, must be approved by the FSA and published if s 85 of the FSMA 2000 applies to the listing (see **Chapter 6**). (Note that LR 2.2.11R refers to the need for listing particulars, rather than a prospectus, if LR 4 applies. This concerns the issue of specialist securities which are not the focus of this book.)

(h)   *Accounts (LR 6.1.3R)*. The company must have published or filed independently audited accounts for at least three years ending not more than six months before the date of the prospectus. The accounts must be consolidated for the company and all of its subsidiaries.

The FSA has discretion to accept accounts for a period of less than three years if satisfied that it is desirable in the interests of investors and that investors have the necessary information to make an informed judgement about the company and its listed shares (LR 6.1.13G).

(i)   *Nature and duration of business activities (LR 6.1.4R)*. The company must carry on an independent business as its main activity, and at least 75% of the company's business must be supported by a three-year trading record, during which the company must have controlled (and must still control, at the time of application for listing) the majority of its assets.

The FSA has discretion to accept a trading record shorter than three years on the basis outlined at (h) above (desirability and investors having necessary information), but it must be satisfied that there is an overriding reason for the company seeking a listing on the Official List as opposed to seeking admission to a market more suited to a company with a trading record of less than three years (such as AIM) (LR 6.1.13G to LR 6.1.15G).

(j) *Working capital (LR 6.1.16R)*. The company and its subsidiaries must have sufficient working capital for the group's requirements for at least 12 months from the date on which the prospectus is published.

(k) *Shares in public hands (LR 6.1.19R)*. Following the flotation, at least 25% of the class of shares to be listed should be 'in public hands' across the European Economic Area (EEA). This is to ensure there is a sufficient market in the shares. Listing Rule 6.1.19(4)R explains what are *not* considered to be 'public hands', including directors, anyone connected with a director (again, as defined by the Listing Rules) and anyone interested in shares which represent 5% or more of that class of share. The current EEA States are named in the definitions section of the Listing Rules at Appendix 1.

The FSA has discretion to accept a percentage below 25% if it considers the market will nevertheless operate properly in view of the large number of shares of the same class and the extent of their distribution to the public (LR 6.1.20G). If sufficient shares are not in public hands even after the IPO, then the FSA has the power to cancel the company's listing. An example of this was the cancellation of Simon Group plc's listing on 22 August 2007 because only 5% of its shares were in public hands. The full reasons for the cancellation were given in the FSA's newsletter, List! No 17 (available on its website).

(l) *Electronic settlement (LR 6.1.23R)*. All shares listed must be capable of electronic settlement (see **2.5.3.1** above).

Application procedure

The Listing Rules set out a detailed application procedure, to which the company must adhere in order to have its shares admitted to listing. In particular, the company and its advisers must publish an important marketing document which gives potential investors information about the company so that they can make an informed decision about whether to invest. This document must comply with the requirements of the Prospectus Rules and be submitted to the FSA in accordance with the Listing Rules. Before the document can be published, the FSA must approve it. The marketing document required for a share issue is called a prospectus (where the issue is of specialist securities – encountered rarely in practice – it is called 'listing particulars'). **Chapter 6** examines the prospectus further.

4.3.1.2 Regulatory requirements for admission to trading

As noted at **4.3.1.1**, LR 2.2.3R provides that shares cannot be admitted to listing without also being admitted to trading. There is a parallel provision in the Guidance to ADS 1.1 of the Stock Exchange's Admission and Disclosure Standards (see **Appendix 1**), which provides that shares cannot be admitted to trading unless they are listed or proposed to be listed. As the two processes are tied together in this way, there is no need for the Stock Exchange to duplicate the onerous regulatory requirements for listing. Instead, the Stock Exchange can 'piggy-back' onto the requirements for listing, and can proceed safe in the knowledge that any company seeking to have its shares admitted to *trading* will have to fulfil the regulatory requirements for *listing* set out in the Listing Rules, and comply with the Prospectus Rules, before its application for admission to trading can succeed.

For this reason there are few formal regulatory requirements for admission to trading. Instead, the Stock Exchange's Admission and Disclosure Standards set out a very straightforward set of conditions (ADS 1), which state that the company must be in compliance with the Stock Exchange's requirements and that the Stock Exchange has discretion to refuse admission in certain circumstances (including the inability to comply with any bespoke condition the Stock Exchange imposes for admission). In effect, therefore, these conditions simply give the Stock Exchange the flexibility to supplement the requirements for listing should it wish. The

Admission and Disclosure Standards also set out a basic admission procedure which is detailed at **5.3.7** and **5.4.3** below.

4.3.2   Commercial requirements

The regulatory requirements detailed in **4.3.1** above obviously exist to ensure that the company is in good shape for the IPO. However, just because a company meets these criteria does not necessarily mean that investors will think the company is an attractive investment. As part of its preparation, the company needs to take an objective view of its business and consider whether, commercially, it is good enough to meet the expectations of potential investors. The sponsor and broker will be able to guide the company through the relevant considerations, but matters to consider include:

(a)   Does the company have a good track record?

(b)   Where is the company headed? Does it have a viable business plan?

(c)   Does the company have an effective board and management team?

(d)   Is there anything about the company which could put off investors? Is the company open to any criticism over corporate governance issues (see **Chapter 8**)? Is there an influential substantial shareholder? Have there been any accounting issues? Will the company be able to withstand the intense scrutiny of the IPO process?

(e)   Are the market conditions right for an IPO?

(f)   Is this the right time in the company's development for an IPO, or would it be better to wait a couple of years?

(g)   Is the Main Market the right market for the company, or would AIM be more suitable?

IPOs ceased in the turmoil of the global financial crisis. As the following article explains, hope is growing for a bumper crop of IPOs in the near future

Equity market upturn puts flotations back on the menu

Jonathan Sibun

Back in November 2007, Sir Richard Branson appointed Goldman Sachs, the US investment bank, to lead a flotation of the Virgin gym business. Some 21 months later Sir Richard is still waiting.

Goldman was appointed after the collapse of Northern Rock, when equity markets were suffering but amid expectations that any downturn in the financial sector would be short-lived and the world would soon return to its former health.

In the months that followed the bank's appointment, it became clear that such hopes were in vain.

Bear Stearns' near collapse, the blow-up of Lehman Brothers and AIG, the insurance giant, in the United States, and finally the part-nationalisation of Britain's banking system left any hopes of a return to normality in tatters. The door was firmly closed to any private companies wanting to take their bow on the public stage.

Sir Richard is not the only one who has been waiting. Private equity firms, who gorged themselves on a diet of cheap and readily available debt in the boom years, bought up

hundreds of British companies with the intention of quickly flipping them off for a profit.

The credit crisis put those plans on ice but now rising equity markets and a growing belief that the worst of the recession could be over are helping to raise hopes that the hiatus might be drawing to an end and buyout firms can get back to business.

Private equity firms across Europe are drawing up plans to bring scores of companies to the equity markets. Virgin Active, part owned by Permira and Bridgepoint, the buyout firms, is likely to be among the candidates but could face competition.

Acromas, the group behind AA, the roadside emergency service, and Saga, the travel and insurance specialist, joins Pets at Home, the retailer, and United Biscuits and Birds Eye, the food companies, as just a handful of those thought to be on the shortlist of possible initial public offering (IPO) candidates.

Historically, private equity firms have avoided flotations, preferring the pricing certainty of selling companies to trade buyers or buyout

firms. But the lack of debt financing available to potential buyers has forced them to consider other options.

"When markets begin to settle down, private equity firms have to start considering exit routes and right now they remain severely limited," says one private equity manager.

Despite the excitement, some in private equity are warning that bankers – eager to generate fees – are getting ahead of themselves.

"It is fair to say that people are thinking about it more seriously and with more optimism than in a long while, but that does not mean we are going to see a flood of deals any time soon," says one partner at a leading private equity firm. "A fair bit of noise is being generated by the banks which have an interest in seeing activity levels rise. That said, there is more happening in the US and that is generating hope of a pick-up over here."

Despite the warning, bankers are pushing hard for IPO mandates and remain genuinely optimistic. Most speak of a list of at least 20 potential

IPO candidates that could each come with flotations of more than €1bn (£847m).

David Wilkinson, IPO team leader at Ernst & Young, says many companies began preparing their flotation plans in May and June as the equity markets started to bounce back.

The timing suggests the first deals could come in the final quarter of this year or the first three months of 2010, as does past history.

"Historically it has been six quarters after the onset of a recession that we have seen signs of IPO activity," Wilkinson says. "The sixth quarter is the back end of this year."

The US economy, thought by some to be further along the path to economic recovery than the UK, has already seen signs of life in the IPO market, giving further succour to hopes of a renaissance in Europe.

Last week, Spectrum Equity Investors, a US buyout firm, unveiled plans to float Ancestry.com, a genealogy website in a $75m (£45m) deal. That came after Silverlake Partners and KKR pushed through the public offering of Avago Technologies, a semiconductors business.

Bankers expect the first IPOs in Europe to come from more conservative businesses. "The early IPOS will come from defensive companies. Investors are unlikely to be willing to pay for future growth as much as stable cash flows," says Georg Hansel, chairman of equity capital markets for Europe, the Middle East and Africa at Deutsche Bank.

Even those companies could face challenges. While equity markets are rising, boosting hopes of a return of IPO activity, that is just one consideration. Also vital will be the valuations that buyout firms can generate. Given that many companies were bought at the top of the economic cycle, at over the odds prices, some assets will remain off limits to buyout firms who will not want to realise losses. Investors are pushing for sales, but not at any costs.

That suggests many of those companies that come to market will not only have to have fared well in the recession, but will also be older investments, bought in 2005 or 2006 when valuations were lower.

The difficulty for private equity firms will be that in order to garner interest from investors, IPOs may have to be priced to sell. That could be difficult if buyout firms do not want to be left with a loss. Many private equity companies will likely dual-track assets – offering them for sale at the same time as preparing them for flotation – to try to protect themselves.

Another difficulty will be growth projections. Given that companies are coming out of a substantial decline in economic activity, it will be difficult to convince investors that growth projections are realistic. "There will be a debate about how performance snaps back," one banker says.

Some investors suggest that even the best companies will not have an easy ride. Rising equity markets have undoubtedly boosted investor confidence and prompted an increase in risk appetite, but that does not mean investors will be giving their money away. There is interest in the IPO market – some investors are looking for better returns than refinancings are likely to offer and historically IPOs at the bottom of the market have provided sizeable profits in the long-run – but interest is germinal.

"Investors are going to be very selective about what they look at," one institutional investor says. "We're only going to be looking at companies we know well and that have a long trading history. If we don't have enough visibility on profit margins, if a company has gone through significant restructuring, or if there are a lack of comparable companies on the public markets, we're not going to be interested."

Bankers appear aware of those concerns, arguing that they will be focusing on companies which have previously traded on the public markets and which investors already know. They are also aware that the success or otherwise of the first clutch of deals will decide the fate of others' plans. However, another investor suggests that may not be enough.

"Are we better off recapitalising a good business that has just got the wrong capital structure or buying into a private equity business on which we do not have full visibility?

Are we better off giving money to strong companies so that they can buy distressed assets at distressed prices or investing in private equity companies and then finding out things are not what they seemed," he says. "The answers suggest the private equity option is going to have to be extremely compelling."

In the wake of the credit crisis, which has left many investors cursing their involvement in companies previously floated by private equity firms, there are some who question whether a change in approach will be necessary.

"We need to feel as though we have the boot properly on our foot this time. We have to be clear that it is going to be good for us," says the institutional investor. "A question for us now is how private equity sees its relationship with us. Do they want to bring companies to market at such a price where it will be good for us and then trust in our support for further deals down the road, or do they take a more aggressive approach?"

Bankers also expect a spate of further recapitalisations in the autumn and those will have to be completed before the IPO market comes alive. Many public companies have avoided the equity markets in the first half of this year because of depressed share prices, but for those with financing commitments in 2010 and 2011, they will have to move soon.

However, all the potential hurdles for IPOs will be irrelevant if equity markets do not continue to rise. Without further strength in the stock markets, private equity firms will be left once again sitting on the sidelines.

"The Pollyanna scenario is one where the FTSE, S&P and Dax all rise another 15pc to 20pc. Then investors will be willing to take greater risks and to underwrite growth," says one banker. "If the recovery is more L-shaped, with markets trading sideways, there will be IPOs but they will be the more defensive companies. But if we find the current rally is a short-term blip before markets head down again, you can forget about any IPOs in the short-term."

For private equity firms, the remainder of the summer will be a FTSE-watching affair.

Source: *The Telegraph*, 8 August 200

4.4 Choosing how to float

The company must choose the most suitable way to float on the Stock Exchange. There are a number of different ways in which a company seeking to float can list its shares, namely by:

(a)   a public offer;

(b)   a placing;

(c)   an intermediaries offer; or

(d)   an introduction.

The method, or methods, chosen will depend on a number of factors, including how much money the company is prepared to spend on the float (some methods are generally cheaper than others), how well-known the company seeking to float is (some methods are less suitable for relatively unknown companies), how much money the company wishes to raise both on flotation and afterwards (some methods favour a certain type of investor who may have deeper and more open pockets than others), what type of investor the company wishes to have initially (some methods will result in mainly institutional shareholders, others will involve the general public), how wide the company wishes its shareholder base to be after the float (some methods will result in a wider spread of shareholders than others, which may affect how easy it is to trade in the shares).

In the first seven months of 2008 there were 52 IPOs on the Stock Exchange's Main Market, of which 21 were public offers, 7 were placings and 24 were introductions. In the first seven months of 2009, by comparison, there were just 18 IPOs, (overwhelmingly foreign companies), of which 6 were public offers and 12 were introductions. It is also important to note from this that the methods of flotation are not mutually exclusive: a combination of methods (usually a public offer and a placing) can be used to effect an IPO, although none were carried out in the past year.

Prior to 1 July 2005 and the reform of the previous listing regime (see **3.1**) the rules contained a list of specific methods by which a company could float. That is no longer the case. Although some of the methods above are referred to in the definitions section (Appendix 1) to the Listing Rules, the Listing Rules now only concentrate on special features of certain methods of flotation rather setting out a definitive list of how companies can float. As a consequence, increasingly you will find that IPOs are described in terms different to those above. These alternative terms are discussed at **4.4.2** below. It should also be noted that there are further ways to list shares once the company has been through the IPO process and is listed on the Stock Exchange (see **17.6**).

4.4.1 Methods of flotation

4.4.1.1 Public offer

A public offer involves an invitation being made to members of the public to buy shares in the company seeking to float. It is usually structured in one of three different ways: as an offer for subscription; as an offer for sale; or as a combination of the two.

An offer for subscription (defined in Appendix 1 to the Listing Rules) is an invitation to the public to subscribe for (ie buy) shares not yet in issue. In other words, on flotation the company will issue new shares and raise new money for the company. This is one of the key advantages to obtaining a listing (see **1.7.2**).

An offer for sale (defined in Appendix 1 to the Listing Rules) is an invitation to the public to subscribe for (ie buy) shares already in issue. In other words, shareholders currently owning a part of the company before the IPO are using the opportunity afforded by the IPO to sell their shares. No new money is raised for the company in this case – all the money goes to the selling shareholders. This allows shareholders (such as venture capitalists or founder shareholders) to realise their investment in the company and is another common reason for a company seeking an IPO.

As mentioned above, it is perfectly possible — in fact it is very common — both for existing shareholders to want to offload some of their shares and for the company to issue new shares at the same time as part of the IPO. This would mean that the public offer would entail both an offer for subscription and an offer for sale.

Although an essential element of a public offer is that it involves private investors buying shares in the company, it does not preclude institutional investors (such as pension funds, insurance companies and investment banks) from participating in the IPO and buying shares in the company at the same time. In fact, in light of the huge resources available to them, the involvement of institutional investors will be essential. The key distinguishing feature of a public offer then is that it involves private investors, but not exclusively so.

The advantages of a public offer are:

(a)   This is usually the most appropriate method to raise large amounts of capital.

(b)   Private investors can purchase shares, rather than just institutional investors. This means that the shareholder base will be broader (there will be more investors, holding fewer shares), which in turn facilitates the trading of the shares on the market (that is, the shares are more 'liquid').

The disadvantages are:

(a)   This is the most expensive method of flotation, partly because it involves underwriting (see **4.2.7** above).

(b)   Due to the involvement of the public, the regulatory burden is more onerous.

4.4.1.2   Placing

A placing (defined in Appendix 1 to the Listing Rules) involves the marketing of shares either already in issue or not yet in issue to specified persons, or clients of the sponsor or other securities house assisting the placing. Typically this involves the sponsor offering the shares in the company seeking to float to institutional investors. Those shares may be new (raising more money for the company), or existing ones being sold by the current shareholders (raising money for the selling shareholders). The definition of a placing in the Listing Rules goes on to state that it does not involve an offer to the public. Great care must be taken here. All this definition seeks to do is to distinguish a placing from a public offer in **4.4.1.1** above for the purposes of the Listing Rules. It will not, therefore, involve a general offer to private investors at large. It has no impact on the separate definition of offer to the public under s 85(1) of the FSMA 2000 regarding the need to prepare a prospectus (see **6.4.1.3**).

The advantages of a placing are:

(a)   This is usually cheaper than a public offer.

(b)   The company has greater discretion to choose its shareholders.

(c)   The company can raise large amounts of capital.

The key disadvantage is that the shareholder base will be narrower (there will be fewer shareholders, holding more shares), which can impede trading in the company's shares (the shares have less 'liquidity').

4.4.1.3   Intermediaries offer

An intermediaries offer (defined in Appendix 1 to the Listing Rules) is similar to a placing (see **4.4.1.2** above). However, the shares can be marketed only to firms who comply with the definition of an intermediary in the FSA Handbook, which broadly means they are offered to stockbrokers independent of the sponsor and any securities house assisting with the IPO. On receipt of the shares, the stockbroker then acts as intermediary and sells them to clients in exchange for a commission.

The advantage of an intermediaries offer is that this method can achieve a wider spread of professional investors than a placing alone.

The disadvantage of an intermediaries offer is that it involves considerable administration and tends to be suitable only in very large IPOs. For this reason, intermediaries offers are quite rare.

4.4.1.4   Introduction

An introduction is not defined in the Listing Rules. It involves a company with shares already held by the public or institutional investors being admitted to listing on the Stock Exchange without offering any further shares. As we have seen, most companies seek to use an IPO to raise money which can be put towards acquisitions of other companies or businesses, paying off debt or investment in the current business. The question therefore arises as to why a company would wish to float on the Stock Exchange and not raise more money. When is an introduction useful? It is used mainly in three situations:

(a)   By overseas companies which already have a wide spread of shareholders. For example, a company may already be listed on the Shanghai Stock Exchange and now wishes to list in London to bring it closer to one of the biggest sources of equity investment in the world.

(b)   Companies quoted on AIM may wish to transfer to the Main Market and take advantage of the higher profile and greater liquidity in shares that this offers. For example, Booker Group plc, the UK's largest food wholesale operator, was introduced to the Main Market from AIM in July 2009.

(c)   An existing listed company may decide to 'demerge' part or all of its business. GUS plc decided to demerge (ie split) its business into two new companies which were both floated on the Stock Exchange, Experian Group plc (the credit reference agency) and Home Retail Group plc (formerly Argos). Both companies were introduced to the Main Market in October 2006. Carphone Warehouse Group plc announced in April 2009 that it is to demerge its retail and broadband internet operations into two separately listed companies on the Main Market. This is expected to take place in 2010.

Generally such a company will have to show a sufficiently wide spread of shareholders, with usually at least 25% being held in public hands as defined under the Listing Rules (see **4.3.1.1**). The theory is that, as the company's shares are already widely held and in public hands, the company has already demonstrated the marketability of its shares.

The advantages of an introduction are:

(a)   this is usually the cheapest method of flotation;

(b)   as it does not usually involve the issue or marketing of any shares, there is no need for underwriting (as underwriting covers the risk that shares offered are not taken up); and

(c)   there is little need for advertising.

The disadvantages of an introduction are:

(a)   it does not of itself afford an opportunity to raise capital (as no shares are being issued, the company receives no consideration); and

(b)   it does not afford the company the same opportunities for publicity as a public offer or placing. This could affect the marketability of the shares after flotation (although as the shares are already widely held in public hands, and are therefore clearly marketable, often this is not an issue).

4.4.2   Other methods

As stated at **4.4** above, you will often see IPOs described in terms different from those set out in **4.4.1**, and these tend to focus on who the offer is aimed at. These include:

(a)   an institutional offer;

(b)   a retail offer;

(c)   a global or international offer;

(d)   an employee offer; or

(e)   a 'friends and family' offer.

Frequently the word 'offering' is used in place of 'offer' here.

It is important to note that usually one or other of the terms above overlaps with the methods of floating a company described in **4.4.1**. This often causes unnecessary confusion. The key really is to remember that these are all simply different ways of explaining the same thing, namely how a company floats on the Stock Exchange. The fact that there is more than one way to describe an offer of shares involving the public (public offer, offer for subscription, offer for sale and retail offer (see **4.4.2.2**)) does not change the practical reality common to them all, that the shares of the company seeking to list on the Main Market will be offered to private investors at large rather than just to institutional investors. Some of the terms may be more specific: for example, public offer and retail offer are wide terms (focusing on the fact that shares are offered to private investors), whereas an offer for sale (being both a public offer and a retail offer) provides additional information in that it highlights that some of the shares being offered to the public will be coming from existing shareholders (and therefore the money raised will not be of benefit to the company). An offer for sale is also specifically addressed in the Listing Rules.

4.4.2.1   Institutional offer

An institutional offer describes an offering of shares on flotation to institutional investors such as investment banks, pension funds and insurance companies. Typically the offer is made by way of a placing, but this is not essential. The key element is the participation of institutional investors in the offer. The institutional offer can be made on a bookbuilt basis or a fixed price basis.

Bookbuilding

The sponsor sends potential investors an invitation to bid for shares before it sets the share price and the size of the offer. Usually the invitation to bid will set out a range of prices. The institutional investor will then bid, stating the number of shares it is willing to buy and at what price, or range of prices. The bids are not binding. The bank will keep a record ('book') of the bids it receives, which helps it to assess the appropriate share price and the likely level of demand for the shares. The thinking is that this process will ensure the highest possible value for the company's shares.

As the offer is not underwritten until all bids have been received, the underwriting risk is reduced to some extent, as the demand for the shares has already been tested among institutional investors, and the period of risk tends to be shorter. This means that usually the offer can be underwritten at a much lower commission rate than with a fixed price institutional offer, thereby saving the company money.

Fixed price

The sponsor and broker use their knowledge of the market to advise on a suitable fixed price per share, which should be attractive to potential investors but which is not too low. Typically the offer will be fully underwritten.

It is currently much more common for such offers to be made on a bookbuilt basis.

4.4.2.2   Retail offer

A retail offer is when the shares are offered to members of the public. This can increase demand for the shares and can raise the profile of the company, because the media will market the IPO to the public. A retail offer is made by way of offer for subscription and/or sale. It is suitable for larger IPOs.

As the public need more protection than institutional investors, a retail offer is more heavily regulated than an institutional offer. Usually a retail offer is made together with an institutional offer.

4.4.2.3 Employee offer

This is when the shares are offered to employees of the company (and often to employees of other group companies). The employees may be given preferential allocation rights for new shares being issued in the company. As referred to at **1.7.6** above, an employee offer allows the company to reward its employees. It also encourages employees to invest in the company, which then ensures they have a vested interest in the ongoing success of the company.

As with a retail offer, an employee offer can increase demand for the shares. The company will set eligibility criteria, such as length of service, to determine which employees can take up the offer. Usually an employee offer is made together with a retail offer, and will mirror its terms.

4.4.2.4 Friends and family offer

This is when the shares are offered to certain individuals. 'Friends and family' captures the essence of the nature of these individuals, but in practice other people, such as suppliers, customers and initial backers, can be offered shares as part of a friends and family offer.

4.4.2.5 Global or international offer

As the name suggests, this is when the offer of shares in the company seeking to float is made to investors not just in the UK but also abroad. Typically it will comprise an offer for subscription and an offer for sale, but the key element is the involvement of overseas investors. A global offer suits larger companies and those with a significant international presence or aspirations to expand internationally.

Depending on how this offer is structured it may require full compliance with local securities laws, which will make the offer even more costly and time-consuming than a pure UK offer. It is usual, though, to set up the offer to take advantage of exemptions under those local laws, for example by limiting the offer overseas to qualifying institutional investors and thereby reducing the foreign regulatory burden.

4.4.3 Combination of different methods

As explained at **4.4** above, it is possible to combine the different methods when a company floats on the Stock Exchange. You will see in the extract from the announcement by moneysupermaket.com, the price comparison website, set out below (and made online), how it describes its then forthcoming IPO in July 2007. Note how the IPO is described as a 'Global Offer', which consists of an offering to institutional investors (ie an institutional offer) both in the UK and overseas, and as a 'Retail Offer' (for private investors) and an employee offer. There is also a reference to intermediaries becoming involved. Furthermore, the announcement states that the Global Offer will consist of new and existing shares. Although not expressly stated, this of course means that the offer will probably take the form of an offer for subscription and sale to private and institutional investors. This was confirmed by details contained in the prospectus subsequently published by the company. (The company re-registered as a plc before the IPO, as required by the Listing Rules (see **4.3.1.1**).)

> **moneysupermarket.com Group Limited has announced it is to trade on the London Stock Exchange (LSE).**
>
> It intends to proceed with an initial public offering ('IPO') of its Ordinary Shares, which are intended to be admitted to the Official List of the FSA and to trading on London Stock Exchange plc's main market for listed securities.
>
> . . .
>
> **Details of the Proposed Global Offer:**
>
> moneysupermarket.com intends to apply for admission of its Ordinary Shares to the Official List of the FSA and to trading on London Stock Exchange plc's main market for listed securities. The Global Offer will consist of an offering of new and existing Ordinary Shares by the Company and certain shareholders respectively (the 'Global Offer'). The proceeds of the Global Offer received

by the Company will principally be used to repay the Group's existing debt facilities and to fund the Group's expected growth. Following the Global Offer the Chief Executive and the senior management team are expected to own a majority interest in the Company.

The Global Offer is expected to comprise an offer to institutional investors in the UK and in certain other jurisdictions as well as an offer to retail investors in the UK, Channel Islands and Isle of Man. The Company also intends to make an employee offer to eligible employees of the Group.

Credit Suisse is acting as Sole Sponsor, Sole Global Coordinator and Bookrunner in connection with the Global Offer; Lehman Brothers International (Europe) and UBS Limited are acting as Co-Lead Managers in connection with the Global Offer.

Details of the Retail Offer:

Retail investors in the United Kingdom, Channel Islands and Isle of Man can register their interest in participating in the Retail Offer through the moneysupermarket.com share offer website, www.moneysupermarket.com/shareoffer. It is expected that registration will be open for less than two weeks. Registration will only be possible on-line. By registering, retail investors will be able to choose their preferred method of application. When the Retail Offer opens, they will be able to apply either online, by downloading an application form or by returning an application form mailed to them. Retail investors may only request an application pack by mail during the registration phase.

Retail investors who register their interest online will be notified directly when the Retail Offer opens.

It is intended that moneysupermarket.com customers (being persons who are current subscribers to the Group's e-mail alerts as at 28 June 2007) as well as persons who register their interest in applying for Ordinary Shares and subscribe to receive the Group's e-mail alerts through www.moneysupermarket.com/shareoffer by 11.59 p.m. on Thursday, 5 July 2007, will receive preferential treatment ('Customer Preference') in the allocation of Ordinary Shares in the Retail Offer, in the event that there is excess demand. As the Retail Offer will only be open for a limited period we recommend that potential investors register their interest online at the earliest opportunity.

Further information on the Company as well as details of how retail investors can register their interest in the Retail Offer are available on www.moneysupermarket.com/shareoffer.

Intermediaries may also participate in the Retail Offer and place orders on behalf of their clients once the Retail Offer opens. Clients of Intermediaries will not be eligible to receive Customer Preference.

4.5 Restructuring the company

It is not always necessary to restructure a company before its IPO. The company seeking to float may be in perfect shape. However, it is important that the company is in good order when it floats, and so in the year or so prior to the IPO the company must consider whether it needs to implement any changes. The following are some of the common areas of concern.

4.5.1 Group structure

In all likelihood the company seeking to float will form part of a wider group of companies. Before the company floats, the lawyers must make sure that this group has a rational structure. The most common structure is for the company seeking the IPO to be the holding company of the group. The other companies will then be subsidiaries, organised in a logical manner. A supermarket chain, for example, might group the companies in its supermarket business together, its banking related companies together and its companies for its mobile phone operations together, as in **Figure 4.1** below.

Figure 4.1: Group structure

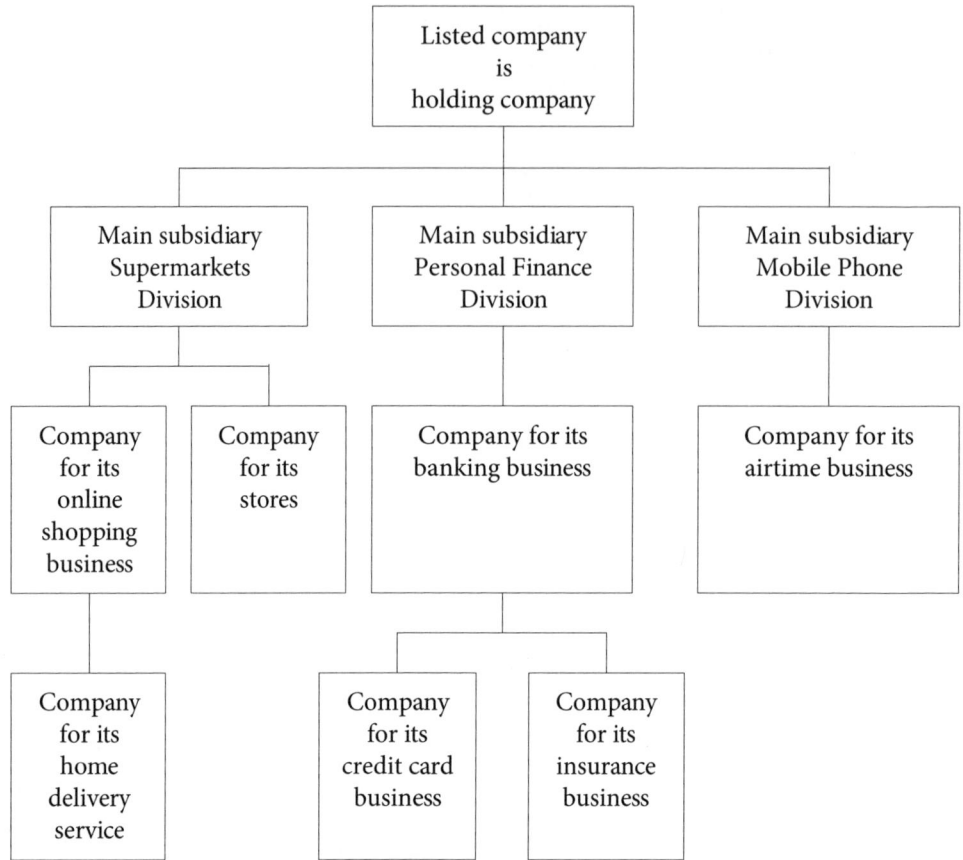

While this seems straightforward, in fact many businesses have grown in an unwieldy fashion through acquisitions and organic growth, with little thought paid to group structure. The company seeking the IPO might be a subsidiary company. Subsidiaries may exist which are now dormant (for example, because all the assets were transferred out of a subsidiary by a previous business sale) and may need to be dissolved. It may be that the company is planning to acquire or dispose of a business or company. If this is the case, the transaction should be completed as soon as possible so that the company structure is stable in the run up to completion. The lawyers need to examine the group structure well in advance of the IPO and effect any necessary changes, possibly by way of share and/or asset sales or purchases, company incorporation and/or dissolution, so that the company forms part of a logical group of companies.

4.5.2   Capital structure

As stated at **4.4.1.1** above, it is important that the offer price of the shares is fixed at the correct level. The share capital of the company may need to be altered to take account of this. For example, imagine that the advisers have stated that the offer price should be between £1.75 and £2.25 per share. However, the company has a current issued share capital of 2,000,000 shares of £1 each (nominal value) and is currently worth £20,000,000. This means that each share has a current value of £10. How could the shares be offered at the advised offer price without the company suffering a huge loss?

There are various solutions which the lawyers can effect. The simplest here would be to subdivide each share of £1 into 5 shares of 20p. This would mean that the company is still worth £20,000,000, but now has an issued share capital of 10,000,000 shares of 20p each, so each share has a current value of £2.00, which is within the acceptable price range.

4.5.3 Company constitution

If the company has not been incorporated as a public company, the lawyers will need to re-register the company as detailed at **1.9.3**. The company's constitution will comprise the articles of association and the memorandum of association. In advance of the IPO, the lawyers need to check these documents to make sure there is nothing in them which is inconsistent with *listed* company status. Usually the company will adopt a completely new set of articles which comply with the requirements for a listed company. Two notable requirements with which the company's existing articles may not comply are:

(a)   there should be no restrictions on the transfer of shares (see **4.3.1.1**, 'Eligibility critera (or "conditions for listing")' above); and

(b)   each class of shares should have the same voting rights (often unlisted companies attach enhanced rights to some, but not all, shares in a certain class).

4.5.4 The board of directors

As explained in **Chapter 8**, the board of directors of a listed company needs to comply with various principles of corporate governance (best practice). The lawyers need to consider whether any changes should be made to the board well in advance of the IPO, so that the company can make the required appointments and/or dismissals. In addition, it may be that the boards of subsidiary companies could be rationalised further (taking the example in **Figure 4.1** above, it may be logical for Ms Y, a key manager in the Supermarkets Division, to sit on the board of each of the companies in the Supermarkets Division), or perhaps the records of board appointments at Companies House need to be updated.

4.5.5 Legal issues

As **Chapter 6** explores further, the IPO process involves considerable disclosure about the company. Any negative news may discourage potential investors. The lawyers will examine the company's history to identify any breaches of the law and, to the extent possible, remedy them (for example, ensure that all filings at Companies House are up to date). However, when the structure of the IPO is being planned, the lawyer also needs to be alert to any issues which may give rise to legal problems. Two potential problems lawyers need to bear in mind at this stage are:

(a)   Might the IPO arrangements give rise to any financial assistance issues (see **Chapter 16**)?

(b)   Section 580 of the CA 2006 provides that no share should be issued at a discount to its *nominal* value (see **13.3.1**).

4.6 What next?

This chapter has outlined the preliminary steps a company can take in advance of the IPO process. While it can take a year (or longer) for the company to prepare for an IPO, the actual IPO process itself is much shorter (usually between three to six months). **Chapter 5** considers the IPO process.

Chapter 5

Initial Public Offerings: The Process

5.1 Introduction

This chapter must be read in conjunction with **Chapter 4**, which explains what an IPO is and the preliminary steps a company seeking to float must take, and **Chapter 6,** which examines the content of the vital marketing document, the prospectus. This chapter considers the IPO process itself, that is, the period of between 12 and 24 weeks before flotation when the company applies to the FSA for admission to listing and to the Stock Exchange for admission to trading. The preparation referred to in **Chapter 4**, which takes place in the year or two before the IPO, is generally referred to as 'pre-IPO preparation' rather than as part of the IPO process itself.

5.2 The IPO process

A simplified version of the IPO process (other than by way of a bookbuilt offer – see **4.4.2.1**) is set out in **Table 5.1** below. The timing of the process is by reference to what is known as 'impact day'. This is the day when the IPO is announced to the market, the offer price is made known and the marketing document, the prospectus (see **Chapter 6**), is advertised. Impact day is not the day the company actually floats. The company floats when the FSA makes an Official List announcement (see **5.4.3.1** below) and the Stock Exchange publishes a London Stock Exchange Notice (see **5.4.3.2** below). Dealing in the company's shares can then begin. This day is known as 'admission day'.

5.3 The lawyers' perspective

Table 5.1 provides an overview of the IPO process. It includes not just the dual applications for listing and trading but also the advisers' roles. As mentioned previously, it is important that the lawyers appreciate not only who the company's other advisers are, but also what they do and when. Of course, there are some areas where the lawyers will have little or no involvement, and other areas where the lawyers' role will be vital. So where does the lawyers' work lie?

5.3.1 Agreeing the timetable and the list of documents

At the beginning of the IPO process the sponsors will draw up a draft timetable for the IPO. Several factors drive the timetable. The FSA and the Stock Exchange have their own rules about timing, which cannot be changed. The company may have particular requirements as to timing, which may be inflexible (such as a desire to dovetail the IPO with a particular point in the company's financial year) or subject to change (for example, if the company's IPO is dependent on the occurrence of a certain event which has no fixed deadline). There are also practicalities to be taken into account, such as the prevailing movement on the stock market and the fact that it is virtually impossible to reduce the IPO procedure to anything less than three months (even on the premise that the advisers require very little sleep). The lawyers will be asked to comment on the draft timetable and agree it. The sponsor will have the task of ensuring that the agreed timetable does not slip. The lawyers need to ensure that:

(a) there are no omissions in the timetable; and

(b) the timetable is viable.

The lawyers will also be involved early in the IPO process in commenting on the list of documents drawn up by the sponsor. The list sets out all the documents required, the parties and who has primary responsibility for producing them. Like the timetable, this will be used as a reference point by all advisers, and so needs to be detailed and accurate.

Table 5.1: The IPO process

24–52 weeks (6–12 months) before impact day	**Pre-IPO preparation.** Company chooses advisers, considers its suitability for an IPO and the most appropriate method of listing its shares, and effects any necessary restructuring (see **Chapter 4**). Company takes decision to proceed with IPO.
12–24 weeks (3–6 months) before impact day	**The IPO process begins.** Company appoints advisers and meets sponsor. Sponsor drafts and advisers agree a timetable. Sponsor informs FSA about intended IPO. First marketing meetings with sponsor and broker. Initial planning meetings with advisers take place. Legal and financial due diligence begins (see **5.3.4**).
6–12 weeks (1.5–3 months) before impact day	**The process gathers momentum.** Key managers of the company work full-time on the IPO. Accountants produce long-form and draft short-form report (see **4.2.5**). Lawyers produce draft prospectus and begin the verification process (see **5.3.5** and **6.8**). Initial drafting meetings with advisers. Sponsor submits draft documentation relating to the approval of the prospectus (including 2 drafts of the prospectus) to the FSA (see **5.3.6.1** and **5.3.6.2**). Pay FSA fee for approval of the prospectus (see **5.3.6.2**). Sponsor and company have first meeting with the Stock Exchange. Initial pricing meetings with sponsor, broker, and any underwriters and sub-underwriters. Valuation of any key assets. Meetings with Financial PR consultants (sponsors, brokers and lawyers present).
2–6 weeks (one month) before impact day	**The process becomes intense.** Detailed drafting meetings, incorporating FSA's comments. Lawyers complete verification. Publish any pathfinder prospectus. Accountants and sponsors review cash-flow statements and any profit forecasts. Convene completion GM of company. Further PR meetings. Ensure any ancillary documentation (re-registering the company, new memorandum and articles) is prepared. First meeting with registrars. Deadline for submitting draft prospectus to the FSA is 20 days before impact day (see **5.3.6.1**). Submit draft application for listing to FSA and draft application for trading to LSE.

The week before impact day	**The preparation peaks.** Completion GM held. Directors' marketing roadshows.
The day before impact day	**All documentation must be signed off:** (a) Verification meeting. (b) Completion board meeting (sometimes known as a pricing meeting). (c) Underwriting agreement signed and held in escrow. (d) Any other agreements (placing, offer for sale) signed and held in escrow. Submit final version of prospectus (and any ancillary documentation referred to in the prospectus) to the FSA. Pricing meeting to agree offer price.
Impact day	**IPO announced.** FSA approves prospectus. Offer price is made public. Bulk print prospectus. Advertise prospectus. Release underwriting agreement from escrow.
The week after impact day	**Attend to formalities.** Continue to publish prospectus and advertise the IPO. Directors' roadshows continue. Submit '48 hour' documents to the FSA (see **5.3.6.3**) and 'Two day' documents to the Stock Exchange (see **5.3.7.2**) to apply for admission to listing and to trading. Pay FSA admission fee (see **5.3.6.3**). **Day of admissions hearings.** Submit 'on the day' documents to the FSA (see **5.3.6.4**). The FSA hears application for admission to listing. The Stock Exchange hears application for admission to trading. Open application lists and receive applications from investors (see **5.4.2.2**). Close application lists (see **5.4.2.2**).
2 weeks after impact day	**Admission week.** Announce basis of allotment of shares. Despatch letters of acceptance/regret to investors. **Admission day.** The FSA makes an Official List announcement that shares have been admitted to listing (see **5.4.3.1**) and the Stock Exchange publishes a London Stock Exchange Notice that shares have been admitted to listing (see **5.4.3.2**). Dealing in shares commences. Stock Exchange invoice raised (see **5.3.7.3**).
3–5 weeks after impact day	**Formalities.** Receive letters of acceptance. Issue share certificates. Lodge information with the FSA (see **5.3.6.5**) and the Stock Exchange (see **5.3.7.4**). Pay Stock Exchange fee (see **5.3.7.3**).

Debenhams meets investors prior to float

Debenhams has begun testing the market for its flotation on the London Stock Exchange, which could see the department store valued at about £3bn, including debt.

The investment banks are now sounding out institutional investors and are expected to launch a formal roadshow in two weeks time.

The initial price range is expected to be set just after Easter, with final pricing at the beginning of May when the company launches on the LSE, paving the exit of the management, buy-out and private equity groups that bought into the group three years ago.

Debenhams will float on the back of half-year figures to the end of February. In the full year ended September, total sales rose 9.7 per cent to £2.09bn. The flotation is expected to be one of the biggest in the UK this year.

Debenhams appointed Citigroup and Merrill Lynch as joint global co-ordinators for the flotation in January and mandated Morgan Stanley and CSFB as bookrunners.

Since January, seven companies raising a total of £2.79bn have joined the UK's main market via initial public offerings - the highest level of activity since the first quarter of 2000 when eight companies floated, raising £524m, according to KPMG.

Debenhams - which is owned by Texas Pacific Group and CVC Capital, the buy-out groups, and the private equity wing of Merrill Lynch - is expected to use part of the proceeds from the float to pay down debt, which was £1.9bn at the end of August 2005.

Last summer, the group completed a £2bn re-financing, its second since it was acquired by the buy-out trio in 2003 for £1.9bn.

Since then, they have received capital repayments of about £1.3bn from Debenhams, more than twice their combined equity investment of £600m.

The management, led by Rob Templeman, the chief executive, owns up to 12 per cent of Debenhams' equity. TPG has 36 per cent, CVC just less than 26 per cent and Merrill Lynch 20 per cent.

The buy-out trio are expected to retain small shareholdings in Debenhams after the flotation.

Since the group was taken private, it has increased the number of stores from 120 to 200 and its market share has risen from 15.2 per cent to 18.6 per cent.

Source: *Financial Times*, 6 April 2006

5.3.2 Drafting documentation

The majority of the lawyers' time will be divided between drafting, meetings (see **5.3.3**) and due diligence (see **5.3.4**). The most important document the lawyers will draft is the prospectus. This is a lengthy, detailed document and **Chapter 6** considers it in more detail.

There will also be ancillary documentation for the lawyers to draft. This could include documents to effect any restructuring (see **4.5** above). It will certainly include board minutes which record the board's progress through the IPO process, and the board's approval of the process and related documentation.

There will also be documentation relating to the method of listing the shares. If it is a public offer by way of an offer for subscription and/or sale (see **4.4.1**), an agreement (between the company, its directors, any selling shareholders and the sponsor) will be required. For a placing (see **4.4.1.2**), a placing agreement is needed (the parties are the same as for an offer for subscription and/or sale agreement).

The lawyers will also produce a sizeable document called a verification note (see **5.3.5** below).

5.3.3 Attending meetings

5.3.3.1 Drafting meetings

So many advisers, as well as the company, need to feed information into the prospectus that it becomes impossible for the adviser with responsibility for the document (the sponsor or the lawyers) to collate and incorporate comments on the draft by e-mail or telephone. Once the draft prospectus is reasonably progressed, there will be numerous drafting meetings, where all the parties can contribute and discuss their comments on the draft. If more than one party has comments on a certain point, those parties can agree revised wording. The meetings are productive, but can be very time-consuming.

5.3.3.2 Completion GM

The completion GM takes place a few days before impact day. The IPO itself does not require shareholder approval, but some matters which are vital to the preparation of the company for the IPO often do require such approval. The completion GM is the forum to obtain this consent. Usually, the lawyers will draft the notice to convene this meeting and ensure that it is sent out within the required time limits in the CA 2006 (at least 21 clear days' notice for all resolutions of a public company unless approval is obtained by the shareholders at an AGM to shorten the notice period to 14 clear days (see **8.6.1**). The company's articles of association may extend this notice period). The lawyers will then draft the necessary resolutions and usually will attend the GM to deal with any issues which may arise on the day. There is little scope for error.

The resolutions which may be necessary depend on the particular requirements of the company, but they may include:

(a)   if the IPO involves an offer of shares by way of subscription (ie, it involves the company issuing new shares):

    (i)   granting authority to allot under s 551 of the CA 2006,

    (ii)   disapplying pre-emption rights under s 561 of the CA 2006 on allotment (see **Chapter 14**);

(b)   reorganising the share capital (see **4.5.2** above); and/or

(c)   adopting new articles of association (see **4.5.3** above).

5.3.3.3   Verification meeting

The verification meeting takes place just before the completion board meeting. The board sign the verification note at this meeting (see **5.3.5** and **6.8** below).

5.3.3.4   Completion board meeting

The completion board meeting takes place the day before impact day. The directors will approve all the IPO documentation and the steps required to float the company. In particular, the board will resolve to:

(a)   approve the terms of the prospectus;

(b)   approve the terms of any ancillary documentation; and

(c)   proceed with the IPO, and in particular the application for admission to listing and the application for admission to trading.

After the completion board meeting the prospectus is submitted to the FSA for final approval.

5.3.4   Due diligence

Due diligence, often referred to as 'DD' or 'due dil', or sometimes called 'legal review' is a time-consuming exercise that begins early on in the IPO process. The aim of due diligence is to investigate the company thoroughly and collate comprehensive information about it, which can then be used in the prospectus, the financial reports and other IPO documentation. The process also helps the advisers to identify the value of the company (and therefore fix the offer price) and any steps which are necessary to prepare the company for the IPO, such as those outlined at **4.5** above.

Due diligence falls into three main categories:

(a)   business due diligence;

(b)   financial due diligence; and

(c)   legal due diligence.

5.3.4.1   Business due diligence

This is an investigation into the commercial aspects of the company, such as its performance, competitors and strategy. The lawyers do not lead this due diligence, but they do need some of the results of it for the legal due diligence exercise (see **5.3.4.3**).

5.3.4.2   Financial due diligence

This is the investigation carried out by the reporting accountants so that they can produce the long form report, the short form report and the working capital report to which **4.2.5** above refers.

5.3.4.3   Legal due diligence

The lawyers have responsibility for the legal due diligence exercise. Trainees are heavily involved in this process. Basic information about the company will be obtained from public registries, such as Companies House, Land Registry and the Land Charges department, the Patent Office, the Trade Mark Registry and the Designs Registry, and the lawyers will also request copies of the company's statutory books. However, the scope of the legal due diligence exercise is very broad, and the lawyers really need access to the company's management to obtain the level of information required.

As should be clear from the timetable in **Table 5.1** above, the company's management are not time-rich during this stage of the IPO process, and so the lawyers need to make the most of the time that management makes available to them. The usual procedure is for the lawyers to draw up a document called a due diligence questionnaire, which has a heading for each area to be investigated and then lists questions requesting information and documentation relating to each area. The usual areas for investigation are:

(a)   corporate – structure and constitution of the company;

(b)   business and trading – including requests for all material agreements;

(c)   assets;

(d)   property;

(e)   environmental matters;

(f)   insurance;

(g)   basic financial information – for example, requests for report and accounts, details of charges and insolvency events (the accountants will request more detailed information as part of the financial due diligence process referred to at **5.3.4.2**);

(h)   intellectual property and information technology;

(i)   employees;

(j)   pensions;

(k)   disputes; and

(l)   any market-specific regulatory issues.

Each question will be given a number, as will each document requested, so that when the deluge of responses arrive, the lawyers can identify the question to which each response relates. It also means that the responses can be filed in an orderly and logical manner. The company can respond to the due diligence questionnaire in a variety of ways. Some responses can be e-mailed or faxed, some need to be discussed face to face. The company may be advised to set up a data room, where all the information provided in response to the questionnaire is kept. This has some advantages for the trainee responsible for due diligence; if there is no data room, often the trainee's office will become the storage place for all the due diligence files.

The lawyers must review all the responses very carefully. This involves disseminating the information to specialist teams of lawyers within the firm (for example, all the information will be received by the corporate lawyer who sent out the questionnaire, but when he or she receives a response relating to pensions, that response will be copied to the pensions department for their comment, and similarly information about employees will be copied to the employment department and so on). The corporate lawyer who co-ordinates the due diligence process must have excellent project management skills.

Once all the information has been reviewed by the appropriate specialists, the corporate lawyer must compile the product of the review into a due diligence report. The level of detail in the report can vary. Some reports focus solely on any problematic issues revealed by the due diligence process, others report in detail on all areas which were reviewed, even if they were problem-free. Either way, the most important part of the due diligence report from the company's point of view is what is known as the 'executive summary'. This is a chapter at the beginning of the report which states succinctly, and in layman's terms, the key issues revealed by due diligence and advises of any steps which are required before or after the IPO in relation to such issues. It is the executive summary which the directors will actually read and act upon. The detail in the rest of the report is still important, however, both for the lawyers (to record that the process was carried out thoroughly and diligently) and for the directors (to record the efforts they have made to ensure that the information in the prospectus complies with the requirements of the Prospectus Rules, the Listing Rules and the FSMA 2000 (see **Chapter 6**)).

5.3.5   Verification

While due diligence is undertaken early in the IPO process, to provide the information which goes into the prospectus, verification does not begin until the first draft of the prospectus is reasonably progressed. Verification is actually part of the due diligence process, but it has evolved into a discrete exercise. Again, trainees are heavily involved in verification. So what is it? Essentially it is a process which produces a written record (called a 'verification note') so that the company can support what it has said in the prospectus. The purpose of verification is to protect those who have responsibility for the prospectus (particularly the directors) from legal liability arising out of its publication (see **6.6** and **6.8** below).

Verification can involve a painstaking line-by-line examination of the prospectus. In the verification note, each statement in the prospectus is phrased as a question, to test that it is true, accurate and not misleading. For example, if there is a line in the prospectus which states, 'We, Cheap as Chips plc, are the largest chain of supermarkets in the world', the verification note would contain a question along the lines of, 'Please confirm that Cheap as Chips plc is the largest chain of supermarkets in the world'. The answer to this question would then be recorded and copies of any supporting documentation would be annexed to the verification note. It may be, of course, that the answer to the question has already been provided as a response to the due diligence questionnaire. If so, management will not appreciate the lawyers asking the same question again. By the time the lawyers carry out verification, therefore, they must be familiar with the responses to the due diligence questionnaire. If the verification process raises questions not dealt with in the due diligence process (which is often not as detailed as the verification process) then the lawyer will send this new list of questions to the company, so management can collate the necessary information before meeting with the lawyers to provide the responses.

Alternatively, the verification process may be limited to ensuring the key selling messages in the prospectus are adequately supported and may ignore the more obvious statements.

The directors and anyone else who has formal responsibility for the prospectus (see **6.5**) cannot be available to all advisers at all times, so in practice they delegate responsibility for answering verification questions to key management (however, they cannot delegate ultimate legal responsibility for the content of the prospectus).

The lawyers must be vigilant in ensuring that the responses the company provides to the due diligence or verification questionnaire really do answer the questions posed. For example, in the example above, a full answer would detail the basis of this pivotal statement: What is the measure of 'largest' – is the company referring to turnover, profits, number of outlets, number of employees?; What constitutes a 'chain' – just two shops, or more?; How is 'supermarket' defined – is it just a shop that sells predominantly food, or does it include those that sell clothes, books, DVDs, personal financial products and petrol?; What is meant by 'world'?; and so on. The verifier must bear in mind all the elements of the statement and ensure that she covers them adequately when drafting her response.

If the lawyers are not satisfied that the company can support the statement sufficiently, they will feed this information into the drafting meetings and the statement in the prospectus will be amended until the lawyers are satisfied that the statement can be supported. For example, the reference in the statement above to the 'largest' might be amended to 'one of the largest'.

As you might imagine, although this process is ultimately for the benefit of those responsible for the prospectus, including the directors, it is often a source of great frustration to those who have to provide the information, and each lawyer involved in the process (often a junior lawyer or a trainee) must have well developed social skills, a good sense of humour and a thick skin to survive the process. Each director, and any other person bearing responsibility for the prospectus (see **6.5**), will sign the verification note in the verification meeting (just before the completion board meeting), and it, together with the due diligence report, will provide reassurance to the directors as they accept responsibility for the prospectus in the completion board meeting itself.

5.3.6   Submission of documentation to the FSA

The sponsor will have the responsibility of ensuring that the documents listed below are submitted to the FSA, and that the documents listed at **5.3.7** below are submitted to the Stock Exchange, in a timely manner. However, each adviser, including the lawyers, needs to be aware of the deadlines.

The documents referred to at **5.3.6.1** (prospectus) and **5.3.6.2** (documents to be submitted with the prospectus) are required by Chapter 3 of the Prospectus Rules as part of the prospectus approval process. The documents referred to at **5.3.6.3** to **5.3.6.5** ('48 hour' documents, 'on the day' documents and information to be lodged after admission day) are required by Chapter 3 of the Listing Rules as part of the listing application procedure.

5.3.6.1   Prospectus

The FSA must approve the prospectus, pursuant to the procedure set out in the Prospectus Rules, before it can be published (PR 3.1.10R and FSMA 2000, s 85(7)). The company must submit two copies of the draft prospectus to the FSA, in hard copy or an agreed electronic format, at least 20 working (ie business) days before impact day (PR 3.1.3R and PR 3.1.4R). The draft must be annotated in the margin to indicate compliance with all applicable requirements of Pt VI of the FSMA 2000 and the Prospectus Rules (this is a common trainee task) (PR 3.1.4R) (see **6.5.2.4**).

The FSA will provide its comments on the draft, and the document will be re-drafted in the light of these comments. In practice, 20 working days would not allow much time to deal with any comments the FSA might make. The earlier the draft is submitted the better, and the sponsor will aim to submit the draft some two to three months before impact day. On receipt of the FSA's comments, the document will be redrafted and resubmitted to the FSA. This process will continue until the FSA confirms it has no further comments. At this point, the prospectus can be printed and submitted in final form to the FSA for approval.

The FSA can approve the prospectus only when it is satisfied that it meets certain criteria set out in s 87A of the FSMA 2000, PR 3.1.7UK and PR 3.1.8G. In practice, the FSA will not give formal approval until impact day itself.

5.3.6.2   Documents to be submitted with the prospectus

The FSA requires that a Risk Information Sheet (available from the UKLA section of the FSA's website) is submitted with the first draft of the prospectus sent to it. As part of the process set out in the Prospectus Rules for approving the prospectus, the draft prospectus, referred to at **5.3.6.1** above, must also be accompanied by the following (PR 3.1.3R):

(a)   completed Form A (available from the UKLA section of the FSA website) in final form;

(b)   the relevant fee (set out in the Fees Manual in the High Level Standards section of the FSA Handbook); and

(c)   drafts of the documents set out at PR 3.1.1R, namely:

   (i)   a cross-referenced list identifying where each item in the PD Regulation (set out, for information, in Appendix 3 of the Prospectus Rules; see **3.5.1.1** and **6.5.2**) can be found in the prospectus (if the order of items in the prospectus does not coincide with the order set out in the PD Regulation – see PR 2.2.10EU, para 4),

   (ii)   a letter identifying any items from the PD Regulation (set out in Appendix 3 of the Prospectus Rules) which are not applicable and so have not been included,

   (iii)   a copy of any document incorporated into the prospectus by reference (annotated to indicate which item of the schedules and building blocks in the PD Regulation it relates to) (see **6.5.2.2**),

   (iv)   information required by PR 2.5.3R (if requesting permission to omit information from the prospectus – see **6.5.2.3**),

   (v)   contact details of individuals, sufficiently knowledgeable about the documents submitted, who can answer queries from the FSA between the hours of 7 am and 6 pm, and

   (vi)   any other information the FSA specifically requires.

5.3.6.3   '48 hour' documents

No later than midday, at least two business days before the FSA hears the company's application for the admission to listing, the company must submit to the FSA, in final form, the documents set out at LR 3.3.2R. These include:

(a)   the Application for Admission of Securities to the Official List;

(b)   the FSA-approved prospectus;

(c)   any circular published in connection with the application;

(d)   any FSA-approved supplementary prospectus; and

(e)   written confirmation of the number of shares to be allotted pursuant to a board resolution allotting the shares (or, if this is not possible, the written confirmation must be provided to the FSA at least one hour before the admission to listing is to become effective).

In addition, LR 3.2.2R provides that a fee becomes payable on the date the company makes its application for listing (set out in the Fees Manual in the High Level Standards section of the FSA Handbook).

5.3.6.4   'On the day' documents

By 9 am on the day the FSA hears the company's application for admission to listing (see **5.4.3**), the company must lodge with the FSA a completed Shareholder Statement, signed by the sponsor (LR 3.3.3R). The form is available from the UKLA section of the FSA website.

5.3.6.5   Information to be lodged after admission day

The company must provide to the FSA written confirmation of the number of shares that were allotted if the actual number was lower than that originally announced, as soon as practicable following the hearing of the application for admission to listing (LR 3.3.5R).

5.3.7 Submission of documents to the Stock Exchange

5.3.7.1 Provisional application for admission to trading

New applicants (that is, all companies seeking to float) must complete an application form (Form 1, available on the Stock Exchange's website) and submit it, together with a draft copy of the prospectus, to the Stock Exchange no later than 12.00 pm at least 10 business days before the requested date for the hearing of the company's application for admission to trading (ADS 2.1, **Appendix 1**). This is treated as a provisional application. A formal application can only be made once the prospectus has been approved by the FSA (see **5.3.7.2**).

5.3.7.2 'Two day' documents

By 12.00 pm on the day which is at least two business days before the Stock Exchange hears the company's application for admission to trading, the company must submit to the Stock Exchange a copy of the documents listed at ADS 2.4.1, **Appendix 1**, namely:

(a)   an application for admission to trading on the finalised Form 1;

(b)   an electronic copy of the prospectus;

(c)   an electronic copy of any circular, announcement or other document relating to the issue of shares;

(d)   an electronic copy of any notice of meeting referred to in any of the documents mentioned above;

(e)   written confirmation of the number of shares to be allotted pursuant to the board resolution (or, if this is not possible, it must be provided to the Stock Exchange by 7.00 am on the expected day of admission); and

(f)   a copy of the Regulatory Information Service announcement relating to the admission.

This deadline will correspond with that for the submission of the '48 hour' documents to the FSA (see **5.3.6.3**).

5.3.7.3 Fee payable on the day of the application hearing

The Stock Exchange will raise an invoice on admission, which the company must pay within 30 days (Guidance to ADS 2.1, **Appendix 1**).

5.3.7.4 Information to be lodged after admission day

The company must lodge a statement of the number of shares which were issued (and, where different, the total number of issued shares of that class) as soon as this information is available (ADS 2.5, **Appendix 1**). This corresponds with the requirement of the FSA referred to at **5.3.6.5** above.

5.4 Key dates

5.4.1 Impact day

By the time of impact day all paperwork will have been finalised and the offer price will have been set (at the previous day's completion or pricing board meeting). The prospectus will have been submitted to the FSA at least 20 working days (probably more) before impact day (see **5.3.6.1** above). Section 87C of the FSMA 2000 provides that the FSA must notify the company whether it has decided to approve the prospectus before the end of the period of 20 working days beginning with the date the application is received. In practice, while the FSA will indicate that is has no further comments on the prospectus, actually it will formally approve the prospectus on impact day itself. Once it is approved, the prospectus must then be filed with the FSA under PR 3.2.1R.

Other ancillary agreements, such as the offer for sale agreement, placing agreement and underwriting agreement, will be dated.

The IPO is 'live' with effect from impact day. Investors can apply to invest in the company. However, the company has not yet floated. Flotation is still conditional upon the FSA admitting the shares to listing and the Stock Exchange admitting the shares to trading, and this will not be done until admission day (see **5.4.3**). The shares in the company are not yet being traded.

5.4.2 Between impact day and admission day

5.4.2.1 Publishing the prospectus

Having been approved by and filed with the FSA, the prospectus can be published. The company must publish the prospectus at least six working days before the end of the offer period (PR 3.2.3R). Prospectus Rule 3.2 governs the publication process.

There are four different ways to publish the prospectus, set out in PR 3.2.4R:

(a)   insert it into one or more newspapers widely circulated in the UK);

(b)   make it available to the public, in printed form, free of charge, at the offices of the Stock Exchange or the company's registered office and at the office of any intermediary placing or selling the shares;

(c)   make it available in electronic form on the company's website and on the website of any intermediary placing or selling the shares; or

(d)   make it available in electronic form on the Stock Exchange website.

Note that the FSA made clear in issue 10 of its newsletter, *List!*, that there is no requirement for the prospectus to be published on the company's website, and that it is possible to publish in hard copy only. However, if the company chooses to publish in electronic form, pursuant to (c) or (d) above, it should be aware that, nevertheless, any investor is entitled to demand a free hard copy under PR 3.2.6R.

5.4.2.2 Applications for shares

Investors who have been impressed by the prospectus and wish to invest in the company will complete the application form attached to the prospectus and send it to the receiving bank (see **4.2.8**). The application form states the deadline by which the form must reach the receiving bank. This is usually 10.00 am on the day following the FSA's admission hearing. This deadline is known as the time the 'lists open'.

If the offer is popular and over-subscribed, the lists will close at 10.01am. The board, advised by the sponsor, will then decide on the basis of allotment. If the offer is over-subscribed, clearly not all applicants will receive all the shares they applied for. The basis of allotment is a formula which decides the proportion of shares each applicant will receive. It varies according to the circumstances of the IPO, but it could be, for example, that each applicant receives, say, two-thirds of the number of shares applied for. On the other hand, it could be that the two-thirds ratio is applied only to those investors applying for significant numbers of shares, and those investors applying for small numbers of shares simply enter into a ballot system where they may be allotted their full quota, or none at all. Once the board has decided the basis of allotment, the company will make a formal announcement of the decision to investors.

With the Standard Life IPO in 2006, applicants for up to £2,000 worth of shares received the full amount they asked for. Those trying to buy more got 70% of the amount they applied for.

If the offer is under-subscribed, the lists will remain open longer. The company will then inform the underwriters how many shares they need to take up.

The receiving bank will cash the applicants' cheques and account to the company, and any shareholders who sold existing shares, for the proceeds. The company will then send share certificates, or letters of acceptance (see **5.4.3.4** below), to the successful investors, and (in the event that the IPO is over-subscribed) will send letters of regret to the investors who applied but have not been successful in buying any or all of the shares for which they applied.

5.4.2.3   Admission hearings

The FSA will hear the application for admission to listing on the same day that the Stock Exchange hears the application for admission to trading. The Listing Rules provide that the FSA can refuse admission to listing in certain circumstances, such as if it considers that admission would be detrimental to investors' interests (LR 2.1.3G and FSMA 2000, s 75(5)). The Admission and Disclosure Standards (ADS 1.5(a), **Appendix 1**) also reserve the right for the Stock Exchange to refuse admission to trading if admission might be detrimental to the orderly operation or integrity of the market. However, by the time the hearings take place, all the hard work on the IPO has been completed. The company and its advisers will have been in regular contact with the FSA and the Stock Exchange throughout the IPO process. It is very rare, therefore, for the FSA or the Stock Exchange to refuse admission at this stage.

5.4.3   Admission day

5.4.3.1   The Official List announcement

When the FSA is satisfied that it is prepared to admit the shares to listing, it must announce the admission through a Regulatory Information Service (LR 3.2.7G). In practice, the Official List issues an announcement, referred to as an Official List announcement or notice, to the Regulatory News Service (RNS) each day at 8am. This announcement refers to all companies which will list securities that day (both new applicants and companies which are already listed but which are listing further securities). The list does not distinguish the new applicants from the applicants which are already listed but which are listing further shares. Once the announcement is made (often referred to as 'going down the wire') the listing is effective, and dealing in the company's shares can begin. The company has floated.

An excerpt from the Official List announcement dated 23 June 2008 (the date Cadogan Petroleum plc, an oil and gas exploration and production company and a new applicant, floated) is set out below:

> **NOTICE OF ADMISSION TO THE OFFICIAL LIST**
>
> 23/06/2008 08:00am
>
> The Financial Services Authority ("FSA") hereby admits the following securities to the Official List with effect from the time and date of this notice:
>
> ABBEYCREST PLC
> 2,600,000   Ordinary Shares of 10p each fully paid   (GB0000037191)
>
> CADOGAN PETROLEUM PLC
> 231,091,734   Ordinary shares of 3p each fully paid   (GB00B12WC938)
>
> IMPAX ENVIRONMENTAL MARKETS PLC
> 659,168   Ordinary Shares of 10p each fully paid   (GB0031232498)
>
> MEARS GROUP PLC
> 73,620,041   Ordinary Shares of 1p each fully paid   (GB0005630420)
>
> MORRISON (WM) SUPERMARKETS PLC
> 661,000   Ordinary Shares of 10p each fully paid   Block Listing (GB0006043169)

5.4.3.2   The London Stock Exchange Notice

Similarly, when the Stock Exchange is satisfied that it wishes to admit the shares to trading, it must announce the admission using its website (Guidance to ADS 2.1). In practice, this will go down the wire at the same time as the Official List announcement.

An excerpt from the London Stock Exchange Notice dated 23 June 2008 is set out below:

NOTICE OF ADMISSION TO TRADING ON THE LONDON STOCK EXCHANGE

23/06/2008 08:00

The following securities are admitted to trading on the LSE with effect from the time and date of this notice:

ABBEYCREST PLC

2,600,000	Ordinary Shares of 10p each fully paid	(0-003-719)(GB0000037191)

CADOGAN PETROLEUM PLC

231,091,734	Ordinary Shares of 3p each fully paid	(B12WC93)(GB00B12WC938)

IMPAX ENVIRONMENTAL MARKETS PLC

659,168	Ordinary Shares of 10p each fully paid	(3-123-249)(GB0031232498)

MEARS GROUP PLC

73,620,041	Ordinary Shares of 1p each fully paid	(0-563-042)(GB0005630420)

MORRISON (WM) SUPERMARKETS PLC

		Block Admission
661,000	Ordinary Shares of 10p each fully paid	(0-604-316)(GB0006043169)

5.4.3.3   Dealings in shares

The company and its advisers will watch the market with bated breath on the first day of dealings. Ideally, the market price will rise a little above the offer price, meaning that the shares are trading at a small premium. This can suggest that the company pitched the offer price correctly. If the market price rises significantly, this may suggest that the offer price was something of a giveaway. If the market price drops below the offer price, the shares are trading at a discount, which may evidence a lack of demand for the shares. Sometimes, however, the first day of dealings can be distorted by market conditions altogether unrelated to the company. Cadogan Petroleum's shares dropped 13% on their first day's trading on the Stock Exchange in June 2008, reflecting the ongoing market turmoil caused by the 'credit crunch'.

5.4.3.4   Letters of acceptance

Sometimes the offer is structured so that initially successful applicants do not receive a share certificate, but a renounceable letter of acceptance. This is a bearer document, and the recipient can transfer title in the shares to someone else simply by handing them the letter (rather than by stock transfer form which is the usual method of transferring shares). Shares can be traded by way of renounceable letter for six weeks from admission day. The company's registrars will enter into the company's register of members whoever holds the letter at the end of that six-week period, and will send them a share certificate.

Letters of acceptance can be a useful method by which shares can be transferred easily at time when there tends to be substantial trading in shares. This also saves the registrars from issuing several new certificates in respect of the same shares.

5.4.4   After admission day

Admission day should not be seen as the end of a process but as the beginning of one. The company is now a listed company. The directors, key managers and the advisers will take the opportunity to celebrate the IPO together, and will then attempt to catch up on the many hours of sleep lost in the previous weeks. Then the company has to get back to business. The directors and management will return to their day-to-day business of running the company. However, life cannot simply return to how it was pre-IPO. There is now a whole new set of rules and regulations for the company to comply with. **Parts II, III** and **IV** of this book consider what life is like for a public company. Before we leave behind the IPO process, however, **Chapter 6** takes a detailed look at the main marketing document for any IPO: the prospectus.

Chapter 6
Initial Public Offerings: the Prospectus

6.1 Introduction

The lawyer must refer to the Prospectus Rules and Pt VI of the FSMA 2000 in order to advise whether a prospectus is required and, if so, what information the document must contain.

6.2 Purpose

The prospectus is the main marketing document for the IPO process. Potential investors will read the document and, it is hoped, the information it contains will encourage them to invest in the company. However, the company cannot be selective about what information to include in the document. The Prospectus Rules and the FSMA 2000 prescribe its contents. The lawyers must make sure that the document complies with all of the legal requirements as to content, but that it also retains the style of a marketing document which will attract investors. The prospectus is vital to the success of the IPO and, as is evident from **Chapter 5**, the drafting of this document takes up a large proportion of the IPO process.

6.3 Prospectus or listing particulars?

Prior to 1 July 2005, the main marketing document for an IPO could have been either a prospectus or listing particulars. Since that date the marketing document required for any IPO involving the issue of shares will be a prospectus. Listing particulars are required only for the issue of certain specialist securities, which, typically, the lawyer will encounter only rarely in practice. As the focus of this book is on the listing of shares, it makes no further reference to listing particulars but focuses on the prospectus.

6.4 The requirement for a prospectus

Prospectus Rule 1.2.1UK and s 85 of the FSMA 2000 provide that a prospectus, approved by the FSA, is required if the company wishes to do either or both of the following events:

(a) *offer* transferable securities *to the public* in *the UK* (s 85(1)); or

(b) request *admission* of transferable securities to *trading* on a regulated market situated or operating *in the UK* (even if there is no offer to the public) (s 85(2)).

This book focuses on IPOs which involve the issue and/or sale of ordinary shares which will be listed on the Official List and admitted to trading on the Main Market. This type of float involves both (a) and (b) above; both s 85(1) and s 85(2) apply, and, subject to any exemptions, a prospectus will be required (one prospectus will suffice, as confirmed in issue 10 of *List!*).

Note that even if the circumstances of an IPO meant that it involved only (a) or (b) above, then, subject to any exemptions, a prospectus would still be required.

The FSMA 2000 includes exemptions to s 85(1) and s 85(2). If these exemptions apply, a prospectus is not required, so the lawyer must be ready to advise how the float might be structured to avoid the need for this time-consuming and costly document.

It is important to recognise that the exemptions are drafted to apply specifically either to s 85(1) (offer to the public) or to s 85(2) (admission to trading). To take the example of our IPO, which involves both an offer to the public and admission to trading, even if it benefits from one of the 'offer to the public' exemptions, it will still require a prospectus unless one of the 'admission to trading' exemptions also applies.

Paragraphs **6.4.1** and **6.4.2** below examine the criteria of s 85(1) and s 85(2), and consider the different exemptions which apply to them.

6.4.1   Section 85(1): offering transferable securities to the public in the UK

Section 85(1) refers to all public offers of shares, including shares not listed on the Official List (such as shares admitted to the AIM).

Section 103 of the FSMA 2000 states that 'offer of transferable securities to the public' has the meaning in s 102B of the FSMA 2000. This in turn provides guidance on the interpretation of some of the key terms used in s 85(1).

6.4.1.1   Offer

There will be an offer if there is a communication to any person which presents sufficient information, on the shares to be offered and the terms on which they are offered, to enable an investor to decide to buy or subscribe for those shares (s 102B(1)). The communication may be made in any form and by any means (s 102B(3)).

A flotation by way of an offer for subscription and/or sale, placing or intermediaries offer will fulfil this criterion.

6.4.1.2   Transferable securities

Section 102A(3) defines 'transferable security' by reference to the Markets in Financial Instruments Directive (MiFID). For our purposes it is enough to note that this term includes ordinary shares. Therefore our example of an IPO involving the issue or sale of ordinary shares will fulfil this criterion.

6.4.1.3   To the public

Section 102B(2) of the FSMA 2000 provides that if the offer is made to 'a person in the United Kingdom' it is made to the public in the UK.

It is likely that an offer for sale or subscription will fulfil this criterion, but that a placing and intermediaries offer will be structured to fall within one of the exemptions, such as the 'qualified investors' or '100 persons' exemption, so that they do not fulfil this criterion. Note that LR Appendix 1.1 defines a placing as *not* constituting a public offer. However, this is unconnected to the definition of a public offer under the FSMA 2000 and so s 85 must still be considered.

6.4.1.4   In the UK

As referred to at **6.4.1.3** above, s 102B(2) of the FSMA 2000 makes clear that this criterion is satisfied if any recipient of the offer is in the UK.

The list of recipients of any offer for subscription and/or sale, placing or intermediaries offer must be analysed to see if this criterion is fulfilled.

6.4.1.5 Exemptions

The exemptions to s 85(1) of the FSMA 2000 (requiring a prospectus for offers to the public) are set out in s 85(5) (which in turn refers to Sch 11A of the FSMA 2000 and PR 1.2.2R) and s 86 of the FSMA 2000. The principal exemptions are as follows:

(a) *Offers to qualified investors (FSMA 2000, s 86(1)(a))*. The FSA maintains a register of qualified investors (the 'QIR') in accordance with s 87R of the FSMA 2000, which it makes available to companies and their agents exclusively for the purpose of making an offer of shares to qualified investors only. The register includes, for example, institutional investors such as insurance companies or investment firms. Certain individuals and small and medium-sized enterprises can self-certify that they are qualified investors.

(b) *Offers to fewer than 100 persons (who are not qualified investors) in each EEA State (FSMA 2000, s 86(1)(b))*. The Treasury has confirmed that there is no need to include the clients of discretionary brokers in calculating the number of persons to whom the offer is made.

(c) *Offers involving significant investment by each investor (FSMA 2000, s 86(1)(c) and (d))*. This will apply where each investor invests a minimum total consideration of €50,000 or where the shares being offered are denominated in amounts of at least €50,000 (or equivalent).

(d) *Small offers*. There are two exemptions relating to small offers. First, s 86(1)(e) of the FSMA 2000 exempts offers where the total consideration for the *transferable securities* cannot exceed €100,000. Secondly, s 85(5)(a) of and para 9 of Sch 11A to the FSMA 2000 exempt offers where the total consideration for the *offer* is less than €2,500,000. The second exemption was inserted into the Directive at a very late stage and there has been little commentary on the interaction between the apparently contradictory two small offer exemptions.

(e) *Share swaps (PR 1.2.2R(1))*. The issue of shares must not involve any increase in the company's issued share capital.

(f) *Offers in conjunction with takeovers (by way of share for share exchange) or mergers (PR 1.2.2R(2) and (3))*. However, a document must be available which contains information which the FSA regards as equivalent to that of a prospectus (referred to as an 'equivalent document').

(g) *Bonus issues and scrip dividends of a class of shares already listed (PR 1.2.2R(4))*. However, a document must be available which contains basic information about the number and type of shares offered, and the reasons for and the detail of the offer.

(h) *Offers by listed companies to employees and/or directors (PR 1.2.2R(5))*.

6.4.2 Section 85(2): admitting transferable securities to trading on a regulated market

6.4.2.1 Transferable securities

The definition of transferable securities is discussed at **6.4.1.2** above. Ordinary shares are transferable securities, so our IPO will fulfil this criterion.

6.4.2.2 Admit to trading

The type of IPO which is the focus of this book involves the admission of shares to trading (on the Main Market) and so fulfils this criterion.

6.4.2.3 Regulated market

This is defined in s 103(1) of the FSMA 2000. This refers to the definition contained in Art 4.1(14) of MiFID. It will probably pay to be seated before attempting to read it.

'Regulated market' means a multilateral system operated and/or managed by a market operator, which brings together or facilitates the bringing together of multiple third-party buying and selling interests in financial instruments – in the system and in accordance with its non-discretionary rules – in a way that results in a contract, in respect of the financial instruments admitted to trading under its rules and/or systems, and which is authorised and functions regularly and in accordance with the provisions of Title III.

Under the Title III referred to, it is up to the FSA to oversee the regulation of such regulated markets, and Art 47 of MiFID requires a list of regulated markets to be produced.

A list of regulated markets can be found on the FSA's and the European Commission's websites. It is far from easy navigating either website to locate this information (it is much easier to Google, particularly for the FSA), and when finally you reach the list it merely refers to 'London Stock Exchange – regulated market'.

What is not apparent from this is that the Main Market of the LSE is a regulated market under MiFID but AIM is not.

Our IPO will therefore involve a regulated market. (Note, however, that an AIM float will require a prospectus only if s 85(1) applies, ie that shares are being offered to the public as defined and no exemptions apply.)

6.4.2.4   Exemptions

The exemptions to s 85(2) of the FSMA 2000 (requiring a prospectus for shares to be admitted to trading on a regulated market) are set out in s 85(6) (which in turn refers to Pt 1 of Sch 11A to the FSMA 2000 and PR 1.2.3R). The principal exemptions are as follows:

(a)   *Admission of shares representing less than 10% of shares of the same class already admitted to trading on the same market (PR 1.2.3R(1)).* This is a *'de minimis'* provision. Issue 10 of the FSA's newsletter *List!* (available in the UKLA section of the FSA's website) confirms that the 10% limit is applied over a rolling 12-month period. This means that any shares admitted over the previous 12 months, which have not benefited from any *other* exemption, would count towards the 10%.

Example

Imagine a company has 1,000 shares in issue on 28 April 2007. On 5 July 2008 it issued 50 shares to employees under the admission to trading exemption referred to at (e) below. On 5 January 2009 it issues a further 50 shares which are placed with institutions, under the offer to the public exemption referred to at (a) in **6.4.1.5** above. The calculation to work out whether the 10% admission to trading exemption applies to this issue of 50 shares is as follows:

$$\frac{\text{Number of shares to be issued (including shares admitted over last 12 mths) which have not benefited from any other exemption)}}{\text{Number of shares of the same class already admitted to trading on the same market}}$$

that is,

$$\frac{50 \text{ (other issue within the last 12 months benefited from another exemption)}}{1,050}$$

that is, 4.7%. This issue of 50 shares would therefore be covered by the 10% exemption.

One month later, the company issues a further 50 shares. The calculation is now:

$$\frac{50 \text{ (this was covered by the 10% exemption, not any other exemption, so counts)} + 50}{1,100}$$

that is, 9.09%, so this issue is covered by the 10% exemption.

One month later, the company issues a further 50 shares. The calculation is:

$$\frac{50 + 50 + 50}{1,150}$$

that is, 13%, so this issue is outside the 10% exemption and will therefore require a prospectus.

(b)   *Share swaps (PR 1.2.3R(2)).* As **6.4.1.5(e)** above.

(c)   *Offers in conjunction with takeovers (by way of share for share exchange) or mergers (PR 1.2.3R(3) and (4)).* As at **6.4.1.5(f)** an equivalent document must be available.

(d)   *Bonus issues and scrip dividends of a class of shares already listed (PR 1.2.3R(5)).* As **6.4.1.5(g)** above.

(e)   *Offers to employees and/or directors of a class already listed (PR 1.2.3R(6)).*

(f)   *Shares of a class already listed resulting from the exercise of exchange or conversion rights (PR 1.2.3R(7)).*

(g)   *Shares already admitted to trading on another regulated market (subject to conditions) (PR 1.2.3R(8)).*

6.4.3 Conclusion

Having analysed the criteria, we can conclude that:

(a)   an IPO;

(b)   involving the offer or sale of ordinary shares;

(c)   which will be listed on the Official List and admitted to trading on the Main Market,

will require a prospectus, *unless* it benefits from *both*:

(d)   an 'offer to the public' exemption; and

(e)   an 'admission to trading' exemption.

In practice, as the table below shows, it is unlikely that an IPO can be structured to benefit from the required combination of exemptions.

Table 6.1

Method of flotation	Public offer under s 85(1)?	Admission to trading under s 85(2)?	Prospectus required?
Public offer	Yes. '100 persons' exemption possible but highly unlikely, given size of most retail offers.	Yes. '10%' exemption irrelevant in context of IPO, as no shares currently admitted to trading.	Yes (s 85(1) and s 85(2)).
Placing	Yes – however, likely to benefit from 'qualified investor' or '100 persons' exemption.	Yes. '10%' exemption irrelevant in context of IPO, as no shares currently admitted to trading.	Yes (s 85(2)).
Intermediaries offer	Yes. Likely to benefit from 'qualified investor' or '100 persons' exemption.	Yes. '10%' exemption irrelevant in context of IPO, as no shares currently admitted to trading.	Yes (s 85(2)).

Method of flotation	Public offer under s 85(1)?	Admission to trading under s 85(2)?	Prospectus required?
Introduction	No. No offer involved.	Yes. '10%' exemption irrelevant in context of IPO, as no shares currently admitted to trading.	Yes (s 85(2)).

6.5 Content

The FSMA 2000 and the Prospectus Rules prescribe the content of a prospectus.

Reading about the content requirements of a prospectus is essential, but there is no substitute for having a look at the real thing. I would recommend checking the websites of companies which have recently floated as, increasingly, companies are posting the prospectus and other documents, such as RNS announcements, on the area of their website aimed at shareholders (sometimes entitled 'investor relations').

6.5.1 General content requirements

As set out in PR 2.1.1UK, s 87A(2), (3) and (4) of the FSMA 2000 provide for the general content requirements of a prospectus. These provisions require that any prospectus must:

(a)   contain information necessary to enable investors to make an informed assessment of the assets and liabilities, financial position, profits and losses and prospects of the company, and the rights attaching to any securities (for our purposes, shares) (s 87A(2)); and

(b)   present the information referred to at (a) above in a form which is comprehensible and easy to analyse (s 87A(3)).

The information must be prepared having regard to the particular nature of the shares and the company (there is not an identical format of prospectus for all companies) (s 87A(4)). The FSA must not approve a prospectus unless it is satisfied that such general content requirements have been met (s 87A(1)).

6.5.2 Specific content requirements

As explained at **3.5.1.1**, the requirements regarding the content of a prospectus (other than the summary – see **6.5.2.1** below) are set out in the articles and annexes of the PD Regulation, the aim being that prospectuses issued by companies across the EU contain the same information in the same circumstances. These requirements are duplicated in the Prospectus Rules (the articles are set out at PR 2.3.1EU and the annexes are replicated at Appendix 3 of the Prospectus Rules).

Prospectus Rule 2.3 sets out the minimum information to be included in a prospectus. This rule refers to the 'schedules' and 'building blocks' of the annexes of the PD Regulation (and therefore of Appendix 3 of the Prospectus Rules), which are defined as follows:

> *Schedule* a list of minimum information requirements adapted to the particular nature of the different types of issuers and/or the different securities involved.
>
> *Building block* a list of additional information requirements, not included in one of the schedules, to be added to one or more schedules, as the case may be, depending on the type of instrument and/or transaction for which a prospectus … is drawn up.

In other words, the Prospectus Rules contain various minimum content requirements which may apply, depending on the type of company issuing shares and the nature of the shares. Not all of the information will be required in every prospectus. It is the lawyer's job to select which minimum content requirements are relevant for the particular transaction.

How can the lawyer find the content requirements required specifically for an IPO? In Annex XVIII of the PD Regulation (again, set out in Appendix 3 of the Prospectus Rules) there is a table which summarises which schedules and building blocks are required, depending on the circumstances of the issue (PR 2.3.1EU, citing PD Regulation, art 21). You should be aware that you will struggle to make sense of this Annex if you access the version in the Prospectus Rules on the FSA's website, as it lacks some essential shading of selected boxes which are needed to identify the content requirements. It is best to view a copy of the original PD Regulation on the EU's website.

For a straightforward IPO of ordinary shares the appropriate schedules will be the share schedules (Annexes I and III) and the pro forma financial information building block (Annex II). (The other annexes are relevant, for example, for the issue of debt securities, derivatives, depositary receipts or guarantees, or if the issuer falls within a certain category, for example it is a Member State.)

6.5.2.1   Format of the prospectus

The company has a choice of how it draws up the prospectus. Either it prepares a single document, or the prospectus may comprise three separate documents (PR 2.2.1R):

(a)   a summary (PR 2.1.2UK);

(b)   a registration document (PR 2.2.2R); and

(c)   a securities note (PR 2.2.2R).

Prospectus Rule 2.2.10EU sets out brief requirements as to the basic format of the prospectus.

It is intended that the option to draw up three separate documents will assist companies who are regular issuers of shares in circumstances which require a prospectus (see **6.4** above), as PR 5.1.4 provides that any approved registration document remains valid for up to 12 months (subject to the requirement to update). This means that once a registration document has been approved, any further issue of shares will require only a new summary and securities note. However, as explained at **6.10**, the new securities note must also update the registration document as to any material changes. This means that due diligence is still required each time the company wishes to use its registration document. As a result of this, and the fact that a bespoke prospectus tends to have advantages from a marketing perspective, to date companies have used the single document format.

The summary, registration document and securities note are considered in more detail below. Note that even if the company chooses the single document format, the document must include an identifiable summary and the information required by the registration document and securities note.

The summary

Prospectus Rule 2.1.2UK provides that in the UK, whichever format of prospectus is selected, the prospectus must include a self-contained summary. This must set out, briefly and in non-technical language, the essential characteristics of, and any risks associated with, the company and the shares to which the prospectus relates.

Prospectus Rules 2.1.4EU to 2.1.7R explain how the content of the summary will be determined. The following are the key requirements:

(a)   It is for 'the issuer, the offeror or the person asking for admission to trading' (usually the company) to decide the content of the summary (PR 2.1.4EU).

(b)   The summary should contain a warning that any prospective investor should read the full prospectus, not just the summary, before deciding to invest (PR 2.1.7R). (In practice, of course, many investors will feel that life is too short to heed this warning.)

(c)   The summary generally should not exceed 2,500 words (PR 2.1.5G), which is a commonsense approach to prevent the summary from becoming unwieldy, but may be difficult to achieve in practice. In issue 10 of *List!*, the FSA commented that a summary could exceed this word limit when the particularly complex nature of the company or the securities would make it difficult to meet the content requirements of the summary within 2,500 words. Even in such circumstances, however, the summary should not exceed excessively the 2,500 word limit.

Note that the summary has particular importance under the passporting procedure (see **6.11** below) as it is the only part of the prospectus which another Member State can request to be translated.

The onerous task of deciding what to include in the summary is relieved somewhat by the knowledge that limited liability attaches to it (see **6.7.1.1**).

The registration document

The registration document must provide information about the company. Prospectus Rule 2.3.1EU provides that it should contain the information set out in Annex I of the PD Regulation (set out at Appendix 3 of the Prospectus Rules). The main content requirements of Annex I are summarised below, but this is intended to provide only a flavour of the content of the prospectus. For comprehensive details of the content requirements, reference must be made to the Prospectus Rules themselves. The numerical paragraph references below correspond to the paragraph numbers of Annex I.

1.   *Persons responsible.* The document must identify all persons responsible for the information given in the registration document, and those persons must declare in the document that:

     having taken all reasonable care to ensure that such is the case, the information contained in the registration document is, to the best of their knowledge, in accordance with the facts and contains no omission likely to affect its import.

     This is referred to as the 'responsibility statement'. (Paragraphs **6.6** and **6.7** below discuss further the issues of responsibility and liability for the document.)

2.   *Statutory auditors.* The document must identify the company's auditors.

3.   *Selected financial information.* Certain financial information must be provided.

4.   *Risk factors.* A section headed 'risk factors' must include prominent disclosure of any and all risk factors which are specific to the company or its industry.

5.   *Information about the issuer.* The document must refer to the company's history and development, including information such as its date of incorporation, the address of its registered office and important events in the development of the company's business. The document must also contain a description of the company's principal investments, existing and future.

6.   *Business overview.* The company's principal activities and markets must be described.

7.   *Organisational structure.* The document must detail if the issuer is part of a group, a brief description of the group and the company's position within that group. It must also identify the company's significant subsidiaries.

8.   *Property, plant and equipment.* The company's existing and planned material tangible fixed assets, such as leased properties, and any encumbrances to which they are subject,

must be listed. The document must also highlight any environmental issues which may affect the company's ability to use such assets.

9. *Operating and financial review.* The document must include a description of the company's financial condition and other information which has materially affected, or could materially affect, the issuer's operations. In each case information is required for each of the years covered by the audited financial statements.

10. *Capital resources.* The document must detail the company's capital resources, including cash flow, borrowing requirements, any restrictions on the use of capital resources and information regarding the anticipated sources of funds for any future investments.

11. *Research and development, patents and licences.* Information must be provided about the company's research and development policy.

12. *Trend information.* Information is required about the most significant trends in production, sales and inventory, costs and selling prices, and any known trends or uncertainties which are reasonably likely to have a material effect on the company's prospects for the current financial year.

13. *Profit forecasts or estimates.* If an issuer chooses to include a profit forecast in the prospectus then it must also provide the information set out in para 13 of Annex I, including a statement setting out the assumptions on which the forecast is based and a report by the company's auditors or independent accountants that the forecast has been properly compiled.

14. *Administrative, management and supervisory bodies and senior management.* The document must provide information about the company's management, particularly the directors, but also potentially any founders (if the company is less than five years' old) and senior managers who are relevant to establishing that the company has appropriate expertise and experience for the management of the company's business. Some of this information could be seen as rather 'personal', such as details of any unspent convictions in relation to fraudulent offences, details of any insolvency events and details of any public criticisms of any director by any statutory or regulatory bodies. Ideally there will be no skeletons hiding in the directors' (or, if relevant, founders' or senior managers') closets which need to be aired in the prospectus (and if there are not, an appropriate 'negative statement' must be made in the document). However, if there are, then the due diligence process should ensure that they come to light sooner rather than later, so that the financial PR consultants have time to consider how they can manage the issues in a way that will not stop potential investors from investing in the company. Details of any conflict of interest between any of the people covered by para 14 must also be disclosed (and if there are none, an appropriate negative statement must be made).

15. *Remuneration and benefits.* Details of the remuneration (for the last full financial year) and benefits of the directors (and, if relevant, founders and senior managers) must be provided.

16. *Board practices.* Certain information about the running of the board, including periods of service, service contract information and corporate governance compliance (see **Chapter 8**), must be included.

17. *Employees.* The document must include information relating to employees, including the number of employees, information regarding their share or share option ownership, and a description of any arrangements for involving the employees in the company's capital.

18. *Major shareholders.* The document must identify any major shareholder of the company (that is, anyone other than a director who has an interest in the company's capital or voting rights which is notifiable under national law (3% in the UK – see **Chapter 15**), and provide other information as to such shareholders, such as whether or not they have different voting rights.

19.   *Related party transactions.* Details of any related party transactions (see **19.5**) must be provided, together with the amount to which such transactions form part of the company's turnover.

20.   *Financial information concerning the issuer's assets and liabilities, financial position and profits and losses.* The prospectus must contain a significant amount of financial information, prepared with the help of the reporting accounts. Paragraph **4.2.5** above refers to some of this information. In particular, the short form report, containing information relating to the profits and losses, assets and liabilities, financial record and position of the group for the period of three years before the IPO, must form part of the document. The document must also include a statement as to whether or not there has been any significant change in the financial or trading position of the group since the date to which the last accounts or interim statements were made up. This paragraph also refers to the inclusion of the 'building block' pro forma financial information required by Annex II.

Information is also required, by para 20.8, about any litigation or arbitration (including any pending or threatened) which might have, or has had, a significant effect on the group's financial position. This can be a very sensitive area for the company, which would not usually consider publicising litigation, or the threat of it. However, the Prospectus Rules are very clear that it must do so, subject to the 'significant effect' qualification. If the company does not consider it has anything to disclose in this regard, it must include a 'negative statement' to that effect.

Information about the company's dividend policy must also be included.

21.   *Additional information.* The document must include information about the company's share capital, such as the authorised and issued share capital, and certain details of the history of the company's share capital. In addition, various information about the company's memorandum and articles of association must be provided, including a description of the company's objects, a description of the rights attaching to each class of existing shares and a description of certain issues in the articles, such as any change of control clause or any conditions governing changes in capital which are more stringent than those required by law.

22.   *Material contracts.* The document should summarise the principal contents of certain contracts referred to as 'material contracts', namely those contracts which have been entered into other than in the ordinary course of business by the company or any member of the company's group:

(i)   in the two-year period preceding the publication of the document (if the contract is material); or

(ii)   at any time (if the contract provides the company or any member of the company's group with any entitlement or obligation which is still material to the company or the group as at the date the prospectus is published).

The lawyers will help the company to identify which documents fall within the definition and draft the summaries of those contracts for inclusion in the document.

23.   *Third party information and statement by experts and declarations of any interest.* If the document includes a statement or report attributed to a person as an expert, it must provide information about the expert. If the document contains any information sourced from a third party, the source of that information must be identified, and confirmation must be provided that the information has been reproduced accurately and that, as far as the issuer is aware, no facts have been omitted which would render the information inaccurate or misleading.

24.   *Documents on display.* The document should include a statement that, for the life of the registration document, certain documents (set out in para 24) are available at a named location for inspection. These documents include the company's memorandum and

articles of association and historical financial information. The lawyers will assist the company in creating and indexing the files of display documents.

25. *Information on holdings.* Information must be provided about any undertakings in which the company holds shares which are likely to have a significant effect on the assessment of the company's finances.

The securities note

The securities note must contain information about the securities (for our purposes, shares) to be offered or admitted. Prospectus Rule 2.3.1EU provides that the securities note should contain the information set out in Annex III of the PD Regulation (set out at Appendix 3 of the Prospectus Rules). The main content requirements of Annex III are summarised below. Again this is intended to provide only a flavour of the content of the prospectus, and for a comprehensive list of the content requirements, you should refer to the Prospectus Rules themselves. The numerical paragraph references below correspond to the paragraph numbers of Annex III.

1. *Persons responsible.* As with the registration document, a responsibility statement must be included; this time by all those responsible for the information given in the prospectus.

2. *Risk factors.* Again, there is a requirement similar to that which exists for the registration document, that the securities note must include prominent disclosure, under the section headed 'risk factors', of risk factors that are material to the shares being offered and/or admitted. This is to enable investors to assess the market risk associated with the shares.

3. *Key information.* The document must include what is referred to as the 'working capital statement', namely a statement that, in the company's opinion, the working capital is sufficient for the issuer's present requirements or, if not, how it proposes to provide the additional working capital it requires. Of course, this ensures the directors address their minds to the ability of the company to thrive, or at least survive, after flotation, and address the likelihood of insolvency problems after the IPO. (The working capital statement is, in effect, a statement that the company is not going to 'go belly up' (ie become insolvent) straight after the IPO.) The document must also include a capitalisation and indebtedness statement. In addition, information must be provided in relation to anyone with any particular interest in the issue/offer of shares (including any conflicting interest), and in relation to the reasons for the offer and how it is intended any proceeds will be used.

4. *Information concerning the securities to be offered/admitted to trading.* Information must be provided about the shares which are to be offered or admitted, including a description of the type and class of shares, the legislation under which the securities were created (until 1 October 2009, the CA 1985; thereafter, the CA 2006), the rights which attach to the shares (such as voting rights, rights to share in capital, dividend rights and pre-emption rights: see **Chapters 13** and **14**). In the case of new issues, the resolutions, authorisations and approvals by virtue of which the shares have been created and/or issued must also be stated (see **Chapter 14**).

5. *Terms and conditions of the offer.* The document must set out detailed terms and conditions of the offer, including the total amount of the offer, the period for which the offer will be open and the circumstances under which the offer can be revoked, and an indication of the offer price. Details of any underwriters and when the underwriting agreement was or will be reached are also required.

6. *Admission to trading and dealing arrangements.* As a prospectus is required for all public offers (unless an exemption applies), there is a requirement to include a statement as to whether the shares offered will be admitted to trading with a view to their distribution on a regulated market. For our purposes, in the context of an IPO the shares will be admitted to trading on the Main Market, a regulated market.

7.   *Selling securities holders.* If the IPO involves an offer for sale of shares (see **4.4.1.1**) then specific details must be provided, including the name and address of the selling shareholders and the number and class of shares being sold by each shareholder.

8.   *Expense of the issue/offer.* The securities note must detail the total net proceeds and an estimate of the total expenses of the issue/offer.

9.   *Dilution.* The amount and percentage of immediate dilution (see **14.6.2**) resulting from the offer must be included in the document.

10. *Additional information.* There is a requirement, to mirror the requirement in para 23 of Annex I relating to the registration document, that if the securities note includes a statement or report attributed to a person as an expert, then it must provide information about the expert. If it contains any information sourced from a third party, the source of that information must be identified, and confirmation must be provided that the information has been reproduced accurately and that, as far as the issuer is aware, no facts have been omitted which would render the information inaccurate or misleading. Other additional information which must be included is a statement of the capacity in which any advisers, referred to in the securities note, have acted, and to identify and reproduce, or summarise, audited information referred to in the document.

6.5.2.2   Incorporation by reference

Information can be incorporated by reference into the registration document or the securities note, in certain circumstances, without, therefore, having to be restated in full. To be incorporated, the information must:

(a)   have been approved by, filed with, or notified to the FSA (PR 2.4.1R);

(b)   be the latest available to the company (PR 2.4.3R);

(c)   be accessible using a cross-referenced list in the prospectus (PR 2.4.5R); and

(d)   not endanger investor protection (PR 2.4.6EU, para 5).

Prospectus Rule 2.4.6EU, para 1 sets out examples of information which can be incorporated by reference, such as information in the audited report and accounts of the company, or the company's memorandum and articles of association. As explained at **5.3.6.2** above, the company must submit to the FSA a copy of any document incorporated into the prospectus by reference (annotated to indicate to which item of the schedules and building blocks in the PD Regulation it relates). To date reference to information incorporated by reference seems to have been made in the rubric on the cover page of the prospectus.

Unlike the registration document and the securities note, the summary cannot incorporate information by reference (PR 2.4.4R).

6.5.2.3   Omission of information

Prospectus Rule 2.5.2UK and s 87B of the FSMA 2000 provide that the FSA has the discretion to authorise the omission of any information required by the Prospectus Rules or s 87A of the FSMA 2000 if:

(a)   disclosure of the information would be contrary to the public interest; or

(b)   disclosure of the information would be seriously detrimental to the company and the omission of the information is not likely to mislead investors in their assessment of the investment; or

(c)   the information to be omitted is of minor importance for a specific offer or admission and is unlikely to influence the investors' ability to make an informed choice as to whether to invest.

As mentioned at **5.3.6.2** above, any request to omit information under PR 2.5.2R must comply with the requirements of PR 2.5.3R.

The lawyers must make the directors aware of this discretion of the FSA, but they must manage the message carefully. As we have seen, the Prospectus Rules and the FSMA 2000 require significant disclosure in the prospectus. The directors may not want certain information to be included in the prospectus, and will ask the lawyers how they can avoid disclosure of that information. The general message is that if the Prospectus Rules, or the general disclosure requirement in s 87A of the FSMA 2000, require such disclosure then the prospectus must contain that information. The FSA will exercise its discretion to omit information only in exceptional circumstances. Indeed, the very fact that directors wish to omit certain information may suggest that they think that such information would deter investors from investing in the company. This means that the information is likely to be highly relevant to investors, and so would not fall within the FSA's discretion in any event. Lawyers need to be firm with directors who try to conceal facts, because ultimately the directors themselves may be personally liable to investors for inaccuracies in or omissions from the prospectus (see **6.7** below).

6.5.2.4 Checking content

Chapter 5 describes how the prospectus is submitted to the FSA for approval. To help the FSA check that the document complies with its content requirements, PR 3.1.4R requires that the draft document must be annotated in the margin to indicate which Prospectus Rule requirement the text complies with. So, for example, the margin opposite the list of directors' names and addresses would be annotated with 'I.14' to indicate that the list fulfils the content requirements of Annex 1, para 14. Subsequent drafts must comply with PR 3.1.5R. In issue 22 of the FSA's Newsletter, *List!*, (available on the UKLA section of the FSA's website) the FSA asks that deleted text should be retained (eg by using 'strike-through') to speed up the approval process.

6.6 Responsibility

It is all very well requiring the production of a prospectus which will usually run to well in excess of 100 pages, but what if any of the information included in the prospectus proves to be incorrect, or what if a relevant piece of information has been omitted? This may lead to investors losing money if they have invested as a result in a company which is in reality not what it appears to be from the prospectus. Can the investors be compensated in such circumstances? The answer is yes. The FSMA 2000 provides the authority to make certain people involved in the preparation of the prospectus take responsibility for the accuracy of its contents. It then makes those responsible liable for any mistakes or omissions which cause investors loss.

6.6.1 Who is responsible for the contents of the prospectus?

The answer lies in the Prospectus Rules as authorised by s 84(1)(d) of the FSMA 2000. Where, as in our case, the prospectus relates to equity securities (ordinary shares) for which the UK is the home Member State, PR 5.5.3R(2) provides that the following people will be responsible for the prospectus:

(a)   the issuer (ie the company) (PR 5.5.3R(2)(a));

(b)   the directors of the company (as at the date the document is published) (PR 5.5.3R(2)(b)(i));

(c)   anyone who has agreed to be named, and is named, in the prospectus as a director, or as having agreed to become a director, either immediately or in the future (after the IPO, for example) (PR 5.5.3R(2)(b)(ii));

(d)   anyone who accepts, and is stated in the prospectus as accepting, responsibility for the prospectus (PR 5.5.3R(2)(c));

(e)   anyone, other than the company, who is offering shares (and if this is another company, the directors of that company at the time the prospectus is published) (PR 5.5.3R(2)(d));

(f)   the person requesting admission to trading of the shares (if not the company) (and if this is another company, the directors of that company at the time the prospectus is published) (PR 5.5.3R(2)(e)); and

(g)   anyone else who authorises the contents of the prospectus (PR 5.5.3R(2)(f)).

Paragraph (e) above will be of particular concern to any selling shareholders if an offer for sale forms part of the IPO. They may well be individuals who would not be comfortable taking such responsibility. However, comfort is at hand. Prospectus Rule 5.5.7R provides that a person will not be responsible under PR 5.5.3R(2)(d) if the shareholder is making the offer in association with the issuer and it is primarily the issuer, or the issuing company's advisers, who draw up the prospectus. This will usually be the case with IPOs, so usually the lawyer will be able to reassure any selling shareholders on the issue of responsibility.

Paragraph (g) above will, for example, cover the accountants (because they have authorised financial information prepared specifically for the prospectus) (Annex I, para 23 and Annex III, para 10 – see **6.5.2.1** above). As a result, they must set out a statement in the prospectus that they are responsible for such content. However, they will not be required to give such a statement in respect of financial information incorporated by reference which was not prepared specifically for the prospectus.

It appears that the FSA does not consider the sponsor to have authorised the prospectus for the purposes of the responsibility regime, as current practice is for sponsors not to provide such a statement under PR 5.5.9R.

Lawyers similarly are covered by the exemption in PR 5.5.9R. They do not have responsibility by reason only of giving advice about the content of the prospectus in a professional capacity.

6.6.2   What does responsibility mean?

The persons with responsibility for the document must ensure that the document complies with the general disclosure obligation imposed by the FSMA 2000 (see **6.5.1** above), the specific content requirements set out in the Prospectus Rules (see **6.5.2** above) and the requirements of the Listing Rules in relation to the listing application to the FSA (see **Chapter 5**). In other words, they must ensure that all relevant information is included in the prospectus. The consequences of this are discussed at **6.7** below.

6.6.3   Practicalities

6.6.3.1   Responsibility statement

As mentioned at **6.5.2.1** above, a responsibility statement must be included in the prospectus pursuant to para 1.2 of both Annex I and Annex III of the Prospectus Rules.

6.7   Liability

As stated in **6.6.2** above, those with responsibility for the prospectus must ensure that it meets the content requirements of the Prospectus Rules and the FSMA 2000, and the rules relating to the application for listing under the Listing Rules. The document must not omit any information or contain information which is incorrect or misleading. The consequence of this is that the persons responsible for the document may incur civil and/or criminal liability in relation to any inaccuracies or misstatements in, or omissions from, the document.

6.7.1 Civil liability

6.7.1.1 Section 90 of the FSMA 2000

This is the liability which a person responsible is most likely to face for problems arising out of the content of the prospectus.

The effect of s 90 of the FSMA 2000 is that those responsible for *listing particulars* must pay compensation to anyone who has acquired shares which are the subject of the listing particulars, and has suffered loss as a result of any inaccurate or misleading statement in the document, or any omission of information which should have been disclosed under s 87A. Section 90(11) (added by para 6 of Sch 1 to the Prospectus Regulations 2005) provides that this applies equally in relation to a *prospectus*. While it includes specific reference to the general disclosure requirement under s 87A of the FSMA 2000, in practice s 90 is construed to apply not only to a failure of the prospectus to meet this requirement, but also to any failure to meet the content requirements of the Prospectus Rules.

Note that s 90(12) provides that a person can be liable for the contents of the summary (see **6.5.2.1**) only if the summary is misleading, inaccurate or inconsistent when read together with the rest of the prospectus.

It may help to consider the issue of liability by way of an example.

Example

Imagine that an investor, Mr X, encouraged by the positive messages in the prospectus, invests in Company A. In fact, the prospectus failed to include information about a very real risk that a rival's new invention could significantly reduce Company A's sales. Imagine that, after the IPO, the rival's new invention goes terribly wrong. Company A continues to prosper and Mr X makes a good profit. Mr X has suffered no loss and the persons responsible for the inaccurate prospectus, through sheer luck, will incur no liability under s 90.

Consider now what would happen if, in fact, the rival's new invention is a huge success, to the extent that Company A loses significant sales and ultimately goes belly up. Mr X loses his entire investment. He has suffered loss and wants compensation. Section 90 of the FSMA 2000 provides that he should obtain compensation from those persons responsible for the incorrect selling document (that is, mainly, the directors).

What is the scope of s 90? There are two particular phrases in the provision which have caused some debate:

(a)   'who has acquired' – s 90 concerns the loss suffered by a person 'who has acquired' securities. Is this restricted to the original investor, or does it include those who buy the shares from that original investor?

(b)   'as a result of' – for any investor to have a claim to compensation under s 90, he must prove that he suffered loss 'as a result of' the deficiencies in the document. Does this mean that the investor must have relied on the document? Must the investor have read the document?

These phrases leave open the possibility that any aggrieved original investor who had not even read the document, or any subsequent purchaser of the shares from the original investor, could try to run the argument that s 90 is wide enough to afford him a claim for compensation.

There are some exemptions from liability under s 90, which are set out in Sch 10 to the FSMA 2000. These exemptions include:

(a)   if, at the time the prospectus was submitted to the FSA, the persons responsible (having made reasonable enquiries) believed the erroneous information was true and not misleading;

(b)   where loss arises as a result of a statement by an expert;

(c)   where a correction had been published before shares were acquired;

(d)   where the erroneous information was reproduced from a public official document; and

(e)   where the person seeking compensation acquired the shares knowing the information was deficient.

6.7.1.2   Liability in tort

The persons responsible for the prospectus may also incur tortious liability under the following heads:

(a)   *Negligent misstatement.* Those with responsibility for the prospectus owe a duty of care to those investing at the time of the IPO. The publication of a deficient document breaches this duty. If an investor relies on a deficient prospectus and suffers loss because of that reliance then, on the basis of *Hedley Byrne & Co Ltd v Heller & Partners Ltd* [1964] AC 465, those responsible for the prospectus will be liable to that investor. Note that, applying *Caparo Industries v Dickman* [1990] 1 All ER 568, the persons responsible for the document would not owe any duty to any subsequent purchasers of the shares. This, and the fact that the investor must have *relied* on the erroneous information or omission, can be contrasted with the position under s 90 of the FSMA 2000 (see **6.7.1.1**) and therefore makes this a less attractive claim for an aggrieved investor.

(b)   *Deceit.* If an investor can prove that any misstatement in the prospectus was made fraudulently, he may have a claim in damages for deceit.

(c)   *Misrepresentation Act 1967.* If an investor chooses to invest in the company on the basis of an incorrect or misleading prospectus, he may be able to rescind the contract for the purchase of shares and/or claim damages from the other party to the contract (see also CA 2006, s 655). Note that the other party will be the issuer of the shares, ie the company (in the case of an offer for subscription) or the selling shareholder (in the case of an offer for sale), rather than the directors.

6.7.1.3   Liability in contract

The prospectus will form either the whole or part of any contract between an investor buying shares and either the company issuing shares to the investor, or any existing shareholder selling shares to the investor (the circumstances will vary depending on the IPO). If the prospectus is deficient, the investor may be able to rescind the contract, or sue the other party to the contract (the company or the selling shareholder) for damages.

6.7.2   Criminal liability

The threat of paying compensation or damages may be bad enough for the persons responsible, but it could get worse. Reflecting the importance of protecting the investing public, there may even be the possibility of criminal liability. Mentioning this sanction does tend to help any director, who is tiring of the legal due diligence or verification process, to re-focus.

6.7.2.1   Section 397 of the FSMA 2000

A director risks criminal liability under the following provisions of the FSMA 2000:

(a)   *Section 397(1) and (2) (misleading statements).* These provisions make it a criminal offence for any director knowingly or recklessly to make a materially misleading, false or deceptive statement, promise or forecast, or to conceal dishonestly any material facts, in order to induce an investor to buy shares.

(b)   *Section 397(3) (market manipulation).* This provision catches anything the director does to create a false or misleading impression as to the market in, or price or value of the shares, if he does so deliberately to induce investors to buy shares.

Section 397 of the FSMA 2000 is considered in more detail at **9.5** below.

6.7.2.2 Theft Act 1968

Section 19 of the Theft Act 1968 imposes criminal penalties on any director who makes false or misleading statements with intent to deceive shareholders. Clearly this could apply to any director who is responsible for a deficient prospectus, if intent can be proved.

6.7.2.3 Section 85(3) of the FSMA 2000

It is a criminal offence for a person to offer shares to the public or request their admission to trading without providing an approved prospectus to the public.

6.7.2.4 Fraud Act 2006

It is a criminal offence under s 2 of the Fraud Act 2006 to dishonestly make a representation and in doing so intend to make a gain or cause a loss. Under s 3 it is a criminal offence for a person to fail to disclose information which he is legally obliged to do and in doing so make a gain or expose another to the risk of loss. Under s 12, if the offence is committed by a company then a director or other officer of the company is (in addition to the company) liable for that offence if he consents or connives in that offence. The penalties for these offences under s 1 are a maximum of 10 years imprisonment and an unlimited fine.

6.7.3 Fines

As seen at **3.6** above, s 91 of the FSMA 2000 provides that the FSA can fine the company for breach of Part 6 Rules, including the Prospectus Rules and, if it can prove that any director or former director was knowingly concerned in the breach, can also fine that director.

6.7.4 Censure

As seen at **3.6** above, s 91 of the FSMA 2000 provides that the FSA may choose privately or publicly to censure the company, or a director or former director knowingly concerned in the breach, as an alternative to a fine.

6.8 Verification

As the range of possible liability set out at **6.7** above makes clear, it is not a good idea for the directors to make incorrect statements in the prospectus, or to omit required material from it. During the IPO process, therefore, great care is taken to ensure that the prospectus meets the requirements of the Prospectus Rules and the FSMA 2000. As **6.6.1** above explains, directors are not the only people with responsibility for the document, but they do have responsibility, and their responsibility is for the entire document. Accordingly, a process has emerged which aims to ensure that the directors make all reasonable enquiries to satisfy themselves that:

(a)   each material statement of fact or opinion in the document is not only true, but also not misleading in the context in which it appears;

(b)   the document as a whole gives a true and fair impression of the history, business and prospects of the company; and

(c)   the document does not omit any information which makes it misleading or which contravenes the Prospectus Rules and/or s 87A of the FSMA 2000.

This process is called verification. It protects the directors by providing evidence that they have taken reasonable care to ensure the information required by s 87A of the FSMA 2000 has been included. It also helps to avoid breaching s 397 of the FSMA 2000 (see **9.5**) and the market abuse regime (see **Chapter 10**), and so provides comfort to the sponsor. The verification process is considered in more detail at **5.3.5** above.

6.9   Types of prospectus

6.9.1   Full

So far, this chapter has considered the document which will ultimately be submitted to the FSA for approval as part of the company's application for admission to listing. This is known as the full prospectus. However, references to other forms of the prospectus may be made during the IPO process. These references are explained below.

6.9.2   Preliminary prospectus

This is virtually identical to the full prospectus. It too has to be approved by the FSA before it can be sent out to prospective investors. The key difference is that the price for the shares being offered will not be specified in the document as a fixed amount, instead there will usually be a price range. It is even possible to issue the preliminary prospectus without a price or the number of shares being offered being mentioned at all. Approval by the FSA means that this document can be sent out to any potential investor. A pricing statement will subsequently be issued setting out the final price before the offer closes under PR 2.3.2R. This statement does not require prior approval by the FSA (possibly with a supplementary prospectus (see **6.9.4** below) if, for example, there has been a material change to the information in the preliminary prospectus).

6.9.3   Pathfinder prospectus

This is a draft of the prospectus which is sent out to prospective investors to stimulate interest in the IPO. A full prospectus will be sent out once expressions of interest have been received. The crucial difference from the preliminary prospectus (see **6.9.2**) is that it is sent to prospective investors without prior FSA approval. This causes a potential problem in that it could result in a breach of s 21 of the FSMA 2000 (see **Chapter 12**). The impact of s 21 is that it is an offence for a company to send out a pathfinder to induce investors to buy shares. The company can avoid this problem by sending the pathfinder only to persons exempt from s 21 (mainly institutional investors) (see **12.9**). In addition, a pathfinder must comply with the rules relating to advertisements set out in PR 3.3 (see **5.3.6.6**), as clarified in Issue 12 of *List!*, the FSA's newsletter (available in the UKLA section of the FSA's website).

Note that under PR 3.2.3R, an approved prospectus (be it full or preliminary) must be made available to investors at least six working days before the close of the offer (see **5.4.2.1**).

6.9.4   Factors to take into account

There are a number of factors to weigh up before the company decides whether to issue a preliminary or pathfinder prospectus.

A pathfinder can be distributed only to limited categories of person (such as institutional investors) whereas a preliminary prospectus can be sent out to any investor, including a member of the public.

If a preliminary prospectus is used, a supplementary prospectus may have to be prepared which will need to be approved by the FSA before it is distributed (see **6.9.5**). This does not arise with a pathfinder, as no prior prospectus relating to the offer is in existence. The publication of a supplementary prospectus grants investors the right to withdraw their acceptance of the offer (FSMA 2000, s 87Q(4)).

Another potential disadvantage of the company choosing to use a preliminary prospectus (which does not arise with a pathfinder) is that investors have the right to withdraw their acceptances of the offer within two working days of the date the company provides the price of the offer to the FSA under s 87A(7) of the FSMA 2000 (FSMA 2000, s 87(Q)(1) and (2)). However, if the prospectus details the method and conditions for determining the price and amount (or, in relation to the price, states a maximum offer price) then this right to withdraw will not arise (FSMA 2000, s 87Q(3)).

Note that under PR 3.2.3R, an approved prospectus (be it full or preliminary) must be made available to investors at least six working days before the close of the offer (see **5.4.2.1**).

6.9.5 Supplementary

Section 87G of the FSMA 2000 and PR 3.4.1UK provide that if, in the period following the approval of the prospectus but before dealings in shares commence, there arises or is noted any significant new factor, material mistake or inaccuracy relating to the information included in the approved prospectus, the company must produce a supplementary prospectus. This document must contain details of the new factor, mistake or inaccuracy, and must be approved by the FSA. As mentioned at **6.9.4** above, investors have the right to withdraw their acceptances of the offer during the two working days following publication of the supplementary prospectus (FSMA 2000, s 87Q(4)), so this is a situation to be avoided if at all possible and demonstrates another reason for having the thorough due diligence process in the period leading up to the IPO.

6.10 Validity

A prospectus is valid for 12 months after its publication, for any further offers or admissions to trading, provided that it is updated by a supplementary prospectus, approved by the FSA (see **6.9.5**) (PR 5.1.1R). As mentioned at **6.5.2.1** above, the registration document is valid for a period of up to 12 months after it has been filed, but this is also subject to updating, using a new securities note, which again requires the approval of the FSA (PR 2.2.5R and PR 5.1.4R).

Given the requirements for FSA approval of any update to either the prospectus (by supplementary prospectus) or the registration note (by a new securities note), any advantage of this extended validity period may be limited, as explained at **6.5.2.1** above.

6.11 Passporting

The Prospectus Directive has ensured that each Member State has the same rules regarding the drawing up of a prospectus. This reflects the principal aim of the European Commission's Financial Services Action Plan (FSAP), to create a single financial market across the EU. It also applies to non-EU EEA states, such as Norway and Iceland. This has enabled the introduction of a 'passporting' procedure, whereby a company will not need to produce a prospectus for an offer of shares to the public, or an admission of shares to trading, in one EEA member state ('MS2') if another EEA member state ('MS1') has already approved and published a prospectus in the previous 12 months. Subject to updating (see **6.10** above), the company simply must translate the summary (not, interestingly, any other part of the prospectus) into a language acceptable to MS2 and obtain a 'certificate of approval' from the competent authority in MS1 (in the UK, the FSA) that the prospectus has been drawn up and approved in accordance with the Prospectus Directive. Prospectus Rule 3.1.6G states that any request for such a certificate should be included with the company's application for approval of the initial prospectus. Prospectus Rule 5.3 and ss 87H and 87I of the FSMA 2000 set out the rules relating to the certificate of approval, and the UKLA Publications Factsheet No 4 (available from the UKLA section of the FSA's website) provides further information on the procedure to be followed.

While the passporting procedure is easier to use than the previous mutual recognition procedure, a potentially lengthy due diligence exercise may still be required to ensure any previously issued prospectus is up to date. In addition, the eligibility criteria for listing are not covered by the Prospectus Directive and so remain diverse in each of the EEA member states (remember that in the UK the conditions for listing are set out in Chapters 2 and 6 of the

Listing Rules – see **4.3.1.1**). The company may have to meet further criteria in order to list shares in MS2 which it did not have to meet to list shares in MS1.

To date, a number of companies in the UK have taken advantage of the passporting procedure for an offer of shares in more than one EEA member state. For example, the prospectus approved for the Royal Bank of Scotland's rights issue (see **17.7**) in 2008 was passported into France, Germany, Ireland, the Netherlands and Spain. Most EEA member states have been requesting that the summary be translated into their national language, although certain EEA member states (such as Austria, Luxembourg, the Netherlands and, in certain cases, Norway) accept the English language version. The Royal Bank of Scotland summary had to be translated into French, German and Spanish, but not into Dutch.

The FSA maintains a database (accessible through the UKLA section of its website) of companies which have passported prospectuses from non-UK EU jurisdictions.

Part II
BEING A LISTED COMPANY

Chapter 7
Continuing Obligations

7.1 Introduction

Chapter 1 explained that, once a company is listed, it becomes subject to continuing obligations. Both the FSA (in the DTRs, the Corporate Governance Rules, the Prospectus Rules and the Listing Rules) and the Stock Exchange (in the Admission and Disclosure Standards) impose continuing obligations on listed companies. As with the IPO process, however, the FSA and the Stock Exchange have worked together to dovetail their requirements.

7.2 Why have continuing obligations?

The continuing obligations exist to protect both existing and potential investors. They seek to ensure that there is an orderly market for investments (stablility being crucial to investors' confidence in the markets) and that all investors have access to information at the same time (in the interests of fairness).

Put into context, it makes sense that listed companies should bear these obligations. Remember that their shareholder base is diverse, and the vast majority of shareholders will not be involved in the management of the company and may know little about its day-to-day running (see **2.6** above). They therefore require increased protection to ensure that their investment in the company is safe.

At first glance, there may seem to be so many continuing obligations that you might wonder why any company would choose to float. Before embarking on the IPO process a company should of course consider, as part of its pre-IPO preparation, whether it is capable of meeting the continuing obligations that will be imposed on it after the IPO. However, the obligations are certainly not meant to deter companies from listing. In practice, once companies have put in place the administrative processes to enable them to deal with the obligations, most find that meeting the continuing obligations simply becomes part of the day-to-day running of the business.

That said, it seems that greater regulation imposed on listed companies trading on stock markets in the US, such as the NYSE and NASDAQ, principally as a result of the Sarbanes-Oxley Act of 2002 (a name guaranteed to get the pulse racing amongst bankers, lawyers, entrepreneurs and investors across the globe), has led to an increase in (particularly non-UK) companies seeking to list in London rather than in the US. Some foreign companies (including UK ones such as lastminute.com) even 'delisted' from US stock markets to avoid the increased liability for directors and the greater cost of compliance with new accounting rules and other new continuing obligations brought in under the Sarbanes-Oxley Act. The Act was introduced in the US as a direct result of the financial scandals involving US listed companies, such as Enron and Worldcom, with the aim of increasing investor protection. The UK has, together with all other EU Member States as part of the FSAP, also strengthened controls on listed companies, particularly regarding the disclosure of financial information, albeit in a more measured fashion. However, this position is under review. In light of the failure of regulators to prevent the global financial crisis and the ability of listed companies, particularly banks, to put themselves in a position which imperilled their very existence, governments throughout the world are calling for tighter controls to be introduced, particularly on banks. It remains to be seen how this will translate into more restrictive continuing obligations on listed companies.

The company will, of course require advice on the continuing obligations from its advisers from time to time. If the company was impressed by the work of its advisers on the IPO, it may well retain those advisers on a permanent basis after flotation. Due to the day-to-day nature of the continuing obligations, the in-house legal department of the listed company will often take responsibility for ensuring that the company meets those obligations. However, where a second opinion is required, or where the in-house solicitors are not available, the company will often call on its external lawyers, who will be expected to know what the continuing obligations are and how to meet them. As is explained below, due to the need to meet the obligations in a timely manner, the company will often require advice on an urgent basis.

7.3   Where to find the continuing obligations

The continuing obligations imposed on listed companies can be found in the CA 2006, Chapters 9–19 of the Listing Rules, the DTRs, the Corporate Governance Rules, PR 5.2.1R and in the Stock Exchange's Admission and Disclosure Standards. Chapters 14–19 of the Listing Rules relate to special types of issuer or security and so fall outside the scope of this textbook. Chapters 10 and 11 of the Listing Rules which deal with transactions, are discussed at **19.4** and **19.5** respectively. The remainder can be tackled more manageably if they are grouped together as follows:

(a)   obligations with continuing application (see **7.4**);

(b)   obligations requiring the disclosure and notification of information about the company (see **7.5**);

(c)   obligations relating to the shareholders of the company (see **7.6**);

(d)   obligations relating to financial information about the company (see **7.7**); and

(e)   obligations in the Admission and Disclosure Standards (see **7.10**).

The Association of General Counsel and Company Secretaries of the FTSE 100 (GC100) produced a set of Guidelines (the GC100 Guidelines) in three parts on 1 June 2007. Part I seeks to assist its members (who are employed by the biggest listed companies) in establishing procedures, systems and controls to ensure that they comply fully with the Listing Rules and the DTRs. The Guidelines are neither legally binding nor part of the FSA's Handbook, although the FSA has agreed to include the following wording in the Guidelines, 'the FSA has seen this material in draft and recognises these Guidelines as a useful contribution to a difficult area'. In practice, therefore, the corporate lawyer needs to be aware of their existence.

7.4   Obligations with continuing application

Listing Rule 9.2 sets out some of the eligibility requirements for listing (see **Chapter 4**) which will continue to apply even after the IPO has taken place.

7.4.1 Admission to trading

You will recall that a condition for listing is that the shares are admitted to trading (LR 2.2.3R) (see **4.3.1.1**). Listing Rule 9.2.1R provides that it is a continuing obligation that the company's shares are admitted to trading at all times. This seeks to ensure that shares in a company are always freely marketable.

7.4.2 Compliance with the Disclosure, Transparency and Corporate Governance Rules

Under LR 9.2.5G and LR 9.2.6R, a listed company must comply with Chapter 2 of the DTRs (that is, the general obligation of disclosure and related matters discussed at **7.5** below).

Under LR 9.2.6AG and LR 9.2.6BR, a listed company must comply with the Transparency Rules (Chapters 4–6 of the DTRs) and the Corporate Governance Rules (Chapter 7 of the DTRs).

These continuing obligations explicitly reinforce compliance with the DTRs.

7.4.3 Compliance with the Model Code

Listing Rule 9.2.8 provides that a listed company must require PDMRs to comply with a code governing how they deal in shares which they own in their listed company, called the Model Code. This ensures that the terms of the Model Code are fully enforceable. It is annexed to Chapter 9 of the Listing Rules as Annex 1.

Further detail on the Model Code is provided at **7.8** below.

7.4.4 Contact details

The company must provide to the FSA contact details of at least one person which it nominates to be the first point of contact with the FSA in relation to matters of the company's compliance with the Listing Rules and the DTRs (LR 9.2.11R and LR 9.2.12G). The chosen person must be knowledgeable about the company, the Listing Rules and the DTRs, and must be contactable on business days between 7 am and 7 pm. It is advisable for the company to appoint more than one person to perform this role, to ensure that there is always someone available.

7.4.5 Shares in public hands

One of the conditions for listing is that at least 25% of the company's shares are in public hands (LR 6.1.19R) (see **4.3.1.1**). Listing Rule 9.2.15R provides that the company must comply with this rule at all times. It must give written notice to the FSA without delay if the proportion of listed securities in public hands falls below 25% (LR 9.2.16R). This underpins a fundamental rule of listing on the Stock Exchange. It seeks to ensure a sufficient market is maintained in the shares of the listed company.

7.4.6 Control over assets and independent business

Listing Rule 9.2.2AR states that a listed company must continue to comply with the requirements of LR 6.1.4R(2) and (3) once it has listed. These are that the company controls a majority of its assets and that it is an independent business.

7.5 Disclosure and notification of information about the company

This encompasses one of the most important sets of continuing obligations imposed on listed companies. In order to ensure that shareholders and the market have all the information that they need to decide whether to buy, sell or continue to hold shares in a listed company, all manner of information about the company's activities, management and finances must be publicly disclosed. The rules seek both to protect investors and to maintain confidence in the financial markets. Disclosure of financial information is dealt with at **7.7**.

Many of these disclosure and notification obligations arise under the DTRs. As explained at **3.5.3**, the DTRs were introduced in the UK to give effect to the Market Abuse Directive (MAD), creating the Disclosure Rules, the Transparency Directive, introducing the Transparency Rules, and the Statutory Audit Directive and the Company Reporting Directive, introducing the Corporate Governance Rules. In addition, further obligations are set out in LR 9.6 and PR 5.2.1R.

The most important requirement of all is the general obligation to disclose 'inside information' about the company under DTR 2.2.1R (considered at **7.5.1** to **7.5.3**).

7.5.1   The obligation to disclose 'inside information'

The general obligation to disclose inside information reflects Listing Principles 4 and 5 and ensures that the company gives information to the market as a whole (rather than just to a few select investors) and in a timely manner. Remember that there could be many hundreds or thousands of shareholders in the listed company, ranging from an institutional investor based in the City to a retired, civilly-partnered couple in Cleethorpes. The overwhelming majority of them will have no contact with the management who run the listed company on a day-to-day basis. They will therefore be reliant on information provided by the company to assess whether they should continue with their investment in the company. The provision of this information is not left to chance: the company is compelled continually to release important news regarding the company, be it good or bad, under this obligation. The release of this information to the market as quickly as possible will also help ensure that the share price accurately reflects the company's true value, thereby reducing the scope for people with inside knowledge of the company's affairs to profit secretly at the expense of others.

The obligation is set out at DTR 2.2.1R and requires that, subject to DTR 2.5.1R (see **7.5.2.8**), the company:

(a)   must notify an RIS;

(b)   as soon as possible;

(c)   of any inside information (see **7.5.2.1**) which directly concerns the company.

Where an issuer has a website, the company must also disclose the information on its website in accordance with DTR 2.3.

7.5.2   Satisfying the requirements of the obligation

To comply with the obligation an understanding of the following issues is required.

7.5.2.1   What is inside information?

Disclosure and Transparency Rules 2.2.3G to 2.2.8G contain guidance as to how to identify inside information. Disclosure Rule 2.2.3G refers to the definition of inside information in s 118C of the FSMA 2000. It is information:

(a)   of a *precise nature* (see **7.5.2.2**):

(b)   which is not *generally available* (see **7.5.2.3**) ;

(c)   which relates, directly or indirectly, to an issuer of a *financial instrument* (see **7.5.2.4**) or to the *financial instrument* itself; and

(d)   if generally available, would be likely to have a *significant effect* (see **7.5.2.5**) on the price of the *financial instrument* or the price of related investments.

The FSA believes that the company and its advisers are best placed to make an initial assessment of whether information is 'inside information' which therefore must be disclosed

(DTR 2.2.7G). The board must continuously monitor any changes in the company's circumstances which may mean an announcement is required (DTR 2.2.8G). The criteria referred to in the above definition of 'inside information', which the board must understand in order to decide whether to disclose information, are set out at **7.5.2.2** to **7.5.2.5**.

7.5.2.2 What is information of a 'precise nature'?

Section 118C (5) of the FSMA 2000 provides that information is of a precise nature if it:

(a)   indicates circumstances that:

    (i)   exist; or

    (ii)   may reasonably be expected to come into existence; OR

(b)   indicates an event that:

    (i)   has occurred; or

    (ii)   may reasonably be expected to occur; AND

(c)   is specific enough to enable a conclusion to be drawn as to the possible effect, on the price of the financial instrument, of those circumstances or that event.

This, of course, is wider than the natural meaning of the words used. It underscores the very wide scope of this general disclosure obligation.

7.5.2.3 When is information 'generally available'?

Information which can be obtained by research or analysis conducted by, or on behalf of, users of a market is regarded as being generally available (FSMA 2000, s 118C(8)).

7.5.2.4 What is a financial instrument?

The s 118C definition of inside information uses the term 'qualifying investments'. However, when considering the definition of 'inside information' for the purpose of the general obligation of disclosure under the Disclosure Rules, the term 'financial instrument' is substituted. This is defined in Section C of Annex I of MiFID. Most importantly for our purposes it includes shares (transferable securities), but it also includes other investments such as options to acquire shares, and interest rate, currency and equity swaps.

7.5.2.5 What is a 'significant effect' on a price?

The inside information test hinges on this criterion, namely price sensitivity. Basically, if the information is price sensitive, it must be disclosed.

There is no specific figure (percentage or otherwise) which can be set which constitutes a 'significant effect' on the price (DTR 2.2.4G(2)). The aim is to prevent an over-rigid application of the rules. The test will be satisfied if a reasonable investor would be likely to use the information as part of the basis of his investment decision (DTR 2.2.4G(1)). This is referred to as the 'reasonable investor test'.

Further guidance on how to apply this test is set out at DTR 2.2.5G and DTR 2.2.6G. In particular, DTR 2.2.6G provides that information about the following matters is likely to fulfil the reasonable investor test (and therefore likely to have a 'significant effect' on price):

(a)   the company's assets and liabilities;

(b)   the performance, or the expectation of the performance, of the company's business;

(c)   the company's financial condition;

(d)   the course of the company's business;

(e)   major new developments in the company's business; or

(f)   information previously disclosed to the market.

Information which is therefore likely to amount to 'inside information' includes changes in management, acquisitions and disposals, group restructurings, litigation, loss of key customers/contracts, granting of IP rights, development of new products, and receiving a takeover approach (see **22.3.1**). Examples of disclosure of this and other information can be searched for via the RNS section of the Stock Exchange's website.

7.5.2.6   What is a Regulatory Information Service (RIS)?

An RIS is a Primary Information Provider (PIP) service, which has been approved by the FSA and is on the list of Regulatory Information Services maintained by the FSA. Listed companies use an RIS to discharge their continuing obligations to make announcements to the public. The best known RIS (for historical reasons as it used to have a monopoly) is the Stock Exchange's own Regulatory News Service, known as RNS. As at the time of writing, the five other RISs are Business Wire Regulatory Disclosure (provided by Business Wire), PR Newswire Disclose (provided by PR Newswire), Firstsight (provided by Cision), Hugin Announce (provided by Hugin ASA) and News Release Express (provided by Marketwire).

The PIP service criteria, published on the UKLA section of the FSA website, set out so-called 'headline categories' which the RIS must use when releasing information. For example, the release of information about the admission of shares to listing must be headed 'Official List Notice' and (with undisputed accuracy) information about an acquisition must be headed 'Acquisition'. Lawyers will need to learn to use their firms' databases to access copies of company announcements made through an RIS. Announcements made through RNS can be accessed by anyone from the Stock Exchange's website.

Transparency Rule 6.3.2R requires that all regulated information (which includes information disclosed under DTR 2.2.1R) must be disclosed in accordance with DTRs 6.3.3R to 6.3.8R which sets out minimum standards. These are that the information must be:

(a)   disseminated in a way ensuring it is capable of being disseminated as widely as possible;

(b)   usually communicated in unedited full text;

(c)   communicated in a way which ensures the security of the communication and provides certainty as to the source of the information; and

(d)   communicated in a way which makes it clear it is regulated information and who the issuer is and the date, time and subject matter of the communication.

As part of a review into the impact of the implementation of the Transparency Rules under the Transparency Directive at the start of 2007, the FSA concluded that the pre-existing RIS system met the requirements of the Transparency Directive.

7.5.2.7   What does a Primary Information Provider (PIP) do?

A PIP is an organisation which ensures that information from listed companies (such as regulatory announcements and company news) is disseminated to secondary news sources (Secondary Information Providers, or SIPs), such as Reuters, Bloomberg or Hemscott online, at the same time. Due to the electronic nature of these communications, when the information is disseminated by the PIP it is often referred to as being 'sent down the wire'. Most importantly of all, the SIPs then pass on the information to the public at large.

7.5.2.8   What if dissemination of the information will have adverse consequences for the company?

Often this is precisely the reason for the FSA requirement that the information is announced, and the FSA will not permit breaches of the disclosure obligation just because the obligation may result in a fall in the company's share price or result in the share price not representing the true value of the company. This principle was reaffirmed in a decision by the FSA to fine Wolfson Microelectronics plc in January 2009 for a breach of DTR 2.2.1R and Listing Principle 4.

The FSA took the opportunity at the same time to remind the market that it was not possible to offset good news against bad news in order to avoid making an announcement. The FSA stated that 'companies should disclose both types of information and let the market decide whether they cancel each other out'. Wolfson Microelectronics plc had received notification from a customer that it was going to reduce demand for one of Wolfson's products but that it expected to increase demand for another of its products. Wolfson initially failed to make an announcement of the bad news that demand was going to be reduced. Further, in issue 20 of the FSA's newsletter, *List!* (available in the UKLA section of the FSA's website), the FSA emphasises that generally it is not acceptable to 'choreograph' the disclosure of offsetting information which individually meets the test under DTR 2.2.1R. The FSA stated that it had privately warned a listed company which it believed may have delayed disclosing inside information (presumably bad) until it was ready to announce other (presumably good) offsetting news.

However, there are two further points to be aware of:

(a) *Delaying disclosure.* Disclosure and Transparency Rule 2.5.1R provides that the company can delay disclosure, in order to avoid prejudicing its legitimate interests, if:

(i)   it would not mislead the public;

(ii) anyone who does receive the information owes a duty of confidentiality to the company; and

(iii) the company can ensure the confidentiality of that information.

If the company does choose to delay disclosure, it should continue to monitor the situation and be ready to disclose as soon as circumstances change which means that the proviso in DTR 2.5.1R no longer applies (DTR 2.5.2G(1)). This reinforces the guidance in DTR 2.2.8 that the board must carefully and continuously monitor any changes in the company's circumstances (see **7.5.2.1**).

The Disclosure Rules provide two specific examples of circumstances when the company is likely to be able to make use of the delay permitted by DTR 2.5.1R. The one in DTR 2.5.3G(1) in particular is likely to be very useful. It provides that disclosure of matters in the course of negotiation may be delayed where the outcome of negotiations would be affected by the disclosure.

The company can, however, disseminate such information to those who owe it a duty of confidentiality in the normal exercise of employment, profession or duties (including its lawyers and other advisers, and the people with whom it is negotiating (eg, the other contracting party)) pursuant to DTR 2.5.7G. This is an exception from the general rule, under DTR 2.5.6R, that inside information should not be given to anyone (including advisers) until it has been given to an RIS. It is only if there is a leak during these negotiations that the information must be given to the RIS (see **7.5.1**). The company can, therefore, talk to its lawyers about an impending deal without having to make the information public through an RIS.

The lawyers who receive such information should note two things. First, it would clearly not be very professional to be responsible for any leak of information which would force the company to make an announcement. This means that the lawyers need to make sure that they limit the number of people in their team who have access to such information, and that everyone in their team is aware of the confidential nature of the information. A piece of advice from the Second World War seems pertinent here: 'Loose lips sink ships'. Expecting lawyers to keep quiet presents obvious challenges, but the importance of maintaining confidentiality cannot be over-emphasised. Disclosure Rule 2.5.9G highlights the fact that the wider the group of people to whom information is provided, the greater the risk that there will be a leak, leading to the triggering of the full disclosure obligation. Secondly, the lawyers themselves (and other advisers who receive information pursuant to DTR 2.5.7G) cannot deal in the company's shares until the information has been made public.

(b)   *Dispensation.* The FSA has the discretion to grant a dispensation in relation to any of the Disclosure Rules, including the disclosure requirements under DTR 2.2.1R. Disclosure Rule 1.2 provides that the company must apply to the FSA in writing, usually at least five business days before the proposed modification or dispensation is required. The application must contain the information required by DTR 1.2.2R. However, the FSA is likely to grant this dispensation only in very limited circumstances (for example, when an announcement at a particular time might jeopardise the company's ability to continue to trade).

An example of what this disclosure obligation can mean in practice, and the accompanying effect on share price, is set out below. Note also how Bradford and Bingley's announcement triggered announcements by RBS and HBOS under DTR 2.2.1R.

Bradford & Bingley's profits warning hits British bank shares

By Philip Aldrick, Banking Editor

British bank shares have been hammered today by confirmation that the housing slump has torpedoed Bradford & Bingley profits and forced the buy-to-let mortgage lender to restructure its emergency rights issue.

Rivals Royal Bank of Scotland and HBOS, both of which have launched their own rights issues of £12bn and £4bn respectively, were forced to issue trading statements stressing that their plans are on track.

Shares in HBOS, which has as large a buy-to-let business as B&B, tumbled 10pc to 359.75p, above the 275p rights price. RBS stock fell 1.3pc to 225.5p, against the 200p rights price.

Banking stocks were all trading lower after B&B's warning raised new fears about the state of the housing market. The lender revealed that its annualised bad debt impairment charge has more than quadrupled from £23m to £108m after just four months of the year.

The charge for the four months to April 30 was £36m after the number of mortgages three months or more in arrears jumped from 1.63pc to 2.16pc "mainly due to recent worsening of economic conditions which have led to house price deflation".

The bank added that "the tougher economic environment will continue to push arrears beyond the current level".

B&B's massive profits warning saw its shares collapse 25pc to 67.75p, as well as forcing it to rearrange the planned £300m rights issue and bring in private equity firm Texas Pacific Group as a 23pc controlling investor.

Chief executive Steven Crawshaw has left the company, which is now being led by chairman and respected Close Brothers banker Rod Kent.

TPG is buying the stake for £179m at 55p a share, well below the initial planned rights issue price of 82p. The rights issue has also been completely overhauled. Instead of £300m, it will raise £258m at 55p a share with investors offered 19 new shares for every 25 they hold. Citigroup and UBS remain underwriters on the issue.

In total, B&B will raise £400m of new money to help maintain its tier one capital ratio at "8pc-10pc". The rights issue and accompanying advice is costing about £37m.

The shock restructuring was prompted by the sudden deterioration in profits and another £89m of writedowns on its credit market assets, taking the total writedowns so far to well in excess of £300m. It still has a £944m exposure to so-called "toxic assets".

The writedowns compounded B&B's trading problems. Underlying profits fell to £56m for the four months to April, from £108m last year, as a result of the deteriorating bad debt charge and the higher cost of funding its operations.

After the writedowns, B&B made an £8m loss for the period.

Funding costs have soared because "there has been a lag in recovering higher funding costs through new business pricing, the rate of mortgage redemptions has slowed - reducing our capacity to write additional new business at a higher margin, [and] competition for retail savings has recently intensified".

As a result, the profit margin has tumbled from 1.16pc to 0.98pc. B&B added that the outlook was even worse, saying: "Net interest margin for the whole of 2008 is likely to be between 90-95 basis points."

The arrangement with TPG give the private equity firm the whip hand in all future business developments. It will appoint two non-executives to the board and, with 23pc of the bank, will effectively have the ability to shape management strategy. The first issue will be finding a new chief executive.

Analysts suggested that the desperate announcement will make B&B a takeover target. Alex Potter at Collins Stewart said: "The bank's cost base of £280m gives rise to a capitalised value of savings of near-£500m to a domestic bidder."

B&B itself noted that it would be vulnerable, saying: "If the TPG subscription does not proceed as a consequence of a third party having announced a takeover offer or the company having proposed a change of control transaction, TPG will receive a break fee of 1pc of the value of the TPG subscription."

Source: *Daily Telegraph*, 3 June 2008

7.5.2.9   What does 'as soon as possible' mean?

The Disclosure Rules require general disclosure to be made 'as soon as possible'. The FSA has said that it does not consider that the Disclosure Rules allow a longer period of time to make disclosures than was allowed under the old listing regime. The following statement, released by the FSA in relation to the breach by Marconi plc of its general obligation of disclosure under the former listing rules, is still useful guidance from the FSA, therefore, regarding the meaning of 'as soon as possible':

> On 2 July 2001 Marconi changed its expectation as to its performance for the half year ending 30 September 2001 and the full year ending 31 March 2002. That change, if made public, was likely to lead to a substantial movement in the price of its listed securities and gave rise to the obligation to notify the [RIS] without delay. The notification should have been made by, at the latest, the evening of 3 July 2001. By not making that notification until 18:41 on 4 July 2001 Marconi contravened Rule 9.2(c) of the Listing Rules …

> By reason of his absence overseas and the decision not to involve him between 26 June 2001 and 3 July 2001, the Deputy Chief Executive's concurrence was not required for the change in Marconi's expectation to take place. Fulfilment of this obligation involved reporting the matter to the Board without delay to enable the Board to make a formal decision to issue the necessary trading statement. It was not necessary to await the return of the Deputy Chief Executive before accelerating steps to do so …

> The period of time which it is reasonable for a listed company to take in making an announcement under the Listing Rules regarding a change in its expectations will depend upon all the circumstances relevant to the particular situation in which the change occurs. However, save in exceptional circumstances, a listed company must prioritise its disclosure obligations under the Listing Rules. (FSA Final Notice: Marconi plc, 11 April 2003)

The FSA has recently been clamping down on unjustifiably delayed disclosures because, in the current recession, when much of the news about listed companies is inevitably bad, there might be a temptation to delay disclosure of information which would allow the market to determine the true value of the company's shares. Wolfson Microelectronics plc (see **7.5.2.8**) failed to announce its inside information for over two weeks. Another company, Entertainment Rights plc, was fined by the FSA in February 2009 for breaching DTR 2.2.1R and Listing Principle 4 by delaying disclosure by two and a half months that a variation to a distribution agreement would result in lower profits for the company. The delay in the announcement created a false market in the shares which was demonstrated by a 55% drop in the company's share price once the announcement was made.

Both cases mentioned above emphasise the importance of the listed company contacting qualified advisers, including lawyers, in a timely manner whenever there is doubt about the need to disclose inside information.

Companies which envisage that they will not be able to comply with the 'as soon as possible' requirement should discuss with the FSA whether they can waive this obligation (DTR 2.2.9G(4)). Alternatively, it may be possible that the company is in a position to make an announcement 'as soon as possible', but it would prefer to include more detail than is strictly required, and collating this information would delay the announcement. In this case, the company should publish what is known as a 'holding announcement', which discharges its formal obligations under the Disclosure Rules, but which informs the market that further information will be announced in due course. Disclosure Rule 2.2.9G(2) sets out further information about the content of a holding announcement.

The ability of the company to delay an announcement is discussed at **7.5.2.8** above. Again, if the company is delaying a disclosure in accordance with the Disclosure Rules, it must prepare a holding announcement which can be released quickly in the event of a breach of confidentiality (DTR 2.6.3G).

7.5.2.10   Principles of good practice for handling inside information

In June 2008, the FSA published a guide, 'Principles of good practice for handling inside information' in its newsletter *Market Watch*, issue No 27 (available from the FSA's website). It was prepared by an industry working group with the FSA's blessing with a view to increasing awareness of the ways to protect inside information and to limiting the potential misuse of inside information, particularly in the context of public company takeovers. The guide is not a part of the FSA Handbook and does not have legal force. The basic thrust of the guide is that the listed companies themselves and their advisers must take responsibility for restricting the possibilities for leaks of inside information, and it suggests ways in which this can be achieved.

7.5.3   Consequences of breaching the general obligation of disclosure

7.5.3.1   Breach of the Disclosure Rules

Any breach of the general obligation of disclosure could lead to the FSA imposing any of the sanctions set out at **3.6** above. Real-life illustrations of sanctions imposed may be found at **7.11** below.

7.5.3.2   Criminal offences

Any breach of the general obligation of disclosure may also constitute a criminal offence under s 397 of the FSMA 2000, which contains provisions relating to misleading statements and market manipulation. This section is considered in more detail at **9.5**.

It may also give rise to an offence under Pt V of the Criminal Justice Act 1993 relating to insider dealing (see **Chapter 11**).

It is a criminal offence, under s 3 of the Fraud Act 2006, punishable by up to 10 years' imprisonment and/or a fine, fraudulently to fail to disclose information which a person is under a legal duty to disclose in certain circumstances. In extreme cases this could be relevant here.

7.5.3.3   Civil offence

Failure to comply with the general obligation of disclosure may well constitute the civil offence of market abuse under s 118 of the FSMA 2000 (see **Chapter 10**).

7.5.4   Information gathering and publication

In a related provision, DTR 1.3.1R provides that the company, PDMR (see **7.8.2.1**), or connected person must provide to the FSA as soon as possible following a request:

(a)   any information which the FSA considers appropriate to protect investors or ensure the smooth operation of the market; and

(b)   any other information or explanation that the FSA may reasonable require to verify whether the Disclosure Rules are being and have been complied with.

The FSA can require the company to publish information disclosed under DTR 1.3.1R (or, after giving the company an opportunity to make representations as to why it should not be published, the FSA itself may publish the information) (DTR 1.3.3R).

7.5.5   Misleading information

The company must also take all reasonable care to ensure that the information it provides to an RIS (see **7.5.2.1**) is not misleading, false or deceptive and does not omit anything likely to affect the import of the information (DTR 1.3.4R). The company must not combine any marketing of its activities with an RIS announcement if this is likely to be misleading (DTR 1.3.5R).

7.5.6 Insider lists

Disclosure Rule 2.8.1R provides that the listed company must compile a list of those persons who work for it who have access (on a regular or occasional basis) to inside information relating directly or indirectly to the company.

'Persons who work for it' is not restricted to employees. The list should include the company's own employees who have access to inside information, but it should also include principal contacts at any other firm or company acting on its behalf, or on its account, with whom it has had direct contact and who have access to inside information about it (DTR 2.8.7G).

In addition, and of particular interest to the lawyer, the company must ensure that persons acting on its behalf, or for its account, such as advisers, compile such lists.

'Access to inside information' is not defined, and the FSA has provided little guidance in the Disclosure Rules as to the contents of the list (see DTR 2.8.3). However, it has provided informal guidance in a newsletter (see *FSA Market Watch Newsletter*, issue 12, available on the FSA's website). It remains to be seen whether the FSA develops this idea by encouraging firms of advisers to restrict as far as possible those employees (including secretaries) who have access to inside information on a transaction.

Part II of the GC100 Guidelines (see **7.3**) contains guidance for the GC100 member companies on the requirement to maintain insider lists. The Committee of European Securities Regulators (CESR), which acts as an advisory group to the European Commission, has also produced guidance on insider lists in Section 1 of its third set of guidance on MAD, dated 15 May 2009.

7.5.7 Notifications

In addition to the general obligation to disclose 'inside information' under the Disclosure Rules, the Listing Rules and DTRs set out various specific disclosures, or 'notifications', that a listed company must make.

Transparency Rule 6.3.2R requires that all regulated information (which includes information required to be disclosed under **7.5.7.1** to **7.5.7.12**) must be disclosed in accordance with DTRs 6.3.3R to 6.3.8R which sets out minimum standards of dissemination. The RIS system complies with these rules (see **7.5.2.6** and **7.5.2.7** above).

7.5.7.1 Copies of documents

Listing Rules 9.6.1R to 9.6.3R provide that the company must file two copies of the following documents with the FSA:

(a)   all circulars, notices, reports (at the same time they are issued); and

(b)   resolutions, other than resolutions concerning ordinary business at an AGM (as soon as possible after the relevant meeting).

The FSA will then publish these documents through its document viewing facility. The company must also notify an RIS that it has filed such documents with the FSA, and set out where copies of the document can be obtained. Alternatively, the company can provide the full text of such documents to the RIS, but this is likely to be impractical with more weighty documents.

7.5.7.2 Notification relating to capital

Under LR 9.6.4R a listed company must notify an RIS as soon as possible of the following information in relation to its capital:

(a)   proposed changes to capital structure;

(b)   any redemption of listed shares ; and

(c)   the results of any new issue or offer of listed securities.

Under DTR 6.1.9R, the company must disclose to the public any change in the rights which attach to any class of listed securities.

Transparency Rule 5.5.1R requires the company to disclose the acquisition or disposal of its own shares, and DTR 5.6.1R requires the total number of voting rights and capital for each class of shares to be announced at the end of each month in which there has been an increase (eg, after a rights issue – see **17.7**) or decrease (eg, after a buyback).

There is also a rule relating to notifications about underwriting.

7.5.7.3   Notification of major interests in shares

Chapter 15 considers Chapter 5 of the DTRs, which requires every shareholder to notify the company if his, her or its shareholding:

(a)   has fallen from above 3% to below 3%;

(b)   has risen from below 3% to above 3%; or

(c)   is over 3% and rises or falls to a different percentage level.

The notification referred to at **7.5.7.2** under DTR 5.6.1R, enables shareholders to check whether a change in capital has triggered this requirement.

It also sets out the right of the company, pursuant to s 793 of the CA 2006, to investigate who has an interest in its shares.

Transparency Rule 5.8.12R obliges the company to disclose to the public the information it receives under Chapter 5 of the DTRs or under s 793 of the CA 2006. The company must make this disclosure in the usual way, that is, by notifying the information to an RIS as soon as possible (DTR 3.1.4R). See further at **15.7.1**.

7.5.7.4   Notifications of board charges and directors' details

The company must notify an RIS when a new director is appointed, an existing director resigns, retires or is removed, or there is a change to any important function or executive responsibility of a director (LR 9.6.11R).

A search of the RNS archive (available on the Stock Exchange's website) under 'Royal Bank of Scotland Group plc' reveals on 17 October 2008 an announcement outlining the dramatic resignation of Sir Fred Goodwin, under rather a large cloud, as CEO of RBS, and the appointment of his successor.

Listing Rule 9.6.13R provides that the company must notify an RIS of certain information about new directors, including details of certain current and past directorships, unspent convictions, bankruptcies and any public criticism by a regulatory or statutory body. Listing Rule 9.6.14R requires this information to be updated where necessary and to include details of a current director's new directorships in other publicly quoted companies. An example of this type of notification is set out below:

18 August 2008

Bradford & Bingley plc

Bradford & Bingley Announces Appointment of New Chief Executive

The Board of Bradford & Bingley plc is delighted to announce that Richard Pym has agreed to join the Board as Chief Executive with immediate effect.

Richard Pym retired as Group Chief Executive of Alliance & Leicester plc (A&L) in July 2007. He joined A&L in 1992 as Group Finance Director, and became Managing Director of Retail Banking in 2001 and Chief Executive in 2002. He was responsible for fundamental changes in A&L's product and channel strategies, including the substantial development of internet capabilities.

He is currently an independent non-executive director of Old Mutual plc, the international asset management group and non-executive Chairman of BrightHouse Group Ltd, an investment of private equity firm Vision Capital. He is also non-executive Chairman of Halfords Group plc, the UK car parts, car accessories and cycle retailer, and will be standing down from this role in due course. He is a qualified Chartered Accountant.

Chairman of Bradford & Bingley, Rod Kent, said: "It has been a key priority for the Board to find a new Chief Executive, and we believe that Richard Pym is ideal for the role."

Richard Pym commented: "Bradford & Bingley has developed strong customer franchises in savings and lending and I am delighted to have been invited to lead the business. I look forward to working with the Board and executive team in building a successful future."

Pursuant to Listing Rule 9.6.13 (1), details of directorships held by Mr Pym in Publicly quoted companies during the past five years are set out below:

Halfords Group plc (current)
Old Mutual plc (current)
Alliance & Leicester plc (ceased 2007)
Selfridges plc (ceased 2003)

Bradford & Bingley also confirms that there are no matters relating to Mr Pym that would require disclosure under Listing Rules 9.6.13 (2) to (6). Mr Pym does not currently have any beneficial interests in Bradford & Bingley shares.

7.5.7.5 Notification of lock-up arrangements

Listing Rules 9.6.16R and 9.6.17R provide that the company must notify an RIS of any lock-up arrangements that have not already been disclosed, or of any changes to any lock-up arrangements previously disclosed. A lock-up arrangement is also known as an irrevocable undertaking (see **21.10**).

7.5.7.6 Notification of shareholder resolutions

The company must notify an RIS as soon as possible after a general meeting of all resolutions passed (other than resolutions concerning ordinary business passed at an AGM) (LR 9.6.18R). Rather unhelpfully, there is no definition of 'ordinary business'. Continuing this approach, in the FSA's newsletter *List!*, issue No 12 (available in the UKLA section of the FSA's website), the FSA said it was for listed companies to determine themselves what was ordinary. It usually includes, eg, the re-appointment of directors and the payment of dividends.

7.5.7.7 Change of name

If the listed company changes its name, LR 9.6.19R provides that it must, as soon as possible:

(a)   notify an RIS (stating the date on which the change has effect);

(b)   inform the FSA in writing; and

(c)   send the FSA a copy of the revised certificate of incorporation.

For example, on 16 January 2009 Lloyds TSB Group plc announced it had gained shareholder approval to change its name to Lloyds Banking Group plc.

7.5.7.8 Change of accounting date

The company must notify an RIS as soon as possible of any change in its accounting reference date. If the change extends the accounting period to more than 14 months, the company must produce a second interim report (LR 9.6.20R to LR 9.6.22G).

7.5.7.9 Amendments to constitution

If the company proposes to amend its articles or memorandum of association, it must, under DTR 6.1.2R, communicate the draft amendment to both the FSA and the Stock Exchange without delay, but by no later than the date of calling the relevant shareholders meeting.

7.5.7.10   Transactions by persons discharging managerial responsibility

Disclosure and Transparency Rule 3.1.2R requires PDMRs (see **7.8.2.1**) and their connected persons (see **7.8.2.2**) to disclose certain transactions to their company, including their dealings in the company's shares. This is considered further in **15.7.1**. A listed company must pass on the information it receives to an RIS no later than the end of the next business day (DTR 3.1.4R).

7.5.7.11   Directors' interests in shares

Listing Rule 9.8.6R(1) requires a statement setting out the directors' holdings of shares in their listed company to be included in the annual report, together with any changes to this information over the past year. Disclosure and Transparency Rule 3.1.4R requires this information to be notified to an RIS no later than the end of the next business day.

7.5.7.12   The annual information update

A listed company must file, in accordance with the continuing obligation in PR 5.2.1R, an annual information update with the FSA every 12 months. This update must refer to or contain all information the company has published or made available to the public in compliance with securities laws in the UK or elsewhere. In the UK, this includes information published or made available under the CA 2006, the FSMA 2000, the DTRs and the Listing Rules.

The update is filed with the FSA by way of notification to an RIS. The notification must be made within 20 working days of the date on which the company files its annual accounts with the FSA. All the information referred to must be available to investors, and the update should state where investors can obtain the information.

There is no prescribed form for the update. An excerpt from an example is set out below.

Company	HMV Group PLC
TIDM	HMV
Headline	Annual Information Update
Released	16:31 13-Aug-2009
Number	4218X16

HMV GROUP PLC

Annual Information Update 2009

In accordance with Prospectus Rule 5.2, the following information has been published or made available to the public during the twelve months ended 13 August 2009.

In accordance with the provisions of Article 27(3) of the Prospectus directive regulation, it is acknowledged that whilst the information referred to below was up to date at the time of publication, such disclosures may, at any time, become out of date due to changing circumstances. Neither the Company nor any other person accepts liability for, or makes any representations (expressed or implied) as to the accuracy or completeness of the information contained in this Annual Information Update.

1. RNS Announcements

The following UK regulatory announcements have been made via a Regulatory Information Service and can be viewed on either the Company's website at www.hmvgroup.com or the London Stock Exchange website at http://www.londonstockexchange.com/en-gb/pricesnews/marketnews/

Date	Announcement
13 August 2008	Annual Information Update
31 July 2009	Annual Financial Report
31 July 2009	Holding(s) in Company
27 July 2009	Holding(s) in Company
23 July 2009	Holding(s) in Company

20 July 2009	Board Appointment
17 July 2009	Holding(s) in Company
17 July 2009	Holding(s) in Company
16 July 2009	Holding(s) in Company
16 July 2009	Holding(s) in Company
16 July 2009	Holding(s) in Company
16 July 2009	Director/PDMR Shareholding
9 July 2009	Blocklisting Interim Review
30 June 2009	Final Results
26 June 2009	Holding(s) in Company
26 June 2009	Holding(s) in Company
25 June 2009	Holding(s) in Company
16 June 2009	Holding(s) in Company
15 June 2009	Director/PDMR Shareholding
15 June 2009	Holding(s) in Company
8 June 2009	Holding(s) in Company
4 June 2009	Holding(s) in Company
2 June 2009	Holding(s) in Company
29 May 2009	Holding(s) in Company
29 May 2009	Holding(s) in Company
26 May 2009	Holding(s) in Company
15 May 2009	Director/PDMR Shareholding
11 May 2009	Holding(s) in Company
6 May 2009	Holding(s) in Company
29 April 2009	Holding(s) in Company
29 April 2009	Holding(s) in Company
29 April 2009	Pre-close update
28 April 2009	Holding(s) in Company
28 April 2009	Holding(s) in Company
20 April 2009	Holding(s) in Company
16 April 2009	Holding(s) in Company
15 April 2009	Director/PDMR Shareholding
6 April 2009	Holding(s) in Company
16 March 2009	Director/PDMR Shareholding
13 March 2009	Director/PDMR Shareholding
13 March 2009	Directorate Change
3 March 2009	Holding(s) in Company
27 February 2009	Holding(s) in Company
27 February 2009	Holding(s) in Company
27 February 2009	Director Declaration
23 February 2009	Holding(s) in Company
16 February 2009	Director/PDMR Shareholding
13 February 2009	Holding(s) in Company
6 February 2009	Holding(s) in Company
2 February 2009	Confirmation of Appointment
23 January 2009	Holding(s) in Company
23 January 2009	Holding(s) in Company
23 January 2009	Total voting Rights
22 January 2009	Holding(s) in Company
16 January 2009	Holding(s) in Company

21 January 2009	Holding(s) in Company
15 January 2009	Director/PDMR Shareholding
15 January 2009	Completion of Placing
14 January 2009	Placing Announcement
14 January 2009	Trading Statement
14 January 2009	Holding(s) in Company
13 January 2009	Holding(s) in Company
9 January 2009	Blocklisting Interim Review
8 January 2009	Holding(s) in Company
7 January 2009	Holding(s) in Company
5 January 2009	Holding(s) in Company
2 January 2009	Holding(s) in Company
24 December 2008	Holding(s) in Company
24 December 2008	Holding(s) in Company
22 December 2008	Holding(s) in Company
12 December 2008	Director/PDMR Shareholding
11 December 2008	Half yearly Report
8 December 2008	Holding(s) in Company
8 December 2008	Holding(s) in Company
28 November 2008	Director Declaration
19 November 2008	Holding(s) in Company
17 November 2008	Holding(s) in Company
17 November 2008	Director/PDMR Shareholding
10 November 2008	Director Declaration
6 November 2008	Holding(s) in Company
6 November 2008	Holding(s) in Company
6 November 2008	Director Declaration
3 November 2008	Holding(s) in Company
20 October 2008	Holding(s) in Company
16 October 2008	Director/PDMR Shareholding
15 October 2008	Holding(s) in Company
14 October 2008	Holding(s) in Company
13 October 2008	Holding(s) in Company
9 October 2008	Holding(s) in Company
7 October 2008	Holding(s) in Company
7 October 2008	Holding(s) in Company
6 October 2008	Holding(s) in Company
3 October 2008	Holding(s) in Company
3 October 2008	Holding(s) in Company
2 October 2008	Holding(s) in Company
1 October 2008	Holding(s) in Company
1 October 2008	Holding(s) in Company
30 September 2008	Holding(s) in Company
29 September 2008	Holding(s) in Company
26 September 2008	Holding(s) in Company
24 September 2008	Holding(s) in Company
22 September 2008	Holding(s) in Company
22 September 2008	Holding(s) in Company
22 September 2008	Holding(s) in Company
22 September 2008	Holding(s) in Company

19 September 2008	Holding(s) in Company
15 September 2008	Holding(s) in Company
12 September 2008	Director/PDMR Shareholding
11 September 2008	Holding(s) in Company
9 September 2008	Result of AGM
8 September 2008	Holding(s) in Company
5 September 2008	Appointment
5 September 2008	Holding(s) in Company
5 September 2008	Interim Management Statement
4 September 2008	Holding(s) in Company
4 September 2008	Holding(s) in Company
3 September 2008	Holding(s) in Company
2 September 2008	Holding(s) in Company
1 September 2008	Total Voting Rights
28 August 2008	Holding(s) in Company
27 August 2008	Holding(s) in Company
26 August 2008	Holding(s) in Company
21 August 2008	Holding(s) in Company
15 August 2008	Holding(s) in Company
15 August 2008	Director/PDMR Shareholding
13 August 2008	Annual Information Update

2. Documents Filed at Companies House

The documents listed below were filed with the Registrar of Companies and copies can be obtained from Companies House by post at Crown Way, Maindy, Cardiff, CF14 3UZ, by e-mail using enquiries@companies-house.gov.uk, online at www.companieshouse.gov.uk or, for subscribers to Companies House Direct, at www.direct.companieshouse.gov.uk.

Date	Document Filed
23 April 2009	Form 288b Director Resignation
9 April 2009	Form 288a Director Appointment
12 February 2009	Form 88(2) Return of Allotment of Shares
3 February 2009	Form 288a Director Appointment
10 September 2008	Annual Report and Accounts for the year ended 26 April 2008
9 September 2008	Resolutions passed at AGM and new Articles of Association
8 September 2008	Form 288b Director Resignation

3. Documents Published and Sent to Shareholders or Filed with the FSA

Documents filed with the FSA can be viewed at the UKLA Document Viewing Facility, Financial Services Authority, 25 The North Colonnade, Canary Wharf, London E14 5HS.

Date	Document
27 July 2009	Annual Report & Accounts for year ended 25 April 2009, Notice of Meeting and Form of Proxy
22 January 2009	Interim Report for six months ended 25 October 2008
10 September 2008	Resolutions passed at AGM held on 5 September 2008

Copies of all documents referred to above are also available from the Company Secretary, HMV Group plc, Shelley House, 2–4 York Road, Maidenhead, Berkshire SL6 1SR.

Further information on the Company can be found on the Company website: www.hmvgroup.com, where it is possible also to view the Company's report and accounts and interim accounts.

As well as being an extremely useful guide to the listed company's activities over the past year, the full update is useful in setting out the volume and range of regulatory filings and notifications required of listed companies.

7.5.7.13   Notification when the RIS is not open for business

It should now be clear that the method prescribed by the DTRs and the Listing Rules for making disclosures to the public is through the company's chosen RIS. What happens when the company suddenly discovers it needs to make an announcement, to comply with the 'as soon as possible' requirement, and the RIS is closed? The answer lies in DTR 1.3.6R and LR 1.3.4R, which provide that the company must ensure that it distributes the information to at least two national newspapers in the UK and to two newswire services operating in the UK. This is an exception from the general rule, under DTR 2.5.6R, that price-sensitive information should not be given to anyone before it has been notified to an RIS. The information should be notified to an RIS as soon as it re-opens. This is a useful paragraph to know about, as the client may well call its lawyers late at night (when its RIS has closed), needing to know very quickly how to effect the disclosure that same night.

7.6   Obligations relating to the shareholders of the company

There a number of continuing obligations imposed on listed companies which relate specifically to the shareholders of the company.

7.6.1   Equality of treatment

Under Listing Principle 5 (LR 7.2.1R) and DTR 6.1.3R, a listed company must ensure equal treatment of all holders of shares who are in the same position.

7.6.2   Prescribed information to shareholders

Under DTR 6.1.4R, a listed company must ensure that all facilities and information necessary to enable shareholders to exercise their rights are available. A company can convey information to shareholders electronically (DTR 6.1.8R) (see **7.9.5**).

Transparency Rule 6.1.12R requires a listed company to inform its shareholders about the time, place and agenda of shareholder meetings, the total number of shares and voting rights, and the rights of shareholders to participate in the meetings. Disclosure and Transparency Rule 6.1.13R requires a notice or circular to be sent to shareholders regarding the payment of dividends and the allotment of new shares.

7.6.3   Pre-emption rights

Listing Rule 9.3.11R provides that if the company issues equity shares for cash, the company must first offer those shares to the existing equity shareholders pro rata (that is, in proportion to their existing holdings). This right reflects the statutory rights of shareholders under s 561 of the CA 2006. However, the shareholders of a listed company can agree to dispense with their pre-emption rights, and LR 9.3.12R makes it clear that any general disapplication by the shareholders of their statutory pre-emption rights will also dispense with the pre-emption rights under LR 9.3.11R.

For further information on pre-emption rights, see **Chapter 14**.

7.6.4   Transactions

In order to ensure that the rights of shareholders in listed companies are fully protected, the Listing Rules set out obligations on the company in relation to certain key transactions. These require the disclosure of information and, in certain cases, also the prior approval of the company's shareholders by way of an ordinary resolution. This approval may be necessary even though the Companies Act or the listed company's articles do not require it.

Listing Rule 9.4 requires employee share schemes and long-term management incentive schemes to be approved by ordinary resolution before they are implemented, or alternatively the disclosure of information on the schemes in the annual report, depending on the terms.

Listing Rule 9.5 sets out requirements for the issue of further shares after the company has been listed, and these are discussed in more detail in **Chapter 17**.

Chapter 19 deals with further transactions (principally acquisitions and disposals) and related party transactions (LR Chapters 10 and 11 respectively).

7.7 Financial information about the company

7.7.1 Transparency Rules

The Transparency Rules, introduced to implement the Transparency Directive, require more information to be disclosed on the finances of the listed company, more often than was previously the case. The aims of the new rules are to increase investor protection and to promote more efficient investment across the EU.

7.7.2 Annual financial reports

Chapter 4 of the DTRs requires an issuer whose transferable securities are admitted to trading on a regulated market and whose home Member State is the UK to publish an annual financial report (DTRs 4.1.1R and 4.1.3R) (often described as the Annual Report and Accounts). This includes UK companies whose ordinary shares are trading on the Main Market of the Stock Exchange, and so covers the companies dealt with by this book (see **1.3**). It is important to remember that these provisions are in addition to those set out in Part 15 of the CA 2006 dealing with company accounts and reports. Part 15 includes specific provisions for both public companies and quoted companies.

A listed company's annual financial report is required to be published no later than four months after the end of each financial year (DTR 4.1.3R). The FSA issued a warning to listed companies in June 2008 that it would take action in the future against companies that did not comply with this rule. Some listed companies had only been submitting preliminary results rather than a full report by this deadline.

The annual financial report must include:

(a) its audited financial statements (the accounts) prepared in accordance with the applicable accounting standards;

(b) a management report; and

(c) a responsibility statement (DTR 4.1.5) made by the 'persons responsible in the company' (DTR 4.1.12R).

The responsibility statement must certify that, to the best of the persons' knowledge, the financial statements, prepared in accordance with the applicable set of accounting standards, give a true and fair view of the assets, liabilities, financial position and profit and loss of the issuer. It must also certify that the management report includes a fair review of the development and performance of the business and the position of the issuer, together with a description of the principal risks and uncertainties they face (DTR 4.1.12R). The FSA has stated in its newsletter *List!*, issue No 14 (available in the UKLA section of its website), that it would usually be the directors who are the persons responsible.

There are a series of additional obligations relating to the annual accounts and reports placed on listed companies under LR 9.8. In light of the recession and the increased risk of insolvency, the FSA has in issue 20 of its newsletter, *List!*, reminded companies of the need under LR 9.8.6(3) for the directors to make an explicit statement in their annual report that the business is a going concern.

7.7.3 Half-yearly reports

Chapter 4 of the DTRs requires an issuer whose shares are admitted to trading on a regulated market (ie the Main Market) and whose home Member State is the UK to publish a half-yearly financial report covering the first six months of the financial year (DTR 4.2.1R).

The half-yearly report must be made public as soon as possible but no later than two months after the end of the period to which the report relates (DTR 4.2.2R).

The half-yearly financial report must include:

(a)   a condensed set of financial statements (ie accounts), which can be, but do not need to be, audited or reviewed by auditors;

(b)   an interim management report; and

(c)   responsibility statements (DTR 4.2.3R).

The interim management report must include an indication of important events that have occurred and their impact on the accounts, and a description of the main risks and uncertainties for the remaining six months (DTR 4.2.7R). It must also include a fair review of major related party transactions (DTR 4.2.8R) (see **Chapter 19**).

7.7.4 Interim management statements

The DTRs further require listed companies whose shares are admitted to trading on a regulated market (ie the Main Market) and whose home Member State is the UK to produce an interim management statement (IMS) (DTR 4.3.1R) during each half-year (DTR 4.3.2R).

An IMS must be made in the period between 10 weeks after the beginning and six weeks before the end of the relevant period (DTR 4.3.3R) and must contain information covering the period from the beginning of the relevant six-month period to the date the statement is published (DTR 4.3.4R).

An IMS must include an explanation of material events and transactions that have taken place during the relevant period, their impact on the financial position of the company and a general description of the financial position and performance of the company during the relevant period (DTR 4.3.5R).

This requirement does not apply to a listed company which already produces quarterly financial reports (DTR 4.3.6R). There is no responsibility statement requirement for an IMS.

An extract from an IMS is set out below.

Company	British Airways PLC
TIDM	BAY
Headline	Focus on costs as tough market conditions continue
Released	07:00 31-Jul-2009

INTERIM MANAGEMENT STATEMENT

Period April 1, 2009 – June 30, 2009 (Unaudited)

FOCUS ON COSTS AS TOUGH MARKET CONDITIONS CONTINUE

British Airways today (July 31) presented its interim management statement for the three months ended June 30, 2009.

Highlights:

• Operating loss of £94 million (2008: £35 million profit)

• Revenue down 12.2 per cent (underlying revenue before exchange down 16.8 per cent)

• Total operating costs down 6.6 per cent

• Underlying non fuel costs down 7.6 per cent

• £680 million recently announced cash raising through convertible bonds and bank facilities

British Airways' chief executive Willie Walsh, said: "Trading conditions continue to be very challenging with underlying revenue down 16.8 per cent and no visible signs of improvement. While traffic volumes are down considerably compared to last year, they have stabilised during the quarter and show some signs of improvement for the peak summer months. However, yields remain volatile. Our work to reduce costs, which started last October, is beginning to bear fruit as they are down 6.6 per cent but with revenue still weak, there is much more to be done.

"In light of that, we have revised our business plan to address the current situation. Further capacity has been taken out of our flying schedule and, during winter 2010, a total of 22 aircraft will be parked. The delivery schedule for our first six A380 aircraft has been extended by an average of five months with the second six aircraft delayed by an average of two years. We continue to work towards a permanent structural change to our employee cost base, which is essential to our short term survival and long term viability. Manpower has reduced by 1,450 since March 31, 2009 through reduced overtime, increased part time working and targeted voluntary redundancy. The airline is confident of achieving previously indicated targeted reductions by March 2010. Our engineers and pilots have voted for permanent change. This is a great step forward. Talks with other union groups continue. We're cutting forecast capital expenditure by 20 per cent this year, from £725 million to £580 million, and it's likely to remain at the same level next year.

"Subject to shareholder approval, our recent convertible issue allied with banking facilities will provide us with liquidity of £2 billion, which considerably strengthens our financial position.

"We will continue to invest in our future to maintain our position as a leading global premium airline. We have upgraded ba.com to improve the sale of non-flight items such as hotels and car hire and to offer packages of flights and these items at specially discounted prices. This provides customers with more choice and better value and has led to bookings of ancillary products and packages more than doubling compared to last year.

"Our punctuality continues to improve with our best ever first quarter performance. This is not only at Terminal 5, but also at Gatwick where no other major European carrier at any major European airport can match our team's record. The strong operational performance is reflected in our customer satisfaction ratings which remain at record levels with more than 75 per cent of customers saying they are extremely or very satisfied with the airline".

Financial review:

Total revenue in the period was down 12.2 per cent.

Passenger revenue was down 12.5 per cent, on capacity down 3.1 per cent. Yields were down 9.7 per cent, 13.3 per cent excluding exchange, as a result of price declines and a shift in the sales mix within cabin class.

Our cargo business continues to be impacted by the worldwide decline in demand for airfreight coupled with significant excess capacity driving lower prices. Cargo revenue decreased by 28.1 per cent, with cargo volumes, measured in cargo tonne kilometres, declining by 11.5 per cent. Cargo yields declined by 18.8 per cent driven by lower levels of fuel surcharges as the oil price fell and significant price declines.

Operating costs were down 6.6 per cent with unit costs down 3.0 per cent. Fuel costs for the period were down 15.6 per cent. Other operating costs, excluding fuel, were down 2.4 per cent, down 7.6 excluding exchange. This decrease sees the continuation of the cost savings that were launched last October.

Our financial position remains strong. Our cash position at the end of June 2009 was £1,258 million, down £123 million on March 2009. The recently announced cash raising through the convertible bonds and bank facilities will increase our liquidity to approximately £2 billion. Net debt improved to £2,268 million, down £114 million from March 2009, primarily as a result of foreign exchange movements.

The retranslation of foreign debt and the marked-to-market movement on fuel and currency hedges have increased reserves by £467 million since March 31, 2009. This reflects a strengthening of sterling and increased fuel prices since the end of the year.

The tax rate for the quarter was 28 per cent.

Business review:

Our four key business priorities remain unchanged.

Upgraded customer experience

Our new lounge for premium passengers opened at Heathrow Terminal 3. The 300-seat Galleries Club Lounge is for eligible customers travelling on British Airways flights from T3.

We are launching flights this winter from Heathrow to Las Vegas and Gatwick to the Maldives, Montego Bay, Punta Cana in the Dominican Republic, Sharm El Sheikh and Innsbruck. Gibraltar, Malaga and Pisa flights will move from Gatwick to Heathrow and flights from Gatwick to New York JFK, Alicante, Barcelona, Krakow, Madrid, Malta and Palma will be suspended.

Capacity

Capacity for this summer will reduce by 3.5 per cent compared to last year with capacity for this winter down 5 per cent versus last year. In addition to the 16 aircraft that will be parked this winter, the remaining three Boeing 757s will be grounded in summer 2010 and a further three Boeing 747s will be grounded during winter 2010.

Competitive cost base

Our permanent change programme which we started last year and is driven by pay and productivity is progressing well. Manpower has reduced by 4,000 in the last 12 months. Around 7,000 employees have volunteered for schemes in support of the airline's cost reduction programme. In addition, we have reduced our external costs by working closely with our top 250 suppliers.

Corporate responsibility

The Aviation Global Deal Group, which British Airways co-founded, last month presented its proposal for a worldwide carbon trading framework to UN negotiators preparing for the UN climate change summit in Copenhagen in December. Carbon allowances would be allocated partly by auctioning, generating up to $5bn a year to fund environmental projects in developing countries. (See website www.agdgroup.org)

Trading outlook

The industry continues to face very difficult trading conditions, with considerable uncertainty over the likely timeframe of the recovery from the global economic downturn.

Underlying volumes and seat factors have stabilised during the quarter and are expected to improve in the peak summer months. Yields will be under pressure from the year on year impact of lower fuel surcharges, exchange movements and mix. Yield uncertainty continues to make revenue forecasting difficult. Based on current fuel prices and exchange rates the full year fuel bill is expected to be between £450 million and £500 million lower than last year.

We continue to focus on excellent customer service and cost reduction initiatives to offset the declines in revenue.

Appendix

Financial Position and Performance for the three months ended June 30, 2009 (unaudited)

		Three months ended June 30		
		2009	2008	Change
Revenue	£m	1,983	2,259	(12.2)%
Operating (loss)/profit	£m	(94)	35	nm
(Loss)/profit before tax	£m	(148)	37	nm
(Loss)/profit after tax	£m	(106)	27	nm
EBITDAR	£m	118	253	(135)
Net debt	£m	2,268	1,104	(1,164)
Cash & cash equivalents	£m	1,258	1,955	(697)
Basic earnings/(loss) per share	P	(9.6)	2.0	nm
Cash (out)/in from operating activities	£m	(29)	285	(314)
Passenger revenue per RPK*	P	6.06	6.71	(9.7)%

* prior year restated for inclusion of frequent flyer passengers
nm: not meaningful

7.7.5 Exemptions

The periodic financial reporting requirements set out at **7.7.2** to **7.7.4** above do not apply in certain circumstances (DTR 4.4). These are not relevant to this book.

7.7.6 Liability

Under s 90A of the FSMA 2000, a listed company will be liable to pay compensation to a person who has acquired shares and suffered loss as a result of any untrue or misleading statement in, or omission from, the annual financial report, the half-yearly report, the IMSs or any preliminary statement published in advance of the annual financial report.

A company will be liable if a PDMR for the publication knew that the statement was wrong or misleading, was reckless as to whether it was or knew any omission was a dishonest concealment of a material fact.

Under s 463 of the CA 2006, directors can be liable to their company for any untrue or misleading statement made in or omissions from the directors' report, the directors' remuneration report (see **8.4** below), and summary financial statements taken from them.

A director will be liable only if:

(a)   he knew the statement to be untrue or misleading, or was reckless as to whether it was untrue or misleading, or

(b)   he knew the omission to be dishonest concealment of a material fact.

Section 1270 of the CA 2006 inserts new ss 90A and 90B into the FSMA 2000, setting out the issuers' liability in damages for disclosures required under the Transparency Directive.

If the company fails to publish the required financial information within the prescribed time limits, the FSA may impose any of the sanctions set out at **3.6** above.

7.8 The Model Code

As stated at **7.4.3**, the company must ensure that its persons discharging managerial responsibilities (PDMRs) (see **7.8.2.1**) comply with the Model Code, which is set out at Annex 1 to chapter 9 of the Listing Rules. The company can, however, impose more rigorous obligations than those required by the Model Code if it wishes (LR 9.2.9G). The Model Code restricts when and how PDMRs can deal in the company's shares. It is in addition to the other rules which apply to dealing by such persons, such as:

(a)   the market abuse provisions of the FSMA 2000 (see **Chapter 10**);

(b)   the insider dealing regime of the CJA 1993 (see **Chapter 11**);

(c)   the notification obligations under DTR 3.1.2R; and

(d)   the statutory duties of directors.

The task of making sure the directors comply with the Model Code is usually dealt with in-house, by the company secretary or an in-house lawyer, because the day-to-day nature of compliance means that it would be administratively difficult (and expensive) for external lawyers to police. For example, the Model Code contains detailed provisions relating to share schemes, trusts and options, which require a detailed knowledge of the company's affairs before they can be applied. To this end, Part III of the GC100 Guidelines offers assistance to the GC100 member companies on compliance with the Model Code. However, external lawyers will be expected to advise on aspects of the Model Code on occasion, for example if they want a second opinion. As always, recourse should be made to the detail of the Model Code itself. However,the following provides a flavour of those parts of the Model Code with which the external lawyer will need to be familiar.

7.8.1   Purpose of the Model Code

Why is so much attention paid to the dealings of PDMRs, over and above the dealings of any other shareholder? Well, PDMRs, including directors, manage the day-to-day business of the company. They are best placed to know when they can trade in shares to make a personal profit. For example, say the directors receive an approach from a bidder with a lucrative offer to take over the company. Imagine at this point that the company's shares are worth £1 each and the offer is that bidder will pay £2 for each share. The shareholders do not know it yet, but they are about to double their money. The PDMRs, however, will know it, so what is to stop them from using their advantage over the other shareholders by suddenly investing huge amounts in the company before the offer becomes public knowledge? Answer: the Model Code (or its equivalent). The integrity of the market and the protection of investors require that directors do not abuse their position in this way. The Model Code, therefore, restricts the ability of PDMRs to deal in the company's shares.

7.8.2   Applicability of the Model Code

The Model Code applies to PDMRs (see **7.8.2.1**).

In addition, the PDMRs must also comply with the following rules in relation to 'connected persons' (Model Code, paras 20 to 22):

(a)   take reasonable steps to prevent any dealings in the company's shares, by, or on behalf of, his connected persons, on considerations of a short-term nature (see **7.8.4.3**) (para 20); and

(b)   seek to prohibit dealings in the company's shares, by, or on behalf of his connected persons (or by an investment manager on the connected person's behalf) during a close period (see **7.8.4.3**) (para 21).

In order to fulfil the obligation set out in paras 20 and 21, the PDMR must comply with para 22 and advise the connected persons and investment managers of:

(a)   the listed company's name;

(b)   the close periods during which they cannot deal; and

(c)   the fact that they must advise the company immediately after they have dealt in the company's shares.

Note that the Model Code will not apply to PDMRs once they leave the company. They will, however, still be caught by the market abuse and insider dealing regimes (see **Chapter 10** and **Chapter 11**). The FSA can also impose a financial penalty on any former director who, while a director, was knowingly concerned in a breach of the Listing Rules (FSMA 2000, s 91(2)).

7.8.2.1   Persons discharging managerial responsibilities

A PDMR is defined in s 96B of the FSMA 2000 as:

(a)   a director; or

(b)   a senior executive of a company who:

    (i)   has regular access to inside information relating, directly or indirectly, to the company; and

    (ii)   has power to make managerial decisions affecting the future development and business prospects of the company.

Practically this will include directors and a few other managers of sufficient seniority to be classified as PDMRs.

7.8.2.2 Connected person

This is defined in Sch 11B to the FSMA 2000 (FSMA 2000, s 96B(2)). Note that the wider definition in s 252 of the CA 2006 does not apply here. The definition includes:

(a) the PDMR's family, that is his:

    (i) spouse,

    (ii) civil partner,

    (iii) child or step-child under 18,

    (iv) relative with whom, as at the date of the transaction, he has shared a house for at least 12 months;

(b) a body corporate with which the PDMR is associated (that is, the PDMR or connected person is a director or senior executive with the power to make managerial decisions affecting the future development of the body coporate, or the PDMR and connected persons control, or can exercise, more than 20% of its voting power in general meeting, or are interested in at least 20% of its equity shares);

(c) the trustee of certain trusts of which the beneficiary or potential beneficiary includes the PDMR, his spouse, civil partner, children or step-children under 18, relative sharing the house or an associated body corporate; and

(d) any partner of the PDMR, or any connected person's partner.

This definition was brought in by the FSMA 2000 (Amendment) Regulations 2009 (SI 2009/246).

7.8.3 Prohibited dealings

The key provision of the Model Code is para 3: a restricted person (that is, a PDMR) must not deal in any of the company's shares unless he obtains advance clearance to deal.

Dealing is defined by para 1(c) of the Model Code. At its simplest, it includes buying and selling shares, or agreeing to buy and sell shares. Paragraph 2 of the Model Code sets out dealings which are not subject to the Model Code.

7.8.4 Clearance to deal

This is dealt with in paras 4 to 7 of the Model Code.

7.8.4.1 Who can give clearance to deal?

Person seeking clearance	Person able to give clearance
Director (other than Chairman or Chief Executive)	Chairman, or other director designated by the board (para 4(a))
Company Secretary	As above
Chairman	Chief Executive (para 4(b)), or the senior independent director, or a committee of the board or a nominated officer
Chief Executive	Chairman (para 4(c)), or the senior independent director, or a committee of the board or a nominated officer
If Chairman and Chief Executive are the same person	Board of Directors (para 4(d))
PDMR (other than a director)	Company secretary, or designated director (para 4(e)).

7.8.4.2   The clearance procedure

The company must:

(a)   keep a written record of the requests for clearance it receives, and of any clearance given (para 6);

(b)   respond within five business days of the request for clearance (para 5); and

(c)   provide a copy of the response and any clearance to the restricted person concerned (para 6).

Once clearance has been given, the restricted person must deal as soon as possible, and in any event within two business days of clearance being received (para 7).

7.8.4.3   Refusal of clearance to deal

Clearance to deal must not be given during a prohibited period or on considerations of a short-term nature. Each is considered in turn below.

During a prohibited period (Model Code, para 8(a))

A prohibited period means:

(a)   any close period (see below); and

(b)   any period during which inside information exists in relation to the company.

Broadly, a 'close period' is the 60-day period prior to publication of the preliminary announcement of the company's annual results or the annual financial report (see **7.7.2**) and the period from the end of the relevant financial period up to the publication of the half-yearly report (see **7.7.3**). (If the company reports on a quarterly basis, the close period is the 30-day period before the announcement of the quarterly results. Note that this does not include the IMSs (see **7.7.4**).) See the definition at para 1(a) of the Model Code for further information.

'Inside information' is as defined by s 118C of the FSMA 2000 (see **7.5.2**, substituting 'qualifying investments' for 'financial instruments'). Remember that, usually, if inside information does exist about the company, it should be disclosed to an RIS under the general obligation of disclosure provided by DTR 2.2.1R (see **7.5.1** above), and so would no longer be inside information. The prohibition on giving clearance while such inside information exists assumes that an exception to the obligation to disclose must exist, for example because the matter is still under negotiation (DTR 2.5.3G(1) – see **7.5.2.8**). The fact that any request for clearance would have to be refused, however, may well flag up, to a restricted person otherwise unaware of it, that there is some inside information – perhaps an acquisition or disposal in the course of negotiation – in existence. (In addition, it is possible that the restricted person might then consult the company's insider list (see **7.5.6**) to see who might well have access to that information, and so who might be interesting to take to lunch to pump for gossip.) For this reason, the lawyer will advise the company to train its restricted persons in relation to the requirements of the Model Code and the DTRs, and the importance of avoiding any breach.

On considerations of a short-term nature (Model Code, para 8(b))

An investment with a maturity of one year or less will always be considered to be of a short-term nature.

Why will clearance to deal not be given in such circumstances? Most shareholders can buy and sell shares as quickly as they like. For example, if you or I invest £100 in Company X tomorrow, and the next day our investment has grown to £1,000, we might well choose to realise our investment that day and treat ourselves to a cheeky long weekend away. We have made what is known as a 'fast buck'. Persons discharging managerial responsibilities subject to the Model Code cannot do this. Why? Directors' shareholdings are seen as a barometer of the company's fortunes. If a director buys shares, it sends a certain message to the market (usually positive).

Similarly, if a director sells shares, it can send a negative message to the market. If a director was buying or selling shares left, right and centre, the market might well lose confidence in the company and the share price might become unstable. The Model Code's aim is to protect investors and maintain the integrity of the market; hence it prohibits such short-term trading.

7.8.4.4 Exception for severe financial difficulty and other exceptional circumstances

Despite the rules set out at **7.8.4.3** above, paras 9, 10 and 11 provide that clearance to sell (but not buy) shares may be given during a prohibited period as restricted under para 8(a) (see **7.8.4.3**) where the restricted person:

(a)   is not in possession of inside information; and

(b)   either:

(i)   is in severe financial difficulty (eg, she has a pressing financial commitment which cannot be satisfied otherwise than by selling the shares, but this would not include a liability to tax unless the person had no other means of satisfying the liability); or

(ii)   is in other exceptional circumstances (eg, there is a court order, or other overriding legal requirement, for the sale).

Ultimately, the person with responsibility for giving clearance to deal must decide whether the exception applies, but FSA guidance can be (and, in the case of exceptional circumstances, should be) sought.

In practice it is likely to be very rare that circumstances will arise permitting the use of this exception.

If the 'exceptional circumstances' exception is used, the company must notify an RIS of the information under DTR 3.1.4R, including the nature of the exceptional circumstances (LR 9.2.10R).

7.8.4.5 Trading plans

Changes were introduced to the Model Code with effect from 6 March 2009 to permit PDMRs to deal in their company's securities during 'prohibited periods' in certain circumstances without breaching the Model Code.

It was difficult for PDMRs to adopt long-term trading strategies in relation to their company's shares without breaching the Model Code due to the significant number of times when there would be a 'prohibited period' during any given year due to the regular release of financial information and the unpredictability of when inside information would arise.

Further, some companies are listed in more than one country, some of which already permitted dealing by PDMRs in circumstances where there would be no suspicion of abusing inside information even during a 'prohibited period'. This meant that a PDMR would be able to deal in the company's shares in one country but breach the Model Code in the UK.

The changes to the Model Code seek to address both issues.

The dealing must occur in line with a pre-determined agreement, known as a trading plan, entered into with an independent third party. The terms of the plan must have been fixed outside of a 'prohibited period'. Due to the independence of the third party and the fact that the terms of dealing have been agreed in advance, there will not be the same concerns about PDMRs abusing inside information.

Entering a trading plan

A PDMR can at any time which is not a 'prohibited period' enter into a 'trading plan' (para 24). This is defined in the Glossary as a written plan between a PDMR and an independent third party setting out a strategy under which the third party will be given authority for the acquisition or disposal of specified securities in the PDMR's company and either it:

(a)   specifies the amount, date and price of securities to be dealt; or

(b)   gives discretion to the independent third party as to when, how many and at what price to deal in the securities; or

(c)   includes a written formula setting this out.

Clearance is required to be given to enter a trading plan in accordance with para 4 of the Model Code. This cannot be given during a 'prohibited period' (para 24).

Dealing under a trading plan

A PDMR can deal in securities of his company during *both* 'prohibited' and non-prohibited periods. Dealing can take place during a 'prohibited period' only if (para 25):

(a)   the trading plan was entered into before the 'prohibited period';

(b)   clearance has been given to the plan in accordance with para 4 before the 'prohibited period'; and

(c)   the trading plan does not allow the PDMR to exert any influence or discretion over the third party as to how, when, or whether to deal in the company's securities.

The PDMR must notify the company at the same time as making the required DTR 3.1.2 notification of the fact that the dealing was under the trading plan and the date the plan was entered into (para 26).

The company must notify an RIS of information provided to it by a PDMR in accordance with para 26 (DTR 3.1.4R(d)).

Amending a trading plan

A trading plan cannot be amended without clearance in accordance with para 4, and this cannot be given during a 'prohibited period' (para 24).

Cancelling a trading plan

A trading plan cannot be cancelled without clearance in accordance with para 4 (para 24).

A trading plan can only be cancelled during a 'prohibited period' in the exceptional circumstances set out in paras 9 and 10 of the Model Code (para 24) (see **7.8.4.4**).

7.8.5   Sanctions for breach of the Model Code

The Model Code forms part of the continuing obligations of the Listing Rules, and is enforceable against the company itself by virtue of LR 9.2.8R. If the company has not required PDMRs to comply with the Model Code and to take all proper and reasonable steps to ensure their compliance, the FSA may impose the sanctions for a breach of the Listing Rules referred to at **3.6** above.

However, it may be that the company has complied with its obligations but a PDMR has still breached the Model Code. If so, the FSA may impose a financial penalty under s 91(2) of the FSMA 2000, but only if the PDMR is a director or former director who was knowingly concerned in a breach of the Listing Rules.

7.9   Communication with shareholders

As we have seen, the Listing Rules, Prospectus Rules and DTRs set out many different circumstances when the company must communicate information to its shareholders.

7.9.1   The circular

The usual way of communicating with shareholders is by way of a document known as a circular. The Listing Rules define a circular as:

> Any document issued to holders of listed securities including notices of meetings but excluding prospectuses, listing particulars, annual reports and accounts, interim reports, proxy cards and dividend or interest vouchers.

Chapter 13 of the Listing Rules, entitled 'Contents of Circulars', prescribes general content requirements for all circulars (LR 13.3) (see **7.9.3**) and specific content requirements for particular types of circular (see **7.9.2**).

7.9.2   When is a circular required?

The Listing Rules set out the circumstances when a circular is required. The following are the most commonly encountered by the lawyer. The Chapter 13 Listing Rule governing the specific content requirements of the required circular is provided in brackets.

- Class 1 transactions (LR 13.4, LR 13.5 and LR 13, Annex 1R) (see **19.6.1**)
- Related party transactions (LR 13.6) (see **19.6.2**)
- Circulars regarding the purchase of own securities ('buyback') (LR 13.7)
- Authority to allot shares (LR 13.8.1R) (see **14.5.6**)
- Disapplying pre-emption rights (LR 13.8.2R) (see **14.6.15**)
- Reduction of capital (LR 13.8.4R)
- Capitalisation or bonus issue (LR 13.8.5R)
- Scrip dividend alternative (LR 13.8.6R)
- Scrip dividend mandate schemes/dividend reinvestment plan (LR 13.8.7R)
- Notices of meetings (including business other than ordinary business at an AGM) (LR 13.8.8R)
- Amendments to the company's constitution (LR 13.8.10R)
- Employees' share scheme arrangements (LR 13.8.11R to LR 13.8.14R)
- Discounted option arrangements (LR 13.8.15R)
- Reminders of conversion rights (LR 13.8.16R)

7.9.3   General content requirements

The basic content requirements of all circulars are prescribed by LR 13.3. To provide a flavour of what is in a circular, a sample of the requirements include:

(a)   a clear and adequate explanation of the subject matter;

(b)   a statement why the shareholder is being asked to vote, or otherwise why the circular is being sent;

(c)   if voting or other action is required:

    (i)   all information necessary to allow the shareholder to make a properly informed decision; and

    (ii)   a heading drawing attention to the importance of the document and advising the shareholder to consult an independent adviser if he is unsure what action to take;

(d)   if voting is required, a recommendation from the board as to how shareholders should vote, indicating whether the proposal is, in its opinion, in the shareholders' best interests.

7.9.4   FSA approval

Some circulars require prior approval by the FSA before the company can circulate them to shareholders, and others do not. The lawyer will need to be able to advise on whether a circular requires prior approval.

Once published, any circular, approved or otherwise, must be sent to FSA for publication on its document viewing facility (see **7.5.7.1**).

7.9.4.1   Circulars which do not require approval

Listing Rule 13.2.2R provides that circulars which do not require prior approval are those which:

(a)   are listed in LR 13.8 (or relate only to a proposed change of name);

(b)   comply with LR 13.3 and any requirements of LR 13.8; and

(c)   have no unusual features.

As can be seen from the list at **7.9.2** above, there are many circulars listed in LR 13.8. They include circulars relating to share capital changes, such as an increase in authorised share capital, the grant of an authority to allot and the disapplication of pre-emption rights.

7.9.4.2   Circulars which require approval

All other circulars require approval (LR 13.2.1R). By definition, these will be circulars which:

(a)   are not listed in LR 13.8R; and

(b)   have unusual features.

Examples include circulars produced in connection with Class 1 transactions (see **19.4**) and related party transactions (see **19.5**).

The approval process is detailed in LR 13.2.4R to 13.2.9G. The company must submit the draft circular to the FSA at least 10 clear business days before the intended publication date.

7.9.5   Electronic communication

The CA 2006 has introduced provisions in ss 308, 309, 333 and 1143 to 1148 which apply to all companies. They permit (but do not compel) documents or information to be sent from the company to the shareholder or *vice versa* electronically (including via e-mail and on a website), provided the conditions in Schs 4 and 5 are met.

These provisions are supplemented for listed companies by Chapter 6 of the DTRs. Transparency Rule 6.1.7G permits (but does not compel) listed companies to communicate with their shareholders by 'electronic means', provided certain conditions are met, the most important of these being (DTR 6.1.8R) the need for prior approval of the shareholders by ordinary resolution and for identification arrangements to be put in place.

'Electronic means' is defined in the DTRs as a 'means of electronic equipment for the processing (including digital compression), storage and transmission of data, employing wires, radio optical technologies, or any other electromagnetic means.' A pretty impenetrable definition for most lawyers (except that rarity the lawyer-geek, who will doubtless be salivating at the prospect of explaining the full extent of these terms to his or her colleagues) – it includes fax, e-mail and websites.

The ICSA has produced a guidance note for electronic communication with shareholders under the CA 2006 and the DTRs (available on its website) setting out recommended best practice. The FSA has also produced guidance on the impact of the CA 2006 provisions in its newsletter *List!* No 17 (available in the UKLA section of the FSA's website).

7.10   The Admission and Disclosure Standards

As stated at **7.1** above, the Admission and Disclosure Standards contain continuing obligations which are additional to those set out in the Listing Rules. These obligations are set out at ADS 3 (see **Appendix 1**), and they include that the company must comply with the Part 6 Rules. The other continuing obligations are mercifully very brief, compared with the requirements of the Listing Rules. They include:

(a)   requirements relating to the timetable for what are referred to as 'corporate actions', that is, payment of dividends, open offers, rights issues and the like (ADS 3.5 to 3.9);

(b)   a requirement that proposed amendments to the company's constitution must be communicated to the FSA and Stock Exchange in draft form, at the latest on the date of calling the relevant GM (ADS 3.11);

(c)   that the Stock Exchange will suspend the admission to trading of any shares which are suspended from admission to listing (ADS 3.15) (this is a mirror image of LR 9.2.1R – see **7.4.1** above); and

(d)   that the company must pay an annual fee to the Stock Exchange (ADS 3.14).

7.11   Sanctions

7.11.1   Sanctions for breach of the Disclosure Rules, the Transparency Rules, the Corporate Governance Rules, the Prospectus Rules or the Listing Rules

Sanctions for breach of the Part 6 Rules are set out at **3.6** above. At the time of writing just three fines had been imposed (the article below gives an example) and no public censure had been issued for breaches of the Part 6 Rules (introduced from 1 July 2005).

Wolfson fined by FSA over disclosure failure

Ian King, Deputy Business Editor

Wolfson Microelectronics, the chip designer, was this morning fined £140,000 by the Financial Services Authority (FSA) for failing to reveal price sensitive information to the market as soon as possible.

The fine, which comes just three weeks after Dave Shrigley stepped down as Wolfson's chief executive, is increasing evidence of the City watchdog's determination to clamp down on companies which are slow to update the market.

The FSA fined Woolworths £350,000 last June for failing to disclose, swiftly enough, that EUK, its distribution arm, had lost a major contract with Tesco. Others have been fined by the FSA during the last four years for similar offences include tour operator MyTravel, Pace Micro, the set-top box maker, Universal Salvage, the vehicle salvage business and electrical parts distributor, Eurodis Electron.

Wolfson's punishment dates back to a profits warning it issued on March 27 last year, when it said a major customer, later revealed to be Apple, would not be requiring it to supply parts for two new products, later confirmed to be the iPod Nano and iPod Touch.

The FSA said that Wolfson had first learned of the news, which clipped $20 million or 8 per cent of its forecast revenue for 2008, as early as March 10 and said that, as the negative news was constituted inside information, it should have been disclosed as soon as possible.

The FSA said that, on March 12 last year, Wolfson had discussed the matter with its investor relations advisors, who wrongly recommended that there was no need to disclose the negative news, causing the company to delay making an announcement.

It said that, at a board meeting on March 20, Wolfson reconsidered the earlier advice and subsequently sought further advice from its lawyers and corporate brokers – who recommended disclosing the news.

When the statement was finally issued to the stock exchange, Wolfson shares fell by 18 per cent.

Sally Dewar, the managing director of wholesale and institutional markets at the FSA, said: "Listed companies must carefully consider what could be inside information and their obligations to disclose it. It is unacceptable for a company not to disclose negative news because it believes other matters are likely to offset it. Doing this hampers an investor's ability to make informed investment decisions and

risks distorting the market value of a company's shares."

Wolfson, whose other customers include Sony and LG, put out a further profit warning in October, cautioning that a slowdown in demand for consumer gadgets had hit demand for its chips.

Mr Shrigley's successor, former Motorola executive Mike Hickey, joined the company at the beginning of the year.

Tim Dolan, a partner at Pinsent Masons, said: "During this financial crisis firms will feel under increased pressure to delay publication of bad news.

"Today's fine simply reinforces the FSA's view that delaying publication of bad news is not acceptable in any circumstance, even if good news is imminent. Firms need to be ensuring that they are keeping the market up to date at all times."

Simon Morris, a partner at CMS Cameron McKenna, said: "This is a large fine for sixteen days' inadvertent non-disclosure. It highlights that acting good faith is no defence to FSA's absolute requirement for prompt announcement of price sensitive information."

Wolfson shares were down 3p at 74p at 15:00.

Source: *The Times*, 20 January 2009

Fines have also been imposed on Woolworths Group plc (£350,000 on 11 June 2008) and on Entertainment Rights plc (£245,000 on 19 January 2009) for breaches of DTR 2.2.1R and Listing Principle 4. A fine of £17 million was imposed on the Shell group of companies in August 2004 for both breaches of the old Listing Rules and market abuse (see **Chapter 10**). The fine was wholly for the market abuse offence, with no extra amount imposed for the Listing Rule breaches. On 2 November 2007 the FSA cancelled the listing of shares in Simon Group plc as it was no longer satisfying its continuing obligations for listing as the percentage of shares in public hands had fallen below 25% in breach of LR 6.1.19R. You can find out more information from issue no 17 of the FSA's newsletter, *List!* (available on the UKLA section of the FSA's website).

7.11.2   Sanctions for breach of the Admission and Disclosure Standards

The sanctions are set out in ADS 3.23. In the event of breach of any continuing obligation, the Stock Exchange may privately or publicly censure a company, fine it, order the company to make a payment to any person, or alternatively cancel the company's admission to trading.

7.12   Future developments

The Committee of European Securities Regulators (CESR), which acts as an advisory group to the EU Commission, suggested in July 2007 that further work is needed to harmonise the requirements for insider lists (see **7.5.6** above) across Member States and that the definition of 'inside information' may need to be revisited.

The European Commission's consultation document on proposals to simplify and improve the application of the Prospectus Directive (see **3.7.1**) included proposals to remove the need for the annual information update.

Chapter 8
Corporate Governance

8.1 What is corporate governance?

Corporate governance refers to how a company is run. This includes not only how a company is directed and controlled, but also how a company is performing, how that performance can be enhanced, and how a company should account to interested parties such as shareholders and employees.

Corporate governance is relevant to all companies, but once a company is listed, those who control the company (directors and controlling shareholders) are not the same as, and therefore may have conflicting interests to, those who own the company (shareholders). This means that corporate governance is a particularly important issue for listed companies.

Corporate governance is also once again very much in the news. It has jumped to the top of politicians' and regulators' agendas worldwide as a result of the global financial crisis which has triggered the deepest recession in over 70 years. Listed companies stood at the heart of the crisis, and post mortems are being conducted, particularly into the poor corporate governance of banks and other financial companies, some of the largest of which are now only functioning thanks to governmental intervention. Although financial services companies are the main focus of many of the proposed changes to corporate governance rules, it is worth noting that in the UK the rules are being reviewed for all listed companies.

8.2 The UK framework

Common law, the CA 2006, the Listing Rules (in particular, the continuing obligations, Model Code and Listing Principles), the Corporate Governance Rules, the Combined Code on Corporate Governance (the 'Combined Code'), the Large and Medium-sized Companies and Groups (Accounts and Reports) Regulations 2008 (SI 2008/401), the FSA's Code of Market Conduct and various non-legal guidelines produced by institutional shareholders (such as the ABI, the NAPF and PIRC) and the accountancy profession all contain provisions which address corporate governance issues. The Combined Code, the Corporate Governance Rules and the 2008 Regulations are discussed further below.

The EU is having increasing influence in this area. Generally the European Commission does not believe in the introduction of an EU-wide corporate governance code. However, it does support the introduction of a limited number of measures to harmonise national codes.

The European Commission has been following its Action Plan on company law and corporate governance (Modernising Company Law and Enhancing Corporate Governance in the EU) since 2003. The Action Plan contains 24 measures, most recently leading to implementation of the Shareholder Rights Directice (2007/36/EC) in the UK in August 2009 (see **8.6**). Other proposals are being discussed as a direct result of perceived deficiencies in corporate governance arising from the global financial crisis.

8.3   The Combined Code

8.3.1   Nature

The Combined Code is the most prominent part of the UK corporate governance framework. It is a codification of best practice in corporate governance. The Combined Code does not have the force of law. Rather, as **8.3.4** below explains in more detail, companies are required to comply with the Combined Code, or, if they do not, to explain their non-compliance. The Combined Code is not included in the Listing Rules but instead is available on the Financial Reporting Council's (FRC) website (and reproduced in this book at **Appendix 4**).

8.3.2   Background

To date there have been four editions of the Combined Code: the original of 1995, revised versions published in 2003 and 2006, and an updated version published in 2008.

8.3.2.1   Background to the original Combined Code of 1995

The provisions of the original Combined Code were based on the findings of three reports, namely the Cadbury, Greenbury and Hampel Reports, which were commissioned in the 1990s to consider corporate governance in detail. The Hampel Committee 'combined' the recommendations of all three reports to produce the original Combined Code. This Combined Code was annexed to the Listing Rules in 1995 and the Listing Rules were amended to refer to compliance with it. In 1999 a further report (the Turnbull Report) was commissioned, to provide guidance to listed companies regarding implementation of the requirements in the original Combined Code relating to internal control.

8.3.2.2   Background to the Combined Code of 2003

In 2002, financial scandals involving Enron (see the article below) and WorldCom put corporate governance in the spotlight again. In the UK, two further reports were commissioned immediately. The Financial Reporting Council commissioned the Smith Report (concerning audit issues) and the DTI commissioned the Higgs Report (concerning non-executive directors and remuneration). Those responsible for compiling these reports worked closely together to propose a consolidated revised code. Some of the proposals proved controversial, however, so the Financial Reporting Council set up a working group to revise the code further. The final text of this revised code was published in July 2003.

Enron: The Countdown to Court
Leader of boys' club culture
The Chief Executive

Before he became the most prominent alleged white collar criminal of his era, Jeffrey Skilling was the quintessential Enron executive.

Perhaps no one at the Houston-based energy company so embodied its combustible corporate culture of brains and arrogance as Mr Skilling, a Harvard Business School graduate and McKinsey & Company alumnus.

Like Kenneth Lay, his Enron boss, Mr Skilling rose from humble roots to become one of the most celebrated - and later reviled - American executives. The son of a salesman, he worked his way through university despite earning a scholarship.

Academia came easy to Mr Skilling, and he demonstrated a brash self-confidence well before he had scaled the heights of the business world.

When asked during his Harvard interview if he was smart, Mr Skilling famously replied: "I'm f***ing smart," according to The Smartest Guys in the Room, a book about Enron by Bethany McLean and Peter Elkind.

After graduation, Mr Skilling moved on to become one of the youngest partners in the history of McKinsey. It was a remarkable achievement at a consulting firm known for its over-achievers.

It was at McKinsey, leading the energy practice, that Mr Skilling encountered Enron, a relatively unexciting pipeline company that had been strung together by a series of mergers.

After years of advising its then chief executive, Mr Lay, he finally moved over full time in 1990. Mr Skilling's phenomenal success at Enron was something known as the Gas Bank, which was an attempt to apply emerging financial techniques to a stubborn patch of the traditional energy business.

His plan was to insert Enron between natural gas buyers and sellers to smooth out the notoriously unpredictable prices for the commodity that were embedded in rigid, long-term contracts, or a wild spot market.

Enron then went on to create a secondary market to trade natural gas contracts in the same way as other commodities to give buyers and sellers even more flexibility. To spur the venture, Mr Skilling convinced the Securities and Exchange Commission in 1992 to allow the gas contracts to be marked-to-market, an accounting treatment that would allow their entire projected value, sometimes over 20 years or more, to be recognised upfront. A decade later, this would prove to be a fateful accomplishment as Enron routinely abused mark-to-market accounting to record billions of dollars of dubious profits that were never likely to materialise.

In the meantime, however, the Gas Bank was an enormous success. It created a robust trading market that boosted the natural gas industry as a whole.

And Enron was at the centre of it all.

Not only did the company reap trading commissions, its own traders were able consistently to bet on the right side of the market.

Part of Mr Skilling's downfall was a stubborn insistence that the Gas Bank's success could be replicated. Under his leadership, Enron shed dependable assets such as its pipelines and instead made markets in everything from paper pulp to broadband internet access.

The results were disastrous. One problem, among many, was that Enron simply did not understand these commodities in the same way it did natural gas, with which it had an intimate history.

As the debacles mounted, Enron executives resorted to ever more aggressive accounting techniques to satisfy Mr Skilling's obsession with hitting Wall Street earnings targets and boosting the share price.

In keeping with many other big companies, this focus on share price and short-term earnings, often to the exclusion of all other business measures, would be a hallmark of the 1990s stock market bubble and its ensuing corporate scandals.

For all his intellectual brilliance, Mr Skilling did not prove to be much of a manager. He favoured raw intelligence over experience in his recruits, and presided over a ruthless compensation system in which top performers were lavishly rewarded while others were tossed out. A boys' club culture prevailed at the company, where a cadre of loyalists such as Andrew Fastow, the former chief financial officer; Lou Pai, the former head of Enron Energy Services; and Ken Rice, the former head of Enron Broadband; joined Mr Skilling on exotic company-paid vacations where they raced off-road vehicles across Mexico.

Meanwhile, internal controls were practically non-existent, and inter-office affairs became de rigeur.

Even as Enron's fortunes, and his own, have collapsed, Mr Skilling has not abandoned his trademark arrogance. At a Congressional hearing two years ago, the former executive declined to exercise his Fifth Amendment right as so many embattled executives had done, including Mr Lay, and remain quiet. Instead, he proceeded to lecture enraged legislators on the intricacies of accounting rules.

It was an audacious performance, and one that Mr Skilling will now have the opportunity to replay with federal prosecutors at an upcoming criminal trial.

Source: *Financial Times*, 20 February 2004

In May 2006 Jeffrey Skilling was convicted on 19 counts of conspiracy and fraud in a joint trial with Kenneth Lay, the former Enron chairman. Skilling was found not guilty of nine counts of insider trading. On 23 October 2006 Skilling was sentenced to 24 years and 4 months in prison.

Kenneth Lay was also convicted of 10 counts of fraud and other related charges, but died of a heart attack in July 2006, prior to sentencing. The guilty verdict against him has now been overturned on the basis that Mr Lay did not have the opportunity to appeal against his conviction before his death.

Enron's former chief financial officer, Andrew Fastow, pleaded guilty to conspiracy to commit wire fraud and securities fraud, and turned informant against Skilling and Lay in return for a more modest sentence of six years in prison.

8.3.2.3 Background to the 2006 Combined Code

In July 2005, the FRC announced a review of the implementation of the 2003 version of the Combined Code. As a result of this review, a small number of changes were incorporated into an updated version of the code published in June 2006.

8.3.2.4 Background to the 2008 Combined Code

The FRC announced a further review of the impact and effectiveness of the Combined Code in April 2007. As a result, it has made a number of changes to the 2006 version of the Combined Code, with the most important being to allow an individual to be the chairman of more than one FTSE 100 company. At the same time, the FRC introduced some changes necessary to comply with the new Corporate Governance Rules (see **3.5.3**). The new Combined Code was published in June 2008 and replaces the 2006 version. It applies to reporting years beginning on or after 29 June 2008. It is included in **Appendix 2**. References in this book to the Combined Code are to the 2008 version.

8.3.3 Structure

The Combined Code consists of 17 main principles of good governance. Each principle is supplemented by a set of supporting principles and code provisions. The supporting principles were drafted with the intention of affording companies an element of flexibility regarding the implementation of the main principles.

The Combined Code is divided into two main sections. Section 1 sets out the main principles relating to:

(a)   directors (para A – seven principles);

(b)   remuneration (para B – two principles);

(c)   accountability and audit (para C – three principles); and

(d)   relations with shareholders (para D – two principles).

Section 2 sets out three main principles relating to institutional shareholders (para E).

In recognition that smaller listed companies can find it difficult to achieve full compliance with the Combined Code, certain provisions have been relaxed for companies below the FTSE 350.

8.3.4 Associated guidance

The following guidance on the Combined Code is also available from the FRC website.

8.3.4.1 The Turnbull Guidance

The Turnbull Guidance was published originally in 1999, to set out best practice on the internal control of companies. Following a review by the FRC, the guidance was updated in October 2005.

8.3.4.2 Good Practice Suggestions from the Higgs Report

Companies are not obliged to follow this guide to best practice in relation to non-executive directors (see **8.3.6.1**), but they may find it helpful. The suggestions, published in June 2006, provide guidance on the role of the Chairman and the non-executive director, a summary of the principal duties of the remuneration and nomination committees, a due diligence checklist for new board members, a sample letter of appointment of a non-executive director, an induction checklist and a performance evaluation guidance.

8.3.4.3   The FRC's Guidance on Audit Committees

The latest version of this guide to best practice in relation to audit committees was published in October 2008. It includes guidance on how to establish a committee, the relationship of the committee with the board, the role and responsibilities of the committee, and how it should communicate with shareholders. As with the Higgs Report suggestions, companies are not obliged to follow the FRC's Guidance.

8.3.5   Compliance

8.3.5.1   Section 1

While any company can choose to follow the provisions of Section 1 of the Combined Code, the Listing Rules provide that, strictly, Section 1 applies only to listed companies incorporated in the UK. Even these companies are not subject to any formal requirement to comply with Section 1. Instead, the requirement is that any such company must include in its annual financial report (ie the annual report and accounts) a statement, known as a 'disclosure statement', which details:

(a)   how it has applied the main *principles* set out in Section 1 (in a way which would enable shareholders to evaluate how the principles have been applied) (LR 9.8.6R(5)); and

(b)   whether it has complied throughout the relevant accounting period with the code *provisions* set out in Section 1 and, if it has not, which provisions it has not complied with, the period of non-compliance, and why it has not complied (LR 9.8.6R(6)).

The disclosure requirements are often referred to as the 'comply or explain' approach. This approach encourages compliance even though strictly it does not require it, because the requirement to disclose any failure to comply carries with it a risk of adverse publicity. The institutional investors have made it clear, however, that they do expect compliance and, in practice, companies which do not comply with Section 1 are often subject to significant pressure from institutional investors such as the ABI, the NAPF and PIRC.

You will see in the extract from a newspaper article below, the limits of this 'comply or explain' approach (together with a typically robust and colourful defence by the chief executive).

In the line of fire

Richard Johnson

. . .
In 2004 Sugar couldn't even drag himself along to the AGM. Pensions Investment Research Consultants (PIRC), an organisation that advises on corporate governance, recommended that the Amstrad shareholders get rid of him – and fast.

It shouldn't bother Sugar – according to the 2005 Sunday Times Rich List, he's worth an estimated £760m. But it does. 'The shareholders are looked after by me,' he says. 'And they should be very thankful. I run Amstrad as if it was my own. They get their accounts every year, their profits and dividends. And if they don't like it, they should sell their shares. But I'll run my – the – company the way I want to. Not the way some ***t in the City wants me to.'

. . .
Sugar's single-mindedness is a strength – if Amstrad is doing the business. But as Amstrad has been struggling of late – total sales fell 21% in the six months to New Year's Eve – analysts have talked of his single-mindedness as a weakness. Sugar has been the chairman and chief executive of Amstrad ever since the former CEO resigned in October 2001. Which isn't considered best practice. And he has a son on the board, even though he sold his shares in November. The balance of power and authority in the company seems to have disappeared. Theoretically, Sugar has too much control.

PIRC voiced its concerns. 'Sir Alan serves as the chairman-chief executive, with a further four executives on the board, including his son. There are also two non-executives, only one of whom we consider to be independent. The risks of a concentration of power at the head of the company and lack of independent representation on the board are well known. As a result, we are recommending opposition to the re-elec-tion of Sir Alan as chairman-chief executive.' In November, the Co-operative Insurance Society (CIS) added to the mounting criticism by awarding Amstrad the wooden spoon for the worst annual general meeting. 'Amstrad's chairman, Sir Alan Sugar, did not attend because he was 'away on business',' said Ian Jones, head of responsible investment at CIS. 'For a plc, what more important business can there be than the annual shareholders' meeting?'

'I think it was the first time in 25 years that I couldn't make an AGM,' says Sugar. 'The AGM has its date set three or four months in advance. And something just came up. I don't have to be at the AGM. It's just some stupid little idiot writing stories again. And he can go and f*** himself. He can stick his bloody share certificate right where the sun don't shine, as far as I'm concerned.'
. . .

Source: *Sunday Times*, 26 March 2006

Amstrad was bought by BSkyB plc in September 2007 and ceased to be a listed company subject to the Combined Code. Alan Sugar resigned in July 2008 as chairman and CEO of the company to concentrate on, amongst other things, 'The Apprentice' television show.

There is no prescribed form of disclosure statement, which, as with other aspects of the corporate governance regime, is intended to afford companies a degree of flexibility.

Listing Rule 9.8.10R(2) provides that, before it publishes its annual report, the company must ensure that its auditors review the disclosure statement in relation to nine provisions of the Combined Code which deal with audit and accountability, and which are objectively verifiable (namely C1.1, C2.1 and C3.1 to C3.7).

Listing Rule 9.8.7R sets out the obligations of any overseas company listed on the Official List, in relation to the matters referred to above. Such companies are not required to 'comply or explain', but they must state their compliance with their domestic corporate governance code or law and explain how their actual practices differ from the Combined Code.

8.3.5.2 Section 2

Section 2 of the Combined Code applies to institutional shareholders rather than companies. Companies do not, therefore, need to comply with, or make a disclosure statement in relation to, Section 2.

8.3.5.3 Disclosure of corporate governance arrangements

In addition to the disclosure statement referred to at **8.3.5.1** above, several of the Combined Code provisions require further disclosure, including in the company's annual report, of other information relating to corporate governance. These provisions are highlighted in Schedule C to the Combined Code.

8.3.5.4 Corporate governance statement

The Corporate Governance Rules (see **3.5.3**) require a listed company to include a corporate governance statement in its directors' report in the company's annual report (DTR 7.2.1R) or in a separate report or on the company's website (DTR 7.2.9R) containing the information set out in DTR 7. It should be noted that there is some overlap with the requirements of DTR 7 and the Listing Rules and the Combined Code. For example, DTR 7.2.4G explains that compliance with LR 9.8.6R(6) (see **8.3.5.1**) satisfies DTR 7.2.2R and 7.2.3R, which together require information about the corporate governance code followed by the company, how the company applies it in practice and an explanation of any non-compliance with the code. As the Combined Code requires this information to be included anyway, these provisions of the DTRs will usually be superfluous. However, where a listed company chooses to 'explain' rather than 'comply' with the Combined Code, it will have to show that it still meets the minimum requirements in DTR 7 (Preamble to Combined Code, para 11).

8.3.5.5 Directors' remuneration

Further, Listing Rule 9.8.8R sets out the information on directors' remuneration which must be included in a report to shareholders in the company's annual report.

8.3.6 Key features

As explained at **8.3.3** above, Section 1 provides guidance for good corporate governance in relation to directors, remuneration, accountability and audit, and relations with shareholders. The key features of the provisions relating to each area are discussed below, to provide a flavour of the issues the Combined Code addresses.

The Combined Code does, of course, go into some detail in relation to each of these, and other, issues; therefore any in-depth analysis must involve recourse to the Combined Code itself (reproduced at **Appendix 4**).

Numerous practical guides are also available. The website of the Institute of Chartered Secretaries and Administrators (ICSA) features guidance notes on how to implement the requirements of the Code, which are useful to lawyers seeking to draft corporate governance documentation. The Institute of Directors has also collated some useful corporate governance information on its website, which is updated regularly, and the Institutional Voting Information Service website of ABI contains a useful monitoring checklist on the Combined Code.

8.3.6.1 Directors

The board

The Combined Code highlights the important role of the board of directors in taking the company forward. It sets out provisions about the appointment, composition and ability of the board. Guidance on the role of the nomination committee is set out in 'Good Practice Suggestions from the Higgs Report' (see **8.3.4.2**). BIS has published on its website a guide to best practice in recruitment and performance in the boardroom, entitled 'Building Better Boards', which, although based on the 2003 version of the Code, is still useful.

The following is a selection of some of the main provisions in the Combined Code regarding the board:

(a)   All companies should be headed by an effective board, which has collective responsibility for the success of the company and which meets regularly (A.1).

(b)   The board should consist of a balance of executive and non-executive directors (in particular *independent* non-executive directors). At least half of the board should comprise independent non-executive directors, unless the company is below the FTSE 350, in which case there should be at least two independent non-executive directors (see '**Non-executive directors**' below) (A.3, A.3.1, A.3.2).

(c)   The procedure for appointment of directors should be formal, rigorous and transparent. A nomination committee, a majority of which are independent non-executive directors, should lead the appointment process (A.4, A.4.1).

(d)   The chairman must ensure that the directors receive adequate induction training, and must provide directors with the necessary resources for developing their knowledge and skills (A.5).

(e)   Directors' performance, both as a board and individually, should be evaluated formally and rigorously every year (A.6).

(f)   All directors should be submitted for re-election at regular intervals (A.7).

Compliance with these requirements of the Combined Code is the reason that companies tend to announce new non-executive director appointments prior to the IPO. As the press announcement below shows, Debenhams appointed five non-executive directors to its board in April 2006, prior to its IPO in May. As a result, on flotation the Debenhams board met the requirement of the Combined Code that at least half the board comprise independent non-executive directors.

Debenhams positions for float
City figures recruited for expanded board
£700m raised by offer will pay down debt

Debenhams' attempts to attract investors to one of this year's biggest stock market floats will gather pace next week when the retailer unveils an expanded board rich with City figures.

Adam Crozier of the Royal Mail; Richard Gillingwater, a former Credit Suisse banker and head of the government's Shareholder Executive; and Paul Pindar, chief executive of support services group Capita, all agreed this month to join the department store group as non-executive directors.

Peter Long, chief executive of First Choice Holidays, and Dennis Millard, former finance director of Cookson, the electronics manufacturer, have also signed up, according to Debenhams' draft prospectus, a copy of which has been obtained by the Financial Times.

The document, titled "Project Delilah", also shows that Debenhams shares are scheduled to be priced and begin conditional dealings on May 4.

The offer will raise £700m that will be used to pay down debt.

Net debt was £1.74bn at the end of the half-year on March 4 and should fall to about £1.1bn by the time of the float. Analysts believe Debenhams could command a market value, excluding debt, of about £1.8bn-£1.9bn.

Details of the indicative price range and the amount of capital to be raised by Debenhams' trio of private equity backers - Texas Pacific Group, CVC Capital and Merrill Lynch's buy-out wing - are expected after Easter when the formal investor roadshow kicks off.

The new non-executives will sit alongside Debenhams' retail executives - John Lovering, chairman, Rob Templeman, chief executive, and Chris Woodhouse, finance director. The three have been involved in a string of lucrative retail buy-out deals, including Homebase, the DIY group, and Halfords, the cycles and car parts retailer.

Potential investors will want to know how long the trio intend to stay at Debenhams and will take a hard look at the group's figures for the first half of its current financial year. These show total sales up more than 9 per cent to £1.22bn in the period to March 4, with like-for-like sales up 0.6 per cent. "The directors believe this exceeded almost all other retailers' performances," the draft prospectus says.

Interim operating profits rose from £144.5m to £153.1m. Debenhams generated more than £200m of cash from operating activities during the half, only £60m below the figure of £264m generated in the 12-month period ended September 2003, Debenhams' last full-year financial period when it was quoted on the London Stock Exchange.

Of the £700m raised by the company, an estimated £20m will go to cover underwriting commissions and other fees.

Source: *Financial Times*, 15 April 2006

The article below shows the level of shareholder frustration with one listed company's alleged lack of compliance with the corporate governance rules on directors.

Shareholders line up to push top two directors out of Photo-Me's picture

Alistair Osborne

The top two directors at accident-prone photographic company Photo-Me International face the boot after activist investors, claiming support from more than 50pc of shareholders, ganged up to oust them.

Chairman Vernon Sankey and chief executive Serge Crasnianski, who have presided over an album's worth of profits warnings, received a requisition for an extraordinary general meeting to vote on their removal.

The call came from two rebel shareholders – Principle Capital, run by activist investor Brian Myerson, and hedge fund Cycladic Capital – which together own 18.2pc of the shares.

They claimed holders of a further 28.2pc, including shares held

via contracts for difference (CFD), had 'expressed support for these resolutions', bringing the total to 46.3pc – a figure believed to have topped 50pc by the end of trading. Photo-Me shares rose 2¼ to 60¼p.

Mr Crasnianski joined Photo-Me as an executive director in 1990 and has been chief executive since 1998. Mr Sankey was put into the company as deputy chairman in 2000 after a previous shareholder revolt, becoming chairman in 2005.

Principle and Cycladic claimed that 'under the current leadership, the company has suffered from unsatisfactory operational performance, a badly managed strategic review process and a lack of credibility with investors'.

Chris Vincent, Principle's senior

analyst, said the strategic review, begun in June 2006, had only just started to generate interest for the company's photo-booth wing.

'The strategic review has been a shambles, the corporate governance situation that Vernon Sankey was put in to sort out has not been resolved – the board is still full of Crasnianski's mates – and the management of the company is not up to scratch,' Mr Vincent said. Photo-Me will hold a board meeting today, with sources arguing that expressions of support, not least from CFD holders, did not count as votes.

Mr Crasnianski would only say: 'We will only talk after the board meeting.'

Mr Sankey did not return calls.

Source: *Daily Telegraph*, 24 August 2007

The two directors subsequently resigned from their positions.

Roles of the Chairman and the Chief Executive

The Chairman and the Chief Executive are both responsible for the leadership of the company, but in different ways. While the Chief Executive is responsible for running the business, the Chairman must ensure that the board runs effectively. Guidance on the role of the Chairman is set out in 'Good Practice Suggestions from the Higgs Report' (see **8.3.4.2**). The ICSA has also published a guidance note on the roles of the Chairman and the Chief Executive.

Some key provisions in the Combined Code relating to these roles are as follows:

(a)   The Chairman's responsibilities (as proposed by the Higgs Report) are incorporated into the Combined Code as a supporting principle (A.2). The part of the Combined Code containing related guidance and good practice suggestions provides further guidance on the Chairman's role (based on the Higgs Report). The emphasis is on the role of the Chairman both as a leader of the non-executive directors and as a channel of communication between the shareholders and the board (D.1.1).

(b)   The role of Chairman and Chief Executive should be held by separate individuals (A.2.1).

(c)   When appointed, the Chairman should be independent, measured against criteria set out at A.3.1 of the Combined Code (A.2.2).

(d)   The Chief Executive should not go on to become the Chairman. This was introduced by the Higgs Report and was controversial, as many listed companies had a tradition of 'sending the Chief Executive upstairs', to be Chairman. This provision can be waived in exceptional circumstances if the board consults with major shareholders first and discloses the reasons behind the decision in the annual report and accounts (A.2.2).

Sometimes even the bluest of blue-chip listed companies are prepared to run the risk of incurring the wrath of their investors by going against this core principle of the Combined Code. Sir Stuart Rose, Chairman and Chief Executive of M&S, survived a shareholder resolution at its 2009 AGM which was proposed for M&S's breach of this principle. 37.7% of shareholders voted against Sir Stuart Rose's dual role while 62.3% voted in favour. Sir Stuart had previously noted that it had even resulted in him being described as the 'Robert Mugabe of retail'. This remains an exceptional step to take, and in M&S's case signified the depth of its worries about its future trading performance in an increasingly tough economic climate.

Non-executive directors

Guidance on the role of the non-executive director (commonly referred to as a NED), and a sample letter of appointment, is set out in 'Good Practice Suggestions from the Higgs Report' (see **8.3.4.2**). These guidelines provide the following useful description of the role of the NED:

> In addition to these requirements for all directors, the role of the non-executive director has the following key elements:
>
> *Strategy.* Non-executive directors should constructively challenge and help develop proposals on strategy.
>
> *Performance.* Non-executive directors should scrutinise the performance of management in meeting agreed goals and objectives and monitor the reporting of performance.
>
> *Risk.* Non-executive directors should satisfy themselves on the integrity of financial information and that financial controls and systems of risk management are robust and defensible.
>
> *People.* Non-executive directors are responsible for determining appropriate levels of remuneration of executive directors, and have a prime role in appointing, and where necessary removing, executive directors and in succession planning.

Some of the main provisions in the Code itself relating to NEDs are as follows:

(a)   Schedule B to the Combined Code provides guidance on the liability of NEDs.

(b)   The NEDs must appraise the performance of the Chairman annually, and scrutinise the performance of the executive directors (A.1, A.1.3).

(c)   To be effective, NEDs ideally should be 'independent'. The board should identify, in the annual report, each NED it considers to be independent. Guidance as to the meaning of 'independent' is provided in para A.3.1.

(d)   The term of appointment of any NED requires careful consideration (A.7.2).

(e)   The role of the NED is set out at supporting principle A.1.

(f)   The Chairman should hold some meetings with the NEDs alone, where the executive directors are not present (A.1.3).

(g)   The board should appoint one of the NEDs to be the senior independent director (A.3.3).

The ICSA has produced a guidance note on the role of the senior independent director.

The role of the NED is not a particularly easy one in today's climate. Companies need to take care to select a suitable NED who will take the role seriously and be able to meet the dramatically increased expectations of their performance in light of the perceived failings of NEDs in preventing the poor decision-making which ultimately led to the global financial crisis. Furthermore, it is likely that, in the near future, the requirements for NEDs, particularly of financial services companies, will be tightened and the duties and legal responsibilities on them increased (depending on the outcome of various reviews – see **8.6**). The website of the Institute of Chartered Accountants maintains a register of independent directors.

It is worth remembering that in company law a NED is treated no differently than an executive director and shares the same potential liability.

8.3.6.2   Remuneration

(a)   While directors need to be paid an amount which will motivate them to perform, their pay should also be related to their performance. The company should avoid paying more than is necessary to attract, retain and motivate directors (B.1).

(b)   Notice periods under service contracts should not exceed one year. The remuneration committee should avoid rewarding poor performance in the event of an early termination of a director's service contract (B.1.5, B.1.6).

(c)   Policy on directors' remuneration should be formal and transparent. A remuneration committee, of at least three (two in the case of a company below the FTSE 350) independent non-executive directors, should determine the remuneration of directors (B.2, B.2.1).

Remuneration, and indeed the remuneration committee, has been creating headlines well beyond the financial pages of the press for some years now. 'Good Practice Suggestions from the Higgs Report' (see **8.3.4.2**) sets out guidance on the role of the remuneration committee. The ICSA has produced specimen terms of reference for the remuneration committee.

The result of the remuneration committees' actions has been a phenomenal rise in the pay of listed company directors (particularly for the largest companies and particularly for men, with the highest paid female director of a FTSE100 company taking home just a tenth of the pay of the highest paid man in 2008). The average remuneration package (including benefits) for a FTSE 100 Chief Executive was £3.1 million in 2008. The average remuneration for FTSE 100 Chief Executives is over 128 times greater than that of the average full-time worker in the UK. Ten years ago it was just 47 times greater. Mining group, Xstrata plc, had the most expensive board of directors of a UK listed company, costing it just over £30 million in 2008.

Pay gap widens between executives and their staff

Ashley Seager and Julia Finch

The pay gap between top bosses and their staff continues to widen as executive remuneration races ahead of staff wage settlements – providing further evidence that the recession is hitting the shopfloor far harder than the boardroom.

The highest-paid boss last year was Bart Becht, chief executive of Reckitt Benckiser, which makes everything from Nurofen to Cillit Bang. The Dutchman, who was the most highly rewarded boss in the FTSE 100, received the same pay as 1,374 average workers at the Slough-based multinational. The huge boss-worker ratio is not a result of Reckitt workers being particularly poorly paid – their average salary is £26,700, in line with the national average – but is a reflection of the huge rewards handed out in pay, perks and share-based incentives to the chief executive. Becht received about £37m last year.

Tesco's boss, Sir Terry Leahy, was paid more than 900 times as much as Tesco's average worker, while Nick Buckles of the security business G4S – the biggest employer quoted on the London Stock Exchange with 585,000 workers in operations ranging from cash collection to landmine clearance – was paid 328 times the company's average staff salary.

Details of the widening gap between boss and workers' pay, revealed in the Guardian executive pay survey, comes as pressure is mounting for the government to tackle the boardroom bonus culture.

According to the left-wing think tank Compass, which has called for a high pay commission to monitor top pay in the same way as the Low Pay Commission advises the government on the national minimum wage, the average ratio of chief executive-to-employee pay has risen from 47 to 128 over the past 10 years.

In a report published today, Compass says a high pay commission would investigate how huge executive rewards affect economic stability and long-term corporate performance, and would consider "the social effects of gross inequality".

The think tank suggests there is substantial public support for change, with 78% of respondents to a YouGov/Compass poll saying that the growing gap between rich and poor was "bad for our society" and 73% saying they would support a government move to impose a new tax on all bonuses of more than £10,000.

Among the think tank's suggestions are wage and bonus caps, an end to guaranteed bonuses – and limits on wage ratios.

The banker John Pierpont Morgan, founder of JP Morgan, once said that no one at the top of a company should earn more than 20 times those at the bottom. Among FTSE-100 companies last year, only two chief executives met Morgan's test. Michael Lynch of the software firm Autonomy had a salary only 9.5 times as large as the firm's average of £64,500, while Andrew Sukawaty at the satellite communications group Inmarsat earned 16 times the firm's average – although that average is a hefty £119,000 a year.

Sir Bill Gammell, head of the oil group Cairn Energy, only just broke the Morgan rule, with a 20.1 ratio. Others nearer their firms' average, on a modest 24 times, are Francis Salway at Land Securities and Michael Grade at ITV. At the other end of the scale, the pay deals of eight bosses suggest their contribution is worth more than that of 200 of their workers.

Many companies with the highest boss-to-worker pay ratios have much of their workforces overseas, where average pay is far lower than in Britain. At Eurasian Natural Resources, which mines iron ore in Kazakhstan but is based in London, the average wage is £4,300. Chief executive Johannes Sittard's salary is 643 times higher. At Kazakhmys, another Kazakhstan mining group, the chairman, Vladimir Kim, is paid 183 times his average worker's £7,773 salary. While Kim has a multimillion-pound fortune from his shareholding in the company, his miners endure some of the most dangerous working conditions in the industry. Last year's annual report shows the number of deaths had risen from 23 in 2007 to 32 last year.

Since the company floated on the London Stock Exchange four years ago, Kazakhmys has admitted its fatality rate "is higher than the usual level in similar operations elsewhere in the world".

The miners' pay and conditions contrast starkly with privileged white-collar workers in City-based and property companies, even in a year of near-meltdown in the financial sector. The average pay at money broker Icap last year topped £200,000 for the first time, while the Man hedge fund paid an average of £198,760. The Guardian survey five years ago showed Man's average was £100,000. Other top payers include fund manager Schroders, private equity firm 3i, the London Stock Exchange and the property firm Hammerson.

Eva Neitzert, of the New Economics Foundation, said the figures were out of all proportion to the value of the jobs. "Remuneration should be about what we value as a society. With the average salary of a FTSE 100 chief executive now being 100 times that of a school teacher, we've lost all sense of proportion."

Source: *The Guardian*, 16 September 2009

For further information on directors' remuneration, see **8.4**.

8.3.6.3 Accountability and audit

As explained at **8.3.4.3** above, it is useful to consult the FRC's Guidance on Audit Committees when considering what the Code has to say on this issue. Some of the key provisions in the Combined Code relating to accountability and audit are as follows:

(a) The board should present a balanced and understandable view of the company's position and prospects (C.1).

(b) The board should ensure there are internal controls in place to safeguard shareholders' investments and the company's assets (C.2).

(c) There should be an audit committee with at least three members (unless the company is below the FTSE 350, in which case there should be at least two members) who are independent non-executive directors. At least one member should have recent and relevant financial experience (C.3, C.3.1, A.3.1).

(d)   The main role and responsibilities of the audit committee should be set out in written terms of reference, which are available both on the company website and on request, and a section in the company's annual report should describe the committee's work in discharging those responsibilities (C.3.2, C.3.3). The lawyer may be required to draft the terms of reference for the audit committee. The ICSA has published standard form terms of reference for audit committees.

(e)   The role of the audit committee is set out at C.3.2.

The implementation of the EC's Statutory Audit Directive in the UK through the Corporate Governance Rules introduced a statutory requirement for an Audit Committee for listed companies including at least one independent member and one member with suitable accounting experience. A statement must be made publicly disclosing which body carries out these functions and how it is comprised. This may be included with the corporate governance statement (see **8.3.5.4**). There is of course an overlap with the provisions of the Combined Code, and the FSA states in DTR 7.1.7G that compliance with the Combined Code's provisions for audit committees will result in compliance with those in the Corporate Governance Rules. It is worth noting that the UK's Combined Code places additional requirements on listed companies beyond those in the EU-inspired Corporate Governance Rules.

8.3.6.4   Relations with shareholders

(a)   The Chairman should ensure that the views of shareholders are communicated to the board (D.1.1).

(b)   The board should use the AGM to communicate with shareholders and to encourage their participation (D.2).

Ashley labels unhappy investors 'cry babies'

Marianne Barriaux

Mike Ashley, the Sports World billionaire, has accused unsupportive investors of being 'cry babies'.

The sports retailer, which owns Lillywhites and Dunlop, has faced accusations of a lack of transparency. Since the group's flotation five months ago, its share price has almost halved.

But Mr Ashley told the Sunday Times: 'I've got balls of steel. Some investors have been great and have been very supportive. But some of these City people act like a bunch of cry babies.'

He said some investors were too focused on the near-term share price, and not on the future prospects of the company.

Source: *The Guardian*, 30 July 2007

8.4   Directors' remuneration

8.4.1   Background

There are rules governing the remuneration of listed company directors in both the Listing Rules (see **8.3.5.5**) and the Combined Code (see **8.3.6.2**). Listed company directors must also comply with the rules set out in Chapters 6 and 9 of Pt 15 of the CA 2006.

In addition, the Large and Medium-sized Companies and Groups (Accounts and Reports) Regulations 2008 (SI 2008/410) supplement the regime regulating the remuneration of directors of listed companies. Finally, the IPCs have produced non-binding guidance for their members on directors' remuneration to assist them in deciding whether to vote in favour or against shareholder resolutions on the matter.

On 14 December 2004 the European Commission published a non-binding Recommendation on fostering an appropriate regime for the remuneration of directors of listed companies.

Member States were invited to implement necessary measures to comply with the Recommendation by 30 June 2006. The UK's regime is very similar to the Recommendation.

8.4.2   Nature of the CA 2006 rules and the 2008 Regulations

The CA 2006 rules and the 2008 Regulations came into force on 6 April 2008 to apply in respect of financial years beginning on or after 6 April 2008.

The CA 2006 rules and the 2008 Regulations (that part which applies to remuneration) apply to 'quoted companies', which are defined by s 385(2) of the CA 2006 as including not only companies admitted to the Official List and the Main Market (referred to as 'listed companies' in this book, see **1.3** above), but also companies listed on certain other markets in Europe and the USA. The scope of the CA 2006 rules and the 2008 Regulations is therefore wider than the scope of the Listing Rules and the Combined Code (see **8.3.5** above). The CA 2006 rules and the 2008 Regulations do not, however, apply to companies quoted on AIM.

8.4.3   Key features

The CA 2006 rules have three key requirements, set out below. Any director of a company which fails to comply with these requirements will be guilty of an offence under the CA 2006 and liable to a fine. A director can also be personally liable to the company for any loss it suffers under s 437 of the CA 2006 for any false or misleading statements in the report, or an omission from it, if he knew or was reckless as to whether the statement was false or misleading or knew the omission to be a dishonest concealment of a material fact.

8.4.3.1   Remuneration report

Under s 420 of the CA 2006, the company must produce an annual directors' remuneration report which contains the information required by Sch 8 to the 2008 Regulations, made under s 421 of the CA 2006, in the form prescribed by the Regulations. The information which the report must disclose (including the company policy on directors' remuneration, details of the directors' service contracts and a company performance graph) is considerable, and goes beyond the disclosure requirements of both the Listing Rules and the Combined Code. In a new requirement under the 2008 Regulations, the report must contain a statement of how pay and employment conditions of employees of the company and of other undertakings within the same group as the company were taken into account when determining directors' remuneration for the relevant financial year. The report forms part of the annual report and accounts and must be filed at Companies House (CA 2006, s 439).

8.4.3.2   Audit of report

Under s 497 of the CA 2006, the company's auditors must, in addition to auditing the company's accounts and financial information, audit the remuneration report and state in its report to shareholders whether the information set out in Part 3 to Sch 8 of the 2008 Regulations relating to the directors' compensation, share options, pension benefits, incentive schemes and other matters in the report has been properly prepared in accordance with the CA 2006.

This is of course part of the control mechanism on listed companies to ensure that they reveal all the necessary information correctly.

8.4.3.3   Shareholder approval

Every listed company must send a copy of its annual accounts and reports (including, under CA 2006, s 471(3), the remuneration report) to every shareholder (CA 2006, s 423). The company must then table the remuneration report at a general meeting (CA 2006, s 437) and obtain approval of the report (by ordinary resolution) of the shareholders (CA 2006, s 439). Note that this requirement does not mean that any specific director's service contract is conditional upon shareholder approval (CA 2006, s 439). If shareholders do not approve the remuneration report the effect is advisory only (in other words, this and the accompanying adverse publicity sends a public message to the board that will be hard to ignore). In light of a public outcry at the bloated bonuses and remuneration packages of some directors of listed companies even when the companies' share price had dropped sharply, institutional investors have become increasingly active in this area. Nonetheless, it is still extremely rare for the remuneration report not to be accepted. Between 2002 and 2008 there was just one example of shareholders rejecting a remuneration report. In 2009, up to the time of writing, there have been three, two of which are mentioned in the article below.

Angry shareholders ambush the top pay bandwagon

Richard Wachman

In the City, a whiff of grapeshot hangs in the air after the unleashing of one of the biggest waves of shareholder anger in recent times. The target companies include big names such as Shell, BP, RBS, Xstrata, Next, Amec and Provident Financial.

All must bear the shame of knowing that their remuneration reports have been opposed by a majority or a sizeable minority of shareholders. Once again, bosses are accused of having their snouts in the trough during a period when capitalism was coming off the rails.

The onslaught comes after politicians, regulators and public opinion identified bonuses and sky-high pay packets as one of the prime causes of the slump. By linking pay with share price performance, managers were encouraged to make foolish short-term decisions that ultimately brought the edifice of capitalism crashing down. Now there is a backlash as shareholders target excessive pay and bonuses sometimes awarded even if a company does badly or misses its performance targets.

Few would disagree that executive pay has been spiralling out of control. According to remuneration specialists, the average FTSE 100 chief executive has seen his rewards jump 125% in the past 10 years, while the heads of smaller quoted firms have seen their pay increase by 80% in the same time span.

So what? That was the stock response in the City when everyone was coining it, but in a recession, things are different. Investors are out of pocket, and besides it's best to be seen to be doing something when politicians are muttering about draconian legislation to cap pay awards once and for all.

Not that fund managers - who act on behalf of pension funds, retail investors and insurance companies - come up smelling of roses. They stand accused of complacency, even collusion, when the good times were rolling. Colin Melvin, at pension fund manager Hermes, speaks for the critics when he says: "My feeling is that the horse has bolted; action should have been taken years ago. Investors have shown that they haven't been good long-term owners of companies."

Many fund managers would strongly disagree, arguing that they had pulled out of the banks, for instance, well before the onset of the credit crunch in the summer of 2007. Legal & General, among others, challenged executives on pay, strategy and high debt levels, but to no avail.

But Melvin is surely right to wonder how long the backlash will last. After all, we have been here before: remember Cedric the Pig in 1995 when the GMB union held aloft pictures of a pig outside British Gas's annual meeting to protest at the pay of chief executive Cedric Brown (although, at £475,000, Brown's pay was modest by today's standards).

Then there was the upswing in shareholder activism after the technology crash at the turn of the millennium when new rules were introduced to strengthen corporate governance. The protests culminated at GlaxoSmithKline, where shareholders threw out the remuneration report amid outrage that former boss Jean-Pierre Garnier was entitled to a £22m golden parachute if he left.

But when recovery took hold, and stock prices headed north, opposition to fat cat pay subsided. Peter Montagnon, head of investment affairs at the Association of British Insurers, recognises the syndrome all too well. "The investment community gets tougher during a downturn and more forgiving when things go well." But he warns that "what has been acceptable up to now may not be acceptable in the future".

The severity of the banking crisis has shaken public confidence, and this cannot be underestimated, he says. "Unless companies behave responsibly, there is a danger people will question the principles that underpin the whole system."

What he fears most, though, is too much regulation, too much socialism: he concedes that the jury is out on capitalism, but says people should not lose sight of the fact that "businesses create wealth for savers". He acknowledges, however, that "the public's faith in capital markets has been shaken and it needs rebuilding". One way to do it is to ensure that executive pay is "based on demonstrable integrity and that it rewards performance, not underperformance and mediocrity".

The latest bout of shareholder activism comes as the European commission is threatening to clamp down on executive pay across the spectrum. In Britain, City minister Lord Myners says things must change and has accused investors of behaving like absentee landlords.

At an Investment Management Association dinner last week, Myners warmed to his theme that short-termist institutional investors - the fund management industry acting on behalf of its pension fund clients - were asleep at the wheel. He said: "We have almost certainly understated the profound challenges faced by the majority of institutional fund managers … they are not set up to act as owners. They are investor-leaseholders rather than freeholders."

Myners has ordered the Financial Reporting Council, as well as a task force led by Sir David Walker, to come up with reforms that could be enshrined in new laws or become part of beefed-up codes of best practice.

Myners even took a swipe at the pension fund industry itself, saying that "short-termism, as practised by pension funds, is self-defeating for those charged with delivering pensions over many decades in the future, yet it remains a dominant form of behaviour".

He added that a focus on shareholder value, as measured by relative share price performance over quite short time periods, "lies at the heart of a number of behaviours which have delivered less than ideal outcomes".

Among these, he lists "a failure to take account of the longer-term consequences of investment activity, including its impact on the broader economy and society".

At Hermes, Melvin argues that pension fund trustees need to take a more proactive role in holding managements to account and institutional investors in general should work together to campaign for better corporate governance.

Despite fears that the City will go back to its bad old ways when the recession lifts, Melvin says there are grounds for optimism because pension funds are beginning to act in unison after losing colossal sums in the crash.

"By acting as a united voice, pension funds [and other long-term investors] are helping to steer companies away from dangerous waters towards the safer shores offered by more accountable, transparent and responsible business practices," he says.

But Pirc, the shareholder activism group, reckons that it will take new City regulations to bring recalcitrant companies to heel. Its managing director, Alan MacDougall, says that if Shell, for instance, fails to put its house in order, ministers will need to "rewrite the corporate governance rulebook" and make majority shareholder votes at annual meetings binding on management.

In one of the biggest investor rebellions over directors' pay, 59% of Shell's shareholders voted down its remuneration report last week. They objected to the discretionary award to executive directors of bonuses for 2006-08 performance, made even though the company failed to meet its targets. The size of the Shell "no" vote has been topped only at RBS, where 80% opposed the company that had angered Britain when it allowed Fred Goodwin to leave with a pension worth £703,000 a year.

Worryingly, Shell has given no indication that the bonuses will have to be repaid. Neither has it reprimanded Sir Peter Job, head of the remuneration committee that decided to pay the bonuses in the first place.

MacDougall says that the Shell vote, as well as clashes at other companies, make this a unique moment for capital-market reforms: "The danger is that when stock prices head up, a lot of this will be forgotten. While we applaud what Lord Myners has said, we want real change. The time to strike is now."

Pirc is proposing that voluntary codes of governance be scrapped in favour of regulation that would be enforced by the Financial Services Authority. It is calling for the compulsory annual re-election of all board directors, and wants shareholders to be allowed to vote on audit reports. Auditors would be forced to resign if their reports were rejected.

MacDougall says: "There are serious structural flaws in the model of capitalism we have grown used to in the UK and these require urgent attention. The steady inflation-busting growth in executive pay while equity markets have see-sawed destroys the myth that we either have remuneration under control or have linked it to performance."

Pirc is by no means alone in its criticism of standards of corporate governance. This month, the Treasury select committee warned that the review on the future of regulation by FSA chairman Lord Turner was too complacent about the role of City pay in the current crisis.

And, for the first time, the committee tackled head-on the murky role of remuneration consultants whose advice on pay levels and bonus packages is regarded as being too readily accepted by the big-company non-execs who staff remuneration committees.

Perhaps it is time for the consultants to emerge from the shadows; there are only a handful that service the major UK companies. Step forward Towers Perrin, Kepler Associates, New Bridge Street, Deloitte, Watson Wyatt, Hewitt, and Mercer. As in other sectors of the City, there is a circle of star performers: among them Carol Arrowsmith of Deloitte, John Carney of Towers Perrin and Vicky Wright of Watson Wyatt.

One leading fund manager says:

"These are well-known names who know a lot about remuneration schemes, but there are concerns. Generally, I would say they are a thoroughly bad influence. They are seen by fund managers as having extreme conflicts of interest: they are effectively paid by the board and are only seen to be doing their jobs if remuneration rises. In theory, remuneration consultants bring a certain level of objectivity to the task, but their existence allows companies to say they have done due diligence on pay, therefore it's not their fault when benefits and performance do not match."

But for evidence that things are looking up, look no further than America, where laissez-faire economics has been taken for granted until quite recently.

In a landmark move, the US Securities and Exchange Commission agreed last week to allow shareholders to nominate company directors. The SEC said it had proposed the rule because the economic crisis called into question whether boards were exercising enough oversight. Analysts were unanimous in saying that publicity about generous pay and the need for taxpayer-funded bailouts have changed the mood. The rule will allow large shareholders such as pension funds to nominate up to a quarter of a company's board members.

Andy Hammerson at Co-operative Asset Management says the crisis has shown that taxpayers ultimately pick up the bill for risky decisions taken by insufficiently accountable companies. He adds: "But then taxpayers get hit by another double whammy: their pensions are cut as the markets fall, and their security is threatened by the prospect of large-scale job losses."

Inflated executive pay does more than rub salt into the wounds, he adds. Rather, it is "symptomatic of a system that has been brought into disrepute and is now crying out for long-overdue reform".

But will any new regulation go far enough? "That's the $64,000 question," says Hammerson.

A fund manager's view: time to stop feeding the habit

In the 14 years since Cedric the Pig became a symbol of boardroom greed at the British Gas annual meeting, a series of reports - Cadbury, Greenbury, Hampel, culminating in the Combined Code - have sought to overhaul Britain's corporate governance system. There have been worthwhile reforms but, as the furore around Shell's remuneration package last week shows, there is still a big problem.

The total earnings of FTSE 100 chief executives grew by more than 11% a year in real terms between 1999 and 2006, compared with 1.4% for the median of all full-time employees. Executives and their remuneration consultants (Ratchet, Ratchet and Bingo, as Warren Buffett called them) have defended this with various arguments: one advanced now that we need to pay up in order to retain the people who can get companies out of the mire.

Shareholders have been prepared to accept arguments for pay growth while there has been evidence of strong profits growth. But the credit crunch has brought pay back on to investors' radar. Problems surrounding appropriate pay have gained most attention in the banking sector, but are far more endemic than that. Shell and BP are two obvious cases - 59% and 40% respectively of their shareholders voted against their recent remuneration reports - but there are many others.

Take housebuilder Bellway. Was it really sensible for the remuneration committee to award bonuses equivalent to 55% of base salaries to three executives at a time when sales had halved and the company was warning of big job cuts?

Having approved many pay packages in the past and thereby fed the bonus habit and culture, shareholders clearly have to take some responsibility. But we are starting to face up to our previous inattention or failure to monitor the actions of remuneration committees.

The key issue has been the break between pay and performance. How, for example, was BT's former chief executive Ben Verwaayen able to take home sizeable bonuses, partly on the back of growth in the company's global services division, yet face no clawback when BT was forced to write down the value of this operation just a few years later? BT is now seeking to include a clause in the contracts of executives to allow it to reclaim cash bonuses.

Companies need to find a way to restore this connection. We want to feel that executives have "some skin in the game", so a robust approach to setting targets, which should apply over the long term, is imperative. Perhaps, for example, any bonus over 100% of base salary should be deferred for three years.

We are looking closely at bonus payments for 2008 and the vesting of awards under incentive schemes. We are placing greater emphasis on base salaries and whether any increases have been awarded in 2009, as variable pay is usually calculated as a multiple of base salary.

There are other steps companies and investors can take to improve governance, although this may take time. One is to stop the vicious circle of short-termism in the City: fund managers are under constant pressure to produce results in the short term, which, in turn, can lead us to put pressure on companies to deliver and therefore encourages short-term thinking with regard to remuneration.

Institutional shareholders do not want to micro-manage executive pay, but company directors and remuneration committees need to wake up and start showing some sensitivity and restraint in the current environment or they risk facing the kind of ignominy and public showdown suffered by Shell.
• Anthony Nutt is head of income and UK equities teams, Jupiter Asset Management

Source: *The Observer*, 24 May 2009

Increasingly, a rejection is seen as a vote of no confidence in the remuneration committee. The chairman of Shell's remuneration committee has resigned although remains on the committee.

At its 2008 AGM, Aegis was still struggling to convince a significant minority of shareholders on the subject of the directors' pay, with over 37% of votes against. The necessary ordinary resolution was, however, still passed.

8.5   Institutional investors

As explained at **8.3.5.1** above, it is really the institutional investors (see **2.6.2**) who enforce the Combined Code by making life difficult for those companies who do not comply. Certain IPCs, such as the ISC, NAPF and PIRC, publish their corporate governance expectations and circulate them to shareholders and listed companies. Recent examples include:

(a)   'The Responsibilities of Institutional Shareholders and Agents – Statement of Principles', published by the Institutional Shareholders' Committee in June 2007 and available from the Institutional Voting Information Service (IVIS) website.

The IVIS website also offers a subscription service, where reports including recommendations for voting at AGMs are provided. A decision is reached dependent on the listed company's compliance with the ABI Guidelines and the Combined Code.

(b)   'Corporate Governance Policy and Voting Guidelines', published in November 2007 by NAPF, the UK representative body for pension providers, on its website, and the 2008/09 updates.

(c)   'Shareholder Voting Guidelines', 13th edn, published in March 2009 by PIRC.

The global financial crisis has led to an increased awareness of the importance of good corporate governance. One side effect has been an increase in shareholder activism particularly by institutional investors and greater turnout and voting at listed companies' AGMs. In the year to 31 July 2009, votes were cast by 67.3% of shareholders at FTSE100 company AGMs. This compares to 63% in 2008 and 53.2% in 2003.

Board shake-up after criticisms over corporate governance

Peter Thal Larsen and Kate Burgess

HSBC shareholders have been grumbling about shortcomings in the bank's corporate governance for years. Now it appears that the lender is responding to some of their criticisms.

The bank yesterday unveiled a boardroom shake-up that will see three long-serving non-executive directors step down at the annual meeting in May.

At the same time, HSBC also revealed that it was introducing a new long-term incentive plan for senior executives.

The three directors who are stepping down - Baroness Dunn, Sir Brian Moffat and Lord Butler - have been criticised because their long tenure on HSBC's board means that they are no longer considered independent.

They are being replaced by two non-executive directors: Safra Catz, the president and chief financial officer of Oracle, the US software group; and Narayana Murthy, one of the founders of Infosys, the Indian IT services group.

HSBC is also elevating three of its most senior executives to the board: Vincent Cheng, chairman of its Asian operations; Sandy Flockhart, its chief executive in Asia; and Stuart Gulliver, head of HSBC's investment banking division.

Separately, Stephen Green, HSBC's chairman, yesterday revealed the bank was consulting shareholders about a new long-term incentive plan for executives. This would measure performance based on return on equity, cost efficiency, capital ratios, and total shareholder return relative to a group of rival banks. Shortcomings in the current plan have been highlighted by Knight Vinke, the activist investor that is agitating for change at HSBC.

Knight Vinke has argued that the lender should include banks in emerging markets, rather than just large US and European banks, when measuring its performance.

Mr Green said it was "likely" that HSBC would update its list of rival banks to reflect a shift in its strategy.

Source: *The Financial Times*, 4 March 2008

8.6   Shareholder Rights Directive

As we have seen, better corporate governance can be achieved by greater shareholder involvement in the running of listed companies. To further this aim the EU Shareholder Rights Directive (2007/36/EC) was adopted in June 2007. It was implemented in the UK on 3 August 2009 by the Companies (Shareholders' Rights) Regulations 2009 (SI 2009/1632) and seeks to improve the way that companies trade on regulated markets in the EU by improving shareholder information and rights to participate in general meetings. The Directive applies to companies on the Main Market but not to those on AIM.

The Regulations amend Part 13 of the CA 2006 and apply to general meetings where the notice is given on or after 3 August 2009. The most important rights are set out below.

8.6.1   Notice period for general meetings

The CA 2006 allowed general meetings of listed companies (not being the AGM) to be held on not less than 14 clear days' notice. Under a new s 307A the notice period must be 21 clear days unless:

(a)   the company offers all shareholders the right to vote electronically (which can be met by the company enabling all shareholders to appoint a proxy via a website); and

(b)   shareholders pass a special resolution each year at the AGM resolving that only 14 clear days notice is required for such meetings, in which case the notice period can be 14 clear days.

8.6.2 Contents of notice

The following additional information must now be included in the notice calling a meeting of a listed company (s 337(3) for (f)(ii) and (iii) below and s 311(2) for the remainder):

(a)   details of the website containing the information relating to the general meeting (see **8.6.3** below);

(b)   a statement that the right to vote is by reference to the Register of Members and the time when the right to vote will be determined;

(c)   details of how to attend and vote including deadlines;

(d)   details of forms for appointing proxies;

(e)   where the company allows voting in advance or electronic voting then the procedure for doing so; and

(f)   if the AGM notice is sent out more than six weeks before the meeting it must contain a statement about the shareholders' rights to:

   (i)   ask questions at the meeting (see **8.6.4** below);

   (ii)   give notice of a resolution at the meeting; and

   (iii)   include a matter in the business of the meeting (see **8.6.5** below).

8.6.3 Publication of information on a website

Section 311A requires a listed company to publish certain specified information in advance of the meeting on a website on or before the date on which notice of a meeting is given including the matters set out in the notice itself and details of the company's share capital. The information must be kept on the website for at least two years.

After the meeting s 341(1A) requires additional information about poll votes to be posted on the website, such as the number of votes for and against and abstentions.

8.6.4 Right to ask questions

There is a new right, under s 319A, for shareholders to ask questions at a meeting which the company must cause to be answered unless an exception applies. The exceptions include if it would involve revealing confidential information and if it is undesirable in the interests of the company or good order of the meeting.

8.6.5 Right to requisition a resolution

In addition to the existing right of shareholders (holding either at least 5% of the voting rights of the company or being at least 100 in number owning shares with an average paid up capital of at least £100 per shareholder) to requisition a resolution at an AGM, they have a new right in s 338A to require the company to include 'a matter' (not being a resolution) in the business of the AGM.

8.6.6 Appointment of proxies

The company must provide an electronic address for the return of proxies (s 333A). Section 327(A1) and s 330(A1) require the appointment and termination respectively of a proxy by a shareholder in a listed company to be in writing. This can be done by electronic means.

8.7 Future developments

Unsurprisingly there has been much soul-searching by governments and regulators as to why existing corporate governance rules were so ineffective in preventing the global financial crisis. Given the role of listed companies in contributing to the crisis, especially those in the financial services industry, and the size of these companies and their importance to the economy, a plethora of reviews has been and continues to be undertaken in the UK, by the EU and elsewhere, all with one aim in mind – never again. A summary of some of the more relevant reviews affecting UK listed companies follows. One consequence of these reviews is that a raft of amendments to existing rules and legislation and the creation of new rules are expected in the coming year and beyond. As lawyers, you will of course be called upon to advise listed companies of the changes. It is therefore imperative that you keep a beady eye on developments in this area.

8.7.1 Combined Code

8.7.1.1 FRC review

At the time of writing the FRC is conducting a fundamental review of the Combined Code. The FRC is inviting comments on all aspects of the Combined Code but in particular on the effectiveness of the board; the composition of the board including finding the right balance between expertise and independence; the responsibilities of the chairman and non-executive directors; remuneration policy; engagement between shareholders and the board; the frequency of directors' election; board information, development and support; the effectiveness of risk management systems and the usefulness of the board's reporting on corporate governance. The ICSA and the GC100 are among those organisations which have already responded.

The FRC will also take account of the Walker review (see below), the European Commission's recommendations on the remuneration of executive directors of listed companies (see below) and the relevant recommendations of the House of Commons Treasury Committee's third report on the banking crisis, before considering whether to make any changes to the Combined Code. It is currently expected to report by the end of 2009, with any changes taking effect in mid-2010.

8.7.1.2 Walker review

As part of the UK Government's response to the global financial crisis, the Prime Minister appointed Sir David Walker in February 2009 to conduct a review of the corporate governance of UK banks (later extended to other financial companies) and to make recommendations (the 'Walker review'). In his report of July 2009 published by HM Treasury, Sir David made 39 recommendations covering board size, composition and qualification; functioning of the board and evaluation of performance; the role of institutional shareholders; remuneration and risk governance. A period of consultation is under way at the time of writing with final conclusions expected in November 2009. From the review it seems most likely that the proposals for change will be incorporated in the Combined Code or require action to be taken by the FSA.

8.7.1.3 FSA review

The FSA is conducting a separate review into the operation of the listing regime (see **3.7.2**). As part of this review the FSA is considering whether to extend the applicability of the Combined Code to overseas listed companies in the same way that it currently applies to UK companies.

8.7.2 Directors' remuneration

8.7.2.1 FSA's remuneration code

A new code of practice will come into force on 1 January 2010 which will apply to certain financial services companies including banks. It will require the companies to have in place remuneration policies that are consistent with effective risk management. The code of practice is designed to ensure that these companies' boards of directors focus more closely both on ensuring that the total amount distributed by a firm is consistent with good risk management and sustainability and that individual compensation practices provide the right incentives. The code is being introduced in an attempt to try and limit the remuneration policies which encourage excessive risk-taking and which are believed to have played a significant role in provoking the global financial crisis. It will probably result in some employment contracts having to be amended.

8.7.2.2 European Commission Recommendation

On 5 May 2009 the European Commission published a further non-binding Recommendation on the remuneration of directors of listed companies, focusing on the structure and determination of directors' remuneration. For example the Recommendation calls on Member States, among other things, to set a limit on directors' termination payments (usually no more than the equivalent of two years of the fixed component of a director's pay) and to provide that termination payments should not be paid if termination is due to inadequate performance.

Member States are asked to implement the necessary measures by 31 December 2009. The Commission will consider whether further measures are required after this date.

Chapter 9

The Financial Services and Markets Act 2000

9.1 Background

The Financial Services and Markets Act 2000 (FSMA 2000) received Royal Assent on 14 June 2000. The majority of the Act, and some of the secondary legislation and rules made pursuant to it, came into force on 1 December 2001. This date is often referred to as 'N2'.

At N2 the FSA became the single regulator for the financial services industry. The FSMA 2000 replaced the Financial Services Act 1986.

9.2 Objectives

Some of the provisions of the FSMA 2000 are complex. They are easier to understand if you consider them in the context of the objectives of the Act. The principal objectives of the FSMA 2000 are set out in s 2. They are:

(a) *market confidence* – maintaining confidence in the financial system;

(b) *public awareness* – raising public understanding of the financial system;

(c) *the protection of consumers* – securing the appropriate degree of protection for consumers; and

(d) *the reduction of financial crime* – reducing the extent to which it is possible for a business to be used for a purpose connected with financial crime.

9.3 Relevance to practice

No corporate finance lawyer can avoid the FSMA 2000. Together with the CA 2006, the 2000 Act will be the most thumbed statute on the lawyer's desk. It affects all professional firms which carry on regulated activities, and also affects how companies, particularly listed companies, conduct their day-to-day corporate and trading activities. The lawyer will have most involvement with the following provisions of the FSMA 2000:

(a) the general prohibition on carrying on a regulated activity in the United Kingdom (s 19);

(b) the financial promotion regulatory framework (s 21);

(c) the rules relating to the official listing of securities (Pt VI and in particular ss 85, 87, 90A and 91);

(d) the market abuse regime (s 118); and

(e) the provisions relating to misleading statements and market manipulation (s 397).

The remainder of this chapter considers (a) and (e) above. **Chapter 12** considers financial promotion; **Chapter 6** explores the rules of the FSMA 2000 relating to the listing of securities; and **Chapter 10** considers market abuse.

9.4   The general prohibition on carrying on a regulated activity

Lawyers must be aware of the general prohibition in s 19 of the FSMA 2000 not only so that they can advise their clients accordingly, but also so that they can ensure that neither they nor their law firm breaches that section.

9.4.1   The general prohibition

Section 19 of the FSMA 2000 prohibits any person from carrying on a regulated activity in the United Kingdom unless he is:

(a)   an authorised person; or

(b)   an exempt person.

This is known as the 'general prohibition'. Contravention of the general prohibition is a criminal offence (s 23). Any agreement which results from a breach of s 19 will be unenforceable (s 26).

9.4.2   Regulated activities

The general prohibition relates to the carrying on of a 'regulated activity'. What is a regulated activity? The actual definition is provided by s 22 of the FSMA 2000. It is:

> an activity of a specified kind which is carried on by way of business and:
>
> (a)   relates to an investment of a specified kind; or
>
> (b)   in the case of an activity of a kind which is also specified for the purposes of this paragraph, is carried on in relation to property of any kind.

This is not particularly helpful. Schedule 2 to the Act, together with a number of statutory instruments, including the Financial Services and Markets Act 2000 (Regulated Activities) Order 2001 (SI 2001/544) ('Regulated Activities Order 2001') (as amended over 15 times!), seeks to clarify the definition. Schedule 2 to the FSMA 2000 provides examples of regulated activities, and the Regulated Activities Order 2001 details the meaning of specified activities (Pt II) and specified investments (Pt III). In practice, recourse should be made to these sources. However, for our purposes it is more useful to consider a few of the more common examples of 'regulated activities' which a corporate finance lawyer might encounter, namely those relating to investments (such as shares). The regulated activities include:

(a)   dealing in investments (Regulated Activities Order 2001, Chapters IV and V) – this includes dealing as principal or agent;

(b)   arranging deals in investments (Regulated Activities Order 2001, Chapter VI) – this includes making arrangements with a view to another person buying or selling shares;

(c)   managing investments (Regulated Activities Order 2001, Chapter VII) – this includes managing someone else's shares;

(d)   advising on investments (Regulated Activities Order 2001, Chapter XII) – this includes giving advice to someone buying or selling shares. It will not include general advice in relation to an investment, or merely explaining the implications of exercising rights. So, for example, explaining the meaning of technical jargon, or advising how to complete an application form will not amount to advising on investments. (It could, however, still amount to arranging deals in investments – see (b) above.)

The definition of 'regulated activities' is wide. The prohibition prevents any person carrying on a regulated activity, unless that person is an authorised person or an exempt person. So who are these persons?

9.4.3 Authorised person

Section 31(1) of the FSMA 2000 defines an 'authorised person'. The most common example of an authorised person is someone who has obtained permission from the FSA to carry on regulated activities (under Pt IV of the Act), such as an accountant or financial adviser seeking to act as a sponsor or broker (see **Chapter 4**). Part IV of the Act contains the detail of how such permission is obtained. From the lawyer's point of view, however, the important issue is that, unless a client is an authorised person or an exempt person, it will be prohibited from carrying out any regulated activity, and the lawyer must advise the client to instruct an authorised person (or, more rarely, an exempt person) to carry out the activity instead.

9.4.4 Exempt person

A person is exempt if he has been granted an exemption order under s 38(1) of the FSMA 2000, or is exempt as an 'appointed representative' under s 39(1) of the Act. In practice, exempt persons are encountered rarely. However, the most common 'exempt person' with which lawyers will be familiar is any recognised investment exchange or recognised clearing house pursuant to s 285 of the FSMA 2000. For example, in certain circumstances (see s 285(2)) the Stock Exchange will be exempt from the general prohibition.

9.5 Misleading statements and market manipulation

As stated at **9.3** above, this is another area covered by the FSMA 2000 in relation to which the lawyer must be able to advise.

9.5.1 Misleading statements

9.5.1.1 The criminal offence

As outlined at **6.7.2.1** above, s 397(1) and (2) of the FSMA 2000 provides that it is a criminal offence for a person to:

(a)   make a statement, promise or forecast which he *knows is* materially misleading, false or deceptive;

(b)   dishonestly conceal any material facts; or

(c)   *recklessly* make (dishonestly or otherwise) a statement, promise or forecast which *is* materially misleading, false or deceptive,

in order to induce (or be reckless as to whether it may induce) another person to:

(i)   enter into, or offer to enter into, or refrain from entering or offering to enter into a *relevant agreement*, or

(ii)   exercise, or refrain from exercising, any rights conferred by a *relevant investment*.

Note that the person who is induced does not have to be the recipient of the statement, promise or forecast. This offence is generally referred to as the restriction on making misleading statements (but clearly it applies equally to promises and forecasts).

9.5.1.2 'Relevant agreement'

A relevant agreement is defined by s 397(9) of the FSMA 2000. The definition refers to 'specified kinds of activity', which are contained in art 3 of the Financial Services and Markets Act 2000 (Misleading Statements and Practices) Order 2001 (SI 2001/3645) ('Misleading Statements Order 2001'). An example of a relevant agreement is an agreement to sell (or not sell) shares.

9.5.1.3 'Relevant investment'

A relevant investment is defined by s 397(10) of the FSMA 2000. Reference is made to 'specified kinds of investment', which are contained in art 4 of the Misleading Statements Order 2001. Shares and bonds are examples of relevant investments.

9.5.1.4 'Reckless'

'Reckless' includes not only someone not giving any thought to the accuracy of a statement, but also someone making a statement when he is aware that he should first make some enquiries as to the accuracy of the statement yet fails to make such enquiries (provided those enquires would have revealed that the statement was false or misleading).

9.5.1.5 The Disclosure and Transparency Rules

Failure to comply with the DTRs, and in particular the general obligation of disclosure set out at DTR 2.2.1R (see **7.5.1**), may constitute the dishonest concealment of material facts for the purpose of s 397 (see **9.5.1.1(b)**).

9.5.1.6 Example

The most common s 397 scenario which a corporate finance lawyer will encounter is where a client makes a misleading statement so that shareholders continue to buy, or do not sell, shares, when if the statement was actually truthful, those shareholders might be tempted not to buy, or to sell, their shares. The article below provides a real-life (and most recent) example of this.

FSA takes directors to court over 'misleading' statement

By Dominic White

THREE former directors of Henley-based software group AIT appeared in court yesterday accused of misleading the financial markets in the first criminal prosecution of its kind brought by the Financial Services Authority.

Carl Rigby, Alistair Rowley and Gareth Bailey were charged with four counts under the Financial Services and Markets Act 2000 when they appeared before City of London magistrates.

Mr Rigby, former chief executive, Mr Rowley, ex-sales director, and Mr Bailey, former finance director, are alleged to have issued a statement about the company's turnover

and profits on the Regulatory News Service, knowing it to be "misleading, false or deceptive".

The statement on May 2, 2002, said turnover and profits were expected to be in line with market expectations. But four weeks later, the company issued a shock profits warning that caused the shares to plunge 80% in a single day.

Soon after the once well-regarded group was forced into a £20.5m rescue refinancing that almost wiped out the existing shareholders.

The men face two similar charges relating to making a statement to the financial markets and two further similar charges of conspiracy.

Mr Rigby, 41, Mr Rowley, 41, and Mr Bailey, 35, all dressed in dark suits, were remanded on unconditional bail to appear before Southwark Crown Court for a preliminary hearing on March 2.

The FSA said it was the first prosecution it had brought using its criminal powers.

Separately, a company secretary who sold shares ahead of a sales warning by his company was yesterday fined £15,000 in the first case of its kind by the City watchdog.

Robert Middlemiss avoided a loss of £6,825 by selling 70,000 shares in publishing and communications company Profile Media Group, according to the FSA.

Source: *Daily Telegraph*, 11 February 2004

On 18 August 2005 the FSA announced that it had secured criminal convictions against the former chief executive and former finance director. The former chief executive was sentenced to three and a half years' imprisonment (reduced to 18 months on appeal). The former finance director was sentenced to two years' imprisonment (reduced to 9 months on appeal). These are the first criminal convictions under s 397(1) of the FSMA 2000.

9.5.2   Market manipulation

9.5.2.1   The criminal offence

This is a separate offence from that of making a misleading statement, although it is also contained within s 397 of the FSMA 2000. Section 397(3) provides that it is a criminal offence to:

(a)   do any act, or engage in any course of conduct;

(b)   which creates a false or misleading impression;

(c)   as to the market in, or the price or value of, any relevant investment (see **9.5.1.3**);

(d)   in order to:

    (i)   create that impression, and

    (ii)   induce another person to deal or not deal in those investments.

This offence is referred to as the restriction on market manipulation.

9.5.2.2   Examples

One scenario in which this offence might arise is as follows. Bidder plc plans to make a takeover offer for Target plc. It therefore seeks to undertake a stakebuilding exercise (see **Chapter 21**). Target plc suspects that Bidder plc is going to make a bid for it, and is not pleased. It arranges for its associate companies to buy shares in Target plc, so that the share price of Target plc rises, which makes Bidder's stake-building exercise more costly. Bidder will have to pay more for its stake. This contravenes s 397(3), because Target plc has deliberately manipulated the market to discourage Bidder plc from dealing in the shares of Target plc.

Two *Daily Mirror* journalists were found guilty of conspiracy to commit market manipulation under the forerunner to s 397(3) of the FSMA 2000. The journalists bought shares in listed companies and then tipped them as a buy in their column in the *Daily Mirror*, 'City Slickers'. The share price rose post-publication and the two men then sold the shares, making a profit. They were aided by a third person (who pleaded guilty to the same charge), who used Internet message boards to stimulate interest in the same companies. As an indication of how serious the offence is, one of the journalists was sentenced to six months' imprisonment, having made approximately £40,000 profit. The second, who co-operated with the investigation, made £15,000 profit and was sentenced to community service. On the steps of the court after sentencing he remarked, 'That was a close one!' The third person was sentenced to three months' imprisonment, having made £17,000.

9.5.2.3   Defence

Section 397(5) provides a defence for a person charged under s 397(3) if he can show that he reasonably believed the act or conduct would not create a false or misleading impression.

9.5.3   Relationship between s 397(1) and s 397(3)

The sections are not mutually exclusive. One act can give rise to charges under both sections.

9.5.4   Sanctions

Section 397(8) of the FSMA 2000 provides that the offences of making a misleading statement or manipulating the market are punishable by imprisonment and/or a fine. On summary conviction, the maximum sentence is six months, and on conviction on indictment the maximum sentence is seven years.

The risk of directors breaching s 397 by making a misleading statement in a prospectus was examined at **6.7.2.1** above. As noted in that paragraph, the verification process is used to try to ensure that s 397 is not breached during the marketing of an IPO, and the threat of a prison sentence is usually enough to focus the directors' attention on this process.

Chapter 10
Market Abuse

10.1 Introduction

As discussed in **Chapter 9**, the market abuse regime is one of the key features of the FSMA 2000. Part VIII (ss 118 to 131A) of the Act sets out that regime. Market abuse is a civil offence which was created by the FSMA 2000. It supplements the criminal offences of:

(a) misleading statements and market manipulation under the FSMA 2000 (see **9.5** above); and

(b) insider dealing under the CJA 1993 (see **Chapter 11**),

which target the same kind of behaviour covered by the market abuse regime.

It is important to note that both the Government and the FSA are treating market abuse as a top priority at the moment in light of the maelstrom which affected the world's financial markets, including of course the London Stock Exchange. In a speech given on 27 April 2009, Margaret Cole, FSA Director of Enforcement, said that the FSA is 'interested in results and headlines because of the demonstration effect'. The authorities' rationale is that uncertain times lend themselves to a greater possibility of market manipulation and the economic damage which can flow from it.

In the last couple of years we have seen some of the world's and the UK's biggest banks driven to failure, nationalisation or a rescue takeover in the space of days by a loss of confidence expressed in part through a collapsing share price. Rumours abounded as to which institution might be next to be in trouble, and this resulted in breathtaking falls and rises in share prices as panic spread and confidence ebbed and flowed depending on the latest developments.

This presents opportunities to make huge amounts of money, not just legitimately (however morally questionable this may be) but also for the unscrupulous at a potentially devastating cost to the companies, investors, employees and ultimately economies involved. Now, more than ever, shoring up investor confidence and reimposing market stability in the UK are seen as critically important in avoiding even worse financial and economic problems, and tackling market abuse is seen as an important part of achieving this. It is of course also one of the FSA's statutory objectives under the FSMA 2000 to try to main efficient, orderly and fair markets.

HBOS: Malicious traders in the City try to topple the Halifax bank

Christine Seib

Stock market manipulators yesterday tried to bring down one of Britain's biggest banks by spreading false rumours through the City.

The Bank of England was forced to issue an unprecedented denial that HBOS was in trouble.

The Financial Services Authority (FSA) said that it would pursue traders guilty of "market abuse" by spreading untrue claims that banks were on the brink of collapse.

The authorities believe that the fear and uncertainty in financial markets are allowing unscrupulous traders to make multimillion-pound profits by whipping up hysteria about the stability of big banks.

Yesterday's drama began at about 8.30am when rumours started spreading through London's stock market that HBOS, which owns Halifax, the UK's biggest mortgage lender, and Bank of Scotland, was about to become another Northern Rock and that it had

begged the Bank of England for a multi-billion-pound emergency loan. Within 20 minutes HBOS's shares had plunged by more than 17 per cent as investors dumped their stakes. An hour later, the Bank of England announced that no bank needed emergency funding, while the FSA issued a statement warning investors to stop spreading false accusations.

It is feared that short-sellers - investors who use falling share prices to make money - were deliberately spooking the market in order to profit from plunging stocks in a practice called trash 'n' cash.

Rumours that the American investment bank Bear Stearns was short of cash contributed to its near-collapse last week after its lenders were scared into demanding that it repay them immediately.

The warning to speculators came as it emerged that the American financial watchdog was investigating similar activity in the trading of

shares of Bear Stearns and Lehman Brothers, another US investment bank heavily exposed to risky American mortgage business.

Andy Hornby, the HBOS chief executive, vehemently denied that the bank needed an emergency loan. He said: "It's categorically untrue that we've approached any central bank for funding."

Sally Dewar, the FSA's managing director of wholesale markets, said that a series of "completely unfounded rumours about UK financial institutions in the London market" had been spread over the past few days, usually accompanied by short-selling of the banks' stocks.

The FSA can listen to office telephone calls and investigate suspicious transactions but has never brought a trash 'n' cash prosecution. HBOS shares closed 7 per cent down at 446.25p.

Source: *Times*, 20 March 2008

10.1.1   The civil offence

The civil offence of market abuse was introduced so that the FSA could catch abusers of the market who might otherwise have escaped punishment for the criminal offences referred to at (a) and (b) above, which were widely considered not to have been terribly effective in practice. It has, at least in theory, the following advantages over the criminal regime:

(a)   it is wider in scope;

(b)   it is easier to prove. The standard of proof in criminal cases is 'beyond all reasonable doubt'. This high standard means that it is very difficult to convict anyone of insider dealing, or of making misleading statements and/or manipulating the market. To date there have been very few convictions for these offences. Market abuse, however, as a civil offence, has a lower standard of proof, namely 'on the balance of probabilities';

(c)   it assesses behaviour according to its effect rather than the intention behind it (although there is an element of intention lurking in the detail of the regime);

(d)   it can be committed by anyone – an individual or a company (contrast insider dealing, which can only be committed by an individual, see **11.7** below);

(e)   a jury is not required to try the offence; and

(f)   it is possible to settle a case of market abuse, unlike with a criminal offence, and the FSA has powers to to offer leniency to wrongdoers, to encourage co-operation where more than one individual is involved.

10.1.2   The Code of Market Conduct

Section 119 of the FSMA 2000 requires the FSA to provide guidance to market users as to what behaviour amounts to market abuse. The FSA has obliged with the Code of Market Conduct (CoMC). The CoMC confirms that the scope of market abuse is wide, and the FSA has significant power to tackle market abusers. It is not binding but it does have evidential weight. The CoMC forms Chapter 1 of the FSA Market Conduct Sourcebook (known as 'MAR'), which is part of the FSA Handbook and can be viewed under 'Business Standards' in the FSA Handbook section of the FSA's website. To follow market practice, references below to 'MAR 1' are to paragraphs of the CoMC.

The FSA also provides information periodically on the market abuse regime through its *Market Watch* publications (available on the FSA's website).

10.1.3   The Market Abuse Directive

The Market Abuse Directive (MAD) came into force in the UK on 1 July 2005, as part of the EU's FSAP.

The MAD was implemented in the UK through:

(a)   the Disclosure Rules;

(b)   amendments to Pt VIII of the FSMA 2000 (made by the MAD Regulations 2005); and

(c)   a new version of the CoMC.

10.2   What is market abuse?

Market abuse, in layman's terms, is certain behaviour (see **10.3.4** below), relating to certain investments which trade, or are seeking admission to trade, on certain markets, which is deemed improper. The offence punishes those who seek to manipulate the market for their own benefit.

10.3   The main offence

Sections 118(1) and 118A(1) of the FSMA 2000 sets out the test which must be satisfied for behaviour to constitute market abuse. The behaviour of the market abuser must:

(a)   occur in the UK;

(b)   occur in relation to:

(i)   a *qualifying investment* admitted to trading on a *prescribed market*, or

(ii)   a *qualifying investment* in respect of which a request for admission to trading on a prescribed market has been made, or

(iii)   (in the case of 'insider dealing' or 'improper disclosure' offences – see **10.3.4** below) an investment *related* to such a qualifying investment; and

(c)   fall within any one or more of the types of behaviour set out at **10.3.4**.

10.3.1   Qualifying investment

This term is defined by the Financial Services and Markets Act 2000 (Prescribed Markets and Qualifying Investments) Order 2001 (SI 2001/996) ('PMQI Order 2001'), which refers to the definition of 'financial instrument' under art 1(3) of the MAD. For our purposes, note that qualifying investments include shares and bonds.

10.3.2   Prescribed market

The PMQI Order 2001 specifies the prescribed markets for the purposes of the market abuse regime. For our purposes, note that both of the Stock Exchange's markets (ie, the Main Market and the AIM) are prescribed markets. Other markets in the UK, such as PLUS, are also included.

10.3.3   Related investments

This term is defined by s 130A(3) of the FSMA 2000 as an investment whose price or value depends on the price or value of the qualifying investment. This includes more complex investments, for example an equity swap on a share traded on the Main Market.

10.3.4   The seven types of behaviour

Section 118(2) to (8) provide that the following types of behaviour will constitute market abuse:

Type 1: Insider dealing (s 118(2))

This is behaviour where an insider (as defined by the FSMA 2000, s 118B) deals, or attempts to deal, in a qualifying investment (see **10.3.1**) or related investment (see **10.3.3**), on the basis of inside information (see the very detailed definition at **7.5.2.1**, substituting 'qualifying investment' for 'financial instrument') relating to that investment. Further guidance is provided in MAR 1.3.

This would cover, for example, the situation where a director of a company is aware of a takeover offer which has not yet been announced, and buys shares in the company with the expectation that the share price will rise on the announcement of the offer.

Remember this is a type of behaviour under the civil offence of market abuse and is quite separate from the criminal offence of insider dealing referred to in **Chapter 11**.

Type 2: Improper disclosure (s 118(3))

This is behaviour where an insider (as defined by the FSMA 2000, s 118B) discloses inside information (see **7.5.2.1**, substituting 'qualifying investment' for 'financial instrument') to another person other than in the proper course of his employment, profession or duties. Further guidance is provided in MAR 1.4.

This would include, for example, a director telling a friend in the gym that her company was going to sell off a major division of the company before it was publicly announced.

Type 3: Misuse of information (s 118(4))

This is behaviour based on information *not generally available* to those using the market, but which, if available to a regular user of the market, would be, or would be likely to be, regarded by him as *relevant* when deciding the terms on which transactions in investments of the kind in question should be effected. (This 'relevant information not generally available' is sometimes abbreviated to RINGA.) The behaviour must fail the regular user test (see **10.3.5** below). Further guidance is provided in MAR 1.5. This type of behaviour may also amount to the criminal offence of insider dealing (see **Chapter 11**).

Note that this provision is due to expire on 31 December 2011. It had been due to expire on 31 December 2009 but was extended by HM Treasury in light of the ongoing review of the market abuse regime at an EU level.

Note also that behaviour falls within type 3 behaviour only if it does not fall within type 1 or type 2 behaviour (s 118(4)).

'Relevant information'

The CoMC (see **10.1.2**) sets out the factors to be taken into account to determine whether information is relevant. The information must relate to matters which regular users would reasonably expect to be disclosed to market users. The CoMC also gives examples of relevant information. Of particular interest to the corporate lawyer is the example of information concerning business affairs or prospects (such as entering into a significant contract with a supplier).

'Not generally available'

The CoMC states that information *is* generally available if it can be obtained by research or analysis conducted by, or on behalf of, users of the market. Information notified to an RIS, or sent to a public registry such as Companies House, would be classed as generally available information.

Type 4: Manipulating transactions (s 118(5))

This is behaviour which effects a transaction (other than for legitimate reasons, in conformity with accepted market practices – as defined by s 130A(3) and MAR 1, Annex 2G) which either:

(a)   gives, or is likely to give, a false or misleading impression as to the supply of, or demand for, or as to the price of, a qualifying investment (see **10.3.1**); or

(b)   secures the prices of such an investment at an abnormal or artificial level.

This offence is most likely to be committed by a market professional, such as a trader. Further guidance is provided in MAR 1.6. It includes two specific situations:

(a)   *An abusive squeeze.* This is perhaps less interesting than it sounds. It describes a situation where a person corners the market and uses that position to distort the market.

(b)   *Price positioning.* This consists of entering into a transaction, or series of transactions, to position the price at a distorted level (that is, materially different to that which reflects the operation of usual market forces).

Type 5: Manipulating devices (s 118(6))

This is behaviour which effects transactions which employ fictitious devices or any other form of deception or contrivance. Again, this is most likely to be committed by a market professional, such as a trader. Further guidance is provided in MAR 1.7. An example of this type of behaviour is a trader who buys shares, then spreads misleading positive information about the shares to increase their price, before selling the shares at a profit (known as a 'pump and dump').

Type 6: Dissemination (s 118(7))

This is behaviour which disseminates information which gives, or is likely to give, a false or misleading impression as to a qualifying investment (see **10.3.1**), by a person who knew, or could reasonably be expected to have known, that the information was false or misleading.

Posting false information on a website about a listed company's financial position would fall under this type of behaviour.

Type 7: Distortion (s 118(8))

This is behaviour which is:

(a)   likely to give a regular user of the market a false or misleading impression as to the supply of, or demand for, or price or value of, a qualifying investment (see **10.3.1**); or

(b)   would be, or would be likely to be, regarded by a regular user of the market as behaviour that would distort, or would be likely to distort, the market in such an investment.

The behaviour must fail the regular user test (see **10.3.5** below). Further guidance is given in MAR 1.9.

Figure 10.1: Section 118 flowchart

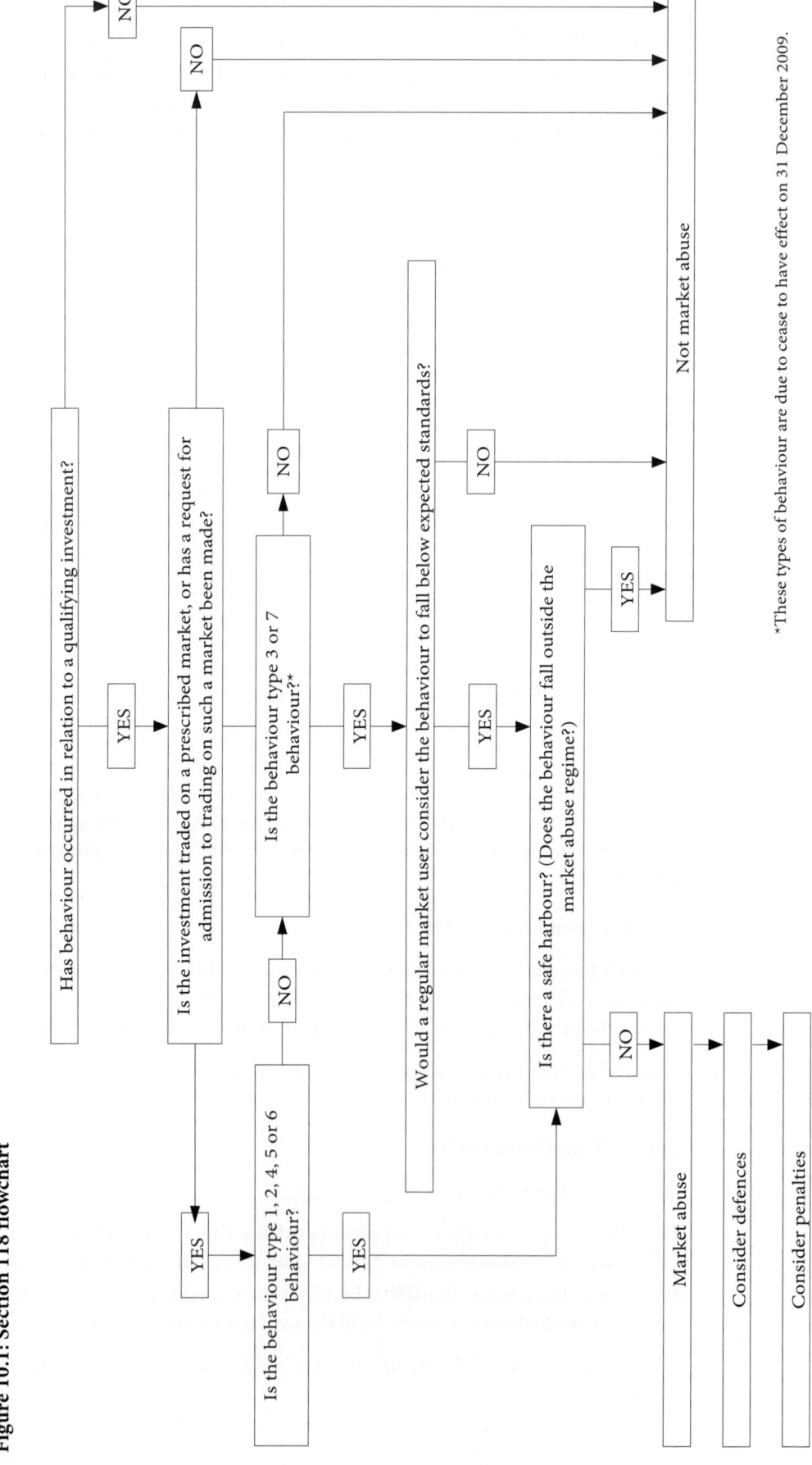

*These types of behaviour are due to cease to have effect on 31 December 2009.

As one part of the strategy to prevent the collapse of the UK's financial system threatened by the global credit crunch, the FSA introduced temporary restrictions on the short selling of securities on the Stock Exchange in September 2008. Short selling is a practice whereby investors seek to profit from the falling price of the shares in listed companies. It was thought that this practice was exacerbating the already considerable problems faced by certain companies, principally banks such as HBOS, now owned by Lloyds Banking Group plc.

A temporary ban was placed on the short selling of UK financial sector companies (defined to include banks and insurance companies amongst others) until 16 January 2009. This was achieved by amending MAR 1.9 to state that such behaviour would in the opinion of the FSA amount to market abuse as type 7 (distortion) behaviour.

There are also rules requiring the public disclosure of short selling arrangements in certain cases, which has again been achieved by amendments to MAR 1.9.

Note that s 118(8) is due to expire on 31 December 2011. It had been due to expire on 31 December 2009 but was extended by HM Treasury in light of the ongoing review of the market abuse regime at an EU level.

Note also that behaviour falls within type 7 (distortion) behaviour only if it does not fall within type 4, 5 or 6 behaviour (s 118(4)).

The Financial Services and Markets Tribunal (on appeal from fines imposed in June 2008 on a market maker, Winterflood, and two of its traders) has held that it is not necessary to have an intention to mislead or distort the market under s 118. This is in keeping with MAR 1.2.3G.

10.3.5   The regular market user test

10.3.5.1   Application

The test applies only to type 3 (misuse of information) and type 7 (distortion) behaviour.

10.3.5.2   The test

The test is whether a regular user of the market would regard the behaviour of the person (let us call him X) as failing to observe the standard of behaviour reasonably expected of a person in X's position. If so, X has failed the regular market user test.

10.3.5.3   The regular market user

The regular market user is 'a reasonable person who regularly deals on that market in investments of the kind in question' (s 130A(3)). There are difficulties in applying this test. It is not easy to identify a hypothetical regular market user, or to identify the standards of behaviour which that user would expect of someone else. Guidance on the application of type 3 and type 7 is set out in the CoMC (see **10.3.4** above).

10.3.6   Summary

The main offence under s 118 of the FSMA 2000 is summarised in **Figure 10.1**.

10.4   The secondary offence

The main offence under Pt VIII of the FSMA 2000 is that of market abuse (under s 118), which is considered at **10.3** above. However, there is also a secondary offence under Pt VIII; that of 'requiring or encouraging market abuse'. Section 123(1)(b) of the FSMA 2000 provides that penalties can be imposed on a person (let us call him A) if, by taking or refraining from taking any action, he 'requires or encourages' another person, X, to engage in behaviour which, if engaged in by A, would amount to market abuse. This secondary offence is designed to catch those people who might otherwise circumvent the market abuse offence by asking someone else to carry out their instructions.

Further guidance is provided in MAR 1.2.22 and 1.2.23. Examples include a director, in possession of relevant and disclosable information which is not generally available, who instructs an employee to deal in qualifying investments in respect of which the information is relevant information. If the director did the dealing, it would constitute market abuse and would be an offence under s 118. Section 123 ensures that the director will still be caught, albeit under the s 123 offence of requiring or encouraging, rather than the s 118 offence of market abuse.

10.5 Behaviour which does not amount to market abuse

10.5.1 Safe harbours under the MAD

A safe harbour is a type of behaviour which will not constitute market abuse, even if it satisfies the test in s 118 of the FSMA 2000. It is therefore equivalent to an exception.

The MAD provides only two safe harbours, one relating to share buyback (s 118A(5)(b) and MAR 1.10.1G(1)) and the other relating to price stabilisation activities (s 118A(5)(b) and MAR 2).

10.5.2 Section 118A(5)

Section 118A(5) of the FSMA 2000 stipulates specific behaviour which will not amount to market abuse. It includes not only the two safe harbours referred to at **10.5.1**, but also behaviour which conforms to a rule which includes a provision to the effect that behaviour conforming with that rule does not amount to market abuse (s 118A(5)(a)). This includes the parts of the Listing Rules (LR 1.4.7R) and the Disclosure Rules (DTR 1.5.2R) which relate to a disclosure, announcement, communication or release of information. In addition, MAR 1.10.2G and MAR 1.10.3G specify that there are no FSA rules or rules in the City Code (relating to takeovers, see **Chapter 21**) which permit or require a person to behave in a way which amounts to market abuse.

In practice, behaviour falling within s 118A(5) will also be referred to colloquially as falling within a 'safe harbour'.

Behaviour on the part of a person acting on behalf of a public authority in pursuit of monetary policies, policies in respect of exchange rates, the management of public debt or foreign exchange reserves will also not amount to market abuse (s 118A(5)(c)).

10.6 Defences

If behaviour falls outside the market abuse regime (see **10.5** above) then it is not market abuse. However, even if behaviour falls within the regime, and is market abuse, the perpetrator may still be able to avoid any penalty, by raising a defence under s 123(2).

10.6.1 Defences to the s 118 offence of market abuse

If the market abuser, X:

(a)   believed, on reasonable grounds, that his behaviour did not amount to market abuse; or

(b)   had taken all reasonable precautions and exercised all due diligence to avoid engaging in market abuse,

then the FSA cannot impose a penalty on X (s 123(2)).

10.6.2 Defences to the s 123 offence of requiring or encouraging

If A, the person requiring or encouraging X to abuse the market:

(a)   believed on reasonable grounds that his behaviour did not require or encourage X to engage in behaviour which, if engaged in by A, would have amounted to market abuse; or

(b)   had taken all reasonable precautions and exercised all due diligence to avoid requiring or encouraging X to engage in behaviour which, if engaged in by A, would have amounted to market abuse,

then, under s 123(2) of the FSMA 2000, the FSA cannot impose a penalty on A.

10.7   Sanctions

If the FSA suspects that market abuse may have occurred, it can use its statutory powers to investigate the issue.

One of the biggest problems in proving market abuse is evidence. In an attempt to tackle this, the FSA now requires the firms it regulates to record telephone conversations and other electronic communications (including fax, email, texts and instant messages) relating to client orders and the conclusion of transactions in the equity and other markets, and keep the records for six months. One glaring lacuna in the new rules is that mobile phone and handheld devices are exempt.

FSA gets tough in fight against insider trading

Michael Herman

The Financial Services Authority (FSA) is becoming increasingly aggressive in its battle against insider trading and market abuse, adopting techniques such as cold calling and demanding comprehensive records of traders' activities.

Since reinforcing its commitment to tackling financial crime in a series of speeches and policy documents late last year, the FSA has begun phoning traders, brokers and investors without notice.

The FSA says this is a longstanding power used as part of a wider battle to curb market abuses, but market sources said the regulator has become more active in using it in recent weeks.

Ian Mason, a partner at law firm Barlow, Lyde & Gilbert, said the FSA was increasingly employing "SEC-type tactics" - a reference to the more aggressive approach to insider trading and other financial crimes adopted by the US Securities and Exchange Commission.

"The FSA are definitely upping the ante and trying to get the evidence while it's hot," Mr Mason, a former head of wholesale enforcement at the regulator, said.

The FSA declined to comment on specific cases of cold calling or whether the policy had been successful. Although regulated firms and individuals have a duty to cooperate with the regulator, they are under no obligation to answer immediate telephone questions.

Investigators will need to identify themselves and warn that the conversation is taking place under caution, which means its contents can be presented as evidence in court.

One adviser described the tactic as the FSA trying to "get in first before legal and compliance get involved and everyone turns shy".

Sources said the FSA has also been making increasing use of powers to write to trading houses such as banks and hedge funds demanding specific details about individuals.

One person who advises banks said: "We're seeing an increasing number of instances where the FSA is identifying a specific individual at a bank - or more commonly a hedge fund - and demanding details of all trades they have carried out, the names of all the counterparties involved plus transcripts of all telephone conversations the trader has made."

Regulated firms are obliged to provide this information within a reasonable period, usually seven days, subject to negotiation. This week the FSA announced formal regulations for brokers to record all telephone calls involving equity, bond, and derivatives trades although the majority of large institutions already do this as standard.

Jonathan Herbst, a partner at Norton Rose, said the FSA was determined to prove that it means business in its fight for cleaner markets. Late last year, the regulator announced specific plans to crack down on hedge funds, many of which it said had unacceptably lax compliance procedures.

News of a more aggressive stance comes just weeks after the FSA launched its first criminal prosecution for insider dealing. In January it charged two employees of TTP Communications with trading company shares ahead of a £103 million bid from Motorola, the US telecoms company, in June 2006.

In November, the FSA made two arrests as part of a crackdown on foreign "boiler room" scams in which personal investors are sold worthless or non-existent shares by overseas brokers.

Source: *Times*, 5 March 2008

Once, though, market abuse has been proved and no defence applies, the FSA can:

(a)   choose not to act (FSMA 2000, s 123);

(b)   impose an unlimited fine (s 123) (see also **3.7.4**);

(c)   make a public statement that the person has engaged in market abuse (s 123). Clearly, the hope here is that 'naming and shaming' will serve as a deterrent;

(d)   apply to the court for an injunction (s 381);

(e)   require the person to pay back profits made, or losses avoided (s 383); or

(f)   require the person to compensate any victims (s 384).

The first case of market abuse concluded since the new regime was introduced on 1 July 2005 resulted in a fine of £85,000 being imposed on John Shelvin on 1 July 2008 for type 1 (insider dealing) market abuse in relation to the shares of Body Shop International plc, a company where he worked in the IT department. The article below is referring to market abuse insider dealing and not criminal insider dealing.

Body Shop 'snoop' John Shevlin fined for insider dealing

Miles Costello

A former IT technician at Body Shop, the ethical retailer, has been fined for market abuse in a rare victory for the Financial Services Authority in its battle against insider dealing.

The City regulator said yesterday that it had fined John Shevlin £85,000 after he was found to have gained inside knowlege by snooping on confidential e-mails between executives.

Mr Shevlin, who worked at the beauty company's head office in London, borrowed more than his annual salary to bet that Body Shop's share price would fall, having obtained a sneak preview of an unexpectedly bleak Christmas trading update.

As an IT technician, it is likely that Mr Shevlin had privileged access to executives' passwords, enabling him to access their computers without their knowledge, the FSA said.

It is not clear whether Mr Shevlin, who joined Body Shop in 1998, had any access to computer equipment operated by Dame Anita Roddick, the company's founder, who died last year.

According to the FSA, Mr Shevlin borrowed £29,000 on January 10, 2006, for short-selling. He offloaded 80,000 shares in Body Shop that he did not own in the hope of buying them back more cheaply at a later

date. His annual salary was £28,000.

The FSA said that he built up a total underlying exposure to the company's share price through contracts for difference (CFDs) of £213,536.

He made a profit of £38,472 by closing out his position a day later, once the disappointing trading update had been circulated to the wider market and Body Shop shares had fallen.

The FSA discovered Mr Shevlin's activities after one of the brokers that he had been using submitted a suspicious transaction report. Mr Shevlin used numerous spread-betters between January 1 and January 10, 2006, including IG Markets, IFX Markets and Squaregain.

Margaret Cole, director of enforcement at the FSA, said: "Mr Shevlin deliberately set out to obtain highly sensitive and valuable information to which he was not entitled. He abused the trust placed in him by his employers and misused his technical skills to gain a financial advantage over other market users."

Last October, Ms Cole unveiled a crackdown on market abuse, stating that the regulator would choose to pursue more criminal convictions rather than chasing civil cases.

Although the FSA admitted that it had failed to establish that Mr Shevlin was guilty of insider dealing, it said information that emerged in the latter stages of its investigation pro-

vided compelling evidence that this had happened.

Mr Shevlin, whose FSA case was civil rather than criminal, no longer works for the Body Shop. He denied any guilt throughout the process, according to the regulator. His solicitor did not return calls seeking comment yesterday. The FSA said that because Mr Shevlin had chosen not to admit to trading using inside information, it had not reduced his fine.

Yesterday's fine represents the first time since last March that the regulator has levied a fine for market abuse.

It is also one of the rare occasions that the regulator has fined an unauthorised individual. It comes as the FSA clamps down on dealers who indulge in market abuse by creating false rumours about a company and then taking a short position in the shares.

Most recently, the FSA attracted controversy by demanding that investors who short shares in companies carrying out rights issues disclose their exposure if it is worth more than 0.25 per cent of the value of a target company.

The move was widely seen as a defence of a £4 billion rights issue under way at HBOS, the mortgage bank, whose shares fell heavily after it was targeted by hedge funds and other aggressive investors.

Source: *The Times*, 2 July 2008

The FSA imposed its largest fine of £17 million for market abuse and for breaches of the Listing Rules on Royal Dutch Shell.

Shell's shame: FSA spells out abuse

Terry Macalister

The Financial Services Authority yesterday accused Shell of 'unprecedented misconduct' for misleading the markets over the reporting of oil and gas reserves.

The searing criticism came alongside confirmation of a £17m fine for 'market abuse' from the FSA plus a further $120m (£67m) from the Securities and Exchange Commission in the United States.

The main part of the two regulatory inquiries is now over, but the FSA said a review 'into other aspects of this matter' was continuing.

The SEC made clear it is also still investigating the behaviour of key individuals, presumably including former Shell chairman Sir Philip Watts.

The Anglo-Dutch group, which controls 1,000 UK petrol stations and 23% of North Sea production, shocked the stock market in January by announcing it had to downgrade its oil reserves by 20% to meet SEC guidelines.

Shell later downgraded these figures a further 5% and then ousted chairman Sir Philip and exploration director Walter van de Vijver after revealing what appeared to be a reserves cover-up.

Shell, which still faces legal action from angry investors and is the subject of takeover speculation, said it would pay all the fines. But it insisted it was making the settlements 'without admitting or denying the findings and conclusions'.

Fadel Gheit, an oil analyst at broker Oppenheimer & Co in New York, said the latest revelations from the regulators proved this was

a corporate scandal of 'historic proportions'. He added: 'Short of Enron, which involved criminality, I have not seen anything like this in 30 years of covering the market.'

Harold Degenhardt, the administrator of the SEC's Fort Worth office, which has been dealing with the scandal, said significant civil penalties were necessary 'to deter Shell and others from engaging in similar misconduct'. Future investigations would 'focus on, among other things, the people responsible for Shell's failures'.

Shell shares closed down 5p at 396.75p yesterday, having taken a pounding since the first reserves announcements were made. Some £3bn was wiped off its value on one day alone in January.

The £17m penalty in Britain, revealed by Shell last month, is small for a firm that makes £1bn in profits every six weeks. But it is still the biggest ever imposed on a UK firm and four times larger than any previous fine. A spokesman for the regulator insisted it was a suitable punishment, even for a company as big as Shell.

'We believe this will send a clear message to others that we will not tolerate this kind of behaviour,' he said.

The FSA accused Shell in a formal statement of making 'false and misleading announcements' in relation to its reserves. A 17-page statement from the regulator gave graphic detail based on internal memoranda regarding how executives were aware of the problems they faced at least four years be-

fore. The regulator details the way in which an internal group reserves auditor's report for 2001 expressed concerns that the company's reserve figures were being artificially ramped up to help secure better financial bonuses for staff.

'The widespread use of reserves targets in score cards affecting variable pay is seen to affect the objectivity of staff in some [operating units] when proposing reserves additions', according to the internal group reserves auditor's report quoted in the regulator's document.

A year earlier the auditor had suggested that proved reserves figures for Nigeria could only be supported through 'significant aspirational upturns in future offtake levels in order to justify their proved reserves figures'.

The FSA report says the auditor raised these issues in each of the next two annual reports without the company doing anything about it.

The regulator concludes: 'By mid-2000, Shell had information indicating that the proved reserves figures reported to the market for at least the previous three years may have been overstated.'

Yesterday Jeroen van der Veer, a Shell board member for many years but now the company's chairman, said Shell had worked hard over the past months to improve its systems to prevent any recurrence.

The oil company wanted to put these issues behind it now 'and continue our efforts to regain and maintain the confidence and trust of our investors, partners, customers and employees'.

Source: *Guardian*, 25 August 2004

There have been a number of other investigations under the market abuse regime, some leading to enforcement action being taken by the FSA. Details can be found on the FSA's website.

10.8   The FSA's current approach

On 17 March 2006 the FSA published an occasional paper called 'Measuring Market cleanliness'. The paper sought to assess the level of market cleanliness by analysing share price movement ahead of regulatory announcements. It concluded that there had been potential market abuse in relation to almost a third of takeovers in 2004. Not surprisingly, the press seized the opportunity to criticise the FSA once more for failing to deal effectively with market abusers (one headline in the *Independent on Sunday* reading 'Sadly we can do sweet FSA about insider dealing'). The negative findings and the negative press comment prompted the FSA to seek to improve its activities in this area.

With the problems arising out of the credit crisis to contend with as well, the FSA has adopted a number of new strategies to tackle market abuse.

Recognising the difficulty of successfully proving market abuse, the FSA is seeking to improve its own systems and those in the firms it regulates in order to try to prevent market abuse arising before it occurs. This includes the FSA devoting more resources to monitoring the markets and enforcement, promoting best practice by liaising with firms, advising and providing guidance in its *Market Watch* publication (for example on the control of inside information on takeovers), undertaking reviews and investigating and bringing more cases and imposing sanctions which have a deterrent effect. It is also commencing criminal insider dealing prosecutions with a renewed vigour (see **Chapter 11**).

One area of particular concern has been the misuse of inside information in relation to takeovers of listed companies. The need for secrecy in preparing a takeover offer, or in agreeing the terms of a takeover by both parties involved, makes takeovers particularly vulnerable to possible market abuse. Following a major review in 2007, the FSA has undertaken a number of steps to address the problem, including publishing a set of non-binding Principles of Good Practice for the Handling of Inside Information, prepared by an industry working group to rise awareness of the need to protect price-sensitive information. More information can be found in Issue 27 of the FSA's newsletter *Market Watch* (available on the FSA's website).

In issue 30 of the FSA's *Market Watch* publication, the FSA has also provided guidance on how to deal with market rumours which can result in market abuse occurring.

The FSA has served notice that it will not tolerate misuse of information or other bad behaviour in the markets. If the preventative measures do not work, it is watching, probing and, armed with an increasing array of powers, ready to spring into action at the first whiff of trouble.

10.9   Future developments

The CESR, which acts as an advisory group to the EU Commission, has suggested, following a review of the MAD in July 2007, that further work needs to be done in developing the list of sanctions under the market abuse regime, to accommodate concerns about the diversity of measures applied in different Member States. It also suggested that further investigations be carried out into splitting the one definition of 'inside information' for both market abuse (see **10.3.4** above) and the obligation on listed companies to disclose 'inside information' under DTR 2.2.1R (see **7.5.1** above).

The European Commission is now conducting a review of the MAD and its implementation, which may result in changes to EU legislation in this area (see **3.7.3**).

The UK Government is proposing to grant the FSA new statutory powers to allow it to grant immunity to witnesses when investigating criminal cases. The provisions are contained in the Coroners and Justice Bill currently before Parliament.

Chapter 11
Insider Dealing

11.1 Introduction

Part V of the Criminal Justice Act 1993 (CJA 1993) contains the insider dealing provisions. These provisions existed before the FSMA 2000 came into force. As explained at **10.1** above, the criminal offence of insider dealing overlaps considerably with the civil offence of market abuse. The market abuse regime, however, does not affect the insider dealing regime. It is therefore possible to commit both the offences of insider dealing under the CJA 1993 and market abuse under s 118 of the FSMA 2000.

Lord Lane explained the reason for the insider dealing regime very effectively in layman's terms as follows: '... the clear intention to prevent, so far as possible, what amounts to cheating when those with inside knowledge use that knowledge to make a profit in their dealing with others' (*Attorney-General's Reference (No 1 of 1988)* [1989] 2 WLR 729).

As part of its new get-tough strategy for market misconduct, the FSA has been using its criminal powers of prosecution for insider dealing as never before. It has brought five cases in 2009 alone (see **11.7**).

11.2 The offence

Section 52 of the CJA 1993 provides that the offence of insider dealing can be committed in three ways, namely, if an *insider*:

(a) *deals* in price-affected securities, when in possession of *inside information*;

(b) *encourages another* to deal in price-affected securities, when in possession of *inside information*, or

(c) *discloses inside information* other than in the proper performance of his employment, office or profession.

Whichever way the offence is committed, there are two common requirements, namely, an 'insider' and 'inside information'.

11.2.1 Insider

An insider is defined by s 57(1) of the CJA 1993. A person is an insider if:

(a) he has information which is *inside information*;

(b) he has received that information *from an inside source*; and

(c) he *knows* (a) and (b).

11.2.2   Inside information

Unlike the market abuse regime and the DTRs, which use the definition under s 118C of the FSMA 2000, the insider dealing regime uses the definition of 'inside information' under s 56 of the CJA 1993. This is information which:

(a)   relates to particular, rather than general, securities or companies;

(b)   is specific or precise;

(c)   has not been made public; and

(d)   is price-sensitive (that is, would be likely to have a significant effect on the price of securities, such as shares, if it were made public).

This definition has been criticised because there is not much guidance about the meaning of the terms used. Until these words are defined, or their meaning falls to be decided by the courts, they must be given their ordinary dictionary meaning. It is not clear, for example, whether a rumour which turns out to be false would be 'specific or precise' (although common sense would suggest it would not).

11.2.2.1   Particular not general

This includes information which may affect a company's prospects (which may be about the sector in which the company operates rather than about the company itself).

11.2.2.2   Specific or precise

As discussed at **11.2.2** above, there is no definition of these terms.

11.2.2.3   Not made public

If information has been made public it is not inside information. Think back to Lord Lane's comments at **11.1** above; how can someone cheat if he is using freely available information? Section 58 provides some guidance as to when information has been made public. Information which a company provides to an RIS has been made public and therefore will not be inside information. Further s 58 provides that information made available only to a section of the public can also be treated as having been made public. It is difficult to see the logic in this. Surely it is unfair if, in order to make a profit, you use information I am unable to access? There is no guidance as to what constitutes a 'section' of the public.

11.2.2.4   Price-sensitive

There is no guidance on what amounts to a 'significant effect' on price, and so this has to be considered on a case-by-case basis.

11.2.3   From an inside source

Section 57(2) provides that a person has information from an inside source if he:

(a)   is an inside source (that is, a director, employee or shareholder) of 'an issuer of securities' (for our purposes, a company (but not necessarily the company whose securities are the subject of insider dealing)); or

(b)   has access to the information because of his employment, office or profession; or

(c)   obtained the information from someone who obtained it by way of (a) or (b) above.

Persons falling within (a) and (b) are known as 'primary insiders'. Persons falling within (c) are known as 'secondary insiders', or 'tippees'. An example of a tippee is a director's relative, who overhears talk about an impending takeover bid and then invests in the target company.

11.3   Three ways the offence can be committed

As explained at **11.2**, the offence can be committed in three different ways.

11.3.1 The dealing offence (s 52(1))

It is an offence to *deal* in price-affected *securities* on a *regulated market*, or by or through a *professional intermediary*.

11.3.1.1 Dealing

Section 55 of the CJA 1993 explains the meaning of 'dealing'. It includes:

(a)   the acquisition, or disposal, of securities;

(b)   any agreement to acquire securities (for example, entering into a share option agreement);

(c)   any agreement to create securities (for example, subscribing for shares), whether as principal or agent; and

(d)   procuring an acquisition or disposal of securities by any other person.

11.3.1.2 Securities

Securities are defined by s 54 of and Sch 2 to the CJA 1993. The definition is wide and includes shares, bonds, warrants and options.

11.3.1.3 Regulated market

Under powers granted by s 60 of the CJA 1993, this has been defined by the Insider Dealing (Securities and Regulated Markets) Order 1994 (SI 1994/187) as including both the Main Market and the AIM, as well as other, lesser known UK markets, such as PLUS. Dealing on a regulated market is referred to as an 'on-market' transaction. If you or I decide to buy shares in Marks and Spencer Group plc through the Stock Exchange, that is an on-market transaction. The dealing offence is concerned with on-market transactions.

11.3.1.4 Professional intermediary

A professional intermediary is a person who carries on a business of acquiring or disposing of securities, or who otherwise acts as a professional intermediary between persons taking part in any dealing in securities (s 59). A stockbroker acting in the normal course of business will be a professional intermediary, but lawyers and accountants acting in their normal course of business will not.

> **Example**
>
> Imagine that B plc is considering making a takeover bid for X plc, a listed company. B's investment bank acquires some shares in X plc on B's behalf, as a preliminary stake-building exercise. The shares are purchased privately, directly from a shareholder in X plc. This is known as an 'off-market' transaction. Although this acquisition has not taken place on a regulated market, B plc made the deal through a professional intermediary, the merchant bank, and therefore the deal has the potential to be within the scope of the dealing offence.

11.3.2 The offence of encouraging another to deal (s 52(2)(a))

It is not necessary for the person who is encouraged to deal either:

(a)   actually to deal; or

(b)   to realise the securities are price-affected.

A simple statement such as 'I cannot tell you why, but now is a good time to buy shares in X plc' could be caught by s 52(2)(a).

11.3.3 The disclosing offence (s 52(2)(b))

This prohibits any individual from disclosing inside information to another person other than in the proper performance of the functions of his employment, office or profession.

> **Example**
>
> Imagine that X plc, a listed company, is a weapons manufacturer. X plc is about to sign a lucrative deal with the Ministry of Defence. D, a director of X plc, knows about the deal. L is the company's lawyer. B is L's brother. Over a family dinner at which much wine is consumed, L mentions to B that this deal is pending. B, D and L all buy shares in X plc on the Stock Exchange before details of the deal have been made public. Who is guilty of an offence (subject to any defences)?
>
> (a)   D is guilty of insider dealing under s 52(1) (see **11.3.1**). He is an insider. He has inside information (he knows about the proposed takeover, which is specific information relating to X plc which has not been made public and is likely to have a significant effect on X plc's share price). D, presumably, knows that he is an insider with inside information. He received the information from an inside source (he has the information as a director of X plc). He has dealt in price-affected securities (the shares) on a regulated market (the Main Market).
>
> (b)   L is also guilty of insider dealing under s 52(1). He is in a similar position to D, although L is an insider because he has information through having access to it by virtue of his profession.
>
> L is also guilty of an offence under s 52(2)(b) (see **11.3.3**) as he has disclosed the information to his brother, which is not in the proper performance of his profession.
>
> If L encouraged his brother to buy shares in X plc, L is also be guilty of an offence under s 52(2)(a) (see **11.3.2**).
>
> L is also guilty of serious professional misconduct and liable to be punished by the Solicitors Regulatory Authority (SRA) for breaches of the Solicitors Code of Conduct 2007, such as breach of his duty of confidentiality.
>
> (c)   B may also be guilty of the dealing offence under s 52(1) (see **11.3.1**). Is he an insider? He is a tippee (see **11.2.3**). The source of the information is a primary insider (his brother, a lawyer) and B knows this. B has inside information. Does B know this? If B does, he will be guilty of the dealing offence.

11.4   Territorial scope

11.4.1   Dealing

Section 62(1) of the CJA 1993 provides that a person is not guilty of the dealing offence unless:

(a)   he was within the UK at the time of dealing;

(b)   the market is a UK regulated market (such as the Main Market, or AIM); or

(c)   the professional intermediary was within the UK at the time he is alleged to have committed the offence.

11.4.2   Encouraging or disclosing

Section 62(2) of the CJA 1993 provides that a person is not guilty of the encouraging or disclosing offence unless:

(a)   he was within the UK at the time of the encouragement or disclosure; or

(b)   the recipient of the encouragement or information was within the UK when he received that encouragement or information.

11.5   Defences

11.5.1   General defences

Section 53 of the CJA 1993 provides defences to each of the three ways of committing the offence.

11.5.1.1   Dealing or encouraging

No offence will be committed if the defendant can prove that:

(a)   he did not expect to gain an advantage. This is a difficult defence to run. The prosecution will have proved already that he was an insider and knew he had insider information;

(b)   he believed the information had been (in the case of the dealing offence) or would be (in the case of the encouraging offence) disclosed widely enough to ensure no-one would be prejudiced; or

(c)   he would have traded anyway, even if he did not have inside information. This could be used, for example, if he had to meet urgent financial commitments.

11.5.1.2   Disclosing

No offence will be committed if the defendant can prove that:

(a)   he did not expect dealing to occur; or

(b)   he did not expect profit to result.

Again, the defence set out at (b) is a difficult defence to run once the prosecution has proved the defendant was an insider who knew he had inside information.

11.5.2   Special defences

Schedule 1 to the CJA 1993 includes some special defences relating to market-makers, market information and price stabilisation.

11.5.2.1   Market-makers

A market-maker (see **2.5.2**) has a special defence to the dealing and encouraging offences (but not the disclosing offence) if he acts in good faith in the course of his business as, or employment by, a market-maker.

11.5.2.2   Market information

There are special defences available to those who have inside information which qualifies as 'market information'. Market information is information consisting of any of the following facts:

(a)   that securities of a particular kind have been, or are to be, acquired or disposed of, or that their acquisition is under consideration or the subject of negotiation;

(b)   the number or price (or range of prices) of those securities;

(c)   the identity of those involved, or likely to be involved, in any capacity in an acquisition or disposal; or

(d)   the fact that securities of a particular kind have not been, or are not to be, acquired or disposed of.

There are two separate defences available. In each case, the defences are only available to an individual charged with dealing and/or encouraging. They are not available in relation to the disclosing offence. The defences are:

(a)   The information which the individual had as an insider was *market information* and it was *reasonable* for a person in his position to have acted as he did, despite having that information as an insider at the time. Paragraph 2(2) of Sch 2 sets out a non-exhaustive list of factors to be taken into account in determining reasonableness (the content of information, the circumstances and the capacity in which the individual first had the information and the capacity in which he now acts).

(b)   The individual acted in connection with an acquisition or a disposal which was under consideration or the subject of negotiation (or in the course of a series of such acquisitions or disposals), and with a view to *facilitating the accomplishment* of the relevant transaction(s). The individual must also show that the information he had was *market information* arising directly out of his involvement in the transaction(s) in question. This is referred to as the 'facilitation defence'. Note that there is no reasonableness element for this defence.

It may help to consider an example of the 'market information' defence.

Example

Imagine that X plc is considering making a takeover bid for Y plc, a listed company. The directors of X plc decide that, as a preliminary to the bid, X plc should purchase shares in Y plc on the Stock Exchange. X plc's directors instruct the company's stockbrokers to buy shares in Y plc. Are the directors guilty of insider dealing?

At the time of dealing the directors are insiders. They have inside information (namely, that X plc is about to make a bid for Y plc). The directors have that information from an inside source (in their capacity as directors). They will know that they have inside information from an inside source. The directors are dealing in price-affected securities (remember that the definition of dealing includes the situation where a person procures an acquisition of securities by another, here X plc (see **11.3.1.1**)) on a regulated market (the Main Market). It would seem that they are guilty of insider dealing under s 52(1).

Nonetheless, in these circumstances, the directors may be able to rely on the market information defence if they can show they acted to facilitate the accomplishment of the takeover of Y plc, and the information they had was solely market information arising directly out of their involvement in the takeover, and not any other confidential price-sensitive information.

11.5.2.3   Price stabilisation

There is a special defence for individuals engaged in price stabilisation operations within any price stabilisation rules made under s 144(1) of the FSMA 2000. Price stabilisation is market activity undertaken to support the price of shares offered on an IPO (see **Chapter 4**) and some secondary issues (see **Chapter 17**), as there is often a disproportionately large amount of selling at these times. The defence is available as the practice is justified on policy grounds (that it encourages equity finance and shores up confidence in the market).

11.6   Sanctions

The offence of insider dealing is punishable in the same way as the criminal offence of making a misleading statement or manipulating the market (under the FSMA 2000 – see **9.4** above), namely by imprisonment and/or a fine. On summary conviction, the maximum sentence is six months, and on conviction on indictment the maximum sentence in seven years.

Note that s 63(2) provides that no contract shall be void or unenforceable solely because an offence has been committed under s 52.

Insider dealing may also amount to a breach of the Model Code (see **7.8** above).

The FSA has responsibility for enforcing the insider dealing provisions of the CJA 1993, and has the power to launch criminal prosecutions in its own right without the need for permission from the Secretary of State of BIS or the Director of Public Prosecutions. A challenge to this power in an action brought by three individuals who were prosecuted for insider dealing failed in the High Court in December 2008.

Net tightens on insider trading

Robert Verkaik

A series of insider dealing scams, involving corporate takeover deals worth millions of pounds have been uncovered in the biggest-ever crackdown on market abuse in the City by its regulator.

Dozens of corporate advisers and executives have already, or will be shortly, interviewed in six separate cases being investigated by the Financial Services Authority (FSA).

The investigations have been prompted by a high number of suspicious trading alerts that identified unusual movements in share prices of companies ahead of almost a third of all merger or takeover announcements.

The FSA has brought just one criminal case of insider dealing since its inception in 2001. But the new crackdown reflects concerns that traders and corporate advisers in the heart of the City have resorted to using confidential information to make illegal profits from mergers and acquisitions markets which have been hit by the recession.

Margaret Cole, head of enforcement at the FSA, the chief City regulator, told The Independent she wanted to send a message to the City that there were no hiding places for those who tried to profit by abusing the financial markets. In the first of the six cases, a man and a woman, one a senior corporate finance adviser, were arrested last week in connection with an ongoing investigation into suspected organised insider dealing.

Ms Cole said that three other cases were being prepared for court this year and three more were being investigated. As part of the latest investigation, search warrants were executed at a number of addresses in Greater London. The operation involved 25 FSA staff, assisted by 11 officers from the City of London Police.

Ms Cole said: "I know of at least three other investigations which we are close to commencing as criminal proceedings. And I know of

several other investigations which are being conducted on a criminal investigative basis." She added that decisions on the remaining cases would depend on what the evidence justified.

Ms Cole, a lawyer who worked for a leading US law firm before joining the FSA, said that according to the FSA's own research into suspicious transactions, insider dealing had "been going on for some time" which, she said, posed a "significant risk" to the City. In one of the cases being investigated, the FSA was given the names of 2,000 people who were or could have been privy to confidential market information.

Criminal prosecutions over insider dealing have had an unhappy history in the UK. The Serious Fraud Office and the Department of Trade and Industry were involved in a series of flawed cases until the responsibility for prosecuting was handed to the FSA in 2001. But the City regulator has fared little better, mounting just one case in almost eight years. That ended earlier this month in the first conviction for Ms Cole and her team.

In a significant breakthrough, a solicitor and his father-in-law were each sentenced to eight months in prison after being found guilty in the FSA's first insider dealing criminal case. The jury at Southwark Crown Court found that the lawyer, Christopher McQuoid, had passed inside information to his father-in-law, James Melbourne, who had traded on the back of it and made a £49,000 profit.

The FSA won a court order freezing the profits made from the trade, which McQuoid and his father-in-law had shared between them.

Ms Cole explained why she thought it had taken so long for a successful criminal prosecution: "You will remember cases where the SFO and DTI prosecuted insider dealing and didn't do very well with it. It was seen as a victimless

crime; it was seen as not doing any harm. It was extraordinarily complex and difficult to get juries to understand and convict on."

The FSA was given powers to prosecute insider trading through the civil courts but found that it was not particularly effective either. It has turned to pursuing criminal prosecutions instead.

Ms Cole said the impact of jailing a 40-year-old solicitor, with an otherwise clean record, would act as a deterrent to those who thought they could get away with trading on confidential information.

But critics argue that until a market professional is sent to prison for insider dealing it will not make a real difference to the attitude towards a crime that is perceived by some as just as a "perk" of working in the City.

"Clearly we do want to deal with market professionals where we find the evidence and clearly we will. I think this case was an important case. We also want to deter the people who do insider dealing on an opportunistic basis. We don't want anyone to think they are under our radar. It would be a mistake for people to think out there that if I do a little bit every now and again I will be OK."

FSA monitoring of the markets has uncovered unusual trading in 29 per cent of cases before takeover or merger announcements were made.

But Ms Cole said: "Don't correlate 29 per cent of movements with 29 per cent of market abuse. We see it as an [indicator] for what we have to look at. All unusual price movements get looked at. We have not seen a massive drop-off yet. We would hope that the work we are doing this year would start translating down the line. But I think we have got a good idea of what's going on - I don't think we are missing anything. We look at all kinds of things and take early views to decide which cases are the promising ones to take forward."

Source: *The Independent*, 6 April 2009

In the FSA's first-ever criminal prosecution for insider dealing in *R v McQuoid and Melbourne* in relation to TTP Communications plc, the two defendants, one a solicitor, were sentenced to eight months imprisonment (one suspended for 12 months) in March 2009. The second, *R v Calvert*, involves a former partner at Cazenove who is charged with 12 counts of insider dealing on the basis of information about planned takeovers. In the third case, *R v Matthew and Neel Uberoi*, the defendants were charged in September 2008 with 17 counts of insider dealing contrary to s 52 of the CJA 1993 in connection with the takeover of NeuTec Pharma plc.

Another prosecution, *R v Power and Carlisle*, started before the FSA got its powers of prosecution, was announced in August 2008 after years of investigations and involved all three offences under s 52 of the CJA 1993 in relation to the takeover of the Belgo Group plc. Mr Carlisle's case was dismissed. Mr Power was given an 18 month suspended prison sentence in March 2009.

The FSA announced in January 2009 that Neil Rollins has been charged with insider dealing and encouraging offences and money laundering offences in relation to the disposal of shares in PM group plc. In the fifth case to be brought by the FSA, Andrew King, a finance director, and Michael Mcfall and Andrew Rimmington, solicitors, were charged in June 2009 with eight counts of insider dealing for disclosing and dealing on the basis of inside information in relation to the proposed takeover of Neutec Pharma plc.

Ex-Belgo director avoids jail for insider trading

Michael Herman

Timothy Power, the former Belgo executive who last month pleaded guilty to insider dealing in shares of the restaurant group, has avoided jail after being given an 18 month suspended sentence.

Power, 43, who made guilty pleas on two counts of insider dealing, was sentenced to 18 months imprisonment suspended for two years at Southwark Crown Court this morning.

Judge James Wadsworth, QC, said: "The offences to which you pleaded guilty are serious because they are a grave breach of trust by someone at the centre of a company which is going to cause sensitive movement on the Stock Exchange and upon which other people are relying on for honesty and transparency, and you went deliberately behind it.

"Matters were made worse because you did it on two separate occasions in respect of two quite separate items of knowledge," the judge said.

The judge added that we was able to suspend Power's sentence because of the exceptional circumstances that the offences were committed 11 years ago and that Mr Power had spent 163 days in custody while awaiting trial.

Power was also disqualified from being a company director for six years.

Outside court, Power, who is "currently in negotiations with a business in Miami", said: "I am pleased it is all over."

Today's case was his third criminal conviction. In 2001 he was sentenced to 120 hours of community service for failing to register a personalised number plate, P9WER, on his £70,000 silver Ferrari 355 convertible.

The following year Power was given two years' jail at Leeds Crown Court for one count of theft and two of obtaining money transfers by deception.

Power pleaded guilty to passing inside information about Belgo to his friend Euan Carlisle, who was alleged to have made tens of thousands of pounds trading off the tips.

Mr Carlisle was tried in the same prosecution but last week a judge directed the jury to find him not guilty on all counts, saying that there was insufficient evidence to convict.

Source: *The Times*, 2 March 2009

Furthermore, in the course of ongoing investigations into major insider dealing rings by the FSA, a number of people have been arrested.

11.7   Scope of the offence

The offence of insider dealing is narrower in scope than the offence of market abuse (see **Chapter 10**). Unlike market abuse, only an individual can commit the offence of insider dealing; a company cannot (although an individual can commit the offence by requiring a company to deal). A company can, however, be convicted of aiding and abetting the offence. Anything done by an individual acting on behalf of a public sector body in pursuit of monetary policies, or policies with respect to exchange rates, the management of public debt or foreign reserves, cannot be the subject of an insider dealing offence.

As the offence is so narrow and subject to the criminal burden of proof and the vagaries of the jury system, it is notoriously difficult to convict anyone of it, and this explains the lack of prosecutions until 2008.

As one of the FSA's leading officials said in a speech on 22 May 2007 to leading financial institutions (available in the library section of the FSA's website):

Insider dealing cases are amongst the most difficult cases we are called upon to prove, they are time consuming and complex and we may not be able to establish all of the facts necessary to support an insider trading charge. Insider dealing may have been conducted by a number of defendants, involved multiple trades over a number of months and have been of a sophisticated nature. The trading may have been conducted through a number of accounts and attempts made to hide the distribution of proceeds. The investigation into such activities increasingly involves a number of foreign jurisdictions.

It is rare to find a 'smoking gun' and often cases hinge on circumstantial evidence. It is quite common for insider traders to come up with alternative rationales for their trading strategies that can be difficult to disprove. In the consultative document preceding the legislation, the Government stated it would be inappropriate to impose criminal penalties if the individual did not realise that the information he had was inside information. This is something which can be very difficult to establish, for example in the face of a defendant who states that he was simply fortunate in the timing of his dealing.

This was one of the reasons, of course, for the introduction of the market abuse regime. However, the FSA's newfound keenness to use the criminal provisions seems to be bearing fruit.

11.8   Future developments

Trials and further charges are expected in the coming year.

Chapter 12

Financial Promotion

12.1 Introduction

As **Chapter 9** stated, the regulation of financial promotion is one of the key features of the FSMA 2000. The main restriction on financial promotion is in s 21 of the Act, but there are two other important sources which provide further detail about the financial promotion regime.

The first is the Financial Services and Markets Act 2000 (Financial Promotion) Order 2005 (SI 2005/1529) ('FPO 2005'), as amended.

The second is Chapter 8 of a regulatory guide, the Perimeter Guidance manual ('PERG'), available in the FSA Handbook section of the FSA's website. The guidance is not legally binding, but may be persuasive.

The FSA's Conduct of Business Sourcebook ('COBS'), in particular Chapter 4, is also relevant, as it contains the rules for authorised persons on financial promotion.

The financial promotion regime is not confined to listed companies. The majority of the provisions referred to in this chapter are equally applicable to unlisted companies, other than the exemptions referred to in **12.9.2**, some of which apply to listed companies only.

12.2 Section 21 of the FSMA 2000

Section 21(1) provides that a person must not, in the course of business, communicate an invitation or inducement to engage in investment activity. This is referred to as the 's 21 restriction'; the criteria are explored in more detail at **12.7** below. Section 21(2) provides that s 21(1) does not apply if:

(a)   the person making the communication *is* an authorised person; or

(b)   the content of the communication *has been approved by* an authorised person.

Section 21(1) will also not apply if the communication is covered by an *exemption* (see **12.9**).

12.3 Consequences of breach

The consequences of a breach of s 21 of the FSMA 2000 are as follows:

(a)   it is a criminal offence punishable by a fine and/or imprisonment (a maximum of six months on summary conviction; two years on conviction on indictment) (s 25);

(b)   any agreement which results from a communication made in breach of s 21 may be unenforceable (s 30);

(c)   any third party to the unenforceable agreement can sue for any loss incurred (s 30);

(d)   there may be an order for an injunction or for restitution (ss 380, 382); and

(e)   there may be an action for damages (s 150).

The FSA has fined 13 firms more than £1.5 million in the last three years for failings that included breaches of the financial promotion rules. The FSA can also take lesser action, such as requiring the amendment or withdrawal of a promotion.

12.4   What is a financial promotion?

Before we proceed, it would be helpful to identify what a financial promotion actually is. The term 'financial promotion' can be confusing. It is the name of an entire regime, yet the term is not actually referred to in the FSMA 2000, other than in the heading and side note to s 21. There is certainly no definition of the term. It does not mean much to the layman, or indeed to the lawyer who has not encountered it before. So what is a 'financial promotion'? Well, consider it as a generic term to refer to a communication covered by s 21. In very basic layman's terms, it is a communication that contains information which might entice someone to invest in a company, or do certain other activities in relation to investments in that company.

The key point to note at this stage is that what amounts to a financial promotion may not be immediately obvious. Of course, some financial promotions should set off alarm bells immediately. Take, for example, the company secretary who calls to inform you that the company is about to place a newspaper advertisement, 'Need extra cash? Invest in us – we are doing really well'. Hopefully, even the most inexperienced lawyer would consider that this might fall foul of s 21. However, consider a company which is planning to run a television advertising campaign to raise its profile. You happen to know that the company is preparing an IPO within the next month. The TV advertising campaign does not mention this at all. Would s 21 spring to mind? Would the company even consider bringing the existence of the campaign to the notice of its lawyers? Perhaps not, but it should, as in the context of the impending IPO, the advertisements might well fall within s 21.

Even advertising on the carrier bags used by sandwich shops for a spread-betting company has been held to be a financial promotion.

Its importance is reflected by the fact that in the first half of 2008 alone approximately £545 million was spent by financial services companies across all media.

12.5   Relevance in practice

In practice, the rules relating to financial promotion mean that, if a client company is proposing to make a communication, the lawyer must check whether that communication will fall within s 21 of the FSMA 2000. If it does then this is not good, for the reasons set out at **12.3** above. The lawyer must advise the client that it needs to ensure that the communication falls outside s 21. The easiest way to do this is to instruct an authorised person (see **9.4.3**) to approve the communication before it is made (see **12.2** above). Sometimes it is not possible for an authorised person to approve the communication (see **12.9.1.1** below), and in such circumstances the lawyer must advise the client not to make the communication at all, or to change it to a form which can be approved. This approach is summarised by the flowchart in **Figure 12.1** below.

To put this into context, it is important for a lawyer advising a listed company to be alert to the types of communication that company might make, and to analyse whether these communications might fall within s 21. For example, if a company is raising funds, as considered in **Chapter 17**, then the company will publish a prospectus, perhaps a preliminary prospectus or a pathfinder document (see **6.9.3**), and a press announcement. If the company is effecting a takeover, as considered in **Chapters 20, 21** and **22**, then the company may seek irrevocable undertakings and will make a r 2.5 announcement, circulate an offer document and announce levels of acceptance. The lawyers must advise as to whether these communications fall within the s 21 restriction or not, and the consequences of this. This advice will depend on the individual circumstances of the communication (which may affect, for example, whether an exemption applies).

Figure 12.1: Financial promotion flowchart

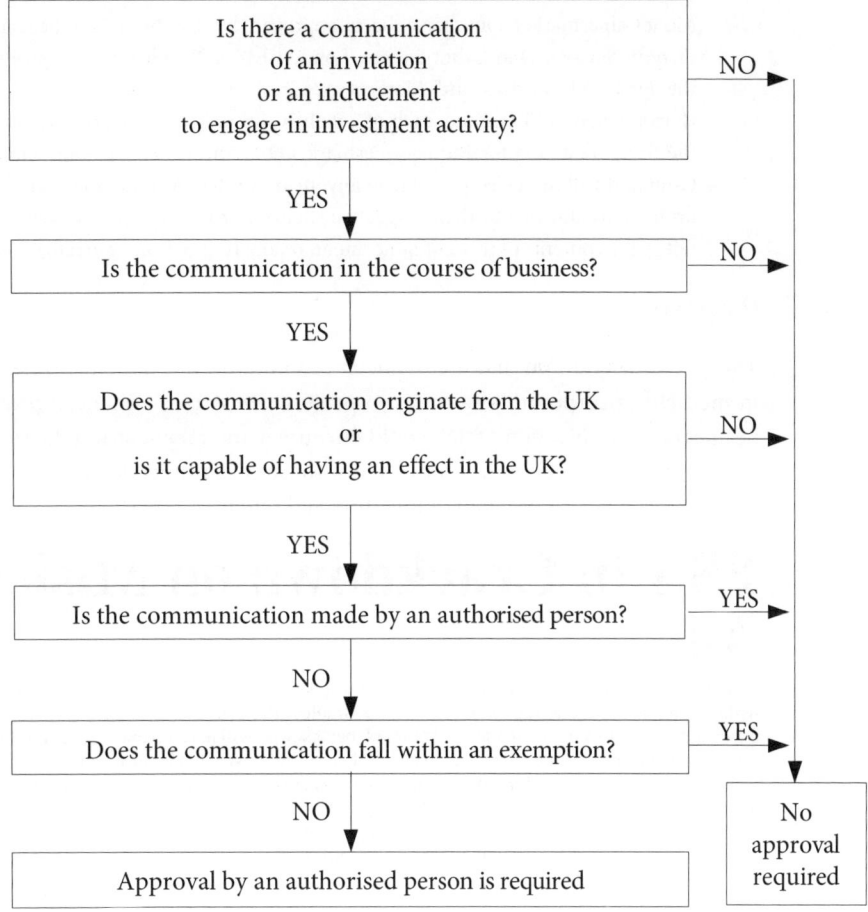

12.5.1   Example

Below is an extract from moneysupermarket.com's announcement of its IPO.

Not for release, distribution or publication into or in directly or indirectly the United States, Australia, Canada or Japan

This announcement is an advertisement and not a prospectus and investors should not subscribe for or purchase any ordinary shares ('Ordinary Shares') referred to in this announcement except on the basis of information in the prospectus to be published by Moneysupermarket.com Group Limited ('Moneysupermarket.com' or the 'Company') in due course following its intended re-registration as a public limited company and change of name to Moneysupermarket.com Group PLC (the 'Prospectus') in connection with the admission of its Ordinary Shares to the Official List of the Financial Services Authority (the 'FSA') and to trading on London Stock Exchange plc's main market for listed securities. Once published, copies of the Prospectus will be available from the Company's registered office at Moneysupermarket.com House, Saint David's Park, Ewloe, Chester CH5 3UZ.

29 June 2007

Moneysupermarket.com Group Limited

Intention to seek admission to trading on London Stock Exchange plc

Moneysupermarket.com Group Limited today announces its intention to proceed with an initial public offering ('IPO') of its Ordinary Shares, which are intended to be admitted to the Official List of the FSA and to trading on London Stock Exchange plc's main market for listed securities. Headquartered in Ewloe, Moneysupermarket.com is the UK's leading finance price comparison website and a leading UK travel price comparison website.

. . .

Important Notice

The contents of this announcement, which have been prepared and are the sole responsibility of Moneysupermarket.com, have been approved by Credit Suisse Securities (Europe) Limited ('Credit Suisse'), One Cabot Square, London E14 4QJ, solely for purposes of section 21(2)(b) of the Financial Services and Markets Act 2000. Credit Suisse, Lehman Brothers International (Europe) and UBS Limited, each of which is authorised and regulated in the United Kingdom by the FSA, are acting for Moneysupermarket.com and no one else in connection with the Global Offer and will not be responsible to anyone other than Moneysupermarket.com for providing the protections afforded to their respective clients, nor for providing advice in relation to the Global Offer, the contents of this announcement, or any transaction or arrangement referred to herein.

12.6 Purpose

The s 21 restriction on making financial promotions, like so many other statutory provisions in the field of corporate finance, is to protect investors. A financial promotion is basically a business communication which could encourage the recipient to take some action in relation to an investment. Section 21 controls how those communications are made and what they say, so that advantage is not taken of investors and potential investors.

FSA in Crackdown on Misleading Ads

JAMES DALEY

THE FSA, the City watchdog, yesterday announced a crackdown on misleading advertising by financial services companies, launching a whistle-blowing hotline and creating a 30-strong department to police financial marketing material.

The move comes after a year that has seen a record number of complaints concerning financial adverts, with almost 600 cases relating to more than 350 firms. Several of the complaints have already led to the Financial Services Authority asking for adverts to be withdrawn or amended, whilst Chase de Vere was fined £165,000 last December for misleading marketing literature concerning "precipice" bonds.

Anna Bradley, the FSA's director of retail themes, who will head up the new division, said: "We hope that firms will make use of the new hotline, as well as consumers. Consumers can pay a heavy price when they buy a financial product as a result of a misleading advert. But the industry also pays a heavy price when their reputation is damaged."

The FSA also revealed yesterday that it had written to the chief executives of companies that sell investments for children, warning them to be especially careful of how they promote the products. It said firms should be very careful to warn of the risks if savings products are linked to the stock market, and should not refer to products as "safe" or "secure" if there was any risk to capital.

It said: "Many consumers may not see the difference between the savings plans' referred to in these promotions, which include an equity-linked element, and safer methods of saving such as regular deposit accounts ... Financial promotions should provide adequate information, which the target audience is able to understand."

The FSA's hotline number is 08457 300168.

Source: *Independent*, 7 July 2004

12.7 The detail of s 21

The following paragraphs consider some of the detail of the s 21 restriction and the exemptions from it. The FSA has provided a lot of guidance on the interpretation of the restriction and the main exemptions in PERG. This does not bind the courts, but it may be persuasive.

12.7.1 Person

'Person' includes a corporate entity such as a company.

12.7.2   Course of business

Section 21(4) of the FSMA 2000 gives the Treasury the power to define this term, but to date it has not done so. This requirement excludes from the ambit of s 21 communications of a personal nature. So, if tonight in the pub I mention that I am going to buy a few shares in company X, and suggest that my friends do the same, my suggestion will not be caught by the s 21 restriction; the communication would not have a commercial nature. Further guidance is provided by PERG 8.5.

12.7.3   Communication

'Communication' means all communication, through whatever medium, so it includes oral and written communication as well as electronic communication (for example, a website announcement). 'Communicate' includes causing a communication to be made (FSMA 2000, s 21(13)). This means that if a company makes an announcement through, for example, financial PRs, and the announcement is in breach of s 21, then, subject to any exemptions which apply, not only the company but also the financial PRs would be responsible for the communication, and therefore caught by the s 21 restriction. PERG 8.6.3 sets out categories of persons whom the FSA does not consider will communicate or cause a communication to be made.

12.7.4   Invitation or inducement

Neither term is defined by the FSMA 2000. 'Invitation' will catch direct invitations to engage in investment activity, such as an invitation to buy shares. It can range from a polite request to an encouragement. A prospectus, together with an application form (see **Chapter 6**) would constitute an invitation to buy shares. 'Inducement' is thought to be wider. The Treasury stated that the term is intended to catch any communication which contains a degree of incitement to engage in an investment activity and that a communication of purely factual information would not amount to an inducement. It is unclear how wide this could be: what if a company embarks on a marketing campaign to raise its profile? It is possible that this could amount to an inducement if it contains any incitement to invest in that company. If the campaign involves putting the company's name onto a few umbrellas, then it would probably not amount to an inducement. PERG 8.4 provides further guidance.

12.7.5   Engaging in investment activity

Section 21(8) and (9) of the FSMA 2000, together with art 4 of and Sch 1 to the FPO 2005, define 'engaging in investment activity' as:

(a)   entering into an agreement which constitutes a 'controlled activity' (such as buying, selling and underwriting shares; see Pt I of Sch 1 to the FPO 2005); and

(b)   exercising any rights conferred by a 'controlled investment' (such as shares and bonds; see Pt II of Sch 1 to the FPO 2005) to buy, sell, underwrite or convert that investment.

This definition could affect how a company chooses to structure transactions. For example, while share sales constitute 'investment activity', asset sales do not.

12.8   Territorial scope

The s 21 restriction will apply to any communication which is:

(a)   made from the UK; or

(b)   made from overseas, but is capable of having an effect in the UK (s 21(3)).

(However there are exemptions, under art 12 of the FPO 2005, for certain communications which are made to a recipient who receives the communication outside the UK, or which is directed only at persons outside the UK.)

Additional guidance is to be found in COBS 4.

12.9   Exemptions

As the s 21 restriction is so wide, to counterbalance this, the FPO 2005 contains over 65 exemptions from the restriction. Remember that while approval by an authorised person brings the communication outside the scope of s 21, it is not an exemption. If an exemption applies, there is no requirement for the communication to be approved by an authorised person.

The exemptions do contain some new terminology, however. The application of certain exemptions depends on the nature of the communication, in particular whether it is 'real time' or 'non real time' and, if real time, whether it is 'solicited' or 'unsolicited'. The meaning of these terms is explained at **12.9.1** below.

The s 21 restriction applies to both listed and unlisted companies. Nevertheless, there are some very useful exemptions which apply to listed companies only. The exemptions are detailed in, and in practice recourse must be made to, the relevant article of the FPO 2005 and PERG. However, the exemptions of particular use to listed companies are summarised at **12.9.2** below.

12.9.1   Terminology

In **12.9.1.1** and **12.9.1.2** below, references to 'art' are references to articles of the FPO 2005.

12.9.1.1   Real time and non-real time communications (art 7)

A real time communication is any communication made in the course of a personal visit, telephone conversation or other interactive dialogue. A non-real time communication is any communication which is not a real time communication. Examples include letters, e-mails and newspaper announcements. Article 7(5) contains a list of indicators that the communication is 'non-real time'.

The reason that the exemptions distinguish real time communications from non-real time communications is that the FSA considers that investors require more protection from real time communications (because people can get carried away in interactive dialogue and there is less opportunity for a cooling-off period). The exemptions which apply to real time communications therefore are narrower in scope than those exemptions which apply to non-real time communications. In fact, it is not possible for even an authorised person to approve real time communications, so care must be taken to ensure that any real time communication does fall within the scope of an exemption.

Further guidance on this issue is provided by PERG 8.10.

12.9.1.2   Solicited and unsolicited real time communications (art 8)

A solicited real time communication is a real time communication which has been initiated by the recipient, or which has been made in response to a request from the recipient. An unsolicited real time communication is a real time communication which is not a solicited communication.

12.9.2   Exemptions useful to listed companies

In **12.9.2.1** to **12.9.2.9** below, references to 'art' are references to articles of the FPO 2005.

12.9.2.1   Communications to shareholders and creditors (art 43)

The s 21 restriction does not apply to non-real time or solicited real time communications made by, or on behalf of, a company to, or directed at, its shareholders, provided that the communication does not relate to an investment (for example, shares) issued, or to be issued, outside the company's group. (However, any individual who sends such a communication, for example the chairman, may be at risk of breaching s 19 of the FSMA 2000; see **9.4**.)

12.9.2.2   Group companies (art 45)

The s 21 restriction will not apply to any communication between a company and any of its group companies.

12.9.2.3   Annual report and accounts (art 59)

The s 21 restriction will not apply to the distribution by a company of its annual report and accounts, provided it meets certain criteria, such as not including any invitation or advice to persons to buy, sell, underwrite or subscribe for any investments.

12.9.2.4   Employee share schemes (art 60)

The s 21 restriction will not apply to any communications by the company, or its group companies or trustees, which are for the purpose of any employee share scheme (see **13.9**).

12.9.2.5   Sale of body corporate (art 62)

This is subject to certain conditions. The intention of this exemption seems to be to enable controlling shareholders of small companies to buy and sell those companies without being caught by the s 21 restriction. However, as drafted, the scope of this exemption is not clear. If read literally, this exemption would apply to takeovers of public companies, which many consider cannot have been intended. The Treasury recognised this issue and, during 2004, drafted proposals to narrow the exemption. It was expected that the exemption would be amended when the FPO 2005 replaced the previous Financial Promotion Order. However, surprisingly, no changes were made, and the Treasury has not clarified why it has not implemented its proposals.

12.9.2.6   Other communications by listed companies (art 69)

The s 21 restriction will not apply to some communications made by listed companies, provided that certain criteria are met.

12.9.2.7   Promotions included in listing particulars, etc (art 70)

The s 21 restriction will not apply to any non-real time communication in a prospectus or supplementary prospectus which has been approved in accordance with the Prospectus Rules, or to any other document required or permitted to be published by the Listing Rules or the Prospectus Rules (except an advertisement within the meaning of the Prospectus Directive). This is because it is presumed that the FSA will provide sufficient protection to investors in these rules, so protection under the financial promotion regime is unnecessary.

The FSA considers that 'permitted' means something which is expressly permitted rather than simply not expressly prohibited (PERG 8.21.14G).

12.9.2.8   Material relating to prospectus for public offer of unlisted securities (art 71)

The s 21 restriction will not apply to any non-real time communication relating to a prospectus or supplementary prospectus, in the circumstances set out in art 71.

12.9.2.9   Investment professionals (art 19), certified high net worth individuals (art 48), high net worth companies (art 49) and certified and self-certified sophisticated investors (arts 50 and 50A)

Section 21 will not apply to communications made to the above-mentioned recipients. This can be useful to a company seeking to raise funds; by targeting these recipients only, the communication will be exempt from the s 21 restriction. There is the problem, of course, of how a company would know that the high net worth individuals and sophisticated investors it targets are certified.

Note that arts 48 and 50A apply only to communications relating to investments in *unlisted* companies.

12.10 Conclusion

Section 21 of the FSMA 2000 is very wide in its application. It covers most of the communications a listed company would make in its day-to-day corporate and trading activities. The exemptions, and the ability of authorised persons to approve non-real time communications, narrow the scope of the s 21 restriction. The exemptions are drafted with the rationale of s 21 in mind (see **12.6** above), namely investor protection. The more inexperienced the recipient, the more likely it is that the exemptions will not apply, and that s 21 will either prohibit the communication, or ensure that the communication is approved by an authorised person, in order to protect that recipient.

Part III
EQUITY FINANCE

Chapter 13
Shares

13.1 Introduction

Shares are not unique to listed companies, or even to public companies. Most companies have limited liability. Most companies with limited liability have a share capital, and are limited by shares rather than by guarantee. So why dedicate a whole chapter of this book to shares? Well, any corporate finance lawyer needs to have a sound understanding of the basic law relating to share capital. **Chapter 1** established that the principal reason most companies choose to float is to take advantage of the opportunities afforded by the market to raise funds, both on an IPO (considered in **Chapters 4, 5** and **6**) and once listed (considered in **Chapter 17**). **Chapter 1** also set out the requirements that a company's share capital has to meet before the company can re-register as a public company. **Chapter 4** explained that the company's share capital has to meet further requirements before the company can seek an IPO. **Part IV** of this book also explains that listed companies often use their share capital as consideration when entering into various transactions, such as acquisitions or takeovers of other companies.

So listed companies are always making changes to their share capital. It is the lawyer's job to make sure they do so in a way permitted by law. **Chapters 13** to **16** explore the law relating to the share capital of a company, with particular focus on the law relating to listed companies.

13.2 What is a share?

A share represents ownership of a company. A person who owns a share owns a bundle of rights in the company, such as the right to receive a dividend and, maybe, the right to vote. This person is referred to as a 'member', or 'shareholder', of that company. This book uses the term 'shareholder', but 'member' means exactly the same thing. The term 'investor' may be used to describe someone who has invested cash in return for shares in a company, but it could also be used to describe someone who has provided a loan to the company. In the former scenario, the investor will be a shareholder; in the latter, she will not.

13.3 Some terms relating to share capital

13.3.1 Nominal value (also known as par value)

Shares must have a fixed nominal value (CA 2006, s 542). A company can have shares with a nominal value of 1p ('1p shares'), 10p ('10p shares') £1 ('£1 shares') – in fact, shares of any nominal value, although the nominal value should not be too high, as, under s 580 of the CA 2006, a company cannot issue a share at a discount to (that is, for any less than) its nominal value. This means, for example, that a company could not issue a £1 share for 80p. If it wanted to issue the share for 80p, the nominal value of that share would have to be equal to or less than 80p.

As stated at **13.3.3** below, the company's memorandum of association must state the nominal value of the company's authorised share value. Note that the nominal value will usually bear no correlation to the current market value of the share (see **13.3.5**). Most shares will be sold at a premium (see **13.3.2**). A share with a nominal value of £1 (a £1 share) could be worth, say, £5 when sold on the market.

13.3.2   Premium

A premium is the difference between the nominal value of the share and the price paid for that share. For example, if I pay £5 for a share which has a nominal value of £1, I have paid £1 nominal value and a premium of £4.

13.3.3   Restrictions on share capital

Under the CA 2006 a company may restrict the number of shares that it can issue by including a provision in the company's articles of association.

Companies formed before 1 October 2009, before the relevant provisions of the CA 2006 came into force, had restrictions on the number of shares they could issue in their pre-CA 2006 memorandum of association (the authorised share capital). Under s 28 of the CA 2006 these provisions are automatically treated as restrictions in the articles with effect from 1 October 2009. The restrictions can be removed by passing an ordinary resolution or by adopting new articles by special resolution with no limit on the issue of shares or authorising the directors to issue shares in excess of the current limit.

Remember that there is a minimum authorised share capital requirement for a public company of at least £50,000 or its euro equivalent (see **1.9.2** and **1.9.3.2** above).

13.3.4   Issued share capital

This is the total nominal value of the shares a company has in issue. It may be equal to the authorised share capital (if all authorised shares are in issue), or less than the authorised share capital (if not all authorised shares are in issue), but it cannot be more than the authorised share capital. Take the example of X plc at **13.3.3** above. If X plc has 75,000 shareholders, who each hold 10 shares of £1 each, then the issued share capital of X plc is £750,000. This means that there are 250,000 shares of £1 each which are authorised but unissued. It may help to think of authorised share capital as a pool of shares from which the company may issue shares. When all the shares in this pool have been issued, the pool must be replenished before the company can issue any further shares. **Chapter 14** considers this process further.

Remember that there is a minimum issued share capital requirement of £50,000 for a public company which is trading (see **1.9.2.2** and **1.9.3.2** above).

13.3.5   Market value

The market value is the price that investors are willing to pay for a share on the market. It usually bears no correlation to the nominal value of the share (see **13.3.1**). By way of example, the ordinary shares in J Sainsbury plc, the supermarket chain, have a nominal value of 28.57p. On 17 September 2009, the closing market value on the Main Market was 334.60p. Market-makers (see **2.5.2**) will set a price at which they are willing to buy shares and a price at which they are willing to sell shares. The market value of shares which are quoted in the newspaper is, in fact, a middle price between these two prices.

13.3.6   Market capitalisation

Market capitalisation is one method of valuing a company. It represents the market value of the company's issued share capital. It is calculated as follows:

number of issued shares × current market value of each share

J. Sainsbury plc had a market capitalisation of (ie was worth) £5,850,736,491 (1,748,576,357 issued shares × 334.60p) at the close of trading on 17 September 2009 (which represented a 40% drop from two years previously).

13.3.7 Fully, nil or part paid

A share is 'fully paid' when the shareholder has paid the company the nominal value of the share together with any premium payable on it. If the shareholder has paid nothing in this regard, the share is 'nil paid'. If the shareholder has made a payment towards this, but has not paid the full amount, the share is 'part paid'.

Remember that there are specific requirements as to the amount which must be paid up on any share if the company is a public company. Each share (other than a share allotted pursuant to an employee share scheme – see **13.9**) must be paid up at least as to one-quarter of its nominal value together with the whole of any premium paid on it (see **1.9.2.2** and **1.9.3.2** above).

13.4 What benefits does a share have?

The share has a number of benefits.

13.4.1 Limited liability

Any shareholder is liable to pay the company the amount due on the share. Once the share is fully paid, the shareholder (together with any person to whom the shareholder transfers that share) will have no further liability to the company. Even if the share is nil paid or part paid (see **13.3.7** above), the shareholder will have liability only up to the balance due on the share.

Why is this relevant? Well, imagine that Marks & Spencer Group plc goes bust tomorrow. I have 100 shares of 25p (nominal value) in the company, for which I paid £270. I am a humble lecturer (from the corporate lawyer's viewpoint) living on the breadline. Should I be worried? Might I have to stand behind the company's debt and help to satisfy all those unpaid suppliers of ladies underwear? No, because my shares limit my liability to the company and to any liquidator of the company. In paying the amount due on the shares, I discharged my liability in full. The only issues that may concern me are that I might have lost some or all of the £270 I paid for my shares (see **13.5.2.3**) and I have lost the potential for further capital growth.

13.4.2 Rights

A share will convey various rights on the shareholder. The rights may be set out in the company's memorandum of association (but this is rare), or in a special resolution, but usually they are set out in the company's articles of association, under the following headings (or similar):

(a) *Income rights.* This is the right to share in the profits of the company, through the right to a dividend.

(b) *The right to receive notice of, attend and vote at meetings.* The right which gives the shareholder the most power is the right to vote.

(c) *Capital rights.* This is the right to share in the capital of a company, on a winding up, after payment of the company's debts. This may be a right to be repaid the capital paid up on the shares (that is, the nominal value and any premium paid for the shares), or an additional right to share in any surplus assets once the amount paid up on all classes of shares has been repaid.

13.4.3 Capital growth

Many investors are attracted to shares because of the opportunity they afford for capital growth. A shareholder will buy shares on the Main Market at a certain price. The price of those shares is likely to change throughout the period the shareholder owns the shares. The shareholder's original investment will rise or fall in value. The shareholder therefore takes the risk of capital gains or losses. Investors hope, of course, that they will be able to weather any storms and sell when their investment has increased in value. The reality, of course, can be very different. Some will remember (and the author's wallet can testify to this) the dotcom 'boom and bust' in the late 1990s, when shareholders who bought shares in dotcom businesses early enough became millionaires overnight. Some of these shareholders had the good sense (or luck?) to sell some shares and bank the profit, but others lost considerable amounts when the dotcom bubble burst in 2000.

Since the summer of 2007, dramatic uncertainty has returned to the world's stock markets. Wild surges in share prices are being caused by the global financial crisis brought on by the collapse in the housing market in the US. At the time of writing, there has been a dramatic recovery in stock markets, with the FTSE 100 Index of the London Stock Exchange's leading companies having risen 50% from its low in the current crisis in March 2009 of 3,500 points.

13.5   Classes of share

Often the company will want to create different types of share, with different rights attaching to each type. The company may, for example, be pre-IPO, and want to attract a venture capital company to invest, in return for shares. Usually, the venture capital company will be in a position to demand enhanced rights over the other ordinary shareholders. Alternatively, perhaps the company wants to reward its loyal employees for their commitment, or the original owners who built up the company, with some shares, but does not want to give them the power to vote, which ordinary shares would convey. The company will create a separate class of shares to issue to the venture capital company, or to its employees. Again, the company's articles will detail the rights attached to each class of share, using the headings set out at **13.4.2** above. The lawyer may well have to draft these rights, and they can be quite complex.

The common classes of shares are discussed below. Note, however, that it is impossible to list all the classes you are ever likely to encounter. That is another advantage of the share; there is an infinite number of permutations. Take care, however, not to presume anything from the name of the class of share; always check the articles for the specific rights, and any restrictions, which attach to a share.

13.5.1   Ordinary shares

Ordinary shares are the most common class of share. Usually listed companies will list their ordinary shares. They may, however, choose not to list other classes of share. Remember that if a company chooses to list a class of shares, it must list all the shares in that class (see **4.3.1.1** above). It is Marks & Spencer Group plc's ordinary shares of 25p that you or I are able to buy on the Main Market.

Typical rights attaching to ordinary shares are examined at **13.5.1.1** to **13.5.1.3** below.

13.5.1.1   Income rights

The holders of other classes of shares might be entitled to a preferential dividend payment before the ordinary shareholders (see **13.5.2.1** below), but usually any profits to be paid out over and above that preferential dividend will be paid entirely to the ordinary shareholders. Shares which carry this unlimited right to income are referred to as equity shares (to draw an analogy with a law firm, equity shareholders are like equity partners; they have an unlimited, but proportionate, right to share in profits). Note, however, that the company is not obliged to declare a dividend. It may not declare one if it has not had a profitable year and there are insufficient profits available for distribution (see **18.2.1**).

13.5.1.2 The right to receive notice of, attend and vote at meetings

The ordinary shareholders are usually entitled to receive notice of, attend and vote at company meetings. Occasionally, however, non-voting ordinary shares are created, for example to raise capital without diluting control of the company. Usually, other classes of share will not afford the right to vote save in very limited circumstances.

13.5.1.3 Capital rights

On a winding up of the company, the company's assets are used, first, in paying off the company's liabilities, then in repaying the capital (that is, the amount paid up) on all the classes of shares other than ordinary shares. Only then will the ordinary shareholders be repaid the amount paid up on their shares. However, if there are any surplus assets once all these payments have been made, they will usually be distributed between the ordinary shareholders.

13.5.2 Preference shares

A preference share is any share which has preferential rights over other classes of share, particular ordinary shares. A company may have more than one class of preference shares, for example it may have 'A' preference shares, with one set of rights, and 'B' preference shares, with another set of rights. Again, the company's articles will list the rights which attach to the shares.

Often, as stated in **13.5** above, preference shares are tailor-made for a particular scenario and with particular preference shareholders in mind. The bargaining position of these shareholders might dictate the rights which attach to the shares. If preference shares are being created as a 'freebie' reward, the company will have a free hand in drafting the rights. However, if the company is keen to bring on board a venture capital company, that venture capital company might well be demanding as to the share rights it obtains in return for its cash injection into the company.

Typical rights which may attach to preference shares are examined at **13.5.2.1** to **13.5.2.3** below.

13.5.2.1 Income rights

Preferential dividend

The holders of preference shares might be entitled to a fixed preferential dividend payment from distributable profits before the ordinary shareholders are entitled to their dividend (see **3.5.1.1** above). This is often expressed as a percentage of the nominal value of the share. For example, a '5% preference share' will entitle a preference shareholder, on the declaration of a dividend, to a fixed payment of 5% of the nominal value of his shareholding before any dividend is paid to ordinary shareholders. To continue the analogy with a law firm from **13.5.1.1** above, preference shareholders are like salaried partners; they have a limited right to share in profits.

If the company does not declare a dividend then, subject to any cumulative rights (see below), the shareholders are not entitled to a dividend payment.

Cumulative right to a dividend

Unless the articles expressly state to the contrary, all preference shares will be 'cumulative'. Usually the articles state expressly that preference shares are cumulative. This means that if the company does not declare a dividend, or if it declares a dividend so small that the preference shareholders do not receive their full dividend, then the dividend (or the shortfall, as the case may be) will be carried forward to the next year automatically; and if there is no dividend that year, it will be carried forward to the following year, and so on.

> ## Example
>
> Imagine that X plc has an issued share capital of £100m, divided into 90 million ordinary shares of £1 each and 10 million cumulative 5% preference shares of £1 each. This means that in any year in which a dividend is declared, the first £500,000 (5% of £10 million, the nominal value of the shares) is payable to the preference shareholders. Any excess is payable to the ordinary shareholders. The table below shows the dividend payments over a five-year period.
>
> | Year | Total dividend | Preference dividend | Ordinary dividend | Preference entitlement carried forward to following year |
> |------|----------------|---------------------|-------------------|--|
> | 1 | £900,000 | £500,000 | £400,000 | Nil |
> | 2 | £400,000 | £400,000 | Nil | £100,000 |
> | 3 | £550,000 | £550,000 | Nil | £50,000 |
> | 4 | Nil | Nil | Nil | £550,000 |
> | 5 | £1,200,000 | £1,050,000 | £150,000 | Nil |
>
> In year 3, although a total dividend of £550,000 is declared, the ordinary shareholders do not receive £50,000. Instead, that is also paid to the preference shareholders, to make up some (but not all) of the £100,000 arrears carried forward from year 2. The rest of the shortfall (£50,000) is not paid to the preference shareholders in year 4; no dividend at all was declared then. Instead, it, together with the arrears of £500,000 from year 4, is made up in year 5, and there is even some left for the ordinary shareholders this year.

Dividend on a winding up

When preference shares are cumulative, the articles should make clear whether any arrears of the preference dividend are payable to the preference shareholders on a winding up of the company. For example, in the example used above, if X plc was wound up in year 4, the articles should clarify whether the £550,000 arrears would be payable to the preference shareholders.

Participating preference shares

Participating preference shares have further rights to a dividend, not just a preferential right to a fixed amount before the ordinary shareholders. Participating preference shares can be cumulative, but they do not have to be. Take again the example above. You can see that once the preference shareholders have taken their 5% dividend, the remainder goes to the ordinary shareholders in their entirety. Take year 5. The remaining £150,000 is paid to the ordinary shareholders. If the preference shares had been participating preference shares, the preference shareholders would have had some right to part of this amount. In other words, they get a second bite at the dividend cherry. The articles will provide what that right is, but it could be, for example, that the ordinary shareholders also take a fixed percentage, then the balance is divided equally between the preference shareholders and the ordinary shareholders. Participating preference shares may also have further rights to capital (see **13.5.2.3** below).

13.5.2.2   The right to receive notice of, attend and vote at meetings

Usually, preference shares will give preference shareholders the right to receive notice of general meetings and to attend meetings. However, they will seldom give preference shareholders the right to vote, other than in relation to certain limited matters, such as on a resolution to wind up the company, or to vary the rights which attach to the preference shares.

13.5.2.3   Capital rights

Just because a preference shareholder has a preferential right to a dividend does not necessarily mean that he will have a preferential right on a return of capital, and vice versa. Often in practice, however, preference shareholders do have preferential rights as to capital. It may be that once the company has repaid its debts, the preference shareholders are repaid their capital before the ordinary shareholders. If there are any surplus assets remaining after even the ordinary shareholders have been repaid, then the preference shareholders may have some rights over the surplus, for example to divide it between themselves and the ordinary shareholders. In this case the preference shares would be participating preference shares. Unless there is an express provision to the contrary, however, this surplus will belong to the ordinary shareholders alone.

13.5.3 Redeemable shares

13.5.3.1 Creation

Under s 684 of the CA 2006, a company can issue shares which will, or may, be redeemed at the option of the company or the shareholder, if the company has in issue other shares which are not redeemable.

For a public company only, the company must be authorised to do this by its articles of association. A private company may include a provision in its articles excluding or restricting its ability to issue redeemable shares.

A company may find it useful to issue redeemable shares if, for example, a venture capital company wishes to invest in the company for a fixed period of time. Any lawyer drafting redeemable share rights should pay particular attention to s 685 of the CA 2006, which provides some guidelines as to the terms and manner of redemption which must be dealt with on creation of the shares.

13.5.3.2 Redemption

The general rule under s 687(2) of the CA 2006 is that redeemable shares can be redeemed only out of either:

(a)   distributable profits of the company; or

(b)   the proceeds of a fresh issue of shares made for the purpose of the redemption.

Any premium payable to redeemable shareholders on redemption must be paid out of distributable profits rather than capital (but see s 687(4) of the CA 2006, which provides that any premium payable in relation to redeemable shares which were issued at a premium may be made out of the proceeds of a fresh issue of shares, up to a certain amount). There is, however, an exception for private companies, which can redeem out of capital, subject to any restrictions in the articles of association and provided the company adopts the procedure in Chapter 5 of the CA 2006 to effect the redemption (s 687(1)). *Business Law and Practice* considers further the law relating to the redemption of redeemable shares.

13.5.3.3 The effect of redemption

Pursuant to s 688 of the CA 2006, the effect of redemption is that the shares are treated as cancelled. This means that the issued share capital of the company will be reduced by the nominal value of the shares redeemed.

13.5.4 Convertible shares

A company may issue convertible shares, which, as their name suggests, can be converted into ordinary shares. The conversion may be at a specified time, or may be triggered by the happening of some event (eg, an IPO). The attractions to a convertible shareholder of converting to ordinary shares may be the acquisition of voting rights, or the fact that the market value of the ordinary shares has risen above the conversion price of the convertible shares.

13.5.5 Bonus shares (also known as 'scrip' or 'scrip issues')

If its articles permit, a company can transfer profits to a fund called its 'capital redemption reserve' and use it to issue 'bonus' shares to the shareholders in proportion to their existing shareholdings. Since the issue may reduce the amount of money available for paying dividends, the term 'bonus' is not really appropriate. The correct term is 'capitalisation of reserves' (or 'capitalisation issue'), but the terms 'scrip', or 'scrip issues' are also used to describe such shares.

13.5.6   Subscriber shares

The memorandum will show the names of the people who agreed to own shares when the company was first registered. These people are called the subscribers, and the shares which were allotted to them on the company's registration are referred to as subscriber shares (see CA 2006, s 8(1)). Section 584 of the CA 2006 provides that in a public company the subscriber shares must be paid up in cash.

13.5.7   Summary

You will now appreciate that, usually, ordinary shares bear the greatest financial risk, because, unlike preference shares, typically they do not afford any prior right to a dividend or return of capital. It is because ordinary shareholders bear this risk that, generally, they also are afforded full voting rights. However, ordinary shares also carry the greatest potential for financial gain, because the rights they do afford in relation to income and capital tend to be unlimited, unlike preference shares, which often afford fixed rights to income and capital.

13.6   Shares or debt?

This book is concerned with equity finance. There is another book in the series which deals with debt finance (see *Banking and Capital Markets*). **Chapter 18** of this book provides an overview of the difference between equity and debt finance.

Some classes of share, which are equity finance, can easily be confused with debt finance. Take, for example, a 5% cumulative redeemable preference share. It will yield a return (the 5% fixed dividend), like interest on a loan, and it is redeemable, so repayable, like a loan. However, a closer inspection reveals that preference shares are in fact equity finance, not debt finance, for the following reasons:

(a)   The 5% return is a dividend, not interest. It will therefore have different tax consequences. It will not be a deductible expense in the calculation of the taxable profits of the company.

(b)   There is no guaranteed right to a dividend. The company will pay a dividend only to the extent that distributable profits are available for that purpose. The cumulative nature of preference shares does not alter this fact, as it is a benefit only if there are distributable profits in the future which are sufficient to cover the arrears of the preference dividend (or if the preference shareholder is afforded a right to arrears on a winding up). Conversely, an investor would expect the company to guarantee interest payments on a loan.

(c)   The fact that the shares are redeemable is not a guarantee that the shareholder will be repaid. The company can redeem the shares only out of distributable profits or a fresh issue of shares (unless it is a private company; see **13.5.3.2** above). If it cannot redeem the shares this way, the shareholder will not be repaid.

13.7   Varying class rights

13.7.1   Introduction

Section 630 of the CA 2006 provides that rights attaching to a class of shares, 'class rights', can be varied. This is good news for a company, as it provides a degree of flexibility, for example to reduce the amount of a preference dividend, or to create a new class of preference shares which rank ahead of an existing class of preference shares.

In both of these examples, however, there will be a class of shareholders who are worse off as a result of the variation of the rights of the existing preference shares, namely, the existing preference shareholders. As you might expect, the CA 2006 provides some protection for these shareholders in the procedures it prescribes for the variation of class rights. The Act provides different procedures, and the procedure the company must follow is dictated by whether the articles of association provide a variation procedure or not.

13.7.2 Class rights-defined in the articles of association

If the articles do not contain a procedure for variation, s 630(4) provides that class rights can be varied if:

(a)   the holders of 75% in nominal value of the issued shares of the class of shares to be varied consent in writing to the variation; *or*

(b)   a special resolution, passed at a separate general meeting of the class in question (known as a 'class meeting'), sanctions the variation (this means that 75% of those who attend the class meeting and vote in person or by proxy must vote in favour of the resolution).

While this affords protection to the holders of the shares whose rights are to be varied, in that a majority of them must agree to the variation, it does mean that the rights attached to the 25% minority of shares can be changed without their owners' consent.

Section 633 of the CA 2006 addresses this. It provides a procedure by which those shareholders who hold, in aggregate, not less than 15% of the issued shares of the class can (provided they did not consent to, or vote for, the variation) apply to the court within 21 days of the consent to, or vote for, the variation to have it cancelled. The court can then choose either to disallow (if satisfied the variation would unfairly prejudice the shareholders), or to confirm the variation. If a s 633 application is made, the variation has no effect until the court confirms it.

13.7.3 Class rights defined in the articles of association

If the articles contain a procedure for varying class rights, s 630(2) states that it is this procedure which should be followed, not the statutory procedure under s 630. The rationale behind this is that the class of shareholders need no extra statutory protection; they had notice of the articles when they became shareholders, and also have power to change the articles.

The articles can specify a procedure for varying class rights which sets a higher or, importantly, a lower standard than the statutory procedure.

The same right to apply to court to have the variation cancelled under s 633 (see **13.7.2**) applies to variations made in accordance with the articles' procedure.

13.8   Registration of share rights

A company must send details of share rights it has created or varied to the Registrar of Companies (that is, to Companies House). This obligation arises under ss 636–640 of the CA 2006.

13.9   Employee share schemes

It was explained at **1.7.6** above that one of the benefits of listing is that companies can issue shares with an identifiable value to their employees to incentivise and reward them. Companies do this through schemes known as employee share schemes, which, if structured correctly, have the following tax benefits:

(a)   for the company – the cost to the company is a deductible expense for corporation tax purposes;

(b)   for the employee – the benefit is not normally subject to income tax or national insurance contributions (if all the criteria of the individual plan are met). The shares do have some tax consequences, however; capital gains tax will be charged when the employee disposes of the shares.

Note that share schemes do not usually create a separate class of share; in fact, this is specifically avoided, as it can mean that the scheme does not attract the beneficial tax treatment outlined above.

The law relating to share schemes is particularly specialised, and firms will often have a discrete team dedicated to advising solely in relation to such schemes. The corporate lawyer will, however, need to know about the existence of any share schemes, because they will be referred to in documents he drafts, such as a prospectus (see **Chapter 6**) or an offer document (see **22.4.1**). A noddy guide to the four share schemes which are currently approved by the Revenue is provided at **13.9.1** to **13.9.4** below. It covers the basics but not much more.

The corporate lawyer should also appreciate the following points about employee share schemes:

(i)   they are exempt from the application of s 551 of the CA 2006 (see **14.5.2**);

(ii)   they do not trigger pre-emption rights under s 561 of the CA 2006, although they do entitle their holders to pre-emption rights (see **14.6.8.2**);

(iii) there is an exception for employee share scheme shares from the prohibition on financial assistance (see **16.5.3**);

(iv)   shares allotted in pursuance of an employee share scheme are also excluded from the requirement, under s 586 of the CA 2006, that shares must be paid up to at least one quarter of their nominal value, together with the whole of any premium (see **13.3.7**); and

(v)   generally a prospectus is not required where shares are offered by a listed company to existing or former directors or employees. Instead, a short document giving details of the company, the offer and the shares will suffice (see **6.4.1.5(h)** and **6.4.2.4(e)**).

13.9.1   Approved savings-related share option scheme or save as you earn (SAYE)

This scheme must be open to all employees. The company grants options to purchase shares in the company. At the time the option is granted, the price of the shares is fixed and the employees start to make regular monthly contributions to savings accounts. When an employee's account matures, the employee can use the proceeds to fund the exercise of the option.

13.9.2   Share incentive plan (SIP)

This scheme must also be open to all employees. There is a number of possible features. The company may:

(a)   issue up to £3,000 worth of shares each year to an individual employee;

(b)   allow an individual to purchase shares each year up to a value of the lower of £1,500, or 10% of salary; or

(c)   issue up to two shares for each share purchased by an individual employee.

13.9.3   Approved company share option plan (CSOP)

This scheme can be made available to selected employees, and so is often used to reward senior executives. The company grants options to purchase shares in the company. As with the approved savings-related share option scheme (see **13.9.1** above), at the time of the option is created, the price for the shares is fixed. However, with this scheme there is no associated savings account; the employee must provide his own funds to exercise the option.

13.9.4 Enterprise management incentives (EMI)

This scheme can also be made available to selected employees, and, like the approved company share option plan (see **13.9.3** above), it is often used to reward key employees. The company grants options to purchase shares in the company. Again, at the time the option is created, the price for the shares is fixed. There is no associated savings account. A number of significant conditions attach to this scheme (for example, the scheme is only available to companies with gross assets not exceeding £30m and fewer than 250 employees).

Chapter 14
Issuing Shares

14.1 Introduction

Chapter 13 explored the concept of the share and the classes of share which may comprise a company's share capital. Once a listed company has created a class of share, it will want to use those shares to raise capital. This will involve issuing shares to shareholders, in return for consideration.

The legislation relating to the issue of shares is relatively easy to apply when the issuing company is a private company. However, the application of those rules to the issue of shares by a public company can be more complex, not because the legislation is fundamentally different (it is not), but because usually public companies have more complex share structures, so it is necessary to delve a little further into the detail of the legislation. In the case of the issue of shares by listed companies, there are other considerations in addition to the legislation to take into account, namely guidelines issued by the ABI, the Statement of Principles issued by the Pre-Emption Group and the requirements of the Listing Rules. This chapter considers share issues by a listed company.

In this Chapter we will only be examining those rules which apply to public companies.

14.2 Terminology

Some terminology, which has the potential to be confusing, is explained below.

14.2.1 Issuing shares or transferring shares?

'Issuing' relates to the issue of a share from the company to a shareholder. It is different to 'transferring' or 'selling' a share, which is when a shareholder transfers a share to another person. On a share issue, the company is party to the transaction and receives money for the share. On a share transfer, the parties will be the shareholder selling the share and the shareholder buying the share, not the company, and so the selling shareholder receives the proceeds and not the company. This chapter considers only the issue of shares. **Chapter 19** considers the transfer of shares.

14.2.2 Allotted shares or issued shares?

When considering the subject of issuing shares, the terms 'allotted' and 'issued' arise frequently. Let us be clear from the outset what they mean and the distinction between them. In practice the terms are used interchangeably and, usually, it is entirely appropriate to do this. However, it is essential for the corporate finance lawyer to be aware of the specific meaning of terminology he uses when advising a client.

14.2.2.1 Allotted

Pursuant to s 558 of the CA 2006, shares are allotted when a person acquires the *unconditional right to be included* in the company's register of members in respect of those shares.

14.2.2.2 Issued

Although there is no statutory definition of the meaning of 'issued', case law suggests that shares are issued when the allottee's name *is registered* in the company's register of members in respect of those shares (*Ambrose Lake Tin and Copper Co, Re (Clarke's Case)* (1878) 8 Ch D 635, CA and *National Westminster Bank plc and Another v IRC and Barclays Bank plc* [1994] 2 BCLC 30, CA).

14.2.2.3 The distinction

The above explanations reveal the minute difference between the two terms. The distinction lies in whether the shareholder's name has been included in the register of members, with allotment preceding issue. Of course, the majority of companies ensure that the register of members is kept up to date. This will remove any distinction between the two terms, as one will equate to the other; as soon as a person has an unconditional right to be entered into the register of members in respect of certain shares, his name will be entered into the register of members in respect of those shares. At that stage, the shares will be both allotted and issued.

14.3 Issuing shares: three vital questions

Now that the terminology is clear, let us turn to the topic of issuing shares. There are three important questions which the lawyer must consider in relation to any issue of shares, namely (and in this order):

(a)   Limit on the number of shares – does the company have a limit in its articles of association on the number of shares that it can issue?

(b)   Authority to allot – do the directors have sufficient authority to allot the shares under s 551 of the CA 2006?

(c)   Pre-emption rights – do the pre-emption rights under s 561 of the CA 2006 apply to the issue and, if so, does the company need to disapply them?

The detail of, and the potential action required by, these questions is considered at **14.4** to **14.6** below.

14.4 Limit on number of shares

The first question the lawyer must consider, then, on a share issue, is whether there is a provision in the company's articles of association which limits the number of shares the company can issue.

Companies formed after 1 October 2009 under the CA 2006 can place a limit in their articles on the number of shares which can be issued.

Companies formed before 1 October 2009, before the relevant provisions of the CA 2006 came into force, were required to have restrictions on the number of shares they could issue in their pre-CA 2006 memorandum of association (known as the 'authorised share capital'). Under s 28 of the CA 2006 these provisions are automatically treated as restrictions in the articles with effect from 1 October 2009.

If there is a limit in the articles and the proposed issue of shares will result in that limit being exceeded then that provision must either be removed or altered to permit the issue.

14.4.1 Checking articles and issued share capital

14.4.1.1 Locating the filings at Companies House

The lawyer should first locate and check the articles to see if there are any restrictions on the issue of shares. In a company formed before 1 October 2009 the lawyer should also check the memorandum of association (as the authorised share capital clause became a limit under the articles on that date).

The lawyer must check back through the records the company has filed at Companies House, to identify the current articles. If these contain a limit on the number of shares then the lawyer must also check the existing issued share capital to see if the new issue of shares will exceed this limit. The easiest way to find the existing issued share capital is to take the figures provided in the latest filed annual return, then to check all the filings made since that annual return to see if any of them alter either the authorised share capital, or the issued share capital. Note that with effect from 1 October 2009 the annual return is known as Form AR01. However, the last annual return you find on file for a company may well be a Form 363 (which was required under the CA 1985). This is because an annual return only needs to be filed once a year, and if a Form 363 was filed in September 2009 it will not be until September 2010 that a Form AR01 is required. You can see a copy of both forms on the Companies House website. The lawyer should then check that the figure on record at Companies House corresponds with the company secretary's records (see **14.4.1.2** below).

Once the lawyer has identified the current figures, and knows how many shares the company is proposing to issue, it should be easy to calculate whether the company needs to remove the limit.

Examples

X plc wants to issue 50,000 shares in return for cash consideration. It has a restriction in its articles limiting its issued share capital to £1m divided into 1 million ordinary shares of £1 each. Let us take a couple of scenarios and analyse whether X plc needs to remove the restriction.

(a)   *Issued share capital is £1m*

It is easy to see that in this case, X plc must remove or increase the limit by £50,000 to £1.05 million.

(b)   *Issued share capital is £500,000*

In this case, X plc can issue a further 500,000 shares; it does not need to remove the limit.

(c)   *Issued share capital is £975,000*

X plc needs to remove the limit or increase it, but only by £25,000 to £1.025 million; as it is currently below the £1 million limit by 25,000 shares.

14.4.1.2 Ensuring filings are up to date

The lawyer should always check that the issued share capital figures on record at Companies House correspond with the company secretary's records. This is to make sure the company is up to date with its filings. If it is not, it will need to make late filings, otherwise this may lead to problems later on in the share issue.

14.4.2 Checking the guidelines

If the company is a listed company, the guidelines issued by the ABI and the Statement of Principles issued by the Pre-Emption Group have a bearing on the extent to which the company can issue new shares. It is preferable to check these guidelines and principles at this stage, to identify from the outset whether they will affect the proposed share issue. If they will, the company may decide not to proceed with the issue, and any preliminary steps, such as removing the limit in the articles on issued share capital. The provisions of the guidelines and principles are considered at **14.5.7** and **14.6.16** below.

14.4.3   Removing the limit on issued share capital

Let us assume that X plc wishes to issue 50,000 shares of £1 each. The records at Companies House reveal the following:

(a)   Issued share capital is £1m, divided into 1 million shares of £1 each.

(b)   The articles contain a restriction preventing the company from issuing shares which would take the issued share capital over £1 million, being one million shares of £1 each.

The company secretary has confirmed that the records at Companies House accord with his records and are up to date. The lawyer has checked, and the issue will be within the guidelines issued by the ABI and the Pre-emption Group (see **14.5.7** and **14.6.16** below).

X plc instructs its lawyer to draft the documentation to remove the limit on its issued share capital in its articles to enable the 50,000 shares of £1 each to be issued. How can this be done?

14.4.3.1   Special resolution

Section 21 of the CA 2006 provides that the company can change its articles by special resolution of the shareholders.

The lawyer must now draft the special resolution. The shareholders must pass this resolution by way of a special resolution in general meeting. The written resolution procedure under s 288 of the CA 2006 is not available to a public company.

If the company is formed before 1 October 2009 and there is an existing limit (see **14.4**) then it can be removed in one of three ways:

(a)   by passing an ordinary resolution to remove the limit; or

(b)   by passing a special resolution to adopt new articles without a limit; or

(c)   by passing a special resolution amending the articles authorising the directors to allot shares in excess of the limit.

Of course if there is no limit in the articles of association in the company concerned then this step can be dispensed with altogether.

14.4.3.2   Notifying Companies House

Under ss 29 and 30 of the CA 2006, a copy of the resolution and the amended articles must be sent to Companies House within 15 days of the date of the resolution (s 30(1)). Failure to comply with s 30 renders the company, and every officer who is in default, liable to a fine (s 30(2) and (3)).

14.4.4   The Listing Rules

The lawyer must also ensure that if the issuing company is a listed company it complies with the continuing obligations of the FSA in relation to communicating with its shareholders about the increase in issued share capital. These requirements are explained at **7.9** above. In particular, the company must publish a circular giving information on the change of articles (if relevant) and on the issue of new securities, including the arrangements for the allotment. The circular does not require the approval of the FSA (LR 13.2.2R). Listing Rule 13.8.10R provides that it must include the following information relating to the new articles (if relevant):

(a)   an explanation of the effect of the proposed amendments; and

(b)   either the full terms of the proposed amendments or a statement that they will be available for inspection:

(i)   from the date of the sending of the circular until the close of the relevant GM at a place in or near the City of London or such other place as the FSA may determine; and

(ii)   at the place of the GM for at least 15 minutes before and during the meeting.

In addition, the circular must contain certain information relating to the directors' authority to allot the new securities (see **14.5.6** below) and the disapplication of pre-emption rights (see **14.6.15** below).

The company must lodge two copies of the resolution and circular with the FSA, and notify an RIS that it has done so (LR 9.6.2R, LR 9.6.1R and LR 9.6.3R) (see **7.5.7.1**). Any proposed alteration of the company's capital structure must be notified to an RIS as soon as possible (LR 9.6.4R(1)).

The aim of the additional rules is, of course, to maximise the protection for shareholders in the listed company and to ensure the markets have all the information on the company as quickly as possible.

14.5   Authority to allot

Once the company has removed any limit (if this is required) on the issue of shares in the articles, the second question the lawyer must consider is whether the directors have authority to allot the shares.

14.5.1   Section 551 of the CA 2006

Section 551 of the CA 2006 applies to public companies (and private companies with more than one class of share). It prohibits directors from allotting 'relevant securities' unless they are authorised to do so by:

(a)   the company's articles of association; or

(b)   ordinary resolution of the shareholders.

14.5.2   Shares

Section 551 applies to:

(a)   the allotment of any type of share (ordinary and preference); and

    (i)   the subscriber shares (s 559), and

    (ii)   shares allotted under an employee share scheme (see **13.9**) (s 549(3)) (limb 1); and

(b)   the grant of any right to subscribe for, or convert to, any type of share *other than* under an employee share scheme (s 551(2)) (limb 2).

The exceptions are clear; no s 551 authority is needed to issue the initial subscriber shares in a company (see **13.5.6**), or to issue employee share scheme shares.

Clearly, most shares fall outside the exceptions referred to at (a)(i) and (ii) above and so are caught by limb 1 of the test; s 551 authority is therefore needed before those shares can be allotted.

What is not so obvious, however, is the effect of limb 2 of the test. Basically, limb 2 brings more than just shares within the ambit of s 551. A few typical examples, which often are the source of some confusion as to *when* s 551 authority is required in respect of them, are considered below.

14.5.2.1   Convertible loan stock

Convertible loan stock is a class of debt security which carries the right to convert into shares.

Is it within s 551?

Yes, provided the stock does not convert to employee share scheme shares.

When is s 551 authority needed?

There are three possibilities. Is it:

(a)   when the debt securities are allotted; or

(b)   when the debt securities are converted into shares; or

(c)   both (a) and (b)?

The answer is (a) – s 549(3). This is important; *at the time the debt securities are allotted* there must be sufficient s 551 authority to cover the ordinary shares into which the debt securities will convert.

14.5.2.2   Options

Is an option within s 551?

The grant of an option to subscribe for shares (other than employee share scheme shares) will fall within s 551.

When is s 551 authority needed?

Section 551 authority is required *at the time of the grant*, not at the time of the exercise, of the option.

14.5.2.3   Convertible preference shares

A convertible preference share is a share which carries the right to convert into ordinary shares.

Is it within s 551?

Yes. In fact, both limbs of s 551 (see above) catch these shares. Limb 1 of the test catches the intial allotment of preference shares. However, the preference shares also carry a right to convert into ordinary shares, and this right is caught by the second limb of the test (see **14.5.2.1** above).

When is s 551 authority needed?

Again, the question is whether s 551 authority is required:

(a)   when the convertible preference shares are allotted; or

(b)   when the shares are converted into ordinary shares; or

(c)   both (a) and (b)?

The answer is (a). Note, however, that, on the basis of the analysis set out above, the s 551 authority will need to cover *both* of the shares comprised in this type of shares, namely, the convertible preference shares and the ordinary shares they will convert into. For example, if the company is issuing 50 preference shares, which carry the right to convert into 50 ordinary shares, *at the time the convertible preference shares are allotted* the directors require authority to allot both share 1 and share 2, so two separate s 551 authorities are required.

A flowchart summarising the application of s 551 is set out at **Figure 14.1** below.

Figure 14.1: Section 551 flowchart

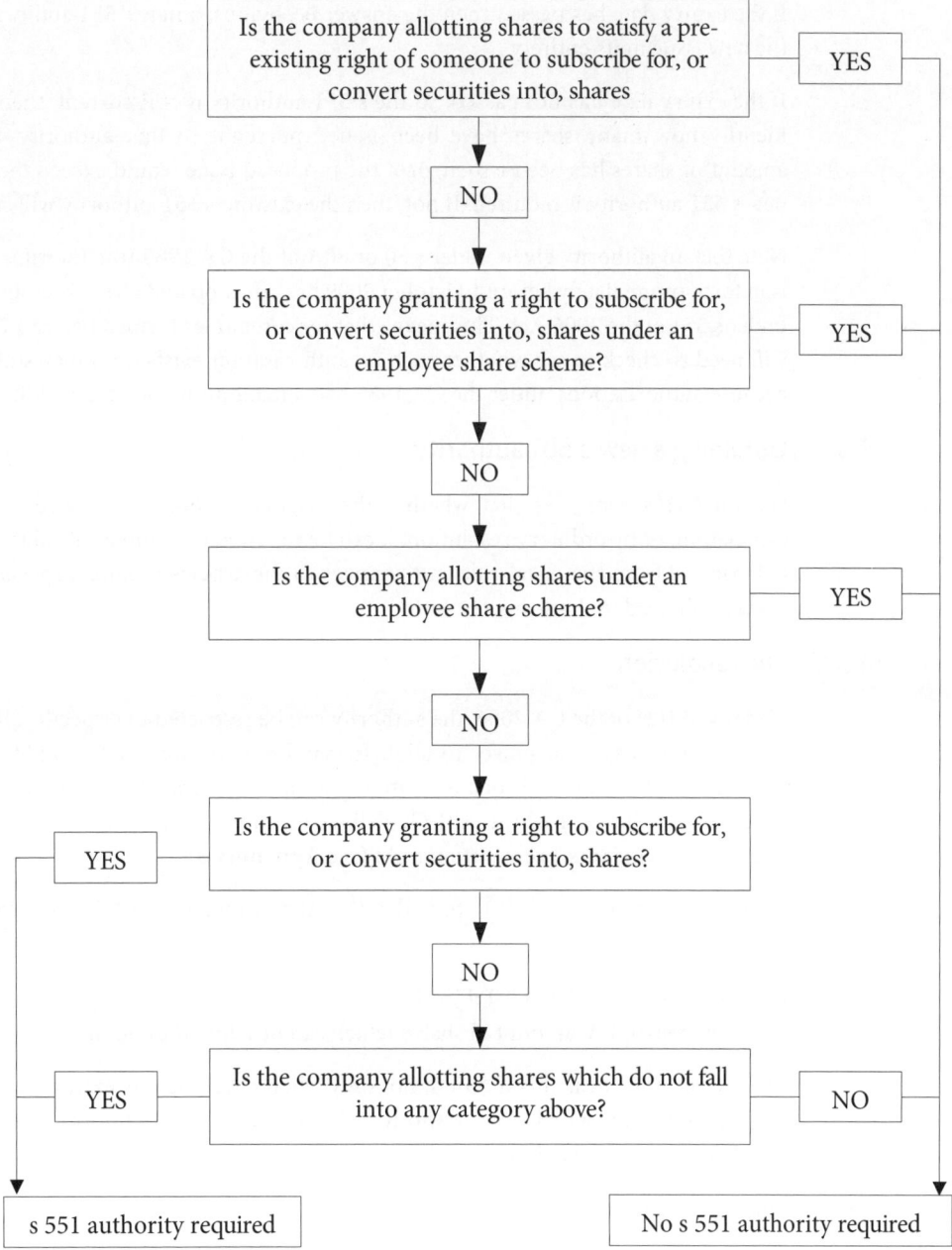

14.5.3 Checking the existing s 551 authority

We now know that it is necessary to examine carefully the nature of the securities to be issued, to determine whether s 551 authority is required. However, our example of X plc wishing to issue 50,000 ordinary shares (see **14.4.3** above) is relatively straightforward. The shares within limb 1 of the s 551 test. Section 551 authority is required. So now what? First the lawyer will need to check the existing s 551 authority, to see whether the directors already have authority to allot the 50,000 shares, or whether a new s 551 authority is required.

As explained at **14.5.1**, any s 551 authority will either be in the articles of association, or in an ordinary resolution. The lawyer must check the articles and the records at Companies House to identify the most recent s 551 authority. The lawyer must then check this authority to identify two key features, namely:

(a)   the date on which it expires; and

(b)   the maximum amount of relevant securities which can be allotted under it.

If the expiry date has passed then the answer is obvious; a new s 551 authority is required for the new issue in its entirety.

If the expiry date has not passed, so the s 551 authority is still current, then the lawyer must identify how many shares have been issued pursuant to that authority. If the maximum amount of shares has been issued, or if the proposed issue would exceed that amount, then a new s 551 authority is required. If not, then the existing s 551 authority will suffice.

Note that an authority given under s 80 or 80A of the CA 1985 (the forerunners to s 551) that is in force immediately before 1 October 2009 has effect on and after 1 October 2009 as if given under s 551 of the 2006 Act. This means that for companies formed before 1 October 2009 you will need to check to see whether such an authorisation exists, as it may still be valid. This is because authorisations under the CA 1985 had a maximum potential validity of five years.

14.5.4   Obtaining a new s 551 authority

Section 551(8) provides that whether the original authority was given in the articles of association, or by ordinary resolution, it can be renewed by ordinary resolution. This is clearly a departure from the usual rule that changes to the articles require a special resolution. The lawyer will need to draft this resolution.

14.5.5   The resolution

Under s 551(2) of the CA 2006, the authority can be restricted to a specific allotment, or it can be drafted as a general power to allot. It may be made subject to conditions, or it can be unconditional. An example of a resolution granting a general, unconditional s 551 authority is set out in resolution 1 of the ABI Guidelines on directors' powers to allot share capital and disapply shareholders' pre-emption right (see **Appendix 3**).

As **14.5.3** explained, s 551(3) provides that the authority must include two key pieces of information:

(a)   the date on which it expires; and

(b)   the maximum amount of shares which can be allotted under it.

The lawyer must bear this in mind, not only when checking any existing s 551 authority, but also when drafting a new s 551 authority. The two key pieces of information are considered at **14.5.5.1** and **14.5.5.2** below.

14.5.5.1   The expiry date

Under s 551(3)(b) of the CA 2006, the expiry date must not be more than five years from either:

(a)   the date on which the company was incorporated (if the authority is contained in the articles of association); or

(b)   the date of the resolution giving the authority.

Clearly (a) is relevant only in relation to drafting the original s 551 authority, and therefore it is (b) which applies in relation to drafting the majority of s 551 authorities. The authority can be for up to a fixed period of five years. In an abundance of caution, this is usually expressed in the resolution as being the fifth anniversary of the resolution, less one day.

Note that in practice, listed companies usually grant the directors a new s 551 authority each year, at the AGM, as a safeguard against inadvertently allowing an authority to expire. Another safeguard in relation to the expiry date which can be drafted into a s 551 authority is to allow the directors to allot shares, even if the s 551 authority has expired, if they do so pursuant to an offer or agreement made by the company before the authority expired (see resolution 1 of the ABI Guidelines in **Appendix 3**).

14.5.5.2 Maximum amount of relevant securities

The s 551 authority must state the maximum amount of shares which can be allotted under it. The amount is usually stated in terms of the maximum nominal amount (for example, £50,000), rather than the number of shares (for example, 50,000 shares of £1 each), so that if the company consolidates or subdivides its shares (for example, into shares of £2 or 10p), it will not need to amend the s 551 authority.

In relation to limb 2 of the s 551 test (see **14.5.2** above), the maximum amount relates to the shares which will be issued on exercise of the right. If the issue were of 10 debt securities, for example, which will be converted to a maximum of 100 ordinary shares of £1 each, then the maximum amount would be £100.

When determining this maximum amount, if the company is a listed company, regard must be had to the ABI guidelines, which impose a limit on the amount. The provisions of the guidelines are considered at **14.5.7** below.

14.5.5.3 Notifying Companies House

Under s 555 of the CA 2006 the company must file with Companies House within one month a return of the allotment together with a statement of capital. These are contained in one Companies House form, Form SH01. Under s 554, directors must register an allotment as soon as practicable, but no later than two months after the allotment, otherwise an offence will have been committed.

The lawyer must also ensure that the s 551 ordinary resolution is filed at Companies House within 15 days of it being passed.

14.5.6 The Listing Rules

Again, if the company issuing the shares is a listed company then it must comply with the continuing obligations of the Listing Rules regarding communications with shareholders (see **7.9** above). In particular, LR 13.8.1R provides that when a listed company sends out the s 551 resolution to its shareholders, the explanatory circular (which does not require approval by the FSA (LR 13.2.2R)) must include the following information:

(a)   a statement of:
    (i)   the maximum amount of relevant securities which the directors will have authority to allot, and
    (ii)   the percentage which that amount represents of the total issued ordinary share capital as at the latest practicable date before publication of the circular;

(b)   a statement by the directors as to whether they have any present intention of exercising the authority, and if so for what purpose; and

(c)   a statement as to whether the authority will lapse.

The circular must also include information relating to any treasury shares held by the company.

The company must lodge two copies of the resolution and circular with the FSA, and notify an RIS that it has done so (LR 9.6.1R, LR 9.6.2R and LR 9.6.3R) (see **7.5.7.1**).

14.5.7 The ABI Guidelines

At the time of writing these guidelines, issued in December 2008, had not been updated to take account of the repeal of the CA 1985 by the CA 2006. This means that the guidelines still refer to the 'authorised' share capital, which has been abolished by the CA 2006. They also refer to s 80 of the CA 1985, which has been replaced by s 551 of the CA 2006. They are unlikely to change substantially when reissued, although only the second requirement ((b) below) will be relevant for most listed companies following the abolition of the requirement for the authorised share capital.

The ABI has issued guidelines (see **Appendix 3**) which restrict the amount of share capital which can be included in a s 80 (now s 551, CA 2006) authority given by listed companies. The ABI Guidelines provide that the 'maximum amount' of relevant securities for which authority can be given is the initially lesser of:

(a)   the authorised but unissued ordinary share capital; and

(b)   one-third of the issued ordinary share capital.

The ABI will accept an authority to allow the allotment of a further one-third of the issued share capital provided that the additional authority is only used for fully pre-emptive rights issues and both the general and additional authorities expire at the next AGM (rather than up to five years for a general authority). Further the entire board of directors must put itself up for re-election at the next AGM if more than one-third of the issued share capital is actually allotted in one year; in other words if recourse is had to the additional authority.

The permission for this additional one-third authority was introduced by the ABI in 2008 in response to the frequency with which some listed companies, principally banks, were having to exceed the original one-third limit to raise sufficient funds from its shareholders to stave off possible insolvency.

Examples

Let us use X plc as an example. X plc is now a listed company and has an authorised share capital of £1.05m and an issued share capital of £1m.

(a)   X plc wants to issue 50,000 shares of £1 each (not by way of rights issue).

    (i)   The authorised but unissued ordinary share capital is £50,000.

    (ii)   The sum equal to one-third of the issued ordinary share capital is £333,333.

    (iii)   £50,000 is the lesser figure, so it is fine to give the directors the s 551 authority for issuing the £50,000 shares.

(b)   Imagine instead that X plc wants to issue 500,000 rather than 50,000 shares (not by way of rights issue). X plc has already increased its authorised share capital to £1.5m. The issued share capital is still £1m.

    (i)   The authorised but unissued ordinary share capital is £500,000.

    (ii)   The sum equal to one-third of the issued ordinary share capital is £333,333.

    (iii)   £333,333 is the lesser figure, so the ABI Guidelines would prevent X plc giving s 551 authority over the entire amount of shares X plc wants to issue, namely £500,000. It could issue only 333,333 shares.

(c)   Imagine instead that X plc wants to issue 500,000 rather than 50,000 shares but this time fully pre-emptively by way of rights issue. X plc has already increased its authorised share capital to £1.5m. The issued share capital is still £1m.

    (i)   The authorised but unissued ordinary share capital is £500,000.

    (ii)   The sum equal to two-thirds of the issued share capital is £666,666.

    (iii)   £500,000 is the lesser figure so the ABI Guidelines would permit X plc to give s 551 authority to issue the number of shares it wants. This is only because the issue will be by way of fully pre-emptive rights issue. The further conditions mentioned above must also be satisfied.

This is why, as stated in **14.4.2** above, it is important to analyse the ABI guidelines upfront.

The ABI Guidelines are non-statutory and designed to prevent the dilution of (principally institutional investors') shareholdings without the shareholders' prior approval. If the company considers that it has good reason to exceed the limit set out in the Guidelines, it can discuss this with the ABI in advance of any allotment.

14.5.8   Sanctions for breach of s 551

Breach of s 551 does not actually invalidate the share allotment (CA 2006, s 549(6)). However, s 549(4) and (5) provide that any director who knowingly and wilfully contravenes, or permits or authorises a contravention of, s 551 is liable to a fine.

14.5.9   Sanctions for breach of the Listing Rules

The sanctions for breach of the Listing Rules are as set out at **3.6** above.

14.6   Pre-emption rights on allotment

Now that X plc has removed any limit in the articles on issuing the 50,000 shares, and the directors have authority to allot the 50,000 shares, what is preventing the company from allotting the shares? Well, there is one final question to consider: do the pre-emption rights under s 561 of the CA 2006 apply to the allotment and, if so, does the company need to disapply them?

(Remember not to confuse pre-emption rights on allotment of new shares with pre-emption rights on the transfer of existing shares. This chapter is considering the issue of new shares, not the transfer of existing shares, and therefore is concerned only with pre-emption rights on allotment.) Any pre-emption rights on transfer will be drafted into the company's articles of association or, if the company has issued any convertible securities, or warrants and options etc, the deeds or agreements setting out the terms of issue may also contain specific pre-emption rights on transfer.)

14.6.1   What is a pre-emption right on allotment?

A pre-emption right on allotment is a right of first refusal for existing shareholders on an issue of shares by a company. This means that when a company wants to issue shares, it must first offer those shares to the existing shareholders in proportion to their existing shareholdings.

14.6.2   Rationale

The right of pre-emption protects the shareholders against the dilution of their shareholdings. If each shareholder takes up the shares offered to him under the right of pre-emption, although the number of shares held by him will increase, his percentage shareholding will be preserved. Of course, the right helps the existing shareholder to preserve his percentage shareholding only if he can afford to buy the shares offered to him.

14.6.3   Where are pre-emption rights on allotment?

The main provisions relating to pre-emption on allotment are in the CA 2006 and the Listing Rules. A company's articles of association may also contain specific provisions relating to pre-emption on allotment. If a listed company has issued any convertible securities, or warrants and options etc, the deeds or agreements setting out the terms of issue may also contain specific pre-emption provisions on allotment.

14.6.4   Obstruction

We are about to consider the complex provisions relating to pre-emption rights. Bear in mind, while you are reading, that from the company's perspective (acting through its directors) pre-emption rights can be a pain. They may prevent, at least initially, the company from issuing shares to those to whom it would prefer to issue and compel the company to offer those shares to existing shareholders. We will come back to this at **14.6.13** below.

14.6.5   Section 561 of the CA 2006

Section 561 of the CA 2006 provides statutory pre-exemption rights on allotment. A company proposing to issue *equity securities* in return for *cash* must first offer the shares to holders of *ordinary shares* in proportion to the nominal value of their existing shareholdings.

Let us be very clear: this means that there are two types of securities we need to analyse:

(a)   equity securities – that is, the shares the company is proposing to issue which might *trigger* pre-emption rights, so that those equity securities must be offered first to those people who have pre-emption rights; and

(b)   ordinary shares – that is, the shares which *entitle* their owners to pre-emption rights, so that their owners are offered first refusal over an issue of equity securities.

These two types of securities are considered further at **14.6.6** and **14.6.8** below.

14.6.6   Equity securities

This term relates to the shares the company is proposing to issue. If the company is proposing to issue an equity security, it will trigger pre-emption rights under s 561. Section 560(1) of the CA 2006 defines 'equity securities'. It does so by reference to the term 'ordinary shares'.

Basically, equity securities are:

(a)   any 'ordinary shares' in the company (see **14.6.8** below) *other than*:
  (i)   a subscriber share (s 577) (see **13.5.6**),
  (ii)   a bonus share (s 564) (limb 1), and
  (iii)   shares held under an employees' share scheme (s 566); and

(b)   any right to subscribe for, or convert securities into, ordinary shares (limb 2).

14.6.7   For cash

Section 565 provides that the pre-emption rights under s 561(1) will apply only if the issue of shares is *wholly* in return for cash. If the consideration for the issue is partly or wholly anything other than cash (for example, shares or land), the s 561 pre-emption rights on allotment will not apply. Section 583 of the CA 2006 defines a payment of cash to include cash or cheque.

14.6.8   Ordinary shares

This term relates to the shares that entitle their owners to benefit from pre-emption rights in the event that the company issues equity securities. Section 560(1) defines 'ordinary shares' as any shares *other than* a share which, in relation to both dividends and capital, carries a right to participate only up to a specified amount (the definition therefore includes shares such as an ordinary share and a non-participating preference share – see **13.5.2.1**).

If you compare the definition of 'equity securities' (see **14.6.6**) with the definition of 'ordinary shares', you will notice several important distinctions between the two.

14.6.8.1   The right to subscribe for, or convert into, ordinary shares

This falls within the definition of equity securities (limb 2), but outside the definition of 'ordinary shares'. This means that while the issue of a right to subscribe for, or convert securities into, ordinary shares will *trigger* the pre-emption rights (see (a) and (b) below for more detail), those rights to subscribe or convert will not *entitle* their owners to pre-emption rights. Let us delve a little further into this by exploring the position regarding two different types of convertible security and whether they *trigger* pre-emption rights:

(a)   *Convertible loan stock.* The loan stock will fall within limb 2 of the definition of 'equity securities' and the issue of convertible loan stock for cash will *trigger* s 561 pre-emption rights.

By 'triggering pre-emption rights' we are saying that the company must first offer the loan stock to existing shareholders *pro rata*. Why? the loan stock is convertible into shares, and if this conversion takes place it will dilute the existing shareholders' ownership if converted shares are held by outsiders.

(b)   *Convertible preference shares.* The issue here is whether the convertible preference shares are participating or non-participating shares. If they are participating, they will be caught by the definition of 'equity securities' (limb 1: they are 'ordinary shares' for these purposes) and will *trigger* s 561 pre-emption rights, assuming they are issued for cash. If they are non-participating, they will fall outside limb 1 (they are not 'ordinary shares'); however, they will be caught by limb 2. The issue of those shares will *trigger* the pre-emption rights, assuming they are issued wholly for cash.

14.6.8.2   Employee share scheme shares

Section 566 states that s 561 pre-emption rights do not apply to shares held under an employees' share scheme (see **14.6.5** above). This means that employee share scheme shares will not trigger the s 561 pre-emption provisions when they are issued, but, once issued, they will *entitle* their owners to pre-emption rights in the event that the company issues equity securities.

Employee share schemes are explored in more detail at **13.9**.

14.6.8.3   Bonus/subscriber shares

Sections 564 and 577 state that the allotment of bonus/subscriber shares will not trigger pre-emption rights, but holders of bonus and subscriber shares will be *entitled* to pre-emption rights provided they are ordinary shares and are not excluded because they carry only a limited right to participate in income and share capital.

14.6.9   How to consider pre-emption rights

When analysing whether s 561 will apply to a share issue, you need to separate your analysis of the securities the company is proposing to issue, which might *trigger* pre-emption rights, from your analysis of the securities which might *entitle* their holders to a pre-emption right on an issue of equity securities.

Now, two pieces of good news. The first is that the summary at **14.6.10** below, and the examples at **14.6.11** below, should simplify the application of s 561. The second is that, if the company decides to disapply the pre-emption rights, you will not need to apply s 561 at all (see **14.6.15** below) (although unfortunately you do need to be capable of applying s 561 to find out whether you need to disapply it in the first place).

14.6.10   Summary of statutory pre-emption rights on allotment

(a)   Equity securities which *can trigger* pre-emption rights when they are issued (that is they must be offered pro rata to the existing shareholders):

    (i)   ordinary shares;

    (ii)   participating preference shares; and

    (iii)   rights to subscribe for, or convert into, ordinary or participating preference shares.

(b)   Securities which are not equity securities and *cannot trigger* pre-emption rights when they are issued:

    (i)   non-participating preference shares;

    (ii)   employee share scheme shares;

    (iii)   any share issued for non-cash consideration;

    (iv)   bonus shares; and

        (v)   subscriber shares.

  (c)   'Ordinary shares' which *entitle* their owners pre-emption rights on an issue of equity securities (these shareholders will expect a pro rata offer of the equity securities being offered):

        (i)   ordinary shares;

        (ii)   participating preference shares;

        (iii)   employee share scheme shares (if they are (i) or (ii) above);

        (iv)   bonus shares (if they are (i) or (ii) above); and

        (v)   subscriber shares (if they are (i) or (ii) above).

  (d)   Shares which *do not entitle* their owners to pre-emption rights on an issue of equity securities:

        (i)   non-participating preference shares;

        (ii)   rights to subscribe for, or to convert into, ordinary or participating preference shares.

14.6.11　Examples

The following examples assume that there is not already in place a disapplication of the statutory pre-emption rights on allotment and that, unless otherwise stated, the consideration for the proposed issue is wholly cash.

Example 1

A plc is proposing to issue ordinary shares. The company's existing share capital comprises ordinary and participating preference shares. The shares to be issued are equity securities and the proposed issue is for cash consideration. Therefore, unless a s 561 disapplication is obtained, the directors must offer the shares first to the holders of the ordinary and the preference shares (both are 'ordinary shares') pro rata to their respective holdings.

Example 2

B plc is seeking to acquire the entire issued share capital of Z plc and is offering Z's shareholders two B plc shares for each of their Z shares. Section 561 does not apply to the issue of B shares because the consideration for them is not cash. The consideration comprises the shares in Z.

Example 3

C plc intends to issue ordinary shares. The existing capital structure comprises ordinary shares and convertible loan stock. This is an issue of equity securities but the new shares will be offered only to the holders of the ordinary shares. Convertible loan stock does not fall within the definition of 'ordinary shares' and so does not entitle its owners to pre-emption rights.

Example 4

D plc intends to issue convertible loan stock. The existing capital structure comprises ordinary shares and non-participating preference shares. The issue of convertible loan stock does amount to an issue of equity securities. On this assumption, s 561 applies. Unless the section is disapplied the directors must offer the convertible loan stock first to the ordinary shareholders. The holders of the non-participating preference shares do not have statutory pre-emption rights as they are not the holders of 'ordinary shares'.

14.6.12　Pre-emption rights on allotment under the Listing Rules

As explained at **7.6.3** above, listed companies must, in addition to the statutory pre-emption rights, comply with pre-emption rights on allotment (LR 9.3.11R). The statutory rights under the CA 2006 apply to all companies registered in the UK, whether public or private. The Listing Rules rights apply just to listed companies. These will usually be UK-registered, but they may also be registered overseas and so not subject to the CA 2006. On an issue of *equity shares for cash*, there is a continuing obligation on a listed company to offer those shares first to the *existing equity shareholders* (of shares of that class, or of another class who are entitled to be offered them) in proportion to their existing holdings.

An issue by a listed company pursuant to the pre-emption rights set out in LR 9.3.11R is known as a 'rights issue' or an 'open offer'. **Chapter 17** considers these in more detail.

These rights of pre-emption on allotment under the Listing Rules reflect the statutory rights of shareholders of any company, listed or not, under ss 561 to 577 of the CA 2006, but the pre-emption rights on allotment under the Listing Rules are not identical. For example:

(a)   The definition of 'equity shares' in the Listing Rules is different from 'equity securities' in the CA 2006. Under the Listing Rules, equity shares are just:

   (i)   ordinary shares; and

   (ii)   participating preference shares.

(b)   Listing Rule 9.3.12R(2) provides that a company does not need to comply with the pre-emption rights in LR 9.3.11R in relation to equity shares which:

   (i)   represent fractional entitlements; or

   (ii)   the directors think it is necessary or expedient to exclude from any offer due to legal problems under the laws of any territory or due to any regulatory body,

   where there is a disapplication in a rights issue or an open offer, used solely in respect of the shares covered by (b)(i) and (ii) above, rather than generally for *all* shares.

   In addition, LR 9.3.12R(3) and LR 9.3.12R(4) provide that the pre-emption rights under the Listing Rules will not apply if the company is selling treasury shares for cash to an employee share scheme, or if the company is an overseas company with a primary listing.

   Section 561 makes no provision for fractional entitlements so, in practice, entitlements are rounded down. Further, in order to comply with s 561 without making an offer in jurisdictions outside the EEA with onerous requirements, companies must follow the procedure under s 562(3) of the CA 2006, known as the 'Gazette route'.

These differences are easier to understand in the context of a rights issue. Their practical effect is considered at **17.7.6** below. Pre-emption rights under the CA 2006 can cause problems on a rights issue in a way that the pre-emption rights under the Listing Rules do not.

Note that there are no pre-emption rights on *transfer* in the Listing Rules. (Indeed, this would be contrary to the requirement that the shares of listed companies should be freely transferable – see **4.3.1.1**.)

14.6.13   What is the problem with pre-emption rights?

By now (perhaps with the help of a cold towel) you should be able to work out whether the proposed issue will trigger pre-emption rights either under the CA 2006, or under the Listing Rules. Let us consider the example of X plc again. X plc is proposing to issue 50,000 ordinary shares. These fall within limb 1 of the 'equity securities' test. The shares are to be issued wholly for cash. They will therefore *trigger* statutory pre-emption rights; they must first be offered to holders of relevant shares and relevant employee shares who are entitled to pre-emption rights.

Does this suit the company's purposes? Well usually no, not really. If pre-emption rights apply, the company must follow the detailed procedure set out in s 562 of the CA 2006, regarding the form the offer must take and the length of time for which it must remain open (14 days from the date the offer is made). Only once this period has expired, or the company has received a reply from each shareholder who benefits from the pre-emption rights, can it allot any shares which have not been taken up through pre-emption.

This usually inconveniences the company, so it will normally disapply the statutory pre-emption rights.

14.6.14   Disapplication of pre-emption rights under the CA 2006

The CA 2006 provides a number of ways in which a company can disapply s 561 when allotting equity securities for cash. Those under ss 567, 568 and 569 are available only to private companies. We are not concerned with private companies, and so will not consider these methods any further.

Public companies can disapply pre-emption rights under ss 570 and 571 of the CA 2006. These sections provide that the company can disapply the s 561 pre-emption rights:

(a)   specifically (see **14.6.14.1**); or

(b)   generally (see **14.6.14.2**).

14.6.14.1   Specific disapplication (s 571)

A disapplication of pre-emption rights in relation to a specific allotment must be effected by a special resolution. However, this is not a popular method because of the requirements of s 571(5)–(7). This provides that before the resolution is proposed, the directors must recommend that the resolution be passed and circulate a written statement setting out:

(a)   their reasons for making the recommendation;

(b)   the amount of consideration for the shares; and

(c)   the justification of that amount.

The statement must be circulated to the members before the general meeting to pass the special resolution. The directors risk up to 12 months' imprisonment or a fine if the statement contains anything which is materially misleading, false or deceptive (s 572).

14.6.14.2   General disapplication (s 570)

This is the most common method of disapplying pre-emption rights, and can be used where there is in place a general authorisation for the purposes of s 551 of the CA 2006. The disapplication can be effected either by special resolution, which is most common, or by a provision in the articles. Unlike under s 571, the directors are not required to make any recommendation in relation to the resolution (see **14.6.14.1**).

14.6.14.3   Duration

Whether the disapplication is specific or general, it will be effective only until the s 551 authority to which it relates expires (s 570(3)). This means that the disapplication cannot last more than five years. Whenever a new s 551 authority is obtained, a new s 570 or 571 disapplication should also be obtained.

14.6.14.4   Example

An example of a general s 570 disapplication, which shows how it relates to the s 551 authority, is set out in resolution 2 of the ABI Guidelines on directors' powers to allot share capital and disapply shareholders' pre-emption right (see **Appendix 3**).

Note that at the time of writing this resolution still referred to the corresponding CA 1985 provisions which have now been replaced by ss 551 and 561 of the CA 2006.

14.6.14.5   Notifying Companies House

The company must file a copy of the s 570 or 571 resolution at Companies House within 15 days of it being passed (s 29(1)(a) and s 30).

14.6.15   Disapplication of pre-emption rights under the Listing Rules

As explained at **7.6.3** above, the shareholders of a listed company can also agree to dispense with their pre-emption rights under the Listing Rules. Listing Rule 9.3.12R(1) makes clear that a general disapplication by the shareholders of their statutory pre-emption rights in accordance with s 570 of the CA 2006 will also dispense with the pre-emption rights under LR 9.3.11R. In practice, most public companies effect a general disapplication of the statutory pre-emption rights at each AGM, at the same time that they take any s 551 authority. Although in theory this also dispenses with the pre-emption rights under the Listing Rules in their entirety, listed companies prefer to state in the resolution that they will nevertheless comply with the pre-emption rights under the Listing Rules. The s 570 disapplication, set out in resolution 2 of the ABI Guidelines on directors' powers to allot share capital and disapply shareholders' pre-emption right (see **Appendix 3**), is a typical example. This allows directors to make small, non pre-emptive issues and rights issues or open offers that follow the pre-emption provisions in the Listing Rules. The rationale for the provision that rights issues and open offers should follow the pre-emption rights under the Listing Rules but not the pre-emption rights under the CA 2006, is explained at **14.6.12** and **17.7.6**.

Again, if the company is listed, it will need to observe the continuing obligations of the Listing Rules relating to communications with shareholders. These obligations are considered at **7.9** above. Listing Rule 13.8.2R provides that a circular should accompany the s 570 or 571 disapplication containing the following information (the circular does not require approval by the FSA – LR 13.2.2R):

(a)   a statement of the maximum amount of equity securities that the disapplication will cover; and

(b)   (in the case of a general disapplication in respect of equity securities for cash made otherwise than to existing shareholders in proportion to their existing shareholdings) the percentage which the amount generally disapplied represents of the total ordinary share capital in issue as at the latest practicable date before publication of the circular.

The company must lodge two copies of the resolution and circular with the FSA, and notify an RIS that it has done so (LR 9.6.2R, LR 9.6.1R and LR 9.6.3R) (see **7.5.7.1**).

14.6.16   The Pre-Emption Group

The institutional investors do not generally support issues of new shares by listed companies other than by way of a rights issue, because otherwise the issue will dilute a shareholder's shareholding, resulting in a smaller share of the company's profit (dividend) and a smaller percentage of voting rights. The original Pre-Emption Group was established in 1987 under the auspices of the Stock Exchange and consisted of representatives of listed companies, institutional investors and corporate finance practitioners. The Group issued Pre-Emption Guidelines advising shareholders not to vote in favour of any annual disapplication of pre-emption rights unless certain conditions were met.

Following concerns that the Guidelines were out of date, and after a Government-sponsored report by Paul Myners in 2005, a new Pre-Emption Group was established in 2005. The Group's members represent listed companies, investors and intermediaries. In May 2006, the Group produced a 'Statement of Principles' to provide guidance to shareholders and companies on the disapplication of pre-emption rights, and which were updated in July 2008. The Principles, supported by the ABI, the NAPF and the IMA, replaced the Pre-Emption Guidelines. They are set out in full at **Appendix 4**. They can also be viewed at the Pre-Emption Group's website (www.pre-emptiongroup.org.uk).

The Principles do not have the force of law, but are stated to be a basis for discussion between companies and their investors. In practice, they reflect the position that the powerful institutional shareholders will take in relation to any s 570 or 571 disapplication. Paragraph 5 of the Statement makes clear that the Principles apply to equity issues for cash, other than on a pre-emptive basis, by UK companies which are listed on the Main Market. AIM companies are encouraged to comply too, although it is recognised that they may require a greater degree of flexibility. Paragraph 5 also makes clear that the Principles do *not* apply to issues of equity securities for cash if the issue is on a pre-emptive basis.

The Pre-Emption Group has stated that it will monitor the application of the Principles.

Note that at the time of writing reference was still being made in the Principles to the provisions of the CA 1985 which were replaced by the CA 2006 on 1 October 2009.

14.6.16.1 Routine disapplications

The Statement recognises that shareholders will consider some requests to disapply pre-emption rights as non-controversial, or 'routine'. While the company needs to explain why the disapplication is required, and notify shareholders of the need for it in good time, shareholders are likely to agree in principle with such requests and will require less in-depth discussion about them. Typically, a routine disapplication can be made by way of an appropriate resolution at an AGM (para 18).

The Statement sets out the following guidance as to what constitutes a 'routine disapplication':

(a)   A request is more likely to be 'routine' when the company is seeking authority to issue non-pre-emptively 5% or less of ordinary share capital in any one year (regardless of how the issue is structured) (paras 8 and 9);

(b)   a company should not issue more than 7.5% of its ordinary share capital for cash, other than to existing shareholders, in any rolling three year period, unless:

(i)   it has consulted suitably in advance; or

(ii)   the matter was specifically highlighted when the disapplication request was made (para 10); and

(c)   the price at which the shares are proposed to be issued is relevant; a discount of greater than 5% is not likely to be regarded as routine (paras 11, 20 and 21).

14.6.16.2 Non-routine disapplications

As recommended by the Myners Report, the Principles recognise that some requests to disapply pre-emption rights might be non-routine but nevertheless in the interests of the company and its shareholders. The Principles emphasise that the limits set out above are intended to ease the granting of authority to routine requests to disapply pre-emption rights, not prohibit the granting of non-routine disapplications. Rather, any request for a non-routine disapplication should be considered by shareholders on a case by case basis.

The Principles set out examples of issues which are likely to be critical to shareholders in terms of voting on any non-routine disapplication, such as the size and stage of development of the company in the sector in which it operates and the extent to which the issue would dilute the value and voting control of existing shareholdings (para 16). Any non-routine disapplication should be made at a specially convened GM, unless the company is in a position to provide all the necessary information to shareholders at its AGM, in which case the request can be made at the AGM (para 18). A disapplication should not be granted for more than 15 months or until the next AGM, whichever is the shorter (para 19).

14.6.16.3 The disapplication procedure

For both routine and non-routine disapplications, the company must communicate with shareholders as soon as possible (para 4). Following the granting of any disapplication, the company should publish in its annual report certain information about the non-pre-emptive issue, such as the level of discount, the amount raised and how it was used (para 22).

> **Example**
> Let us apply the Statement of Principles to our example of X plc. The issued ordinary share capital at the date of the last published accounts was £1m. 5% of £1m is £50,000, so the disapplication required relating to the issue of 50,000 shares of £1 is 'routine', provided X plc has not made any other issues in the last three years which would exceed the 7.5% cumulative total referred to at **14.6.16.1(b)**. The lawyer needs to check that the consideration complies within the requirement set out at **14.6.16.1(c)**, then, finally, X plc will be in a position to issue shares.

Note that at the time of writing reference was still being made to the forerunners to the CA 2006 provisions under the CA 1985 which ceased to be in force on 1 October 2009.

14.6.17 Sanctions for breach of s 561

A breach of s 561 will not invalidate or cancel an allotment. However, s 563 of the CA 2006 provides that the company and any director who knowingly permitted the breach are jointly and severally liable to compensate any person to whom the shares should have been offered under the pre-emption rights.

14.6.18 Sanctions for breach of the Listing Rules

The sanctions for breach of the Listing Rules are as set out at **3.6** above.

14.7 Issuing the shares

Once the three questions listed at **14.3** above have been considered and the appropriate action taken, the company is in a position to issue the shares. However, the lawyer must check that the circumstances of the issue do not trigger any other legal problems. The areas to check are as follows.

14.7.1 Directors' duties

The directors must issue the shares in accordance with their statutory obligations under the CA 2006 and the remaining common law and fiduciary obligations. In particular, they must:

(a)   act in a way they consider, in good faith, would be most likely to promote the success of the company for the benefit of the company as a whole (CA 2006, s 172); and

(b)   act in accordance with the company's constitution and only exercise their powers for their proper purpose (CA 2006, s 171).

14.7.2 Financial assistance

There is a general prohibition on a company providing financial help to anyone acquiring its shares. This can cause problems on a share issue, and the lawyer must analyse the terms of the issue carefully to identify any potential problems relating to financial assistance. **Chapter 16** considers this topic in detail.

14.7.3 Consideration

'Consideration' means the price paid for the shares. Generally, this does not have to be cash; a subscriber may pay cash, but may also pay in money's worth, such as with other shares (if the subscriber is a company) or other assets. However, where the issuer of shares is a public company, s 585(1) of the CA 2006 provides that it cannot accept consideration in the form of an undertaking:

(a)   to do work; or

(b)   to perform services.

In addition, a public company cannot allot shares as fully or partly paid up otherwise than in cash, if the consideration is or includes an undertaking which will, or may, be performed more than five years after the date of the allotment (s 587(1)). This is referred to as a 'long-term undertaking'.

14.7.4 Issuing shares at a discount

As explained at **13.3.1** above, s 580 of the CA 2006 provides that no company, public or private, listed or unlisted, can issue a share at a discount to its nominal value. The company can, of course, issue a share which is partly paid, but, as discussed at **13.3.7** above, in the case of a public company, each share (other than a share allotted pursuant to an employee share scheme – see **13.9**) must be paid up at least as to one-quarter of its nominal value together with the whole of any premium paid on it.

Finally, as **14.6.16** above explained, the Pre-emption Group's Principles provide that a listed company should not issue any share under a s 570 or 571 disapplication (on a non pre-emptive basis) at a discount of more than 5% of its market value. This restriction does not apply, however, if the pre-emption requirements of the Listing Rules are followed.

14.7.5 Valuation of non-cash consideration

Section 593(1) of the CA 2006 provides that if the consideration for the allotment is not cash ('non-cash consideration'), the consideration must be independently valued, and a report of the valuation must be given to the company and the subscriber. There are some exceptions to this rule, however, and one important exception relates to a 'share-for-share exchange', that is, when the consideration for the issue of shares by one company is shares in another company. In this case no valuation is required (s 594). Note that the European Commission's proposed directive to amend the second Company Law Directive suggests limiting this requirement (see **16.8**).

14.7.6 Class rights

The procedure required to vary rights which attach to a certain class of shares was examined at **13.7** above. The lawyer must examine the rights attaching to the shares the company proposes to issue, to check that the issue will not, in fact, vary any existing class rights (for example, if the shares to be issued are a new class which will rank above an existing class in terms of dividend rights). If they will vary class rights, the procedures detailed in **13.7** above will need to be followed.

14.7.7 The Prospectus Rules

The lawyer must analyse the terms of the share issue to check whether a prospectus is required. **Chapter 17** considers this in relation to listed companies which are seeking to issue further shares.

14.7.8 Filing details of the issue

The company must notify the Registrar of any allotment of shares within one month of the allotment, by completing and delivering Form SH01 to Companies House. Note that the form must include a brief description of the consideration for which the shares were allotted. If the consideration was other than for cash, a simple description of the asset which comprises the consideration will suffice, such as '100 ordinary shares of £1 in Z Limited' if the consideration for the issue is shares. A statement of capital (contained in the form) must also be completed.

14.8 Conclusion

This chapter has shown that, while it is common for a company to issue shares, it can cause a few headaches for the lawyer. However, a methodical approach will ensure that all the required checks are made, and appropriate action taken. Do not forget, either, that while the lawyer should consider the three vital questions outlined at **14.3** above in relation to all issues of shares, not all issues will require action to be taken in relation to all three questions. For example, it may be that the company does not have a restriction in its articles on the number of shares it can issue, the directors already have authority to allot those shares, and the pre-emption rights have already been disapplied.

Also, the introduction to this chapter stated that it is not that the legislation which applies to listed companies is any more onerous than that applying to private companies, it is simply that the share capital of listed companies tends to be more complex. We have considered some of the more complex classes of securities that a listed company may have, such as convertible debt securities and convertible preference shares, in the context of whether an issue of such securities would require a s 551 authority, or trigger, or entitle recipients to, s 561 pre-emption rights on allotment. However, often listed companies will be issuing ordinary shares, like our example of X plc, where the process is much more straightforward because it is easier to determine whether the shares fall within the definitions in the CA 2006.

Chapter 15

Disclosure of Interests in Shares

15.1 Introduction

People become shareholders of a company, public or private, in one of two ways. They either subscribe for shares which the company issues (see **Chapter 14**), or they buy shares from existing shareholders (see **Chapter 19**). In both cases, the new shareholder will identify himself (or itself) to the company, so that the company can record the shareholder's details in its register of members and send out a share certificate.

This chapter considers the rules which require certain shareholders of public companies to disclose their interests in shares to the company, and why, despite the seemingly adequate process outlined above, a public company requires this extra protection.

15.2 Nominee shareholders

A 'nominee' shareholder is the registered owner of a share, but he holds that share on trust for the benefit of another person, the 'beneficial owner'. The nominee will hold the legal title to the share but will have no beneficial interest in that share. Usually the beneficial owner will require the nominee to execute a declaration of trust in respect of the share, in which the nominee will give various undertakings to the beneficial owner, such as:

(a) to account to the beneficial owner for dividends and other income received in respect of the share;

(b) to exercise rights attaching to the share, such as voting rights, as the beneficial owner directs; and

(c) to transfer the share as the beneficial owner directs.

For example, stockbrokers use companies to act as nominee shareholders, to manage the accounts of their clients more efficiently. We have also seen an example with the CREST system of holding shares in listed companies in electronic form (see **2.5.3.1**).

15.3 The register of members

All companies must maintain a register of members, pursuant to s 113 of the CA 2006. However, s 126 of the CA 2006 prohibits a company from recording notice of any trust in the register of members. This means that the register will record details of the holder of the legal title only. It will not record any details of the holder of the beneficial title. In some cases, of course, this is one and the same person. If I buy a share in Marks and Spencer Group plc tomorrow, I will own both legal and beneficial title to it. However, anyone who buys shares through a nominee will remain off the register; it is the nominee's details which the register will record.

15.3.1   Advantages of s 126

The purpose of s 126 is to make the company's administration easier, because the company does not have to concern itself with matters of beneficial entitlement to shares. The company has no obligation to identify the beneficial owner, or to involve itself in the detail of what a nominee shareholder can or cannot do in relation to the shares. As far as the company is concerned, no one has an interest in the share other than the person entered in the register of members. This is so helpful to a company that it will often reiterate this provision in its articles of association.

15.3.2   Disadvantages of s 126

Section 126 does have its disadvantages. It means that the company is not aware of who has beneficial ownership of its shares. Why is this a problem? For private companies it does not tend to be problematic. Often in private companies the shareholders are a relatively small group of people who know each other.

However, with public companies whose shares are traded on the Stock Exchange this is not the case. There are many shareholders. Nominee shareholders can be useful to market abusers or insider dealers seeking to hide their true identities (see **Chapter 10** and **11**). The value of those companies whose shares are traded on the Stock Exchange means that they are often targets for a takeover offer (see **Chapters 20** to **23**). If the company is not aware of the beneficial ownership of its shares, what is to stop a potential bidder secretly building up a large shareholding in the target company by buying shares through a nominee? These shares would come in very useful when it comes to securing acceptance of the offer from target company shareholders.

For these reasons, there are rules which require the disclosure to the company of certain interests in shares. Some of them should be familiar, as we encountered them briefly in **Chapter 7** when we examined the continuing obligations of listed companies.

15.4   Rules requiring the disclosure of share interests

In implementing the Transparency Directive in the UK (see **3.1** and **3.5.3** above), Chapter 5 of the DTRs was introduced with effect from 20 January 2007, requiring major shareholdings to be disclosed to the company. Chapter 5 is considered at **15.5** below.

Part 22 of the CA 2006, through provisions brought into force on 20 January 2007, concerns a public company's right to investigate who has a beneficial interest in its shares. This is examined at **15.6** below.

There are certain other provisions under the DTRs and the City Code which also require the disclosure of the beneficial ownership of a public company shares in particular circumstances. These requirements are discussed at **15.7**.

15.5   Notification of the acquisition or disposal of major shareholdings

The Transparency Directive requires rules to be in place in every EU Member State relating to the notification of the acquisition or disposal of major shareholdings in certain companies. The relevant provisions were introduced by Pt 43 of the CA 2006, which enacted new provisions in Pt VI of the FSMA 2000. Pursuant to these provisions the Transparency Rules were drawn up by the FSA. Chapter 5 contains the particular rules relating to the notification of major shareholdings. Chapter 5 applies to companies whose shares are admitted to trading on a *regulated* market (such as the Main Market). The rules therefore apply to the companies considered by this book. In addition, Chapter 5 of the DTRs applies to companies whose shares are admitted to trading on a *prescribed* market. This includes AIM. Chapter 5 is therefore the only part of the DTRs which extends beyond Main Market companies to include AIM-quoted companies. Chapter 5 requires a shareholder of such companies to disclose his shareholding to the company in certain circumstances. Paragraph **15.3.2** above explains why this protection extends only to certain public companies.

In looking at these rules for this book we shall only consider the position of a UK plc which has its shares admitted to the Official List and admitted to trading on the Main Market. We shall not be considering either AIM-quoted companies or non-UK companies. There is detailed guidance provided by the FSA on the application of the rules for all types of company in its newsletter *List!*, No 14 updated.

15.5.1 Purpose

The purpose of Chapter 5 of the DTRs is to ensure that companies whose shares are traded on the Stock Exchange are made aware of the identity of the beneficial owners of their shares, and therefore who controls voting rights in the company. As explained in **15.3.2** above, this is particularly helpful in terms of assisting the company to expose insider dealing or market abuse and to defend against a possible unwanted takeover bid.

15.5.2 When the obligation arises

The obligation to disclose interests in shares is triggered when the percentage of voting rights a person holds either as a shareholder, or directly or indirectly through his holding of financial instruments, crosses certain thresholds, the lowest of which is 3% (DTR 5.1.2R). Although 3% may not seem like a major shareholding, it is worth remembering that companies whose shares are trading on the Stock Exchange are the biggest in the country. A 3% stake in BP, one of the Stock Exchange's largest companies, is worth approximately £3 *billion* at the time of writing. So a shareholder with such a stake in the company has influence well beyond the apparently unimportant percentage, as so few shareholders will be able to reach this level.

15.5.3 The thresholds triggering disclosure

The applicable thresholds depend on two factors:

(a)   whether the company is a UK company or a non-UK company; and

(b)   the type of person holding voting rights in a company.

15.5.3.1 UK company

A person must notify a UK company if the percentage of voting rights he holds reaches, exceeds or falls below 3% and every whole percentage above 3% up to 100% (DTR 5.1.2R(1)).

It is important to note that a decrease as well as an increase in voting rights may be caught by the obligation to notify. Also, DTR 5.1.2R requires further changes, up or down, in the whole percentage figure of voting rights held by the person after an initial notification to be notified.

Example

Miss C buys 2% of listed UK company Z plc in January 2010. No obligation to notify arises (she has not reached 3%). In March 2010 she buys a further 1%. She must make a notification under DTR 5.2.1R as she now owns 3% of Z plc. Miss C buys a further 2% in June 2010. She must make a further notification under DTR 5.1.2R as she now owns 5% and her voting rights have changed by a whole percentage figure from 3% to 5%. In July 2010 Miss C sells 1% of her shares in Z plc. Again, as her voting rights have changed by a whole percentage figure (from 5% to 4%), she must make another notification.

15.5.3.2 Specialist holders of voting rights

Certain institutional investors (such as an asset manager) need make a notification only at 5% and 10% and every whole percentage above 10% for certain types of share (DTR 5.1.5R).

15.5.3.3   Change in voting rights

Under DTR 5.6.1R, a listed company is obliged, at the end of each month during which there has been an increase or decrease in the number of its issued voting shares, to publish a statement of the new total number of voting rights in the company through an RIS. An increase can occur, for example, after a rights issue or an issue of shares under an employee share scheme. A decrease can occur, for example, after a buyback of shares by the company. The importance of this is that the percentage voting rights of a person who owns, say, 10 shares in a company with 100 issued shares (10%) changes if the number of issued shares in that company increases to 1,000 shares (now 1%) or decreases to 50 shares (now 20%) and that person does not buy or sell any shares.

Transparency Rule 5.1.2R(2) therefore obliges a person whose voting rights reach or cross one of the required thresholds by virtue of a change in the company's issued share capital, to make the necessary notification. This is a logical extension of the basic rule, for even though the person has not bought or sold any shares, his relative voting power (as shown in the example above) has now changed, and 3% is still 3% of the voting rights in the company even if it arose without any shares being bought or sold by the holder.

An example of an announcement made under DTR 5.6.1R is set out below.

Company	Prudential PLC
TIDM	PRU
Headline	Total Voting Rights
Released	12:35 02-Oct-08
Number	9450E12

TOTAL VOTING RIGHTS AND ISSUED SHARE CAPITAL

In accordance with the provisions of the Financial Services Authority's Disclosure and Transparency Rules, Prudential would like to notify the market of the following:

As at 9am on 2 October 2008 Prudential's issued share capital consists of 2,496,881,682 ordinary shares of 5p each and which are admitted to trading. Each ordinary share carries the right to one vote in relation to all circumstances at general meetings of Prudential. Prudential does not hold any ordinary shares in treasury.

Therefore, the total number of voting rights in Prudential is 2,496,881,682.

This figure (2,496,881,682) may be used by shareholders (and others with notification obligations) as the denominator for the calculations by which they will determine whether they are required to notify their interest in, or a change to their interest in, Prudential under the Financial Services Authority's Disclosure and Transparency Rules.

15.5.3.4   Percentage level

For the purposes of calculating whether any of the percentage thresholds in **15.5.3.1** and **15.5.3.2** has been reached, exceeded or fallen below, the percentage figure shall be rounded down to the next whole number (DTR 5.1.1R(6)): 3.5% therefore becomes 3% for the purposes of Chapter 5 of the DTRs; 14.99% becomes 14%; 6.07% becomes 6%, and so on. What this means is practice is that the notification obligation kicks in only when a whole percentage number changes. A person who buys more shares in a company, resulting in a change in voting rights from 3.2% to 3.9%, does not need to make a notification. Both figures are rounded down to the whole number 3% (that person will of course have made a notification on first crossing the 3% threshold). However, a person who sells shares, resulting in a drop in voting rights from 8.1% to 7.9%, must make a notification. The 8.1% is rounded down to 8% and 7.9% is rounded down to 7%. So although the sale represents a drop of only 0.2% in actual voting rights in the company, for the purposes of Chapter 5 it is a drop of whole percentage, thereby triggering a notification under DTR 5.1.2R.

15.5.3.5   Indirect holdings of voting rights

Under DTR 5.1.2R, for the purposes of calculating whether any of the percentage thresholds in **15.5.3.1** and **15.5.3.2** has been reached, exceeded or fallen below, a person must include any indirect holdings of voting rights (by virtue of the definition of 'shareholder' in the Glossary to the FSA Handbook). Direct holdings, which we have considered up to now, are those in shares fully owned in the name of the person concerned. Indirect holdings are specified in DTR 5.2.1R. They cover scenarios where a third party has ownership of the shares but another person is entitled to acquire, exercise or dispose of the voting rights in certain circumstances. Three examples are set out below.

Controlled companies

Disclosure and Transparency Rule 5.2.1R(e) includes voting rights held by a company which another person controls. So, for example, if Mr T owned 2.5 % of the voting shares in A plc in his own name, no notification obligation would arise as he owns below 3% of the voting rights. If, though, a company, ACME Limited, owned 100% by Mr T, subsequently bought 1% of the shares in A plc then this indirect holding would be aggregated with Mr T's direct holding and take him to 3.5%, and therefore require him to make a notification under DTR 5.1.2R.

Proxies

Where the Chairman of a company is given proxy votes to exercise at his discretion at a general meeting then this too will amount to an indirect shareholding, and if totalling 3% or more of the voting rights will have also have to be notified (DTR 5.2.1R(h)).

Concert parties

Disclosure and Transparency Rule 5.2.1R(a) covers people who have an agreement to adopt a lasting common policy towards the directors of the company by the exercise of their joint voting rights. If such people hold 3% or more of the shares in a company then they must make a notification. This would catch people otherwise seeking to avoid the disclosure thresholds by clubbing together to acquire voting rights in a company, but with each holding of voting rights falling below the relevant threshold. For example, if G, H and J each own 2.5% of V plc's shares individually they have no notification obligation. However, if they had an agreement in accordance with DTR 5.2.1R(a) then the obligation would arise. This is particularly useful for a company in defending it against a surprise takeover bid. The rule seeks to ensure that the company is aware not only of a potential bidder's stake in the company (if it breaches 3%), but also of the group companies and the financial advisers of the bidder who may also be buying up shares.

15.5.3.6   Holdings of qualifying financial instruments

Under DTR 5.1.2R and DTR 5.3.1R, for the purposes of calculating whether any of the percentage thresholds in **15.5.3.1** and **15.5.3.2** has been reached, exceeded or fallen below, a person must consider not only direct holdings of voting rights and indirect holdings of voting rights (**15.5.3.5**), but also direct or indirect holdings in qualifying financial instruments which give the right to acquire shares with voting rights in the company. Transparency Rule 5.3.2R gives examples of such instruments, which could include convertible loan stock, options, etc.

15.5.4   Procedure for the making the notification

We now know what the disclosure obligation is and when it must be made. The question now arises as to how the holder of voting rights fulfils his obligation.

15.5.4.1   Who is notified and how?

The person must notify the company in which he holds the voting rights (DTR 5.1.2R and DTR 5.8.2(2)R). Furthermore, a copy of the notification must also be sent to the FSA (DTR 5.9.1 and 5.8.2(2), and *List!*, No 14 updated).

In accordance with DTR 5.8.10R and DTR 5.9.1R, the notification must be made on Form TR1 (available on the FSA's website) and the copy sent to the FSA must be submitted electronically. The content of the Form TR1 can be seen in the example at **15.5.4.3** below.

15.5.4.2   Deadline for making the notification

The notification must be made by the relevant person to the company and the FSA within two trading days after the day when the person became aware, or should have become aware, of the acquisition or a disposal, or possibility of exercising voting rights (DTR 5.8.3R). This deadline is also triggered by the publication of a statement of a change in voting rights made under DTR 5.6.1R. The FSA provides a link to a calendar of trading days through its website (DTR 5.8.9G). Basically, weekends and public holidays are excluded.

15.5.4.3   Content of the notification

The notification must include the information in DTR 5.8.1R for a notification of a direct or indirect holding of voting rights in shares, and DTR 5.8.2R sets out the required contents for a notification of voting rights in qualifying financial instruments. As explained at **15.5.4.1** above, a Form TR1 should be used. An example of a Form TR1 is set out below. Note that in the copy sent to the FSA only there must be an additional Annex containing contact details (DTR 5.9.1R and *List!*, No 14 updated).

Company	Trinity Mirror PLC
TIDM	TNI
Headline	Holding(s) in Company
Released	13:29 15-Sep-2009
Number	0893Z13

TR-1: NOTIFICATION OF MAJOR INTERESTS IN SHARES

1. Identity of the issuer or the underlying issuer of existing shares to which voting rights are attached:	Trinity Mirror plc

2. Reason for the notification (please tick the appropriate box or boxes):

An acquisition or disposal of voting rights	✔
An acquisition or disposal of financial instruments which may result in the acquisition of shares already issued to which voting rights are attached	
An acquisition or disposal of instruments with similar economic effect to qualifying financial instruments	
An event changing the breakdown of voting rights	
Other (please specify):	

3. Full name of person(s) subject to the notification obligation:	Aviva plc & its subsidiaries

4. Full name of shareholder(s) (if different from 3.):	Registered Holder:
	BNY Norwich Union Nominees Limited **2,861,241***
	Chase (GA Group) Nominees Limited **20,157,976***
	Chase Nominees Limited **425,039***
	CUIM Nominee Limited **208,118***
	Vidacos Nominees Limited **24,744***
	*denotes direct interest
	Chase Nominees Limited **964,756**
	Vidacos Nominees Limited **970,034**
5. Date of the transaction and date on which the threshold is crossed or reached:	11 September 2009
6. Date on which issuer notified:	14 September 2009
7. Threshold(s) that is/are crossed or reached:	10% to <10% Change at Combined Interest Level

8. Notified details:

A: Voting rights attached to shares

Class/type of shares if possible using the ISIN CODE	Situation previous to the triggering transaction		Resulting situation after the triggering transaction				
	Number of shares	Number of voting rights	Number of shares	Number of voting rights		% of voting rights	
			Direct	Direct	Indirect	Direct	Indirect
Ordinary Shares GB0009039941	26,129,184	26,129,184	25,611,908	23,677,118	1,934,790	9.19%	0.75%

B: Qualifying Financial Instruments

Resulting situation after the triggering transaction

Type of financial instrument	Expiration date	Exercise/ conversion period	Number of voting rights that may be acquired if the instrument is exercised/converted	% of voting rights

C: Financial Instruments with similar economic effect to Qualifying Financial Instruments

Resulting situation after the triggering transaction

Type of financial instrument	Exercise price	Expiration date	Exercise/ conversion period	Number of voting rights instrument refers to	% of voting rights	
					Nominal	Delta

Total (A+B+C)	
Number of voting rights	Percentage of voting rights
25,611,908	9.94

9. Chain of controlled undertakings through which the voting rights and/or the financial instruments are effectively held, if applicable:
The voting rights are managed and controlled by **Aviva Investors Global Services Limited**, with the following chain of controlled undertakings:-
Aviva Investors Global Services Limited:
• Aviva plc (Parent Company)
• Aviva Group Holdings Limited (wholly owned subsidiary of Aviva plc)
• Aviva Investors Holdings Limited (wholly owned subsidiary of Aviva Group Holdings Limited)
• Aviva Investors Global Services Limited (wholly owned subsidiary of Aviva Investors Holdings Limited)

Proxy Voting	
10. Name of the proxy holder:	See Section 4
11. Number of voting rights proxy holder will cease to hold:	
12. Date on which proxy holder will cease to hold voting rights:	

13. Additional information:	Figures are based on a total number of voting rights of 257,690,520
14. Contact name:	Neil Whittaker
15. Contact telephone number:	01603 684220

15.5.5   The company's response to the notification

The notification made to the company concerned must be made public through an RIS by the end of the next trading day following receipt, in accordance with DTR 5.8.12R. The FSA provides a link to a calendar of trading days through its website (DTR 5.8.9G). The company must comply with DTR 6.3 when releasing the information. There is no set format for such an announcement, but if the Form TR1 is published the Annex must be removed (*List!*, No 14 updated).

15.5.6   Sanctions for breach

The FSA can impose the following sanctions for breaches of Chapter 5 of the DTRs:

(a)   private or public censure;

(b)   an unlimited fine;

(c)   require the relevant information to be disclosed to it (FSMA 2000, s 89H); and

(d)   may suspend or prohibit trading in the shares (FSMA 2000, s 89L).

15.6   The company's power to investigate beneficial ownership

We have already established that direct and indirect major owners of shares (and certain financial instruments) in companies whose shares are trading on the Stock Exchange must disclose certain levels of voting rights to the company. Part 22 of the CA 2006 supplements

Chapter 5 of the DTRs by allowing public companies (whether listed or not) to be proactive and investigate the beneficial ownership of its shares in certain circumstances either:

(a)   on its own initiative, pursuant to s 793 of the CA 2006; or

(b)   because a shareholder has compelled it to do so, under s 803 of the CA 2006.

This power reflects just how important it is considered to be that a public company, particularly one trading on the Stock Exchange, is able to identify the ultimate ownership of its shares. The aim is to enable the company to identify any shareholder who may have predatory intentions toward the company and may be considering or seeking to launch a takeover bid. This power has become all the more important due to the increasing use of nominee shareholder accounts in CREST (the dematerialised system for owning shares in listed companies – see **2.5.3.1**).

15.6.1   Section 793 notice

If a public company knows, or has reasonable cause to believe, that a person:

(a)   is interested; or

(b)   has been interested, at any time within the last three years,

in the company's shares, the company can serve a s 793 notice on that person, requesting him to confirm whether or not he does have such an interest, details of those interests and certain other relevant information. The noticed may be served in writing or electronically. Section 793 details the specific information which the company can request, but it also includes, for example, details of any concert party arrangements (see **15.5.3.5** above). In fact, the company can request information which is not covered by the disclosure obligation; for example, even if the recipient of the notice has interests which are less than 3%, the recipient can still be requested to disclose his interests.

The s 793 notice must specify a reasonable time within which the recipient must respond. This is not defined. In practice, this seems to be interpreted as two days in an emergency situation (such as when the company suspects it is the target of an impending takeover bid), and five days in all other circumstances.

Of course, s 793 is particularly welcome when a company suspects it is about to be the target of an unwanted takeover bid. Imagine that the share price of X plc has been falling dramatically and that the press has speculated that now would be a good time for one of X plc's competitors to launch a takeover bid. The company secretary of X plc will send out s 793 notices in order to expose any prospective bidder. In the event that the bidder then makes the bid, the company secretary will continue to send out s 793 notices, to monitor the level of acceptances. Of course, the bidder should also comply with the disclosure obligations under Chapter 5 of the DTRs and notify the company whenever its shareholding increases by a percentage level.

In practice, while the company secretary will often draft the notice (as it is the company secretary who will have daily contact with the company's registrars), he will often consult the company's lawyers about the interpretation of aspects of the legislation, for example what the current practice is as to the minimum 'reasonable time' within which the company can demand a reply.

The CA 2006 does not specify a format for a s 793 notice, but in light of the minimal changes to the position under the CA 1985, there is a specimen notice available on the BIS website (formerly the DBERR), under s 212 of the 1985 Act, which is still instructive. At the time of writing, BIS had yet to update this specimen.

15.6.2   Shareholders' s 803 requisition

Section 803 of the CA 2006 provides that shareholders who hold at least one-tenth of the company's paid-up voting share capital can requisition the company to use its powers under s 793. The requisition must:

(a)   be in hard copy or electronic form;

(b)   state that the company is requested to exercise its powers under s 793;

(c)   give reasonable grounds for requiring the company to exercise its powers in that way;

(d)   be authenticated; and

(d)   be served in accordance with Pt 37 of the CA 2006.

Section 805 provides that the company must respond by carrying out the requested investigation and compiling a report of its findings, which it must make available at the company's registered office or at a place specified under regulations to be made in accordance with s 1136 of the CA 2006.

The company must act on the request within certain time limits set out in s 805. If it fails to do so, sanctions may be imposed (see **15.6.3.2**).

15.6.3   Sanctions

15.6.3.1   Criminal penalties

It is a criminal offence under s 795(2) of the CA 2006 to fail to comply with a s 793 notice, or knowingly or recklessly to make a false statement in reply. The offence is punishable with up to two years' imprisonment and/or a fine.

Fines can be imposed under s 798 of the CA 2006 for attempts to evade the restrictions placed under a s 794 order (see **15.6.3.2** below).

Fines can also be imposed for a failure to comply with a s 803 shareholder requisition, and for failing to meet various requirements relating to the obligation to provide a report under s 805 and allow access to it.

15.6.3.2   Imposing restrictions on shares

Section 794 of the CA 2006 allows the company to apply to court to have restrictions placed on shares covered by a s 793 notice where the recipient of the notice has failed to respond in time. Section 797 of the 2006 Act sets out the consequences of such an order if it is made:

(a)   any transfer of the shares is void;

(b)   no voting rights are exercisable in respect of the shares;

(c)   the shareholder cannot benefit from any rights given by his shares to receive new shares in the company (such as a bonus or rights issue); and

(d)   except on liquidation, no payment can be made of any sums due from the company on the shares, such as a dividend.

These restrictions are onerous, and are intended to prevent the person in breach of the s 793 notice from taking advantage of the breach, such as by launching a surprise takeover bid (the shares acquired could not be used to vote in favour of the bid) or by profiting from insider dealing or market abuse (the transfer is void). The company or any aggrieved person can apply to court for the removal of the restrictions under s 800 of the CA 2006. The court shall remove the restrictions only if it is satisfied that the relevant facts about the shares have been disclosed to the company and that no unfair advantage has accrued to anyone as a result of the breach of the disclosure obligation, or the shares are sold and the court approves the transfer.

15.6.4 The register of share interests

Section 808 of the CA 2006 provides that the company must keep a separate register which records interests disclosed to it pursuant to a s 793 notice. The company must keep the register, and the public have the right to inspect this register under s 811 of the CA 2006.

Section 817 of the CA 2006 provides protection for anyone who has been entered into the register who does not consider they should be in that register. It can arise in the process of complying with the s 793 notice that a shareholder identifies another person as being interested in shares. Section 817 provides a process whereby that person can insist on being removed from the register, provided the information which has been supplied is incorrect.

15.7 Other requirements

There are further disclosure requirements under the DTRs and the Listing Rules. Both sets of rules apply only to listed companies.

15.7.1 Transactions by PDMRs and their connected persons

As mentioned at **7.5.7.10** above, DTR 3.1.2R requires PDMRs and their connected persons to disclose to the company all transactions conducted on their own account in the shares of the company (or derivatives or any other financial instruments relating to those shares). This must be done within four business days of the day on which the transaction occurred. The PDMR must include in the disclosure the information required by DTR 3.1.3R.

A listed company must then notify an RIS of the information it receives under DTR 3.1.2R (DTR 3.1.4R(1)(a)). The company must include the information required by DTR 3.1.3R (DTR 3.1.5R), and provide the information to the RIS as soon as possible, and in any event no later than the end of the business day following the receipt of the information (DTR 3.1.4R(2)).

An example of such a notification is set out below. They can be found on the RNS section of the Stock Exchange's website under the heading 'Director/PDMR shareholding'.

Company	Tesco PLC
TIDM	TSCO
Headline	Director/PDMR Shareholding
Released	17:24 30-Sep-08
Number	7612E17

DIRECTORS' SHAREHOLDINGS

On 30 September 2008, the following Director exercised an option over Ordinary shares of 5p each in the Company under the Tesco Executive Share Option Scheme and sold a total of 28,240 Ordinary shares at a price of 369.2p.

Director	Number of Shares Acquired	Option Price
T P Leahy	126,832	164.00p

This announcement is made in accordance with the requirements of DTR 3.1.4.

15.7.2 Directors' interests in shares

As mentioned at **7.5.7.11** above, LR 9.8.6R(1) requires a statement, setting out the directors' holdings of shares in their listed company, to be included in the annual report, together with any changes to this information over the past year. Disclosure Rule 3.1.4R requires this information to be notified to an RIS no later than the end of the next business day.

15.7.3   The Model Code

As explained at **7.8** above, PDMRs and their connected persons are required to seek clearance before dealing in shares they own in their listed company.

15.7.4   Takeovers

15.7.4.1   Application of the City Code

Chapter 20 explores this in more detail, but, broadly speaking, the City Code applies during the offer period for a takeover of, for example, a UK plc listed on the Stock Exchange (see **22.3.4**). If the City Code does apply, it applies to everyone participating in the takeover, such as the offeror (the bidder) and the offeree (the target company), and their directors and any advisers.

15.7.4.2   Nature of the City Code

The City Code has the force of law under the Takeover Directive which has now been implemented in the UK. It exists to ensure that all takeovers are conducted fairly and in an orderly manner (see **Chapter 20**).

15.7.4.3   The obligation

Disclosure of issued shares (r 2.10)

The main disclosure obligation is under r 8 of the City Code and relates to dealings in shares during the offer period. However, as a precursor to that disclosure obligation, those companies whose securities will be subject to that disclosure obligation must notify the market, via an RIS, of the exact number of relevant securities which are in issue during the offer period.

Rule 2.10 of the City Code provides that:

(a)   as soon as possible after the commencement of the offer period (and in any event by 9.00 am on the next business day) the target company; and

(b)   by 9.00 am on the business day after any announcement of a firm intention to make an offer (unless it has already stated that its offer will be, or is likely to be, solely in cash) the bidder, or a potential named bidder,

must each announce details, through an RIS, of all classes of relevant securities it has in issue, together with the numbers of such securities in issue.

Relevant securities are defined as:

(a)   voting shares in the target company;

(b)   any other shares in the target company which are the subject of the offer;

(c)   equity share capital in the target company and the bidder;

(d)   securities of the bidder which carry substantially the same rights as any to be issued as consideration for the offer; and

(e)   any securities in the target company and the bidder which are convertible into, or carry subscription rights over, any of the shares referred to at (a) to (c) above.

Disclosure of dealings (r 8)

Rule 8 of the City Code provides that, once the offer period has commenced:

(a)   the offeror;

(b)   the offeree company; and

(c)   any associates of the offeror or offeree company,

must disclose any dealings (as defined by the City Code) in relevant securities (see above) to an RIS and the Takeover Panel no later than 12 noon on the business day following the date of the transaction.

There is no complete definition of 'associate', because the City Code considers that it is not possible to cover all the possible permutations, which depend on the structure of the offer. However, the term is clearly intended to cover those who have an interest in the outcome of the offer. The Code gives the following examples of persons who typically will be associates:

(a) the offeree group companies and the offeror group companies (and their associated companies, being companies in which they have a shareholding of 20% or more);

(b) connected advisers of the offeree company and the offeror (and any members of the connected adviser's groups);

(c) directors (and their close family and related trusts) of the offeree group companies and the offeror group companies;

(d) pension funds of the offeree or the offeror group companies;

(e) any investment company, unit trust or other person whose investments are managed by an associate on a discretionary basis;

(f) employee benefit trusts of any of the companies referred to at (a) above; and

(g) companies which have material trading agreements with the offeree company or the offeror.

1% shareholders (r 8.3)

Rule 8.3 of the City Code provides that if a person is interested or, as the result of any transaction, will be interested (directly or indirectly), in 1% or more of any class of relevant securities of an offeror or offeree, then he must disclose his dealings in any relevant securities of that company, as well as the dealings of any other person through whom he derives his interest. The disclosure must be made by 3.30 pm on the business day following the date of the transaction (Note 3).

If disclosure is required under r 8.1(a) or (b)(i), then the same information does not also need to be disclosed under r 8.3 (Note 5).

The aim is therefore to ensure maximum transparency in share dealings by parties involved in a takeover. It is very important that the offeree company is aware of how big a stake the offeror has in it and when it changes.

15.7.4.4 Content of the notification

The 'Disclosure Forms' section of the Takeover Panel's website contains a specimen disclosure form which sets out the format a r 8 notification should follow. An abbreviated, real-life example of a r 8.1 notification is set out below.

Company	HBOS PLC
TIDM	HBOS
Headline	Rule 8.1- Lloyds TSB Group plc
Released	13:07 03-Oct-08
Number	0601F13

FORM 8.1
DEALINGS BY OFFERORS, OFFEREE COMPANIES OR THEIR ASSOCIATES FOR
THEMSELVES OR FOR DISCRETIONARY CLIENTS
(Rules 8.1(a) and (b)(i) of the City Code on Takeovers and Mergers)

1.   KEY INFORMATION

Name of person dealing (Note 1)	HBOS plc and its subsidiaries
Company dealt in	Lloyds TSB Group plc
Class of relevant security to which the dealings being disclosed relate (Note 2)	Ord 25p
Date of dealing	2 October 2008

2.   INTERESTS, SHORT POSITIONS AND RIGHTS TO SUBSCRIBE

(a)   Interests and short positions (following dealing) in the class of relevant security dealt in (Note 3)

	Long	Short
	Number (%)	**Number (%)**
(1) Relevant securities	72,341,335 (1.211%)	
(2) Derivatives (other than options)		
(3) Options and agreements to purchase/sell		
Total	72,341,335 (1.211%)	

* Difference in position of 1,250 shares due to transfers in and out

3.   DEALINGS (Note 4)

(a)   Purchases and sales

Purchase/sale	Number of securities	Price per unit (Note 5)
Purchase	750	£2.650
Purchase	650,358	£2.650
Purchase	108,290	£2.660
Purchase	346,530	£2.680
Sale	14,170	£2.510

15.8 Summary

The table below summarises the key notification obligations, relating to the disclosure of interests in shares, covered by this chapter. The table is intended to be an overview only, and recourse should be made to the text for the specific detail of the rules.

Rule	Notifier	Notifiee	Interest	Deadline
DTR 5.1.2R	Shareholder of public company	Company	Acquires 3% (or further increase beyond whole percentage point), or falls by a whole percentage point or below 3% (see **15.5.3** for detail)	2 trading days after they become aware of interest
DTR 5.8.12R	Listed company	RIS	Information received under DTR 5.1.2R	By end of trading day following the day the company receives the information
DTR 3.1.2R	PDMRs of listed company (and their connected persons)	Company	All transactions conducted on their own account in the company's shares (or derivatives or any other financial instruments relating to those shares)	4 business days of day on which transaction occurred
DTR 3.1.4R (1)(a)	Listed company	RIS	Information received under DTR 3.1.2R	By end of the business day following the day the company receives the information
City Code Rule 2.10	Offeror, offeree company and associates	RIS	Number of relevant securities in issue	By 9am on the next business day after the start of the offer period (offeree) By 9am on business day after announcement of firm intention to make offer (offeror)
City Code Rule 8	Offeror, offeree company and associates	RIS and Takeover Panel	Any dealings in relevant securities	12 noon on business day following date of transaction

Chapter 16
Financial Assistance

16.1 Introduction

So far, **Part III** of this book has considered the concept of shares: what they are; the different classes of share; the law relating to share issues; and how a company can find out who owns its shares. This chapter considers a potential problem which can arise on the *acquisition* of shares; the problem that, subject to certain exceptions, a public company cannot give 'financial assistance' for the purchase of its shares. With effect from 1 October 2008, the former prohibition on *private* companies giving financial assistance was repealed under the CA 2006.

In its simplest form this means that if I want to buy shares in X plc, X plc cannot give me any financial help to buy those shares.

The rule itself is straightforward enough. So why is it described as a problem? In practice, financial assistance can arise in ways which are not easy to spot. In addition, the lawyer is often removed from the detail of the funding arrangements and is concentrating, instead, on the negotiation of the transaction. These two factors can conspire to make financial assistance an area that can inject an element of last-minute panic into a share acquisition that is otherwise running quite smoothly.

16.2 Rationale

To achieve a good understanding of the financial assistance rules, it can help to consider the rationale behind those rules. Why is financial assistance prohibited?

Let us consider a practical example of financial assistance. I am a financier and I want to buy a company. I lack significant funds. I find a company, X plc, which has substantial cash reserves and easily realisable assets (that is, they can be sold for cash readily). I agree to buy X plc for cash consideration. I am the buyer, and the shareholders of X plc are the sellers. I structure the transaction so that X plc uses its cash reserves, and cash realised from selling some of its assets, to advance me the cash I need to pay consideration to the shareholders of X plc. I then buy the company, but in effect X plc has funded the transaction.

The question is, who has lost out in this transaction? X plc's creditors. Their security is that X plc is cash-rich. This cash is now lining the pockets of the shareholders who sold shares in the company. It is no longer in X plc. X plc has misused its assets.

The prohibition on financial assistance would not permit the transaction described above. The reason? To protect creditors.

16.3   The financial assistance prohibition

Sections 678 and 679 of the CA 2006 contain the prohibitions on financial assistance. Section 678 prohibits the giving of financial assistance for the acquisition of shares in a public company. Section 679 prohibits the giving of financial assistance by a public company subsidiary for the acquisition of shares in its private holding company. Each section contains two prohibitions. The difference between them is:

(a)   s 678(1) and s 679(1) apply to financial assistance given *before or at the same time as* the acquisition of shares; and

(b)   s 678(3) and s 679(3) apply to financial assistance given *after* the acquisition of shares.

16.3.1   Financial assistance given before or at the same time as the acquisition of shares

We will start by looking at s 678(1), which provides that:

(a)   where a person is acquiring or *proposing to acquire* shares in a *public* company;

(b)   it is not lawful for the company;

(c)   or any of the company's *subsidiaries*;

(d)   to give financial assistance;

(e)   directly or indirectly;

(f)   *for the purpose* of that acquisition;

(g)   before or at the time the acquisition takes place.

The following points are of interest here:

(i)   Section 678(1) only applies to the acquisition of shares in a *public* company (whether listed or not).

(ii)   'Proposing to acquire' means that there does not actually have to be an acquisition of shares for s 678(1) to apply; it is the fact that the person *intends* to acquire shares which is important.

(iii)   The person giving the financial assistance (Assistor) does not necessarily have to be the company whose shares are being acquired (Target); if the Assistor is a subsidiary of Target, s 678(1) will apply even if it is a private company.

(iv)   'For the purpose' (see (f) above) means that this is a purpose-based, not a results-based, test. It is not sufficient simply that financial assistance results in the acquisition, or is somehow connected with the acquisition. The Assistor must have *intended* to facilitate the transaction by giving the assistance. It is vital, therefore, to identify why the Assistor has provided the assistance.

For the s 679(1) prohibition, the test is broadly the same as in (a)–(g) above, but in (a) substitute 'private' for 'public', and (b) and (c) will read 'it is not lawful for a public company that is a subsidiary of that company'.

16.3.2   Financial assistance given after the acquisition of shares

Once again we will start by considering s 678(3), which provides that:

(a)   where a person has acquired shares in a *public* company;

(b)   and a *liability has been incurred* (by that, *or any other*, person) for the purpose of that acquisition;

(c)   it is not lawful for the company;

(d)   or any of the company's *subsidiaries*;

(e)   to give financial assistance;

(f)   directly or indirectly;

(g)   *for the purpose* of *reducing or discharging the liability incurred*.

Again, note the following points:

(i)   Section 683(2) provides that 'incurring a liability' includes a change in financial position (there is no indication that this change must be for the worse). The obvious example of this is someone borrowing money to fund an acquisition.

(ii)   The liability does not have to have been incurred by the person acquiring the shares.

(iii)   As with s 678(1), the Assistor does not have to be Target; if the Assistor is a subsidiary of Target, s 678(3) will apply even if it is a private company.

(iv)   As with s 678(1), the words 'for the purpose' feature in s 678(3) too. This means that the financial assistance does not actually have to reduce or discharge the liability incurred, as long as it was *intended* to reduce or discharge that liability. As with s 678, it is vital to identify why the Assistor has provided the assistance.

(v)   Section 683(2) provides that 'reducing or discharging the liability incurred' includes wholly or partly restoring a person's financial position to what it was before the acquisition.

For the s 679(3) prohibition, the test is broadly the same as in (a) to (g) above, but in (a) substitute 'private' for 'public', and (b) and (c) will read 'it is not lawful for a public company that is a subsidiary of that company'.

16.4   What is financial assistance?

Section 677 of the CA 2006 defines 'financial assistance' as:

(a)   financial assistance given by way of gift (that is, where the Assistor transfers an asset of value for nil consideration);

(b)   financial assistance given by way of:

(i)   guarantee, security, indemnity (subject to a limited exception); or

(ii)   release or waiver; or

(c)   financial assistance given by way of loan (or certain other types of agreement such as credit); or

(d)   any other financial assistance given by a company:

(i)   the net assets (defined by s 677(2) as the actual value of assets less liabilities) of which are thereby reduced to a material extent (this is not defined, but appears to be a de-minimis level), or

(ii)   which has no net assets.

You will note that the 'definition' of financial assistance actually uses the words 'financial assistance'. Section 677(1) therefore does not really define what financial assistance is, rather it gives examples of financial assistance.

Nethertheless, this definition makes clear that financial assistance is not limited to the more obvious situations, such as where the Assistor makes a gift or loan to the buyer to fund the acquisition of shares. Assistance of an indirect nature, such as when a bank gives a loan to the buyer to fund the acquisition, but the Assistor guarantees that loan or gives any type of security for it, will also constitute financial assistance. As mentioned in the introduction to this chapter at **16.1** above, these less obvious examples of financial assistance can cause problems for the corporate lawyer.

Example

Imagine a typical day in practice. The chief executive of X plc calls you, its lawyer, to instruct you in relation to a share disposal. X plc is selling the entire issued share capital of its wholly-owned subsidiary, Target plc, to Buyer plc. The acquisition must be completed urgently. X plc needs the cash consideration from the sale by the end of the month (three days' time) or it will go bust.

You download your firm's precedent agreement and launch yourself into a series of meetings, first with your client, X plc, to find out the detail of the transaction, then with Buyer plc and its lawyers, to thrash out a deal.

Can you imagine how easy it is, in that first meeting with your client, for the client to say to you, 'We are selling all the shares in our subsidiary, Target plc. The buyer, Buyer plc, is paying a good price; it has secured a loan on really good terms from the bank', for you to make a note of this, then move on to more pressing areas of detail, such as the structure of the deal and the warranties X plc is prepared to give?

Forty-eight hours later you have an agreement ready to sign. At that point, you receive a call from a colleague in your firm's banking department, who says she has just received a call from the assistant company secretary of Target plc, asking her to review the form of guarantee Target plc is giving to Buyer plc's bank.

Suddenly you have a problem. Target plc cannot give Buyer's bank a guarantee, as this would be financial assistance and prohibited under s 677(1). The bank will not provide the loan to Buyer plc unless it receives the guarantee from Target plc it was promised. Without the bank loan, Buyer plc cannot purchase the shares in Target plc. Without the consideration, X plc will go bust. You have to explain this problem to X plc.

How could this situation have been avoided? Well if, at that first meeting, you had probed a little more into the funding arrangements with Buyer plc's bank, you might have prompted the client to mention the bank guarantee. This is clear with hindsight, but can be very easy to miss in the rush to make a start on the acquisition agreement within the time constraints imposed.

16.5   What is not financial assistance?

The CA 2006 provides three categories of exceptions to the financial assistance prohibition. These exceptions are considered below.

16.5.1   The purpose exceptions

It was explained at **16.3.1** and **16.3.2** above that purpose and intention are important when considering the prohibition on financial assistance. It should come as no surprise, then, to find that one of the exceptions to the financial assistance prohibition is concerned with purpose.

Section 678(2) and s 679(2) provide that s 678(1) and s 679(1) respective (that is, pre-acquisition financial assistance) do not prohibit the Assistor from giving financial assistance if:

(a)   either:

    (i)   the Assistor's *principal purpose* is not to give the financial assistance for the purpose of the acquisition (principal purpose exception), *or*

    (ii)   the giving of the financial assistance for the purpose of the acquisition was only an incidental part of some *larger purpose* of the Assistor (larger purpose exception); *and*

(b)   the Assistor gives the financial assistance in good faith in the interests of the Assistor.

Section 678(4) and s 679(4) provide principal purpose and larger purpose exceptions for financial assistance under s 678(3) and s 679(3) respectively too (that is, post-acquisition financial assistance), but the words 'the acquisition' (see (a)(i) and (ii) above) are replaced with 'reducing or discharging the liability which has been incurred'.

The 'principal purpose' and 'larger purpose' exceptions are somewhat vague, and it is difficult for the lawyer to be able to state definitively that they will apply. The decision in *Brady v Brady* [1989] AC 755 has made the application of the purpose exceptions even less clear.

16.5.1.1   *Brady v Brady*

In this case, an arrangement was made in good faith to divide a family company's assets into two new companies, so that the two brothers who ran the family company could go their separate ways. The arrangement involved the family company giving financial assistance, as Assistor. At first instance, it was held that while the arrangement was prohibited by the forerunner to s 678(1), it was saved by the larger purpose exception; the Assistor's giving of the assistance for the purpose of the acquisition was only an incidental part of the Assistor's *larger purpose*. The House of Lords, however, did not agree that the exception applied.

16.5.1.2   The principal purpose exception

In *Brady v Brady*, Lord Oliver explained that, for this exception to apply, there must be a principal and a secondary purpose behind the giving of the financial assistance. For example, if the principal purpose of the Assistor is to obtain an asset that it really wants, but the secondary purpose is to put the person who is willing to sell the asset in a position to acquire shares in the company, then, as long as the Assistor genuinely enters into the transaction in the belief that it is in the Assistor's best interests, the transaction will fall within the exception. There may be difficulties, however, in proving that the secondary purpose was not, in fact, the primary purpose.

16.5.1.3   The larger purpose exception

This exception covers transactions where the financial assistance is intended but it is incidental to the Assistor's 'larger purpose'. As outlined at **16.5.1.1** above, the House of Lords has interpreted this exception very narrowly and, as such, it is not relied upon in practice.

16.5.2   Section 681: unconditional exceptions

Section 681(2) permits the following (which all involve removing value from the company) on the basis that they are not anything against which creditors require protection:

(a)   (i)   a dividend lawfully made – this would allow, for example, the Assistor to pay a pre-sale dividend to its shareholders before its shares are sold (this may have tax benefits, as it allows shareholders to take some of the value of the company as income not capital);

     (ii)   a distribution in a winding up;

(b)   the allotment of bonus shares;

(c)   a reduction of capital under Chapter 10 of Part 17 of the CA 2006;

(d)   a lawful redemption or purchase of own shares;

(e)   schemes of arrangement made pursuant to a CA 2006, s 899 court order;

(f)   anything done pursuant to an arrangement under s 110 of the Insolvency Act 1986 (this will cover a liquidator accepting shares as consideration for property sold in a winding up); and

(g)   anything done pursuant to a voluntary arrangement made between the company and its creditors.

16.5.3   Section 682: conditional exceptions

Section 682(2) provides the following exceptions:

(a)   the lending of money by money lending companies in the ordinary course of their business;

(b)   where the financial assistance is given in good faith to fund an employee share scheme; and

(c)   loans to bona fide employees (not directors) to allow them to buy shares in the company, or its holding company (no share scheme is required for the exception to apply).

The s 682(1) proviso

Section 682(1) adds an important proviso to the application of the s 682(2) exemptions where the Assistor is a public company. If the Assistor is a public company, it can rely on the s 682(2) exemptions only if the company has *net assets*:

(a)   which are not thereby reduced; or

(b)   to the extent those assets are thereby reduced, the assistance is provided out of distributable profits.

Note that net assets are defined as the *book value* of assets less liabilities (that is, their value for accounting purposes). This is different to the definition of net assets for the purposes of s 677(1) (see **16.4** above), where the definition is the *actual value* of net assets less liabilities. (Liabilities are defined by s 682(4)(b) and distributable profits by s 683(1).)

16.6   Avoiding the restrictions

There is always the option of re-registering a public company as a private company, under s 97 of the CA 2006), so that the company is a private company at the time the financial assistance is given, and that financial assistance can then be given. This is, of course, a little extreme, and certainly would not be appropriate in the case of a listed company.

16.7   Sanctions

16.7.1   Criminal sanctions

Section 680 provides that breach of the prohibition on financial assistance is a criminal offence. The company is liable to a fine, and any officer in default is liable to a fine and/or imprisonment.

16.7.2   Consequences for the share acquisition

The acquisition will be void and unenforceable (*Brady v Brady*) unless the offending term can be severed from any acquisition agreement (*Carney v Herbert* [1985] AC 301).

If the provision of financial assistance breaches the directors' duty to act in good faith in the way most likely to promote the success of the company (CA 2006, s 172) and the breach has not been ratified by a shareholder resolution, the directors may have to compensate their company for any loss it has incurred.

Any third party who received the financial assistance may be required to account for any cash or assets received in breach of s 678 or s 679 (*Belmont Finance Corp Ltd v Williams Furniture Ltd (No 2)* [1980] 1 All ER 393).

16.8   Conclusion

The prohibition on financial assistance has the potential to cause serious problems with share acquisitions involving public companies.

The key is to consider the issue of financial assistance as soon as possible in any share acquisition transaction. This will involve asking questions about how the transaction is funded and, if necessary, making any necessary changes to the structure of the deal.

Chapter 17

Equity Finance

17.1 Background

Part I of this book considered the IPO process, that is (for the purposes of this book) how a company can admit its shares to listing on the Official List and to trading on the Main Market.

As was seen at **4.4** above, a company seeking to float can do so in a number of different ways:

(a) a public offer (encompassing an offer for subscription and/or sale);

(b) a placing;

(c) an introduction; or

(d) an intermediaries offer.

These methods were considered in some detail in **Chapter 4**.

Chapter 1 explained that one of the advantages of an IPO is that, after it has taken place, a listed company can raise further finance through issuing new shares ('equity finance') in a way that an unlisted company cannot. This chapter explores the various methods by which a listed company can seek a listing for further share capital, in order to raise equity finance.

17.2 What is equity finance?

Equity finance involves a company using its equity, namely securities (and more specifically for our purposes, shares), in order to raise finance. An example of a company raising equity finance is when it issues new shares in return for cash, or in exchange for an asset.

As you will realise on reading this chapter, equity finance involves both:

(a) the issue of shares; and

(b) the admission of those shares to listing and to trading on the Main Market of the Stock Exchange.

It is the dual admissions of those shares which gives them their value. The issue and admissions of shares in a listed company in this way is often referred to as a 'secondary issue'. The 'primary issue' is when the company floats and its issued shares are listed for the first time. Subsequent issues of new shares, and the listing of those shares, are therefore 'secondary issues'. (Be aware that this terminology can be confusing, as sometimes the term 'primary issue' is used to describe any issue of shares by the company, and the term 'secondary issue' is used to refer to a sale (transfer) by a shareholder of existing shares. However, for the purposes of this book, the terminology is given the meanings outlined above: a 'primary issue' is an issue of shares by the company on an IPO; and a 'secondary issue' is any subsequent issue of shares by the company.)

When a company raises equity finance, then, the lawyer must be aware of, and be able to apply, not only the law which relates specifically to the raising of equity finance, but also the wider set of rules and regulations which apply to listed companies:

(a)   generally;

(b)   on the issue of shares; and

(c)   on the admission of those shares to listing and trading.

This chapter looks at the law which relates specifically to the raising of equity finance. However, at **17.4** below there below is a brief reminder of the other rules and regulations which relate to (a), (b) and (c) above, and an indication of where you can read about them in this book.

As an indication of the importance of this topic, note that for the period 1 January to 31 August 2009 companies listed on the Main Market raised £56,108,000,000 through secondary issues.

17.3   Why a company needs equity finance

There are numerous reasons why a company might want to raise equity finance. Just like us, it needs money. It may want to pay off debt, buy something, or just make its bank balance look a little healthier. It may be concerned about gearing (its ratio of debt to equity). By increasing the amount of share capital in issue, the company will improve its gearing ratio without having to repay any debt. This may enhance the company's ability to borrow in the future. The company will also have the option to use the cash proceeds from the rights issue to pay off debt, which will improve the company's gearing even more. **Chapter 18** considers the concept of gearing. It also considers briefly the concept of debt finance, and examines the issues a company will take into account in deciding whether to raise equity or debt finance.

In the second half of 2008 and in the first half of 2009 many billions of pounds have been raised on the Stock Exchange by listed companies, initially by banks as they desperately scrambled to access whatever money they could to fend off their collapse as a result of the powerful shockwaves emanating from the global financial crisis. It included a rights issue by the Royal Bank of Scotland Group plc, which raised £12 billion in June 2008 to ensure it had sufficient capital, particularly as its risk to bad debt was thought to be in excess of £5 billion. This was followed by the UK's largest ever rights issue by HSBC Holdings plc which raised £12.5 billion in March 2009. The money was raised to cover losses from a disastrous acquisition of a US company involved in the US sub-prime mortgage market. More recently, the continued lack of availability of debt finance has led companies in other business sectors to turn to rights issues to raise money.

17.4   Listed company rules and regulations

17.4.1   General rules

The general rules relating to listed companies are set out in **Part II** of this book. The general obligation of disclosure under the Disclosure Rules (see **7.5.1**) and the continuing obligations of the Listing Rules, relating to the disclosure of new issues (see **7.5.7** above) and communicating with shareholders in relation to new issues (see **7.9** above), are particularly relevant to any company seeking to raise equity finance. The lawyer must also be alert to any suggestion that the issue might fall foul of the rules relating to corporate governance (see **Chapter 8**), misleading statements and market manipulation (see **Chapter 9**), market abuse (see **Chapter 10**) or insider dealing (see **Chapter 11**). Finally, the lawyer must ensure that the issue is not marketed in a way which would breach the financial promotion rules of the FSMA 2000 (see **Chapter 12**).

17.4.2 Issuing shares

Part III of this book considers the rules of the CA 2006), the Prospectus Rules, the Listing Rules, the City Code, and the ABI Guidelines and the Pre-Emption Statement of Principles which relate to the issue of shares. The following are particularly important, from the company's perspective, when raising equity finance.

17.4.2.1 The Companies Act 2006

Chapters 2 to 4 of Part 17 of the CA 2006 are all relevant to the issue of shares (see **Chapter 14**). The 2006 Act also sets out the procedure which companies must follow if a share issue will vary the class rights of any existing shares. Again, this may be relevant in an equity finance transaction (see **13.7** above). Finally, the issue must be structured in a way which does not cause the company to fall foul of the prohibition on financial assistance (see **Chapter 16**).

17.4.2.2 The Listing Rules

Listing Rules 9.3.11R and 9.3.12R set out the pre-emption rights provisions which are relevant on an issue of shares (see **14.6.12** above).

17.4.2.3 Guidelines and Principles

Institutional investors such as the ABI impose their own requirements relating to the issue of shares. These requirements do not have the force of law, but they are significant because listed companies do not want to get on the wrong side of their largest shareholders. **Chapter 14** considers the ABI Guidelines (see **14.5.7**) and the Statement of Principles of the Pre-Emption Group (see **14.6.16**) which are relevant on an issue of shares.

17.4.3 Admitting new shares to listing and trading

Part I of this book considered the admission of shares on an IPO. Many of the issues addressed by **Part I** are also relevant to the admission of shares on a secondary issue.

It was explained at **4.3.1.1** above that a company cannot choose to list only part of a class of shares. It must list all of the shares in a class. So, if a listed company proposes to issue more shares *of a class which is already listed*, it must seek admission to listing on the Official List and admission to trading on the Main Market in respect of those shares. As mentioned above, this is not only a requirement of the Listing Rules, it also makes the issues commercially attractive, as a listing gives the shares value.

In relation to the listing aspects of a secondary issue, the lawyer must be aware of the following rules and regulations:

(a) *The FSMA 2000.* Part VI of the FSMA 2000 sets out the rules relating to the listing of shares. Sections 87A (general duty of disclosure) and 90 (compensation for loss) are particularly important. See **Chapter 6**.

(b) *The Prospectus Rules.* The requirement for a prospectus under the Prospectus Rules (and s 85 of the FSMA 2000) is discussed at **17.5.1** below. The requirement for a prospectus on an IPO was considered in **Chapter 6**. The prospectus and accompanying documents must be submitted to the FSA as required by the Prospectus Rules (see **5.3.6.1** and **5.3.6.2** above; but note that the submission date for a secondary issue is 10 working days before the prospectus is due to be published (impact day), rather than the 20 working days required for an IPO).

(c) *The Listing Rules.* A formal application for admission of the shares to the Official List must be made to the FSA under the Listing Rules. This involves a process very similar to that set out at **5.3.6.3** to **5.3.6.5** above, in the context of an IPO, namely the submission of:

(i)   '48 hour' documents;

(ii)   'on the day' documents (note the documents differ on a secondary issue to those required for an IPO; a Pricing Statement, rather than a Shareholder Statement signed by the sponsor, is required – see LR 3.3.3R); and

(iii) certain information following admission.

Where the requirements are the same as those for an IPO, see **5.3.6** for further detail. Any raising of equity finance will be made conditional upon admission to listing on the Official List. Admission will be effective when the FSA makes its Official List announcement (see **5.4.3.1**).

(d)   *The Admission and Disclosure Standards.* A formal application for admission of the shares to the Main Market must be made to the Stock Exchange under the Admission and Disclosure Standards. Again, the process involved practically mirrors that required for the application for admission to trading set out in **5.3.7** in relation to an IPO, namely (under ADS 2) the submission of:

(i)   an application for admission to trading – Form 1 (note that for a secondary issue this is submitted with the other two-day documents, rather than 10 days in advance, as on an IPO);

(ii)   various two-day documents in electronic form;

(iii) written confirmation of the number of securities to be allotted;

(iv)   a copy of the RIS announcement relating to the admission; and

(v)   certain information following admission.

Where the requirements are the same as those for an IPO, see **5.3.7** for further detail. Any raising of equity finance will be made conditional upon admission to trading on the Main Market. Again, admission will be effective when the Stock Exchange makes an announcement on its website (see **5.4.3.2**).

Note that, in the context of a rights issue, once the shares have been admitted to listing and trading nil paid, no further application is required to admit the shares fully paid (see **17.7.3.2** below).

17.5   Equity finance documentation

The lawyer spends much of his time drafting, and therefore any lawyer will need to know what documentation is required on a secondary issue. Specific documentation required for each method of raising equity finance considered by this chapter is detailed at **17.7** to **17.11** below. However, the reason these documents are required is explained below.

17.5.1   Prospectus

As referred to at **6.4**, the effect of PR 1.2.1UK and s 85 of the FSMA 2000 is that, if the company wishes to do either or both of the following:

(a)   *offer* transferable securities *to the public* in *the UK* (s 85(1)); or

(b)   request *admission* of transferable securities *to trading* on a regulated market situated or operating *in the UK* (even if there is no offer to the public) (s 85(2)),

an FSA-approved prospectus is required.

Section 85(5) of the FSMA 2000 (which in turn refers to Sch 11A to the FSMA and PR 1.2.2R) and s 86 of the FSMA 2000 set out various circumstances when an *offer to the public* will not require a prospectus. Section 85(6) (which in turn refers to Sch 11A to the FSMA and PR 1.2.3R) sets out the circumstances when an *admission to trading* will not require a prospectus.

These rules apply equally to a secondary issue as they do to an IPO (see **6.4** above). As set out at **6.5.2** above, the content requirements are prescribed by the articles and annexes of the PD Regulation (which are set out at PR 2.3.1EU and PR Appendix 3). For a secondary issue of ordinary shares the appropriate schedules will be the share schedules (Annexes I and III) and the pro forma financial information building block (Annex II), so the level of disclosure required in any prospectus relating to a secondary issue of ordinary shares is exactly the same as for a prospectus relating to an IPO of ordinary shares. An approved supplementary prospectus (see **6.9.4**) will also be required if, for example, during a rights issue, there arises or is noted any significant new factor, material mistake or inaccuracy relating to the information included in the approved prospectus. This supplementary prospectus will trigger statutory withdrawal rights under s 87Q of the FSMA 2000 (see **6.9.4**). Issue 11 of *List!* confirms that the right to withdraw will cease when shareholders pay up their subscription in full.

The only difference is that exemptions, which may not apply in the context of an IPO (see **6.4**), may apply on a secondary issue, depending on its circumstances, with the effect that a prospectus is not required. Clearly, if the lawyer can structure a secondary issue so that no prospectus is required, this will save the company considerable time and expense. **Table 17.1** below analyses whether the exemptions are likely to apply to the key methods of raising money via a secondary issue (see **17.6**): a rights issue, open offer, placing, acquisition issue or vendor consideration placing. As you can see, it is likely that only a placing, acquisition issue or vendor consideration placing can be structured in a way which avoids the need to prepare a prospectus.

Table 17.1

Method of equity finance	Public offer under s 85(1)?	Admission to trading under s 85(2)?	Prospectus required?
Rights issue	Yes. Unlikely to benefit from any exemption. (As a pre-emptive offer made to all shareholders, is unlikely to benefit from the '100 persons' or 'qualified investors' exemptions).	Yes, however small rights issues may be structured so that '10%' exemption applies.	Yes.
Open offer	As for rights issue.	As for rights issue.	As for rights issue.
Placing	Yes ; however, likely to benefit from 'qualified investor' or '100 persons' exemption.	Yes, however small placings may be structured so that '10%' exemption applies.	Yes, unless structured so that is exempt from the requirement for a prospectus.

Method of equity finance	Public offer under s 85(1)?	Admission to trading under s 85(2)?	Prospectus required?
Acquisition issue	May benefit from 'qualified investor' or '100 persons' exemption, depending on target shareholder profile.	Yes, however small rights issues may be structured so that '10%' exemption applies.	Yes, unless structured so that is exempt from the requirement for a prospectus. (Where shares are issued in the context of a takeover, the publication of a document the FSA deems to be 'equivalent to' a prospectus will suffice – see **22.4.4.2**.)
Vendor consideration placing	As for acquisition issue.	As for acquisition issue.	As for acquisition issue.

17.5.2   Circular

The Listing Rules require the company to communicate to its shareholders by way of circular on a new issue (see **7.6.2** above). This may take the form of a notice of GM, and incorporate by reference information in any prospectus. The circular must conform with the requirements of LR 13.3 (see **7.9.3**).

In practice, often the requirement for the circular is met by the prospectus, which will contain all the information required to be in the circular. However, the prospectus also contains an offer of securities, which can cause problems with regard to very strict securities law in certain overseas jurisdictions. One solution is not to send the prospectus to such jurisdictions but a circular. If there are overseas shareholders therefore, the company may prepare both a prospectus and a separate circular. Also, if time is of the essence, the company may (with the permission of the FSA) send out a brief circular outlining the main reasons for the issue, together with a notice of GM, and then send out the prospectus once the document has been completed (as happened, for example, with Bradford and Bingley's £400 million rights issue in the summer of 2008).

17.5.3   RIS notification/press announcement

Any new issue of listed securities must be notified to an RIS under the specific disclosure requirements of the Listing Rules (see **7.5.7.2** above). This will usually take the form of a press announcement to announce the issue to the market. It will contain all material information about the issue, and any related acquisition. Further announcements will be required as the rights issue progresses.

17.5.4   Sale and purchase agreement

If the company is issuing shares as consideration for the acquisition of a non-cash asset, such as shares in another company, then a sale and purchase agreement (also referred to as an acquisition agreement, an S&P or an SPA) will be required for the transfer of that asset.

17.5.5 Underwriting agreement

The concept of underwriting in the context of an IPO was introduced at **4.2.7** above. It is also relevant on a secondary issue. In return for a fee, the underwriters will agree to take up any shares which are not subscribed for. The underwriting agreement will record the agreement between the company and the underwriter.

17.5.6 Placing agreement

If the chosen method of raising equity finance involves a placing of shares, a placing agreement will also be necessary (see **4.4.1.2** above).

17.6 Methods of raising equity finance

As **17.1** above explained, a company can float in a number of different ways. However, once listed, a company can bring securities to listing using a wider variety of methods.

The main methods by which a company can raise equity finance once it is listed are:

(a)   a rights issue (LR 9.5.1R to LR 9.5.6R);

(b)   an open offer (LR 9.5.7R to LR 9.5.8R);

(c)   a placing (Appendix 1 to the Listing Rules);

(d)   an acquisition issue ; and

(e)   a vendor consideration placing (LR 9.5.9R).

These methods are considered in detail at **17.7** to **17.11** below, and we examine why a company might choose one method rather than another. As with an IPO, however, more than one method may be combined, depending on the circumstances (such as the combined placing and open offer by Barclays plc in the summer of 2008 which raised £4.5 billion). Specific documentation required for each method is also set out.

Note that some of the less common methods of raising equity finance are not discussed in detail in this chapter. Two of these, an offer (for subscription and/or sale) and an intermediaries offer, are considered in **Chapters 4** and **6**, albeit in the context of an IPO rather than a secondary issue.

Chapter 9 of the Listing Rules contains the rules relating to the methods by which secondary issues can be listed.

17.7 Rights issue

17.7.1 What is a rights issue?

A rights issue was referred to at **14.6.12** above, when considering pre-emption rights. Appendix 1.1 of the Listing Rules defines a rights issue. Basically, it is:

(a)   an offer to issue new shares or transfer existing shares (or other securities);

(b)   to existing shareholders (or security holders) in proportion to their existing holdings;

(c)   made by way of the issue of a renounceable letter;

(d)   which may be traded 'nil paid' for a period before payment for the shares (or other securities) is due.

The aim is to raise money for the company by issuing new shares. For example, a company could offer to issue two shares to each shareholder for every one share that shareholder already holds (known as a '2-for-1' offer). There is no magic to this figure. The key calculation is how much money the company wishes to raise. It considers how many shares are in issue and then makes the offer accordingly, because of course all shareholders must be offered the right to buy the new shares. In March 2009 HSBC Holdings plc had a '5-for-12' rights issue; shareholders were entitled to buy 5 new shares for every 12 existing shares held.

In the period 1 January to 31 August 2009, over £34.5 billion was raised by companies on the Main Market through rights issues, the most popular means of raising equity finance through secondary issues. As stated above, some were banks seeking funding to try to weather the global financial crisis (HSBC (£12.5 billion)). Other companies which were financially sound took the opportunity of a rights issue to cut the costs of their debt payments. In January 2009 Xstrata plc raised £4.1 billion to repay debt incurred in its £21 billion takeover of Prodeco Coal.

17.7.2   Price

The shares are usually allotted for cash, at a discount to the market price of the existing shares. Why is that? Well, if the company is going to raise finance, it requires shareholders to take up their rights under the rights issue and pay the cash consideration for the shares to the company. This means that the price for the shares must be better (that is, cheaper) than the price of buying shares on the open market. If it is not, the shareholders might choose to buy shares on the market instead, in which case they will pay the selling shareholder, not the company, for the shares.

Increasingly, a company will make what is known as a 'deep-discount rights issue', when it issues shares at a substantial discount to market value. Originally this was done so that the company did not have to pay for the issue to be underwritten (because no shareholder is likely to refuse to take up the rights) (see **17.7.5**), or because the company had an urgent need for the new money, although it is becoming increasingly common for even deeply discounted rights issues to be underwritten where certainty of funds is important (eg, the HSBC rights issue in 2009). Issuing shares at a deep discount will make the issue more attractive to shareholders, so it can increase the chances of success of the rights issue, particularly in a weak market (which, in turn, can help to reduce any underwriting costs, as the company may be able to negotiate lower fees with the underwriter to reflect the reduced risk that shareholders will not take up the shares).

Note that, as long as the price exceeds the nominal value of the share (CA 2006, s 580), there is no legal limit to the discount at which the company can sell the shares. As explained at **14.6.16**, the Pre-Emption Group's Statement of Principles does not apply if the company observes the pre-emption requirements of the Listing Rules. In practice, the rule of thumb is that companies can usually discount by up to 50%, a typical discount being 15–20%, and a deep discount being 40–50%. HSBC's rights issue in 2009 was at a deep discount of 47.5% to the then market price of the shares. However, in these financially uncertain times, some companies are so desperate for money that they have even exceeded the 50% threshold. Johnston Press plc announced in May 2008 a deep discount rights issue of 61% to the market price of its shares. As with humans, so with companies – desperation is often eye-catching but never pretty.

One disadvantage of the discount applied to shares is that it tends to cause a drop in the market value of the shares for a period following the rights issue.

17.7.3   Structure

17.7.3.1   The PAL

The offer to shareholders of the right to buy new shares in the company is made by way of a renounceable letter, known as a provisional allotment letter (PAL). This does exactly what its name suggests: it provisionally allots to the shareholder her pro rata entitlement of shares. At this stage no money has changed hands. The company has given the shareholder a document which sets out her *right* to buy the new shares. The PAL will provide details of the rights issue, including the number of shares to which the shareholder is entitled and the price of those shares. The PAL is a temporary document of title, and as such it must comply with the requirements of LR 9.5.15R. (It is not a permanent document of title such as a share certificate, because so far the shareholder has not paid for the shares offered to her.)

On receiving the PAL, the shareholder then has a number of options. She can:

(a)   take up the rights, by subscribing for the shares (see **17.7.3.2** below);

(b)   renounce the rights and sell them on to a third party, nil paid (see **17.7.3.3** below);

(c)   combine (a) and (b), by taking up some rights and renouncing the rest (**17.7.3.4** below); or

(d)   do nothing (**17.7.3.5** below).

17.7.3.2   Taking up the rights to subscribe

Before the end of the offer period (as **17.7.4** below explains, the offer must be open for at least 14 days) the shareholder who holds the rights to subscribe, and who wishes to exercise them, must submit the consideration and the PAL to the company's receiving agents. (At the end of the offer period, this right will lapse.) This means that the shareholder will have bought the new shares and ensure her existing percentage shareholding is not diluted.

17.7.3.3   Renouncing the rights to subscribe

Rationale

As we have seen in **17.7.3.2** above, if the shareholder takes up the rights, she ensures that her existing percentage shareholding is not diluted. However, if the shareholder renounces the rights, her shareholding will be diluted, meaning a smaller share of the company's profits and a lower percentage share of the voting rights. So why would a shareholder renounce the right to subscribe for shares? As ever with listed companies, usually the motivation is financial.

Example

Imagine that shares in X plc have a current market value of £2 each. X plc gives its shareholders the right to subscribe for more shares, in proportion to their existing shareholdings, for £1.60 per share (that is, at a discount of 20%). The right to subscribe has a value, therefore, of 40p per share. However, the fact that the market value in the shares is likely to drop (see **17.7.2** above) must be taken into account. Imagine that the market value drops to £1.95. If the shareholder renounces her rights and sells them for 35p each, she will have made a profit of 35p per share (less any dealing costs). If the shareholder has, say, 1,000 shares, she can make £350 with no capital outlay. She might consider that this makes diluting her shareholding worthwhile.

(Note, however, that the shareholder may incur an immediate capital gains tax charge if she sells her rights. If she exercised the rights, however, capital gains tax would arise only on a subsequent disposal of the shares.)

The shareholder wishing to renounce and sell rights should not find it too difficult to find a buyer for those rights, as the buyer will be able to buy shares from the shareholder at the market value, here £1.95. The buyer will pay £1.60 per share to the company under the rights issue, plus 35p per share to the shareholder for the right to subscribe. Of course, the risk to the buyer is that the market price drops further.

Example

Imagine the market price of shares in X plc drops not to £1.95, but to £1.50. The buyer has already paid 35p per share to the selling shareholder for the right to subscribe and must pay an additional £1.60 to the company for shares he can buy in the market for £1.50. In this case, the buyer will probably cut his losses; while he cannot claim back the price he has paid to the selling shareholder for the right to subscribe, he can avoid paying the remaining £1.60 to the company simply by not exercising the right, and letting it lapse.

Nil paid dealings

So how does the shareholder renounce and trade her rights to subscribe? The PAL is negotiable, which means that it can be transferred by delivery (ie it can be bought and sold). As **17.7.4** below explains, the offer must be open for at least 14 days. 'Nil paid dealings' can take place during this 14-day period. This means that a shareholder can trade the rights to subscribe simply by signing the PAL and passing it on to someone else. These dealings are referred to as 'nil paid dealings' because trading takes place before any subscription monies have been paid for the shares represented by the PAL. The third party can then exercise the right to subscribe in the manner described at **17.7.3.2** above and will become the owner of the new shares mentioned in the PAL. It is on the admission of the shares to trading in nil paid form that the FSA will grant admission of the shares to the Official List (LR 9.5.3G). (Once the shares are paid up, and the allotment becomes unconditional, there is no need for a further listing application).

17.7.3.4   Taking up some rights and renouncing the rest

Alternatively, the shareholder may choose to take up some rights (using the procedure outlined at **17.7.3.2**) and renounce the remainder (using the process outlined at **17.7.3.3**). This may be used where the shareholder has insufficient funds to buy the whole allocation or does not wish to take up all her rights. The proceeds received from trading some of the rights may help to finance the purchase of the balance of these rights (known as 'tail swallowing').

17.7.3.5   Doing nothing

Shareholders who do nothing are known as 'lazy shareholders'. Even lazy shareholders can benefit from a rights issue, because arrangements are made for the sale of any shares not taken up. Even if a shareholder does not take up the shares and does not trade the PAL, she may still receive a cash payment to the extent that the shares which were provisionally allotted to her are sold in the market for more than their subscription price and the proceeds exceed £5 (LR 9.5.4R). (As explained in **17.7.3.3**, the nil paid rights have a value.)

17.7.4   Timing

Changes were introduced to the statutory and Listing Rules provisions relating to the timing of rights issues in 2009 as result of a Government review of the law.

The Rights Issue Review Group (RIRG) reported to HM Treasury in November 2008. A copy of its report is available on HM Treasury's website. The review group comprised various representative bodies including law firms.

The RIRG's remit was to look at the problems encountered in 2008, particularly in connection with some of the more high profile rights issues involving financial sector companies and 'learn lessons' from them.

Generally speaking the RIRG identified that the length of time taken to complete rights issues under the then existing English law had resulted in a number of problems, particularly the following:

(a)   The opportunities for investors to develop strategies for short selling, often followed by a catastrophic decline in the share price of the company to levels at or below what were already heavily discounted offer prices (eg HBOS's rights issue), and consequent allegations of market abuse aimed at the short sellers.

(b)   The rapidly deteriorating economic conditions had forced some companies (eg Bradford & Bingley) into revising the original terms of the offer proposals at considerable expense and further prolonging the rights issue process.

(c)   Concerns over termination provisions in underwriting agreements – the length of time rights issues take to complete in volatile market conditions, resulting in increased likelihood of MAC (material adverse change clauses) and force majeure clauses being triggered.

The RIRG came up with a range of proposals concentrating on reducing the time taken to complete a rights issue. Some have already been implemented and are included in the following discussion.

The FSA does not allow shares in listed companies to be allotted provisionally on a conditional basis (LR 2.1.5G). This means that if any shareholder approvals are required in relation to the issue (such as to give the directors authority to allot – see **Chapter 14**), the PALs can be posted only after all necessary shareholder approvals have been obtained at the GM. Once the PALs are posted, LR 9.5.6R provides that the offer must remain open for at least 10 business days. Section 562(5) (as amended by the Companies (Share Capital and Acquisition by Company of its Own Shares) Regulations 2009) states that the offer must be open for 14 days. This section will only be relevant if s 561 is not disapplied. If s 561 does apply then the listed company must still also comply with the 10 business day requirement under LR 9.5.6R. This matters because this will be slightly longer than the 14 days period under s 562(5). The 14 days includes the day of posting the PAL (ie the day of making the offer) whereas the 10 business day period under LR 9.5.6R begins on the day after posting the PAL (due to the definition of business day in the Listing Rules).

The combination of the time required for the GM notice (14 clear days for a special resolution at a GM (and not an AGM) under the CA 2006 provisions assuming the conditions in s 307A of the CA 2006 – see **8.6.1** – are met), added to the subsequent minimum offer period of 10 business days (under the Listing Rules), means that the rights issue could take weeks to complete.

17.7.5 Underwriting

The role of underwriters on an IPO was explored at **4.2.7** above. The process of underwriting is equally relevant to a secondary issue. The underwriters (usually an investment bank or a broker) basically guarantee that the company will receive the equity finance it seeks, by agreeing to take up, at no less than the subscription price under the rights issue, any shares which are not taken up by shareholders and which cannot be sold in the market (including fractional entitlements if s 89 has been disapplied – see **17.7.6.1**). These shares are referred to as 'the rump'. As explained at **17.7.3.5**, any premium received over the subscription price must be given to the person to whom the shares were provisionally allotted.

The underwriters must buy any of the rump which is left (that is, which they have been unable to sell). These leftover shares are referred to as 'the stick'. The stick represents the underwriter's risk, and the underwriter will try to predict what the stick, and therefore the risk, will be, in calculating his commission (see **17.7.5.1** at (a) below). As with an IPO, it is common for a secondary issue to be sub-underwritten either in part, or in its entirety (see **4.2.7**).

Events in the second half of 2008 demonstrated in stark terms both the need for underwriting arrangements and the risks involved for underwriters. The article below shows the effect of HBOS's disastrous rights issue which left the underwriters and sub-underwriters having to pay almost £2.5 billion to buy the stick. Of course such failures are extremely rare and reflect the turmoil caused by the problems in the financial markets and the collapse of the share price of banks listed on the Stock Exchange.

HBOS rights issue flops

**Julia Kollewe and
Jill Treanor**

Underwriters to HBOS's £4bn rights issue have been left with almost £3.8bn of shares after investors shunned its cash call in one of the biggest fund-raising flops in UK history.

Shares in HBOS dropped 6% to 265p in early trading, below the offer price of 275p.

Investors took up just 8.3% of shares at 275p, even fewer than expected. The level of support is one of the lowest ever registered for a rights issue and deals a blow to HBOS's management.

When HBOS announced the rights issue on April 29, it was priced at a near-50% discount to its then market price of just under 500p.

Shareholders subscribed to buy 124m shares in the rights issue, leav-ing underwriters Morgan Stanley and Dresdner Kleinwort with 1.375bn shares. The banks have until 4.30pm tomorrow to offer them to new and existing shareholders. If the shares are not placed in the market, the underwriters pass them on to other financial institutions which have agreed to "sub-underwrite" the issue.

The two investment banks keep the leftovers and it is thought they could end up with a maximum of £1bn worth each as a quarter of the bank's shareholder base is made up of retail investors who do not tend to support corporate cash calls.

The rights issue has cost HBOS £160m, including paperwork and underwriting fees.

HBOS's shares fell below 275p in the days before the offer deadline and plunged to 225p at one point. They ended the week at 282p - above the rights issue price but the rally came too late to entice shareholders to the cash call.

Barclays didn't fare much better in its cash call on Friday - with shareholders taking up only 19% of shares offered in a £4.5bn fundraising, forcing "anchor" investors including the Qatar Investment Authority to come to its rescue.

Royal Bank of Scotland and Bradford & Bingley have also tried to raise fresh funds to shore up their balance sheets in the face of the credit crunch. It took B&B three attempts to get through a £400m fundraising, which was finally approved at a special shareholders' meeting last week.

Source: *The Guardian*, 21 July 2008

17.7.5.1   The underwriting agreement

The underwriting arrangements will be recorded in an underwriting agreement, which typically includes the following:

(a)   *Details about the commission payable.* Underwriting costs increase with the length of time for which the underwriter is 'on risk' to take up shares, because the longer the period, the less certain the underwriter can be about how the market in those shares will move. The higher the risk for the underwriter, the more the underwriter will charge for his services. With a rights issue, the underwriter is 'on risk' for a considerable period of time (see **17.7.4** above); therefore the underwriting costs can be high. Traditionally, a typical underwriting agreement might provide, for example, that the underwriter's fees will be 2% of the amount underwritten for the first 30 days of the rights issue, and a further commission of 0.125% of the aggregate amount raised in respect of any further period (although the amount and formula will vary depending on factors such as the amount of the rights issue and the amount of discount).

(b)   *Conditions.* These will include the passing of any necessary resolutions at a GM and the admission of the shares to the Official List and the Main Market, nil paid (known as the 'admission condition'). In other words, the agreement is a conditional contract. If these conditions are not met, the underwriter can walk away from the agreement.

(c)   *Representations and warranties from the company.* Breach of these may give rise to the right to terminate the agreement, in addition to damages.

(d)   *Material adverse change (MAC) clause and force majeure clause.* These clauses will allow the underwriter to terminate the agreement in very limited circumstances.

As stated at **17.7.4**, the FSA does not allow shares in listed companies to be allotted provisionally on a conditional basis. This means that underwriters should not have any right to terminate their underwriting obligation once the nil paid rights have been admitted, because once this point is reached shareholders will begin trading in the rights. Issue 12 of *List!* states that the FSA has been asking companies to confirm that their underwriting arrangements do not allow the underwriters to invoke withdrawal rights (see **6.9.4** and **17.5.1**) under any circumstances.

17.7.6   Pre-emption rights

A rights issue is a pre-emptive offer, that is, it is in accordance with the statutory pre-emption rights on allotment under s 561 of the CA 2006; the company is issuing *equity securities* (for our purposes, ordinary shares) to holders of *ordinary shares* in proportion to the nominal value of their existing shareholdings, in return for cash consideration (see **14.6.5**). This therefore accords with the rationale behind pre-emption rights, namely to allow existing voting shareholders to protect their proportionate share of the votes at the company's GM and of the profits paid by way of dividend.

As the issue is in accordance with s 561, there is no requirement to disapply s 561; however, the company must also comply with s 562 of the CA 2006, which sets out how to make the offer. In particular, the offer:

(a)   must be in hard copy or electronic form (s 562(2));

(b)   must state a period of not less than 14 days during which it can be accepted (s 562(5)) (see **17.7.4**); and

(c)   such period begins:

    (i)   for an offer made in hard copy, with the date on which the offer was sent or supplied; or

    (ii)   for an offer made electronically, with the date on which the offer was sent.

However, having said that there is no *legal requirement* to disapply s 561 for a rights issue, *in practice* s 561 is often disapplied, for the reasons set out at **17.7.6.1** to **17.7.6.3** below. As explained at **14.6.15**, for this reason typically listed companies effect a general disapplication of the statutory pre-emption rights (that is, s 561) at each AGM, in a way which allows directors to make small rights issues provided they follow the pre-emption rights in the Listing Rules (see **17.7.6.5**). Remember, however, that any existing s 561 disapplication will relate to an existing s 551 authority (see **14.6.14.3**). If the rights issue requires a new s 551 authority (because the existing s 551 authority has expired in terms of time or number of shares) then the existing s 561 disapplication will be of no use. If this is the case, the company will need to pass a new s 561 disapplication specifically for the issue if the statutory procedure is not to be followed.

The differences outlined below should be familiar to you from **14.6.12**.

17.7.6.1   Fractional entitlements

If the company offered shareholders their exact proportional entitlements under a rights issue, the calculation may entitle some shareholders to fractions of shares. The CA 2006 is unclear as to how a company should deal with fractional entitlements, so, in practice, the company rounds down each shareholder's entitlement to the nearest whole share. The fractional entitlements which have not been offered have the potential to raise further finance, if the company can aggregate them and sell the aggregate. Unfortunately, the CA 2006 is not clear as to whether fractional entitlements are covered by s 561. Selling the aggregate might infringe the existing shareholders' pre-emption rights. However, if those pre-emption rights are disapplied, the company can sell the aggregate fractional entitlements. The company will take both the subscription price and any premium over the subscription price which it receives.

> **Example**
>
> The company has 500,000 shareholders. One of them, X, holds 302 shares. The company announces a '1 for 3' rights issue, that is 1 new share is offered for every 3 shares held. Strictly X is entitled to 100 shares plus two-thirds of a share (302 divided by 3).
>
> However, as the CA 2006 is unclear as to whether fractional entitlements can be allocated, the company rounds down X's entitlement to 100 shares. This leaves two-thirds of a share unissued. A similar situation has arisen for most of the other 499,999 shareholders, so that, together with X's two-thirds of a share, there is an aggregate of, say, 200,000 shares unissued.
>
> If s 561 applies to the issue, it is thought that selling these 200,000 shares to a third party may infringe the pre-emptive right of X (to his two-thirds of a share) and of each of the other existing shareholders (to their respective fractional entitlements), so the company cannot do anything with these shares.
>
> However, if s 561 is disapplied, these shares can be sold to one or more third parties, raising further finance for the company. The company will take the subscription price for the 200,000 shares and any premium received.

17.7.6.2   Overseas shareholders

Certain jurisdictions, such as Japan, Canada and the USA, have very strict laws concerning the offering of securities. These laws mean that it can be so expensive and time-consuming to make an offer of securities in those jurisdictions that many companies prefer not to make an offer there. If the pre-emption rights have not been disapplied and the company has shareholders in those jurisdictions, the company has a problem. Section 561 of the CA 2006 does provide for this situation; it allows companies to make an offer to those overseas shareholders by way of a notice in the *Gazette* (known as the '*Gazette* route'). However, companies often prefer instead to disapply the pre-emption rights, and arrange for the entitlements of those shareholders to be aggregated and sold in the market, nil-paid. Any premium the company receives over the subscription price will then be given to those overseas shareholders in accordance with LR 9.5.4R.

Note that the FSA will not usually permit the exclusion of shareholders in another EU Member State from a rights issue on the grounds of local securities laws. In such cases it encourages companies to take advantage of the procedure for the 'passporting' of prospectuses (see **6.11**).

17.7.6.3   Convertible securities

If a company has issued securities and the terms of those securities state that they will entitle the holder to pre-emption rights, but under the CA 2006 the holder is not entitled to pre-emption rights (because the securities do not fall within the definition of 'ordinary shares': see **14.6.8** above), the company must disapply s 561. This will ensure that the company will be able to make the rights issue to those holders, in accordance with the terms of the securities.

> **Example**
>
> The company has in issue convertible loan stock. The terms of the loan stock state that the holders of the stock are entitled to pre-emption rights on any rights issue. However, under s 561, convertible loan stock does not fall within the definition of ordinary shares (it is not a share), and so, under s 561 the loan stock does not entitle its holders to pre-emption rights. There is a conflict. It would be very difficult to change the terms of the stock, so instead s 561 is disapplied to resolve the conflict; and the rights issue is offered to the holders of the convertible loan stock.

17.7.6.4   Pre-emption rights under the Listing Rules

As **14.6.12** explained, the pre-emption rights under the Listing Rules are slightly more flexible than the pre-emption rights under the CA 2006, and they do not raise the problems listed at **17.7.6.1** and **17.7.6.2** above (although, they do raise similar problems relating to convertible securities). When the company disapplies s 561, although this also disapplies the pre-emption rights under the Listing Rules (see LR 9.3.12R and **14.6.15**), the company will nevertheless still offer the rights pre-emptively (except to overseas shareholders and fractional entitlements) as envisaged by the Listing Rules. This removes the practical problems of the statutory pre-emption rights in relation to fractional entitlements and overseas shareholders, but keeps the IPCs happy.

17.7.6.5 The IPCs

If the statutory pre-emption rights are disapplied, does this mean that the Pre-emption Group will no longer support the issue? No. As explained at **14.6.16** above, para 5 of the Pre-Emption Group's Statement of Principles makes clear that the Principles do not apply to issues of equity securities on a pre-emptive basis. Paragraph 16 of the Pre-Emption Group's Statement of Principles (see **14.6.16**) evidences the IPC's preference for pre-emptive issues. It states that the choice of financing options (that is, the method of raising equity finance) is one of the critical considerations relating to a request for a non-routine disapplication (see **14.6.16.2**). The Group notes that a wide variety of financing options are now available to companies, and if a non-pre-emptive issue of shares is the most appropriate means of raising capital, companies should explain why that is, and why other financing methods have been rejected.

17.7.7 Timetable

Table 17.2 below is an example of a basic rights issue timetable, assuming that a GM is required. Please note that in practice most documents are submitted to the FSA and to the Stock Exchange in draft form well before the required deadline. Similarly, applications may be made in advance of the date required by the regulatory rules. Remember also that the timetable will be dependent on the particular circumstances of the listed company involved. The timings may therefore vary from rights issue to rights issue.

Table 17.2

Date	Event
1.5 to 3 months (deadline is 10 working days) before impact day.	Submit draft prospectus and related draft documentation to FSA for approval under the Prospectus Rules.
Day before impact day	Board meeting to approve rights issue. Underwriting agreement signed and held in escrow.
Impact day	Press announcement released. Underwriting agreement released from escrow. Prospectus published, containing notice of GM. (PALs cannot be sent out until after GM.)
2 business days before D day (LR 3.3.2R)	Apply for admission of shares, nil paid, to the Official List and Main Market (by submitting '48 hour' documents to FSA under the Listing Rules, and 'two- day' documents to the Stock Exchange under the Admission and Disclosure Standards).
14 clear days after impact day (assuming a GM (and not an AGM) held) (s 307A and s 360, CA 2006)	GM to pass shareholder resolutions (eg grant directors authority to allot, disapply s 561, create a new class of shares, alter articles of association, and/ or approve any related acquisition). PALS sent out immediately after GM.

Date	Event
One business day after GM (**'D day'**)	Submit 'on the day' documents to the FSA under the Listing Rules (LR 3.3.3R).
	Shares admitted to Official List and Main Market, nil paid.
	Statement made by FSA to an RIS and statement published by the Stock Exchange on its website.
	'Admission condition' in underwriting agreement is satisfied.
	Nil paid dealings in shares begin.
	Sale of overseas shareholders' shares and fractional entitlements (if s 561 pre-emption rights disapplied).
10 business days (LR 9.5.6R) after posting of PALs ('Close of offer')	End of nil paid dealing period.
	Deadline for acceptance and payment in full.
1 business day after close of offer	Dealings in shares commence, fully paid.
	Notify underwriters of acceptances.
	Underwriters try to sell rump.
2 business days after close of offer	Identify stick.
	Final confirmation of acceptances announced.
	Announce result of rights issue to RIS see **7.7.11** below.
Week after close of offer	Underwriters pay company consideration for the stick, if any.
	Company receives net proceeds of the issue and despatches share certificates to shareholders.

17.7.8   Advantages of a rights issue

A rights issue has the following advantages:

(a)   *Price.* If the issue is in accordance with the pre-emption requirements of the Listing Rules, there is no limit on the level of discount at which the company can issue the shares (save that the shares must not be issued at a discount to their nominal value in breach of s 580 of the CA 2006).

(b)   *The IPCs.* The IPCs are more likely to support this pre-emptive method of raising equity finance (see **17.7.6.6**).

17.7.9   Disadvantages of a rights issue

A rights issue has the following disadvantages:

(a)   *Cost.* The costs of underwriting can be high.

(b)   *Market value.* The shares issued under a rights issue are usually issued at a discount. This can cause the market value of the shares to fall.

(c)   *Timing.* The offer period is 10 business days under LR 9.5.6R, which cannot run concurrently with the GM notice.

(d)   *Pre-emption.* Even though the offer is on a pre-emptive basis, a s 561 disapplication is often required (see **17.7.6** above).

17.7.10   Is a rights issue appropriate?

When considering whether a rights issue is the most appropriate method to raise equity finance, the following questions will be useful:

(a)   Is the company concerned about underwriting costs? If so, a rights issue may not be the best method.

(b)   Does the company need to raise finance quickly? If so, a rights issue may not be the best method.

(c)   Does the company need flexibility in the amount by which it can discount shares? If so, a rights issue has some advantage over the other methods of equity finance in this regard.

17.7.11   Documentation

The following documentation may be required for a rights issue:

(a)   press announcement of rights issue on impact day and of the results of the issue, issued via an RIS and satisfying the need for an RIS notification (LR 9.5.5R and LR 9.6.6.R);

(b)   underwriting agreement;

(c)   PAL;

(d)   notice of GM;

(e)   prospectus;

(f)   perhaps, a separate circular (see **17.5.2**);

(g)   documents required for admitting shares to listing and to trading (see **17.4.3**);

(h)   if the rights issue involves CREST shareholders, additional documents to enable dealing in the rights; and

(i)   Gazette notice (for overseas shareholders).

17.8   Open offer

17.8.1   What is an open offer?

Appendix 1.1 of the Listing Rules defines an open offer. Like a rights issue (see **17.7** above), an open offer is:

(a)   an offer to issue new shares, or transfer existing shares (or other securities);

(b)   to existing shareholders (or security holders) in proportion to their existing holdings.

Again, the offer is usually for cash. However, unlike a rights issue, the offer is not made by means of a PAL (see **17.7.3.1** above), but by an application form. The structure of the offer is considered at **17.8.3** below.

17.8.2   Price

The shares are offered at a discount, but the discount tends to be less than that for a rights issue (see **17.7.2** above). The default position is that an open offer cannot be priced at a discount of more than 10% of market value (LR 9.5.10R(1)). Listing Rule 9.5.10R(3) provides that this rule does not apply if:

(a)   the company's shareholders have specifically approved the terms of the open offer at a discount of more than 10%; or

(b)   the shares are being issued for cash consideration under a pre-existing general authority to disapply s 561 of the CA 2006.

Note that any shares issued under the exception at (b) above will render the disapplication 'non-routine' under the Pre-Emption Group's Statement of Principles, which advocate limiting any discount to 5%, unless the issue is in accordance with the pre-emption requirements of the Listing Rules (see **14.6.16**).

17.8.3   Structure

The company sends a personal application form to each shareholder. Unlike the PAL used in a rights issue, this form simply offers shares; it does not provisionally allot them. The shareholder can either take up the offer, or do nothing. No shareholder can assign or sell the benefit of the offer. There is no trading in rights. In addition, no arrangements are made for the sale of shares which shareholders do not take up. This is bad news for the 'lazy shareholder'; in contrast to a rights issue (see **17.7.3.5** above), if a shareholder does nothing in relation to the offer, he will receive nothing under the offer.

The structure of an open offer gives shareholders less flexibility than on a rights issue (the shareholder cannot trade the rights nil paid, and the lazy shareholder receives nothing) and open offers tend to be cheaper for companies than rights issues. The IPCs have stated, informally and not through formal guidance, that if an issue represents more than 15–18% of a company's issued share capital , or if the discount is greater than 7.5%, this may cause them concern (if the issue does not otherwise protect shareholders adequately). In such circumstances, the IPCs prefer a rights issue to an open offer.

17.8.4   Timing

Listing Rule 9.5.7R provides that the offer period for an open offer must be approved by the RIE on which the shares are traded. For the Stock Exchange, the approved period is 10 business days from the date of posting the application forms (Admission and Disclosure Standards, ADS 3.9 – see **Appendix 1**). The offer period is therefore the same for a rights issue.

In addition, and of more significance to timing, is the fact that, unlike with a rights issue, the application forms do not provisionally allot shares. This means that the problem with provisionally allotting shares on a conditional basis does not arise. Therefore, if a GM is required in order to obtain the consent of the shareholders in connection with the share issue (to increase the company's share capital and such like – see **Chapter 14**), the offer period can run concurrently with the GM notice. This means that, compared to a rights issue, the underwriting commission is less and the company will receive its cash sooner.

17.8.5   Advantages of an open offer

An open offer has the following advantages for the company:

(a)   *Timing.* The offer period can run concurrently with the GM notice.

(b)   *Cost.* The default position is that shares cannot be offered at a discount of more than 10%. Unless the offer is structured to fall within one of the exceptions to this, the open offer will be cheaper for the company (but see **17.8.6(b)** below).

17.8.6   Disadvantages of an open offer

An open offer has the following disadvantages for the company:

(a)   *Pre-emption.* Even though the offer is on a pre-emptive basis, a s 561 disapplication is usually required, because the statutory pre-emption rights have the potential to cause problems (as they do on a rights issue; see **17.7.6**).

(b)   *Flexibility.* The default position is that shares cannot be offered at a discount of more than 10%. Unless the offer is structured to fall within one of the exceptions to this, an open offer might be less attractive to shareholders than a rights issue.

(c)   *The IPCs.* The IPCs prefer rights issues to open offers in certain circumstances (see **17.8.3**).

17.8.7   Documentation

The following documentation may be required for an open offer:

(a)   press announcement/RIS notification;

(b)   underwriting agreement;

(c)   notice of GM;

(d)   prospectus;

(e)   perhaps, a separate circular (see **17.5.2**); and

(f)   other documents required for admitting shares to listing and to trading (see **17.4.3**).

HSBC asks shareholders for £12.5bn as profits tumble

Katherine Griffiths

HSBC this morning announced plans to ask shareholders for £12.5bn, joining the long list of banks seeking to strengthen their financial position in the teeth of the worst global recession in decades.

The bank plans to raise the money through selling shares to existing shareholders at 254p each, a deep discount to the closing price of 491p on Friday evening.

Alongside the cash call, HSBC also revealed a 62pc drop in profits for last year to $9.3bn. While its operations in Europe, Asia and Latin America were all profitable in the year, it was America that proved its achilles heel.

HSBC racked up a loss of $15.5bn at Household Finance Corporation, which specialised in the troubled US sub-prime mortgage business that helped trigger the global financial crisis.

The bank acknowleged today that nothing can be salvaged from the huge specialist finance business it splurged $15bn on in 2003, briefly making it the biggest sub-prime lender in America. The closure of Household will lead to more than 6,000 job cuts in the US.

Stephen Green, chairman of HSBC, admitted today that "with the benefit of hindsight, this (Household) is an acquisition we wish we had not undertaken." Shares in HSBC fell on today's news and were down more than 6pc at 460p in early London trading.

In light of the decline in profits, none of HSBC's board directors, including chief executive Michael Geoghegan and Mr Green, will take a bonus for last year.

Unlike other banks across the world which have appealed to governments for cash, HSBC is raising its extra capital in the market. The move will also differ from Barclays' fundraising, which was mainly from a group of Middle Eastern investors, as HSBC is appealing to all of its shareholders equally.

Mr Green said the extra money will "enhance our ability to deal with the impact of an uncertain economic environment and to respond to unforeseen events."

HSBC has come under pressure from activist investor Eric Knight to sell or spin off Household. Mr Knight yesterday warned that the money from the rights issue may be needed to meet repayments on Household's debt held by bondholders.

Source: *The Telegraph*, 2 March 2009

17.9   Placing

A placing is one of the methods by which a company can float (see **4.4.2** above). It is also a method which can be used for a secondary issue.

In the period January to August 2009 over £20 billion was raised by companies on the Main Market through full or partial placings, making this the second most popular form of secondary issue after rights issues (see **17.7**).

17.9.1   What is a placing?

The formal definition of a placing is in Appendix 1.1 of the Listing Rules. Basically, a placing is:

(a)   an offer by the company to issue new shares and/or an offer by existing shareholders to transfer existing unlisted shares (or other securities);

(b)   to specified persons or clients of any financial adviser assisting in the placing;

(c)   which does not involve an offer to the public or to existing holders of the company's securities.

Again, a placing is usually for cash. The key distinguishing feature is therefore that a placing involves a much smaller number of people than a rights issue or an open offer, and they are usually institutional investors.

17.9.2   Price

Paragraph 11 of the Pre-Emption Group's Statement of Principles (set out at **Appendix 6**) provides that a request for a discount of more than 5% of market value is not likely to be regarded as 'routine' (see **14.6.16**).

Listing Rule 9.5.10R also provides that a placing, as with an open offer, cannot be priced at a discount of more than 10% of market value unless it is structured to fall within either of the exceptions set out at LR 9.5.10R(3)(a) or (b) (see **17.8.2**).

17.9.3   Advantages of a placing

The advantage of a placing is its cost. The limitations on the discount that can be applied (see **17.9.2**) mean that a placing can be cheaper for the company than a rights issue. As soundings will be taken from the market as to likely demand and an acceptable price, underwriting fees, if any, are likely to be lower than on a rights issue.

17.9.4   Disadvantages of a placing

A placing is not a pre-emptive offer, so:

(a)   a s 561 disapplication is required; and

(b)   the Pre-Emption Group's Statement of Principles will restrict the number of shares which can be issued (see **14.6.16** above) (and the discount which can be applied – see **17.9.2**).

17.9.5   Documentation

The following documentation may be required for a placing:

(a)   press announcement/RIS notification;

(b)   placing agreement;

(c)   underwriting agreement;

(d)   prospectus, unless the placing is exempt (see **17.5.1**);

(e)   if the placing is exempt, or possibly if overseas shareholders, a separate circular (see **17.5.2**); and

(f)   other documents required for admitting shares to listing and to trading (see **17.4.3**).

17.9.6   Example

Standard Chartered plc completed a placing in August 2009 which raised £1.02 billion to support the development and growth of the company's business in Asia, Africa and the Middle East.

17.10   Acquisition issue

17.10.1   What is an acquisition issue?

An acquisition issue is also known as a 'share-for-share exchange', or a 'securities exchange offer'. It is:

(a)   an issue of new shares by the company;

(b)   to the seller(s) of an asset or assets (which includes shares);

(c)   in consideration for the acquisition by the company of that asset or assets.

17.10.2   Structure

An acquisition issue does not involve marketing shares, as in the case of a rights issue, an open offer or a placing. Instead, it consists of the offer of shares as consideration for an acquisition.

Example

Imagine that X plc wants to buy the entire issued share capital of another company, Y Ltd. The buyer is X plc. The sellers are all the shareholders of Y Ltd. The sellers will transfer the shares they hold in Y Ltd to X plc. X plc will then issue shares in itself to the shareholders of Y Ltd, as consideration. See **Figure 17.1** below.

Figure 17.1: Acquisition issue

Before the acquisition

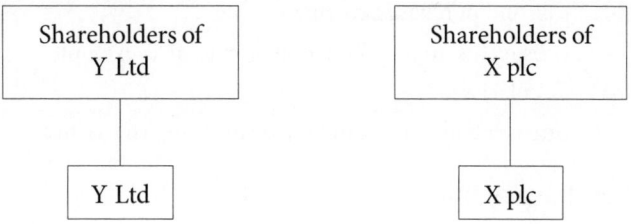

The acquisition

1. Shareholders in Y Ltd *transfer* all the shares in Y Ltd to X plc, so X plc becomes the sole shareholder of Y Ltd.

2. X plc *issues* shares in itself to the shareholders of Y Ltd, as consideration for the transfer, so the former shareholders of Y become additional shareholders of X plc.

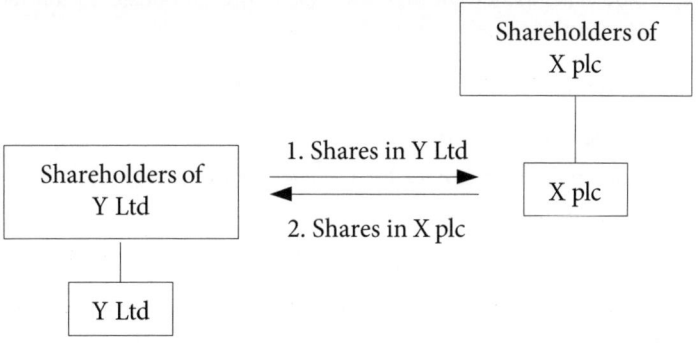

After the acquisition

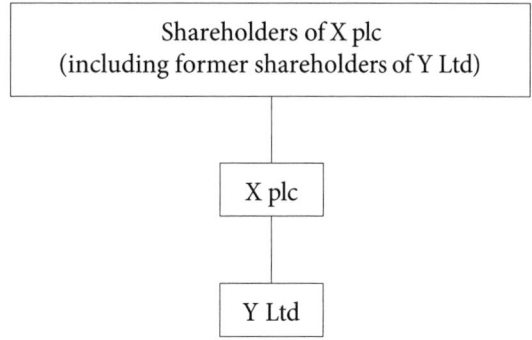

17.10.3   Advantages of an acquisition issue

An acquisition issue has the following advantages:

(a) *Timing.* There are no significant timetabling issues.

(b) *Cost.* An acquisition issue is inexpensive.

(c) *Pre-emption.* The issue is not for cash, so s 89 pre-emption rights are not triggered.

17.10.4 Disadvantages of an acquisition issue

An acquisition issue has the disadvantage that a valuation may be required under s 59 of the CA 2006 (see **14.7.5** above), if the asset to be acquired is anything other than shares.

17.10.5 Documentation

The following documentation may be required for an acquisition issue:

(a)   press announcement/RIS notification;

(b)   sale and purchase agreement;

(c)   prospectus, unless the acquisition issue is exempt;

(d)   circular; and

(e)   other documents required for admitting shares to listing and to trading (see **17.4.3**).

17.11 Vendor placing

17.11.1 What is a vendor placing?

A vendor placing (also known as a 'vendor consideration placing') is used in the context of an acquisition only. It is useful when:

(a)   the company wants to make an acquisition; but

(b)   the company does not have sufficient cash to buy the company or business; and

(c)   the seller is not willing to accept non-cash consideration (so that an acquisition issue (see **17.10** above) is not appropriate).

Instead, the vendor placing is structured so that:

(a)   there is an acquisition issue; then

(b)   the company arranges for its investment bank to place the shares it has issued to the seller as consideration; then

(c)   the company's investment bank gives the proceeds of the placing, in cash, to the seller.

So the listed company acquires the company or business it wants. The seller gets the cash *it* wants.

17.11.2 Price

Listing Rule 9.5.10R provides that, as with an open offer and a placing, a vendor placing cannot be priced at a discount of more than 10% of market value unless it is structured to fall within either of the exceptions set out at LR 9.5.10R(3)(a) and (b) (see **17.8.2**). The vendor placing is not an issue of shares for cash, so it will not fall within the exception at LR 9.5.10R(3)(b).

17.11.3 Advantages of a vendor placing

(a)   *Cost.* The limitation on the discount that can be applied (see **17.11.2**) means that a vendor placing can have cost advantages for the company.

(b)   *Pre-emption.* A vendor placing is not an issue for cash. The company issues the shares for non-cash consideration (it exchanges them for shares). The pre-emption rules do not apply, therefore, so no s 561 disapplication is required. However, the ABI has issued guidelines which provide that vendor placings:

    (i)   of over 10% of the company's issued equity share capital; or

    (ii)   at more than 5% discount,

must be placed on a basis which gives existing shareholders the right to 'claw back' their pro rata share of the issue. The claw-back is usually offered by way of an open offer (vendor placing with open offer), but it can also be made by way of rights issue (vendor consideration rights issue). The ABI Guidelines relating to claw-back are set out at Pt B of **Appendix 5**.

17.11.4 Disadvantages of a vendor placing

A valuation may be required under s 593 of the CA 2006 (see **14.7.5** above), if the asset to be acquired is anything other than shares.

17.11.5 Documentation

The following documentation may be required for a vendor placing:

(a)   press announcement/RIS notification;

(b)   sale and purchase agreement;

(c)   placing agreement;

(d)   underwriting agreement;

(e)   prospectus, unless the vendor placing is exempt;

(f)   circular; and

(g)   other documents required for admitting shares to listing and to trading (see **17.4.3**).

17.12 Future developments

The RIRG (see **17.7.4**) has also proposed further changes to the rights issue regime over the medium term:

(a)   working at the EU level for the adoption of a short form prospectus for rights issues;

(b)   the possible increased use of shelf registration for equity issues including rights issues;

(c)   the FSA to consider further a basis for conditional dealing in rights issues to allow the general meeting notice period and the rights issue subscription period to be run in parallel;

(d)   the FSA to undertake further informal discussions on the usefulness of progressing with further work to introduce more accelerated rights issue models including for this purpose the Australian RAPIDS model; and

(e)   FSA market consultation on a more permanent position on short selling in rights issues.

Further details of these proposed changes can be found in the RIRG's report on HM Treasury's website.

Chapter 18
Equity Finance or Debt Finance?

18.1 Introduction

Chapter 17 considers that, when a company needs finance to provide working capital, reduce borrowings, fund a specific acquisition, or, indeed, for any other reason, it may decide to raise equity finance. This involves the company issuing shares in return for cash or assets. Another book in the series, **Banking and Capital Markets**, discusses another way in which a company may raise finance – debt finance. This involves the company using debt to obtain the cash or assets it requires.

The remainder of this chapter provides a brief overview as to why a company might choose to raise equity finance rather than debt finance, and vice versa. It then examines why most companies, regardless of their size, are financed by a combination of both debt and equity, and considers the key to the right combination.

18.2 Income

18.2.1 Equity finance

A company does not have to declare a dividend. If it does not, the shareholders will not receive any income from their investment. The company does not have to pay any interest to the shareholders. The shareholders do not have a *right* to income.

However, in the real world, any listed company will be aware that if it does not declare a dividend, it risks both losing the support of its shareholders and damaging its reputation as a good investment. It is not a good idea, therefore, for a company to perceive a dividend as something which it can withhold without good reason.

To the extent a company does declare a dividend, the shareholders will share in the profits of the company. For equity shareholders, this right is infinite (see **13.5.1.1**).

18.2.2 Debt finance

Lenders will negotiate a rate of interest with the company. The cost of debt to the company depends on the interest rate which a lender charges. The company will have to pay interest regardless of profits (unlike a dividend). Interest provides lenders with income from their investment (unlike a dividend, this income is finite).

The term 'leverage' is often used in this regard. Leverage is the opportunity to create profit by financing a business through debt which is entitled to a finite return. Imagine that you and nine of your friends own a company; you are its shareholders. You have no more cash to invest.

If you finance the business solely through equity, you need to bring on board other shareholders who are willing and able to inject cash into the company in return for shares. All the profits of the company will now be shared not just between you and your nine friends, but between all the other shareholders too. Now imagine that you decided to finance the company solely through debt. Any profits which are surplus, once the interest on the debt has been paid, will be shared just between you and your nine friends.

18.3 Capital

18.3.1 Equity finance

On a winding up of the company, the company repays its debts first, then it pays to the shareholders the nominal value of their shares, together with any premium they paid on those shares. The shareholders do not have a *right* to capital. This risk, that shareholders will lose their capital, is balanced by the opportunity, described at **18.2.1** above, to share in the profits of the company without limit, and the potential, described at **18.4** below, for capital growth.

18.3.2 Debt finance

Ultimately, the company must repay the capital to the lender. The holders of debt securities will be paid in priority to shareholders on a winding up.

18.4 Capital growth

18.4.1 Equity finance

There is scope for capital growth. The share value will reflect the success of the company. This can help a successful company to market shares.

18.4.2 Debt finance

There is no scope for capital growth. The lender has a right to be repaid only the capital sum, plus interest, no matter how well the company is performing.

18.5 Taxation

18.5.1 Equity finance

Dividends are not a deductible expense in calculating the company's corporation taxation liability.

18.5.2 Debt finance

Interest payable on a loan is tax deductible.

18.6 Rights

18.6.1 Equity finance

When a company issues shares, unless it issues such shares in proportion to the existing shareholders' shareholdings, the issue will dilute those shareholdings.

If the issue is of voting shares, the balance of power within the company could change. This may be a high price to pay for raising finance.

18.6.2 Debt finance

Debt finance will not affect the power structure of the company, nor afford the lender any right to vote in the company.

18.7   Investors

The differences between debt and equity considered above mean that investors have different priorities, depending on how they intend to invest in a company.

The extent to which a potential investor will investigate a company before choosing to invest will differ, depending on whether the investor is seeking to invest by way of equity or debt.

18.7.1   Equity investors

Substantial equity investors include pension funds and other similar financial institutions. Potential equity investors will analyse not only the company's current financial position, but also how the company is placed in the long term, by considering the business sector in which the company operates, the company's expenditure on research and development for new products (R&D), and the company's future earning potential. This reflects the fact that once equity investors invest in a company, they pass the point of no return. They have no right to recover their cash, unless they can sell the shares. They risk losing all their capital.

18.7.2   Debt investors

Substantial debt investors include banks and finance houses. Potential lenders tend to confine their analysis to whether the company can service a loan (and any other loans taken out by the company which would rank ahead of, or equal with, the investor's loan) from current earnings.

This reflects the fact that lenders are entitled to be repaid their capital, and also that it is common for the lender to negotiate the right to monitor the financial position of the company through a series of tests known as 'financial covenants' (which relate to issues such as the net worth, cash flow and gearing (see **18.9.1** below) of the company).

18.8   The problem

It should now be clear that equity finance and debt finance both bring advantages and disadvantages for a company.

With equity finance, there comes the significant risk for shareholders that they will lose capital. This risk usually means that it is impossible for a company to find enough shareholders with sufficient funds to enable it to finance itself solely through equity. Even if it could, a company would still be likely to use debt finance in order to achieve some leverage.

Why not finance the company entirely through debt, to achieve complete leverage, as in the example at **18.2.2** above? The company must repay debt on a regular basis, regardless of the profits the company has made. Imagine what happens if there is a downturn in business. Perhaps the company's major customer goes bust and cannot repay its debts to the company, or perhaps interest rates rise dramatically, or there is a world event which adversely impacts on trading (consider, for example, the impact on the travel industry of the terrorist attacks of recent years). If a business is financed through too much debt, any of these events might mean that the company cannot generate enough cash to enable it to pay its debts as they fall due. (With equity, of course, the company would not have to declare a dividend.)

18.9   The solution

The solution is for a company to achieve a proper balance between debt and equity finance. What is a 'proper balance'? The company needs:

(a)   sufficient equity to provide a cushion against any unexpected problems with the business and/or cash flow; and

(b)   sufficient debt to achieve appropriate leverage and an appropriate return to the equity shareholders.

18.9.1 Gearing

The ratio of a company's debt to equity is referred to as 'gearing'. The higher the proportion of debt, the higher the gearing will be.

Prospective investors in the company will be interested in the company's gearing. In particular, lenders will consider the company's gearing before they negotiate the terms of a loan. If the gearing is high, then, as considered above, there is a greater risk that unexpected problems with the business and/or cash flow will render the company unable to service its debt. This means that there is a higher risk of the company going bust. A lender will demand a higher interest rate, therefore, for a loan to a company which is highly geared.

18.9.2 Articles of association

A company seeking to raise equity finance must involve its shareholders in the decision at some point in the process (for example, to authorise the directors to allot shares). However, the decision whether a company should enter into a loan is usually reserved to the board.

A company's articles of association can protect shareholders in this regard. The articles can provide that, while the ratio of debt to equity is at a certain level, the company can borrow without having to seek permission from the shareholders, but that, once gearing reaches a certain level, the company will require the authorisation of the shareholders in order to borrow.

18.10 Conclusion

A public company must think carefully about whether it should use debt or equity to raise the finance it needs. The company needs to monitor its gearing carefully. Not only might a highly geared company bear a greater risk of going bust, but prospective investors will also scrutinise a company's gearing before deciding whether to invest in the company. It is important, therefore, that the company gets it right.

There are, very rarely, periods of time when it is difficult for a listed company to raise money, by way either of debt or equity. The summer of 2007 was one such rare occasion. The so-called 'credit crunch' in the financial markets, brought on by the housing crisis in the US caused by excessive mortgage lending to the highest credit risk (so-called 'sub-prime' mortgages) and the subsequent problems of borrowers defaulting on repayments, led to banks across the world dramatically cutting back on their lending to one another. This in turn led to the supply of money for lending (including to companies) temporarily drying up. The ability of companies to raise money through equity finance was also affected by the uncertainty of the impact of the losses incurred by financial institutions.

At the time of writing, there was still virtually no debt for companies to access, although increasing numbers of secondary issues in the equity market (see **Chapter 17**) were taking place.

Part IV
LISTED COMPANY TRANSACTIONS

Chapter 19
Acquisitions and Disposals

19.1 Introduction

Chapters 10 and 11 of the Listing Rules regulate 'transactions' by listed companies. This term is defined in LR 10.1.3R (see **19.4.1**). The definition refers principally to acquisitions and disposals by the listed company. **Chapters 20** to **23** discuss the specific rules relating to takeovers and mergers. This chapter considers the main issues which arise when a listed company enters into an acquisition or a disposal.

19.2 Basic considerations

The basic issues which a listed company must consider when it is proposing to enter into a transaction are no different to those an unlisted company would consider. They are:

(a) Structure – purchasing/selling assets or shares?

(b) Consideration – cash or non-cash?

(c) Finance – existing cash, equity or debt?

(d) Due diligence – how much?

(e) Contractual protection – warranties and indemnities?

The Legal Practice Guide, *Acquisitions* explores these basic issues.

However, if a listed company is involved in the transaction, the approach of the company to these issues may differ in the following ways:

(a) *Consideration*. As **Chapter 17** explained, if the buyer is a listed company, it has the option of using its shares as consideration.

(b) *Finance*. Even if the seller does not want shares in the buyer as consideration, if the buyer is a listed company it can choose from a variety of methods (not available to an unlisted company) to raise equity finance (see **Chapter 17**).

(c) *Due diligence*. If the target company is a listed company, there will be information about it in the public domain, which will assist the due diligence process.

(d) *Contractual protection*. If the target company is a listed company and its shares are widely held by members of the public or institutions, they, as sellers, will not provide much (if any) contractual protection to any buyer. (Would you be willing to vouch for anything Vodafone Group plc might warrant about its business in a sale and purchase agreement, just because you own a few ordinary shares?)

As well as having a different approach to the basic issues of a transaction, a listed company will also have some additional considerations. These are examined at **19.3** below.

19.3 Listed company considerations

Most of the additional considerations for listed companies should be familiar to you already, as they have been explained in the preceding chapters of this book. A summary of the main issues follows.

19.3.1 Consideration

If the company is:

(a)   issuing shares as consideration; or

(b)   using equity finance to raise cash to use as consideration

for the acquisition, then the rules and regulations considered in **Chapter 17** will be relevant.

19.3.2 The continuing obligation of disclosure

The general obligation of a listed company, under DTR 2.2.1R, to disclose major new developments in its sphere of activity if the information is not already public knowledge and may lead to substantial movement in its share price, is discussed in **Chapter 7**. This obligation will require companies to disclose significant acquisitions and disposals. An exception to this rule – that a company does not need to disclose information about matters in the course of negotiation, unless there is a breach of confidence during those negotiations – is examined at **7.5.2.8** above. These rules are relevant during an acquisition or disposal, to make sure the company discloses the transaction, through an RIS, in a timely manner as soon as the DTRs require.

19.3.3 The disclosure of interests in shares

Chapter 15 considers the obligation of a listed company:

(a)   under DTR 5.8.12R, to disclose to the public the information it acquires under Chapter 5 of the DTRs (see **15.5.5**);

(b)   under DTR 3.1.4R, to disclose to the public certain transactions by PDMRs and their connected persons (see **15.7.1**);

(c)   under DTR 3.1.4R, to disclose to the public a statement on directors' holdings in their listed company (see **15.7.2**); and

(d)   under the City Code, to disclose its interest in shares to the public once its shareholdings exceed a certain level (see **15.7.4**).

These requirements can be particularly relevant in the context of acquisitions or disposals of shares.

19.3.4 Misleading statements, market manipulation, market abuse and insider dealing

Chapters 9, **10** and **11** consider the civil offence of market abuse and the criminal offences of making misleading statements, manipulating the market and insider dealing. These offences can be relevant on an acquisition or a disposal. The acquisition or disposal of shares by a listed company has the potential to increase that company's value. There is scope for the company's directors, and others, to abuse their inside knowledge that the transaction will take place, by investing in shares which will increase in value once the transaction becomes public knowledge.

19.3.5 Financial regulation

As **Chapter 9** explains, anyone who carries out regulated activities in the process of the transaction must be either authorised, or (less likely) exempt.

19.3.6 Financial promotion

Any communication which persuades someone to do something in relation to an investment must comply with the rules of the FSMA 2000 relating to financial promotion. This is discussed in more detail in **Chapter 12**.

19.3.7 Financial assistance

Chapter 16 explains that the lawyer must always check the structure of any share acquisition, to make sure that it does not give rise to financial assistance problems. There may be further scope for such problems if the consideration also involves shares (that is, the consideration is the issue of shares, or the consideration has been raised through equity finance).

19.3.8 The Model Code

Chapter 7 considers the Model Code. As explained at **7.8.4.3**, directors will not obtain clearance to deal in the company's shares if an acquisition or a disposal has not been made public and the announcement of the transaction would be likely to lead to a significant movement in the company's share price, unless the trading takes place under a 'trading plan'.

19.3.9 The classification of transactions

The remainder of this chapter examines:

(a)   how acquisitions and disposals by listed companies are classified under the Listing Rules; and

(b)   the consequences for the listed company of that classification.

19.4 The classification of transactions

19.4.1 What is a 'transaction' under the Listing Rules?

Listing Rule 10.1.3R defines 'transaction'. It includes all agreements entered into by a listed company or any of its subsidiaries, other than:

(a)   a transaction of a revenue nature entered into in the ordinary course of business (eg, a foreign exchange company buying more currency, or a travel agency selling a holiday);

(b)   an issue of shares, or a transaction to raise finance, which does not involve the acquisition or disposal of any fixed asset of the listed company or subsidiary (eg, a rights issue or open offer);

(c)   a transaction between a listed company and its wholly-owned subsidiary, or between its wholly-owned subsidiaries (that is, certain intra-group transactions).

It also includes the grant of certain options.

Listing Rule 10.1.4G provides general guidance as to the FSA's intention regarding the Chapter 10 regime. It states that it is intended to cover transactions that are outside the ordinary course of a company's business and may change a shareholder's (or other security holder's) economic interest in the company's assets or liabilities (whether or not any change is registered in the balance sheet). This clarifies that the regime is focused on the potential impact of the transaction on the company

Broadly, 'transaction' means acquisitions and disposals of assets or shares. This would therefore cover a listed company buying or selling another company or a business.

19.4.2 The classification regime

Chapters 10 and 11 of the Listing Rules contain rules relating to the classification of transactions. The rules in Chapter 10 divide transactions into four different classes, according to the size of the transaction compared with the size of the listed company. This comparison is made using four calculations referred to as the 'class tests', set out at LR 10, Annex 1 (see **19.4.3**). Each calculation results in a figure which is expressed as a percentage and referred to as a 'percentage ratio'. The percentage ratios determine how the transaction is classified (see **19.4.5.1**, **19.4.6.1**, **19.4.7.1** and **19.4.8.1**).

Why is this classification necessary? As ever, it is to protect shareholders. The purpose of classifying a transaction is so that the Listing Rules can determine the extent to which the transaction needs to be regulated, in order to protect the interests of shareholders. Chapter 10 regulates transactions on the basis of size. If a transaction is of a significant size, it is classified in a way which means that the company must follow strict procedural requirements before it can complete the transaction (for example, the company must seek shareholder approval of the transaction). On the other hand, if a transaction is not so significant, it is classified in a way which means that the company does not have to follow such strict procedural requirements. This reflects the practical reality that the bigger the transaction (say, the acquisition of a new company), the greater the risk to the purchasing listed company and its shareholders.

19.4.3   The class tests

If the thought of taking figures and applying percentage ratio tests to them brings unwelcome flashbacks of school and makes you break out in a cold sweat, do not worry. The company's financial advisers and its reporting accountants will actually apply the tests to the relevant figures. However, the lawyer must be aware of and understand the need for, and the principles behind, the class tests. In particular, the lawyer must make sure that the company considers these class tests at an early stage in the transaction in light of the implications for timing, certainty and cost which the results of these class tests may bring.

So, the first stage is to apply all of the relevant class tests. The class tests, set out in LR 10, Annex 1, are as follows:

(a)   Gross assets test (para 2R)

$$\frac{\text{Gross assets which are the subject of the transaction}}{\text{Gross assets of the listed company}} \times 100\%$$

(b)   Profits test (para 4R)

$$\frac{\text{Profits attributable to the assets which are the subject of the transaction}}{\text{Profits of the listed company}} \times 100\%$$

(c)   Consideration test (para 5R)

$$\frac{\text{Consideration for the transaction}}{\text{Aggregate market value of the listed company's ordinary shares}} \times 100\%$$

(d)   Gross capital test* (para 7R)

$$\frac{\text{Gross capital of the company or business being acquired}}{\text{Gross capital of the listed company}} \times 100\%$$

*This test is to be performed only for the acquisition of a company or business and not for a disposal (para 7R(2)).

Annex 1 to LR, Chapter 10 provides further guidance on the application of the class tests.

The 'listed company' referred to in the class tests is the listed company who is party to the transaction and whom you are advising. If both parties to the transaction, that is, buyer and seller, are listed companies, then the transaction will need to be classified twice, once from the buyer's perspective, where the buyer's details will be the 'listed company' referred to above (which will establish the formalities the buyer needs to comply with to make the acquisition), and once from the seller's perspective, where the seller will be the 'listed company' referred to above (this will establish the formalities the seller needs to comply with to make the disposal).

It is possible that one transaction can fall within two different classes, depending on from whose perspective the transaction is classified. For example, a disposal by small listed company A of a third of its assets is likely to be a really significant transaction for company A, probably Class 1. However, for the buyer, huge listed company B, the acquisition is less significant, say Class 2.

Note that in share sales the sellers are the shareholders rather than the company itself, so, even if the target is a listed company, the transaction will need to be classified from one perspective (the listed company buyer's) only.

Listing Rule 10, Annex 1, para 10G provides that the FSA can modify the class tests, to substitute other relevant indicators of size, in the event that they produce an anomalous result, or if the calculation is inappropriate to the activities of the listed company.

Listing Rule 10.2.10R provides that, for the purposes of the calculations, the transaction must be aggregated with certain other transactions (broadly those involving the same parties, the acquisition or disposal of shares in the same company, or which, taken together, result in a substantial involvement in a new business activity) which took place in the preceding 12 months. The aim is to ensure that a series of transactions over a relatively short space of time, which cumulatively may have the same risks for the listed company and its shareholders as one big transaction, are subjected to the same regulatory protection. The FSA also has discretion to aggregate in other circumstances (LR 10.2.11G). The FSA has provided further information on how it aggregates transactions in issue 22 of its newsletter, *List!*, available on the UKLA section of the FSA's website.

In practice, typically the consideration test proves to be the key test.

19.4.4   The classification of transactions

Ordinarily three class tests will be applied for a disposal, and all four on an acquisition (see **19.4.3**). This will produce either three or four separate percentage ratios. These figures determine the class of the transaction, but what classes are there? There are four classes of transaction under Chapter 10 of the Listing Rules, namely:

(a)   Class 1 transaction;

(b)   Class 2 transaction;

(c)   Class 3 transaction; and

(d)   reverse takeover.

As mentioned at **19.4.2** above, the purpose of classifying a transaction is to determine the level of procedural safeguards which the Listing Rules will impose to protect the shareholders. Let us now consider:

(a)   the percentage ratios required for the class to apply; and

(b)   the requirements of Chapter 10 of the Listing Rules in relation to transactions of that class.

19.4.5 Class 3

19.4.5.1 Percentage ratios

If *all* of the percentage ratios are less than 5%, the transaction will be a Class 3 transaction (LR 10.2.2R(1)). Class 3 transactions are the smallest, least significant transactions.

19.4.5.2 Chapter 10 requirements

Listing Rules 10.3.1R and 10.3.2R provide as follows:

(a)   If the transaction involves an acquisition and the consideration includes the issue of shares which the company is seeking to list, the company must notify an RIS, as soon as possible after the terms of the acquisition have been agreed, of the information set out in LR 10.3.1R(2).

(b)   If the transaction is any other Class 3 transaction and the company releases details of the transaction to the public, the company must notify an RIS of the information set out in LR 10.3.2R(2).

(c)   If the transaction is a Class 3 transaction which does not fall within (a) or (b) above, Chapter 10 does not impose any procedural requirements on the company at all.

These limited requirements reflect the small size of Class 3 transactions.

An example is ICI plc, the chemicals conglomerate, which made a Class 3 announcement via the RNS on 16 August 2007 that it had acquired an American firm, AAA. The announcement specifically noted, 'no regulatory approvals are needed to complete this transaction'.

19.4.6 Class 2

19.4.6.1 Percentage ratios

If *any* of the percentage ratios is 5% or more, but *each* percentage ratio is less than 25%, the transaction will be classified as a Class 2 transaction (LR 10.2.2R(2)). Class 2 transactions are, therefore, more significant transactions than Class 3 transactions.

19.4.6.2 Chapter 10 requirements

Listing Rule 10.4.1R(1) provides that the company must notify an RIS as soon as possible after the terms of any Class 2 transaction are agreed. The announcement (referred to as a 'Class 2 announcement') must contain the information prescribed by LR 10.4.1R(2), which is more detailed than the information required in an announcement relating to a Class 3 transaction.

If the company later becomes aware that:

(a)   there has been a significant change which affects any matter in the Class 2 announcement; or

(b)   a significant new matter has arisen which the company would have been required to mention in the Class 2 announcement if it had arisen at the time it was preparing that announcement,

the company must make a supplementary announcement through an RIS without delay (LR 10.4.2R(1)).

19.4.7 Class 1

19.4.7.1 Percentage ratios

If *any* of the percentage ratios is 25% or more, the transaction will be classified as a Class 1 transaction (LR 10.2.2R(3)). For example, imagine that X plc, a listed company, is acquiring Y Ltd. The profits of X plc are £100m. The profits of Y Ltd are £30m. The percentage ratio resulting from the profits class test is 30% (30/100 × 100%). The transaction is a Class 1 transaction.

19.4.7.2   Chapter 10 requirements

Listing Rule 10.5.1R provides that the company must:

(a)   comply with the Class 2 requirements, that is, make an announcement through an RIS which complies with LR 10.4.1R(1) (note that, in practice, this is still referred to as a Class 2 announcement, even when it relates to a Class 1 transaction), and make a supplementary announcement, if required;

(b)   send an explanatory circular, approved by the FSA, to shareholders in the form prescribed by LR 13 (Class 1 circular: see **19.6.1** below);

(c)   obtain the shareholders' approval of the transaction (by ordinary resolution in general meeting) before completing the transaction (the notice of GM will be sent out with the circular referred to at (b) above); and

(d)   ensure that, if the agreement is to be entered into before shareholder approval is obtained, completion of the transaction is conditional on shareholder approval being obtained.

These are significant additional procedural steps imposed on the listed company. They will require the calling and holding of a GM if the AGM is not conveniently timed. The requirement for shareholder approval, however, is the best form of protection, as it gives the shareholder a veto over what is, in relation to the listed company, a large transaction and therefore a bigger risk for their investment.

The following (very brief) extract from the required RIS announcement released by Xchanging plc demonstrates this in practice.

Company	Xchanging PLC
TIDM	XCH
Headline	Acquisition
Released	07:00 06-Oct-08
Number	1123F07

XCHANGING PLC ("XCHANGING")

PROPOSED ACQUISITION OF CAMBRIDGE SOLUTIONS LIMITED ("CAMBRIDGE SOLUTIONS")

KEY HIGHLIGHTS

- Xchanging announces that it has today agreed to acquire 75% of the fully diluted share capital of Cambridge Solutions from a group of Cambridge Solutions' major shareholders (the "Acquisition"). Cambridge Solutions, with approximately 4,500 employees, is an international BPO and IT services provider with a global presence through offices in eight countries across four continents. Cambridge Solutions provides its services to a blue-chip customer base and is listed on the Bombay, National, Madras and Ahmedabad stock exchanges in India.

- The consideration for the Acquisition will be approximately £83 million, comprising Rs 3,712 million in cash (equivalent to approximately £45 million at current rates) and the issue of 15,249,998 New Xchanging Shares. The New Xchanging Shares amount to 7% of the Company's current issued ordinary share capital.

. . .

- The Acquisition is conditional on receiving the approval of Xchanging Shareholders. Details of a meeting convened to seek this approval will be set out in a circular which will be sent to Xchanging Shareholders in due course.

. . .

1. INTRODUCTION

...

In view of its size, the Acquisition constitutes a Class 1 transaction for Xchanging for the purposes of the Listing Rules and accordingly Completion of the Acquisition is subject to, amongst other things, Xchanging Shareholder approval which will be sought at a general meeting of Xchanging shareholders to be convened in due course.

19.4.7.3   Waiver of the requirements to prepare a circular and obtain shareholder approval

If the company is making a Class 1 disposal (not acquisition) because it is in severe financial difficulty, then LR 10.8.1G provides that the FSA may waive the requirement for a circular and shareholder approval referred to at **19.4.7.2(b)** and **(c)** above. If the company wants to make use of this waiver, it must demonstrate to the FSA that it is in severe financial difficulty and must satisfy the conditions in LR 10.8.2G to LR 10.8.6G. The conditions are onerous, and include:

(a)   the company demonstrating to the FSA that it could not reasonably have entered into negotiations earlier (thereby allowing time to seek shareholder approval);

(b)   the sponsor confirming that the company is in severe financial difficulty and will not be in a position to meet its obligations as they fall due unless the disposal takes place according to the proposed timetable;

(c)   the company's finance providers confirming that further finance or facilities will not be made available and, unless the disposal is effected immediately, current facilities will be withdrawn; and

(d)   the company making a full announcement to an RIS, no later than the terms of the disposal are agreed, containing the information set out in LR 10.8.4G and LR 10.8.5G.

A very rare example of this waiver being granted is set out in the article below relating to the disposal of a business by a listed company, JJB Sports. It also demonstrates how in practice a listed company often needs advice from lawyers of differing legal expertise at the same time. This matter will involve employment law (eg the dismissal), property law (eg the leases), debt finance (eg standstill agreement) and insolvency law (eg possible CVA) as well as company law.

JJB sells gyms and fires chief executive

Jonathan Russell and Rowena Mason

Retailer JJB Sports has sold its chain of fitness clubs to Wigan Athletic chairman Dave Whelan and confirmed it has sacked its chief executive Christopher Ronnie for gross misconduct.

In a widespread shake-up of the struggling sports retailer, finance director David Madeley has also resigned, while the company is to seek an agreement with its landlords over changing the terms of leases on its outlets.

In a statement on Wednesday night, the company said it had agreed to sell the 55-strong fitness club chain to Mr Whelan, the founder of JJB Sports, for £83.4m.

Proceeds from the sale will initially be used to prop up the indebted company. Although Mr Whelan announced the purchase of the chain of gyms on Wigan Athletic's website in the afternoon, it wasn't until six hours later that it was confirmed by JJB Sports.

The company had to seek a waiver from the UK Listing Authority, available to companies in "severe financial difficulty", to conduct the sale without seeking shareholder approval.

A standstill agreement between JJB Sports and its banks expired on Tuesday, before the sale had been completed, to help the struggling retailer pay down some of its debt.

JJB Sports is believed to owe its lenders – Lloyds and Barclays – around £50m.

Following on from the disposal of the fitness club chain, the company has agreed new short and medium-term debt facilities with its banks.

Sir David Jones, JJB executive chairman, said: "In announcing our series of measures today, we have taken the first step in securing JJB's long-term future after months of speculation."

As part of the restructuring, JJB is also seeking a company voluntary arrangement to settle claims of landlords against 140 closed retail stores and to vary the terms of leases on the company's remaining 250 trading stores.

It is understood Mr Ronnie was sacked for failure to disclose details of loans relating to the ownership of his shares.

In January the company warned of losses of up to £10m when it publishes its full-year results in April.

Its shoe businesses, Qube and the Original Shoe Company, have already fallen into administration with the loss of 400 jobs.

Source: *The Telegraph*, 26 March 2009

19.4.7.4   The sponsor's role

It is a requirement that a listed company must obtain guidance from a sponsor as to the application of Chapter 10 if the transaction could be a Class 1 transaction (or a reverse takeover) (LR 8.2.2R).

19.4.7.5   Specific transactions

In addition to the acquisition and disposal of a company or a business, the rules can also result in the following specific types of transactions being classified as Class 1 transactions:

(a)   *Joint ventures.* On entering a joint venture, a company should consider the exit provisions of the venture, to determine whether they result in the transaction being classified as a Class 1 transaction (see LR 10.8.9G).

(b)   *Reverse takeovers.* Listing Rule 10.2.3R provides that a reverse takeover (see **19.4.8** below) will be treated as a Class 1 transaction if it meets the conditions set out in that rule.

(c)   *Indemnities.* It is common, in a sale and purchase agreement, for a buyer to seek an indemnity from the seller, to cover specific areas of risk. An indemnity is an undertaking by the seller to meet a specific potential legal liability of the buyer. The indemnity will entitle the buyer to a payment from the seller if the event giving rise to the indemnity takes place. Unlike a claim for breach of warranty, there is no need for the buyer to establish that he has suffered loss.

Listing Rule 10.2.4R provides that certain exceptional indemnities, where the maximum liability is unlimited, or equal to or more than 25% of the average of the company's profits for the last three financial years, will be treated as Class 1 transactions. (The FSA has discretion to substitute other indicators of the size of the indemnity, in the event that this calculation gives an anomalous result.) Listing Rule 10.2.5G sets out the types of indemnity which are not exceptional (including indemnities customarily given in connection with sale and purchase agreements).

(d)   *Break fees.* A break fee is a fee payable by a company if certain specified events occur which cause the transaction to fail, or which materially impede a transaction (see LR, Appendix 1). It acts as a financial incentive to get the deal done.

Listing Rule 10.2.7R provides that any break fee payable in respect of a transaction will itself be treated as a Class 1 transaction if the total value of break fees in aggregate exceeds 1% of the value of the company, calculated by reference to the offer price (where the company is being acquired) or 1% of the company's market capitalisation (in all other circumstances).

(e)   *Issues by major subsidiary undertakings.* Listing Rule 10.2.8R provides that if a major *unlisted* subsidiary of a listed company issues shares:

(i)   for cash;

(ii)   in exchange for other securities, or

(iii) to reduce indebtedness,

which will cause a dilution with an economic effect equivalent to the sale of 25% or more of the group, then the share issue will be classified as a Class 1 transaction.

19.4.8   Reverse takeover

19.4.8.1   Percentage ratios

If:

(a)   a listed company acquires:

(i)   a business,

(ii)   an unlisted company, or

(iii)   assets; *and*

(b)   either:

(i)   *any* percentage ratio is 100% or more, *or*

(ii)   the transaction will result in:

–   a fundamental change in the business, or

–   a change in the board, or in voting control of the listed company,

then the transaction will be a reverse takeover (LR 10.2.2R(4)). What this means, in layman's terms, is that the listed company is acquiring a company which is either bigger than it is (on the basis of the class tests), or will, in any event, cause fundamental changes to the listed company's business, or, the balance of power at either board or shareholder level. In other words, it is a really significant transaction.

In practice, reverse takeovers can be a useful way for an unlisted company to list shares when it might otherwise not meet the criteria of the Listing Rules considered in **Chapters 4, 5** and **6**. In effect, the unlisted company 'reverses into' a listed company.

Example

Imagine that X plc, our listed company, has fallen on hard times. A large private company, Z Ltd, is doing very well. The shareholders of Z Ltd negotiate a deal, whereby they will sell Z Ltd to X plc in return for an issue of shares in X plc. The shareholders in Z Ltd will become shareholders in X plc, a listed company. The original shareholders of X plc hope that the acquisition by X plc of the successful company, Z Ltd, might help X plc back on its feet.

Figure 19.1 below shows the reverse takeover process in simplified form, using the details in the example above.

Figure 19.1: Reverse takeover

Before the reverse

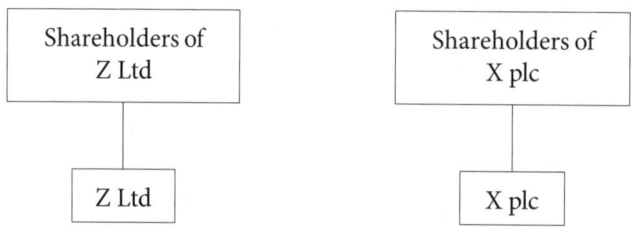

The reverse

1.   Shareholders in Z Ltd *transfer* shares in Z Ltd to X plc

2.   X plc *issues* shares in itself to the shareholders of Z Ltd, as consideration for the transfer.

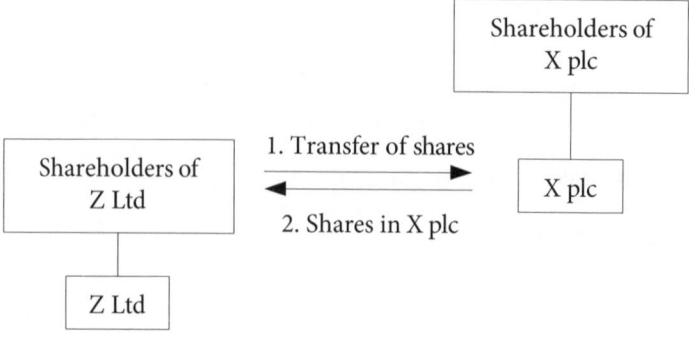

Conclusion

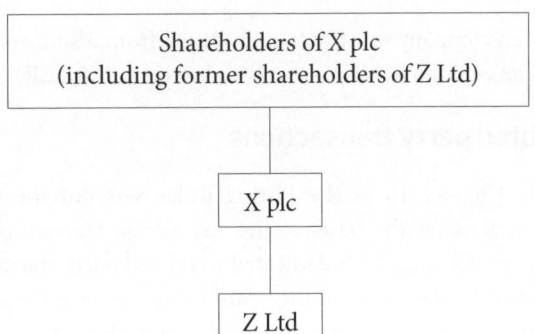

19.4.8.2   Chapter 10 requirements

Listing Rule 10.6.1R provides that the company must comply with the Class 1 requirements. In addition, LR 10.6.2G provides that generally the FSA will cancel the listing of the company's shares. The company must then reapply for the listing of those shares and satisfy the relevant conditions for listing (other than one requirement relating to the company's accounts).

This reflects the reality that a listed company is, in effect, being used as a 'Trojan horse' by the unlisted company's shareholders to gain a listing. As we saw in **Chapter 4**, the directors and the company are normally scrutinised intensely before a company can float on the Stock Exchange. To prevent this process being circumvented by a reverse takeover, the company under new ownership must reapply for listing of the company's shares.

Under LR 10.6.3G, generally the FSA will suspend the listing on its announcement, but it is not compulsory.

Eddie Stobart reverses on to stock market

Graeme Wearden

EDDIE STOBART, the haulage company with its own fan club, is going public through a reverse take-over deal that values the business at £138m. It is merging with the quoted Guernsey property firm Westbury, creating a road, rail and port transport company with assets of more than £250m.

Eddie Stobart is the largest privately owned haulage group in the UK, with a fleet of more than 1,500 trailers and 900 trucks, each with a female name. They are nicknamed 'Stobbies', while lorries in the livery of its French rival Norbert Dentressangle are dubbed 'Nobbies'.

Fans can pick up a wealth of official Eddie Stobart memorabilia from socks and toy lorries to duvet covers and car stickers. There is even a series of children's books featuring a lorry called Steady Eddie.

'For many, the metamorphosis of Eddie Stobart to a publicly listed company will mean that they can now invest and own a part of the company,' the firm said yesterday.

Westbury, which owns Port of Weston in Runcorn, Cheshire, will sell the rest of its property portfolio and be renamed Stobart Group. It is

also buying the rail freight handling business O'Connor for £23m.

William Stobart, the managing director of Eddie Stobart, will become chief operating officer of the new firm. Andrew Tinkler, co-owner of the company, will be chief executive. It is understood that the new company is keen to grow through acquisitions, as well as organically.

'We believe the future of industrial logistics is about the integration of all modes – linking roads with rail, ports and waterways and, in time, air freight,' William Stobart said. 'We believe the merger of our company with one that has a complementary strategy to ours, a strong balance sheet and an experienced board will enable us to invest and grow to benefit our customers, shareholders and staff.'

The company was set up in Cumbria by Eddie Stobart senior, who handed the haulage business on to his son Eddie in 1970. Eddie junior's brother William Stobart and Mr Tinkler took control of the company in 2003.

Yesterday's deal is an asset swap under which Westbury will buy Eddie Stobart for £138m. In return,

William Stobart and Mr Tinkler will buy Westbury's property assets for £142m. The pair will own 28% of Stobart Group.

Analysts have predicted that Stobart Group will have revenues of some £250m in its first year, and pre-tax earnings of around £25m.

It was reported in April that Eddie Stobart was in talks over a possible takeover by Norbert Dentressangle. 'Stobart has clearly been looking for external shareholders, but has not wanted to be sold,' a source close to the company said.

Backstory

Eddie Stobart turned his father's business into Britain's largest privately owned road haulage firm. From eight lorries in 1980, when it moved to Carlisle to be near the M6, it grew to a fleet of nearly 1,000 vehicles and by 1997 its annual turnover exceeded £100m. But the company recorded losses in 2001 and 2002, and in 2003 Eddie junior sold the firm to a company partly owned by his brother William, who had previously worked for the firm as a driver.

Source: *The Guardian*, 16 August 2007

19.4.8.3   The sponsor's role

A listed company must obtain guidance from a sponsor as to the application of Chapter 10 if the transaction *could* be a reverse takeover (LR 8.2.2R).

19.5   Related party transactions

While Chapter 10 of the Listing Rules sets out the rules relating to the classification of transactions on the basis of the *size* of the transaction compared to the size of the listed company, Chapter 11 is dedicated to related party transactions. Related party transactions are classified by the *nature* of the relationship between the parties to the transaction, one of which will be the listed company or one of its subsidiaries.

The rationale behind the related party classification is the same as that behind the Chapter 10 classifications: the protection of investors. Related party transactions are subject to certain safeguards which are designed to prevent those who have considerable power over a listed company from taking advantage of their position.

19.5.1   What is a related party transaction?

A related party transaction is defined by LR 11.1.5R as:

(a)   a transaction (other than a revenue transaction in the ordinary course of business) between a listed company (or any of its subsidiary undertakings) and a related party;

(b)   any arrangements pursuant to which a listed company (or any of its subsidiary undertakings) and a related party each invests in, or provides finance to, another undertaking or asset; or

(c)   a transaction (other than a revenue transaction in the ordinary course of business) between a listed company (or any of its subsidiary undertakings) and any person, the purpose and effect of which is to benefit a related party.

If the transaction falls within any of the above definitions, it will be a related party transaction, regardless of the size of the transaction. However, the transaction does still need to be classified by size, using the Chapter 10 classification system. This is because one of the consequences of a transaction being a related party transaction is that the company must publish a circular to its shareholders, and some of the content requirements of that circular depend on whether the related party transaction is a Class 1 transaction or not (see **19.6.2** below). The size of the related party transaction can also affect whether the transaction is exempt from, or subject to more relaxed requirements than, the usual rules (see **19.5.4** below).

19.5.2   Who is a related party?

A 'related party' means a substantial shareholder, director or shadow director, a person exercising significant influence and any of their associates (LR 11.1.4R).

19.5.2.1   Substantial shareholder

This is defined in LR Appendix 1 and refers to anyone who is (or, at any time in the 12 months before the transaction, was) entitled to exercise, or control the exercise of, 10% or more of the votes at a general meeting of either the listed company, *or any other company in the listed company's group* (but see **19.5.4.1** below in relation to insignificant subsidiaries).

The definition extends to those who were substantial shareholders at any time in the 12 months before the transaction, in order to prevent a shareholder circumventing the procedural requirements of the Listing Rules by reducing his shareholding to just below 10% the day before the transaction.

19.5.2.2 Director or shadow director

This refers to anyone who is (or, at any time in the 12 months before the transaction, was) a director or shadow director of the listed company, or of *any other company in the listed company's group* (but see **19.5.4.1** below in relation to insignificant subsidiaries). The Listing Rules define 'shadow director' as anyone who falls within the definition of a director in s 417(1)(b) of the FSMA 2000. This covers anyone in accordance with whose directions or instructions the directors of the company are accustomed to act. There is, however, some protection for the likes of lawyers; a person will not be a shadow director just because the directors act in accordance with advice he provides in a professional capacity.

19.5.2.3 Person exercising significant influence

This is a person who exercises significant influence over the company.

19.5.2.4 Associate

This means anyone who, at the time of the transaction, was an associate of the substantial shareholder, director, shadow director, or person exercising significant influence, referred to at **19.5.2.1** to **19.5.2.3** above. 'Associate' is defined in LR Appendix 1.1 as follows:

- In relation to a director, substantial shareholder, or person exercising significant influence, who is an individual:

  (1) that individual's spouse, civil partner or child (together 'the individual's family');

  (2) the trustees (acting as such) of any trust of which the individual or any of the individual's family is a beneficiary or discretionary object (other than a trust which is either an occupational pension scheme or an employees' share scheme which does not, in either case, have the effect of conferring benefits on persons all or most of whom are related parties);

  (3) any company in whose equity securities the individual or any member or members (taken together) of the individual's family or the individual and any such member or members (taken together) are directly or indirectly interested (or have a conditional or contingent entitlement to become interested) so that they are (or would on the fulfilment of the condition or the occurrence of the contingency be) able:

    (a) to exercise or control the exercise of 30% or more of the votes able to be cast at general meetings on all, or substantially all, matters; or

    (b) to appoint or remove directors holding a majority of voting rights at board meetings on all, or substantially all, matters.

  For the purpose of paragraph (3), if more than one director of the listed company, its parent undertaking or any of its subsidiary undertakings is interested in the equity securities of another company, then the interests of those directors and their associates will be aggregated when determining whether that company is an associate of the director.

- In relation to a substantial shareholder, or person exercising significant influence, which is a company:

  (1) any other company which is its subsidiary undertaking or parent undertaking or fellow subsidiary undertaking of the parent undertaking;

  (2) any company whose directors are accustomed to act in accordance with the substantial shareholder's, or person exercising significant influence's directions or instructions;

  (3) any company in the capital of which the substantial shareholder, or person exercising significant influence and any other company under (1) or (2) taken together, is (or would on the fulfillment of a condition or the occurrence of a contingency be) interested in the manner described in (3) above.

As you can see, the definition is not particularly user-friendly. It may help to consider an example of who is an associate:

Example

Mr A is a non-executive director (NED) of X plc, a fashion retailer. He also owns 30% of Y Ltd, a marketing company. X plc decides to acquire the business (ie all of the assets) of Y Ltd, to provide an in-house marketing facility for its business.

Y Ltd is an associate of Mr A. This is because Mr A is a director of X plc, and an individual. Y Ltd is caught by para (3) of the appropriate part of the definition; it is a company in whose equity securities Mr A is directly interested and in which he can exercise 30% of the votes.

As a result of Y Ltd being an associate of a director of X plc, Y Ltd is also a related party of X plc. The acquisition by X plc of the business of Y Ltd is not a revenue transaction in the ordinary course of business (retailers do not buy marketing businesses on a day-to-day basis). The acquisition therefore is a related party transaction. There is a risk that Mr A could abuse his position as a director of X plc, for example in negotiating the price, and so the shareholders of X plc will be afforded extra protection under Chapter 11 of the Listing Rules.

19.5.3   Chapter 11 requirements

Subject to the exceptions referred to at **19.5.4** below, the following 'related party rules' apply. The listed company must:

(a)   make a Class 2 announcement (see **19.4.6.2** above), which must also contain the name of the related party and details of the nature and extent of the related party's interest, and make a supplementary announcement, if required (again, do not be confused by the fact that the announcement is still referred to as a Class 2 announcement even though it is being made in relation to a related parties transaction) (LR 11.1.7R(1));

(b)   send an explanatory circular, approved by the FSA, and containing the information prescribed by LR 13.3 and LR 13.6, to shareholders (see **19.6.2** below) (LR 11.1.7R(2));

(c)   obtain the shareholders' approval of the transaction (by ordinary resolution in general meeting before completing the transaction – the notice of the GM will be sent out with the circular referred to at (b) above) (LR 11.1.7R(3)(a));

(d)   if the agreement is to be entered into before shareholder approval is obtained, ensure that completion of the transaction is conditional on shareholder approval being obtained (LR 11.1.7R(3)(b)); and

(e)   ensure that the related party does not (and takes all reasonable steps to ensure that its associates do not) vote on any resolution to approve the transaction (LR 11.1.7R(4)).

19.5.4   Exceptions

There are two categories where the related party rules referred to at **19.5.3** above will not apply. The first is a full exception, where none of the related party rules will apply. The second is a limited exception, where the rules which apply are substantially more relaxed than the full related party rules.

19.5.4.1   When the related party rules will not apply

Listing Rule 11.1.6R provides that the related party rules will not apply if the transaction or arrangement is:

(a)   a small transaction (defined by LR 11, Annex 1R, para 1 as any transaction where each of the Chapter 10 class tests (see **19.4.3** above) results in percentage ratios which are equal to or less than 0.25%); or

(b)   a transaction of a kind referred to in LR 11, Annex 1R, paras 2 to 10, provided it does not have any unusual features.

This includes the following transactions:

New issues (LR 11, Annex 1R, para 2)

The rules will not apply to any issue of new securities to a related party:

(a)   pursuant to a pre-emptive offering; or

(b)   pursuant to the exercise of conversion or subscription rights attaching to listed securities.

The rationale behind this exception is that the shareholders have been protected by other means.

Employees' share schemes (LR 11, Annex 1R, para 3)

The rules will not apply to various awards made pursuant to an employees' share scheme.

Directors' indemnities (LR 11, Annex 1R, para 5)

The rules will not apply to the grant of an indemnity to a director of a listed company or any of its subsidiaries, if the terms of the indemnity are in accordance with those specifically permitted under the CA 2006.

Underwriting (LR 11, Annex 1R, para 6)

The rules will not apply to the underwriting by a related party of certain share issues by the listed company or any of its subsidiaries, provided the consideration to be paid to the underwriter:

(a)   is no more than the usual commercial underwriting consideration; and

(b)   is the same as will be paid to any other underwriters.

Insignificant subsidiaries (LR 11, Annex 1R, para 9)

The rules will not apply if the related party is a related party only through being a substantial shareholder, director or shadow director of an insignificant subsidiary of the listed company (or the associate of any such person). An insignificant subsidiary is a subsidiary which has:

(a)   contributed less than 10% of the profits, and

(b)   represented less than 10% of the assets of,

the listed company for each of the three financial years preceding the date of the transaction for which accounts have been published (or for each financial year for which accounts have been published, if the insignificant subsidiary has been part of the group for less than three years).

Note that this exception will not apply in certain circumstances, such as if the insignificant subsidiary has been part of the group for less than one year, or if the insignificant subsidiary itself is party to the transaction and the ratio of consideration to market capitalisation is more than 10%.

19.5.4.2   When the related party rules will be relaxed

The rules will be relaxed, rather than not apply at all, in relation to any transaction where each of the Chapter 10 class tests (see **19.4.3** above) results in percentage ratios which are less than 5%, but where one or more exceeds 0.25%. In other words, the related party transaction is small, but not small enough to benefit from the full exception referred to at **19.5.4.1** above. How are the rules relaxed? The following rules apply instead of the rules referred to at **19.5.3** above (LR 11.1.10R). The company must:

(a)   inform the FSA in writing of the details of the proposed transaction;

(b)   provide the FSA with written confirmation, from an independent adviser acceptable to the FSA, that the terms of the proposed related party transaction are fair and reasonable so far as the shareholders of the company are concerned; and

(c)   undertake in writing to the FSA to include details of the transaction in the company's next published annual accounts.

Compared to the time and effort required to comply with the usual related party rules by making a Class 2 announcement, publishing a Class 1 circular, and seeking shareholder approval, these rules are much less demanding of the company.

19.5.5   The sponsor's role

A listed company must obtain guidance from a sponsor as to the application of Chapter 11 if the transaction *could be* a related party transaction (LR 8.2.3R).

19.5.6   The Companies Act 2006

The Listing Rules operate alongside the statutory provisions of the CA 2006. In the event of a related party transaction, the following sections of the CA 2006 may also be relevant.

19.5.6.1   Sections 177 and 182 of the CA 2006

These sections require directors to declare their interests in a transaction.

19.5.6.2   Section 190 of the CA 2006

This section requires shareholder approval of substantial property transactions between directors (but not substantial shareholders) and the company.

19.5.7   The memorandum and articles

The company's memorandum and articles may also contain provisions regulating transactions between the company and its directors.

19.6   The circular

As explained in **Chapter 7**, the circular is a means by which a company communicates with its shareholders, particularly where the company requires the shareholders to approve a transaction. The circular should provide enough information to shareholders to allow them to make an informed decision whether to vote for or against the transaction. The circular will also contain the notice of GM, convening the meeting at which the shareholders will vote on the transaction.

Chapter 13 of the Listing Rules prescribes the content of a circular. Listing Rule 13.3 sets out the content requirements for circulars generally (see **7.9.3**); specific content requirements for specific types of circular are then prescribed by other chapter 13 Listing Rules. For example, LR 13.4, LR 13.5 and LR 13, Annex 1R set out the specific requirements, over and above the general LR 3.3 requirements, for a Class 1 circular, and LR 13.6 sets out the specific content requirements for a related party circular.

Just as the Prospectus Rules allow information to be incorporated by reference into a prospectus (see **6.5.2.2** above), so LR 13.1.3R allows information in a prospectus, or other published document filed with the FSA, to be incorporated into a circular.

It was explained at **7.9.4** above that the FSA categorises circulars either as requiring approval prior to being sent out to the listed company's shareholders, or as not requiring prior approval. The Class 1 circular and related party circular both require FSA approval.

Once a circular has been finalised and approved, LR 9.6.1R provides that the company must lodge two copies with the FSA, at the same time it sends the circular to shareholders and it must announce that it has done so through an RIS (LR 9.6.3R(1)). The FSA will then publish the circular through its document viewing facility.

Note that the preparation of the circular can be very time-consuming and costly in light of the information required to be included, and may also delay the timing of the transaction to which it relates (see **19.7** below).

19.6.1 The Class 1 circular

19.6.1.1 Content

As explained at **19.6**, LR 13.3 sets out the general requirements, and LR 13.4, LR 13.5 and LR 13, Annex 1R the specific requirements for a Class 1 circular. Listing Rule 13, Annex 1R cross-refers to Annex 1 and Annex 3 of the PD Regulation (replicated at Appendix III of the Prospectus Rules). This aligns the content requirements of a circular with some of the content requirement for a prospectus (see **6.5.2**). Some of the information in LR 13, Annex 1R must be provided not only for the listed company buyer or seller, but also for the company the subject of the transaction. The requirements of the rules referred to above include the following:

(a) *General disclosure* (LR 13.3.1R(3)). All information necessary for shareholders to be able to make a properly informed decision on the proposal.

(b) *Recommendation* (LR 13.3.1R(5)). A recommendation to shareholders from the directors as to how they should exercise their votes for each resolution, and a statement from the directors as to whether they consider the proposal to be in the shareholders' best interests.

(c) *The directors' responsibility statement* (LR 13.4.1R(4)). A statement by the directors, in the form set out at LR 13.4.1R(4), that they take personal responsibility for the circular.

(d) *Major interests in shares* (LR 13, Annex 1R). The names of the shareholders holding 3% or more of the company's shares (or an appropriate negative statement if there are none).

(e) *Material contracts* (LR 13, Annex 1R). See **6.5.2.1** above.

(f) *Litigation* (LR 13, Annex 1R). See **6.5.2.1** above.

(g) *Significant changes* (LR 13, Annex 1R). A statement about any significant change since the last published accounts, in respect of the listed company, any other company in the listed company's group and the target company.

19.6.1.2 The sponsor's role

As explained at **19.4.7.4** above, the company must obtain the guidance of a sponsor before it enters into a Class 1 transaction. The sponsor has various obligations under the Listing Rules relating to a 'sponsor service', the definition of which includes a company preparing a Class 1 circular. The obligations include the following:

(a) The sponsor owes a general duty of skill and care and taking reasonable steps to ensure that the company understands its obligations under the Listing Rules and the Disclosure Rules (LR 8.3.3R and LR 8.3.4R).

(b) Listing Rule 8.4.12R provides that, before the sponsor submits the Class 1 circular to the FSA for approval, it must be of the opinion, having made due and careful enquiry, that:

    (i) the company has satisfied all requirements of the Listing Rules relevant to the production of a Class 1 circular;

    (ii) the transaction will not have an adverse impact on the company's ability to comply with the Listing Rules or the DTRs; and

    (iii) the directors have a reasonable basis on which to make the working capital statement required by LR 13.4.1R.

The requirement at (ii) above is particularly onerous from the sponsor's point of view.

(c) Listing Rule 8.4.13R sets out further tasks for the sponsor, including:

(i)   submitting to the FSA a Sponsor's Declaration for the Production of a Circular (on the day the circular is to be approved, but before such approval has been given); and

(ii)   ensuring that all matters known to it, which, in its reasonable opinion, should be taken into account by the FSA in considering the transaction, have been disclosed with sufficient prominence in the documentation or otherwise in writing to the FSA.

The proforma Sponsor's Declaration for the Production of a Circular is available from the UKLA section of the FSA's website.

19.6.2   The related party circular

Listing Rule 13.3 lists the general content requirements, and LR 13.6 the specific content requirements, of a related party circular. These requirements include:

(a)   *Full particulars* (LR 13.6.1R(3)). Full particulars of the transaction, including the name of the related party and the nature and extent of that party's interest in the transaction.

(b)   *The fair and reasonable statement* (LR 13.6.1R(5)). A statement by the board that the transaction is fair and reasonable so far as the shareholders of the company are concerned, and that they have been so advised by an independent adviser acceptable to the FSA.

If the percentages ratios reveal that the related party transaction is the size of a Class 1 transaction, LR 13.6.1R(7) provides that the circular must also contain all the information which must be included in a Class 1 circular (see **19.6.1** above), and, if the acquisition or disposal is of an asset for which appropriate financial information is not available, an independent valuation of that asset is also required (LR 13.6.1R(4)).

On receipt of the circular, the shareholders will have all the information to hand to enable them to make an informed decision as to whether or not to approve the transaction by ordinary resolution at the general meeting to be held (**19.5.3** above).

19.6.3   Verification

The verification process in the context of an IPO is explained at **5.3.5** and **6.8** above. Verification is also required in relation to other documents published by listed companies, such as circulars, to protect directors against claims from shareholders on the basis set out at **6.7** above.

19.7   The transaction timetable

The requirements of Chapter 10 and Chapter 11 of the Listing Rules can have a significant effect on the transaction timetable. The detail of an acquisition or disposal timetable for any company, listed or unlisted, is considered in another book in the series (see LPC Guide, *Acquisitions*).

The skeleton timetable below should provide a basic understanding of how the requirements for listed companies impact on an acquisition timetable. The listed company requirements are italicised. Remember, however, that not every listed company will need to follow these requirements; whether it does depends on the classification of the transaction.

(a)   Sign heads of agreement.

       This document will include legally binding provisions. It will contain important provisions about confidentiality and exclusivity.

(b)   Sign the (*conditional*) agreement.

If the transaction is a Class 1, reverse takeover or related party transaction, the agreement must be conditional upon shareholder approval.

(c)   *Make a Class 2 announcement.*

If the transaction is a Class 2, Class 1, reverse takeover or related party transaction, the company must make a Class 2 announcement through an RIS. In certain circumstances the company must also announce a Class 3 transaction.

(d)   *Post the circular and the GM notice.*

If the transaction is a Class 1, reverse takeover or related party transaction, a circular is required.

(e)   *Hold a GM.*

If the transaction is a Class 1, reverse takeover or related party transaction, shareholder approval is required.

(f)   Completion.

Company/business finally bought/sold.

Note that there are several steps in between steps (b) and (f) for a listed company. Usually an unlisted company can sign and complete a sale and purchase agreement simultaneously.

19.8 Conclusion

The Listing Rules regulate the process by which a listed company can make acquisitions and disposals. Depending on the size of the transaction and the relationship between the parties to the transaction, the Listing Rules can require a company to notify an RIS of the transaction and, for more significant transactions, circulate an explanatory circular and obtain shareholder approval of the transaction. These requirements can impact significantly on the timing and cost of the transaction, but reflect the pervasive aim of the regulation of listed companies: to protect investors.

Chapter 20

Takeovers: Regulation

20.1 Introduction

Chapters 21 and **22** consider the detail of a takeover offer (also known as a 'takeover bid'). The purpose of this chapter is to introduce the regulation which will be relevant to any lawyer who advises on such an offer.

20.2 The Panel

The Panel on Takeovers and Mergers (the 'Panel') was established in 1968 as a non-statutory body with the support of the Bank of England. Since then it has supervised the regulatory aspects of takeovers. On 20 May 2006 it was designated as the statutory supervisory authority to carry out certain regulatory functions in relation to takeovers pursuant to the Takeovers Directive (see **20.3**), and on 20 April 2007 it gained statutory powers to regulate takeovers beyond the Takeovers Directive under Chapter 1 of Pt 28 of the CA 2006.

20.2.1 What does the Panel do?

The Panel is an independent body with two roles:

(a)   *Rule-making.* The Panel issues and administers the City Code, the rulebook relating to takeovers (see **20.5** below).

(a)   *Judicial.* The Panel supervises and regulates takeovers and other matters dealt with in the City Code.

20.2.2 Who is on the Panel?

The Panel comprises a maximum of 34 members. It self-appoints a Chairman, up to two Deputy Chairmen and a maximum of 20 other members. Certain financial institutions and professional bodies such as the ABI, the CBI and the NAPF appoint the remaining members.

20.2.3 The Panel Executive

The full Panel itself meets rarely. Instead the Panel Executive carries out the day-to-day work of the Panel, monitoring takeovers and interpreting, consulting on and giving rulings on the City Code. The Panel Executive is headed by the Director General, typically an investment banker seconded to the Panel, and is staffed not only by employees, but also by secondees, including accountants, brokers, investment bankers and, significantly, corporate lawyers. In practice, the term 'Panel Executive' is rarely used; if a lawyer is consulting the Panel Executive, he will invariably refer to this as 'consulting the Panel'. Further information about the Panel Executive is contained in para 5 of the Introduction to the City Code and is available on the Panel's website.

Tempus takeover

THE Clifford Chance partner Jeremy Sandelson has been advising the Takeover Panel over its decision on the recent appeal by WPP plc – the company wanted to challenge the executive's refusal to allow it to invoke a "material adverse change" condition so as to lapse its bid for Tempus. Unusually, the panel and executive were each legally advised: for the latter was Anthony McCaulay of Herbert Smith. Both Sandelson and McCaulay had been seconded to work on the executive panel in the early 1990s. One banker commented: "Blimey – there are more lawyers here than bankers – no doubt as a result of the Human Rights Act."

Source: *The Times*: 13 November 2001

20.2.4   The Panel Committees

The Panel operates principally through the following committees.

20.2.4.1   The Code Committee

The Code Committee, comprising up to 12 members appointed by the Panel, carries out the rule-making role of the Panel (see **20.5**). This Committee is responsible for reviewing and amending the City Code. Typically, the Committee will announce a period of public consultation before amending the Code. The Public Consultation Papers ('PCPs') are published on the Panel's website. Paragraph 4(b) of the Introduction to the City Code provides further detail on the Code Committee.

20.2.4.2   The Hearings Committee

The Hearings Committee carries out the judicial role of the Panel (see **20.2.1**). The Committee reviews the Panel Executive's rulings, and also hears any disciplinary proceedings (which the Panel Executive instigates – see **20.5.7.4**), relating to breaches of the City Code. Usually the secretary to the Hearings Committee is a senior lawyer (such as a partner in a law firm). Paragraphs 4(c) and 7 of the Introduction to the City Code provide further detail on the Hearings Committee.

There is a right to appeal to the Takeover Appeal Board in relation to a decision of the Hearings Committee (Introduction to the City Code, para 8). The Takeover Appeal Board is a separate organisation from the Panel. Further information can be found at www.thetakeoverappealboard.org.uk.

Paragraph 4(d) of the Introduction to the City Code ensures that membership of the Committees are kept separate: a member of the Code Committee (see **20.2.4.1**) cannot be or become a member of the Hearings Committee or the Takeover Appeal Board.

20.2.4.3   The Nomination Committee

The Nomination Committee monitors the size, composition and balance of the Panel. It will therefore doubtless be aware of the fact that (at the time of writing) there is only one woman on the full Panel of 27 and on the Hearings Committee, and that the Panel Executive is led by a man and three male deputies. Only in the Support Group do women predominate, and even here the Office Manager is a man.

20.2.5   The nature of the Panel

Until recently, the Panel was a wholly non-statutory body. In cases such as *R v Panel on Takeovers and Mergers, ex p Datafin plc and Another (Norton Opax plc and Another intervening)* [1987] 1 All ER 564 and *R v Panel on Takeovers and Mergers, ex p Guinness plc* [1989] 1 All ER 509, the courts marvelled at the unique nature of the Panel, which in practice had enormous power as a regulator of some of the largest, most expensive transactions in the financial industry, despite its lack of actual statutory powers. For example, when Guinness breached r 11 of the City Code during its offer for Distillers, the Panel had the power to force

Guinness to pay a considerable sum to the former Distillers shareholders, despite its non-statutory footing at the time (see the article in **Chapter 21**).

However, on 20 May 2006, the implementation of the Takeovers Directive in the UK (see **20.4**) placed the exercise of the Panel's powers on a statutory footing in relation to takeover offers to which the Takeovers Directive applies (see **20.3**). This was extended on 20 April 2007 to include other takeovers covered by the City Code but outside the Takeovers Directive.

20.3 The Takeovers Directive

The Directive on Takeover Bids (Directive 2004/25/EC) (the 'Takeovers Directive') came into force on 20 May 2004 after 20 years of trying to reach agreement in the EU. It aims to impose minimum adequate takeover regulation across the Member States. Each Member State had to implement the Directive into its own law by 20 May 2006.

20.3.1 Application

The Directive applies to takeover *offers* of companies whose shares are admitted to a *regulated market*.

20.3.1.1 Offers

Article 2.1(a) of the Directive states that the Directive applies only to public offers to acquire control of a company. Therefore the Directive does not apply to takeovers effected by way of scheme of arrangement (see **21.12**) (although the City Code does – see **20.4.2**).

20.3.1.2 Regulated market

The reference to a regulated market is to a market within the meaning of art 1(13) of the Investment Services Directive. A list of regulated markets within the EEA is maintained on the website of the European Commission. UK regulated markets are listed on the websites of the Takeover Panel and the Financial Services Authority. For the purposes of this book it is important to note that the Main Market is a regulated market, but AIM is not.

To summarise, the Directive applies to takeovers of companies listed on the Main Market (the focus of this book), but not to takeovers of unlisted public companies or companies quoted on AIM (which are not regulated markets), or takeovers made by way of a scheme of arrangement (which does not involve an offer).

20.3.2 Implementation

In the UK, the original intention was to implement the Takeovers Directive through Pt 28 of the CA 2006. However, the 2006 Act progressed through Parliament more slowly than originally anticipated and was not enacted in time to meet the Directive's implementation date of 20 May 2006. As an interim measure, therefore, the Takeovers Directive (Interim Implementation) Regulations 2006 (SI 2006/1183) were drawn up specifically to implement the Takeovers Directive in the UK on a temporary basis, to remain in force until Pt 28 of the CA 2006 was brought into force. This happened on 6 April 2007, and the Regulations were repealed at the same time.

20.4 Part 28 of the Companies Act 2006

This is now the legal basis for the Panel exercising certain statutory powers in relation to public company takeovers in the UK. Section 942 of the CA 2006 grants the Panel the power to do anything it thinks is necessary or expedient to carry out its functions.

Section 943 of the CA 2006 gives the City Code a statutory basis (formerly it operated without statutory backing, as an informal set of rules which in practice all listed companies observed). The Panel must make rules governing certain matters required by the Takeovers Directive (which are now in the City Code) and it has also been given the power to make rules for takeovers other than those covered by the Takeovers Directive. As discussed in **20.5.1**, the City Code extends well beyond such takeovers and these rules now have statutory effect.

The CA 2006 has also given the Panel statutory powers of investigation and the right to impose sanctions for breaches of the City Code (see **20.5.7**).

20.5   The City Code

The main source of regulation of takeovers is called the City Code on Takeovers and Mergers. This is often referred to as the 'Takeover Code', or the 'City Code'. This book refers to it as the City Code. It may be viewed in full on the Panel's website. (It is also known, in practice, as the 'Blue Book', not for any particularly titillating content but with unquestionable accuracy in describing the colour of the book containing the City Code.)

20.5.1   When does the City Code apply?

The application of the City Code is set out in para 3 of the Introduction to the City Code. It applies to offers (see **20.5.1.2**) for certain companies (see **20.5.1.1**).

20.5.1.1   Companies within the City Code

It is the nature and nationality of the *offeree* company (the company which the offeror is looking to buy) which is important for determining whether the City Code will apply.

The City Code will apply if the offeree company is:

(a)   a public company, or Societas Europaea, with its registered office in the UK, the Channel Islands or the Isle of Man, whose securities are admitted to trading on a *regulated market* in the UK (such as the Main Market, which is the focus of this book, but not AIM) or on any stock exchange in the Channel Islands or the Isle of Man; or

(b)   any other public company, or Societas Europaea (including quoted on AIM and unlisted public companies), or, in limited circumstances, a private company (namely a private company which during the last ten years has had its securities admitted to the Official List, or advertised dealings for a six-month continuous period, or been required to file a prospectus, or had securities subject to a CA 2006, s 693(3) marketing arrangement) which:

(i)   has its registered office in the UK, the Channel Islands or the Isle of Man, and

(ii)   in the Panel's opinion, has its place of central management and control in the UK, the Channel Islands or the Isle of Man.

The City Code uses the word 'offeree company' to describe the target company (or potential target company) whose shares are the subject of the offer (or potential offer). However, you must remember that in fact the offeror will make the offer not to the target company, but to that company's shareholders. In practice, the offeree company is frequently referred to as the 'target'.

In summary, then, it is the offeree company's status as a *public* company (or former public company) which is important for the purposes of the City Code, regardless of whether the offeree company happens to be listed or unlisted. The City Code therefore generally excludes offers for private companies. These are subject to contract law and certain statutory provisions.

Where the company is registered in the UK but its shares are admitted to trading elsewhere in the EEA (or vice versa) there is provision for shared jurisdiction with takeover regulators in other Member States.

20.5.1.2 Offers within the City Code

The City Code applies to 'offers' for those companies mentioned at **20.5.1.1** above. 'Offer' is defined to include those transactions set out in para 3(b) of the Introduction to the City Code. These are principally 'takeover bids and merger transactions however effected, including by means of statutory merger or scheme of arrangement'. (The City Code does extend to less common and more technical transactions as well, but these are beyond the scope of this textbook.) Usually such a transaction will involve the offeror seeking control of the offeree company. 'Control' is defined in the City Code as 30% or more of the voting rights in the offeree company. This textbook concentrates on the most common situation in practice, of an offeror seeking to gain 100% control of the offeree company.

It is worth noting that sometimes it can be difficult to pin down whether a transaction is a 'takeover' or a 'merger'. A merger denotes a union of equals, but frequently the term is used in practice when a takeover (one company taking ownership of another) is occurring. This use of 'merger' is usually done for PR reasons to give the impression that the offeree company is not being swallowed up by the offeror. Ultimately this has no impact on the application of the City Code as it covers both situations.

The Code even applies to transactions which are in contemplation but not yet announced. For example, there are strict rules governing secrecy in r 2 of the City Code (see **21.3**) and dealing in shares (r 4, see **21.8.10.1**) which apply even if a takeover offer has not yet been firmly decided upon.

Note also that the City Code will apply regardless of how the takeover is carried out. For example, it applies to a takeover effected by way of a general offer or by way of a scheme of arrangement – see **21.12**. Again, the City Code is broader than the Takeovers Directive, which, for example, does not apply to schemes of arrangement (see **20.3.1**).

20.5.1.3 The offeror/bidder

There are no rules in the City Code regarding the status or nature of the offeror (also known as the bidder) making the offer. The offeror may be any company, listed or unlisted, public or private, UK or foreign registered. It could be a partnership or limited liability partnership, UK or foreign registered. It could even be an individual or group of individuals. As mentioned in **20.5.1.1** above, it is the status of the *offeree company* which is important. In practice, the offeror may also be referred to as the 'bidder'.

20.5.2 To whom does the City Code apply?

Paragraph 3(f) of the Introduction to the City Code confirms that the Code applies to everyone who is involved in a transaction to which it applies. This includes not only the offeror and the offeree company, but also the directors of the offeror and the offeree company, and their respective professional advisers. The lawyers advising on the transaction, therefore, will be subject to the City Code.

20.5.3 The purpose of the City Code

The Introduction to the City Code explains, in para 2, that its purpose is to:

(a)   ensure fair and equal treatment of all shareholders in relation to takeovers;

(b)   provide an orderly framework within which takeovers are conducted; and

(c)   promote the integrity of the financial markets.

Importantly, the City Code is *not* concerned with the commercial advantages or disadvantages of a takeover. For example, whether the offer price fairly reflects the offeree company's true value. These are matters for the directors and shareholders of the offeree company to decide upon. The City Code also is not concerned with other regulatory issues, such as competition policy, which are subject to their own sets of rules and regulatory bodies (see **20.7**).

20.5.4   The nature of the City Code

As discussed at **20.4** above, s 943 of the CA 2006 gives statutory effect to the previously non-statutory City Code.

The City Code comprises six general principles (see **20.5.5**), 38 rules which are based on, and develop, these principles, and seven Appendices. The rules must be read in conjunction not only with the general principles but also with the accompanying notes, which give practical guidance on the applicability of the rules.

The six general principles are taken directly from the Takeovers Directive and are essentially statements of standards of commercial behaviour.

The City Code is an interesting creature from the common law lawyer's perspective, as, under para 2(b) of the Introduction, it is the *spirit*, and not just the letter, of both the general principles and the rules which is to be applied. This means that the Panel Executive may be willing to modify or relax the wording of the rules, on a case-by-case basis, if this is consistent with the underlying purpose of the rules. This, of course, is a significant departure from normal practice and clearly affects how the lawyer must advise in relation to the Code (see **20.5.6** below).

20.5.5   The general principles

The general principles are the key to understanding the spirit of the City Code. They are the cornerstone of the Code, and they may apply in situations which the rules of the City Code do not cover expressly. The six general principles are set out below, together with (the author's) summaries to help reinforce the essence of each principle:

1.   All holders of the securities of an offeree company of the same class must be afforded equivalent treatment; moreover, if a person acquires control of a company, the other holders of securities must be protected.
     Summary: shareholders should be treated equally and fairly.

2.   The holders of the securities of an offeree company must have sufficient time and information to enable them to reach a properly informed decision on the bid; where it advises the holders of securities, the board of the offeree company must give its views on the effects of implementation of the bid on employment, conditions of employment and the locations of the company's places of business.
     Summary: sufficient information should be made available to shareholders in a timely fashion, to enable them to decide whether to accept or reject the offer.

3.   The board of an offeree company must act in the interests of the company as a whole and must not deny the holders of securities the opportunity to decide on the merits of the bid.
     Summary: Directors have duties of fairness in relation to takeovers.

4.   False markets must not be created in the securities of the offeree company, of the offeror company or of any other company concerned by the bid in such a way that the rise or fall of the prices of the securities becomes artificial and the normal functioning of the markets is distorted.
     Summary: Parties should not commit market abuse, etc.

5.   An offeror must announce a bid only after ensuring that he/she can fulfil in full any cash consideration, if such is offered, and after taking all reasonable measures to secure the implementation of any other type of consideration.
     Summary: The bidder must be in a position to pay for the offeree company's shares.

6.   An offeree company must not be hindered in the conduct of its affairs for longer than is reasonable by a bid for its securities.

Summary: The offer timetable should not drag on.

The practical effect of these general principles is considered in **Chapters 21** and **22**.

20.5.6   The City Code in practice

If there is any doubt as to how the City Code might apply in a certain situation, the parties and their advisers should consult the Panel Executive, who will provide a ruling on the issue. In fact, para 6(b) of the Introduction to the City Code states expressly that legal advice is not an appropriate alternative to obtaining a ruling from the Panel Executive. Does this mean that the lawyer does not need to know anything about the City Code? Far from it. In fact, the lawyer plays a pivotal part in the interpretation of the Code.

First, the lawyer will be involved in trying to identify a 'third way', in circumstances where the company will struggle to comply with the letter of the City Code, but there is a possibility of an alternative approach which would not compromise the spirit of the City Code. The Panel Executive is likely to be much more receptive to a company which approaches it in the hope of modifying the interpretation of a rule if the company has a well thought-out suggestion for such modification. Obviously the lawyer's knowledge and experience, of previous occasions when the Panel Executive has been willing to modify the interpretation of rules of the City Code, will assist in this role.

The second role of the lawyer in relation to the City Code is that, together with certain of the company's other advisers, he will have regular contact with the Panel Executive during the takeover process.

20.5.6.1   Practice Statements

The Panel Executive publishes Practice Statements, which it posts, in date order, on its website. These statements provide informal guidance on how the Panel Executive interprets and applies the City Code in certain circumstances. The Practice Statements do not form part of the City Code, and so are not binding and no substitute for consulting the Panel Executive.

20.5.7   Enforcement of the City Code

The City Code has the force of law in relation to all takeovers to which it applies.

20.5.7.1   Monitoring powers

The Panel has powers to monitor the progress of a takeover. Those dealing with the Panel must do so in an open and cooperative way, and disclose all relevant information (subject to legal professional privilege) (Introduction to the City Code, para 9(a)). The Panel also has the power to require documents and information from persons dealing with the Panel (CA 2006, s 947 and Introduction to the City Code, para 9(b)).

20.5.7.2   Enforcement powers of the Panel

Anyone reporting a breach to the Panel must do so promptly, otherwise the Panel may exercise its discretion to disregard the complaint (Introduction to the City Code, para 10(a)).

Once it is certain that the Code has been breached, the Panel has several powers of enforcement, set out below.

Compliance rulings

The Panel has the power to make a compliance ruling, either to prevent a breach of the Code (if there is a reasonable likelihood of a breach of the City Code or a Panel ruling) or, if the breach has already occurred, to ensure the breach is remedied (Introduction to the City Code, para 10(b)).

Compensation rulings

The Panel has a limited power to make a compensation ruling to order a party to compensate any offeree company shareholders who have suffered financially as a result of a breach of the Code (Introduction to the City Code, para 10(c)). The Panel can exercise this power only in relation to breaches of those rules which deal with the offer consideration (namely rules 6, 9, 11, 14, 15, 16 and 35.3). The effect of a compensation ruling is to put the shareholders into the position they would have been had the breach not occurred. The Panel can also order that simple or compound interest be paid to the shareholders.

Enforcement by the courts

The Panel can ask the courts to enforce the City Code (CA 2006, s 955 and Introduction to the City Code, para 10(d)). The Panel has stated that it will exercise this power only as a last resort, or in urgent cases.

Bid documentation rules

For offers to which the Takeovers Directive applies only (see **20.3.1**), there is a criminal offence under s 953 of the CA 2006 for non-compliance with the 'bid documentation rules'. These are defined in the Introduction to the City Code, para 10(e), and set out in Appendix 6.

The bid documentation rules relate to the content requirements of the main takeover document, known as the offer document (see **22.4.1**) (the 'offer document rules'), and any defence documents (see **22.4.2**) (the 'response document rules'). In the event that the documents do not comply with the rules, a criminal offence is committed (in the case of a breach of the offer document rules) not only by the offeror but also by any director, officer or member of the offeror who caused the document to be published, and (in the case of a breach of the response document rules) by any director or officer of the offeree company if they knew, or were reckless as to whether, the document did not comply with the Code, and failed to take all reasonable steps to ensure compliance. The offence is punishable by a fine. The offence applies only to those takeover offers which are subject to the Takeovers Directive (see **20.3.1**), namely those covered by this book, ie takeovers of companies listed on the Official List and trading on the Main Market (so not to schemes of arrangement or to offers for unlisted companies, or companies listed on AIM).

In certain circumstances, disciplinary action may be taken (see **20.5.7.4**).

20.5.7.3   Enforcement powers of the FSA

Under the Introduction to the City Code, para 11, the Panel can request the FSA to take enforcement action against any person authorised by the FSMA 2000 who contravenes the City Code or a ruling of the Panel. The definition of 'authorised person' is considered at **9.4.3**. In practice, this will cover the stockbroker (see **21.5.3**) and the financial adviser (see **21.5.1**) acting for the company in relation to the takeover. The stockbroker and financial adviser will not continue to act unless the takeover complies with the City Code, as otherwise they risk the sanctions listed below. Note that the FSA can also take enforcement action against an 'approved person', for example a director of an authorised firm.

The FSA can take the following enforcement action in the event of a breach of the City Code:

(a)   public censure;

(b)   fine;

(c)   the removal of authorisation under the FSMA 2000;

(d)   injunction; and

(e)   order for restitution.

Note also the requirement, referred to at **20.5.7.4(e)** below, that the rules of the FSA prohibit a person authorised by the FSMA 2000 from acting for any offender.

20.5.7.4   Disciplinary powers

Paragraph 11 of the Introduction to the Code outlines the power of the Panel Executive to institute disciplinary proceedings before the Hearings Committee (see **20.2.4.2**). If the Committee finds that there has been a breach of the City Code, it can impose the following sanctions:

(a)   private reprimand;

(b)   public statement of censure;

(c)   suspension or withdrawal of, or the imposition of conditions on, any exemption, approval or other special status the Panel has granted;

(d)   reporting the offender's conduct to another regulatory body such as the DBERR, the Stock Exchange or the FSA; or

(e)   publishing a Panel Statement indicating that the offender is unlikely to comply with the City Code. This can trigger other requirements of the FSA and certain professional bodies which oblige their members, in certain circumstances, not to act for the offender in a transaction to which the City Code applies.

There is an example of (b) in Panel Statement 2007/6, available on the Panel's website. The Panel publicly and severely criticises NM Rothschild & Sons, financial advisers, for actions during a takeover of PlusNet by BT plc. This in turn prompted BT plc to announce that it was reviewing the fees it paid Rothschild for acting as financial adviser on the deal.

The Panel Executive has set out, in the 'compliance' section of its website, the issues it will take into account when considering whether to take disciplinary action.

20.6   Other rules and regulations

Chapter 17, which considers the methods of raising equity finance, and **Chapter 19**, which considers listed company acquisitions and disposals, explain that the specific subject matter of those chapters cannot be considered in a vacuum; most of the rules and regulations examined in this book are relevant to the specific areas of law those chapters consider. The same can be said of takeovers. In addition to the City Code, takeovers are subject to other rules and regulations, all of which are considered in this book. They are summarised below.

20.6.1   Consideration

If the company is:

(a)   issuing shares as consideration, or

(b)   using equity finance to raise cash to use as consideration,

for the acquisition, then the rules and regulations considered in **17.4** above will be relevant.

20.6.2   Acquiring shares

A takeover is, after all, just an acquisition of shares. This means that all the rules and regulations summarised at **19.3** above are relevant, including rules under the CA 2006, the Listing Rules, the DTRs, FSMA 2000 and the Model Code.

20.6.3   Merger control

The takeover of a UK company can give rise to merger control issues in the UK under the EA 2002, or in the EU under the EC Merger Regulation. **Chapter 23** considers this issue further.

20.6.4 Sector-specific regulatory controls

Certain sectors have their own specific regulatory provisions. Examples include the defence, travel and broadcasting industries. The lawyer may need to take advice from his client as to the sector-specific regulations which may apply to any takeover transaction.

20.6.5 Compulsory acquisition of minority shareholdings

The provisions of ss 974 to 991 of the CA 2006, which are important in the context of a takeover, are discussed at **22.7** below.

20.7 Regulatory bodies

The rules and regulations which may apply to a takeover, and which are considered in this chapter, mean that the following regulatory bodies may become involved in a takeover bid:

(a)   The Panel, which administers the City Code (see **20.2** above).

(b)   The FSA, which has powers of enforcement in relation to the City Code (see **20.5.7.3** above).

(c)   The FSA (acting in its capacity as UKLA). If the offeror is listed and is issuing new shares as consideration, or to raise cash consideration, those shares must be admitted to listing on the Official List by the FSA. Also, if the acquisition is a Class 1 transaction, the FSA will need to approve the Class 1 circular (see **19.6** above).

(d)   The Stock Exchange. If the offeror is listed and is issuing new shares as consideration, or to raise cash consideration, those shares must be admitted to trading on the Main Market by the Stock Exchange.

(e)   The OFT, the Competition Commission and the European Commission. If the takeover raises competition issues, these bodies may become involved (see **Chapter 23**).

(f)   Sector-specific regulatory bodies. This will depend on the sector in which the parties to the takeover specialise. For example, the Civil Aviation Authority is likely to be involved in the takeover of an airline company, to check the company holds an ATOL licence.

Chapter 21
Takeovers: Preparation

21.1 Introduction

Chapter 20 introduces the concept of a takeover and considers the rules and regulations which the lawyer will need to apply in relation to a takeover. In particular, it explains that the City Code contains the key rules relating to takeovers, and that the unique nature of the Code means that the lawyer will need to consult the Panel Executive (referred to in this chapter as 'the Panel') to determine how the City Code might apply in the circumstances of a particular takeover.

It is very exciting to be instructed in relation to a takeover. Of all the listed company issues considered in this book, it is the takeover which arrests the attention not only of your client, but also, once announced, of shareholders, your colleagues, the press and the general public.

Chapter 22 considers the takeover process once the bid has been announced. However, the lawyer's work begins long before that. This chapter considers the work which the lawyer undertakes prior to the announcement of a takeover bid.

Note that, as explained in **Chapter 20**, in practice the terms 'offer' and 'bid' are used interchangeably, as are the terms 'offeror' and 'bidder', and 'offeree' and 'target'. The City Code uses the terms 'offer', 'offeror' and 'offeree'.

21.2 Recommended or hostile?

Rule 1 of the City Code provides that the offeror must make the offer first to the directors (or advisers) of the offeree company. The most significant factor which will determine the nature of the offeror's preparation is whether the takeover is intended to be recommended or hostile. They could not be more different.

21.2.1 The recommended offer

If the directors of the offeree company consider that the offer is in the best interests of the company's shareholders, employees and (if the company's solvency is in issue) creditors, they must recommend the offeree's shareholders to accept the offer. The offer is described as 'recommended'. Remember, it is the shareholders of the offeree company who own it and who ultimately will determine the success of the offer, in other words, whether to sell their shares to the offeror or not.

Bear in mind that a takeover often results in a change in management. The directors of the offeree company risk losing their jobs, or being relocated, if the takeover goes ahead. The culture of the business may change. However, the directors of the offeree company must not allow personal considerations to influence the exercise of their duties to the company when considering whether to recommend the offer.

With a recommended offer, both the offeror and the offeree company have a common aim in ensuring the takeover goes ahead. A recommended offer to acquire all the securities in a company is the most straightforward form of takeover. The boards of directors of both companies will act consensually to try to achieve that takeover. It has the best chance of success, and it can be completed in the shortest period of time.

EDF agrees takeover of British Energy

Holly Williams

French group EDF today agreed a £12.5 billion takeover of British Energy in a move set to kick-start the UK's nuclear power strategy.

The state-owned utility giant will pay 774p a share, 9p higher than the price offered in July which was rejected as too low by major British Energy shareholders.

British Gas parent Centrica is also in talks to buy a 25% stake in the new British Energy following the deal, it was confirmed today.

Prime minister Gordon Brown welcomed news of the takeover as "good value for the taxpayer and a significant step towards the construction of a new generation of nuclear stations".

Today's deal will see EDF take control of all of British Energy's (BE) nuclear power stations and play a leading role in the development of new stations in the UK, which are likely to be built on BE's existing sites.

It will also allow the UK Government to bank a multi-billion pound windfall from its 36% stake in the firm.

EDF said today it planned to build four new nuclear reactors in the UK and would maximise the potential of British Energy's eight nuclear power stations.

But the Government has stressed that it wants other players in Britain's nuclear power industry.

British Energy employs around 6,000 staff and produces around a sixth of the UK's electricity.

EDF pledged to "recognise and appreciate" the importance of BE employees and said it would safeguard their employment and pension rights.

Pierre Gadonneix, chairman and chief executive of EDF, said: "For EDF, this is an historic milestone in our strategic development plans in Europe and enables the EDF Group top develop significantly in the UK one of its key markets.

"For British Energy it places it at a the vanguard of new nuclear build in the UK and at the centre of the global nuclear renaissance."

Dougie Rooney, national officer of Unite, said: "We welcome the end of a long sales process. EDF was the only potential purchaser. Our job now is to ensure that EDF keep the existing plants open and maintain or improve investment."

Mr Rooney said it was vital that supply companies in the UK were involved in future investment in the nuclear industry which he said would help create thousands of skilled jobs.

Paul Noon, general secretary of Prospect, which represents around 2,000 managerial workers in British Energy, also welcomes the announcement.

He said: "I hope it gives security to the future of workers' jobs as well as Britain's energy supply.

"We have a good relationship with EDF and we are keen to ensure that will continue."

EDF wants to construct and operate two reactors each at Hinkley Point in Somerset and Sizewell in Suffolk, with the first new reactor on-stream by the end of 2017, the Government confirmed.

The group has also agreed with the Government to sell land to other potential nuclear operators in certain pre-agreed circumstances.

EDF's four new reactors could generate electricity to meet more than 13% of the UK's forecast energy demand by the early 2020s, saving more than 14 million tonnes of CO_2 emissions a year, said the Department for Business and Enterprise and Regulatory Reform.

The Prime Minister said: "New nuclear is becoming a reality.

"Nuclear is clean, secure and affordable. Its expansion is crucial for Britain's long-term energy security, as we reduce our oil dependence and move towards a low-carbon future."

British Energy chairman Sir Adrian Montague said his company spent the last six weeks working with EDF to secure the new terms and seal a deal.

He told BBC Radio 4's Today programme: "This new transaction is regarded by the board as good for the shareholders, good for our staff, good for the nuclear industry and also good for the country.

"In the short term I think you will find a stronger supplier of energy in the UK as we bring together British Energy's generating capability with EDF's strength of the supply business.

"And I think that the other key issue here is that we are positioning the company as the lynchpin of a new nuclear future, and we are bringing together two very strong companies in the nuclear industry.

"EDF is a huge supplier of nuclear energy in France, and of course we have been a big supplier in the UK and together we want to build a new nuclear future."

Sir Adrian said the deal would help increase Britain's energy security, saying: "The new nuclear enterprise will be good for the country because it will increase the proportion of electricity that we generate here in a way that is not dependent on international oil and gas prices."

EDF - majority-owned by the French government and the world's biggest nuclear power provider - said the deal had the support of British Energy's largest shareholder, Invesco, which owns a 14.9% stake.

It is thought that the July offer from EDF was scuppered by opposition from institutional investors such as Invesco, which are said to have argued that the price undervalued BE at a time when the value of energy assets was rising.

Oil's slide from July's 147 US dollar peak is thought likely to have persuaded some investors to be more flexible over price demands.

The Government also announced it had committed to accept the EDF deal.

EDF plans to build longer-lasting EPR reactors in the UK, which are a type of pressurised water reactor, similar to those already in operation in nuclear industry-reliant France.

They are believed to last for 60 years compared with the normal 40-year lifespan.

Centrica said it was hoping to take part in EDF's new nuclear builds in the UK under negotiations to take an investment in the new BE.

It is also looking to secure a deal to take at least 25% of the energy output from BE's existing fleet of stations.

BE operates eight nuclear sites in the UK and has land around them where new reactors could be built.

Its eight nuclear power stations are Dungeness B in Kent, Hartlepool, Heysham 1 and 2 in Lancashire, Hinkley Point B in Somerset, Hunterston B in Ayrshire, Sizewell B in Suffolk and Torness in East Lothian.

The group also owns a coal-fired power station at Eggborough, North Yorkshire.

Speaking on Sky News, Mr Brown said: "The reason for this announcement is £25 billion of investment in nuclear power stations and we will start to lead the world in the new generation of nuclear power stations.

"They will probably be able to announce they are building four new nuclear power stations.

"It is exactly what I want to see, and that is, that we have the dependence upon oil reduced, that we are doing something that is more in tune with climate change, we are getting investment in nuclear power... this is a French-British deal in the end that will happen."

Source: *The Independent*, 24 September 2008

21.2.2   The hostile offer

If, having been approached under r 1 by the offeror, the board of the offeree company advises its shareholders not to accept the offer, it is described as a 'hostile' offer. The offeror and the offeree company have diametrically opposed aims. The offeror wants the takeover to be successful, while the offeree company will do everything in its power to ensure the offer fails so that it maintains its independence. For both sides there is much at stake. For the offeror, the takeover could be central to the company's strategy of expansion. The shareholders of the offeree company, who ultimately decide whether to accept the offer, need to balance the fact that their board is advising them to reject the offer against the claims of the offeror about how attractive the offer is, in terms of the consideration they will receive in exchange for their shares in the offeree company. The stakes are raised still further by the offer being played out in the public arena, with hard-won reputations on the line.

21.2.3   The effect on preparation

If the offeror has an existing relationship with the offeree company, it may know in advance whether the offeree company will recommend the offer or not. If so, the offeror can prepare accordingly. However, if the offeror does not have an existing relationship with the offeree company, it has a choice: it can either approach the offeree company with a view to negotiating a recommended offer (and consider whether it is prepared to 'go hostile' in the event the offeree company decides not to recommend an offer), or it can launch a surprise hostile offer for the offeree company without discussing this first with the offeree company.

Whether the offer is intended to be recommended or hostile, the offeror must also plan for the possibility that another offeror may make a rival offer for the offeree company.

21.3   The need for secrecy

Rule 2.1 of the City Code provides that it is vital that the existence of the offer is kept secret until the offer is announced to the public under r 2.4 or r 2.5 (see **22.3**). In practice, this means that the lawyer must advise his client company, together with all advisers who are instructed to work on the transaction, of the importance of secrecy and security (Note 1 to r 2.1). The number of people to whom confidential information is given should be kept to a minimum. Anyone who receives confidential information can pass it on only if it is necessary to do so, and they must ensure that they inform the recipient of any information of the need for secrecy in relation to that information. For the lawyer, this translates into ensuring that:

(a)   the team working on the transaction is no larger than it needs to be;

(b)   each member of the team is aware of the secrecy obligation;

(c)   due diligence (see **21.6**) is carried out discreetly;

(d)   documents relating to the takeover are kept confidential (for example, not left lying around on the printer); and

(e)   the transaction and each of the parties to the transaction are referred to by way of code name rather than their actual names. The code names should not be too obvious. The client may already have code names which it used while carrying out its initial research into the offeree company as a potential target. To take a facile example (although in real life the code names do tend to be facile), imagine a takeover of a company which has an American chairman. The transaction might be code-named 'Project Baseball', the offeror code-named 'Bat' and the offeree company code-named 'Ball'. This means that, in all conversations, meetings, telephone calls, documentation and such like, the code names will be used rather than the real names. The documentation will then be amended, to replace the code names with the real names, just before it is published. All very MI5!

To the layman (and, indeed, to a trainee who has not come across the concept before) this can all seem a little dramatic. It can also result in rather awkward situations for the lawyers. There will be a distinct buzz of activity around the offices of the team of lawyers who are working on a takeover. This can draw inquisitive comments from colleagues, regarding what the team is working on. The effect of r 2.1 is that those colleagues must be rebuffed in as polite a manner as you can manage. This can be particularly difficult for any trainee working on the takeover, who will not be able to discuss the transaction even with more senior lawyers who enquire what the trainee is doing. These measures, however, are vital. A leak can have disastrous consequences for the bid (see **22.3.3.2** and **22.3.3.3** below). While the secrecy obligation can be frustrating for the lawyer, consider just how much more embarrassing it would be if a leak was traced back to him.

The Panel has reiterated the importance of r 2.1 in Practice Statement 2008/20, and expresses its support for the FSA's attempts to tackle the problem of misuse of inside information in takeovers.

21.4 An example

Obviously, the work involved for a lawyer advising on a takeover depends on whether he is advising the offeror or the offeree company. This book examines the takeover principally from the point of view of the offeror. To make sense of what **Chapter 20** and **Chapter 21** have covered so far, let us consider an example.

21.4.1 The facts

Imagine that we advise X plc, a company whose shares are admitted to listing on the Official List and to trading on the Main Market, which is seeking to make an offer for the entire issued ordinary share capital of Y plc, also a company whose shares are admitted to listing on the Official List and to trading on the Main Market. The share price of X plc is looking healthy. Y plc, however, has had some bad press lately. It has been underperforming compared to its main rivals (which include X plc) and its share price is at an all-time low. The press have been speculating about whether Y plc is ripe for a takeover.

21.4.2 The analysis

The transaction is a takeover which is subject to the provisions of the City Code. X plc is seeking to acquire 100% of the shares in a UK company whose securities are admitted to trading on a regulated market (ie the Main Market) (see **20.5.1.1** above), Y plc. X plc is the offeror. Y plc is the offeree company.

Note that the fact that X plc, the offeror, is a listed company is, in fact, irrelevant in terms of the application of the City Code, where it is the identity of the offeree company which is important. It is, however, relevant in terms of applying the class tests and other continuing obligations imposed on listed companies, and in terms of the ability of X plc to offer shares as consideration, or raise cash consideration through the issue of shares.

For the purposes of the application of the City Code, it is worth remembering (see **20.5.1.1**) that Y plc need not be listed. The takeover of *any* public company will fall under the City Code.

21.4.3 Code names

The company secretary of X plc has decided that the code name for the transaction is Project Gotham. The code name of X plc is Batman. The code name of Y plc is Robin.

21.4.4 The parties

The main parties involved in Project Gotham will be as follows:

(a)   The offeror, Batman.

(b)   The offeree company, Robin.

(c)   The board of Batman.

(d)   The board of Robin.

(e)   The shareholders of Batman. The shareholders of Batman may need to be involved for two reasons:

  (i)   if the transaction is a Class 1 acquisition or a reverse takeover, Batman will require shareholder approval before it can complete the acquisition (see **Chapter 19**); and

  (ii)   if Batman decides to issue Batman shares to Robin's shareholders as consideration, the shareholders may need to increase Batman's authorised share capital and/or give the directors authority to allot the consideration shares under s 551 of the CA 2006. Batman shareholders would not need to disapply s 561 of the CA 2006 in these circumstances, as the shares are to be issued for non-cash consideration (see **14.6.7**, which sets out the position under the CA 2006).

(f)   The shareholders of the offeree, Robin. The shareholders of Robin own the shares which Batman wants to acquire. The fate of the takeover rests on whether they decide to accept the offer or not. Ultimately, they are the most important people in the takeover.

(g)   The advisers to both Batman and Robin. See **21.5** below.

21.5   Appointing a team of advisers

As with an IPO, a takeover involves not only lawyers, but a wider team of advisers, who must all work together seamlessly to advise either the offeror or the offeree on all aspects of the transaction.

21.5.1   Financial advisers

Rule 3 of the City Code provides that the offeree must have an independent financial adviser. In practice, the offeror will also have an independent financial adviser. An investment bank will usually adopt the role of financial adviser. In relation to advising the offeror, it will use its experience of other transactions, and its knowledge of the regulatory environment and the City Code, to:

(a)   plan and coordinate the takeover (although increasingly the lawyers are leading coordination of the documentation);

(b)   advise the board in relation to tactics, such as:

  (i)   when to make the offer,

  (ii)   the level of consideration to be offered (including when to raise the level in the event that the offer is not well received),

  (iii)   the type of consideration to be offered (if equity finance is required to raise cash consideration, the financial advisers will advise on the method of equity finance to be used);

(c)   be the offeror's principal point of contact with the Panel, to discuss any provisions of the City Code which are causing concern;

(d)   issue and approve the offer documentation under s 21 of the FSMA 2000 (unless an exemption applies);

(e)   underwrite any cash offer or cash alternative;

(f)   report on profit forecasts (r 28) and merger benefits statements (r 19.1, note 8); and

(g)   advise in relation to any information released during the offer (r 19.1) (see **22.4.5.1**).

21.5.2 Lawyers

The offeror will require lawyers as, of course, will the offeree. However, the financial adviser of the offeror may also be advised, separately from the offeror, by a further team of lawyers.

The lawyers will advise in relation to the rules and regulations considered in **Chapter 20**. They will also be involved in speaking to the Panel in relation to the interpretation of the City Code, and in drafting and, increasingly, coordinating the documentation for the takeover.

21.5.3 Stockbrokers

The investment bank acting as financial adviser will often take on the role of stockbroker. The stockbrokers play an important part in deciding tactics. They are able to do this because of the unique relationship they have with shareholders. Stockbrokers have day-to-day contact with key representatives of institutional shareholders. Remember that institutional shareholders have large stakes in public companies. Usually, therefore, the stockbrokers will have the 'inside track' on the appetite of the offeree company shareholders, and the market, for the offer. This is particularly important in a hostile bid, where the offeror will have to convince offeree company shareholders to accept the offer even though the offeree company board has advised them not to.

The stockbrokers will use this knowledge to:

(a)   monitor market purchases and rumour;

(b)   advise the offeror on the likely reaction of:

    (i)   its shareholders (see **21.4.4**) to the proposed acquisition, and

    (ii)   the offeree company's shareholders to the nature and amount of consideration to be offered; and

(c)   arrange meetings with the offeree company's principal shareholders, before the offer is announced, to explain the basic terms of the offer and to see if those shareholders will commit irrevocably to accept the offer once it is made (see **21.10** below).

21.5.4 Accountants

The accountants will gather the financial information which must be included in the takeover documentation. They will also give comfort to the board in relation to financial information in the takeover documentation, and report on any profit forecast or merger benefits statement (or working capital or indebtedness statement in any prospectus or equivalent document).

21.5.5 Financial public relations consultants

The role of the public relations adviser is to liaise with the press to secure good coverage of the offer, and to ensure that the key messages in connection with the bid are published accurately. The 'Lex' column of the *Financial Times* will comment on high-profile takeovers, as will the business editors of other national daily newspapers, websites and TV channels. The offeror, particularly on a hostile takeover, will hope that the media comment favourably on the offer, so that they might persuade offeree company shareholders to accept the offer.

21.5.6 Registrars or receiving bankers

The registrars or receiving bankers (often the same institution) will receive the forms of acceptance from the shareholders of the offeree company who want to accept the takeover offer. They will monitor the level of acceptances to determine whether the critical level necessary to allow the offer to be declared unconditional as to acceptances has been reached (see **22.4.7.1** below). If a meeting of the shareholders of the offeror is required (see **21.4.4** above), the registrars or receiving bankers will also receive and monitor the return of proxies for that meeting. Appendix 4 of the City Code sets out a code of practice for receiving agents.

21.5.7 Printers

The role of the printers on a takeover is not unlike that on an IPO (see **4.2.11**). The takeover documentation will be created by word processor at the outset of the transaction, but ultimately the final version will be professionally printed. Once each document is substantially in final draft form, therefore, it will be taken to print, and thereafter each draft will be printed (referred to as 'proof printing'). The printers need to process the documentation quickly, accurately and securely.

21.6   Due diligence

21.6.1 The requirement for due diligence

The effect of General Principle 5 (see **20.5.5** above) and r 2.5(a) of the City Code is that an offeror should announce a takeover offer only after the most careful and responsible consideration, when it has every reason to believe that it can and will implement the offer. This means that the offeror must undertake some careful planning and investigation before it announces an offer.

21.6.2 What is 'due diligence'?

The concept of due diligence in the context of an IPO was explained at **5.3.4** above. The concept is not so different on a takeover. While due diligence on an IPO involves investigating the company seeking to float, and collating comprehensive information about the company which can then be used in the prospectus, due diligence on a takeover seeks to investigate the offeree company (and, in certain circumstances, such as if shares in the offeror are to be issued as consideration, the offeror) so that this information can be used in the offer document (**22.4.1**). However, the effect of the secrecy obligation outlined at **21.3** above, means that the due diligence exercise is more limited on a takeover than on an IPO.

21.6.3 The purpose of due diligence

Due diligence is used to discharge the offeror's obligations under General Principle 5 and r 2.5(a) of the City Code (see **22.3.3.1**). For example, the Panel will not look too kindly on an offeror who announces an offer, only to discover that it does not have enough cash to fund it.

The information the offeror will require includes the following:

(a)   Is the offeree company really an attractive acquisition?

    (i)   How has it been performing lately?

    (ii)   What are its main assets and liabilities?

    (iii)   Where is it located?

    (iv)   What do its latest report and accounts reveal?

(b)   Can the offeror successfully integrate the offeree company into its business? What costs savings could be made after the takeover?

(c)   How should the offer be structured?

    (i)   Might the offeree company be willing to recommend the offer?

    (ii)   If not, is the offeror willing to proceed on a hostile basis?

    (iii)   Should the offeror offer cash or shares as consideration?

    (iv)   If offering shares, does the offeror have sufficient unissued authorised share capital, and do the directors have sufficient authority to allot those shares?

    (v)   If not, will the offeror's shareholders be willing to pass the necessary resolution(s)?

    (vi)   Will the offer constitute a Class 1 acquisition, or a reverse takeover? If so, will the offeror's shareholders be willing to approve it?

(vii)   Are there any issues which might affect the timing of the offer; for example, should the offeror company wait until the offeree company's next annual report or accounts are published?

(d)   What are the chances of success?

(i)   Who are the main shareholders of the offeree company, whom the offeror would need to persuade to accept the offer?

(ii)   How many offeree company shareholders might be willing to provide irrevocable undertakings? (See **21.10** below.)

(iii)   How many shares does the offeror hold which it can vote in favour of the bid? (See **21.8** below.)

(iv)   Is anyone else interested in the offeree company: might there be a more attractive competing bid?

(v)   Are there any competition or regulatory issues which could jeopardise the bid? (See **Chapter 23**.)

21.6.4   The due diligence process

21.6.4.1   If the offer is recommended

The offeror will undertake some initial due diligence itself, using publicly available information, before it approaches the offeree company. If the offeree company is receptive to the offer, it will then assist the offeror with its due diligence exercise and provide the information the offeror requires. However, the offeree company must be careful. Rule 20.2 requires any information provided to an offeror to be provided to a competing offeror (should one arise). While the original offeror might have been welcomed by the offeree, the competing offeror may be unwanted, and sensitive information on the offeree, given to the original offeror, will have to be revealed to this new, unwelcome suitor.

21.6.4.2   If the offer is hostile

If the offer is hostile, the offeror will not receive the help from the offeree company which is outlined above. However, as noted at **21.6.4.1**, if the offeree company has provided information to any competing offeror, then r 20.2 of the City Code provides that the offeree company must provide the same information on request to all other offerors or potential offerors. In practice, however, it is probable that a hostile offeror will want to launch a 'surprise' offer on the offeree company, so it will not avail itself of its rights under r 20.2 until its hostile offer has been announced, by which time it should already have completed its due diligence exercise, in order to comply with General Principle 5 and r 2.5(a) of the City Code (see **22.4.5.4**).

21.6.5   Publicly available information

The following information about the offeree company should already be in the public domain:

(a)   articles of association (Companies House);

(b)   details of directors (Companies House, annual report and accounts, RIS disclosures, the offeree's register of directors);

(c)   details of shareholders and share capital (Companies House, annual report and accounts, RIS disclosures, the offeree's register of members and register of directors' interests);

(d)   financial information (annual report and accounts). Section 415 of the CA 2006 provides that a company must prepare a directors' report as part of its annual report and accounts, which contains the information required by Chapter 5 of Part 15 of the CA 2006. The report must contain a business review (CA 2006, s 417), which must contain a fair review of the company's business and a description of the principal risks and uncertainties facing the company. The review should be a balanced and comprehensive review of the development and performance of the business of the company during the financial year and the position of the company's business at the end of that year;

(e)   the directors' remuneration report (see **8.4.3.1**);

(f)   any published prospectus (Companies House); and

(g)   any analyst research (available from investment banks).

Plenty of other information will be available on the company's website, in trade magazines, and possibly in the newspapers.

Section 992 of the CA 2006 requires additional information to be disclosed in the directors' report for companies whose voting shares are admitted to trading on a regulated market (ie the Main Market but not AIM). This implements provisions of the Takeovers Directive. Although the requirements are not limited to companies which are the subject of a takeover offer, the effect of the additional disclosure is to ensure that more information on the share structure of the company, including any share transfer or voting restrictions which might be triggered on a takeover, becomes public information.

21.7   Financing the offer

The offeror must know, before announcing a takeover offer, how it will finance that offer. This is not only a practical consideration; it is a requirement of General Principle 5 and r 2.5(a) of the City Code.

The choices available to the offeror are as follows.

21.7.1   Cash consideration

21.7.1.1   Debt finance

The offeror could obtain a loan to fund the takeover. However, as **Chapter 18** explained, this will affect the company's gearing and so may not be desirable. It will also depend on the prevailing bank interest rates and the prevailing economic climate. Currently, of course, debt finance is very difficult to come by.

21.7.1.2   Equity finance

The offeror could obtain the funds from its existing shareholders, using one of the methods described at **17.7** to **17.9** above. This depends on the existing shareholders being willing to subscribe to a fresh issue of shares.

21.7.2   Paper consideration

21.7.2.1   Debt finance

The company could offer loan notes to the shareholders of the offeree company rather than cash.

21.7.2.2   Equity finance

The company can offer shares (often referred to as 'paper') as consideration rather than cash. This is discussed at **17.10** above.

21.7.3   The option to take cash or shares

It is relatively common for an offeror to offer the offeree company's shareholders the option to take either cash or shares in the offeror in return for their shares in the offeree company. This sounds complicated, but in fact the method by which a company does this should be familiar to you already. This is achieved through a vendor placing, described at **17.11** above. The offeror will actually issue only shares as consideration, but the issue will be on the basis that, for those shareholders in the offeree company who want to take up the cash alternative, the offeror will have those shares placed, and the shareholders will receive the cash proceeds of that placing.

The idea behind this is to make the offer as appealing as possible to the offeree shareholders who decide the success of the offer. Some shareholders may be more likely to accept the offer if they receive cold, hard cash rather than shares in the offeror. Other shareholders may prefer to receive shares rather than cash, for tax reasons.

In some offers, the offeror may offer the offeree shareholders *both* cash and shares. This may be accompanied by a 'mix and match' election, where the shareholders can choose to vary the split of cash and shares being offered. Say that X plc offered offeree shareholders three shares in X plc and £1 in cash for every one share in the offeree. The offeror may allow the offeree shareholders to take four shares in X plc and 50p in cash, or any other combination, so long as the total value paid for each offeree share remains the same.

21.8 Stakebuilding

21.8.1 What is stakebuilding?

Stakebuilding is the strategic purchase of shares in the offeree company by the offeror, in the period before the announcement of an offer, and during the offer period (see **22.3.4**).

21.8.2 The purpose of stakebuilding

The key to the success of the offer depends on reaching a minimum threshold of just over 50% of the voting rights in the offeree company. Once that level is reached, the offeror controls the offeree company. Of course the offeror often wants 100% control, but just over 50% is the minimum required (City Code, r 10). If the offeror buys shares in the offeree it reduces the number of shares required to reach the level necessary to complete the offer and successfully take over the offeree company.

21.8.3 Advantages of stakebuilding

The advantages of stakebuilding are as follows:

(a)   Rule 10 of the City Code provides that the offer can be declared unconditional as to acceptances (see **22.4.7.1**) once the offeror holds over 50% of the voting rights in the offeree company. In other words, the offeror has won control of the offeree. Imagine, then, that an offeror already has a stake of 25% in the offeree company. The offeror would only need to persuade the owners of just over 25% of the offeree company shares to accept the offer in order to be able to declare the offer unconditional as to acceptances.

(b)   The offeror can acquire shares at the market price before the offer is announced. Once the offer is announced the price of the shares in the offeree will rise, often substantially, to reflect the fact that the offeror wants to buy all the shares and they have therefore become more valuable.

(c)   The offeror does not need to alert the offeree to the acquisition if it acquires the shares before it announces the offer and it acquires fewer than 3% of the shares (remember that the disclosure of interest obligations under Chapter 5 of the DTRs would require disclosure of the offeror's interest once that interest reached 3% (see **Chapter 15**)) – but see **21.8.4(e)** below.

(d)   If the offeror has a substantial shareholding by the time it announces the offer, other shareholders may be more inclined to accept the offer.

21.8.4 Disadvantages of stakebuilding

The disadvantages of stakebuilding are as follows:

(a)   The offeror will own the shares even if the offer fails. The offeror will usually want all or nothing – total control of the offeree company, not just to be a minority shareholder.

(b)   If anyone finds out about the strategic purchase (and this is likely given the requirement for the company to pass on to an RIS information it receives under Chapter 5 of the DTRs – see **Chapter 15**), market rumour about a possible takeover may raise the market price of the offeree company's shares. As the consideration for a takeover offer is usually at a premium to the market price, this may make the offeror's intended offer price less attractive.

(c)   The increase in price and/or rumour referred to at (b) above may trigger an announcement under r 2.2 (see **22.3**), thereby removing any element of surprise.

(d)   Purchases prior to the posting of the offer document do not count towards the 90% compulsory acquisition threshold (see **22.7.2** below).

(e)   The purchase may dictate the level or nature of the consideration the offeror must pay pursuant to the offer, under r 6 and r 11 (see **21.8.10.4**), or trigger a mandatory offer under r 9 (see **21.8.10.3**).

21.8.5   Rules and regulations relating to stakebuilding

Some of the rules relating to stakebuilding are considered at **21.8.6** to **21.8.11** below. **Table 21.1**, at **21.9** below, summarises the various stakebuilding thresholds.

The lawyer must be familiar with these rules in order to advise an offeror client whether there are any reasons why it cannot build a stake in the offeree company, or whether it is restricted in building its stake in any particular way. (Note also that the provisions of any standstill letter (see **21.13.4**) will also affect the offeror's ability to build a stake in the offeree company.)

21.8.6   Insider dealing

The fact that the offeror is buying shares in the offeree company at a time when the takeover bid is not public knowledge might suggest that the directors of the offeror are guilty of insider dealing (by requiring the offeror to buy shares; remember that the offeror, as a company, cannot commit the offence – see **11.7**). However, as **11.5.2.2** above explains, in fact the directors may be able to make use of the 'market information' defence.

21.8.7   Market abuse

Again, you could be forgiven for thinking that the offeror's stakebuilding exercise might fall foul of the market abuse regime under the FSMA 2000 (see **Chapter 10**). However, the Code of Market Conduct provides protection which is similar to the defence that exists for insider dealing. MAR 1.3.17C provides that an offeror should not be prevented by the market abuse regime from acquiring shares in a potential target with a view to pursuing a takeover offer, simply because the offeror knew that it would be making an offer.

21.8.8   The Listing Rules

If the offeror seeks to acquire a large stake, consideration must be given to how the acquisition of the stake would be classified under the Listing Rules, and to related requirements of the Listing Rules (see **Chapter 19**).

21.8.9   Disclosure requirements

Stakebuilding can trigger the disclosure requirements under Chapter 5 of the DTRs and (during the offer period – see **22.3.4**) the City Code, as set out in **Chapter 15**.

21.8.10   The City Code

The following rules of the City Code may affect any attempt to acquire a stake in an offeree company.

21.8.10.1 Rule 4.1: prohibited dealings

Rule 4.1(a) prevents anyone other than the offeror from building a stake in the offeree where they have confidential price-sensitive information about an intended offer, until the offer, or approach, is announced. Note 1 to r 4 also prohibits the offeror, and 'other persons', from dealing before an announcement if the offeree company has given the offeror confidential price-sensitive information in the course of offer negotiations.

To prevent a would-be stake builder avoiding this rule simply by asking someone else to buy the stake on his behalf, r 4.1(b) prohibits anyone who has confidential price-sensitive information about an intended offer from recommending to another person to buy offeree company shares.

21.8.10.2 Rule 5.1: acquiring 30% or more

Subject to exceptions, this rule prevents the offeror (or anyone acting in concert with it – see **22.6.1.2**) acquiring any interest in offeree company shares (see **21.8.10.5**), which, when aggregated with the offeree company shares in which he is already interested, would carry 30% or more of the voting rights in the offeree company. Paragraph 5 of the definition of 'interests in securities' and the preamble to r 5 confirm that irrevocable undertakings count towards the 30% threshold for the purpose of r 5.1 (see **21.10**).

The City Code considers that a 30% shareholding represents 'control' of a company (see 'Definitions' section of the City Code). The aim of r 5.1 is to prevent a person gaining control of an offeree company without making a full takeover bid for that company, governed by the City Code with all its protection for offeree company shareholders.

Rule 5.2 sets out the exceptions to r 5.1 referred to above. This rule provides that r 5.1 does not apply to an acquisition of an interest in shares:

(a) from a single shareholder, when it is the only acquisition within a 7-day period (r 5.2(a)). (Note that the offeror cannot then make any further acquisitions, other than pursuant to the exceptions below (r 5.3), and details of the acquisition must be disclosed (r 5.4));

(b) immediately before (and conditional upon) the r 2.5 announcement (see **22.3.3.1**) of a firm intention to make a *recommended* offer (r 5.2(b));

(c) after a r 2.5 announcement (see **22.3.3.1**) of a firm intention to make a bid (not subject to a pre-condition), and:

    (i) the offeree company board has agreed to the acquisition,

    (ii) the offeree company board has recommended the offer, or a competing offer,

    (iii) the first closing date of the offer, or a competing offer, has passed (at least 21 days after posting the offer document; see **22.5.2**) and the offer, or competing offer, has been cleared on competition grounds (see **Chapter 23**), or

    (iv) the offer is unconditional in all respects (see **22.4.7**) (r 5.2(c));

(d) by way of acceptance of the bid (r 5.2(d)); or

(e) which is permitted by Note 11 to r 9.1 or Note 5 to the Dispensations from r 9 (r 5.2(e)).

In the context of a *hostile* offer (see **21.2.2**) these exceptions tend to prevent the offeror from building a stake of more than 29.9% until after the first closing date (see **22.5.2**).

21.8.10.3 Rule 9: mandatory offer

Rule 5.1 of the City Code provides that a person can acquire an interest in shares carrying between 30% and 50% of the voting rights in the offeree company only if the acquisition falls within an exception to that rule. What happens if one of the exceptions to r 5.1 applies and the potential offeror does acquire such an interest? The answer is that r 9 will apply, and for the offeror the consequences of this can be serious.

Rule 9 provides that if:

(a)   a person acquires an interest in shares (see **21.8.10.5**) in a company which results in that person holding 30% or more of the voting rights of that company; or

(b)   a person already interested in shares carrying between 30% and 50% of the voting rights in a company for someone in concert with that person acquires an interest in any other voting shares of that company;

that person must make an offer to acquire all the equity share capital and all other transferable voting capital of that company on the terms set out in r 9.

If r 9 applies, therefore, not only is the potential offeror forced to make a takeover offer, but he cannot even choose the terms of that offer. The terms imposed by r 9 are not favourable to the offeror. Consideration must be cash, or there must be at least a cash alternative. The consideration must be at a level which is equal to the highest price paid by the offeror (or any person acting in concert with the offeror – see **22.6.1.2**) for any interest in shares of that class in the 12 months preceding the announcement of the offer (r 9.5(a)). If the offeror acquires shares above the offer price during the course of the r 9 offer, then it must increase its offer to the highest price it has paid for the shares (r 9.5(b)). The only conditions which can be attached to the offer are that over 50% of the offeree company shareholders must vote in favour of the offer, and that the offer will lapse if referred on competition grounds. It is explained at **22.4.7** why relying on just these conditions is not ideal. However, as set out in the extract from the regulatory announcement below, sometimes an offeror is happy to follow this route.

The reason for r 9 is that same as that for r 5; if r 9 is triggered, the offeror has acquired 'control', that is 30%, of the offeree company, and so must make a full takeover offer for the company, governed by the City Code.

Note that, in contrast to r 5; irrevocable undertakings do not count towards the 30% threshold for the purposes of r 9 (see **21.10** below).

Company	St James Holdings Limited
Headline	Offer for Newcastle United
Released	14:12 23-May-07
Number	1114X

For immediate release

NOT FOR RELEASE, PUBLICATION OR DISTRIBUTION IN, INTO OR FROM AUSTRALIA, CANADA, JAPAN OR THE UNITED STATES

**Cash Offer
by
St James Holdings Limited
for
Newcastle United PLC**

Summary

- St James Holdings Limited (SJHL) (a company formed at the direction of Mike Ashley) announces that it has today acquired 55,342,223 Newcastle United Shares, representing approximately 41.6 per cent. of the issued share capital of Newcastle United, from Wynyard (Guernsey) Limited, Cameron Hall Developments Limited and Cameron Hall Developments Limited Executive Pension Scheme (the ultimate beneficial owners of each of which are all members of Sir John Hall's family) at a price of 100 pence for each Newcastle United Share.

- SJHL is a UK private limited company which is wholly-owned by Mike Ashley and which has been incorporated for the specific purpose of acquiring Newcastle United Shares and making the Offer.

- In accordance with the provisions of Rule 9 of the City Code, SJHL also announces the terms of a cash offer to be made for all of the issued and to be issued share capital of Newcastle United which is not already owned by SJHL. SJHL intends to seek a recommendation of the Offer from the board of Newcastle United.

- The Offer will, when formally made, be conditional only upon the receipt of acceptances in respect of Newcastle United Shares which, together with the Newcastle United Shares acquired or agreed to be acquired before or during the Offer, will result in SJHL holding Newcastle United Shares carrying more than 50 per cent. of the voting rights in Newcastle United.

- The Offer will be **100 pence in cash for each Newcastle United Share**, valuing the entire issued share capital of Newcastle United at £133.1 million

- The Offer represents:

  — a premium of approximately 19 per cent. to the Closing Price of 84 pence for each Newcastle United Share on 22 May 2007; and

  — a premium of approximately 50 per cent. to the average Closing Price of 66.9 pence for each Newcastle United Share in the three month period up to and including 22 May 2007,

  22 May 2007 being the last business day prior to the announcement of the acquisition.

21.8.10.4 Rule 11 and rule 6: consideration

The offeror cannot consider stakebuilding in isolation from the takeover offer itself. The acquisition of a stake may dictate the level (in the case of r 6), or the nature (in the case of r 11) of the consideration the offeror must pay for shares in the offeree company pursuant to the takeover offer. The rationale for these rules is General Principle 1, which provides that shareholders should be treated similarly.

Example

Imagine that A plc, seeking to make a takeover bid for Y plc, acquires a stake in Y plc from Shareholder 1 on Monday at £2.00 per share. A plc then announces a takeover offer on Tuesday for the entire issued ordinary share capital of Y plc at a price of £1.95 per share. Shareholder 1 has clearly been given an advantage over the other shareholders. What if A plc had announced a takeover offer on Tuesday for the entire issued ordinary share capital of Y plc where the consideration was shares in A plc? Again, Shareholder 1 has received special treatment. The effect of r 6 and r 11 is to prevent an offeror breaching General Principle 1.

Rule 11

Rule 11.1: cash consideration

The consideration the offeror might offer to the offeree's shareholders is examined at **21.7** above. However, r 11.1 provides that in certain circumstances the offeror *must* offer cash consideration (or a cash alternative).

If:

(a) the offeror (or any concert party) purchased interests in shares in the offeree company, of a class which is now under offer, during the offer period or within 12 months prior to the start of the offer period, and:

   (i)   the purchase was *for cash*, and

   (ii) the shares carry 10% or more of the voting rights currently exercisable at a meeting of that class; or

(b) the offeror (or any concert party) purchased interests in voting or non-voting shares in the offeree company, of a class which is now under offer, during the offer period, and the purchase was *for cash*; or

(c) the Panel considers that cash consideration is required in order to give effect to General Principle 1, then, unless the Panel otherwise agrees, the offer for that class of shares must be in cash, or accompanied by a cash alternative (see **21.7.3**), at not less than the highest price paid by the offeror (or any concert party) for those shares.

Note that the words 'for cash' are very widely defined. Note 5 to r 11 provides that they actually include the situation where the offeror acquired interests in shares in exchange for *securities*, provided the seller of the offeree shares (or the other party to the transaction giving rise to the interest, if the interest is not the sale of the share itself) is not subject to selling restrictions, such as being required to hold the securities received in exchange for the interest in the offeree shares until the offer has lapsed, or the offer consideration has been posted to accepting shareholders. If the offer falls within this meaning of 'for cash' then, unless the offeror or its associates arranged the immediate placing of those shares, it must also comply with the provisions of r 11.2 (see below).

Example

Imagine that A plc intends to make an offer for the entire issued ordinary share capital of Y plc, offering two A plc shares as consideration for each Y plc share. A plc's lawyers will advise that A plc needs to consider whether it has purchased Y plc shares in the past. A plc provides information about its previous purchases of Y plc shares. It acquired a 4% stake at £3 per share 11 months ago, and a 6% stake at £4 per share 8 months ago. The lawyer must advise A plc that the consideration under the offer cannot be two A plc shares as consideration for each Y plc share, as A plc intended. It must be £4.00 per share, in cash, or at least include a cash alternative.

There follows a real-life example (a cause célèbre of its day) under a previous version of the City Code, but which is still instructive today.

Guinness Told to Pay £85m to Former Distillers Shareholders

Philip Coggan

The Takeover Panel has ordered Guinness to make compensation payments totalling £85m to former shareholders of Distillers, which the brewing and spirits group acquired in 1986.

Mr Anthony Tennant, chairman of Guinness, said "the settlement of this matter on these terms is in the best interests of the company and its shareholders."

Guinness has accepted the decision and appointed Deloitte Haskins & Sells, the accountancy firm, as claims administrator. Advertisements will be placed in national newspapers on July 24 inviting claims.

Argyll – the supermarkets group from which Guinness wrested control of Distillers – and its advisers, which owned shares in the course of the bid, will be entitled under the ruling to payments of £7M and £35M respectively.

Guinness argued that it should not make those payments in view of the pending legal action between itself and Argyll.

The latter is claiming compensation for its failure to win control of Distillers.

Instead, Guinness suggested that payments should be made into an escrow account, but the Panel decided that Argyll should be treated as any other shareholder. Argyll said it "was pleased that the matter has been brought to a satisfactory conclusion."

The compensation payments arise from a breach of Rule 11, which the Panel has decided occurred in the course of the Distillers bid. Rule 11 requires bidders who buy more than 15 per cent of their target to make a general cash offer to all shareholders at the highest price they paid in the market.

On April 17 1986, at a time when Guinness and its bankers owned 14.9 per cent of Distillers, a Swiss company called Pipetec acquired 3 per cent of Distillers at 731p. The Panel ruled that this purchase was associated with Guinness and thus under Rule 11, Guinness should have made a cash offer of 731p per share.

However, the cash alternative to

the Guinness share offer was only 630.3p per share. The Panel has ruled that those who accepted the Guinness cash alternative at the time should be compensated for the difference between the offer and the price paid by Pipetec - that is, 100.7p per share.

Guinness' share offer did not reach a value equivalent to 731p per share until August 21 1986. The Panel ruled that those Distillers shareholders who accepted the share offer and then sold their shares before August 21 1986 will be entitled to the difference between the sale price and 731p.

Those Distillers shareholders who sold their shares in the market between April 15 and August 21 will be entitled to the difference between their sale price and 731p. All those being compensated will also receive interest at the rate of 10 per cent per annum.

Seven men are awaiting trial accused of criminal offences in connection with the takeover, including Mr Ernest Saunders, the former Guinness chairman.

Source: *Financial Times*, 15 July 1989

Rule 11.2: paper consideration

Rule 11.2 provides that if:

(a)   the offeror (or any concert party) purchased interests in shares in the offeree company, of a class which is now under offer, during the offer period or within three months prior to the start of the offer period; and

(b)   the purchase was *in exchange for securities*; and

(c)   the shares carry 10% or more of the voting rights currently exercisable at a meeting of that class,

then those securities must be offered to all other holders of shares of that class. As detailed above, an obligation will also arise, under r 11.1, to make an offer in cash, or to provide a cash alternative, unless the exchange falls outside the wide definition of 'for cash' in Note 5 to r 11.1 (because there are some selling restrictions on the seller of the offeree company shares, or, in the case of an interest in offeree company shares, the other party to the transaction giving rise to the interest).

Rule 6: minimum consideration

Rule 6.1

Rule 6.1 provides that, unless the Panel otherwise consents, if:

(a)   an offeror (or a person acting in concert with the offeror) (see **22.6.1.2** for the meaning of 'in concert');

(b)   has acquired an interest in the offeree company shares (see **21.8.10.5**);

(c)   within three months before the beginning of an offer period (see **22.3.4** for the meaning of 'offer period');

(d)   or during the period (if any) between the commencement of the offer period and a r 2.5 announcement (see **22.3.4** below),

then the offer to shareholders of the same class must be on the same, or better, terms.

Let us consider the example of A plc bidding for Y plc, referred to above. The effect of r 6 is that A plc will not be able to fix the offer price at £1.95 per share. Instead, A plc must offer the Y plc shareholders at least £2.00 per share under the takeover offer.

Note that the Panel has discretion to extend the three-month period if it considers it is necessary to give effect to General Principle 1 (r 6.1(c)).

Rule 6.2

While r 6.1 covers acquisitions the offeror makes *before* the offer period, r 6.2 covers acquisitions the offeror makes *during* the offer period. Rule 6.2 provides that, if:

(a)   an offeror (or a person acting in concert with the offeror);

(b)   has acquired an interest in the offeree company shares (see **21.8.10.5**) above the offer price;

(c)   after a r 2.5 announcement (see **22.3.3.1**) has been made but before the offer closes for acceptance,

then the offeror must increase its offer to equal the highest price it has paid for the interest in those shares, and, immediately after the purchase, it must announce that the revised offer will be made.

Note that while the example below involves cash consideration, neither r 6.1 nor r 6.2 requires the offer to be in cash. However, any paper consideration offered must, as at the date the offer is announced, have a value equal to the highest price the offeror has paid for the relevant prior purchase of offeree shares. (Note, however, that if r 9 or r 11 also apply, the offer does have to be in cash (or accompanied by a cash alternative); see **21.8.10.3** and below.)

> **Example**
>
> Imagine that A plc, having been advised that the offer price must be £2.00, pursuant to r 6.1, announces an offer for Y plc at a price of £2.00 per share on Tuesday. On Wednesday, A acquires some Y shares from Shareholder 2 at a price of £2.00 per share. On Thursday, A acquires some Y shares from Shareholder 3 at £2.05 per share. In breach of General Principle 1, Shareholders 1 and 2 have been treated differently to Shareholder 3. A plc must make an announcement, immediately after it acquires the shares from Shareholder 3, that a revised offer will be made in accordance with r 6.2. Shareholders 1 and 2 will get an unexpected bonus. They will receive the higher, revised price of £2.05 per share, not just £2.00 which they had originally expected.

Overlap between rules 11 and 6

Note that there is clearly the potential for overlap between r 6 and r 11, as both may apply where the offeror has purchased offeree shares *for cash*. Rules 6.1 and 6.2 provide that, in such a case, usually compliance with r 11 will be regarded as sufficient to satisfy the requirements of r 6.

21.8.10.5   Derivatives and options

In relation to disclosure and stakebuilding, the Code applies to dealings in derivatives referenced to shares and options over shares, as well as actual shares themselves. These terms are explained below. The effect of this is that the acquisition of 'interests in shares', and not just actual shares, are taken into account for the purposes of rr 5, 6, 9 and 11. In relation to r 4, the definition of 'dealing' includes the taking, granting, acquisition and disposal of an option over securities and a derivative referenced to securities, so if the rule applies, no interests in shares can be acquired.

Derivative

This term is defined in the City Code. Broadly, it is a financial product whose value depends on the performance of an underlying security. An example of a derivative is a contract for differences ('CFD') under which the holder of the CFD benefits from a change in the price of a company's securities from the reference price agreed at the time the CFD is entered into.

Option

An option is the right to buy or sell a share at a fixed price within a particular time-frame.

Interests in shares

This term is defined in the City Code (under 'interests in securities'). It includes:

(a)   ownership of shares (para 1, definition of 'interests in securities');

(b)   the right to exercise or direct, or having general control of, the voting rights attached to shares (para 2, definition of 'interests in securities');

(c)   the right, option, or obligation to acquire shares (para 3, definition of 'interests in securities');

(d)   being party to certain derivatives in relation to shares (para 4, definition of 'interests in securities'); and

(e)   for the purposes of r 5 only (see **21.8.10.2**), irrevocable commitments (see **21.10**) in relation to shares (para 5, definition of 'interests in securities').

21.9   Stakebuilding thresholds

As the rules relating to stakebuilding are complex, **Table 21.1** below sets out a summary of the significant thresholds, and the consequences for the stakebuilder of acquiring certain stakes.

Table 21.1: Stakebuilding thresholds and consequences

Voting rights in target	Consequences for the stakebuilder
Any amount	Must disclose if issued with a notice under s 793 of CA 2006 (see **15.6**).
	If within three months prior to, or during, the offer period, any offer must not be on less favourable terms (r 6) (see **21.8.10.4**).
	If in exchange for cash, during the offer period, and these shares are now under offer, offer must be in cash, or accompanied by a cash alternative (r 11.1) (see **21.8.10.4**).
	Disclose dealings during an offer period (r 8.1) (see **15.7.4.3**).
1%	Disclose dealings during an offer period (r 8) (see **15.7.4.3**).
3%	Disclose interests to the offeree company (DTR 5 – see **15.5**) and disclose subsequent movements through another percentage point level, or if the interest falls below 3%.
10% or more in exchange for cash in the 12 months prior to an offer period and during the offer period	If shares are voting shares, offer must be in cash, or accompanied by a cash alternative (r 11.1) (see **21.8.10.4**).
10% or more, in exchange for securities, in the 3 months prior to an offer period and during the offer period	Must offer those securities (r 11.2). May also need to make a cash offer, or provide a cash alternative under r 11.1 (see **21.8.10.4**).
25% + 1	Power to block special resolutions.
30%	May be prohibited from dealing (r 5) (see **21.8.10.7**).
	May have to make mandatory bid for the offeree (r 9) (see **21.8.10.3**).
50%	Power to block ordinary resolutions.
More than 50%	Power to pass ordinary resolutions.
	Offer capable of becoming unconditional as to acceptances (r 10) (see **22.4.7.1**).
	City Code generally no longer applicable.
	A subsidiary as defined in CA 2006, s 1159.
75%	Power to pass special resolutions.
90% (applies to each class separately)	May be forced to buy the shares of offeree minority shareholders under s 983 of CA 2006 (see **22.7.3**).
90% of shares subject to the offer (applies to each class separately)	Power to purchase minority shareholdings under s 979 of CA 2006 (see **22.7.2**)

21.10 Irrevocable undertakings

How a potential offeror can acquire interests in shares in order to secure some votes in favour of the takeover offer is considered at **21.8** above. As you will appreciate, the restrictions set out at **21.8.6** to **21.8.10** above mean that it is not easy for the potential offeror to do this. In practice, stakebuilding is usually restricted to an acquisition from a single shareholder, or made immediately before the announcement of a recommended offer (see **21.8.10.2**), so that it falls within the exceptions in the City Code.

A more widely used technique, which also enables the potential offeror to improve the chances of success of the takeover offer, is the irrevocable undertaking (also known as an 'irrevocable commitment' or 'lock-up'). This is where the potential offeror obtains undertakings from certain offeree company shareholders (often major shareholders and directors who hold shares), in advance of the announcement of the offer and with the consent of the Panel (r 4.3), that they will accept the offer if it is made (and, sometimes also that they will vote in favour of any resolution that the offeree company may require to progress the offer).

While with stakebuilding the potential offeror knows that certain shares will vote in favour of the offer (because he owns interests in those shares), with irrevocable undertakings the potential offeror knows that certain shares will vote in favour of the offer because he has irrevocable undertakings from the shareholders which confirm that they will vote in favour.

Irrevocable undertakings fall into two categories:

(a)   Hard irrevocables, which remain binding even if a higher offer is made for the offeree.

(b)   Soft irrevocables, which will fall away to allow the shareholder to accept a higher offer which is made (typically one which is at least 10% higher than of the value of the offer to which the irrevocable relates).

The consideration for providing an irrevocable is the promise of the potential offeror to make the offer. As a safeguard against the irrevocable being held void for lack of consideration, the lawyer should ensure that any irrevocable is entered into by way of deed (see **21.10.4**).

If the offeror (or any associate of the offeror – as defined by the City Code) obtains an irrevocable undertaking during an offer period (see **22.3.4**), it must disclose this through an RIS. The details it must disclose are set out in r 8.4(a) of the City Code.

The effect of irrevocables on certain other public company issues is considered below.

21.10.1 Stakebuilding

Paragraph 5 of the definition of 'interests in securities' (which also covers 'interests in shares') and the preamble to r 5 confirm that, while irrevocable undertakings will not count towards the 30% shareholding threshold for the purposes of r 9 (see **21.8.10.3** above), they will count towards the 30% threshold for r 5 (see **21.8.10.2** above). Rule 5, therefore, acts as a cap on the level of undertakings the offeror can obtain. If one of the exceptions to r 5 applies, an offeror can obtain irrevocable undertakings over 30% or more of the offeree shares without triggering the r 9 mandatory bid provisions.

Is an irrevocable undertaking an 'interest in shares' for the purposes of rr 5, 6, 9 and 11? The effect of para 9(b) of Note 9 to the definition of 'interests in securities' is that the receipt of an undertaking falls outside the para 3 'right to acquire' category of interests (see **21.8.10.5(c)**). However, if the undertaking allows the offeror general control of the voting rights attached to the shares, the offeror will be treated as interested in those shares under para 2 of the definition of 'interests in securities' (see **21.8.10.5(b)**).

21.10.2 Financial promotion

Seeking an irrevocable undertaking may be capable of comprising an inducement or invitation to enter into investment activity. This means that any communication the company makes in order to persuade someone to provide such an undertaking will constitute a financial promotion under s 21 of the FSMA 2000 (see **Chapter 12**). Therefore the company must ensure that the communication either falls within an exemption (for example, because it is made to a professional investor under art 19 of the FPO 2005, or is a communication in relation to the sale of a body corporate under art 62 of the FPO 2005 – if takeovers do fall within this exemption), or that the communication is made by or authorised by an authorised person.

21.10.3   Insider dealing and market abuse

Giving an irrevocable undertaking may also amount to insider dealing (see **Chapter 11**); however, usually the market information defence (see **11.5.2.2**) will apply, unless the person providing the undertaking has confidential price-sensitive information other than simply knowledge that a takeover is proposed. Similarly, the provision of an irrevocable undertaking can amount to market abuse, but is likely to fall outside the regime under MAR 1.3.17C.

21.10.4   Squeeze-out provisions

Shares which are the subject of irrevocable undertakings are not considered to be shares already held by the bidder. Therefore they are 'shares to which the offer relates' and count towards the 90% threshold (see **22.7**) provided that they are entered into by way of deed, or for no consideration, for consideration of negligible value or for no consideration other than the promise of the potential offeror to make the offer (CA 2006, s 975(2)).

21.10.5   Acting in concert

A person who provides an irrevocable undertaking usually is not treated as acting in concert with the offeror or offeree company (Note 9 to the definition of 'acting in concert'). However, if the undertaking allows the offeror or the offeree company to exercise voting rights, or allows the person providing the undertaking to acquire shares, then the Panel should be consulted before the undertaking is given. In its Practice Statement 2008/22, the Panel has advised that where an undertaking on how to vote is given with an irrevocable commitment, it will not normally be acting in concert, provided it is limited to the duration of the offer at the latest and is limited to matters which relate to ensuring that the offer is successful.

21.11   Non-binding indications of intention to accept

Some shareholders, as a matter of policy, will not provide irrevocable undertakings. Sometimes, however, those shareholders will provide non-binding indications of their intention to accept the offer (also known as 'letters of intent'). While these indications are not legally binding, they can provide further reassurance to the potential offeror that the offer will be successful.

If the offeror (or any associate of the offeror – as defined by the City Code) obtains a letter of intent during the offer period (see **22.3.4**) then, as with an irrevocable undertaking (see **21.10**), it must disclose this through an RIS under r 8.4(a) of the City Code.

21.12   General offer or scheme of arrangement?

The bidder must decide how to structure the takeover. A takeover can be effected by:

(a)   a general offer; or

(b)   a scheme of arrangement under Part 26 of the CA 2006.

21.12.1   General offer

This involves the offeror (or the investment bank, on behalf of the offeror) making an offer to acquire shares in the offeree for consideration. As set out at **21.7**, the consideration can take several forms, such as cash, loan notes, shares or other securities. Sometimes the offer gives the offeree shareholders a choice of consideration, such as cash or shares (and under r 9 and, in certain circumstances, r 11.1, the offeror must provide a cash alternative – see **21.8.10** above). The shareholder accepts the offer by returning a form of acceptance (see **22.4.2**).

This structure is suitable for use with both recommended and hostile offers. This book, and in particular **Chapter 22**, focuses on this structure. EDF's £12.5 billion recommended takeover of British Energy Group plc in 2008 was conducted by way of an offer.

21.12.2   Scheme of arrangement

An alternative way of structuring a recommended takeover is by a scheme of arrangement pursuant to Part 26 of the CA 2006. They are currently very much in favour as an alternative to a recommended takeover by way of general offer. Some of the largest recommended takeovers in the last few years were proposed as schemes of arrangement.

The £12.2 billion takeover of HBOS plc by Lloyds TSB Group in 2008 was effected by a scheme of arrangement, as was the £7.6 billion takeover of Scottish & Newcastle plc by Heineken NV and Carlsberg A/S, also in 2008.

21.12.2.1   What is a scheme of arrangement?

A scheme of arrangement is a court-sanctioned arrangement between a company and its shareholders or creditors. It is a statutory procedure governed by Part 26 (ss 896 to 901) of the CA 2006. Section 895 of the CA 2006 does not limit the subject matter of the arrangement (although the court's approval must be obtained). There is, therefore, considerable scope for using a scheme (for example, to effect a reorganisation or return or capital). While the section was not drafted with the takeover in mind, it has also come to be used as a way of effecting a takeover.

There are two forms of scheme, namely a reduction scheme and a transfer scheme. A reduction scheme involves the cancellation of the existing offeree shares and the issue of new offeree shares to the offeror in exchange for the payment of consideration by the offeror to the offeree shareholders. A transfer scheme involves the transfer of the existing offeree shares to the offeror, in exchange for the payment of consideration by the offeror to the offeree shareholders.

In theory, the consideration offered by the offeror to the offeree shareholders under a scheme can take any form, as with a general offer. However, given the longer overall timetable of a scheme, underwritten cash offers can prove too expensive.

As the scheme is arranged by, and so requires the cooperation of, the offeree, a scheme is suitable only for a recommended takeover.

Sections 896 to 899 of the CA 2006 set out the following main requirements for a scheme:

(a)   *Members' meeting (s 896(1))*. The court will (after an application to the Companies Court by the company) convene a meeting of the offeree shareholders (or the offeree company shareholders of the relevant class, as appropriate). At this meeting, the scheme must be approved by (s 899(1)):

   (i)   a majority in number;

   (ii)   representing 75% in value of the offeree company shareholders, or class of offeree company shareholders, voting at the meeting (in person or by proxy).

   The resolution to approve the scheme must be by way of a poll in order to calculate whether the test referred to at (ii) above has been satisfied. Neither the offeror, nor any shareholder connected with the offeror, can vote. This means the offeror cannot increase its chances of success by stakebuilding and/or obtaining irrevocable undertakings.

(b)   *Explanatory statement (s 897(1) and (2))*. The offeree company must send an explanatory statement to its shareholders together with the notice of meeting. The statement should explain the effect of the scheme, and set out any material interests of directors and the effect of the scheme on those interests. The statement must be fair and, as far as possible, give all information reasonably necessary to enable the offeree shareholders to make an informed decision how to vote.

(c)   *Court approval (s 899).* The scheme must obtain not only the approval of the offeree company shareholders, referred to at (a) above, but also the approval of the court. A copy of the court order must be filed at Companies House before the scheme can take effect. The scheme will then bind the offeree company, its shareholders and the offeror (who will have agreed to be bound by it).

21.12.2.2   The City Code

Paragraph 3(b) of the Introduction to the City Code confirms that the City Code governs a scheme of arrangement. Typically certain modifications to the Code will be required for a scheme (for example, as the scheme requires the involvement of the court, it may not be possible to adhere strictly to the timetable requirements set out in the City Code). Appendix 7 of the City Code sets out the modifications to the City Code which apply as a result of the takeover being effected by way of a scheme. It also lists those provisions of the City Code which do not apply to a scheme.

21.12.2.3   Advantages of a scheme

A scheme has the following advantages over a general offer:

(a)   A scheme requires a smaller percentage of offeree shareholder support (see **21.12.2.1(a)**), in order to obtain 100% control of the offeree company, than a general offer (where the offeror must acquire not less than 90% in value of the shares to which the offer relates – see **22.7.2.1**).

(b)   Once the requisite majority of shareholders has approved the scheme, all shareholders are bound by it (with a general offer the offeror must compulsorily acquire the remaining 10% under s 979 of the CA 2006.

(c)   Usually a scheme is quicker than a general offer in reaching the stage where all offeree company shareholders are bound. In the case of a general offer, the compulsory acquisition procedure can increase the timetable considerably. (However, overall, a scheme tends to take longer to effect – see **21.12.2.4(c)**.)

(d)   A scheme is not deemed to be an offer to the public for the purposes of s 85(1) of the FSMA 2000 (but nevertheless a prospectus will be required if the offeror shares will be admitted to trading and none of the exemptions to s 85(2) apply).

(e)   A reduction scheme can offer stamp duty savings (but see **21.12.2.4(g)**).

21.12.2.4   Disadvantages of a scheme

(a)   A scheme cannot be used with a hostile offer (the application to court is made by the offeree company).

(b)   It is more difficult to revise a scheme than a general offer, given the requirement for court approval.

(c)   The requirement for court approval, filed at Companies House, means it can takes longer to effect the takeover than with a general offer (but see **21.12.2.3(c)**).

(d)   There is more time for a competing bidder to intervene (unlike a general offer, a scheme cannot be declared unconditional on Day 21 – see **22.5.2**).

(e)   Stakebuilding and irrevocable undertakings will not increase the offeror's chances of success (see **21.12.2.1(a)**).

(f)   The offeree company controls the timing and implementation of the scheme (this may be a disadvantage from the offeror's perspective).

(g)   A scheme involves greater costs (but see **21.2.2.3(e)**).

21.13   Deal protection

If the offer is recommended, then the lawyer will be involved in drafting various documents to try to ensure that the takeover completes, and to protect their client's interest in the event that it does not. The documents are as follows:

(a)   heads of agreement;

(b)   exclusivity agreement;

(c)   confidentiality agreement;

(d)   standstill agreement; and

(e)   break fee letter.

The exclusivity, confidentiality and standstill agreements are often incorporated into one agreement. Brief details of the documents are set out at **21.13.1** to **21.13.5** below.

21.13.1   Heads of agreement

This agreement is also referred to as heads of terms, a letter of intent or a memorandum of understanding. It is not legally binding, but aims to record the parties' agreement in relation to certain fundamental issues at an early stage in negotiations. Key issues which it addresses include:

(a)   the parties;

(b)   the shares which are to be acquired;

(c)   consideration;

(d)   the extent of the due diligence exercise;

(e)   major terms and conditions;

(f)   timing; and

(g)   choice of law and jurisdiction.

21.13.2   Exclusivity agreement

This agreement is also referred to as a lock-out agreement. Its aim is to prevent a party negotiating with a third party for a certain period. In *Walford v Miles* [1992] 2 WLR 174, it was held that while this type of agreement is enforceable, an agreement which seeks to force a party to negotiate (a 'lock-in' agreement) would not be enforceable. This means the effect of an exclusivity is persuasive only; it will encourage (but not compel) a party to persevere with negotiations rather than start negotiations with another third party who may appear offering a better deal (as the agreement will prevent such negotiations within a certain time).

21.13.3   Confidentiality agreement

This agreement will set out the terms to govern the passing of confidential information from one party to another. It will provide what happens to the information if the deal falls through (usually that the information and any copies must be returned, but sometimes that it must be destroyed), and what will happen in the event of a breach of the agreement.

21.13.4   Standstill letter

A standstill agreement aims to prevent a recommended offeror from being able to launch a hostile offer. It will provide that the potential offeror will not buy any shares in the offeree for a specified period without the offeree's consent.

21.13.5   Break fee letter

Unlike the exclusivity, confidentiality and standstill arrangements referred to above, which are often recorded in a single agreement, the break fee arrangements will be entered into as a separate agreement (usually a letter executed by both parties). Also known as an inducement fee, a break fee is a sum paid by one party to another on the occurrence of a specified event leading to the deal falling through, such as the directors of the offeree company failing to recommend the offer, or the offeree company shareholders failing to pass any necessary resolutions. The lawyer must be aware of the law relating to directors' statutory, common law and equitable duties, the financial assistance provisions of s 678 of the CA 2006 (see **Chapter 16**), r 21.2 of the City Code and LR 10.2.7R (see **19.4.7.5(d)**) when drafting a break fee arrangement. Guidance on the application of r 21.2 to break fees can be found both in the notes to r 21.2 and in Practice Statement 2008/23. Details of any break fee must also be provided in the r 2.5 announcement of the offer (see **22.3.3.1(g)**).

A recent example of this is shown in the September 2008 £12.2 billion takeover of British Energy Group plc, listed on the Stock Exchange, by EDF. Each party agreed to pay a break fee of £50 million to the other. British Energy's fee was payable in two instalments. The first instalment of £20 million was payable if the directors did not unanimously recommend acceptance of EDF's offer or withdrew their recommendations or recommended a competing offer. The second instalment of £30 million would have been payable if a competing offer was successful.

21.14 Future developments

The Panel is consulting on changes to the City Code regarding the disclosure of ownership and dealings in relevant securities during offer periods. It is considering extending the current disclosure requirements. Any amendments to the City Code are expected to take effect in early 2010.

Chapter 22

The Takeover Process

22.1 Introduction

Chapter 20 considered the rules and regulations which can apply to a takeover. **Chapter 21** explained that a substantial part of the lawyer's work on a takeover is undertaken before the offer is announced, to ensure that, once announced, the offer will run smoothly. This chapter looks at what happens after that.

22.2 Timetable

Table 22.1 below sets out a typical timetable for a takeover offer. Note that the events which typically relate to hostile bids only are italicised. This chapter explains in more detail what happens at each stage, but it is useful to consider the timetable at the outset, as it provides an overview of the process.

The City Code sets out the timetable of the offer by reference to the date on which the offeror publishes the offer document. There are three situations which might alter this timetable, namely:

(a) a rival offer is launched (note 4 to r 31.6 provides that, usually, the timetable of the original offer will default to that of the later offer);

(b) no competition authority decision has been reached by Day 39 (the Panel will usually grant permission to freeze the timetable until the decision is announced); and/or

(c) if the Panel exercises any discretion given to it under the City Code to extend any time periods.

Note also that if the offer is referred to the Competition Commission, or if the European Commission initiates Phase II proceedings, r 12.2 of the City Code provides that the offer period will end (see **23.2.1**).

22.3 Announcing the offer

The lawyers will have worked extremely hard to plan the bid. The culmination of this work is when the offer is ready to announce. This is an exciting time, but again the lawyers need to make sure that the announcement is made pursuant to the provisions of the City Code.

22.3.1 Timing

Chapter 21 explained that a considerable amount of the work required to plan a takeover happens behind closed doors. How does an offeror know when to open those doors and announce the bid?

Table 22.1: Timetable for a takeover offer

Date	Event	Rule
Before the announcement	Due diligence by offeror Approach offeree board Draft documents Obtain any irrevocable undertakings Build stake in offeree company Possibly make r 2.4 announcement (if so, the offer period will begin)	1 and 2.2 to 2.8
D – 28	Announce the offer under r 2.5 (earliest date) (if no prior r 2.4 announcement, the offer period will begin)	2.2 to 2.8
DAY 0	**Offeror publishes, displays, sends and announces offer document (and forms of acceptance) (normally within 28 days of r 2.5 announcement)** Market purchases now count towards CA 2006, s 979	30.1
D + 14	*Offeree dispatches, displays and announces first defence document if offer is hostile (latest date)*	30.2
D + 21	First closing date (earliest date)	31.1
By 8.00 am, the business day after first closing date	Announce acceptance levels Announce any extension of the offer	17.1
D + 39 (or 2nd day after any competition decision is announced, if later)	*Latest date for offeree to release any material new information*	31.9
D + 42 (assuming first closing date is D + 21)*	*Accepting shareholders can withdraw acceptances if offer not yet declared unconditional as to acceptances (earliest date)*	34
D + 46	*Latest date for offeror to improve offer*	32.1
By midnight, D + 60	Latest date for offeror to fulfil acceptance condition and declare the offer 'unconditional as to acceptances' (ie wins control)	31.6
D + 74 (assuming offer declared unconditional on D + 60)	Earliest date offer can close	31.4
D + 81 (assuming offer declared unconditional on D + 60)	Latest date for offeror to fulfil other conditions	31.7
14 days after offer becomes unconditional in all respects	Latest date to post consideration to offeree shareholders	31.8

*This rule also applies to recommended offers but in practice is rarely an issue.

Rule 1 provides that, when the offeror is ready to announce the bid, it must first put forward the offer to the offeree board. Rule 2.2 then provides that where a serious source has notified the board of the offeree company of a firm intention to make an offer which is not subject to a pre-condition, this triggers the requirement for an announcement. The announcement must be made to an RIS (r 2.9). Note that a 'firm intention' excludes mere expressions of interest by a possible offeror. The obligation to announce arises only when, in accordance with r 2.5, the offeror has every reason to believe it can proceed with the offer. Financing must therefore be in place before this can be achieved. Subject to DTR 2.5.1R (see **7.5.2.8**), an announcement will also be required pursuant to the general obligation under DTR 2.2.1R (see **7.5.1**). In practice, the announcement required by r 2.2 will satisfy both obligations.

If everything goes to plan, the offeror will notify the offeree company board and then the offer will be announced under r 2.5 once it has been put together. In these circumstances, it is the offeree company's obligation to make the announcement (r 2.3). In a hostile bid (see **21.2.2**), typically the offeror will seek to keep the amount of time, between putting the offer to the board and releasing the press announcement, to a bare minimum, and will telephone the offeree company's chairman just minutes before releasing the r 2.5 press announcement. This ensures that the offeree company is as ill-prepared as possible to deal with the takeover offer (and the offeree company's lawyers will have to get up to speed with the details of the offer from a standing start).

The obligation to announce the offer under r 2.2 can also arise in other circumstances, namely:

(a)   there is an acquisition which gives rise to a r 9 mandatory bid (see **21.8.10.3** above);

(b)   if the offeror has approached the board (but has not notified the offeree company board of a firm intention to make the offer) and the offeree company is then the subject of rumour and speculation, or there is an 'untoward' movement in its share price (the Panel will interpret 'untoward') (this is dealt with further in r 2.4 – see **22.3.3.2**);

(c)   if the offeror has not even approached the board, but the offeree company is the subject of rumour and speculation, or there is an untoward movement in its share price, and there are reasonable grounds for concluding that it is the potential offeror's actions which have led to the situation (this is dealt with further in r 2.4 – see **22.3.3.2**);

(d)   negotiations are about to be extended beyond the parties and their immediate advisers (see **21.3** above); or

(e)   the offeree company is seeking a buyer for an interest or interests in 30% or more of its voting shares and there is either rumour and speculation, or an 'untoward' movement (as determined by the Panel) in the share price, or the number of potential purchasers approached is about to exceed a very restricted number.

You will note that rumour and speculation can lead to the need for the offer to be announced. This explains why secrecy is paramount in the preparation of any bid (see **21.3**), as the offeror will want to avoid having to announce its intentions before it is ready.

Note 1 to r 2.2 provides that parties should consult the Panel if they are in doubt as to whether an announcement is required. It is common for the Panel to be consulted in relation to (d) above in particular, as parties may wish to seek irrevocable undertakings (see **21.10**) or non-binding indications of intention to accept (see **21.11**) without triggering an obligation to announce the offer.

The Panel has reprimanded publicly financial advisers who have decided that no announcement is necessary without first consulting the Panel (see, for example, Panel Statement 2004/9, criticising Nabarro Wells & Co, financial adviser to Transcomm plc, which became the subject of a bid by British Telecommunications plc). However, if it is obvious that an announcement is required, the parties should not use consultation as a delaying tactic (see Panel Statement 2008/20).

22.3.2 Responsibility

Who is responsible for making the announcement in the circumstances listed at (a) to (e) above? Rule 2.3 of the City Code provides that if the announcement is required before the offeror has approached the offeree company (which most likely will arise under r 2.2(c) due to rumour and speculation), or a r 9 obligation has arisen (see (a) above), responsibility for making the announcement lies with the offeror. If the announcement is required after the offeror has approached the offeree company, then responsibility lies with the offeree company. However, Panel Statement 2008/20 provides that if the offeror's approach has been rejected before the announcement is required, usually responsibility for making the announcement will revert back to the offeror.

22.3.3 Method

Rule 2.2 requires that an announcement should be made. To what type of announcement does this refer? There are two options:

(a)   the announcement of a firm intention to make an offer (r 2.5); and

(b)   the announcement of a possible offer (r 2.4).

22.3.3.1 The announcement of a firm intention to make an offer

The ideal scenario is that the announcement triggered by r 2.2 will be of a firm intention to make an offer. This is often referred to as the 'Rule 2.5 announcement', or the 'press announcement'. The potential offeror can make this announcement only after the most careful and responsible consideration, and only if it has every reason to believe that it can, and will continue to be able to, implement the offer (r 2.5(a)). It must also be certain that it can fulfil any cash consideration, and has taken all reasonable measures to secure the implementation of any other type of consideration (General Principle 5); in other words, it must have decided what consideration it will offer, and its financing arrangements must be in place. If it has any doubts, it must make a r 2.4 announcement rather than a r 2.5 announcement (see **22.3.3.2** below).

The r 2.5 announcement is a key document. Typically, it is the first public document to contain details of the offer. It is vital, therefore, that it contains the right message. As well as complying with r 2.5, there are certain conventions as to the matters which the announcement will address.

Content

Rule 2.5 sets out the content requirements of the announcement. The requirements include:

(a)   the terms of the offer;

(b)   the identity of the offeror;

(c)   details of any relevant securities (as defined by the City Code; see **15.7.4.3**) in the offeree company:

    (i)   in which the offeror, or any concert party has an interest, or right to subscribe;

    (ii)   in respect of which the offeror or any associate has procured an irrevocable commitment (see **21.10**);

    (iii)   the offeror or any concert party has borrowed or lent;

(d)   the conditions of the offer (including details of any circumstances where the offeror cannot invoke the conditions);

(e)   details of any indemnity;

(f)   a summary of r 8 (see **15.7.4.3**);

(g)   details of any inducement fees; and

(h)   if the offer is for cash, or includes an element of cash, confirmation by the offeror's financial adviser that the offeror's resources are sufficient to make the offer (known as the 'cash confirmation').

Publication

Rule 2.9 governs the publication of any r 2.5 announcement. The announcement must be typed and faxed or emailed to an RIS. If the announcement is submitted outside business hours, it must also be distributed to at least two national newspapers and two newswire services in the UK.

Rule 2.6 sets out what must be done following the publication under r 2.9. The offeree company must send a copy of the announcement (or a circular summarising the terms and conditions of the offer, together with a r 8 summary – see **15.7.4.3**) promptly to its shareholders, persons with information rights under s 146 of the CA 2006 and the Panel (r 2.6(b)(i)). In practice, the offeree company tends to send the announcement itself rather than a circular, so will arrange for a glossy version of it to be published for this purpose.

The offeror and offeree company must also make the announcement (or circular) available to their respective employee representatives (or, if there are none, to their employees) (r 2.6(b)(ii)). If the company has chosen to distribute a circular rather than the announcement itself, nevertheless the announcement must be made readily available to them (perhaps by posting it on the offeror or offeree company's website) (Note 1 to r 2.6).

Where necessary, the offeror or offeree company, as the case may be, should explain the implications of the announcement and, for an offeree company, the fact that contact information may be provided to the offeror (to enable it to send information) (r 2.6(c)).

If there has been no r 2.4 announcement then the publication of the r 2.5 announcement will start the offer period and the offeree company must make the disclosure required by r 2.10 (details of all classes of relevant securities issued by the offeree company). The offeror must also do this unless the offer is wholly for cash (see **15.7.4.3**).

Effect

Once the offeror has made a r 2.5 announcement, r 2.7 provides that it must proceed with the offer (unless the offer is stated to be subject to a pre-condition which has not been met, or is subject to a condition which could be invoked if the offer were made). In other words, once the r 2.5 announcement is made, usually there is no going back. The only way an offer can be withdrawn is with the consent of the Panel, which will be given only in exceptional circumstances. Panel Statements 2007/25, 2007/23 and 2007/13 give an example of how strictly this rule is applied in practice. An offeror's attempt to withdraw its offer for Freeport plc was rejected by the Panel, which ordered an offer to be made. However, in October 2007, the Panel did allow the offeror for Telent plc the right to withdraw its offer. This was due to exceptional intervention by the Government in the offeree to protect Telent plc's pension fund. Ultimately, the offeror proceeded with the offer.

22.3.3.2   The announcement of a possible offer

If the potential offeror must issue an announcement under r 2.2 but is not in a position to issue a r 2.5 announcement then, as a temporary measure, it, or the offeree company, may issue what is known as a 'possible offer announcement' or a 'holding announcement' under r 2.4.

Content

An example of a holding announcement is set out below. As you can see, the announcement will contain limited information, such as a potential offeree company announcing that talks are in progress with a potential offeror (which does not have to be named), or a potential offeror announcing that it is considering making an offer for a potential offeree company (which, again, can remain anonymous). The announcement should also include a summary of the provisions of r 8 (see **15.7.4.3**) unless the Panel consents to waive this requirement.

Company	HBOS PLC
TIDM	HBOS
Headline	HBOS in Talks with LLoyds TSB
Released	13:25 17-Sep-08
Number	6588D13

In the light of market speculation, the Board of HBOS plc confirms that it is in advanced talks with Lloyds TSB Group plc which may or may not lead to an offer being made for HBOS.

A further announcement will be made when appropriate.

Publication

A r 2.4 announcement must be published under r 2.9 in exactly the same way as a r 2.5 announcement (see **22.3.3.1**).

As the r 2.4 announcement will start the offer period (see **22.3.4**), the offeree company must also:

(a)   send the announcement to its shareholders, persons with information rights under s 146 of the CA 2006 and the Panel under r 2.6(a); and

(b)   make the disclosure required by r 2.10 (see **15.7.4.3**). (The offeror must also do this unless the offer is wholly for cash.)

Effect

A typical example of when a holding announcement is required is if there has been a leak which breaches the secrecy requirement under r 2.1, and which starts rumours that trigger the requirement for an announcement under r 2.2.

Even though the leak may have occurred at a very early stage in planning the offer, once the potential offeror or offeree has made a r 2.4 announcement, the offeree can request the Panel, under r 2.4(b), to require the offeror to 'put up or shut up'. This means that the Panel can impose a time-limit within which the potential offeror must make either a r 2.5 announcement (ie that it definitely will proceed with an offer for the offeree company), or a statement under r 2.8 that it does not intend to make an offer. This can leave an under-prepared offeror with little choice but to make a r 2.8 statement. An example of a 'put up or shut up' notice is set out below.

THE TAKEOVER PANEL 2008/39

LONMIN PLC ("LONMIN")

XSTRATA PLC ("XSTRATA")

Following recent representations made by the advisers to Lonmin, the Panel Executive has been considering the application of Rule 2.4(b) of the Code to the announcement made by Xstrata, on 6 August 2008, in respect of Lonmin. Following discussions with both parties' advisers, the Panel Executive has ruled that, unless the Panel Executive consents otherwise, Xstrata must, by 5.00 p.m. on 2 October 2008, either announce a firm intention to make an offer for Lonmin under Rule 2.5 of the Code or announce that it does not intend to make an offer for Lonmin. In the event that Xstrata announces that it does not intend to make an offer for Lonmin, Xstrata and any person(s) acting in concert with it will, except with the consent of the Panel Executive, be bound by the restrictions contained in Rule 2.8 of the Code for six months from the date of such announcement.

Each of the parties has accepted this ruling.

3 September 2008

Xstrata announced its decision a day before the deadline as set out in the attached article.

Xstrata drops Lonmin bid amid market turmoil

David Robertson

Xstrata scrapped its £5 billion offer for Lonmin yesterday, while BHP Billiton's proposed acquisition of Rio Tinto faced setbacks as the world's two biggest takeover bids were sent reeling by the turmoil in the credit markets.

The Anglo-Swiss mining group said that it had dropped a £33-a-share offer for Lonmin because the debt terms it had arranged were no longer attractive. BHP has a $55 billion (£32 billion) debt facility available to complete its $120 billion offer for Rio Tinto, but bankers have given warning that the cost of borrowing this money could double.

The reduced availability and higher cost of debt is making merger and acquisition deals extremely difficult to put together, even for cash-rich mining companies.

Xstrata had planned to raise $10 billion to finance its purchase of Lonmin, the FTSE 100-listed platinum producer, plus an additional $5 billion to refinance other debt. It successfully negotiated a three-year term for the $5 billion package but the $10 billion funding would have required refinancing in 12 months. Xstrata was unwilling to risk the possibility that credit might then be even more expensive.

Mick Davies, Xstrata chief executive, said: "The lack of clarity and certainty regarding the future availability of credit introduces significant risks into the financing package."

Xstrata made its £33-a-share offer three months ago and acquired nearly 11 per cent of Lonmin's stock at that price. The Takeover Panel had given Xstrata until today to make a formal offer but the company has decided to walk away.

It will be able to rebid only if another buyer emerges or if a friendly deal is arranged. Otherwise, Xstrata must wait six months before it can make a higher offer and 12 months if it wants to make a lower one.

The withdrawal of Xstrata, combined with a halving of the platinum price in the past three months, led to a sharp fall in the value of Lonmin's shares. The stock fell £4.61 to £18.13 yesterday and Xstrata took the opportunity to increase its stake. It bought 14.2 per cent at an average of £19.79, taking its total holding to 24.9 per cent. Xstrata is understood to want regulatory clearance to raise that to 29.9 per cent, the maximum allowed by UK authorities.

Analysts said that the fall in Lonmin's share price would send a "strong message" to the board. Lonmin has been criticised for a series of production downgrades this year and Brad Mills, the chief executive, was ousted on Monday.

Sir John Craven, chairman of Lonmin, said: "Although recent unprecedented developments in world financial and economic markets are having a substantial impact on platinum and other commodity prices, the long-term demand fundamentals for platinum remains positive."

Despite any financing setbacks, BHP's bid for Rio received a boost yesterday when Australian competition regulators cleared the deal. BHP has already received approval from the United States and is only waiting for European Union backing before making a formal offer.

The company has raised $55 billion from a syndicate of banks including Goldman Sachs, Barclays, HSBC and Citibank. It will not draw on the facility before the EU gives its verdict on January 15. Bankers said the price of the debt facility was about 60 basis points when arranged but could double or triple if credit markets remained chaotic.

Source: *The Times*, 2 October 2008

22.3.3.3   Statement of intention not to make an offer

The effect of a r 2.8 statement is that the potential offeror (or any concert party) must 'down tools'. It will not be able to:

(a)   make another offer for the offeree company;

(b)   acquire any interest in shares in the offeree company which would trigger a r 9 mandatory bid (see **21.8.10.3** above);

(c)   acquire any interest in, or procure an irrevocable undertaking (see **21.10**) in respect of, shares in the offeree company which, when aggregated with the shares of other concert parties, would carry 30% or more of the voting rights in the offeree company;

(d)   make any statement which raises or confirms the possibility that an offer might be made for the offeree company; or

(e)   take any steps to prepare a possible offer for the offeree company where knowledge of the possible offer might extend beyond the offeror and its immediate advisers,

for six months from the date of the r 2.8 statement, unless:

(i)   it has the consent of the Panel;

(ii)   there is a material change of circumstances; or

(iii)   an event has occurred which the potential offeror specified in the r 2.8 statement as an event which would enable the statement to be set aside.

These requirements are onerous (in fact, they are the same as those which apply under r 35.1 to a failed bid (see **22.6.1.1**), albeit for a shorter period.

Much can happen to the fortunes of a potential offeror and offeree company during this six-month period, and of course the potential offeror can no longer launch a surprise offer, so a r 2.8 statement can mean the end of any takeover offer plans. Now it may be clearer why so much care is taken to ensure that the r 2.1 secrecy obligation (see **21.3**) is not breached.

Rule 2.8 will apply to any statement to the effect that the company does not intend to make an offer. The lawyer should advise the board not to make such a statement, simply with a view to keeping its intentions secret, if in fact it does intend to make an offer (and, in particular, warn about the severe implications of r 2.8 before the board members give interviews to the media).

Company	Adecco Int Fin B.V.
TIDM	0HK1
Headline	No offer for Michael Page at this stage
Released	06:01 16-Sep-08
Number	HUG1251627

No offer for Michael Page at this stage

Adecco remains financially disciplined

Zurich, Switzerland, September 16, 2008: Adecco S.A. ('Adecco'), the worldwide leader in HR services, today announces that it is no longer considering making an offer for Michael Page International PLC ('Michael Page') at this stage and remains financially disciplined.

Adecco's stated strategy is to expand its professional operations in the US, Europe and Asia as well as looking at specialized general staffing companies. Adecco believes that a combination with Michael Page could have benefited both companies and their respective shareholders and so approached Michael Page in May 2008. Since that time the response from Michael Page and its advisers has indicated that a recommended transaction would not be achievable on terms satisfactory to Adecco.

Adecco is focused on value-based management and considers acquisition targets with financial discipline. Accordingly, Adecco has concluded that it will not be able to agree a combination on terms acceptable to both Adecco and the board of Michael Page at this time.

For the purposes of Rule 2.8 of The City Code on Takeovers and Mergers ('Code'), Adecco reserves the right to make or participate in an offer for Michael Page, or to take any other action which would otherwise be precluded under Rule 2.8 of the Code, within the six months following the date of this announcement:

(i)   with the agreement or recommendation of the board of Michael Page; or

(ii)   following the announcement of an offer by a third party for Michael Page; or

(iii)   following the announcement by Michael Page of a 'whitewash' proposal for the purposes of Rule 9 of the Code or of a reverse takeover, as defined in the Code; or

(iv)   if there is a material change in circumstances.

22.3.4 The offer period

The offer period will begin:

(a)   when the offeror makes either a r 2.5 announcement of a firm intention to make an offer (see **22.3.3.1**), or a r 2.4 announcement of a possible offer (see **22.3.3.2**); or

(b)   when a company announces that shares carrying 30% or more of the voting rights in the company are for sale, or that the board is seeking potential offerors.

When an offer begins, the offeree company and, unless the offer is wholly for cash, the offeror, must make the disclosure required by r 2.10 (see **15.7.4.3**).

The offer period will end:

(a)   on the first closing date (a minimum of 21 days from the date the offeror posts the offer document – see **22.5.2**); or

(b)   if later, the date the offer becomes or is declared unconditional as to acceptances (see **22.5.3**) or lapses (see **22.4.7** and **22.5.7**).

The Disclosure Table on the Panel's website lists all the companies which are currently in an offer period.

22.4 The offer

22.4.1 The offer document

The offer document is the principal document that the lawyer must draft in relation to a takeover offer.

22.4.1.1 Nature

The offer document is addressed to the offeree shareholders. It makes the formal contractual offer to acquire their shares in the offeree. It will constitute a financial promotion under s 21 of the FSMA 2000 (see **Chapter 12**) and will therefore have to be approved by a financial adviser who is an authorised person (see **12.2**).

22.4.1.2 Timing

While the offer period can begin with either a r 2.4 or a r 2.5 announcement, the timetable will start to run with effect from the r 2.5 announcement. Rule 30.1(a) provides that the offeror normally has 28 days from the date of the r 2.5 announcement in which to send the offer document to shareholders and persons with information rights under s 146 of the CA 2006. In practice, however, it is unlikely that the offeror will want to leave 28 days between making the announcement and sending the offer document. This is because the offeror will want the offeree company shareholders to be reading *its* offer document, not that of any other offeror who announces a rival offer and sends an offer document during this 28-day period.

As the timetable at **Table 22.1** shows, the day the offer document is sent is referred to as 'D day', and other dates in the offer timetable are calculated from this day.

22.4.1.3 Publication

Before it is published the document must be sent in hard copy and electronic form to the Panel (r 19.10). In Response Statement 2005/5 the Code Committee confirmed that it will continue to be acceptable where, under the direction of a financial adviser, the document is sent to the Panel at the same time it is posted to the offeree shareholders.

The offer document is then published. The City Code requires the offeror to:

(a) send the offer document to the offeree company shareholders and persons with information rights under s 146 of the CA 2006 (r 30.1(a));

(b) put the offer document on display, in accordance with r 26, on the date it sends the document to offeree company shareholders (r 30.1(a));

(c) announce to an RIS, in accordance with r 2.9, that it has displayed the document, and where (r 30.1(a));

(d) make the document available to its employee representatives, and if there are none, to its employees (the offeree company must also do this) (r 30.1(b)); and

(e) send the document in hard copy and electronic form to the advisers of the other parties to the offer (r 19.10(a)).

Note that under r 19.8 a document, announcement or other information (including the offer document) is deemed sent to a person under the City Code if it is sent in hard copy or electronic form to him or it is published on a website provided a notification of website publication is sent to that person. This applies to both the offeror and the offeree. There are a number of exceptions to this:

(a)   The Note to Rule 19.8 states that only hard copy versions are acceptable for acceptance forms (see **22.4.3**), withdrawal forms (see **22.5.5.1**), proxy forms and other forms required in the offer.

(b)   Rule 19.9 allows persons sent documents electronically or by website publication to request that the documents be sent to them in hard copy.

(c)   Certain rules, such as r 19.10, expressly state the method of communication, in that case hard copy and electronic. Website publication would therefore not be sufficient.

However, when an offeror or offeree sends the document, announcement or information, it must put a copy on its website under r 19.11 by midday of the next business day (subject to certain exemptions in Note 5). The document must be in a 'read-only' format to prevent alterations being made (Note 2).

Rule 30.3 extends the obligation to sending documents to shareholders outside the EEA unless there is an objectively good reason not to.

22.4.1.4   Content

Rule 24 (and, for a recommended offer, r 25) sets out the detailed content requirements of the offer document. Typically, it will include the following:

(a)   a section (sometimes in the form of a letter from the Chairman of the offeror), which explains the rationale of the offer and urges the offeree shareholders to accept it;

(b)   a letter from the Chairman of the offeree company (under r 30.2 of the City Code), which recommends the offer to the offeree shareholders (if the offer is recommended: if not, see **22.4.2** below);

(c)   a formal letter from the offeror making the offer and setting out the principal terms and other important information. Following the implementation of the Takeovers Directive in the UK and the criminal offence under s 953 of the CA 2006 for a breach of the bid documentation rules (see **20.5.7.2**) by the person making the bid (amongst others), it is no longer common for the financial advisers to make the offer on the offeror's behalf;

(d)   a detailed appendix setting out the full terms and conditions of the offer;

(e)   a detailed appendix setting out the information relating to the offeror which is required by r 24 of the City Code and, if the offer is recommended, the information relating to the offeree company which is required by r 25 of the City Code; and

(f)   information about how the offeree company shareholders can accept the offer.

An example of the front page of an offer document is set out below.

22.4.2   The defence document

22.4.2.1   Nature

If the offer is recommended, the views of the board of the offeree company will usually be included in the offer document. However, if the offer is hostile, the offer document will have been prepared by the offeror only. Rule 25.1(a) requires the board of the offeree company to communicate with its shareholders and persons with information rights under s 146 of the CA 2006 by way of circular, which is often referred to as a 'defence document'.

Once the defence document has been sent, the offeror will usually send a further document, to respond to the arguments raised in the defence document and draw the attention of the offeree company shareholders once more to the merits of the offer. The offeree may then send a further defence document to the offeree shareholders in response to the offeror's latest claims, and so on.

22.4.2.2 Timing

Rule 30.2 provides that the offeree company board must publish a circular containing its opinion on the offer as soon as practicable following publication of the offer document and normally within 14 days. For lawyers advising a company which is the subject of a surprise hostile offer, this will involve some swift drafting and several late nights.

22.4.2.3 Publication

The defence document is also a public document. The City Code requires the offeree company to:

(a) send the defence document to its shareholders (r 30.2(a)(i));

(b) put the defence document on display, in accordance with r 26, on the date it sends the document to offeree company shareholders (r 30.2(a));

(c) announce to an RIS, in accordance with r 2.9, that it has displayed the document, and where (r 30.2(a));

(d) make the document available to its employee representatives, and if there are none, to its employees (r 30.2(a)ii)); and

(e) send the document to the Panel and to the advisers to all other parties to the offer electronically and in hard copy (r 19.10(b)).

As mentioned at **22.4.1.3** above, r 30.3 extends the obligation in relation to sending documents to shareholders outside the EEA.

THIS DOCUMENT IS IMPORTANT AND REQUIRES YOUR IMMEDIATE ATTENTION. If you are in any doubt as to the action you should take, you are recommended to seek your own personal financial advice immediately from your stockbroker, bank manager, solicitor, accountant or other independent professional adviser duly authorised under the Financial Services and Markets Act 2000 if you are resident in the UK or, if not, from another appropriately authorised independent financial adviser.

If you have sold or otherwise transferred all of your Amstrad Shares, please forward this document, together with the Form of Acceptance, at once to the purchaser or transferee or to the stockbroker, bank or other agent through whom the sale or transfer was effected, for onward transmission to the purchaser or transferee. However, these documents should not be forwarded or transmitted in or into any jurisdiction in which such act would constitute a violation of the relevant laws of such jurisdiction. If you have sold or otherwise transferred only part of your holding of Amstrad Shares, you should retain these documents and consult the stockbroker, bank or other agent through whom the sale or transfer was effected.

The distribution of this document into jurisdictions other than the United Kingdom may be restricted by the laws of those jurisdictions and therefore any person into whose possession this document comes should inform themselves about, and observe, any such restrictions. Failure to comply with any such restrictions may constitute a violation of the securities law of any such jurisdiction.

Recommended Cash Offer

by

Sky Digital Supplies Limited

a wholly-owned subsidiary of

British Sky Broadcasting Group plc

for

Amstrad plc

Your attention is drawn to the letter of recommendation from the Chairman of Amstrad, set out on pages 3 to 7 of this document, which explains why the Amstrad Directors are unanimously recommending acceptance of the Offer.

The procedure for acceptance of the Offer is set out on pages 15 to 18 of this document and in the Form of Acceptance. If you hold Amstrad Shares in certificated form, to accept the Offer, the Form of Acceptance should be completed, signed and returned in accordance with the instructions printed on it as soon as possible and, in any event, so as to be received by Capita Registrars no later than 3:00 p.m. on 21 August 2007. If you hold Amstrad Shares in uncertificated form, to accept the Offer, you should comply with the procedure for acceptances set out on pages 16 to 18 of this document and ensure that an electronic acceptance is made which settles no later than 3:00 p.m. on 21 August 2007. If you are a CREST sponsored member, you must refer to your CREST sponsor as only your CREST sponsor will be able to send the necessary TTE instruction to CRESTCo.

Merrill Lynch is acting exclusively as financial adviser to Sky and Sky Digital Supplies and no one else in connection with the Offer and the matters referred to in this document. Merrill Lynch will not be responsible to any person other than Sky and Sky Digital Supplies for providing the protections afforded to customers of Merrill Lynch, nor for providing advice in relation to the Offer or any other matters referred to in this document.

Rothschild is acting exclusively for Amstrad and no one else in connection with the Offer and the matters referred to in this document. Rothschild will not be responsible to any person other than Amstrad for providing the protections afforded to customers of Rothschild, nor for providing advice in relation to the Offer or any other matters referred to in this document.

The Loan Notes will not be listed on any stock exchange and have not been, and will not be, registered under the United States Securities Act of 1933, as amended, or under any relevant securities laws of any state of the United States and the relevant clearances have not been, and will not be, obtained from the regulatory authority of any province or territory of Canada. In addition, no prospectus in relation to the Loan Notes has been, or will be, lodged with or registered by the Australian Securities and Investments Commission and no steps have been, nor will be, taken to enable the Loan Notes to be offered in compliance with the applicable securities laws of Japan, New Zealand or any other country or jurisdiction outside the United Kingdom. The Loan Notes will not be offered, sold, resold, delivered or distributed, directly or indirectly, in or into the United States, Canada, Australia, New Zealand or Japan or any other jurisdiction if to do so would constitute a violation of the relevant laws in such jurisdiction.

Reproduced by kind permission of BSkyB plc.

22.4.2.4 Content

The content of the defence document is prescribed by r 25.1. The information the offeree company must set out includes:

(a)   the substance of the advice it has received from its r 3 advisers (see **21.5.1**);

(b)   the board's reasons for forming its opinions and its views on:

    (i)   the effects of the offer on the offeree company's interests (including, specifically, employment); and

    (ii)   the offeror's strategic plans for the offeree company and their likely repercussions on employment and the locations of the offeree company's place of business; and

(c)   an opinion from its employee representatives on the effects of the offer on employment (provided the representatives provide the opinion in good time) (r 30.2(b)).

The defence document will seek to make clear to the offeree company shareholders that the offeror's offer is poor (for example, it undervalues the offeree company, or the premium offered is too low) and will advise the offeree company shareholders to reject the offeror's offer. As acceptance of the offer involves offeree company shareholders relinquishing their offeree company shares to the offeror, the defence document tends to focus on the benefits to the shareholder of keeping their shares. However, it must be careful not to make a profit forecast unless it is willing to report on that forecast (see **22.4.5.1**). If the consideration for the offer is shares in the offeror (a securities exchange offer), the defence document may also attack the worth of the offeror, further fanning the flames of the hostile bid.

22.4.3   The forms of acceptance

The offeree company shareholder must complete a form of acceptance and return it to the offeror's registrars in order to accept the offer. These forms are of crucial importance, and the lawyer will make sure that they are as clear and straightforward as possible. They must be sent in hard copy (Note to r 19.8).

22.4.4   Other documentation

As you will now be aware, the lawyer cannot consider the takeover in isolation from the other rules relating to listed companies. While the main documents relating to the takeover itself are the r 2.5 announcement and the documents considered at **22.4.1** to **22.4.3** above, the following circumstances will also call for further documentation.

22.4.4.1   Class 1 transaction

The takeover is an acquisition of shares, and if the offeror is a listed company then the acquisition must be classified under the Listing Rules and the offeror must comply with the requirements which attach to that classification (see **Chapter 19**). It is likely that a large takeover will constitute a Class 1 transaction. This means that the offeror must make a Class 2 announcement, send a circular to its own shareholders (that is, the offeror shareholders) and obtain the prior consent of those shareholders to the takeover by ordinary resolution.

22.4.4.2   Securities exchange offer

If the offeror is offering shares as consideration then, if that class of shares is listed (which is likely, as a listing gives shares an identifiable value), the consideration shares will also need to be listed. This means that the offeror must prepare a marketing document.

The rule is that a prospectus will be required for a takeover unless the exemption in connection with takeovers applies. This exemption, referred to at **6.4.1.5(f)** and **6.4.2.4(c)** above, is that a prospectus is not required if the takeover involves a share-for-share exchange (that is, the consideration for the takeover is shares) and a document is available containing information regarded by the FSA as being 'equivalent to' a prospectus. Issue 10 of *List!* provides further information about this exemption. In order to decide whether a document is 'equivalent to' a prospectus, the FSA will fully vet the document, which must be submitted at least 10 days before approval is required (PR 3.1.14R and PR 3.1.15R).

There is a disadvantage to using an equivalent document; it will not benefit from the passporting rights referred to at **6.11** above. However, if an equivalent document is used, then there is no obligation to produce a supplementary prospectus, so it has the advantage that it will not raise the potential problem of withdrawal rights outlined at **22.5.5**.

The prospectus (or equivalent document) will be published as a separate document, but sent out to shareholders at the same time as the offer document. Much of the information which would normally be included in the offer document will be contained in the prospectus (or equivalent document). WPP Group plc used an equivalent document in its £1 billion offer for Taylor Nelson Sofres plc in July 2008.

Finally, it is possible that the offeror will need the consent of its own shareholders to authorise the directors to allot shares under s 551 of the CA 2006. Remember that no disapplication of s 561 is required if the issue is for non-cash consideration. (See **Chapter 14**.)

22.4.4.3   Resulting extra documentation

As a result of either of the circumstances discussed at **22.4.4.1** and **22.4.4.2** above, the offeror might need to produce:

(a)   a circular (which contains the Class 1 information, if appropriate, information relating to any required increase in share capital and/or the s 551 authority, and the notice of the GM which convenes the meeting where the shareholders of the offeror can vote on these issues); and

(b)   a prospectus, or 'equivalent document'.

There will also be various r 17.1 press announcements (for example, of the level of acceptances (see **22.5.3**), or notifying an extension to the bid) during the course of the offer.

22.4.5   Standard of information

The City Code sets high standards for any information provided to shareholders and persons with information rights under s 146 of the CA 2006 during an offer. As noted at **22.4.1.4**, the specific requirements regarding this information are contained in rr 24 and 25. However, the City Code also sets out the following general rules about the nature and quality of that information.

22.4.5.1   Rule 19.1: accuracy of information

Rule 19.1 provides that:

(a)   any document or advertisement issued, or statement made, during the course of an offer must be prepared with the highest standard of care and accuracy; and

(b)   the information given must be adequately and fairly presented.

Again, the lawyers will use the verification process to help to protect the board in this regard.

The notes to r 19.1 provide valuable drafting guidance to the lawyer. They advocate the use of unambiguous language, citing sources for any material facts stated (typically this is done in a 'sources and bases' section in the document), and warn against using quotations out of context.

Note 1 to r 19.1 highlights certain areas of particular sensitivity, including profit forecasts, on which comment should be avoided. A profit forecast is any statement which puts a floor under, or a ceiling on, the expected profits for a certain period (for example, 'don't accept the bid as we are going to be much more profitable next year in any event'). As is the case with an IPO (see **6.5.2.1**), any profit forecast made during the course of a takeover must be reported on (r 28). Typically, a forecast will not be made unless it has already been decided that the benefit of making a forecast outweighs the work necessary to report on that forecast. This may be the case, for example, if the offer falls late in the financial year, and the most recent published accounts appear a little dated. Even then, as recognised by Note 1, it should not be the subject of media comment.

The Panel considers that the financial adviser is responsible for ensuring that its client complies with this rule (see **21.5.1(g)**). This can lead to something of a strain in relationships between the financial adviser, who needs to advise caution in making media statements, and the financial public relations consultants (see **21.5.5**), who want to deliver powerful messages to the media.

22.4.5.2   Rule 19.2: the responsibility statement

Rule 19.2 makes clear that it is the directors who must ensure that these standards are met. Each document issued to shareholders and persons with information rights under s 146 of the CA 2006, or advertisement published in connection with an offer, must contain what is referred to as a 'responsibility statement' from the directors of the offeror and/or, where appropriate, the offeree. The information that must be included in the statement is provided by r 19.2. Typically, the statement is drafted as follows:

> The directors of [the company], whose names appear on page [   ], accept responsibility for the information contained in this [document/advertisement]. To the best of the knowledge and belief of the directors (who have taken all reasonable care to ensure that such is the case) the information contained in this document is in accordance with the facts and does not omit anything likely to affect the import of such information.

In a recommended bid, the offer document will include a responsibility statement from the directors of the offeror in relation to the information provided about the offer and about the offeror. However, it will also include a responsibility statement from the directors of the offeree company in respect of the information it includes about the offeree.

In a hostile offer, the directors of the offeree company will not usually have provided the offeror with any of the information which is included in the offer document. The offer document will include a responsibility statement from the directors of the offeror only. However, any defence documents circulated by the offeree company must include a responsibility statement tfrom the directors of the offeree company (see **22.4.2** above).

The wording of the responsibility statement should be familiar. As explained at **6.5.2.1** above, Appendix 3 of the Prospectus Rules requires a similar responsibility statement in a prospectus. You will remember that the purpose of the IPO verification process is to make sure that the directors are in a position to make this statement. The position on a takeover is no different. The junior lawyer will be involved in the process of ensuring that each statement in the offer document is properly verified, and will produce a verification note. The verification process is discussed in more detail at **5.3.5** above.

22.4.5.3   Rule 19.3: unacceptable statements

Rule 19.3 provides that the parties to the offer and their advisers must take care not to issue statements which, while not factually incorrect, may mislead shareholders and the market, or which may create uncertainty. In particular, the offeror should not make a statement which hints that it may improve the offer or that it may make a change to the structure, conditionality or the non-financial terms of its offer, without committing itself to doing so and specifying the improvement. To see an example of a breach of r 19.3 (by Standard Life plc), see Panel Statement 2007/35.

22.4.5.4   Rule 20: equality of information

Rule 20.1

Rule 20.1 develops General Principle 1 (see **20.5.5**). It provides that information about companies involved in an offer must be made equally available to all offeree company shareholders as nearly as possible at the same time and in the same manner.

Note 3 to r 20.1 provides guidance in relation to meetings the board may have with shareholders, analysts, brokers or other investment professionals prior to the announcement of the offer, and during the offer itself. It provides that the directors must not disclose, in the case of a meeting prior to the announcement of the offer, any material new information or significant new opinions that will not be in the r 2.5 announcement and, in the case of a meeting during the offer period, any material new information or significant new opinions at all. Again, a profit forecast is capable of falling within r 20.1.

Of course, the board is very keen to enthuse the audience at such meetings with just the type of statements that r 20.1 seeks to prevent. The financial adviser or corporate broker of the party convening any such meeting must be present at the meeting and has the happy task of providing written confirmation to the Panel, by midday the following day, that the restrictions were complied with. The lawyers tend not to attend these meetings: the risk of soaring blood pressure is too high.

If any material information or significant new opinion is released at the meeting, a circular must be sent to shareholders and persons with information rights under s 146 of the CA 2006 (in the final stages of an offer, an advertisement in a newspaper may be required). If the information or opinion cannot be substantiated, this must be made clear and it must be withdrawn formally. This, of course, would be a public relations nightmare.

Rule 20.2

Rule 20.2 seeks to level the playing field for any competing offeror. It provides that the offeree, on request, must provide the same information to each offeror or genuine potential offeror, no matter how unwelcome that offeror's offer is.

The problem which r 20.2 can cause to an offeree company is illustrated well by the takeover of Midland Bank plc in 1992. Midland had provided information to its preferred offeror, HSBC Holdings Ltd (HSBC) (a subsidiary of the Hong Kong and Shanghai Banking Corporation). Lloyds Bank plc, a high street rival, then stated that it was also 'considering' making an offer for Midland. A pre-condition of Lloyds' offer was the receipt by Lloyds of all the information that Midland had provided to HSBC. Midland objected, on the grounds that it was not fair to oblige it to give commercially sensitive information to one of its arch rivals. Lloyds argued that, without the information, it would not be able to progress its offer and so the shareholders of Midland would lose out on an offer from Lloyds. The Panel upheld Lloyds' request. It saw no reason to modify or relax r 20.2. Lloyds was a genuine potential offeror, and it was in the best interests of Midland shareholders that Midland provide the information to Lloyds. It follows that an offeree company should exercise caution when revealing information, even to a preferred offeror.

Two practical points are worthy of note here. First, the potential offeror must specify the information it requires from the offeree company; it cannot simply ask the offeree company to provide everything which it gave to the preferred offeror. Secondly, r 20.2 is usually of use only once the rival bid is public. As many hostile bids are launched as surprise attacks, and all the preparation and due diligence is undertaken in secret, the usefulness of r 20.2 is limited.

Note also that r 20.2 extends to site visits and meetings with the offeree's management. So, if one bidder has met the offeree's directors, the competing offeror should, if it requests this, be given equivalent access.

22.4.5.5   Rule 23: sufficiency of information

Rule 23 relates to the documents which the offeror and the offeree company prepare during an offer. The rule embodies General Principle 2 of the City Code (see **20.5.5** above) and provides that the offeree shareholders must be given sufficient information and advice, in a timely manner, to enable them to reach a properly informed decision as to the merits or demerits of the offer, and that no relevant information should be withheld from those shareholders.

Note 1 to r 23 recognises that a takeover, particularly a hostile one, can take some time to complete. It provides that if there has been any material change in any information previously published during the offer period, then any subsequent documentation must either detail the change or provide an appropriate negative statement. Rule 27.1 sets out specific matters which must be updated, including irrevocable undertakings and letters of intent, interests and dealings in shares and changes to directors' service contracts.

22.4.5.6   Bid documentation rules

As detailed at **20.5.7.2**, the failure to comply with the bid documentation rules in Appendix 6 of the City Code is a criminal offence punishable by a fine.

22.4.6   Consideration

In certain circumstances the City Code will dictate the level and type of consideration which must be offered (see **21.8.10.4** above).

22.4.7   Conditions of the offer

The offeror will make the offer subject to certain conditions. The r 2.5 announcement and the offer document will set out the detailed terms of these conditions. If the conditions are not fulfilled, the offer will lapse, unless the offeror can waive the conditions.

There will always be a condition as to the number of offeree company shares which the offeror must acquire in order for the offer to succeed (the 'acceptance condition'; see **22.4.7.1** below), but usually there will be other conditions too. The City Code regulates the conditions which the offeror can impose. Rule 13 provides that the offer must not normally be subject to conditions which depend solely on subjective judgements by the directors of the offeror, or the fulfilment of which is in their hands.

The most common conditions which may be attached to an offer are set out at **22.4.7.1** to **22.4.7.7** below. Note, however, that if the offeror seeks to rely on the non-fulfilment of a condition as justification for lapsing the offer, and invoke that condition, it must consult the Panel (Panel Statement 1999/14). In particular, it must satisfy the Panel that the issue in question could not have been discovered through the due diligence exercise carried out before the offer was announced (if the offer was recommended) and that the issue is genuinely material to the offeror. The exception to this rule is if the offer will lapse because any of the conditions referred to at **22.4.7.1**, **22.4.7.4** or, in practice, **22.4.7.2** below are not fulfilled.

Usually, the offeror will reserve the right to waive conditions (other than those set out at **22.4.7.2** and **22.4.7.3** below, which, in practice, must be fulfilled), and the acceptance condition cannot be waived in its entirety; see **22.4.7.1**). This means that the offeror can choose to declare an offer unconditional despite certain conditions not being fulfilled, if it so chooses.

22.4.7.1   Acceptance

This is a key condition which must reflect r 10 of the City Code. Rule 10 provides that the offeror must have acquired, or agreed to acquire, shares carrying over 50% of the voting rights in the offeree company. Once the offeror has acquired such shares it can declare the offer 'unconditional as to acceptances'. In other words, it has won legal control of the offeree company.

However, in practice, the offer condition is usually drafted so that it will be fulfilled only if the offeror acquires 90% of the shares to which the offer relates. This is to enable the offeror to acquire the remaining 10% of shares by invoking s 979 of the CA 2006 (see **22.7** below). Typically the offeror will not want to be left with troublesome minority shareholders whom it is not entitled to buy out.

Usually the condition will specify that the offeror can waive the condition at a level of acceptances below 90% (but not 50% or below as this would breach the minimum acceptance requirement of r 10).

As explained at **22.5.5.1**, until the offer is declared unconditional as to acceptances, shareholders who have already accepted the offer can withdraw their acceptances (typically from Day 42 of the offer). However, once the offer is declared unconditional as to acceptances, such shareholders are bound by their acceptances, subject to the fulfilment of any other conditions to which the offer is subject.

22.4.7.2   Admission of consideration shares to listing and trading

If the offeror is issuing shares of a class which is already listed as consideration then, as explained at **17.4.3** above, in order to:

(a)   comply with the requirements of the Listing Rules; and

(b)   give value to the shares,

these shares must be admitted to listing on the Official List and to trading on the Main Market.

In this case a condition will be included which states that the offer will become wholly unconditional only once the consideration shares are effectively admitted to listing and to trading.

A similar condition is also required if the offeror is issuing shares in order to raise cash consideration for the offer (see Note to rr 13.1 and 13.3).

22.4.7.3   Offeror shareholder approval

If the takeover is a Class 1 transaction then the Listing Rules require the transaction to be approved by the offeror shareholders (see **Chapter 19**). In addition, the offeror shareholders may need to authorise the increase of share capital and the issue of shares (if the offeror is offering its shares as consideration). Again, if the offeror is issuing shares to raise cash consideration, then it will need to include a condition regarding any required shareholder approval, relating to issues such as increasing the share capital, issuing the shares and/or disapplying pre-emption rights (Note to rr 13.1 and 13.3).

It is usual for the offer to be conditional upon the passing at a GM of the offeror of all resolutions that are necessary to implement the offer.

22.4.7.4   Merger control clearance

Rule 12.1(c) of the City Code allows an offeror to make the offer conditional on a decision being made that there will be no reference to the Competition Commission (see **23.4.3**), or, in the case of a takeover which falls within the scope of the EC Merger Regulation, that the European Commission will clear the offer within Phase I (see **23.3**). (Rule 12.1 of the City Code also provides that it must be a *term* of the offer that it will lapse if the Competition Commission or the European Commission take certain action in relation to the offer – see **23.2.1**.) While the offeror can waive any condition relating to merger control, and proceed without clearance from the relevant UK or EC competition authority, it cannot waive the term imposed by r 12.1.

22.4.7.5   Authorisations

This condition states that all authorisations for carrying on the business of the offeree company and other offeree group companies are in full force and effect.

22.4.7.6   Material litigation

This condition provides that no material litigation or arbitration proceedings have been instituted or threatened against the offeree group.

22.4.7.7   Material adverse change

This condition (the 'MAC condition') states that there are no material adverse changes in the offeree company's financial or trading position, other than those which the offeree has already disclosed. In 2001, the Panel refused to allow an offeror, WPP, to invoke its MAC condition on the basis that a material adverse change had taken place in the prospects of the offeree company, Tempus, after the announcement of WPP's offer on 10 September 2001 and, in particular, following the terrorist attacks in the US on 11 September 2001. The Panel stated that a change in economic, industrial or political circumstances will not normally justify the withdrawal of an announced offer.

WPP gives up attempt to halt Tempus deal

RAYMOND SNODDY Media Editor

WPP, the advertising group, hoisted the white flag in its battle to renege on a £432 million takeover bid for Tempus Group, its rival, yesterday.

Sir Martin Sorrell, the WPP chairman, has decided not to appeal against a ruling by the Takeover Panel that the company should proceed with its 555p-a-share cash offer for Tempus.

Sir Martin had sought to cancel the deal by citing "a material adverse change" after the September 11 terrorist attacks caused a sharp downturn in demand for advertising services.

However, the Panel, whose judgment was made public yesterday, said that Sir Martin had "failed by a considerable margin" to make the case for the deal to be scuppered.

Tempus, which had earlier opposed the WPP takeover, subsequently advised its shareholders to accept the offer.

The deal has been dubbed the City's first ever "hostile sale".

The Panel ruled that the temporary effect on profitability of an event such as September 11 was not enough to justify frustration of a legal contract.

The Panel also noted that Sir Martin had accepted that there were strategic and financial benefits in the deal. In the days following the attacks WPP actually increased its Tempus shareholding, making it more difficult for any counter-offer from a third party.

WPP shares fell 18p to 647p yesterday, while Tempus rose 11½p to 535p.

Source: *The Times*, 7 November 2001

22.4.8   Frustrating action

This is relevant only in connection with a hostile bid. If an offeree company receives an unwelcome takeover offer, the directors may be tempted to frustrate the offer by taking some action which will make the offeree company more difficult to acquire, or less attractive to the offeror. Rule 21 expands General Principle 3 of the City Code (see **20.5.5** above) by providing that directors of an offeree company cannot undertake frustrating action without the approval of the offeree company shareholders. Remember that an offer which may be unwelcome from the offeree company board's point of view may be very welcome from the offeree company shareholders' perspective. Account must also be taken of the offeree company's directors' statutory duties.

A non-exhaustive list of frustrating actions is set out in r 21.1(b). It includes:

(a)   the issue of, or granting of options over, unissued shares;

(b)   the sale, disposal or acquisition of assets; and

(c)   the entering into of contracts other than in the ordinary course of business (such as amending a director's service contract to improve his terms without justification).

22.4.9   Poison pills

A poison pill is a general term used to describe defensive measures a company may take even before a bid is imminent (when the City Code rules on frustrating action described at **22.4.8** do not apply). An example of a poison pill is drafting change of control clauses into key agreements (for example, Marks & Spencer Group plc inserting a clause into its contracts with suppliers of all socks and underwear that such contracts would terminate if anyone made a takeover offer for Marks & Spencer Group plc, thus leaving an offeror potentially with a much less valuable offeree company). These are common in the UK, but in practice do not tend to pose too much of a deterrent to a hostile offeror (who may have its own contacts with whom to contract, or indeed have good relations with the party subject to the change of control clause in any event).

When considering whether to adopt a poison pill, the board must take care not to breach its fiduciary duty to the company. *Criterion Properties plc v Stratford Properties UK plc and Others* [2004] UKHL 28 provides some guidance on this issue. In that case, Criterion Properties plc ('Criterion') had entered into a joint venture agreement with Stratford Properties UK plc ('Oaktree') under which Oaktree had a put option, namely the option to require Criterion to purchase Oaktree's shares, in the event that there was a change of control of Criterion, or if two named directors left the Criterion board. The purchase price was so high that it guaranteed Oaktree a minimum return of 25% pa on the investment. Obviously, the effect of the change of control clause was to deter any potential offeror from making an offer for Criterion. Criterion applied to the court to set aside the agreement.

The House of Lords found that the case turned on whether the Criterion directors had authority to enter into the contract. If the directors had actual or apparent authority, the agreement would be valid. If they did not, the court discussed whether the directors had ostensible authority. The court noted that this issue raised a question of considerable public importance, namely whether the directors of a public company have the power to authorise the signing of a poison pill agreement intended to deter third parties from making offers to purchase the company's shares and, in particular, whether they had authority to do so when the deterrent consisted of divesting of some of the company's assets.

Unfortunately, the court of first instance and the Court of Appeal had not considered the issue of authority, and so the House of Lords could not resolve the issue further; however, the case contains some useful commentary on poison pills.

22.4.9.1 Breakthrough provisions

Article 11 of the Takeovers Directive (see **20.3**) sets out what it refers to as 'breakthrough provisions'. These provisions provide that, on a takeover, the offeror can override some poison pills in certain circumstances. Article 11 specifies the types of poison pill which can be overridden. It includes restrictions on transferring shares which are contained in the company's articles or contracts, and restrictions on voting rights.

However, the breakthrough provisions proved so controversial that art 12 of the Directive permits Member States to opt out of art 11. In the event that a Member State does opt out, however, the Directive provides that companies must be able to opt back into (and, if required subsequently, back out of) the breakthrough provisions if they so choose.

In the UK, the Government has opted out of art 11. It prefers to leave to shareholders the decision on whether to have enforceable poison pills. Under s 966 of the CA 2006 a UK company must opt into (and, if required, then opt to back out of) the breakthrough procedures.

In order to opt in, the company must, under s 966(1) of the CA 2006, pass a special resolution, and fulfil the following conditions:

(a)   the company must have voting shares admitted to trading on a regulated market (see **20.3.1**) (that is, it must be a potential offeree company in a takeover to which the Directive applies (see **20.3**)) (s 966(2));

(b)   the company's articles of association must not contain (s 966(3)):

(i)   any of the restrictions on share transfer or voting rights which are listed in art 11 (or if they do, they must fall away in the same circumstances as they would under the breakthrough provisions); or

(ii)   any other provisions that would be incompatible with art 11 of the Directive; and

(c)   no shares conferring special rights in the company can be held by a Government minister, his nominees or any company he directly or indirectly owns or controls (s 966(4)).

Under s 970(1) and (2) of the CA 2006 the company must notify the Panel of any special resolution passed to opt in to (or subsequently opt out of) the breakthrough provisions, within 15 days after the passing of that resolution. Section 968 sets out the consequences of opting in, and in particular which poison pills will be invalid.

22.5 Accepting the offer

Once the offer documents and any defence documents have been posted, the fate of the offer will be determined by whether the offeree shareholders choose to accept it.

22.5.1 Method of acceptance

The offeree company shareholders accept the offer by completing the forms of acceptance (referred to at **22.4.3**) and returning them to the company's registrars, who will then count the votes (as explained at **21.5.6**).

22.5.2 First closing date

Most forms of acceptance will urge shareholders to vote by a specified time and date, known as the 'first closing date'. Rule 31.1 provides that the offer must be open for a minimum of 21 days from the date the offeror publishes the offer document. The offeror will be keen to complete the takeover as soon as possible, and therefore the first closing date is usually the 21st day following the publishing of the offer document, but it can be a longer period. Most offers are extended beyond the first closing date, but the offeror could use the acceptance condition to lapse the offer at this date if it no longer wished to proceed.

Institutional shareholders may delay casting their votes, to see if anything happens to change their decision to vote for or against the offer (such as a rival offeror announcing a better offer, or a dramatic change in market conditions).

22.5.3 Announcing the level of acceptances

Rule 17.1 provides that the offeror must announce the level of acceptances by 8.00 am on the business day after the first closing date.

If the bid is recommended, the offeror will expect to be able to declare the offer unconditional as to acceptances on the first closing date. However, if the offer is hostile, the offeror is unlikely to have received the required level of acceptances (see **22.4.7.1** above), as shareholders may wait to see if the offeror will improve the offer, or whether another rival offer will be made.

The level of acceptances must also be announced, under r 17.1, after any further closing date and after any extension or revision of the offer (see **22.5.4**).

22.5.4 Extending and revising the offer

If the conditions of the offer, including the condition as to acceptances, have not been met by the first closing date, the offeror can withdraw the offer. Rule 31.3 provides that the offeror is not obliged to extend the offer. However, usually the offeror will extend the offer in the hope that it will eventually receive a sufficient level of acceptances. The offeror may also improve the terms of the offer. Typically the offeror will announce the extension or revision of the offer at the same time that it announces the level of acceptances.

If the offeror does decide to revise its offer, it must do as it did with the original offer (see **22.4.1.3**), namely:

(a)   send a revised offer document to the offeree company shareholders and persons with information rights under s 146 of the CA 2006. This must comply with the content requirements of r 24, and also with r 27, which provides that any documents sent to shareholders after the offer document must contain details of any material changes to the documents published previously during the offer period (or state that there are no such changes) (r 32.1(a));

(b)   put the revised offer document on display, in accordance with r 26, on the date it posts the document to offeree company shareholders (r 32.1(a));

(c)   announce to an RIS, in accordance with r 2.9, that it has displayed the document, and where (r 32.1(a));

(d)   make the document available to its employee representatives, and if there are none, to its employees (the offeree company must also do this) (r 32.7(a)); and

(e)   send the document to the Panel and to the advisers to all other parties to the offer electronically and in hard copy (r 19.10(b)).

As mentioned at **22.4.1.3** above, r 30.3 extends the obligation in relation to sending documents to shareholders outside the EEA unless there is an objectively good reason not to.

Rule 32.1(b) provides that the revised offer must be open for at least 14 days following the publishing of the revised document. The effect of this requirement, together with the final day rule, referred to at **22.5.7** below, is that the offer cannot be revised after the 46th day following the publishing of the announcement of the original offer document. Usually this is relevant only on a hostile takeover.

Rule 32.3 provides that any shareholder who accepted the original offer is entitled to receive the revised consideration.

In the event of a revised offer, the offeree company must do as it did with the defence document (see **22.4.2.3**), namely:

(a)   send a circular to its shareholders and persons with information rights under s 146 of the CA 2006 setting out its views on the revised offer, as required by r 25.1(a), drawn up in accordance with rr 25 and 27 (see **22.5.4(a)**) (r 32.6(a)). The offeree company must append to the circular an opinion from its employee representatives on the effects of the offer on employment (provided the representatives provide the opinion in good time) (r 32.6(b));

(b)   put the circular on display, in accordance with r 26, on the date it posts the document to offeree company shareholders (r 32.6(a));

(c)   announce to an RIS, in accordance with r 2.9, that it has displayed the circular, and where (r 32.6(a));

(d)   make the circular available to its employee representatives, and if there are none, to its employees (r 32.7(b)); and

(e)   send the document to the Panel and to the advisers to all other parties to the offer electronically and in hard copy (r 19.10(b)).

Again, r 30.3 extends the obligation in relation to sending documents to shareholders outside the EEA unless there is an objectively good reason not to.

22.5.5   The right of withdrawal

22.5.5.1   Withdrawal rights under the City Code

Any shareholder who has accepted the offer can change his mind and withdraw that acceptance at any time after the date which is 21 days after the first closing date (so, usually, any time after the 42nd day following the announcement of the offer) until the date the offer has become, or is declared, unconditional as to acceptances.

This is why so much importance is attached to the offer becoming or being declared unconditional; once this has happened, shareholders who have accepted the offer are bound by this acceptance, and cannot withdraw.

In a hostile offer, the offeree company will send withdrawal forms to its shareholders to encourage them to take advantage of these rights.

22.5.5.2   Withdrawal rights under the FSMA 2000

We have just noted that, under the City Code, usually withdrawal rights cease to be available after an offer has become or has been declared unconditional. As explained at **6.9.4** above, however, s 87Q of the FSMA 2000 provides that investors have the right to withdraw their acceptances during the two days following publication of any supplementary prospectus (referred to as a 'statutory withdrawal period'). So what happens if a takeover is made by way of share-for-share exchange, and a supplementary prospectus is required? Can withdrawal rights arise under the FSMA 2000 after the offer has become or has been declared unconditional, meaning that the offeror's acceptance level could drop below 50%? Neither the FSMA 2000 nor the City Code are clear on this point. The Panel has addressed this issue in Panel Statement 2005/29. It states that it has received legal advice that the new FSMA 2000 provisions can be interpreted as meaning:

(a)   that the period for withdrawal by an acceptor of an offer ends once the offer has become or has been declared wholly unconditional and the relevant securities have been unconditionally allotted (that is, wholly unconditional bids, where the unconditional allotments of securities have been made, could not be reopened through the exercise of withdrawal rights); and

(b)   that the withdrawal rights under the FSMA 2000 will not arise if a share-for-share offer is made by way of an 'equivalent document' (see **22.4.4.2**) rather than a prospectus.

The FSA confirmed, in Issue 11 of *List!*, that it agrees with this view. Until the courts ultimately decide this matter, practically it is prudent for the offeror to make use of the Panel Statement and either:

(i)   make the offer by way of an equivalent document rather than a prospectus (but see **22.4.4.2** for the disadvantages in this approach); or

(ii)   take steps to avoid becoming or being declared unconditional as to acceptances when a statutory withdrawal period is running, or when there is a possibility that a supplementary prospectus may be required (possibly by organising matters so that the offer becomes wholly unconditional at the same time the offer becomes or is declared unconditional as to acceptances, which is already common practice); and/or

(iii)   include an extra condition to the offer which it can invoke should the exercise of withdrawal rights under the FSMA 2000 result in acceptance levels dropping below 50% after the offer has become or been declared unconditional as to acceptances.

22.5.6   Day 39

Rule 31.9 provides that the offeree company should not, without the consent of the Panel, announce any material new information after the 39th day following the publication of the initial offer document. If any relevant competition authority has not given its decision by this time, the Panel will usually grant permission to extend the deadline until the second day after the decision is announced.

22.5.7   Day 60: the final day rule

For reasons of the offeree's stability (and the advisers' sanity), the takeover process is not allowed to continue indefinitely. Rule 31.6 provides that, except with the consent of the Panel, the offer will lapse if the offeror cannot declare the offer unconditional as to acceptances by midnight on the 60th day after the initial offer document was published. The circumstances when the Panel will grant consent to an extension of this period are set out in r 31.6(a)(i) to (v). For example, if a competing offeror launches a bid for the offeree company, the timetables for both offers will be co-ordinated and run from the posting of the competing offeror's offer document, which will inevitably lead to an extension of Day 60 for the original offer.

22.5.8   Day 74: earliest date the offer can close

Rule 31.4 provides that, after the offer has become or been declared unconditional as to acceptances, it must still remain open for further acceptances for at least 14 days after the current closing date. As explained at **22.5.7**, the latest closing date will tend to be Day 60, and so, if this is the case, the earliest date the offer can close will be Day 74.

Rule 31.2 provides that if the offer remains open for acceptances beyond Day 70, the offeror must give at least 14 days' written notice to all offeree company shareholders who have not accepted the offer.

In practice, typically the offeror keeps the offer open until further notice, and then runs the offer in parallel to the compulsory acquisition procedure (see **22.7**).

22.5.9   Day 81: last date to fulfil other conditions

Rule 31.7 provides that, except with the consent of the Panel, the other conditions of the offer must be fulfilled or waived within 21 days of either the first closing date, or the date on which the offer becomes unconditional as to acceptances (whichever is the later), otherwise the offer will lapse.

The Panel's consent to the extension of this period will be granted only if the outstanding condition involves a material official authorisation or regulatory clearance relating to the offer, and it has been impossible to obtain an extension under r 31.6.

The effect of r 31.6 and r 31.7 is that the latest date on which the other conditions may be satisfied is the 81st day after the posting of the initial offer document. However, in practice most offers are declared wholly unconditional at the same time they are declared unconditional as to acceptances.

22.6   Success or failure?

22.6.1   The failed offer

22.6.1.1   The 12-month restriction

If the offeror withdraws the offer, or the offer lapses, r 35.1 of the City Code provides that, without the consent of the Panel, neither the offeror nor any concert parties (see **22.6.1.2**) can:

(a)   make another offer for the offeree company;

(b)   acquire any interest in shares in the offeree which would trigger a r 9 mandatory bid (see **21.8.10.3** above);

(c)   acquire any interest in, or procure an irrevocable undertaking (see **21.10**) in respect of, shares in the offeree company which, when aggregated with the shares of other concert parties, would carry 30% or more of the voting rights in the offeree company;

(d)   make any statement which raises or confirms the possibility that an offer might be made for the offeree company; or

(e)   take any steps to prepare a possible offer for the offeree company where knowledge of the possible offer might extend beyond the offeror and its immediate advisers,

for at least 12 months from the date the offer is withdrawn or lapses. The rationale for this rule is to promote certainty in the market and avoid companies becoming embroiled in an endless takeover battle (as reflected in General Principle 6). Note that the requirements to 'down tools' are the same as those that apply following a r 2.8 statement (see **22.3.3.3**), albeit for a longer period.

The note to r 35.1 of the City Code sets out the usual circumstances when the Panel will waive the 12-month restriction imposed by r 35.1 These include:

(a)   if the offeror wants to announce a new offer which is recommended;

(b)   if the offeror wants to announce a new offer to compete with another offer; or

(c)   if the original offer lapsed in accordance with r 12.2 (see **23.2.1**) and the offeror wants to announce a new offer following competition clearance.

22.6.1.2   Acting in concert

The City Code defines 'persons acting in concert' as persons:

> who, pursuant to an agreement or understanding (whether formal or informal), co-operate to obtain or consolidate control of a company or to frustrate the successful outcome of an offer for a company.

Affiliated persons (such as a majority shareholder; see Note 2 to the definition) are deemed to be acting in concert with each other.

Certain persons, such as directors and other companies in the same group, are presumed to be acting in concert unless the contrary is established.

22.6.1.3   Restrictions on dealings

If an offer has lapsed which was one of two or more competing offers, then, until the other competing offer(s) have also lapsed, or become wholly unconditional, r 35.4 prevents the failed offeror from acquiring any interest in shares of the offeree company on terms more favourable than under its lapsed offer.

22.6.2   The successful bid

Once the offer is declared wholly unconditional, the offeror can breathe a sigh of relief: the takeover has been successful. However, r 31.4 of the City Code provides that the offer must still remain open for acceptance for not less than 14 days. This affords offeree company shareholders, who did not accept the offer before the offer was declared unconditional as to acceptances, an opportunity to accept the offer once the offeror has acquired control of the offeree.

Ideally, an offeror will want to acquire 100% of the offeree company's shares, to avoid being left to cope with unfriendly minority shareholders (see **22.7.1**). If the offeror has received acceptances in respect of at least 90% of the shares to which the offer relates, it can compel the other offeree company shareholders to sell their shares to the offeror using the compulsory acquisition procedure under s 979 of the CA 2006 (see **22.7** below). However, if the offeror cannot invoke the compulsory acquisition procedure, it must abide with the minority shareholders who rejected the offer. After six months following the closure of the original offer, however, the offeror may be able to buy the shares of this minority by offering them more favourable terms than those of the original offer.

22.7   Buying out minority shareholders

22.7.1   The problem with minority shareholders

The typical offeror will not want to become the majority shareholder of the offeree company alongside minority shareholders who did not accept the offer. Minority shareholders can be problematic for various reasons, including their ability to disrupt GMs and create bad publicity for the company. The presence of a minority can also prevent the company from carrying out its day to day business effectively (for example, the minority may be able to block special resolutions if they hold more than 25% of the company's shares, or prevent a GM from being held on short notice if they hold more than 5%).

The minority shareholders, too, may be less than happy to find themselves holding a minority stake in a company which is controlled by the offeror. In particular, if the offeror decides to take the company private after the takeover, the minority may struggle to find a market for their shares in order to exit from the company.

For the reasons outlined above, once the majority of shareholders have accepted the offer, ss 979 and 983 of the CA 2006 give a statutory right respectively:

(a)   to the offeror, to buy out the minority shareholders, and so acquire 100% of the offeree company (referred to as a 'squeeze-out' right); and

(b)   to each minority shareholder who has refused the takeover offer, to require the offeror to purchase his shares (referred to as a 'sell-out' right).

22.7.2   The right of the offeror to buy out minority shareholders ('squeeze-out')

22.7.2.1   The conditions

Two conditions must be satisfied before the offeror can invoke the compulsory acquisition provisions:

(a)   the takeover offer condition; and

(b)   the 90% squeeze-out threshold condition.

The takeover offer condition

There must be a 'takeover offer', which is defined by s 974 of the CA 2006 as:

(a)   an offer to acquire all the shares in the offeree company (or, where there is more than one class of shares, all the shares of one or more classes) other than the offeree company shares already held by the offeror, or contracted to be acquired by it; and

(b)   where the terms of the offer are the same in relation to all the shares to which the offer relates.

Note that, in relation to overseas shareholders, under s 978 of the CA 2006 the offer can constitute a 'takeover offer' for the purposes of the CA 2006 even if the offer is not communicated to an overseas shareholder, provided:

(a)   the shareholder does not have a registered UK address;

(b)   the offer is not made to the shareholder in order to avoid contravening the law of an overseas territory; and

(c)   the offer is either:

(i)   published in the *Gazette*; or

(ii)   available for inspection at, or can be obtained from, a place in an EEA State, or a website, and notice of this is published in the *Gazette*.

The 90% squeeze-out threshold condition

The rules differ according to whether the offer falls within the Takeovers Directive or not. Only the position under the Takeovers Directive has been considered (see **20.3**).

Under s 979 of the CA 2006 the offeror must have acquired or unconditionally contracted to acquire, by virtue of acceptances of the offer, not less than 90% in value of all the shares *to which the offer relates* and, where the shares to which the offer relates are voting shares, not less than 90% of the voting rights carried by those shares (or, if the offer is for more than one class of share, not less than 90% in value and, where voting shares, not less than 90% of voting rights, for any of the classes to which the offer relates). Note that under s 974(2) of the CA 2006 any shares acquired by the offeror or its associates *before* the offer document was posted do not count towards the 90% threshold, but any shares acquired *after* the document was posted will count towards the threshold (CA 2006, s 979(8)–(10)).

For example, if the offeror already owned 25% of the offeree company's shares before the offer document was posted, the offer relates to only 75% of the offeree company's share capital. The offeror must, therefore, secure acceptances in respect of 90% (in both value and voting rights) of this 75%.

Under s 975(2) of the CA 2006, shares which are the subject of irrevocable undertakings (see **21.10**) as at the date of the offer (which is the date the offer document is published) do count towards the 90% threshold. Shares which the offeror's 'associates' hold or have contracted to acquire as at the date of the offer (CA 2006, s 975(4)) do not count towards the 90% threshold.

Section 986(9) of the CA 2006 provides that the offeror can apply to the court for an order which allows it to serve a squeeze-out notice (see **22.7.2.2**) even though it has not acquired the 90% threshold, if it can prove that:

(a) after reasonable enquiry the offeror has been unable to trace one or more of the persons holding shares to which the offer relates;

(b) if account were taken of the shares of these missing persons, the 90% threshold would be reached; and

(c) the consideration offered is fair and reasonable.

However, the court will make such an order only if it considers it just and equitable to do so, having regard to the number of shareholders who have been traced but who have rejected the offer.

22.7.2.2   The squeeze-out notice

Provided the offeror has acquired or unconditionally contracted to acquire 90% of the shares to which the offer relates and 90% of the voting rights before the expiry of three months after the last day on which the offer can be accepted, the offeror can give notice to those offeree company shareholders who did not accept the offer that it wishes to acquire their shares by the deadline just mentioned.

The squeeze-out notice under s 981 of the CA 2006 entitles, and also obliges, the offeror to acquire the offeree company shareholder's shares on the same terms as those of the takeover offer. For example, if the offer gave shareholders a choice of paper or cash consideration, the same choice must be given to shareholders who did not accept the offer. However, there are some exceptions, for example for certain overseas shareholders. Also, where a cash alternative was due to be provided by a third party who can no longer provide it (eg, through a vendor placing), the offeror must pay a cash equivalent to the offeree shareholder.

The notice must make clear:

(a) that the shareholder must make his choice of consideration known to the offeror, in writing, within six weeks of the notice; and

(b) the default consideration that the shareholder will receive if he does not make his choice known to the offeror.

The offeror must copy the first notice (they are usually distributed in the order they appear on the register of members) to the board of offeree company, together with a statutory declaration that the conditions referred to at **22.7.2.1** above have been satisfied.

22.7.2.3   The acquisition

Six weeks after serving the notice (CA 2006, s 981(6) and (7)) the offeror must send to the offeree:

(a) a copy of all the squeeze-out notices;

(b) a stock transfer form executed by a person the offeror nominates on behalf of the shareholder; and

(c)   the consideration for the shares.

The offeree will then:

(a)   register the offeror as the holder of the shares to which the s 979 notice relates (s 981(7)); and

(b)   hold the consideration on trust for the relevant shareholders (s 981(9)).

Section 982(4) and (5) provide what should happen on the rare occurrence that a shareholder cannot be traced.

22.7.2.4   Preventing the acquisition

Section 986(1) of the CA 2006 provides that any shareholder who receives a s 979 notice can apply to the court, within six weeks of the date on which the notice was given, for an order preventing the acquisition or allowing the acquisition on such terms as the court thinks fit (ie on different terms). However, the courts are unlikely to be willing to investigate the merits of an offer which has already been endorsed by at least 90% of shareholders, unless there is a compelling reason to do so.

22.7.3   The right of minority shareholders to be bought out ('sell-out')

Section 983 of the CA 2006 provides a mechanism whereby an offeree company shareholder who has refused the takeover offer may be able to 'sell out', that is, force the offeror to purchase his shares.

22.7.3.1   The conditions

Two conditions must be satisfied before an offeree company shareholder can require the offeror to take his shares:

(a)   the takeover offer condition; and

(b)   the 90% sell-out threshold condition.

The takeover offer condition

This condition is the same as for squeeze out (see **22.7.2.1**).

The 90% sell-out threshold condition

A shareholder can compel the offeror to buy his shares only when the offeror has obtained an interest in 90% in value carrying 90% of the voting rights of *all the shares in the offeree company* (or the class of shares to which the shares of the minority shareholder belong). Note that the 90% sell-out threshold is different to the 90% squeeze-out threshold (see **22.7.2.1**). For squeeze-out purposes, only shares *to which the offer relates* are included. For sell-out, *all shares* in the offeree are included. Shares held by the offeror before the offer document was posted will count, therefore, towards the 90% sell-out threshold but not towards the 90% squeeze-out threshold (as they would not be shares to which the offer relates). Irrevocable undertakings and shares held by any associate of the offeror also count towards the sell-out threshold.

The effect of this difference is that the offeror may meet the 90% sell-out threshold before it meets the 90% squeeze-out threshold.

Example

Imagine that the offeror acquired a 25% stake in the offeree before it posted the offer document. For squeeze-out, the offeror must acquire 90% of the remaining 75%, which will be triggered once the offeror has acquired an aggregate of 92.5 (90% x 75% + the existing 25%). For sell-out, the offeror must acquire only 90%, and the 25% already acquired will count towards this.

22.7.3.2   The sell-out notice

The average shareholder of an offeree company is unlikely to be aware of his sell-out rights. Therefore, within one month of reaching the 90% threshold, the offeror must notify those shareholders who have not accepted the offer of their sell-out rights (under CA 2006, s 984(3)). If the sell-out notice is served before the end of the offer period, it must state that the offer is still open for acceptance.

The offeror must specify the period within which the shareholder can take up his sell-out rights. Under the CA 2006 procedure, they must be exercised within three months from the last date on which the offer could be accepted or, if later, the date on which the offeror serves the sell-out notice.

Of course, if (as is usual) the offeror has already served a squeeze-out notice to acquire the minority shareholders' shares, the offeror does not need to notify the shareholders of their sell-out rights. For this reason, sell-out notices are not common.

If the minority shareholder exercises his sell-out rights, the offeror must acquire those shares on terms which are the same as the terms of the takeover offer, or on such other terms as may be agreed. If the offer included a choice of consideration, the position is similar to that under squeeze-out: if the chosen consideration is not available, the shareholder will receive the cash equivalent. The court has an overriding jurisdiction, on the application of either the shareholder or the offeror, to determine the terms on which the shares will be acquired.

22.7.3.3   The notice from the shareholder

The shareholder must give the offeror written notice of his desire to sell out. If there is a choice of consideration under the offer, the shareholder must state his choice of consideration.

22.8   Future developments

The Panel is consulting on various minor amendments to the City Code. This affects rr 12.2, 25.3, 26, 27.1, 36 and the Notes to rr 2.7, 9.1 and 16.

Chapter 23
Takeovers: Merger Control

23.1 Introduction

It is difficult to define exactly what constitutes a merger and, from a legal perspective, the distinction between a takeover and a merger is not particularly important. It follows that the law relating to *merger* control can, in fact, apply to a *takeover*.

Why would the competition authorities be concerned with a takeover? Imagine that a supermarket chain, with a 40% market share, decides to make an offer for the entire issued share capital of one of its rivals, which also has a 40% market share. If the takeover is successful, the result will be a supermarket chain with a substantial share of the market. It will have considerable bargaining power and is likely to be able to source produce on very competitive terms. It is possible that other, smaller supermarket chains might be squeezed out of the market, and that others who wanted to break into the market would not be able to do so. The probable result of all of this is that consumers on their weekly shop will have less choice and may have to pay more. This is why the competition authorities will keep a close eye on any takeover offer.

Practically, the corporate lawyer will enlist the help of his colleagues who specialise in competition law, who will then advise in relation to any merger control issues relevant to the takeover. However, this means that the corporate lawyer must be aware of the merger control rules to know when he should consult such colleagues; and, as always, the corporate lawyer will need to know enough about the process to follow discussions at meetings and to understand the impact it may have on the takeover offer. This chapter aims to introduce the corporate lawyer to the basics of merger control.

23.2 Merger control provisions in the City Code

23.2.1 Rule 12

23.2.1.1 Rule 12.1

Rule 12.1 of the City Code provides that it must be a term of the takeover offer that the offer will lapse if, before the first closing date, or the date the offer becomes or is declared unconditional as to acceptances (see **Chapter 22**), whichever is later:

(a) the offer is referred to the Competition Commission for investigation under the Enterprise Act 2002 (EA 2002) (see **23.4**); or

(b) the offer gives rise to a concentration with a Community dimension within the scope of the EC Merger Regulation (see **23.3**), and the European Commission either:

    (i) commences Phase II proceedings under art 6(1)(c) of the EC Merger Regulation (see **23.3.6**), or

    (ii) refers the matter back to the UK under art 9 of the EC Merger Regulation and there is then a reference to the Competition Commission (see **23.3.7**).

23.2.1.2   Rule 12.2

If the offer, or possible offer, is referred to the Competition Commission, or if the European Commission initiates Phase II proceedings, the offer period will end. A new offer period will begin when the 'competition reference period' ends. The competition reference period is defined in the City Code. It covers the period between the date a reference is made, or Phase II proceedings are initiated, and the date the authorities reach a decision on the matter. The rationale for this is due to the fact that the investigation by the relevant competition authorities will usually take a substantial period of time. It would be unreasonable to leave the offeree company subject to the uncertainty of a bid, possibly for many months, which may or may not be permitted once the authorities reach a decision.

23.2.2   Rule 35.1

The effect of r 35.1 of the City Code is that, if the offer has lapsed under r 12 (see **23.2.1**), the offeror cannot make another offer for the offeree for at least 12 months from the date of lapse, unless the Panel consents. The Panel will usually provide such consent if the offer lapsed under r 12 but subsequently received competition clearance.

23.3   EU merger control

On 1 May 2004 the Regulation on the control of concentrations between undertakings (EC Council Regulation 139/2004) (the 'EC Merger Regulation') came into force.

The EC Merger Regulation will apply if the takeover constitutes a *concentration* with a *Community dimension*. If the takeover fulfils these criteria then, subject to limited exceptions (see **23.3.7** below), the Regulation will apply to the exclusion of any national competition law rules and the takeover will fall within the exclusive jurisdiction of the European Commission. This is intended to relieve the burden on the parties to the takeover, by reducing the number of regulatory authorities to which they are subject. For this reason the Regulation is often referred to as 'the one-stop shop'.

If the takeover does not fulfil these criteria, then it falls outside the scope of the EC Merger Regulation, but it may still be caught by domestic merger control rules (see **23.4**).

23.3.1   Concentration

Article 3 of the EC Merger Regulation provides that a concentration can arise on:

(a)   the merger of two or more independent undertakings;

(b)   the acquisition of direct or indirect control of the whole or part of an undertaking or undertakings; or

(c)   some joint ventures.

This definition reflects the fact that the EC Merger Regulation is drafted to catch more than simply takeovers. It is category (b) which may bring a takeover within the EC Merger Regulation. Note, however, that (b) can also can also catch acquisitions which do not constitute a takeover, for example the acquisition of assets.

'Control' in the context of the EC Merger Regulation is wider than the definition of 'control' in the City Code. In this context, 'control' means more than just voting control. It includes, for example, where one party can exercise 'decisive influence' (art 3). An 18% shareholding was considered insufficient to confer control (EDF/AEM/Edison Case COMP/M.3729), whereas in Aker Maritime/Kvaerner Case COMP/M.2117 a 26.7% share constituted control for the purposes of the EC Merger Regulation.

23.3.2 Community dimension

Article 1 provides that a concentration will have a Community dimension if, subject to the two-thirds rule (see **23.3.3** below), it fulfils certain turnover criteria. There are two alternative sets of criteria, namely:

(a) the aggregate *worldwide* turnover of *all* parties exceeds €5,000m (approx. £4,000m); and

(b) the aggregate *Community-wide* turnover of *at least two* of the parties exceeds €250m (approx. £200m);

or

(a) the aggregate *worldwide* turnover of *all* parties exceeds €2,500m (approx. £2,000m);

(b) the aggregate *Community-wide* turnover of *at least two* of the parties exceeds €100m (approx. £80m); and

(c) in at least three Member States:

    (i) the aggregate *national* turnover of *all* the parties exceeds €100m (approx. £80m), and

    (ii) the aggregate *national* turnover of *at least two* of the parties exceeds €25m (approx. £20m).

Even if the takeover does not have a Community dimension, art 4, para 5 of the EC Merger Regulation provides that, if the takeover is capable of being reviewed under the national competition laws of at least three Member States, the parties can request the European Commission to take jurisdiction over the offer instead of the national authorities.

23.3.3 The two-thirds rule

A concentration will not have a Community dimension if each of the parties achieves more than two-thirds of its Community-wide turnover within the same Member State. This means, practically, that if the main impact of the takeover is within one Member State, it will not have a Community dimension. It could, of course, still be caught by the national competition rules of that Member State.

Practically, when calculating whether a takeover falls within the jurisdiction of the Commission, it is helpful to check whether the two-thirds rule applies *before* applying the 'Community dimension' test referred to at **23.3.2** above. If the two-thirds rule applies then there is no need to apply the 'Community dimension' test; the Commission will not have jurisdiction.

23.3.4 Notification

If the takeover constitutes a concentration with a Community dimension then the EC Merger Regulation provides that the parties must notify the European Commission before completion. The takeover cannot complete until the European Commission clears it. The notification should answer the Commission's questionnaire, Form CO, which requires considerable information about the parties and the transaction. Form CO is annexed to Regulation 802/2004/EC, which implemented the EC Merger Regulation.

23.3.5 Phase I

Article 10 provides that the Commission has 25 working days from the date of notification to decide that it:

(a) does not have jurisdiction because the offer does not fall within the scope of the EC Merger Regulation;

(b) will clear the offer (because it does not create or strengthen a dominant position in any relevant Community market);

(c)   will allow the offer to proceed, subject to conditions (for example, the parties agreeing to dispose of part of the business);

(d)   will investigate the offer further (because it has serious doubts whether it creates or strengthen a dominant position in any relevant Community market); or

(e)   will refer the offer back to a Member State under art 9 (because the offer threatens to affect significantly competition in a distinct market within that Member State; see **23.3.7**).

This period of 25 days is referred to as Phase I. Phase I can be extended to 35 working days in certain circumstances, such as where remedies are offered, or where a Member State makes a request for an art 9 reference (see **23.3.7** below).

If the Commission decides (d) above, and commences a Phase II investigation, or decides (e) above, and refers the offer back to the OFT and there is then a subsequent reference to the Competition Commission, the takeover offer will lapse under r 12.1 of the City Code (see **23.2.1.1(b)**).

23.3.6   Phase II

If, at the end of Phase I, the Commission decides to investigate the offer further (option (d) above), that period of investigation is referred to as Phase II. As explained at **23.2.1**, if the European Commission initiates Phase II proceedings, the offer period will end. Phase II can last up to 90 working days. It can be extended by 20 working days at the request of the parties or the Commission (if the parties so consent). Phase II will automatically be extended by 15 working days where the parties offer remedies after the 54th day of the Phase II investigation.

At the end of Phase II, the Commission can:

(a)   clear the takeover; or

(b)   allow the takeover to proceed subject to certain conditions; or

(c)   block the takeover.

23.3.7   Exceptions

As **23.3** explains, the EC Merger Regulation is intended to be a 'one-stop shop' and applies to the exclusion of any national competition laws. However, a Member State can intervene to request repatriation of a case if it can demonstrate to the Commission that a reference back to the national authorities is necessary:

(a)   to protect legitimate interests (such as national security) (art 21); or

(b)   because the takeover threatens to affect significantly competition in a distinct market within that Member State (art 9).

For an example of (a), Spain imposed conditions on E.ON's and Enel and Acciona's bids for Endesa, the Spanish energy company, even though the European Commission had cleared both bids, arguing that it was necessary to protect Spain's national interests. The ECJ ruled that Spain had broken EU law by not withdrawing conditions on E.ON's bid (*Commission v Spain* (E.ON/Endesa) Case C-196/07). Separately, Poland launched infringement proceedings against the European Commission claiming that it had failed to take account of its interests in clearing the Unicredito/HVB merger (Case COMP/M.3894).

For an example of (b), in 1996, under the original EC Merger Regulation, the European Commission granted the UK's request for an art 9 reference with regard to the offer by a German pharmaceuticals company for Lloyds Chemists.

Ryanair to appeal ruling on Aer Lingus bid

Russell Hotten

Michael O'Leary, chief executive of Ryanair, said he would appeal a European Union ruling to block his airline's €1.48bn (£1bn) bid for rival Aer Lingus. Yesterday, Brussels' Competition Commissioner Neelie Kroes said a Ryanair takeover would create a monopoly and be bad for the consumer.

Mr O'Leary said the ruling was a 'nakedly political decision' to support the Dublin government which is against an Aer Lingus takeover and still retains a 25.3pc stake in the privatised airline.

Ms Kroes began investigating the proposed takeover in December, following Ryanair's hostile bid in October. She said yesterday the combined airline would dominate routes between London and Dublin, and said Ryanair's offer to sell take-off and landing slots was not enough.

'What we're doing is preventing a monopoly from emerging in air transport,' Ms Kroes said. 'Ireland, being an island, depends heavily on air transport.' The decision is the first merger veto since December 2004, when she blocked plans by EDP-Energias de Portugal SA to take joint control of Gas de Portugal.

Mr O'Leary said he was confident of getting the ruling overturned, claiming that a merger would guarantee fare reductions of more than €100m annually for consumers. Ryanair said the Commission was wrong to block its takeover when they had cleared others between Air France and KLM and between Lufthansa and Swissair.

But Ms Kroes said her decision was 'legally sound' and will 'bear the scrutiny' of the courts.

Ryanair offered to sell up to two-thirds of Aer Lingus's slots at Heathrow, and offered the disposal of slots at other European airports, still leaving the airline with about 80pc of the market at Dublin's airport.

'The slots were not enough,' Ms Kroes said.

Source: *The Telegraph*, 28 June 2007

23.4 UK merger control

The EA 2002 governs merger control in the UK. The merger control provisions of the EA 2002 will apply to a takeover if:

(a) it is a *relevant merger situation*; and

(b) it results, or may be expected to result, in a *substantial lessening of competition*.

23.4.1 Relevant merger situation

A takeover will constitute a 'relevant merger situation' if:

(a) it is not caught by the EC Merger Regulation (see **23.3** above);

(b) two or more enterprises cease to be distinct;

(c) the time limit for a reference to the Competition Commission has not yet expired; and

(d) either:

    (i)   the turnover test, or

    (ii) the share of supply test,

    is fulfilled.

Let us now consider each criterion in turn.

23.4.1.1 Not caught by the EC Merger Regulation

As stated at **23.3** above, if the takeover constitutes a *concentration* with a *Community dimension* then, subject to limited exceptions (see **23.3.7** above), the Regulation will apply to the exclusion of any national competition law rules. It is only if the takeover falls outside the EC Merger Regulation that the provisions of the EA 2002 may apply.

23.4.1.2 Two or more enterprises cease to be distinct

Enterprise

Section 129(1) of the EA 2002 provides that an 'enterprise' is the activities, or part of the activities, of a business. 'Business' in this context includes an undertaking carried on for gain or reward, or in the course of which goods or services are supplied otherwise than free of charge.

At least one of the enterprises must be carried on in the UK (or by, or under the control of, a body corporate which is incorporated in the UK).

Ceasing to be distinct

Enterprises cease to be distinct under s 26 of the EA 2002 if they are brought under common ownership or control. An offeror will acquire 'control' for these purposes if:

(a)   it can materially influence the policy of the offeree ('influential control');

(b)   it can control the policy of the offeree ('de facto control'); or

(c)   it has a controlling interest (that is, more than 50% of the voting rights) in the offeree ('legal control').

The OFT has produced guidelines to assist in the determination of (a) and (b). BSkyB Group plc's 17.8% acquisition in ITV plc in 2006 was held to amount to 'influential control' by the Competition Commission. This was because, in practice, it would enable BSkyB to block special resolutions (due to average ITV shareholder turnout), BSkyB was the only significant industry shareholder and it could get board representation due to its shareholding. It was ordered in 2008 to cut its shareholding to 7.5%, although this is still being challenged. BSkyB has launched an appeal against the decision at the Court of Appeal.

23.4.1.3   The time limit for a reference has not expired

Section 24 of the EA 2002 provides that the takeover must either:

(a)   not have completed; or

(b)   have completed less than four months ago (unless the takeover completed without a public announcement, and the OFT was not notified, in which case the four-month period will start from the time the takeover comes to the attention of the OFT).

23.4.1.4   The turnover test and the share of supply test

To qualify for investigation the takeover must satisfy at least one of the following tests:

Turnover test

This test (EA 2002, s 28(1)) will be fulfilled if the value of the *UK* turnover of the *offeree* exceeds £70m.

Share of supply test

This test (EA 2002, s 23) will be fulfilled if:

(a)   after the takeover, the offeror will supply, or be supplied with, at least 25% of a defined class of goods or services which are supplied in the UK (or a substantial part of it (see below)); or

(b)   if this was already the case before the takeover, then after the takeover the offeror acquires an even greater share of the market.

Example

If X plc, which controls 20% of the market for the supply of cars, makes a bid for Y plc, another car manufacturer with a market share of 10%, this would fulfil the market share test, because after the takeover X plc would own at least 25% of the UK car market. Even if X plc owned 25% of the car market before the takeover, the takeover of Y plc would still qualify for a reference as it would increase further X plc's market share.

Note that the example above assumes that the car market is a distinct market. In practice it can be difficult for lawyers to predict what is a distinct market. Ultimately, the OFT has the discretion to determine what the criteria are for determining the market. For example, it may consider the number of units sold, the value of goods sold, or the number of employees engaged in the manufacture or supply of the goods.

In a case (decided under the Fair Trading Act 1973, the predecessor of the EA 2002) involving bus companies in the north of England, the House of Lords held that South Yorkshire, which amounts to 1.65% of the area of the UK and which contained 3.2% of the population, was a substantial part of the UK for the purposes of the EA 2002 (*South Yorkshire Transport Ltd and Another v Monopolies and Mergers Commission and Another* [1993] 1 All ER 289).

23.4.2   A substantial lessening of competition

The EA 2002 does not define this term, which is referred to in practice as an 'SLC'. However, the explanatory notes to the EA 2002 state the following:

> Similar language is used in the legislation controlling mergers in a number of other major jurisdictions including the US, Canada, Australia and New Zealand. The concept is an economic one, best understood by reference to the question of whether a merger will increase or facilitate the exercise of market power (whether unilateral or through co-ordinated behaviour), leading to reduced output, higher prices, less innovation or lower quality of choice. A number of matters may be potentially relevant to the assessment of whether a merger will result in a substantial lessening of competition. These matters include, but are not limited to:
> - market shares and concentration
> - extent of effective competition before and after the merger
> - efficiency and financial performance of firms in the market
> - barriers to entry and expansion in the relevant market
> - availability of substitute products and the scope for supply – or demand – substitution
> - extent of change and innovation in a market
> - whether in the absence of the merger one of the firms would fail and, if so, whether its failure would cause the assets of that firm to exit the market, and
> - the conduct of customers or of suppliers to those in the market.

In fact, the OFT ('Mergers: Substantive Assessment' (OFT 516), May 2003) and the Competition Commission ('Merger References – Competition Commission Guidelines') produce their own guidance for determining whether or not there has been an SLC.

HMV cleared by watchdog to bid for Ottakar's

The competition watchdog gave the green light yesterday for the bookseller Waterstone's to swallow its smaller, independent rival Ottakar's.

The provisional verdict of a three-month investigation by the Competition Commission – that a takeover by HMV, the owner of Waterstone's, will not reduce competition by much – is likely to dismay authors, if not the City.

When HMV's £96.8m bid was accepted by Ottakar's in September, a flurry of publishers and high-profile writers claimed the deal would narrow the choice of titles available on the high street.

The commission disagreed, finding an amalgamation of the two would not create any "substantial lessening of competition", even in towns with a Waterstone's and an Ottakar's.

Diana Guy, who led the inquiry, said in a statement: "There is growing competition from supermarkets and internet retailers in terms of both price and range, so the merged company would have little ability to raise prices either on bestsellers or other titles."

The commission also agreed with HMV that such a deal would see Waterstone's heavier distribution clout push a wider range of books into Ottakar's shops.

HMV's offer of 440p per Ottakar's share lapsed in December, when the proposal was referred to the commission by the Office of Fair Trading. The high street music group had trumped a management buyout attempt, led by the managing director James Heneage, pitched at 400p a share.

HMV, advised by the Swiss investment bank UBS, is expected to keep its powder dry until the commission publishes its final findings on 22 May. Then it is likely to return with another offer, significantly lower than before, since Ottaker's trading has deteriorated significantly since HMV first made its interest known. Nick Bubb, an analyst at the investment bank Evolution Group, thought HMV need not pay more than 300p a share to secure an agreed takeover with Ottakar's board.

Other experts, including Richard Ratner at Seymour Pierce, told clients HMV would not need to bid more than 400p a share unless a rival predator, such as WH Smith, emerged.

He, like HMV, applauded the commission's decision, congratulating the watchdog for rejecting "hypocritical" arguments that a combined group would choke the availability of less popular books. "The publishers have been shedding crocodile tears for the authors and the public," he said. "At the same time, they are supplying Amazon and the supermarkets at lower prices than the specialist booksellers are getting."

The prospect of a second bid from HMV spurred Ottakar's shares 25.75p to 350.75p, valuing it at £71.8m. HMV shares eased 0.25p to 173.75p.

HMV has the been the subject of takeover interest from the private equity group Permira. Talks broke down over price.

Source: *The Independent*, 31 March 2006

23.4.3   The competition authorities

The EA 2002 is administered by the following authorities:

23.4.3.1   The Office of Fair Trading ('OFT')

The OFT is the government department which conducts the initial merger control investigation. If the OFT decides that:

(a)   the takeover constitutes a relevant merger situation (see **23.4.1** above); and

(b)   the takeover has resulted, or may be expected to result, in an SLC within any UK market(s) for goods or services (see **23.4.2** above),

then s 33(1) of the EA 2002 provides that it must refer the case to the Competition Commission (see **23.4.3.2** below). In *OFT v IBA Health Limited* [2004] EWCA Civ 142, concerning the takeover by iSoft plc of Torex plc, the Court of Appeal clarified the meaning of 'or may be expected to result'.

The Court ruled that the relevant test is whether the OFT itself believes that a takeover may be expected to result in an SLC. The OFT does not have to predict what the Competition Commission might decide. The OFT's belief must be more than a mere suspicion, and must be reasonable and objectively justified. If the OFT believes the probability of the takeover resulting in an SLC is over 50%, it should refer. If it believes the probability is less than 50%, but more than fanciful, the OFT has discretion as to whether to refer.

As stated at **23.2.1** above, if the OFT does refer to the Competition Commission a takeover which is subject to the City Code, the takeover must lapse.

23.4.3.2   The Competition Commission

The Competition Commission is a statutory body which is independent of the Government. It must investigate takeovers which the OFT refers to it. In doing so, under ss 35 and 36 of the EA 2002 it must decide:

(a)   whether the takeover has resulted, or will result, in an anti-competitive outcome. Note that this involves deciding whether it is more likely than not that the takeover has resulted, or will result, in a substantial lessening of competition. The OFT, in contrast, only had to reasonably believe that there had been, or might be, an SLC; and

(b)   (if there is, or will be, an anti-competitive outcome) what remedies are appropriate.

The Competition Commission has the power to require attendance of witnesses and production of documents. It must take into account any representations made to it by those with a substantial interest in the subject matter of the reference.

Within 24 weeks from the date of the reference, the Competition Commission must consider the reference and make its decisions. In exceptional circumstances the 24-week period can be extended by up to a further eight weeks. It will then publish a report on its assessment of the takeover, the remedies it recommends and the reasons for its decisions. The report will be made available on the Competition Commission's website.

A guidance note, 'Merger References – Competition Commission Guidelines', which sets out how the Competition Commission will assess cases, is also available on its website.

23.4.3.3   The Secretary of State for Business, Innovation and Skills

The Secretary of State's power to intervene in merger control decisions is limited to mergers involving particular public interest issues. In such cases, the Secretary of State, rather than the OFT, can decide, first, whether to refer the merger to the Competition Commission and, secondly, whether to follow the Competition Commission's decision.

In the first use of this power under the EA 2002, the Secretary of State intervened in relation to BSkyB Group plc's acquisition of 17.9% of the shares of ITV plc. The Competition Commission subsequently held the purchase to be anti-competitive and ordered the sale of just over 10% of the shareholding. This decision is still being litigated and is due to be heard by the Court of Appeal.

23.4.4   Notification

23.4.4.1   Clearance

Unlike the EC merger control process, outlined at **23.3.4** above, under the EA 2002 there is no obligation on the parties to notify a merger or proposed merger to the OFT. However, most parties to a takeover choose to notify the OFT in advance in order to seek formal confirmation that it will not be referred to the Competition Commission. This is referred to as a 'clearance'. The takeover process is expensive in terms of both time and money, and the parties will want to be certain that they are not going to make such an investment only for the Competition Commission to block the takeover at a later stage in the process.

There are two methods by which the parties to a takeover can seek clearance:

(a)   *Informal submission.* The offeror (possibly jointly with the offeree) submits a memorandum, together with supporting documentation, to the OFT, explaining why a Competition Commission reference is not required and why clearance should be given.

(b)   *Pre-notification by statutory merger notice.* This method is for pre-notification only, ie, it can only be used for a takeover which has been announced but not yet completed. The parties file a merger notice which answers questions about the takeover and which markets it may affect.

23.4.4.2   Informal advice

In its guidance, 'Mergers – jurisdictional and procedural guidance' of June 2009, the OFT, as an alternative to the offeror seeking clearance, will consider applications for informal advice on competition and jurisdictional issues arising out of a prospective merger situation that has not yet been made public. This procedure is only available to confidential transactions where there is a good faith intention to proceed, and where the OFT's duty to refer to the Competition Commission is a genuine issue. Details of this guidance are available from the OFT website.

23.4.5   Undertakings

If the OFT concludes that, having considered the two issues referred to at **23.4.3.1** above, it is under an obligation to make a reference to the Competition Commission, the parties may be able to provide certain undertakings with the effect that the takeover will not result in an SLC and so no reference is necessary. A good example of the use of undertakings was in the bid by Morrison for Safeway, which was cleared when Morrison provided an undertaking (referred to as a 'divestment undertaking') that it would sell 53 Safeway stores (see the article below).

Note that the provision of undertakings can have an impact on the takeover timetable (see **Table 22.1** above), so any party seeking to provide such undertakings must keep the Panel informed and seek any necessary extensions to the timetable.

Safeway ruling gives Morrison pole position

By SUSANNA VOYLE, Retail Correspondent

SIR KEN Morrison was last night in pole position to buy Safeway and turn his regional supermarket chain into a national group after a government ruling barred larger rivals from bidding and tied the hands of financial buyers.

Patricia Hewitt, trade and industry secretary, yesterday said she had accepted the findings of the Competition Commission which blocked any bid for Safeway by the big three supermarkets – Tesco, Asda/Wal-Mart and J. Sainsbury.

Wm Morrison Supermarkets. however, was cleared to bid as long as it agrees to sell 53 Safeway stores.

The ruling will he seen as a triumph for Sir Ken, who has emerged triumphant after a tough, costly and protracted auction. He built-up Morrison from market stalls run by his father in Bradford in the 1940s.

Competition experts said the wording of the ruling – which stressed the need to maintain four strong national groups and prevent the big three from getting bigger –

blocked any attempt by financial bidders to buy Safeway and break it up.

Shares in Safeway fell heavily, closing down 20½p at 276p, fractionally below the now-lapsed 277½p-a-share offer made by Morrison in January.

Philip Green, the only financial bidder left in the running, said he was studying the commission's findings. "We have got to read the report over the weekend," he said.

However, people close to Mr Green admitted that the findings limited his room for manoeuvre. "For a financial buyer, selling stores to the big three supermarket groups is the main tool in your kitbag," said one

Analysts said any financial bidder would have to buy Safeway to run it – but would be unlikely to bid as much as Morrison, which will achieve cost savings from merging the businesses.

The commission's report said any bid by the three biggest supermarket operators would reduce competition and could lead to higher prices for consumers. It also ex-

pressed concern about the effects on suppliers.

Tesco, Asda/Wal-Mart and Sainsbury said that they were disappointed but accepted the findings and would study the 500-page report to see how many stores they might pick up.

Asda has all but ruled out the possibility of seeking a judicial review.

The commission has set down strict rules about the disposal of the 53 stores. Ironically, it appears that Tesco, Britain's biggest retailer, stands to get the most. It qualifies to buy 21, Sainsbury 20 and Asda just 12.

Tesco was the only supermarket group to see its shares rise yesterday – up 6p at 241p – as investors took the view that its dominance of the market had been set in stone for years to come.

Shares in Morrison fell 8¼p to 211¾p – meaning a retabled bid at the same level would value Safeway at £2.95bn.

Source: *Financial Times*, 27 September 2003.

23.4.6   The lawyer's role

The competition lawyer's role will include the following:

(a)   giving preliminary advice on the likelihood of the takeover being referred to the Competition Commission;

(b)   co-ordinating other advisers who may be needed to formulate arguments in favour of the offeror, such as economists and, perhaps, political consultants;

(c)   preparing submissions on behalf of the offeror, and representing the offeror at hearings before the Competition Commission; and

(d)   negotiating undertakings to ensure the takeover falls outside the scope of the EA 2002.

23.4.7 EC v UK merger regimes

The relationship between the two merger control regimes is illustrated in the case of the takeover of Midland by HSBC (see **22.4.5.4**). After HSBC made its initial offer for Midland, Lloyds announced that it would make a rival offer subject to certain pre-conditions. One of the pre-conditions was that the merger authorities would treat the rival bids alike.

The HSBC offer amounted to a concentration with a Community dimension, and so fell within the scope of the EC Merger Regulation's one-stop shop. However, the European Commission cleared the takeover, as HSBC and Midland competed in only a few sectors and, even after the takeover, intense competition in those sectors would remain.

The proposed Lloyds offer, however, did not fall within the scope of the EC Merger Regulation. Instead, it became apparent that it would be referred under the UK merger control regime. Lloyds therefore withdrew its offer, and the takeover by HSBC was successful.

23.5   Future developments

The European Commission has undertaken a review of the EC Merger Regulation and prepared a report in June 2009. This report found that generally the EC Merger Regulation was working well and generally allocating mergers correctly either to the European or national regulator. There were some concerns about the cumbersome and lengthy referral process and disparities in national laws governing merger control. The Commission will assess at an unspecified future stage whether it is appropriate to make amendments to the current system.

Part V
AIM

Chapter 24
AIM

24.1 Background to this chapter

The focus of Parts I to IV of this book is the company which has its shares admitted to listing on the Official List and admitted to trading on the Main Market. However, in recent years much of the IPO activity in the UK has been on the Alternative Investment Market (AIM). As a result, it would be impossible to practice corporate law in today's climate without at least a basic understanding of AIM, how it compares to the Main Market, and the perceived advantages and disadvantages of an admission to AIM. This chapter seeks to help provide that basic understanding.

24.2 An introduction to AIM

In 1995 the Stock Exchange established the AIM as its international market for smaller and growing companies. The Stock Exchange states that its objective 'was to offer smaller and companies – from any country and any industry sector – the chance to raise capital on a market with a pragmatic and appropriate approach to regulation. With this in mind, AIM was designed to be a highly flexible public market offering many unique attributes both for companies and investors'.

The AIM has proved a great success. In fact, until recently it was the most successful growth market in the world. Since its launch in 1995, over 3,000 companies have joined the market (now known simply as 'AIM'), raising more than £62 billion between them. As at August 2009, 1,365 companies were trading on AIM, with a total market capitalisation in excess of £51 billion. The market's appeal is not limited to the UK. The popularity of AIM with overseas companies has risen sharply in the last few years before the onset of the recession. In 2001, 16 overseas companies joined AIM; this rose to 124 in 2006, but fewer international companies are now joining, with only one new admission in the year 2009 up to August, reflecting the global recession. However, there were still some 317 overseas companies trading on AIM as at August 2009. That said, AIM is certainly feeling the effects of the recession currently. In the first half of 2009, around 150 companies de-listed or left the market. Some went insolvent, a couple transferred to the Main Market, but for the majority it seems that the costs of being on AIM (LSE and professional advisers' fees) and the tighter regulatory controls outweighed the benefits of being on AIM. How long this trend will continue remains to be seen. Typically it is the smaller companies who list on AIM, particularly natural resources, technology and fast-growing companies. Some AIM companies are household names, such as Tottenham Hotspur FC, Majestic Wine and Coffee Republic.

The AIM is regulated by the Stock Exchange. The Listing Rules do not apply to AIM companies (see **3.5.2**). Instead, AIM companies are governed by a set of rules helpfully titled the 'AIM Rules'. The AIM Rules are drafted with smaller companies in mind; they do not contain much legal or technical jargon, and this allows them to be applied flexibly and comprehensively. The AIM Rules are available from the AIM section of the Stock Exchange website.

24.3   Why AIM?

The advantages of listing, set out at **1.7** above, apply equally to AIM as they do to the Main Market. As, typically, it is the smaller, emerging companies who join AIM, the accessible market, easy access to capital and acquisition opportunities and employee incentives AIM offers are a particular draw.

So why join AIM rather than the Main Market? In addition to the benefits referred to above, the following aspects of AIM can render it more attractive than the Main Market, particularly for smaller companies:

(a)   AIM is easier to access:

   (i)   it has reduced eligibility requirements (see **24.4**); and

   (ii)   the role of the 'Nomad' (see **24.4.1**) means the admission process is more straightforward.

(b)   AIM has a more relaxed regulatory regime. In particular:

   (i)   there are reduced disclosure requirements;

   (ii)   shareholder approval is required only for a reverse takeover (see **24.6.2.3**) and a disposal resulting in a fundamental change of business (see **24.6.2.4**). (However the company may still require shareholder approval for ancillary matters relating to other transactions, such as a disapplication of s 561 pre-emption rights);

   (iii) the brevity of the AIM Rules means that the day-to-day regulatory work required for an AIM company costs less than that for a Main Market company; and

   (iv)   the requirement for a prospectus is confined to circumstances where there is a public offer; s 85(2) of the FSMA 2000 does not apply to AIM companies (see **24.5.1**).

(c)   AIM offers tax advantages for investors which the Main Market does not.

24.4   Eligibility criteria

The minimum requirements for admission to AIM are different from those of the Main Market (set out at **4.3.1.1** above). For example, unlike the Main Market, there are no requirements in respect of market capitalisation, the number of shares in public hands, or a three-year trading record.

In order to seek admission to AIM, a company must comply with the following minimum requirements:

(a)   *Incorporation.* The company must be legally established under the laws of its place of incorporation and be able to offer shares to the public. (For UK companies this means being a public company – CA 2006, s 755.)

(b)   *Transferability.* Shares admitted to AIM must be freely transferable (AIM Rules, r 32).

(c)   *Whole class to be listed.* All issued shares of the same class must be admitted (AIM Rules, r 33).

(d)   *Electronic settlement.* All shares admitted must be eligible for electronic settlement (AIM Rules, r 36).

(e)   *Accounts.* The company (if it is incorporated in an EEA country) must have published accounts which conform with International Accounting Standards ('IAS') (AIM Rules, r 19).

(f)   *Nominated adviser.* A nominated adviser (known as a 'Nomad') (AIM Rules, r 1) and broker must be appointed and retained at all times (AIM Rules, r 35) (see **24.4.1**).

In the event that the company's main activity is a business that has been generating revenue and/or been independent for less than two years prior to its admission to AIM, it is subject to a condition that all directors (and their families) and employees who hold an interest in the company and certain substantial shareholders must agree not to dispose of their interests for at least one year following admission to AIM (AIM Rules, r 7).

24.4.1   The Nomad

One of the most significant differences between the Main Market and AIM is the role of the Nomad. The Stock Exchange attributes the success of AIM largely to the role of the Nomad, whose role is to guide a company first through the admission process and then through its life as a publicly quoted company. Rule 1 of the AIM Rules requires every AIM company to retain a Nomad at all times. The Stock Exchange will suspend trading in the securities of any AIM company which ceases to have a Nomad, and cancel their admission if a replacement Nomad is not appointed within one month.

24.4.1.1   Duties and responsibilities

Under r 39 of the AIM Rules the Nomad must comply with a separate set of rules, the AIM Rules for Nominated Advisers (the 'Nomad Rules', available in the AIM section of the Stock Exchange website). These separate rules for Nomads were introduced on 20 February 2007 and strengthen the regulatory regime for AIM-quoted companies.

The Nomad owes its responsibilities solely to the Stock Exchange.

The Nomad must:

(a)   ensure that the company is suitable for admission to AIM; and

(b)   advise and guide the company through the admission process and, once quoted on AIM, on its on-going responsibilities; and

(c)   most importantly, confirm to the Stock Exchange that any admission document or prospectus (see **24.5**) complies with the requirements of Sch 2 to the AIM Rules.

Schedule 3 to the AIM Rules for the Nominated Adviser sets out more detailed responsibilities which the Nomad must perform. These are split into three categories: Admission Responsibilities; Ongoing Responsibilities; and Engagement Responsibilities. Only the first two are relevant to a Nomad acting for a new applicant to AIM.

A list of Nomads is available on the AIM section of the Stock Exchange website.

These various Responsibilities are presented as a group of overriding principles accompanied by supporting 'actions'. The Nomad must comply with the principles in all cases. The 'actions' provide examples of how the principles translate into practice.

For example, principle AR1 requires the Nomad to gain a sound understanding of the company and its business before admission to AIM. One of the listed actions states that usually this requires the Nomad to visit the material places of operation of the company and to meet the directors. This ensures a business trip to Qatar, Kazakhstan, China or Wigan, depending on the company concerned.

There are two points to note about these actions. First, they are not an exhaustive list of actions the Nomad should take and, secondly, although the Stock Exchange usually will expect all the actions listed to be taken, a Nomad can take alternative action if it feels it is better suited to achieving the principle.

24.4.1.2   Admission Responsibilities

In preparation for admission of the new applicant company to AIM the Nomad is obliged, in addition to AR1 mentioned at **24.4.1.1** above, to assess the suitability of the board of directors (individually and collectively), oversee the due diligence procedure leading up to flotation, satisfy itself that the admission document complies with Sch 2 to the AIM Rules, and ensure that procedures are in place for the new company and its directors to comply with the AIM Rules.

24.4.1.3   Ongoing Responsibilities

Once the company has been admitted to AIM, the Nomad must consult regularly with the company, review announcements before they are released to the market, monitor trading in the company's shares, particularly when there is unpublished, price-sensitive information in existence, and advise on any changes to the board of directors to the company and their impact.

In July 2009 the LSE publicly censured and fined Astaire Securities plc £225,000 for breaches of the AIM Rules and Nomad Rules for failing adequately to assess an AIM company's appropriateness for AIM and for not correcting misleading announcements made by the company once it had joined AIM.

24.4.2   The broker

An AIM company must retain a broker at all times (AIM Rules, r 35). If there is no registered market maker (see **2.5.2**), the broker must use its best endeavours to find a matching business. Any member firm of the Stock Exchange can act as broker, subject to any required authorisation by any other regulator. A list of member firms is available on the AIM section of the Stock Exchange website, together with a separate list of brokers which AIM companies have appointed.

24.5   The marketing document

When a company applies for admission to AIM, or is raising further equity finance on AIM then, subject to exemptions (see **24.5.1.1**), the company must produce a prospectus or admission document.

24.5.1   Prospectus or admission document?

Chapter 6 sets out in detail when a company is required to publish a prospectus pursuant to the Prospectus Rules and s 85 of the FSMA 2000. As stated at **3.5.1** above, the Prospectus Rules apply to AIM companies as well as to Main Market companies. A prospectus is required when a company either:

(a)   offers transferable securities to the public in the UK (s 85(1)); or

(b)   requests admission of transferable securities to trading on a regulated market situated or operating in the UK (s 85(2)).

The AIM is a Stock Exchange regulated market. This is not the same as a 'regulated market' for the purposes of s 85(2), so s 85(2) does not apply to an AIM company, or a company seeking admission to AIM. Nevertheless, if an AIM company, or a company seeking admission to AIM, is offering transferable securities to the public in the UK then, subject to any applicable exemptions, a prospectus is required under s 85(1).

As a company seeks admission to AIM because of its more flexible and pragmatic regulation, typically AIM companies will seek to structure any public offer to fall within one of the exemptions set out in s 85(5) and s 86 of the FSMA 2000.

If a prospectus is not required, the company must instead produce an admission document, which must comply with a more relaxed version of the Prospectus Rules (see **24.5.3**). An admission document does not require approval by the FSA.

24.5.1.1 Exemptions to the requirement to produce a prospectus

The exemptions to s 85(1) are set out at **6.4.1.5** above. The most common exemptions relied upon by AIM companies are those set out at **6.4.1.5(a)** (offers to qualified investors), **6.4.1.5(b)** (offers to fewer than 100 persons in each EEA State who are not qualified investors), **6.4.1.5(c)** (offers involving significant investment by each investor), **6.4.1.5(d)** (small offers) and **6.4.1.5(f)** (offers in conjunction with takeovers by way of share for share exchange).

If any of the FSMA 2000 exemptions to s 85(1) apply, a prospectus will not be required (remember that s 85(2) is not relevant in relation to AIM). In practice, any sizeable rights issue or open offer to raise further finance will tend to be to more than 100 persons per EEA State (as is the case with the Main Market), and therefore in these circumstances it will be necessary to draft a prospectus and have it approved by the FSA.

24.5.2 Responsibility

The directors take overall responsibility for a prospectus or admission document (although a third party may take responsibility for a specific part of the document). The directors are responsible for ensuring compliance with the AIM Rules.

24.5.3 Content requirements

24.5.3.1 Prospectus

The content requirements of a prospectus are as set out in the Prospectus Directive (see **6.5**).

24.5.3.2 Admission document

The Stock Exchange has carved out certain requirements of the Prospectus Rules in relation to the content requirements of an admission document. The carve-outs reflect the nature of AIM and the companies admitted to it.

The content requirements for what lawyers refer to as 'an AIM-PD: compliant admission document' are set out in Sch 2 to the AIM Rules (which includes Annexes I–III of the Prospectus Rules, as amended by the AIM Rules).

24.6 Continuing obligations

24.6.1 The general obligation of disclosure

As stated at **3.5.3**, the Disclosure Rules do not apply to AIM companies. The AIM Rules set out continuing obligations of AIM companies. The primary obligation is a general duty of disclosure, set out in r 11. This provides that every AIM company must announce, without delay, any new developments which:

(a)   are not public knowledge; and

(b)   concern a change in its financial condition, its sphere of activity, performance of its business, or its expectation of its performance; and

(c)   if made public, would be likely to cause a substantial movement in the price of its securities.

The company must make the announcement through an RIS. Rule 10 of the AIM Rules requires that the company must take reasonable care to ensure that any information it notifies is not misleading, false or deceptive, and does not omit anything likely to affect the import of such information.

24.6.2   Specific disclosure obligations

In addition to the general obligation to disclose price-sensitive information, there are specific obligations of disclosure in relation to the following:

(a)   substantial transactions (AIM Rules, r 12 – see **24.6.2.1** below);

(b)   related party transactions (AIM Rules, r 13 – see **24.6.2.2** below);

(c)   reverse takeovers (AIM Rules, r 14 – see **24.6.2.3** below);

(d)   any disposal resulting in a fundamental change of business (AIM Rules, r 15 – see **24.6.2.4** below);

(e)   changes to significant shareholders (DTR 5 and AIM Rules, r 17 – see **24.6.2.5** below);

(f)   dealings by directors (AIM Rules, r 17);

(g)   changes in directors, directors' details, Nomad or broker (AIM Rules, r 17);

(h)   any material change in the company's actual trading performance or financial condition and between any profit forecast or estimate included in the company's admission document, or which is otherwise in the public domain (AIM Rules, r 17); and

(i)   other matters set out in r 17 of the AIM Rules, including any change to the accounting reference date, registered office address or legal name; and

(j)   an AIM company must also disclose certain key information on its website, including its current constitutional documents and the number of AIM securities in issue (AIM Rules, r 26).

24.6.2.1   Substantial transactions

An AIM company must disclose details of any substantial transactions. A transaction is substantial if it exceeds 10% of any class test contained in Sch 3 to the AIM Rules (which are similar to the class tests set out in Chapters 10 and 11 of the Listing Rules; see **19.4**).

Schedule 3 sets out a comparison between the size of the transaction and the company itself in respect of the following:

(a)   gross assets;

(b)   profits;

(c)   turnover;

(d)   consideration to market capitalisation; and

(e)   gross capital (in acquisitions of a company or business).

If a transaction is revenue in nature and occurring in the ordinary course of the business of the company, or if it has undertaken to raise finance that does not involve a change in the fixed assets of the company, it will not constitute a substantial transaction.

If the transaction exceeds 10% of any of the Sch 3 class tests, and so constitutes a substantial transaction, an announcement must be made pursuant to Sch 3, which must include the prescribed information set out in Sch 4. However, there is no requirement for shareholder approval, or for a circular (unless required under another AIM rule). Directors of AIM companies often cite this as a reason for choosing AIM over the Main Market.

24.6.2.2   Related party transaction

If the transaction is with a related party (as defined by the AIM Rules) and exceeds 5% in any of the Sch 3 class tests referred to at **24.6.2.1** above, an announcement containing prescribed information as set out in Sch 4 to the AIM Rules is required. The announcement must include a statement that the directors (excluding any director involved directly in the transaction) having consulted with the company's Nomad, consider that the terms of the transaction are fair and reasonable.

Where the class test exceeds 0.25%, the company must include details of any related party transaction in the company's annual audited accounts (see **24.6.3**).

24.6.2.3   Reverse takeover

A transaction (or transactions) over a 12-month period which either:

(a)   exceeds 100% of any of the class tests sets out in Sch 3 to the AIM Rules (see **24.6.2.1**); or

(b)   results in a fundamental change to the AIM company's business, board or voting control (or, in the case of an investing company (as defined by the AIM Rules), departs substantially from the investing strategy set out in its prospectus or admission document),

constitutes a reverse takeover under r 14 of the AIM Rules.

The company must:

(a)   obtain shareholder approval (by ordinary resolution) for any reverse takeover (and any agreement relating to a reverse takeover must be conditional upon such approval);

(b)   prepare a prospectus or admission document, which must describe the circumstances and details of the transaction and convene the shareholders' general meeting to approve the transaction; and

(c)   make an announcement of the reverse takeover via an RIS without delay, disclosing the information specified by Sch 4 to the AIM Rules.

Trading in the company's securities will be cancelled. The enlarged entity must seek admission in the same manner as any other AIM company which is seeking admission for the first time.

24.6.2.4   Disposal resulting in a fundamental change of business

Any disposal which, when aggregated with any other disposal or disposals over the previous 12 months, exceeds 75% in any of the class tests set out in Sch 3 to the AIM Rules (see **24.6.2.1** above), is a disposal which results in a fundamental change of business ('DFCB') (AIM Rules, r 15).

A DFCB must be conditional on shareholder approval (by ordinary resolution). A circular containing the information specified in Sch 4 to the AIM Rules (and r 13 insofar as the disposal is to a related party) and a notice of GM will also be required. Where the proposed disposal will divest the company of all, or substantially all, of its trading business activities, the circular must state the company's investing strategy going forward.

The Company must notify an RIS of the DFCB without delay, disclosing the information specified by Sch 4 to the AIM Rules. If the transaction involves a related party, the information required by r 13 of the AIM Rules must also be disclosed.

The company must make the acquisition (or acquisitions) constituting a reverse takeover under r 14 of the AIM Rules within 12 months of receiving the consent of its shareholders.

24.6.2.5   Changes to significant shareholders

Under r 17 of the AIM Rules, any changes of 1% or more in the holdings of 'significant shareholders' must be notified to an RIS as soon as possible. A significant shareholder is one who holds at least 3% of the AIM company's issued share capital.

In addition, DTR 5 applies to AIM companies incorporated under the Companies Act or who have their principal place of business in the UK (see **15.6**).

Generally compliance with DTR 5 will satisfy r 17 of the AIM Rules, but the Stock Exchange has pointed out that whereas DTR 5 requires the disclosure to be made as soon as possible on receipt of a notification and by no later than the end of the third trading day following notification (DTR 5.8.12R), under r 17 it must be made without delay, which is a stricter standard.

24.6.3   Financial information

The AIM Rules supplement the financial obligations in the CA 2006 with more specific obligations.

The AIM Rules require companies incorporated in an EEA country to publish annual accounts in accordance with International Accounting Standards ('IAS'). The company must send the accounts to shareholders within six months of the end of the financial year to which they relate (AIM Rules, r 19). The accounts must disclose any transaction with a related party (see **24.6.2.2**), whether or not previously disclosed under the AIM Rules, where any of the class tests in Sch 3 to the AIM Rules exceed 0.25%, and specify the identity of the related party and the consideration for the transaction.

The AIM Rules also require listed companies to prepare interim reports in respect of the first six months of the company's financial period. The company must publish the interim reports within three months of the end of this half-year period and must notify an RIS that they have been published (AIM Rules, r 18).

In addition, although not mandatory, it is best practice for an AIM company to include a statement in its annual report which discloses the extent to which it has complied with the principles set out in the Combined Code (see **24.7**).

24.6.4   Share dealing code

Rule 21 of the AIM Rules prohibits dealings by directors and other key employees in the company's securities in certain circumstances, such as when they are in possession of unpublished price sensitive information, or during specified periods. Generally, companies admitted to AIM will adopt a share dealing code which complies with this Rule.

24.7   Corporate governance

The Combined Code does not apply to AIM companies, although they are encouraged to comply with it. In February 2007, the Quoted Company Alliance ('QCA') published corporate governance guidelines for AIM companies. The guidelines are available to order from the QCA website.

Appendices

Appendix 1

The Admission and Disclosure Standards

Note: The Admission and Disclosure Standards dated 7 September 2009 are reproduced below. Please check the Stock Exchange website for any updates.

Admission and Disclosure Standards

Admission

Conditions

1.1 An **application** for **admission to trading** of any **class** of **securities** must:

    (a) relate to all **securities** of that **class**, issued or proposed to be issued; or

    (b) if **securities** of that **class** are already **admitted to trading** on the **Exchange's** markets, relate to all further **securities** of that **class**, issued or proposed to be issued.

    Guidance to Rule:

    *For UK incorporated **issuers** that are subject to the **Listing Rules**, an **application** for **admission to trading** of any **class** of **securities** must relate only to **securities** which are **listed** or proposed to be **listed** or equivalent.*

1.2 An **issuer** must be in compliance with the requirements of:

    (a) any **securities regulator** by which it is regulated; and /or

    (b) any stock exchange on which it has **securities** admitted to trading.

1.3 In the case of **transferable securities**, all such **securities** must be **freely negotiable**.

1.4 **Securities** that are **admitted to trading** on any **regulated market** operated by the **Exchange** must be capable of being traded in a fair, orderly and efficient manner.

1.5 The **Exchange** may refuse an **application** for the **admission to trading** of **securities** if it considers that:

    (a) the **applicant's** situation is such that **admission** of the **securities** may be detrimental to the orderly operation of the **Exchange's** markets or to the integrity of such markets; or

    (b) the **applicant** does not or will not comply with the **Standards** or with any special condition imposed upon the **applicant** by the **Exchange**

1.6 **Issuers** must confirm that they meet the criteria and requirements of the market to which they are applying.

Guidance to Rule:

Issuers *are required to tick the relevant box on **Form 1** to indicate the market to which they are seeking **admission**.*

*In addition to 1.5, as per our obligations under **MiFID** Article 40(1), the **Exchange** has the right to refuse an **application** for the **admission to trading** of **securities** to a <u>certain market or segment</u> if it considers that the **securities** are better suited to another of the **Exchange's** markets or segments.*

Settlement

1.7   To be **admitted to trading**, **securities** must be eligible for electronic **settlement**. The **issuer** must inform the **Exchange** at the time of **application** of the chosen **settlement** mechanism and if **settlement** restrictions will apply to any **securities** to be considered for **admission**.

Guidance to Rule:

*The **Exchange** requires that an appropriate **settlement** solution is in place, dependent upon the trading platform on which the **securities** are to be traded. Accepted **central security depositaries** include Euroclear UK & Ireland, Euroclear Bank, or Depository Trust Clearing Corporation (DTCC). Other **central securities depositaries** will be considered on a case-by-case basis.*

Issuers *should note that certain of the **Exchange's** trading platforms have trades cleared by **central counterparties**. In these cases, the **securities** have to be eligible for the **central counterparty** as well as the central **securities** depositary. In addition, the **central counterparties** may restrict where **settlement** can occur.*

Communication

1.8   An **issuer** must identify a contact within their organisation who will be responsible for communications between the **Exchange** and the **issuer**, and the **Exchange** must be notified in writing of any changes thereafter. An **issuer** may also wish to use a **nominated representative**.

Guidance to Rule:

*The contact should be fully conversant with the **issuer's** responsibilities under these **Standards** and will be either a director or senior employee of the **issuer** in a position to act as the **Exchange's** point of contact. At the **issuer's** discretion, a **nominated representative** from another organisation may also be selected to act as the primary day-to-day contact point with the **Exchange** on regulatory matters. Details of the **issuer's** contact and any **nominated representative** must be provided to the **Exchange** at the time of*

*the **application** for **admission to trading** and the **Exchange** must be notified in writing of any changes thereafter.*

1.9   An **issuer** must ensure that all information provided in connection with the **application** for **admission to trading** is in all respects accurate, complete and not misleading. An **issuer** must be open, honest and co-operative in all dealings with the **Exchange**.

Admission process

1.10   An **issuer** proposing to admit **securities** that will be the subject of an **application** for **admission to trading** must agree the timetable for the **admission to trading** of those **securities** <u>in advance</u> with **Issuer Implementation**.

1.11   The **issuer** must contact the **Exchange** no later than ten **business days** before the **application** is to be considered.

Application

Provisional application

2.1   To ensure the **Exchange** can properly consider any **application** for **admission to trading** the **issuer** must:

- For new **issuers**, submit the **Form 1** and a draft copy of the **prospectus** to the **Issuer Implementation** team by no later than 12:00 at least ten **business days** prior to the day on which the **issuer** is requesting that the **Exchange** consider the **application** for **admission to trading**.

- The submission of **Form 1** shall be provisional. Formal **application** will only be deemed to be made when a **prospectus** relating to the **securities** to be **admitted to trading** has been approved.

- The final **application** form and supporting documentation must be submitted in accordance with 2.4.

Guidance to Rule:

Admission of securities becomes effective only when the decision of the Exchange to admit the securities to trading has been announced by the Exchange via an RNS announcement. (Should RNS suffer an outage; a notice will be made available at the Exchange's ground floor reception).

Except where otherwise agreed by the Exchange, applications for admission to trading are considered on business days between the hours of 09:00 and 17:30.

The Exchange will not, except in exceptional circumstances, admit securities to trading until each of the documents and items listed in 2.4 have been lodged with the Exchange (marked for the attention of Issuer Implementation) in so far as they are relevant. All documents submitted to the Exchange must be written in English and submitted electronically.

An invoice for the admission fee will be raised on admission. The admission fee is calculated in accordance with the Exchange's scale of fees (see 3.14). Payment of the admission fee must be received no later than 30 days after the date of this invoice.

2.2   When further issues of **securities** are allotted of the same **class** as **securities** already **admitted to trading** on our markets, **issuers** must assess whether a **prospectus** or **listing particulars** is required. If applicable, these must be submitted to the relevant **EEA competent authority** for review and approval in accordance with its rules. **Application** for **admission** of such further **securities** must be made at the same time as the **application** for **listing**, but no later than 48 hours before the **application** is to be considered.

2.3   If a request for **when issued dealing** is to be considered:

- A provisional "**when issued dealing application** form" (which can be found at the **Exchange's** website: www.londonstockexchange.com/mainmarket/usefuldocuments) must be received with the provisional **Form 1**.

- The final "**when issued dealing application** form" must be submitted (with a draft **stabilisation** notice if appropriate) at least two **business days** prior to the day on which the **issuer** is requesting that the **Exchange** consider the **application** for **when issued dealing.**

    Guidance to Rule:

    *The **Exchange** reserves the right to refuse **when issued dealing.***

    *Where applicable, we reserve the right to only allow unconditional dealing when confirmation has been received that **admission to trading** on a **regulated market** and/or **listing** is effective.*

Documents

Before admission

2.4   Except as set out in paragraphs 2.1, 2.2, 2.3 or 2.7, or as otherwise agreed by the **Exchange**, the following documents must be submitted to the **Issuer Implementation** team by no later than 12:00 at least two **business days** prior to the day on which the **issuer** is requesting that the **Exchange** consider the **application** for **admission to trading**:

2.4.1 **Issuers** not covered by 2.4.2 or 2.4.3 below:

- an **application** for **admission to trading** on the finalised **Form 1** issued by the **Exchange** signed by a duly authorised officer of the **issuer**; and

- an electronic copy of any **prospectus, listing particulars, passport**, circular, announcement or other document relating to the issue, together with copies of any notice of meeting referred to in such documents; and

- written confirmation of the number of **securities** to be allotted or issued pursuant to the board resolution should be provided and must be received by the **Exchange** no later than 16:30 on the day before **admission** is expected to become effective. By prior arrangement this may be extended 07:00 on the day of **admission**. The **applicant** should keep a copy of the resolution on its records for six years; and

- a copy of the **Regulated Information Service** announcement relating to the **admission.**

Guidance to Rule:

*For **issuers** for whom the **EEA competent authority** is the **FSA**:*

*If the **FSA** has considered an application for **listing** and the **securities** the subject of the **application** are not all allotted and **admitted** following the initial allotment of the **securities** (for example, under an **offer for subscription**), further allotments of **securities** may be **admitted** if, before 4pm on the day before **admission** is sought, the **Issuer Implementation** team has been informed and the **FSA** has been provided with the information required under **Listing Rule** 3.3.4 A R.*

2.4.2   **Issuers** of **covered warrants** and **Listed Structured Products**:

- a finalised **Form 1**, a pricing supplement, indicative price and a completed trading form (depending on the number of products being launched simultaneously) and any additional forms, as appropriate. If products are to be launched under a new **prospectus** then it must also be provided. The relevant form(s) are available at:
www.londonstockexchange.com/mainmarket/usefuldocuments

2.4.3   **Issuers** of **ETFs** or **ETCs** or similar products:

- a finalised **Form 1**, a static data form and Pricing Supplement. If products are to be launched under a new **prospectus**, then it must also be provided. For **ETFs**, written confirmation must be provided that the **ETF** is **listed** by an **EEA competent authority**. The relevant form(s) are available at:
www.londonstockexchange.com/mainmarket/usefuldocuments

After admission

2.5   Where relevant, a statement of the number of **securities** which were, in fact, issued and, where different from the number which were the subject of the **application**, the aggregate number of **securities** of that **class** in issue must be lodged with the **Exchange** (marked for the attention of **Issuer Implementation**) as soon as it becomes available.

techMARK™ and techMARK mediscience™

2.6   An **issuer** may also seek **admission** to techMARK™ or **techMARK mediscience**™. The process and criteria for such **applications** are set out in the relevant **Eligibility Criteria**, which is updated from time to time and is available from our website (www.londonstockexchange.com/techMARK)

Block admission

2.7   Where an **issuer** admits **securities** that will not be allotted prior to **admission** and that do not require a **prospectus** or **listing particulars**, the **issuer** may make an **application** for a **block admission**. These **admissions** may be pursuant to employee share schemes or the exercise of options.

Guidance to Rule:

*Where an **issuer** wishes to admit **securities** on a regular basis, they may make an **application** for a **block admission**. **Block admissions** will usually be for the reasons stated in rule 2.7 but the Exchange will consider requests for other reasons. The Exchange will monitor the correct usage of this facility and the number of **block admission applications** per **issuer**.*

Issuance programmes

2.8   Where **specialist securities** or **certificates representing shares** are issued under an issuance programme, an **applicant** must submit a subsequent **application** for **admission to trading** in the case of an increase in the maximum number of **securities** which may be in issue and **listed** at any one time under an issuance programme.

If the **Exchange** approves the **application**, it will **admit to trading** all **securities** which may be issued under the programme within 12 months after the publication of the **prospectus** or **listing particulars**, subject to the **Exchange** receiving:

(a) advice of the final terms of each issue;

(b) electronic copies of any supplementary **prospectus** or **listing particulars**; and

(c) confirmation that the **securities** in question have been issued.

2.9   The final terms of each issue which is intended to be **admitted to trading** must be submitted in writing to the **Exchange** as soon as possible after they have been agreed and in any event no later than 14:00 on the day before **admission** is required to become effective. The final terms may be submitted by the **issuer** or its **nominated representative**.

Continuing obligations

General

3.1   In order for its **securities** to be **admitted to trading** and to remain on the **Exchange's markets**, **issuers** must be in compliance with:

   (a) the requirements of any **securities regulator** by which it is regulated; and/or

   (b) the requirements of any stock exchange on which it has **securities** admitted to trading, and

   (c) the provisions set out in the **Standards**, including any modification to the application of the **Standards** which has been notified via our website.

3.2   **Issuers** must notify the **Exchange** without delay of any change of status of the information provided under 2.1-2.2, in respect of the **listing** or **admission to trading** (or cancellation from trading) of the **issuer's securities** on any other exchange or trading platform, where such **admission** or cancellation is at the application or agreement of the **issuer.**

3.3   The **Exchange** may make additions to, dispense with or modify the application of the **Standards** (either unconditionally or subject to conditions) in such cases and by reference to such circumstances as it considers appropriate.

3.4   **Issuers** and their **nominated representatives** must provide to the **Exchange** any information or explanation that the **Exchange** may reasonably require for the purpose of verifying whether the **Standards** are being or have been complied with or which relates to the integrity or orderly operation of the **Exchange's** markets.

   Guidance to Rule:

   *Where an issuer has a website where it regularly publishes company information, they should inform the **Stock Situation Analysis Team** of the website address.*

Timetable for corporate actions

3.5   An **issuer** must contact the **Stock Situation Analysis Team** in advance of any announcement of the timetable for any proposed action affecting the rights of existing holders of its **securities** traded on our markets. Except in the case of a dividend timetable notification (which are subject to rule 3.8), the reference to 'in advance' means that the **Exchange** should receive the proposed timetable by no later than 09:00 on the day before the proposed announcement.

3.5 - 3.9 do not apply to **issuers** of **depositary receipts** or **specialist securities**. **Issuers** of **depositary receipts** must observe their obligations under 3.10.

3.6   The Exchange may require amendments to the timetable, as and when considered necessary. The **Stock Situation Analysis Team** will liaise with the **issuer** and its advisors as appropriate.

A timetable which has not been cleared in advance with the **Stock Situation Analysis Team** but which has been announced to the market, may be subject to change if required by the **Stock Situation Analysis Team**. If this situation occurs a further correcting announcement must be made to the market.

3.7   Any proposed amendments to a timetable, including amendment to the publication details of any announcement, must be immediately notified to the **Stock Situation Analysis Team**.

Guidance to Rules:

Rules 3.5 – 3.7 relate to proposed timetables for all corporate actions for ***securities admitted to trading*** *on the* ***Exchange's*** *markets, for example:*

- *Corporate actions where an* ***ex date*** *is required (dividends,* ***scrip dividends, DRIPs,*** *dividend* ***currency elections, open offers, rights issues, bonus issues, capitalisation issues, return of capital/cash, demergers, enfranchisements).***

- *Other events for which clearance of timetables is required are:*
  - *tender/repurchase offers,*
  - *consolidations, subdivision,*
  - *capital reorganisations,*
  - *schemes of arrangement/ schemes of reconstruction,*
  - *some types of conversions/redemptions, or*
  - *any other corporate event which could affect the rights of existing holders of* ***securities admitted to trading on our markets.***

3.8   Where applicable, dividend payments must follow the procedures set out in the guidance below:

Guidance to Rule:

A dividend timetable which follows the guidelines set by the Dividend Procedure Timetable, published on the ***Exchange's*** *website at www.londonstockexchange.com/mainmarket/usefuldocuments, need not be notified to the* ***Exchange*** *in advance, provided the announcement of the dividend includes:*
- *the amount of the dividend (should state whether the dividend is net or gross); and*
- *the record and payment dates; and*

- the availability of any **scrip dividend, DRIP** or **dividend currency option;** and
- publish the election date.

Dividends outside of the guidelines detailed in the Dividend Procedure Timetable must be agreed by the **Stock Situation Analysis Team** in advance of the announcement of the dividend. The **Scrip Dividend** and **DRIP** documentation must also be lodged with the **Stock Situation Analysis Team**.

The term 'dividend' includes all interest payments for **debt securities** (excluding **specialist securities**). An announcement is not required for interest payments, but the **Exchange** must receive notification of any payment no later than seven **business days** prior to the **record date**. This notification must include:

- the appropriate net or gross amount; and
- the record and payment dates; and
- any conversion period details.

Where fixed payment details are available, the **issuer** may use one timetable to inform the **Exchange** of all future payments, providing any subsequent amendments are notified to the **Exchange** immediately.

When an issuer publishes details of future interest payments, they must notify the **Stock Situation Analysis team.**

Timetable for open offer

3.9   The timetable for an **open offer** must ensure that valid claims through the market can be promptly satisfied and must comply with the following:

- there must be a minimum period of at least ten **business days** from the date of posting of the **application** forms to shareholders (or from the date on which the existing **securities** were made 'ex' if that is earlier) until the close of the offer. The **business days** must exclude the **'ex' date** but may include the **application** closing date where the time for closing is no earlier than 11:00. Where the **'ex' date** is earlier than the date of posting, **application** forms must be posted no less than eight **business days** before the close of the offer; and

where possible, the **open offer record date** should be the **business day** before the expected **'ex' date**. A **record date** preceding the **'ex' date** by more than three **business days** will only be approved in exceptional circumstances.

As per 3.5 and 3.6, an **issuer** must contact the **Stock Situation Analysis Team** in advance of any announcement of the timetable for any **open offer**. The reference to 'in advance' means that the **Exchange** should receive the proposed timetable by no later than 09:00 on the day before the proposed announcement. The **Exchange** may require amendments to the timetable,

as and when considered necessary. The **Stock Situation Analysis Team** will liaise with the **issuer** and its advisors as appropriate.

A timetable which has not been cleared in advance with the **Stock Situation Analysis Team** but which has been announced to the market, may be subject to change if required by the **Stock Situation Analysis Team**. If this situation occurs a further correcting announcement must be made to the market.

Continuing obligations for depositary receipt issuers

Timetable for corporate actions for Depositary Receipts

3.10   An **issuer** or its **depositary bank** should contact the **Stock Situation Analysis Team** in advance of any announcement of a timetable for any proposed action affecting the rights of existing holders of its **securities** traded on our markets. The reference to "in advance" means that the **Exchange** should receive the proposed announcement by no later than 9:00 on the day before the proposed announcement.

The **Exchange** may require amendments to the timetable, as and when considered necessary. The **Stock Situation Analysis Team** will liaise with the **issuer** or **depositary bank** as appropriate.

Any proposed amendments to an agreed timetable, including amendment to the published details of any announcement, should immediately be notified to the **Stock Situation Analysis Team**.

3.10 and related guidance must be adhered to by an **issuer** or its **depositary bank** unless otherwise specifically agreed with, and confirmed by, the **Exchange**.

Guidance to Rule:

*3.10 relates to proposed timetables for all corporate actions for **securities admitted to trading** on the **Exchange's** markets, for example: corporate actions where an '**ex date**' is required (**bonus issues**, stock distributions, **rights issues**, **demergers** /spin offs).*

*Issuers will have regard to their domestic regulatory requirements and should discuss possible conflicts between those and **the Standards** with **Stock Situation Analysis Team** in advance, as **issuers** deem necessary.*

*Wherever possible the **record date** should be announced in advance and the '**ex' date** for any of the above corporate actions will be determined by the **Exchange**, dependent on the information received and the type of the corporate action proposed.*

Other events for which clearance of timetables is required are:

- stock splits,
*- **tender/repurchase offers**,*
*- **capital reorganisations**,*
*- or any other corporate action which could affect the rights of existing holders of **securities admitted to trading** on our markets.*

Dividends

*Dividends for **depositary receipts** should be notified to the **Stock Situation Analysis Team** by 09:00 at least three **business days** prior to the dividend **record date**, to allow the **depositary receipt** to be marked Ex Dividend in the normal way, two **business days** prior to the **record date**.*

*In most circumstances the dividend **record date** for the **depositary receipt** will be in line with that of the underlying security. In the event of late notification of the **record date** for the underlying security, or where notice is not received three days prior to the **record date**, the **depositary bank** will be required to set a separate **record date** for the **depositary receipt** to allow the security to be marked Ex Dividend in line with the above timetable.*

*Dividend notifications for **depositary receipts** should include the following details, where available:*

- name of company declaring dividend
- ISIN or CUSIP number
- whether dividend is an approximate or final rate
- amount of the dividend (should state whether the dividend is net or gross and include both rates (if available)
*- **record date***
- payment dates
- any relevant fees or tax charges
*- name of **depositary bank** announcing dividend (including contact details).*

Amendments to constitution

3.11   If an **issuer** of **transferable securities** that have been **admitted to trading** on a **regulated market** (or are the subject of an **application** for **admission to trading** on a **regulated market**) proposes to amend its constitution it must communicate the draft amendment to: (a) the **FSA**; and (b) the **regulated market** on which its **securities** have been **admitted to trading**[3].

In order to fulfil part (b) of this obligation, **issuers** should email details of the amendments to our **Issuer Implementation** team: issuerimplementation@londonstockexchange.com

The communication must be effected without delay but at the latest on the date of calling the general meeting which is to vote on, or be informed of, the amendment.

Guidance to Rule:

*The document should be sent to us when the **issuer** is satisfied it is ready to do so and this should form a part of its communications plan.*

***Issuers** may also choose to make an announcement to the market, via a **Regulated Information Service**, including any draft amendment.*

ETFs

3.12   **Issuers** of **ETFs** for whom the **UKLA** is not the **listing** authority:

(i) must comply with the **listing** rules of the **EEA** state in which they are **listed;**

(ii) must notify a **Regulated Information Service** as soon as possible of all circulars, notices, reports (as required by the **listing** rules of the **EEA** state in which they are **listed**), at the same time as any such documents are issued;

Unless the full text of the document is provided to the **Regulated Information Service**, the notification must set out where copies of the relevant document can be obtained.

(iii) must appoint a registrar in the UK if: (a) there are 200 or more holders resident in the UK; or (b) 10% of more of the equity securities are held by persons resident in the UK.

(iv) must notify a **Regulated Information Service** on a daily basis of the number of outstanding shares and the Net Asset Value per share.

---

[3] **DTR** 6.1.2

Guidance to Rule for issuers of ETFs for whom the UKLA is not the listing authority:

*An issuer must consider its obligations under the **Disclosure and Transparency Rules**. For example, the **Market Abuse Directive** will apply to **ETFs** traded on a **regulated market** and **FSA DTR** 1 and **DTR** 2 will apply to **ETFs admitted to trading** on a **regulated market** in the UK, even if **UKLA** is not the **listing** authority.*

*An **issuer** must also obtain fund recognition from the **FSA** and adhere to the continuing obligations contained within the UCITS Directives[4].*

Settlement

3.13   The **Exchange** requires that the **securities** continue to be eligible for electronic **settlement**, as set out in the Guidance to Rule 1.7.

Fees

3.14   An **issuer** with **securities admitted to trading** shall pay to the **Exchange** all applicable charges set out in the document "Fees for issuers". This publication, as updated from time to time, can be found on our website: www.londonstockexchange.com/mainmarket/usefuldocuments

Suspension

3.15   The **Exchange** will suspend the **admission** to and trading of any **securities** on its markets if a **listing** of such **securities** is suspended.

3.16   The **Exchange** may suspend trading of such **securities** with effect from such time as it may determine, and in such circumstances as it thinks fit where the ability of the **Exchange** to ensure the orderly operation of its markets is, or may be, jeopardised, even if only temporarily.

3.17   Any request by an **issuer** to suspend trading of its **securities** must be confirmed to the **Exchange** in writing by the **issuer** or its **nominated representative**.

3.18   Where trading has been suspended, the **Exchange** may impose such conditions as it considers appropriate prior to resumption of trading.

---

[4] 1 Council Directives 85/611/EEC and 85/611/EEC, as amended.

3.19   An **issuer** must continue to comply with the **Standards**, even when **admission** of its **securities** to trading is suspended, unless the **Exchange** otherwise agrees.

Cancellation

3.20   An **issuer** that wishes the **Exchange** to cancel the right of any of its **securities** to be traded must advise the **Exchange** in writing, not later than 20 **business days** before the date it intends trading in its **securities** to be discontinued. An **issuer** is also required to announce the intended cancellation of any of its **securities** through a **Regulated Information Service**. If agreed, the **Exchange** will announce the intention to cancel individual **securities** through the **Reference Data Service** and the intention to cancel issuers through a **Regulated Information Service**.

3.21   Cancellation will only be effective subject to the **issuer** complying with any legal or regulatory obligation and providing the **Exchange** with appropriate confirmation. Cancellation will only be effective once all outstanding subscriptions, charges, fees or other sums due to the **Exchange** have been paid in full.

Compliance and Appeals

3.22   Where the **Exchange** considers that an **issuer** has contravened the **Standards** and considers it appropriate to impose any sanction as set out in paragraph 3.23, it will follow the procedure set out in the **Compliance Procedures**.

3.23   If an **issuer** has contravened the **Standards**, one or more of the following actions may result:

    a) censure of the **issuer** and, in addition, publication of such censure;

    b) a fine;

    c) an order that the **issuer** make restitution to any **person** (when the **issuer** has profited from a breach of the **Exchange**'s rules at that **person**'s expense);

    d) cancellation of the right of the **issuer** to have its **securities,** or any **class** of its **securities**, traded on the **Exchange's** markets.

3.24   An **issuer** may appeal against a decision of the **Exchange** in relation to the application and interpretation of the **Standards**. The procedures for such appeals are set out in the Compliance Procedures.

Appendix 2
The Combined Code on Corporate Governance
June 2008

PREAMBLE

1. Good corporate governance should contribute to better company performance by helping a board discharge its duties in the best interests of shareholders; if it is ignored, the consequence may well be vulnerability or poor performance. Good governance should facilitate efficient, effective and entrepreneurial management that can deliver shareholder value over the longer term. The Combined Code on Corporate Governance ('the Code') is published by the FRC to support these outcomes and promote confidence in corporate reporting and governance.

2. The Code is not a rigid set of rules. Rather, it is a guide to the components of good board practice distilled from consultation and widespread experience over many years. While it is expected that companies will comply wholly or substantially with its provisions, it is recognised that noncompliance may be justified in particular circumstances if good governance can be achieved by other means. A condition of noncompliance is that the reasons for it should be explained to shareholders, who may wish to discuss the position with the company and whose voting intentions may be influenced as a result. This 'comply or explain' approach has been in operation since the Code's beginnings in 1992 and the flexibility it offers is valued by company boards and by investors in pursuing better corporate governance.

3. The Listing Rules require UK companies listed on the Main Market of the London Stock Exchange to describe in the annual report and accounts their corporate governance from two points of view, the first dealing generally with their adherence to the Code's main principles, and the second dealing specifically with non-compliance with any of the Code's provisions. The descriptions together should give shareholders a clear and comprehensive picture of a company's governance arrangements in relation to the Code as a criterion of good practice.

4. In relation to the requirement to state how it has applied the Code's main principles, where a company has done so by complying with the associated provisions it should be sufficient simply to report that this is the case; copying out the principles in the annual report adds to its length without adding to its value. But where a company has taken additional actions to apply the principles or otherwise improve its governance, it would be helpful to shareholders to describe these in the annual report.

5. If a company chooses not to comply with one or more provisions of the Code, it must give shareholders a careful and clear explanation which shareholders should evaluate on its merits. In providing an explanation, the company should aim to illustrate how its actual practices are consistent with the principle to which the particular provision relates and contribute to good governance.

6. Smaller listed companies, in particular those new to listing, may judge that some of the provisions are disproportionate or less relevant in their case. Some of the provisions do not apply to companies below the FTSE 350. Such companies may nonetheless consider that it would be appropriate to adopt the approach in the Code and they are encouraged to do so. Externally managed investment companies typically have a different board structure, which may affect the relevance of particular provisions; the Association of

Investment Companies's Corporate Governance Code and Guide can assist them in meeting their obligations under the Code.

7.   In their turn, shareholders should pay due regard to companies' individual circumstances and bear in mind in particular the size and complexity of the company and the nature of the risks and challenges it faces. Whilst shareholders have every right to challenge companies' explanations if they are unconvincing, they should not be evaluated in a mechanistic way and departures from the Code should not be automatically treated as breaches. Institutional shareholders should be careful to respond to the statements from companies in a manner that supports the 'comply or explain' principle and bearing in mind the purpose of good corporate governance. They should put their views to the company and be prepared to enter a dialogue if they do not accept the company's position. Institutional shareholders should be prepared to put such views in writing where appropriate.

8.   Companies and shareholders have a shared responsibility for ensuring that 'comply or explain' remains an effective alternative to a rules-based system. Satisfactory engagement between company boards and investors is therefore crucial to the health of the UK's corporate governance regime. Although engagement has been improving slowly but steadily for many years, practical obstacles necessitate a constant effort to keep the improvement going.

9.   Companies can make a major contribution by spreading governance discussion with shareholders outside the two peak annual reporting periods around 31st December and 31st March and by raising further the general standard of their explanations justifying non-compliance. Shareholders for their part can still do more to satisfy companies that they devote adequate resources and scrutiny to engagement.

10.   References to shareholders in this Preamble also apply to intermediaries and agents employed to assist shareholders in scrutinising governance arrangements.

11.   This edition of the Code applies to accounting periods beginning on or after 29 June 2008, and takes effect at the same time as new FSA Corporate Governance Rules implementing European requirements relating to audit committees and corporate governance statements. The relevant sections of these Rules are summarised in Schedule C. There is some overlap between the content of the Code and the Rules, and the Rules state that in these areas compliance with the Code will be deemed sufficient also to comply with the Rules. However, where a company chooses to explain rather than comply with the Code it will need to demonstrate that it nonetheless meets the minimum requirements set out in the Rules.

12.   The Code itself is subject to periodic reviews by the FRC, the latest of which was conducted in 2007 and was generally reassuring about the Code's content and impact. In the normal course of events the next review will take place in 2010.

Financial Reporting Council

June 2008

SECTION 1 COMPANIES

A. DIRECTORS

A.1   The Board

Main Principle

Every company should be headed by an effective board, which is collectively responsible for the success of the company.

Supporting Principles

The board's role is to provide entrepreneurial leadership of the company within a framework of prudent and effective controls which enables risk to be assessed and managed. The board should set the company's strategic aims, ensure that the necessary financial and human resources are in place for the company to meet its objectives and review management performance. The board should set the company's values and standards and ensure that its obligations to its shareholders and others are understood and met.

All directors must take decisions objectively in the interests of the company.

As part of their role as members of a unitary board, non-executive directors should constructively challenge and help develop proposals on strategy. Non-executive directors should scrutinise the performance of management in meeting agreed goals and objectives and monitor the reporting of performance. They should satisfy themselves on the integrity of financial information and that financial controls and systems of risk management are robust and defensible. They are responsible for determining appropriate levels of remuneration of executive directors and have a prime role in appointing, and where necessary removing, executive directors, and in succession planning.

Code Provisions

A.1.1 The board should meet sufficiently regularly to discharge its duties effectively. There should be a formal schedule of matters specifically reserved for its decision. The annual report should include a statement of how the board operates, including a high level statement of which types of decisions are to be taken by the board and which are to be delegated to management.

A.1.2 The annual report should identify the chairman, the deputy chairman (where there is one), the chief executive, the senior independent director and the chairmen and members of the nomination, audit and remuneration committees. It should also set out the number of meetings of the board and those committees and individual attendance by directors[1].

A.1.3 The chairman should hold meetings with the non-executive directors without the executives present. Led by the senior independent director, the non-executive directors should meet without the chairman present at least annually to appraise the chairman's performance (as described in A.6.1) and on such other occasions as are deemed appropriate.

A.1.4 Where directors have concerns which cannot be resolved about the running of the company or a proposed action, they should ensure that their concerns are recorded in the board minutes. On resignation, a nonexecutive director should provide a written statement to the chairman, for circulation to the board, if they have any such concerns.

---

1.   Provisions A.1.1 and A.1.2 overlap with FSA Rule DTR 7.2.7 R; Provision A.1.2 also overlaps with DTR 7.1.5 R (see Schedule C).

A.1.5 The company should arrange appropriate insurance cover in respect of legal action against its directors.

A.2   Chairman and chief executive

Main Principle

There should be a clear division of responsibilities at the head of the company between the running of the board and the executive responsibility for the running of the company's business. No one individual should have unfettered powers of decision.

Supporting Principle

The chairman is responsible for leadership of the board, ensuring its effectiveness on all aspects of its role and setting its agenda. The chairman is also responsible for ensuring that the directors receive accurate, timely and clear information. The chairman should ensure effective communication with shareholders. The chairman should also facilitate the effective contribution of non-executive directors in particular and ensure constructive relations between executive and non-executive directors.

Code Provisions

A.2.1 The roles of chairman and chief executive should not be exercised by the same individual. The division of responsibilities between the chairman and chief executive should be clearly established, set out in writing and agreed by the board.

A.2.2 The chairman should on appointment meet the independence criteria set out in A.3.1 below. A chief executive should not go on to be chairman of the same company. If exceptionally a board decides that a chief executive should become chairman, the board should consult major shareholders in advance and should set out its reasons to shareholders at the time of the appointment and in the next annual report[2].

A.3   Board balance and independence

Main Principle

The board should include a balance of executive and non-executive directors (and in particular independent non-executive directors) such that no individual or small group of individuals can dominate the board's decision taking.

Supporting Principles

The board should not be so large as to be unwieldy. The board should be of sufficient size that the balance of skills and experience is appropriate for the requirements of the business and that changes to the board's composition can be managed without undue disruption.

To ensure that power and information are not concentrated in one or two individuals, there should be a strong presence on the board of both executive and non-executive directors.

The value of ensuring that committee membership is refreshed and that undue reliance is not placed on particular individuals should be taken into account in deciding chairmanship and membership of committees.

No one other than the committee chairman and members is entitled to be present at a meeting of the nomination, audit or remuneration committee, but others may attend at the invitation of the committee.

---

2.   Compliance or otherwise with this provision need only be reported for the year in which the appointment is made

Code provisions

A.3.1 The board should identify in the annual report each non-executive director it considers to be independent[3]. The board should determine whether the director is independent in character and judgement and whether there are relationships or circumstances which are likely to affect, or could appear to affect, the director's judgement. The board should state its reasons if it determines that a director is independent notwithstanding the existence of relationships or circumstances which may appear relevant to its determination, including if the director:

- has been an employee of the company or group within the last five years;

- has, or has had within the last three years, a material business relationship with the company either directly, or as a partner, shareholder, director or senior employee of a body that has such a relationship with the company;

- has received or receives additional remuneration from the company apart from a director's fee, participates in the company's share option or a performance-related pay scheme, or is a member of the company's pension scheme;

- has close family ties with any of the company's advisers, directors or senior employees;

- holds cross-directorships or has significant links with other directors through involvement in other companies or bodies;

- represents a significant shareholder; or

- has served on the board for more than nine years from the date of their first election.

A.3.2 Except for smaller companies[4], at least half the board, excluding the chairman, should comprise non-executive directors determined by the board to be independent. A smaller company should have at least two independent non-executive directors.

A.3.3 The board should appoint one of the independent non-executive directors to be the senior independent director. The senior independent director should be available to shareholders if they have concerns which contact through the normal channels of chairman, chief executive or finance director has failed to resolve or for which such contact is inappropriate.

A.4   Appointments to the Board

Main Principle

There should be a formal, rigorous and transparent procedure for the appointment of new directors to the board.

Supporting Principles

Appointments to the board should be made on merit and against objective criteria. Care should be taken to ensure that appointees have enough time available to devote to the job. This is particularly important in the case of chairmanships.

The board should satisfy itself that plans are in place for orderly succession for appointments to the board and to senior management, so as to maintain an appropriate balance of skills and experience within the company and on the board.

Code Provisions

A.4.1 There should be a nomination committee which should lead the process for board appointments and make recommendations to the board. A majority of members of the

---

3.   A.2.2 states that the chairman should, on appointment, meet the independence criteria set out in this provision, but thereafter the test of independence is not appropriate in relation to the chairman.

4.   A smaller company is one that is below the FTSE 350 throughout the year immediately prior to the reporting year.

nomination committee should be independent non-executive directors. The chairman or an independent non-executive director should chair the committee, but the chairman should not chair the nomination committee when it is dealing with the appointment of a successor to the chairmanship. The nomination committee should make available[5] its terms of reference, explaining its role and the authority delegated to it by the board.

A.4.2 The nomination committee should evaluate the balance of skills, knowledge and experience on the board and, in the light of this evaluation, prepare a description of the role and capabilities required for a particular appointment.

A.4.3 For the appointment of a chairman, the nomination committee should prepare a job specification, including an assessment of the time commitment expected, recognising the need for availability in the event of crises. A chairman's other significant commitments should be disclosed to the board before appointment and included in the annual report. Changes to such commitments should be reported to the board as they arise, and their impact explained in the next annual report.

A.4.4 The terms and conditions of appointment of non-executive directors should be made available for inspection[6]. The letter of appointment should set out the expected time commitment. Non-executive directors should undertake that they will have sufficient time to meet what is expected of them. Their other significant commitments should be disclosed to the board before appointment, with a broad indication of the time involved and the board should be informed of subsequent changes.

A.4.5 The board should not agree to a full time executive director taking on more than one non-executive directorship in a FTSE 100 company nor the chairmanship of such a company.

A.4.6 A separate section of the annual report should describe the work of the nomination committee, including the process it has used in relation to board appointments[7]. An explanation should be given if neither an external search consultancy nor open advertising has been used in the appointment of a chairman or a non-executive director.

A.5   Information and professional development

Main Principle

The board should be supplied in a timely manner with information in a form and of a quality appropriate to enable it to discharge its duties. All directors should receive induction on joining the board and should regularly update and refresh their skills and knowledge.

Supporting Principles

The chairman is responsible for ensuring that the directors receive accurate, timely and clear information. Management has an obligation to provide such information but directors should seek clarification or amplification where necessary.

The chairman should ensure that the directors continually update their skills and the knowledge and familiarity with the company required to fulfil their role both on the board and on board committees. The company should provide the necessary resources for developing and updating its directors' knowledge and capabilities.

Under the direction of the chairman, the company secretary's responsibilities include ensuring good information flows within the board and its committees and between senior management

---

5.   The requirement to make the information available would be met by including the information on a website that is maintained by or on behalf of the company.

6.   The terms and conditions of appointment of non-executive directors should be made available for inspection by any person at the company's registered office during normal business hours and at the AGM (for 15 minutes prior to the meeting and during the meeting).

7.   This provision overlaps with FSA Rule DTR 7.2.7 R (see Schedule C).

and nonexecutive directors, as well as facilitating induction and assisting with professional development as required.

The company secretary should be responsible for advising the board through the chairman on all governance matters.

Code Provisions

A.5.1 The chairman should ensure that new directors receive a full, formal and tailored induction on joining the board. As part of this, the company should offer to major shareholders the opportunity to meet a new nonexecutive director.

A.5.2 The board should ensure that directors, especially non-executive directors, have access to independent professional advice at the company's expense where they judge it necessary to discharge their responsibilities as directors. Committees should be provided with sufficient resources to undertake their duties.

A.5.3 All directors should have access to the advice and services of the company secretary, who is responsible to the board for ensuring that board procedures are complied with. Both the appointment and removal of the company secretary should be a matter for the board as a whole.

A.6   Performance evaluation

Main Principle

The board should undertake a formal and rigorous annual evaluation of its own performance and that of its committees and individual directors.

Supporting Principle

Individual evaluation should aim to show whether each director continues to contribute effectively and to demonstrate commitment to the role (including commitment of time for board and committee meetings and any other duties). The chairman should act on the results of the performance evaluation by recognising the strengths and addressing the weaknesses of the board and, where appropriate, proposing new members be appointed to the board or seeking the resignation of directors.

Code Provision

A.6.1 The board should state in the annual report how performance evaluation of the board, its committees and its individual directors has been conducted. The non-executive directors, led by the senior independent director, should be responsible for performance evaluation of the chairman, taking into account the views of executive directors.

A.7   Re-election

Main Principle

All directors should be submitted for re-election at regular intervals, subject to continued satisfactory performance. The board should ensure planned and progressive refreshing of the board.

Code Provisions

A.7.1 All directors should be subject to election by shareholders at the first annual general meeting after their appointment, and to re-election thereafter at intervals of no more than three years. The names of directors submitted for election or re-election should be accompanied by sufficient biographical details and any other relevant information to enable shareholders to take an informed decision on their election.

A.7.2 Non-executive directors should be appointed for specified terms subject to re-election and to Companies Acts provisions relating to the removal of a director. The board should set out to shareholders in the papers accompanying a resolution to elect a non-executive director why they believe an individual should be elected. The chairman should confirm to shareholders when proposing re-election that, following formal performance evaluation, the individual's performance continues to be effective and to demonstrate commitment to the role. Any term beyond six years (e.g. two three-year terms) for a non-executive director should be subject to particularly rigorous review, and should take into account the need for progressive refreshing of the board. Non-executive directors may serve longer than nine years (e.g. three three-year terms), subject to annual re-election. Serving more than nine years could be relevant to the determination of a non-executive director's independence (as set out in provision A.3.1).

B. REMUNERATION

B.1   The Level and Make-up of Remuneration

Main Principles

Levels of remuneration should be sufficient to attract, retain and motivate directors of the quality required to run the company successfully, but a company should avoid paying more than is necessary for this purpose. A significant proportion of executive directors' remuneration should be structured so as to link rewards to corporate and individual performance.

Supporting Principle

The remuneration committee should judge where to position their company relative to other companies. But they should use such comparisons with caution, in view of the risk of an upward ratchet of remuneration levels with no corresponding improvement in performance. They should also be sensitive to pay and employment conditions elsewhere in the group, especially when determining annual salary increases.

Code Provisions

Remuneration policy

B.1.1 The performance-related elements of remuneration should form a significant proportion of the total remuneration package of executive directors and should be designed to align their interests with those of shareholders and to give these directors keen incentives to perform at the highest levels. In designing schemes of performance-related remuneration, the remuneration committee should follow the provisions in Schedule A to this Code.

B.1.2 Executive share options should not be offered at a discount save as permitted by the relevant provisions of the Listing Rules.

B.1.3 Levels of remuneration for non-executive directors should reflect the time commitment and responsibilities of the role. Remuneration for nonexecutive directors should not include share options. If, exceptionally, options are granted, shareholder approval should be sought in advance and any shares acquired by exercise of the options should be held until at least one year after the non-executive director leaves the board. Holding of share options could be relevant to the determination of a non-executive director's independence (as set out in provision A.3.1).

B.1.4 Where a company releases an executive director to serve as a nonexecutive director elsewhere, the remuneration report[8] should include a statement as to whether or not the director will retain such earnings and, if so, what the remuneration is.

---

8.   As required under the Directors' Remuneration Report Regulations 2002.

Service Contracts and Compensation

B.1.5 The remuneration committee should carefully consider what compensation commitments (including pension contributions and all other elements) their directors' terms of appointment would entail in the event of early termination. The aim should be to avoid rewarding poor performance. They should take a robust line on reducing compensation to reflect departing directors' obligations to mitigate loss.

B.1.6 Notice or contract periods should be set at one year or less. If it is necessary to offer longer notice or contract periods to new directors recruited from outside, such periods should reduce to one year or less after the initial period.

B.2   Procedure

Main Principle

There should be a formal and transparent procedure for developing policy on executive remuneration and for fixing the remuneration packages of individual directors. No director should be involved in deciding his or her own remuneration.

Supporting Principles

The remuneration committee should consult the chairman and/or chief executive about their proposals relating to the remuneration of other executive directors. The remuneration committee should also be responsible for appointing any consultants in respect of executive director remuneration. Where executive directors or senior management are involved in advising or supporting the remuneration committee, care should be taken to recognise and avoid conflicts of interest.

The chairman of the board should ensure that the company maintains contact as required with its principal shareholders about remuneration in the same way as for other matters.

Code Provisions

B.2.1 The board should establish a remuneration committee of at least three, or in the case of smaller companies[9] two, independent non-executive directors. In addition the company chairman may also be a member of, but not chair, the committee if he or she was considered independent on appointment as chairman. The remuneration committee should make available[10] its terms of reference, explaining its role and the authority delegated to it by the board. Where remuneration consultants are appointed, a statement should be made available[11] of whether they have any other connection with the company.

B.2.2 The remuneration committee should have delegated responsibility for setting remuneration for all executive directors and the chairman, including pension rights and any compensation payments. The committee should also recommend and monitor the level and structure of remuneration for senior management. The definition of 'senior management' for this purpose should be determined by the board but should normally include the first layer of management below board level.

B.2.3 The board itself or, where required by the Articles of Association, the shareholders should determine the remuneration of the non-executive directors within the limits set in the Articles of Association. Where permitted by the Articles, the board may however delegate this responsibility to a committee, which might include the chief executive.

B.2.4 Shareholders should be invited specifically to approve all new long-term incentive schemes (as defined in the Listing Rules) and significant changes to existing schemes, save in the circumstances permitted by the Listing Rules.

---

9.   See footnote 4.
10. This provision overlaps with FSA Rule DTR 7.2.7 R (see Schedule C).
11. See footnote 5.

C. ACCOUNTABILITY AND AUDIT

C.1   Financial Reporting

Main Principle

The board should present a balanced and understandable assessment of the company's position and prospects.

Supporting Principle

The board's responsibility to present a balanced and understandable assessment extends to interim and other price-sensitive public reports and reports to regulators as well as to information required to be presented by statutory requirements.

Code Provisions

C.1.1 The directors should explain in the annual report their responsibility for preparing the accounts and there should be a statement by the auditors about their reporting responsibilities.

C.1.2 The directors should report that the business is a going concern, with supporting assumptions or qualifications as necessary.

C.2   Internal Control[12]

Main Principle

The board should maintain a sound system of internal control to safeguard shareholders' investment and the company's assets.

Code Provision

C.2.1 The board should, at least annually, conduct a review of the effectiveness of the group's system of internal controls and should report to shareholders that they have done so[13]. The review should cover all material controls, including financial, operational and compliance controls and risk management systems.

C.3   Audit Committee and Auditors[14]

Main Principle

The board should establish formal and transparent arrangements for considering how they should apply the financial reporting and internal control principles and for maintaining an appropriate relationship with the company's auditors.

Code provisions

C.3.1 The board should establish an audit committee of at least three, or in the case of smaller companies[15] two, independent non-executive directors. In smaller companies the company chairman may be a member of, but not chair, the committee in addition to the independent non-executive directors, provided he or she was considered independent on appointment as chairman. The board should satisfy itself that at least one member of the audit committee has recent and relevant financial experience[16].

---

12. The Turnbull guidance suggests means of applying this part of the Code. Copies are available at www.frc.org.uk/corporate/internalcontrol.cfm
13. In addition FSA Rule DTR 7.2.5 R requires companies to describe the main features of the internal control and risk management systems in relation to the financial reporting process (see Schedule C).
14. The Smith guidance suggests means of applying this part of the Code. Copies are available at www.frc.org.uk/corporate/auditcommittees.cfm
15. See footnote 4.
16. This provision overlaps with FSA Rule DTR 7.1.1 R (see Schedule C).

C.3.2 The main role and responsibilities of the audit committee should be set out in written terms of reference and should include[17]:

- to monitor the integrity of the financial statements of the company, and any formal announcements relating to the company's financial performance, reviewing significant financial reporting judgements contained in them;

- to review the company's internal financial controls and, unless expressly addressed by a separate board risk committee composed of independent directors, or by the board itself, to review the company's internal control and risk management systems;

- to monitor and review the effectiveness of the company's internal audit function;

- to make recommendations to the board, for it to put to the shareholders for their approval in general meeting, in relation to the appointment, re-appointment and removal of the external auditor and to approve the remuneration and terms of engagement of the external auditor;

- to review and monitor the external auditor's independence and objectivity and the effectiveness of the audit process, taking into consideration relevant UK professional and regulatory requirements;

- to develop and implement policy on the engagement of the external auditor to supply non-audit services, taking into account relevant ethical guidance regarding the provision of non-audit services by the external audit firm; and to report to the board, identifying any matters in respect of which it considers that action or improvement is needed and making recommendations as to the steps to be taken.

C.3.3 The terms of reference of the audit committee, including its role and the authority delegated to it by the board, should be made available[18]. A separate section of the annual report should describe the work of the committee in discharging those responsibilities[19].

C.3.4 The audit committee should review arrangements by which staff of the company may, in confidence, raise concerns about possible improprieties in matters of financial reporting or other matters. The audit committee's objective should be to ensure that arrangements are in place for the proportionate and independent investigation of such matters and for appropriate follow-up action.

C.3.5 The audit committee should monitor and review the effectiveness of the internal audit activities. Where there is no internal audit function, the audit committee should consider annually whether there is a need for an internal audit function and make a recommendation to the board, and the reasons for the absence of such a function should be explained in the relevant section of the annual report.

C.3.6 The audit committee should have primary responsibility for making a recommendation on the appointment, reappointment and removal of the external auditors. If the board does not accept the audit committee's recommendation, it should include in the annual report, and in any papers recommending appointment or re-appointment, a statement from the audit committee explaining the recommendation and should set out reasons why the board has taken a different position.

C.3.7 The annual report should explain to shareholders how, if the auditor provides non-audit services, auditor objectivity and independence is safeguarded.

---

17. This provision overlaps with FSA Rules DTR 7.1.3 R (see Schedule C).
18. See footnote 5.
19. This provision overlaps with FSA Rules DTR 7.1.5 R and 7.2.7 R (see Schedule C).

D. RELATIONS WITH SHAREHOLDERS

D.1   Dialogue with Institutional Shareholders

Main Principle

There should be a dialogue with shareholders based on the mutual understanding of objectives. The board as a whole has responsibility for ensuring that a satisfactory dialogue with shareholders takes place[20].

Supporting Principles

Whilst recognising that most shareholder contact is with the chief executive and finance director, the chairman (and the senior independent director and other directors as appropriate) should maintain sufficient contact with major shareholders to understand their issues and concerns. The board should keep in touch with shareholder opinion in whatever ways are most practical and efficient.

Code Provisions

D.1.1 The chairman should ensure that the views of shareholders are communicated to the board as a whole. The chairman should discuss governance and strategy with major shareholders. Non-executive directors should be offered the opportunity to attend meetings with major shareholders and should expect to attend them if requested by major shareholders. The senior independent director should attend sufficient meetings with a range of major shareholders to listen to their views in order to help develop a balanced understanding of the issues and concerns of major shareholders.

D.1.2 The board should state in the annual report the steps they have taken to ensure that the members of the board, and in particular the non-executive directors, develop an understanding of the views of major shareholders about their company, for example through direct face-to-face contact, analysts' or brokers' briefings and surveys of shareholder opinion.

D.2   Constructive Use of the AGM

Main Principle

The board should use the AGM to communicate with investors and to encourage their participation.

Code Provisions

D.2.1 At any general meeting, the company should propose a separate resolution on each substantially separate issue, and should in particular propose a resolution at the AGM relating to the report and accounts. For each resolution, proxy appointment forms should provide shareholders with the option to direct their proxy to vote either for or against the resolution or to withhold their vote. The proxy form and any announcement of the results of a vote should make it clear that a 'vote withheld' is not a vote in law and will not be counted in the calculation of the proportion of the votes for and against the resolution.

D.2.2 The company should ensure that all valid proxy appointments received for general meetings are properly recorded and counted. For each resolution, after a vote has been taken, except where taken on a poll, the company should ensure that the following information is given at the meeting and made available as soon as reasonably practicable on a website which is maintained by or on behalf of the company:

---

20.   Nothing in these principles or provisions should be taken to override the general requirements of law to treat shareholders equally in access to information.

- the number of shares in respect of which proxy appointments have been validly made;
- the number of votes for the resolution;
- the number of votes against the resolution; and
- the number of shares in respect of which the vote was directed to be withheld.

D.2.3 The chairman should arrange for the chairmen of the audit, remuneration and nomination committees to be available to answer questions at the AGM and for all directors to attend.

D.2.4 The company should arrange for the Notice of the AGM and related papers to be sent to shareholders at least 20 working days before the meeting.

SECTION 2   INSTITUTIONAL SHAREHOLDERS

E. INSTITUTIONAL SHAREHOLDERS[21]

E.1   Dialogue with companies

Main Principle

Institutional shareholders should enter into a dialogue with companies based on the mutual understanding of objectives.

Supporting Principles

Institutional shareholders should apply the principles set out in the Institutional Shareholders' Committee's "The Responsibilities of Institutional Shareholders and Agents – Statement of Principles"[22], which should be reflected in fund manager contracts.

E.2   Evaluation of Governance Disclosures

Main Principle

When evaluating companies' governance arrangements, particularly those relating to board structure and composition, institutional shareholders should give due weight to all relevant factors drawn to their attention.

Supporting Principle

Institutional shareholders should consider carefully explanations given for departure from this Code and make reasoned judgements in each case. They should give an explanation to the company, in writing where appropriate, and be prepared to enter a dialogue if they do not accept the company's position. They should avoid a box-ticking approach to assessing a company's corporate governance. They should bear in mind in particular the size and complexity of the company and the nature of the risks and challenges it faces.

---

21. Agents such as investment managers, or voting services, are frequently appointed by institutional shareholders to act on their behalf and these principles should accordingly be read as applying where appropriate to the agents of institutional shareholders.

22. Available at www.institutionalshareholderscommittee.co.uk.

E.3   Shareholder Voting

Main Principle

Institutional shareholders have a responsibility to make considered use of their votes.

Supporting Principles

Institutional shareholders should take steps to ensure their voting intentions are being translated into practice.

Institutional shareholders should, on request, make available to their clients information on the proportion of resolutions on which votes were cast and non-discretionary proxies lodged.

Major shareholders should attend AGMs where appropriate and practicable. Companies and registrars should facilitate this.

Schedule A: Provisions on the design of performance related remuneration

1. The remuneration committee should consider whether the directors should be eligible for annual bonuses. If so, performance conditions should be relevant, stretching and designed to enhance shareholder value. Upper limits should be set and disclosed. There may be a case for part payment in shares to be held for a significant period.

2. The remuneration committee should consider whether the directors should be eligible for benefits under long-term incentive schemes. Traditional share option schemes should be weighed against other kinds of long-term incentive scheme. In normal circumstances, shares granted or other forms of deferred remuneration should not vest, and options should not be exercisable, in less than three years. Directors should be encouraged to hold their shares for a further period after vesting or exercise, subject to the need to finance any costs of acquisition and associated tax liabilities.

3. Any new long-term incentive schemes which are proposed should be approved by shareholders and should preferably replace any existing schemes or at least form part of a well considered overall plan, incorporating existing schemes. The total rewards potentially available should not be excessive.

4. Payouts or grants under all incentive schemes, including new grants under existing share option schemes, should be subject to challenging performance criteria reflecting the company's objectives. Consideration should be given to criteria which reflect the company's performance relative to a group of comparator companies in some key variables such as total shareholder return.

5. Grants under executive share option and other long-term incentive schemes should normally be phased rather than awarded in one large block.

6. In general, only basic salary should be pensionable.

7. The remuneration committee should consider the pension consequences and associated costs to the company of basic salary increases and any other changes in pensionable remuneration, especially for directors close to retirement.

Schedule B: Guidance on liability of non-executive directors: care, skill and diligence

1.   Although non-executive directors and executive directors have as board members the same legal duties and objectives, the time devoted to the company's affairs is likely to be significantly less for a non-executive director than for an executive director and the detailed knowledge and experience of a company's affairs that could reasonably be expected of a non-executive director will generally be less than for an executive director. These matters may be relevant in assessing the knowledge, skill and experience which may reasonably be expected of a non-executive director and therefore the care, skill and diligence that a non-executive director may be expected to exercise.

2.   In this context, the following elements of the Code may also be particularly relevant.

(i)   In order to enable directors to fulfil their duties, the Code states that:

   •   The letter of appointment of the director should set out the expected time commitment (Code provision A.4.4); and

   •   The board should be supplied in a timely manner with information in a form and of a quality appropriate to enable it to discharge its duties. The chairman is responsible for ensuring that the directors are provided by management with accurate, timely and clear information. (Code principle A.5).

(ii)   Non-executive directors should themselves:

   •   Undertake appropriate induction and regularly update and refresh their skills, knowledge and familiarity with the company (Code principle A.5 and provision A.5.1)

   •   Seek appropriate clarification or amplification of information and, where necessary, take and follow appropriate professional advice. (Code principle A.5 and provision A.5.2)

   •   Where they have concerns about the running of the company or a proposed action, ensure that these are addressed by the board and, to the extent that they are not resolved, ensure that they are recorded in the board minutes (Code provision A.1.4).

   •   Give a statement to the board if they have such unresolved concerns on resignation (Code provision A.1.4)

3.   It is up to each non-executive director to reach a view as to what is necessary in particular circumstances to comply with the duty of care, skill and diligence they owe as a director to the company. In considering whether or not a person is in breach of that duty, a court would take into account all relevant circumstances. These may include having regard to the above where relevant to the issue of liability of a non-executive director.

Schedule C: Disclosure of Corporate Governance Arrangements

Corporate governance disclosure requirements are set out in three places:

   •   FSA Listing Rule 9.8.6 (which includes the 'comply or explain' requirement);

   •   FSA Disclosure and Transparency Rules Sections 7.1 and 7.2 (which set out certain mandatory disclosures); and

   •   The Combined Code (in addition to providing an explanation where they choose not to comply with a provision, companies must disclose specified information in order to comply with certain provisions).

These requirements are summarised below. The full text of Listing Rule 9.8.6 and Disclosure and Transparency Rules 7.1 and 7.2 are contained in the Listing, Prospectus and Disclosure section of the FSA Handbook, which can be found at http://fsahandbook.info/FSA/html/handbook/.

There is some overlap between the mandatory disclosures required under the Disclosure and Transparency Rules and those expected under the Combined Code. Areas of overlap are summarised in the Appendix to this Schedule. In respect of disclosures relating to the audit committee and the composition and operation of the board and its committees, compliance with the relevant provisions of the Code will result in compliance with the relevant Rules.

Listing Rules

Paragraph 9.8.6 R of the Listing Rules states that in the case of a listed company incorporated in the United Kingdom, the following items must be included in its annual report and accounts:

- a statement of how the listed company has applied the Main Principles set out in Section 1 of the Combined Code, in a manner that would enable shareholders to evaluate how the principles have been applied;
- a statement as to whether the listed company has:
    - complied throughout the accounting period with all relevant provisions set out in Section 1 of the Combined Code; or
    - not complied throughout the accounting period with all relevant provisions set out in Section 1 of the Combined Code and if so, setting out:
        (i)   those provisions, if any, it has not complied with;
        (ii)   in the case of provisions whose requirements are of a continuing nature, the period within which, if any, it did not comply with some or all of those provisions; and
        (iii) the company's reasons for non-compliance.

Disclosure and Transparency Rules

Section 7.1 of the Disclosure and Transparency Rules concerns <u>audit committees or bodies carrying out equivalent functions</u>.

DTR 7.1.1 R to 7.1.3 R sets out requirements relating to the composition and functions of the committee or equivalent body:

- DTR 7.1.1 R states that an issuer must have a body which is responsible for performing the functions set out in DTR 7.1.3 R, and that at least one member of that body must be independent and at least one member must have competence in accounting and/or auditing.
- DTR 7.1.2 G states that the requirements for independence and competence in accounting and/or auditing may be satisfied by the same member or by different members of the relevant body.
- DTR 7.1.3 R states that an issuer must ensure that, as a minimum, the relevant body must:
    (1)   monitor the financial reporting process;
    (2)   monitor the effectiveness of the issuer's internal control, internal audit where applicable, and risk management systems;
    (3)   monitor the statutory audit of the annual and consolidated accounts;
    (4)   review and monitor the independence of the statutory auditor, and in particular the provision of additional services to the issuer.

DTR 7.1.5 R to 7.1.7 R explain what disclosure is required:

- DTR 7.1.5 R states that the issuer must make a statement available to the public disclosing which body carries out the functions required by DTR 7.1.3 R and how it is composed.
- DTR 7.1.6 G states that this can be included in the corporate governance statement required under DTR 7.2 (see below).
- DTR 7.1.7 R states that compliance with the relevant provisions of the Combined Code (as set out in the Appendix to this Schedule) will result in compliance with DTR 7.1.1 R to 7.1.5 R.

Section 7.2 concerns corporate governance statements. Issuers are required to produce a corporate governance statement that must be either included in the directors' report (DTR 7.2.1 R); or in a separate report published together with the annual report; or on the issuer's website, in which case there must be a cross-reference in the directors' report (DTR 7.2.9 R).

DTR 7.2.2 R requires that the corporate governance statements must contain a reference to the corporate governance code to which the company is subject (for listed companies incorporated in the UK this is the Combined Code). DTR 7.2.3 R requires that, to the extent that it departs from that code, the company must explain which parts of the code it departs from and the reasons for doing so. DTR 7.2.4 G states that compliance with LR 9.8.6R (6) (the 'comply or explain' rule in relation to the Combined Code) will also satisfy these requirements.

DTR 7.2.5 R to 7.2.7 R and DTR 7.2.10 R set out certain information that must be disclosed in the corporate governance statement:

- DTR 7.2.5 R states that the corporate governance statement must contain a description of the main features of the company's internal control and risk management systems in relation to the financial reporting process. DTR 7.2.10 R states that an issuer which is required to prepare a group directors' report within the meaning of Section 415(2) of the Companies Act 2006 must include in that report a description of the main features of the group's internal control and risk management systems in relation to the process for preparing consolidated accounts.
- DTR 7.2.6 R states that the corporate governance statement must contain the information required by paragraph 13(2)(c), (d), (f), (h) and (i) of Schedule 7 to the Large and Medium-sized Companies and Groups (Accounts and Reports) Regulations 2008 (SI 2008/410) where the issuer is subject to the requirements of that paragraph.
- DTR 7.2.7 R states that the corporate governance statement must contain a description of the composition and operation of the issuer's administrative, management and supervisory bodies and their committees. DTR 7.2.8 G states that compliance with the relevant provisions of the Combined Code (as set out in the Appendix to this Schedule) will satisfy the requirements of DTR 7.2.7 R.

The Combined Code

In addition the Code includes specific requirements for disclosure which are set out below:

The annual report should record:

- a statement of how the board operates, including a high level statement of which types of decisions are to be taken by the board and which are to be delegated to management (A.1.1);
- the names of the chairman, the deputy chairman (where there is one), the chief executive, the senior independent director and the chairmen and members of the nomination, audit and remuneration committees (A.1.2);

- the number of meetings of the board and those committees and individual attendance by directors (A.1.2);

- the names of the non-executive directors whom the board determines to be independent, with reasons where necessary (A.3.1);

- the other significant commitments of the chairman and any changes to them during the year (A.4.3);

- how performance evaluation of the board, its committees and its directors has been conducted (A.6.1);

- the steps the board has taken to ensure that members of the board, and in particular the non-executive directors, develop an understanding of the views of major shareholders about their company (D.1.2).

The annual report should also include:

- a separate section describing the work of the nomination committee, including the process it has used in relation to board appointments and an explanation if neither external search consultancy nor open advertising has been used in the appointment of a chairman or a non-executive director (A.4.6);

- a description of the work of the remuneration committee as required under the Directors' Remuneration Report Regulations 2002, and including, where an executive director serves as a non-executive director elsewhere, whether or not the director will retain such earnings and, if so, what the remuneration is (B.1.4);

- an explanation from the directors of their responsibility for preparing the accounts and a statement by the auditors about their reporting responsibilities (C.1.1);

- a statement from the directors that the business is a going concern, with supporting assumptions or qualifications as necessary (C.1.2);

- a report that the board has conducted a review of the effectiveness of the group's system of internal controls (C.2.1);

- a separate section describing the work of the audit committee in discharging its responsibilities (C.3.3);

- where there is no internal audit function, the reasons for the absence of such a function (C.3.5);

- where the board does not accept the audit committee's recommendation on the appointment, reappointment or removal of an external auditor, a statement from the audit committee explaining the recommendation and the reasons why the board has taken a different position (C.3.6); and

- an explanation of how, if the auditor provides non-audit services, auditor objectivity and independence is safeguarded (C.3.7).

The following information should be made available (which may be met by placing the information on a website that is maintained by or on behalf of the company):

- the terms of reference of the nomination, remuneration and audit committees, explaining their role and the authority delegated to them by the board (A.4.1, B.2.1 and C.3.3);

- the terms and conditions of appointment of non-executive directors (A.4.4) (see footnote 8 on page 10); and

- where remuneration consultants are appointed, a statement of whether they have any other connection with the company (B.2.1).

The board should set out to shareholders in the papers accompanying a resolution to elect or re-elect directors:

- sufficient biographical details to enable shareholders to take an informed decision on their election or re-election (A.7.1);

- why they believe an individual should be elected to a non-executive role (A.7.2); and
- on re-election of a non-executive director, confirmation from the chairman that, following formal performance evaluation, the individual's performance continues to be effective and to demonstrate commitment to the role, including commitment of time for board and committee meetings and any other duties (A.7.2).

The board should set out to shareholders in the papers recommending appointment or reappointment of an external auditor:

- if the board does not accept the audit committee's recommendation, a statement from the audit committee explaining the recommendation and from the board setting out reasons why they have taken a different position (C.3.6).

Additional guidance

The Turnbull Guidance and Smith Guidance contain further suggestions as to information that might usefully be disclosed in the internal control statement and the report of the audit committee respectively. Both sets of guidance are available on the FRC website at http://www.frc.org.uk/corporate/.

APPENDIX

OVERLAP BETWEEN THE DISCLOSURE AND TRANSPARENCY RULES AND THE COMBINED CODE

DISCLOSURE AND TRANSPARENCY RULES	COMBINED CODE
D.T.R 7.1.1 R Sets out minimum requirements on composition of the audit committee or equivalent body.	**Provision C.3.1** Sets out recommended composition of the audit committee.
D.T.R 7.1.3 R Sets out minimum functions of the audit committee or equivalent body.	**Provision C.3.2** Sets out the recommended minimum terms of reference for the committee.
D.T.R 7.1.5 R The composition and function of the audit committee or equivalent body must be disclosed in the annual report *DTR 7.1.7 R states that compliance with Code provisions A.1.2, C.3.1, C.3.2 and C.3.3 will result in compliance with DTR 7.1.1 R to DTR 7.1.5 R.*	**Provision A.1.2:** The annual report should identify members of the board committees. **Provision C.3.3** The annual report should describe the work of the audit committee. Further recommendations on the content of the audit committee report are set out in the Smith Guidance
D.T.R 7.2.5 R The corporate governance statement must include a description of the main features of the company's internal control and risk management systems in relation to the financial reporting process. *While this requirement differs from the requirement in the Combined Code, it is envisaged that both could be met by a single internal control statement.*	**Provision C.2.1** The Board must report that a review of the effectiveness of the internal control system has been carried out. Further recommendations on the content of the internal control statement are set out in the Turnbull Guidance.
DTR 7.2.7 R The corporate governance statement must include a description of the composition and operation of the administrative, management and supervisory bodies and their committees. *DTR 7.2.8 R states that compliance with Code provisions A.1.1, A.1.2, A.4.6, B.2.1 and C.3.3 with result in compliance with DTR 7.2.7 R.*	This requirement overlaps with a number of different provisions of the Code: **A.1.1**: the annual report should include a statement of how the board operates. **A.1.2**: the annual report should identify members of the board and board committees. **A.4.6**: the annual report should describe the work of the nomination committee. **B.2.1**: a description of the work of the remuneration committee should be made available. [Note: in order to comply with DTR 7.2.7 R this information will need to be included in the corporate governance statement]. **C.3.3**: the annual report should describe the work of the audit committee.

Appendix 3

The ABI Guidelines for Directors' Powers to Allot Share Capital and Disapply Shareholders' Pre-emption Rights

The ABI Guidelines are available on the website of the Institutional Voting Information Service (IVIS).

Note: The references to the CA 1985 are now historic. Check the IVIS website to see whether these guidelines have been updated.

The requirement on companies to obtain shareholder authorisation of powers both for the general allotment of new shares and any disapplication of pre-emption rights is embodied in law (currently the Companies Act 1985). This guidance sets out the expectations of institutional investors in this regard. Model resolutions are included in Annex 1.

This guidance, which replaces that previously issued by the ABI, addresses the particular recommendation of the 'Rights Issue Review Group' that the overall allotment headroom that shareholders should normally be invited to approve be increased from one-third to two-thirds of an issuer's issued share capital. The ABI Investment Committee recognises, in particular, the case for ensuring that the routine S.80 headroom should allow for capital raising when made by way of a fully pre-emptive rights issue within an overall value headroom of one third by reference to the company's prevailing market value rather than the quantity of shares issued.

The guidance will be reviewed after three years of operation. In the meantime the ABI will monitor the use by companies of the additional headroom.

S.80 General Power to Allot

ABI Members will regard as routine a request for authorisation to allot new shares in an amount of up to one third of the existing issued share capital[1].

In addition they will regard as routine requests to authorise the allotment of a further one third. Such additional headroom shall be applied to fully pre-emptive rights issues only and the authorisation shall be valid for one year only.

Where an additional authority of this kind is taken and where

- the aggregate actual usage of the authority exceeds one third as regards nominal amount and also,

- in the case of issuance being in whole or part by way of a fully pre-emptive rights issue, monetary proceeds exceed one third (or such lesser relevant proportion) of the pre-issue market capitalisation,

ABI Members will expect that all members of the Board wishing to remain in office will stand for re-election at the next Annual General Meeting of the company following the decision to make the issue in question.

---

1. It is emphasised that this recommended level is not an absolute limit on the amount of share capital the directors may allot: it will merely require the board to return to shareholders if the company proposes significantly to increase the amount of issued share capital.

S.95 General Power to Disapply Pre-emption Rights

The terms of the resolution to disapply pre-emption rights are designed to accord with the provisions of the Pre-Emption Group's Statement of Principles with regard to routine disapplications. It will assist shareholders if, when seeking such authorisations, companies take the opportunity to confirm their intention to adhere to the provisions in the Principles regarding cumulative usage of authorities within a rolling 3-year period where the Principles provide that usage in excess of 7.5% should not take place without prior consultation with shareholders.

ANNEX 1

The attached example resolutions are intended to assist companies and their advisers in understanding the limitations which ABI member Offices have indicated they would expect to see placed on the directors' authority to allot share capital under S.80 of the Companies Act 1985 and the general authority to disapply shareholders' pre-emption rights under S.95.

Resolution 1 (S.80 General Power to Allot)

The figure inserted at 'A' in each of (i) and (ii) should be the lesser of

(a)   the unissued Ordinary share capital or

(b)   a sum equal to one-third of the issued Ordinary share capital[2].

To the one-third figure can be added amounts for which the company requires further additional powers under Section 80. For example, further powers may be required to allot shares in respect of deferred consideration or options.

If the resolution contains a figure greater than one-third of the issued Ordinary share capital (by reference to the total issued Ordinary share capital as disclosed in accordance with the Listing Rules) it is important to explain clearly in the supporting documents the basis on which the figure is calculated, including the nature of any amounts which have been specifically added to the basic one-third figure.

Resolution 2 (Section 95 General Power to Disapply Pre-emption Rights)

The figure inserted at 'B' should not be more than 5% of the issued Ordinary share capital of the company. If the resolution contains a figure greater than five per cent of the issued Ordinary share capital (by reference to the total issued Ordinary share capital as disclosed in accordance with the Listing Rules), it is important to explain clearly in the supporting documents the basis on which the figure is calculated.

Ordinary Resolution

1(i)   **THAT** the board be and it is hereby generally and unconditionally authorised to exercise all powers of the company to allot relevant securities (within the meaning of Section 80 of the Companies Act 1985) up to an aggregate nominal amount of £...A... provided that this authority shall expire on ....*...... save that the company may before such expiry make an offer or agreement which would or might require relevant securities to be allotted after such expiry and the board may allot relevant securities in pursuance of such an offer or agreement as if the authority conferred hereby had not expired, and further,

(ii)   **THAT** the board be and it is hereby generally and unconditionally authorised to exercise all powers of the company to allot equity securities (within the meaning of Section 94 of the said Act) in connection with a rights issue in favour of Ordinary shareholders where the equity securities respectively attributable to the interests of all

---

2.   However, to the extent that the S.80 authority sought for general purposes is less than one third, the S.80 authority reserved for rights issues only may be increased commensurately to provide a rights issue headroom of up to two thirds by reference to the nominal value of the share capital being issued compared to that outstanding.

Ordinary shareholders are proportionate (as nearly as may be) to the respective numbers of Ordinary shares held by them up to an aggregate nominal amount of £...A... provided that this authority shall expire on the date of the next annual general meeting of the company after the passing of this resolution save that the company may before such expiry make an offer or agreement which would or might require relevant securities to be allotted after such expiry and the board may allot relevant securities in pursuance of such an offer or agreement as if the authority conferred hereby had not expired.

* Where an authority is sought in respect of both (i) and (ii) the date of expiry specified should be the date of the next annual general meeting. Where an authority is sought in respect of (i) only, a period up to 5 years is acceptable

Special Resolution

2   **THAT** subject to the passing of the previous resolution the board be and it is hereby empowered pursuant to Section 95 of the Companies Act 1985 to allot equity securities (within the meaning of Section 94 of the said Act) for cash pursuant to the authority conferred by the previous resolution as if sub-section (1) of Section 89 of the said Act did not apply to any such allotment provided that this power shall be limited

(i)   to the allotment of equity securities in connection with a rights issue in favour of Ordinary shareholders where the equity securities respectively attributable to the interests of all Ordinary shareholders are proportionate (as nearly as may be) to the respective numbers of Ordinary shares held by them and,

(ii)   to the allotment (otherwise than pursuant to sub-paragraph (i) above) of equity securities up to an aggregate nominal value of £...B...

and shall expire {on the date of the next annual general meeting of the company after the passing of this resolution } save that the company may before such expiry make an offer or agreement which would or might require equity securities to be allotted after such expiry and the board may allot equity securities in pursuance of such an offer or agreement as if the power conferred hereby had not expired.

Appendix 4

Pre-emption Group: Disapplying Pre-emption Rights: A Statement of Principles

OVERARCHING PRINCIPLES

1. Pre-emption rights are a cornerstone of UK company law and provide shareholders with protection against inappropriate dilution of their investments. They are enshrined in law by the 2nd Company Law Directive and the Companies Act 1985, which provides that they may be disapplied only by a special resolution of shareholders at a general meeting of the company.

2. Whilst not undermining the importance of pre-emption rights, a degree of flexibility is appropriate in circumstances where new equity issuance on a non-pre-emptive basis would be in the interests of companies and their owners.

3. The principles set out in this paper aim to provide clarity on the circumstances in which flexibility might be appropriate and the factors to be taken into account when considering the case for disapplying pre-emption rights and making use of an agreed authority for a non-pre-emptive share issue.

4. Companies, institutional investors and voting advisory services all have an important role to play in ensuring the effective and flexible application of this guidance:

   - Companies have a responsibility to signal an intention to seek a non-pre-emptive issue at the earliest opportunity and to establish a dialogue with the company's shareholders. They should keep shareholders informed of issues related to an application to disapply their pre-emption rights.

   - Shareholders have a responsibility to engage with companies to help them understand the specific factors that might inform their view on a non-pre-emptive issue by the company. They should review the case made by companies on its merits and decide on each case individually using the usual investment criteria. Where a shareholder does intend to vote against a resolution to disapply preemption rights, the Institutional Shareholders' Committee Statement of Principles[1] on the responsibilities of shareholders makes clear that it is best practice to explain in advance the reasons for the decision.

   - While companies should in any case consult their main shareholders, advisory services should be prepared to receive representations from companies. In such circumstances the advisory services should explain any recommendations made in light of the reasons provided. This should involve setting out the pros and cons of the proposal so that the ultimate decision maker can take an informed view.

APPLICATION OF THE PRINCIPLES

5. The principles set out here relate to issues of equity securities for cash other than on a pre-emptive basis pro rata to existing shareholders by all UK companies which are primary listed on the Main Market of the London Stock Exchange. Companies quoted on AIM are encouraged to apply these guidelines but investors recognise that greater flexibility is likely to be justified in the case of such companies.

6. These principles are supported by the ABI, NAPF and IMA as representatives of owners and investment managers. These associations hope that the guidance they contain will

---

1. 'The Responsibilities of Institutional Shareholders and Agents – Statement of Principles'; Institutional Shareholders' Committee, June 2007 [available at: http://www.institutionalshareholderscommittee.org.uk/library.html]

be helpful to companies in approaching requests for disapplication and in gauging the likely reaction of shareholders to proposals they may wish to make.

ROUTINE DISAPPLICATIONS

7   In a significant number of situations a request for disapplication is likely to be considered non-controversial by shareholders. While this does not reduce the importance of effective dialogue and timely notification, routine requests are less likely to need in-depth discussion and shareholders will be more inclined in principle to support them.

8   Requests are more likely to be routine in nature when the company is seeking authority to issue non-pre-emptively no more than 5% of ordinary share capital in any one year.

9   This principle applies whatever the structure of the proposed issue. For example, an issue of shares which contains both a pre-emptive and non-pre-emptive element ('combination issues') would normally be considered routine provided that the non-preemptive element met the criteria specified for routine applications within these guidelines. This would include issues that comprised a placing of shares with a partial clawback by existing shareholders.

10   In the absence of (a) suitable advance consultation and explanation or (b) the matter having been specifically highlighted at the time at which the request for disapplication was made, companies should not issue more than 7.5% of the company's ordinary share capital for cash other than to existing shareholders in any rolling three year period.

11   Where a request is made for the disapplication of pre-emption rights in respect of a specific issue of shares, the price at which the shares are proposed to be issued will also be relevant. Shareholders' approach to the pricing of non-pre-emptive issues is set out in paragraphs 18 and 19 below. Companies should note that a discount of greater than 5% is not likely to be regarded as routine.

12   Treasury shares issued for cash will be counted within the guideline levels set out in paragraph 8, but not those in paragraph 10.

13   Convertible instruments will be counted within the guideline levels set out in paragraphs 8 and 10, and should be counted at the point when authority to issue the instruments is sought, not the point at which they are converted to ordinary shares.

14   **These principles are intended to ease the granting of authority below those figures, not to rule out approvals above them. Requests which, if granted, would exceed these levels should be considered by shareholders on a case by case basis.** In these instances it is particularly important that there is early and effective dialogue, and that the company is able to communicate to shareholders the information they need in order to reach an informed decision. The considerations set out in the following section are critical to making a decision.

CRITICAL CONSIDERATIONS RELATING TO NON-ROUTINE REQUESTS FOR DISAPPLICATION

15   It is neither possible nor desirable to define all the circumstances in which shareholders might be willing to agree to disapply pre-emption rights above the level set out in paragraphs 8 and 10 above. Nevertheless, there are some general considerations that are likely to be relevant in the majority of cases; these are set out below. Companies should ensure they are in a position to communicate such information to shareholders to help them make an informed decision.

16.   The critical considerations are likely to include:

- **the strength of the business case:** In order to make a reasoned assessment shareholders need to receive a clear explanation of the purpose to which the capital raised will be put and the benefits to be gained - for example in terms of product development or the opportunity cost of not raising new finance to exploit new commercial opportunities -and how the financing or proposed future financing fits in with the life-cycle and financial needs of the company.

- **the size and stage of development of the company and the sector within which it operates**. Different companies have different financing needs. For example, shareholders might be expected to be more sympathetic to a request from a small company with high growth potential than one from a larger, more established company.

- **the stewardship and governance of the company**. If the company has a track record of generating shareholder value, clear planning and good communications, this may give shareholders additional confidence in its judgement.

- **financing options**. A wide variety of financing options are now available to companies. Companies should explain why a non-pre-emptive issue of shares is the most appropriate means of raising capital, and why other financing methods have been rejected.

- **the level of dilution of value and control for existing shareholders.** If there would be no resulting dilution, for example if an investment trust sought authority to issue shares at a premium to the underlying net asset value per share, this would not normally raise any concerns;

- **the proposed process following approval:** Companies should make clear the process they would follow if approval for a non-pre-emptive issue were to be granted, for example how dialogue with shareholders would be carried out in the period leading up to the announcement of an issue.

- **contingency plans:** Company managers should explain what contingency plans they have in place in case the request is not granted, and the implications of such a decision.

TIMING OF REQUESTS FOR DISAPPLICATION

17   Companies should signal the possibility of their intention to seek a non-pre-emptive issue at the earliest opportunity. For example if, at the time of the initial public offering, a company is aware that it is likely to have a need relatively quickly for additional cash, it should alert potential investors to this in the prospectus. In other cases it might be appropriate for the company to signal a potential request in its annual report. In some cases it may be appropriate for companies to consult a small number of major shareholders before making any announcement. Companies and shareholders should be mindful of the possible legal and regulatory issues in doing this.

18   Authority to disapply pre-emption rights following a 'routine' request would normally be granted by shareholders' approval of an appropriate resolution at an AGM. As discussed above, shareholders will not generally agree to a non-routine disapplication request without a sufficiently strong business case for this course of action. Thus, non-routine requests would be made at an AGM only when the company is in a position to justify this approach by providing relevant information such as that set out in paragraph 16; otherwise a specially convened EGM would be needed.

19   Authorities should be granted for no more than 15 months or until the next AGM, whichever is the shorter period.

OTHER CONSIDERATIONS RELATING TO NON PRE-EMPTIVE ISSUES

20   Companies should aim to ensure that they are raising capital on the best possible terms, particularly where the proposed issue is in the context of a transaction likely to enhance the share price. Any discount at which equity is issued for cash other than to existing shareholders will be of major concern. Companies should, in any event, seek to restrict

the discount to a maximum of 5% of the middle of the best bid and offer prices for the company's shares immediately prior to the announcement of an issue or proposed issue.

21   Where an issue is priced on a date after the announcement date, the level of discount should be assessed at the time of pricing rather than the time of announcement. Companies should also have regard to any adverse impact on the share price of the earlier announcement, which may create the potential for a significant loss or transfer of value, in deciding whether to proceed with an issue in such circumstances.

22   The principles and critical considerations set out above apply to requests for the disapplication of pre-emption rights. Once a request to disapply pre-emption rights has been approved, shareholders expect companies to discharge and account for this authority appropriately. It is recommended that the subsequent annual report should include relevant information such as the actual level of discount achieved, the amount raised and how it was used and the percentage amount of shares issued on a non-pre-emptive basis over the last year and three years.

ROLE OF THE PRE-EMPTION GROUP

23   The Pre-Emption Group will monitor the development of practice in relation to disapplying pre-emption rights. It expects that this Statement of Principles will inform the way in which all interested parties participate in this process. It will monitor and report annually on the application of these principles. The Pre-Emption Group will not express a view on or otherwise intervene in specific cases.

APPENDIX

DEFINITIONS

Clawback

Clawback as it is referred to in paragraph 9 is the right of existing shareholders to subscribe for a share of an issue at the pre-agreed price. This differs from a full rights entitlement since it is non-renounceable and therefore does not permit the shareholder to sell this entitlement to another investor.

Discounts

In general terms, the 'discount' (paragraphs 20 and 21) is defined as the aggregate of (a) the amount by which the offering price differs from the market price, and (b) expenses directly relevant to the making of the issue. In the case of issues of a new class of deferred equity in the form of convertibles, warrants or other deferred equity, the amount of the opening market price above the issue price and any difference at point of pricing of the instrument to underlying fair value will be regarded as part of the discount.

Market Movements

Where the pricing takes place at a time later than that of the announcement of the proposed issue (paragraph 21), it is recognised that the achievable price of the placing may vary in accordance with general market conditions. For the purposes of these guidelines the measurement of discount therefore relates to the time and date of the pricing rather than the time and date of the announcement of the issue.

Appendix 5
Websites

The following websites are referred to in this book:

BBC News	news.bbc.co.uk
BIS	www.bis.gov.uk
Competition Commission	www.competition-commission.org.uk
Euroclear UK & Ireland	www.euroclear.com
European Commission	www.ec.europa.eu/index_en.htm
Financial Reporting Council	www.frc.org.uk
FSA	www.fsa.gov.uk
FSA Handbook	fsahandbook.info/FSA/html/handbook
Hermes	www.hermes.co.uk
Institute of Chartered Secretaries and Administrators	www.icsa.org.uk
Institutional Voting Information Service	www.ivis.co.uk
London Stock Exchange	www.londonstockexchange.com
OFT	www.oft.gov.uk
Pre-Emption Group	www.pre-emptiongroup.org.uk
Quoted Companies Alliance	www.quotedcompaniesalliance.co.uk
Takeover Appeal Board	www.thetakeoverappealboard.org.uk
Takeover Panel	www.thetakeoverpanel.org.uk

The following websites may also be of interest:

ABI	www.abi.org.uk
CBI	www.cbi.org.uk
Companies House	www.companieshouse.gov.uk
EEA	www.efta.int
European Union	www.europa.eu
HM Treasury	www.hm-treasury.gov.uk
Institute of Chartered Accountants in England and Wales	www.icaew.com
Institute of Directors	www.iod.com
NAPF	www.napf.co.uk
NASDAQ	www.nasdaq.com
New York Stock Exchange	www.nyse.com
PIRC	www.pirc.co.uk
RNS (Regulatory News Service)	www.londonstockexchange.com

Bibliography

The Prospectus Rules, the Listing Rules and the Disclosure and Transparency Rules (Financial Services Authority)

The City Code on Takeovers and Mergers (The Panel on Takeovers and Mergers)

Practical Law Company (online)

Butterworths *LexisLibrary* (online)

Westlaw (online)

Index